About the Editor

Azim A. Nanji is professor and chair of the Department of Religion at the University of Florida, where he also holds an associate appointment in the Center for African Studies. He was born in Kenya and attended schools in Kenya and Tanzania; he received his undergraduate education from Makerere University in Kampala, Uganda. After coming to North America in 1967 to study at Harvard University and begin graduate study at McGill University in Montreal, Canada, he obtained his M.A. in 1970 and Ph.D. in 1972.

Along with his academic duties, Nanji has participated in international conferences and lectures in Australia, Canada, China, Europe, Mexico, Russia, and the United States and in many of the countries of the Muslim world. He is a member of the Religion and Philanthropy Committee of the Council on Foundations in Washington, D.C. and is on the editorial board of the Journal of the Academy and its International Directions Committee. He also served as co-chair of the Islam section of the American Academy of Religion. His academic and research interests in Islamic studies is combined with the development of educational programs in the study of Islam at colleges, universities, and schools. He is involved in projects on the development of integrated education in *madrasa*-based programs in East Africa. Phillips Academy in Andover, Massachusetts has sought Nanji's advisement on integrating the study of Muslim cultures and societies into their global curriculum; he has also created similar projects in Canada, England, and the United States.

Nanji has authored, co-authored, and edited several books including: *Building for Tomorrow* (1994); *The Religious World, Third Edition* (1993); *The Nizari Ismaili Tradition* (1976); and the forthcoming *Mapping Islamic Studies* (1996). He has also contributed articles and chapters to *The Encyclopedia of Religion, The Encyclopedia of Islam, The Oxford Encyclopedia of the Islamic World, A Companion to Ethics,* and to various academic journals and books.

Besides being a consultant, academician, and author, Nanji has been the recipient of fellowships and grants from the Canada Council, the National Endowment for Humanities, and the Rockefeller Foundation. In 1995, he was invited to give the baccalaureate commencement address at Stanford University—the first Muslim scholar to be so honored.

THE
MUSLIM
ALMANAC

THE
MUSLIM
ALMANAC

A Reference

Work on

the History,

Faith, Culture,

and Peoples

of Islam

Azim A. Nanji,

Editor

 **Gale Research Inc.**

An International Thomson Publishing Company

I(T)P
An ITP Information/Reference Group Company

NEW YORK • LONDON • BONN • BOSTON • DETROIT • MADRID
MELBOURNE • MEXICO CITY • PARIS • SINGAPORE • TOKYO
TORONTO • WASHINGTON • ALBANY NY • BELMONT CA • CINCINNATI OH

Gale Research Inc. Staff

Lawrence W. Baker, *Managing Editor*
Kenneth Estell, Jane Hoehner, Rebecca Nelson, *Developmental Editors*
Jolen M. Gedridge, Camille Killens, *Associate Editors*
Andrea Kovacs, Jessica Proctor, *Assistant Editors*
Mary Beth Trimper, *Production Director*
Evi Seoud, *Assistant Production Manager*
Shanna Heilveil, *Production Assistant*
Cynthia Baldwin, *Product Design Manager*
Barbara J. Yarrow, *Graphic Services Manager*
Mary Krzewinski, *Cover Designer*
Arthur Chartow, *Page Designer*
Pamela A. Hayes, *Photography Coordinator*
Randy Bassett, *Image Database Supervisor*
Robert Duncan, *Scanner Operator*
Benita L. Spight, *Data Entry Supervisor*
Gwendolyn S. Tucker, *Data Entry Coordinator*
Nancy K. Sheridan, *Data Entry Associate*
Cover calligraphy by: Mohamed Zakariya. Translation: "There is no divinity except God, Muhammad is his Messenger."

Library of Congress Cataloging-in-Publication Data
The Muslim almanac/edited by Azim Nanji
     p. cm.
     Includes bibliographical references (p.   ) and index.
     ISBN 0-8103-8924-X (alk. paper)
     1. Islam. 2. Islamic countries. I. Nanji, Azim.
     BP40.M83 1995   95-17324
     297—dc20   CIP

The trademark ITP is used under license.

1 0 9 8 7 6 5 4 3 2

"In the name of God, Most Gracious, Most Merciful."

Contents

Preface

The history and culture of the Muslim peoples of the world are part of the shared heritage of humankind. In recent years, the historical experience of Muslims has taken on major significance in world affairs. This heightened awareness, unfortunately, has in many cases, led the media and the popular imagination of Westerners to a distorted view of Islam. In explaining current events in the world, Muslims are often portrayed in homogenized fashion; their rich diversity and heritage has remained unrecognized or unrepresented. By focusing on the turbulent regions of the Muslim world and its radical leaders, who are adherents for a restored vision of early Islam, an image has been created which represents Muslims to be violently opposed to other values, particularly those of the West. This imagined and fictitious contrast distorts and misrepresents the variety in present-day and historical life of the Muslim world; overlooks the lengthy exchanges and fruitful interaction that have taken place between Muslims, other cultures, and civilizations, including the West, reduces its meaning to the realm of romance and stereotype; and confirms and reinforces ancient prejudices.

This book provides a perspective on the historical formations of the worldwide Muslim community from Arabia to the Philippines; it portrays the intellectual, spiritual, and institutional pluralism that has developed during a history of over fourteen centuries. *Muslim Almanac* examines particular regional developments showing the evolution of Muslim societies within local and global contexts, revealing the diversity that exists among individual Muslims, traditions, and various periods of Muslim history. It explores the process of its permeation and interaction in the different cultures of the world and examines the multiple expressions, as well as conflicts and tensions that have occurred in Muslim history to the present.

This publication allows the reader to build on the foundations of Islam by tracing Muslim history through its various geographical contexts and to understand the specific nature of Islam in each of its regional expressions. The study of each realm and region provides an interconnected setting for an overview of the intellectual and cultural achievements in Islamic contexts. These include the study of theology, law, philosophy, and science; the arts and literature; education and learning; and architecture.

Dramatic changes have taken place in the Muslim world within the last two centuries. The chapters on Muslims in modern times explore these changes and their implication for all facets of Muslim life and society.

The writers of various chapters of *Muslim Almanac* are scholars—each specializing in the subject in which they have contributed. Their work represents the academic study of Islam; their insights are based not only on research, but also from personal experiences from living in different parts of the Muslim world. This provides an indepth look at the faith and culture of Islam, the history, and achievements of a world religion, whose traditions and civilization continue to play an influential role in our world.

Acknowledgements

A project of this magnitude and international scope would not have been possible without the advice, assistance and cooperation of many individuals and institutions.

The quality of *Muslim Almanac*'s illustration has been made possible by the following institutions and individuals: the Smithsonian Institution; Harvard University Art Museums; the Hartford Seminary; the Institute of Ismaili Studies Library; Suha Ozkan, Farrokh Derakshani, Jack Kennedy, and William O'Reilly—the Aga Khan Trust for Culture; Katherine Hinckley—the Aga Khan Foundation; Ahmad Nabal—the MIT Visual Archives of the Aga Khan Program in Islamic Architecture; Frederick M. Denny; Hasan-Uddin Khan; Carl Ernst; Rebecca Gearhart; Tania Kamal Eldin; Vernon Schubel; Vasudha Narayanan; Michael Dillon; Stephen Harmon; John Waterbury; Walter Denny; Sheila S. Blair; and Jonathan M. Bloom. Their generosity and cooperation is greatly appreciated.

Many others have also been very helpful including: the Board of Advisors–Esin Atil, Frederick M. Denny, Nurcholish Madjid, Sulayman Nyang, Abdulaziz Sachedina, and Ismail Serageldin; Farhan Nizami—director of the Oxford Center for Islamic Studies; Sara Smith—the Visual Resources Center of the College of Fine Arts—University of Florida; Cornell Fleischer—University of Chicago; Susan Lewis—research assistant and project coordinator; Julia Smith; and Annie Newman. My wife Razia, cautioned me about the enormity of the task; however, as always, she gave her unstinting support to all aspects of the development and completion of the project.

Additional gratitude goes to Gale Research's editors Rebecca Nelson, Jane Hoehner, and Kenneth Estell for their patience and guidance of this publication to its completion.

Advisory Board

Esin Atil is a specialist in the arts and cultures of Islam at the Freer and Sackler Galleries, the Smithsonian Institution, in Washington, D.C. She received her Ph.D. in Islamic Art in 1969 from the University of Michigan. She has authored twenty books on the artistic and cultural traditions of the Islamic world and has curated exhibits in America and Muslim-oriented countries. Her publications include: *Islamic Art Patronage Treasures From Kuwait* (1990); *Age of Sultan Suleyman the Magnificent* (1987); *Suleymanname the Illustrated History of Sule* (1986); *Kalila Wa Dimna: Fables From a Fourteenth Century Arabic Manuscript* (1981); and *Ceramics From the World of Islam* (1973).

Frederick M. Denny is a professor in the Department of Religious Studies at the University of Colorado at Boulder. He received his Ph.D. in Islamic Studies and History of Religions from the University of Chicago in 1974. He also studied at the American University in Cairo. He travels throughout the Muslim world and lectures extensively on subjects related to Islam and the History of Religions. Denny is the editor of the series *Studies in Comparative Religion*,—a highly acclaimed collection of studies in the field. He has written several publications on Islam including: *An Introduction to Islam, Second Edition* (1994); *Islam and the Muslim Community* (1987); *The Holy Book in Comparative Perspective* (1985); and *Islamic Ritual Practices* with co-editor Abdulaziz Sachedina. He serves on the Board of Directors for the American Academy of Religion and is actively involved in promoting education about Islam in the public school systems in the United States.

Nurcholish Madjid is a leading scholar of Islam and History of Religions in Indonesia. He received his Ph.D. in 1984 from the University of Chicago where he trained under the late Professor Fazlur Rahman. Madjid has held academic positions at the State Institute of Islamic Studies in Jakarta and the Indonesian Academy of Sciences. He is currently the director of the Paramadina Foundation in Jakarta and a participant in international conferences and meetings on all aspects of Islam, its role in modern society, and relation to other religious and cultural traditions.

Sulayman Nyang obtained his Ph.D. from the University of Virginia in 1969. After serving as assistant professor and acting director of African Studies at Howard University in Washington, D.C., he was appointed deputy ambassador and head of chancery at the Embassy of the Gambia in Saudi Arabia. He returned to Howard University in 1978 where he was appointed professor and department chairperson of African Studies. Nyang has a particular interest in African and Muslim thought and their implication for social and political change on the African continent. His publications include: *Islam, Christianity and African Identity* (1984); and *Religious Plurality in Africa: Essays in Honor of John Mbiti* (1993) with co-editor Jacob Olupona.

Abdulaziz Sachedina is a professor in the

Department of Religious Studies at the University of Virginia. He received his early education in East Africa, Pakistan, and Iran; he also obtained his Ph.D. in Islamic Studies in 1974 from the University of Toronto, Canada. Besides being a teacher and lecturer in the Muslim world, Europe, and North America, he has been considered an expert commentator on Muslim affairs and issues. Sachedina served on the editorial board of *The Oxford Encyclopedia of the Modern Islamic World*. His publishing ventures include: *The Just Ruler in Shiite Islam* (1988); *Islamic Messianism: The Idea of the Mahdi in Twelver Shiism* (1981); *Human Rights and the Conflict of Cultures: Western and Islamic Perspectives on Religious Liberty* (1988); and *Islamic Rituals and Practices* with co-editor Frederick Denny.

Ismail Serageldin is vice president for Environmentally Sustainable Development at the World Bank in Washington, D.C., where he has worked since 1972. Within the World Bank he specializes in designing and managing poverty-focussed projects and environmentally sustainable programs in the developing world. He works extensively in Sub-Saharan Africa, North Africa, Europe, and the Middle East. He received his education at Cairo University and Harvard University where he earned his Ph.D. Serageldin is an author on the aspects of development and culture, with a particular interest in architecture and development in the Muslim world. His most recent publications include: *Development Partners: Aid and Co-operation in the 1990s* (1993); *Friday Morning Reflections at the World Bank: Essays on Values and Development* (1991); and *Space for Freedom: The Search for Architectural Excellence in Muslim Societies* (1989).

Contributors

Sharifah Zuriah AlJefri, is a Malaysian artist and writer who lives in Kuala Lumpur where she is associated with several cultural and women's organizations. She has shown her work in several exhibits and believes in putting her art to the service of charity and other worthy causes.

Sajida Alvi, Ph.D., is a professor and chair of Urdu Languages and Culture at McGill University in Montreal, Canada. Her most recent book is *Advice on the Art of Governance: An Indo-Islamic Mirror for Princes* (1989).

Peter Antes, is head of the Study of Religions Department at the University of Hannover in Germany. He has been a member of the International Association of the History of Religion (IAHR) Executive Committee since 1985. His most recent publication appears in *Religion in Europe, Contemporary Perspectives* (1994).

Mohammed Arkoun, Ph.D., is a professor emeritus of the History of Islamic Thought at the Sorbonne. He is a leading modern Muslim thinker and associated with several think tanks in Europe and America. Among his many publications, his most recent work is *Rethinking Islam* (1993).

Ali Asani, Ph.D., is a professor and specialist of Indo-Muslim Cultures at Harvard University. He is the author of *The Bujh Niranjan* (1991) and of a forthcoming study on poetry in praise of the Prophet.

Mahmoud Ayoub, Ph.D., is a professor of religion at Temple University, specializing in Islamic studies and inter-faith relations. His most recent project is a series of ongoing studies on *The Quran and Its Interpreters.*

Aida Bamia, Ph.D., is a professor of Arabic languages and culture at the University of Florida. Her most recent research focusses on women's writings in the Arab world. She has written several books in Arabic.

C. E. Bosworth, Ph.D., is a professor emeritus in Arabic and Islamic studies at Manchester University in England. A widely published author, his most recent work is *The History of Saffarids of Sistan and the Maliks of Nimruz* (1994); he is an editor of *The Encyclopedia of Islam.*

Thomas Burman, Ph.D., is an associate professor of history at the University of Tennessee at Knoxville. He is the author of *Religious Polemic and the Intellectual History of the Mozarabs* (1994) and *Spain's Arab Christians and Islam* (1994).

Juan Campo, Ph.D., is an associate professor of religious studies at the University of California, Santa Barbara. He is the author of *The Other Side of Paradise* (1991).

Farhad Daftary, Ph.D., is head of Graduate Studies and Research at the Institute of Ismaili Studies in London. He is the author of *The Ismailis* (1990) and *The Legends of the Assassins* (1994).

Alnoor Dhanani, Ph.D., teaches Muslim philosophy and thought at Harvard University. He is the author of *The Political Theory of Kalam* (1994).

Michael Dillon, Ph.D., is a lecturer of modern Chinese history at the University of Durham in England. His current research focuses on Muslims in China.

Carl Ernst, Ph.D., is a professor of religious studies at the University of North Carolina, Chapel Hill. His most recent publication is *Eternal Garden: Mysticism, History and Politics at a South Asian Sufi Center* (1992).

Sibel Erol, Ph.D., is an assistant professor of Turkish in the Department of Asian and Near Eastern Languages at Washington University in St. Louis. Her research focuses on Turkish literature.

Aziz Esmail, Ph.D., is dean of the Institute of Ismaili Studies in London. His research concentrates on philosophical issues in the modern world, particularly as they affect Muslims and other philosophical traditions.

Zayn Kassam-Hahn, Ph.D., is an assistant professor of religion at Pomona College, California. Her research deals with the comparative religious texts in Islam and Hinduism.

Shakeel Hossain, is a visiting scholar at the Harvard/MIT Aga Khan Program for Islamic Architecture. He specializes in the role of icons and images in Indian culture and is organizing an exhibit on Islam in India.

Marcia Hermanesen, Ph.D., is a professor of Islamic studies in the Department of Religious Studies at San Diego State University, California. Her most recent work centers on women and gender and literary issues in Islam. She has published previously on the Sufi tradition in Islam.

Hasan Uddin Khan, is an architect currently associated with Harvard/MIT Aga Khan Program in Islamic Architecture. He was editor-in-chief of *Mimar,*— a journal of architecture and development and is co-editor of *The Mosque* (1994).

Ahmet Karamustafa, Ph.D., is an associate professor of Islamic thought and Turkish literature at Washington University, St. Louis. He is the author of *God's Unruly Friends* (1994).

Bruce Lawrence, Ph.D., is a professor in the Department of Religion and director of Comparative Area Studies at Duke University. His most recent books are *Nizam al din Awliya: Morals for the Heart* (1991) and *Defenders of God: The Fundamentalist Revolt Against the Modern Age* (1989).

Kamal Abdul-Malek, Ph.D., teaches comparative literature at Brown University. He is the author of *A Study of the Vernacular Poetry of Ahmad Fuad Nigm* (1990).

Lawrence Mamiya, Ph.D., holds the Mattie M. Paschall Davis Chair in Religion at Vassar College, New York and is also a professor and chairperson of the Department of Religion. He has written *The Black Church in the African-American Experience* with co-author C. Eric Lincoln. They are currently working on their next project on African-American Muslims.

Khalid Masud, Ph.D., is a professor at the Islamic Research Institute, International Islamic University in Islamabad, Pakistan. He is the author of *Islamic Legal Philosophy* (1977) and *Iqbal's Concept of Ijtihad* (1985).

Margaret Mills, Ph.D., is a professor in the Department of Folklore and Folklife at the University of Pennsylvania. Besides being a Guggenheim Fellowship holder, she is the author of *Rhetoric and Politics in Afghan Traditional Storytelling* (1991) and *Gender, Genre and Power in South Asian Expressions* (1991).

Razia Jinha Nanji is a librarian, specializing in reference literature and Africana materials at the University of Florida. She is the author of the forthcoming *Historical Dictionary of Islam*.

Gordon Newby, Ph.D., is a professor and chair of Near East Studies at Emory University. He is the author of *Making of the Last Prophet* (1989) and *The History of the Jews of Arabia* (1988).

Kevin Reinhart, Ph.D., is an associate professor of religion at Dartmouth College, New Hampshire. He is the author of *Before Revelation: The Boundaries of Muslim Moral Thought* (1995).

M. Ruthven, is a writer and a consultant on Middle East affairs, who was for several years with the BBC's Arabic Service in London. He teaches currently at the University of Aberdeen in Scotland and is the author of *A Satanic Affair: Salman Rushdie and the Rage of Islam* (1990) and *Islam in the World* (1984).

Fariyal Ross-Sheriff, Ph.D., is a professor of social work at Howard University in Washington, D.C. with extensive research and field experience on refugee populations and issues. She is co-author of *Mental Health and People of Color: Curriculum Development and Change* (1983).

Daniel Schroeter, Ph.D., is an associate professor of history at the University of California Davis and author of *Merchants of Essouira* (1988).

Vernon Schubel, Ph.D., is an associate professor of religion at Kenyon College, Ohio. He is the author of *Religious Performance in Contemporary Islam Shii Devotional Ritual in South Asia* (1993).

Michael Sells, Ph.D., is an associate professor of Islam and Comparative Religion and Chairperson of the Department of Religion at Haverford College, Pennsylvania. He is the author of *Mystical Languages of Unsaying* (1994) and *Desert Tracings* (1989).

James Steele, is a teacher of architecture at the University of Southern California. His publications include a monograph on Hasan Fathy; he has also edited *Architecture for a Changing World* (1992).

Farouk Topan, Ph.D., is a lecturer of Swahili at the School of Oriental and African Studies, University of London. He is the author of *A Taste of Heaven* (1980).

Chronology of Major Events

570 Birth of the Prophet Muhammad. "Year of the Elephant." Invasion of Mecca fails.

595 Muhammad's marriage to Khadija.

610 Muhammad receives first revelation; beginning of the Prophetic mission.

613 The period of public preaching begins; mounting opposition to Muhammad's message.

615 A group of Muslims leave for Abyssinia to escape persecution and to seek the protection of its Christian ruler, the Negus.

616–618 Boycott of the Prophet's family by leaders of the *Quraysh* opposed to him.

620 Death of Khadija. Death of Abu Talib, the Prophet's uncle.

622 The *Hijra*. Establishment of an Islamic community in Medina. The Prophet undertakes social and economic reforms. Beginning of the Muslim lunar calendar.

624 Battle of Badr; Muslims are victorious over Meccan *Quraysh*.

625 Battle of Uhud. Fatima marries Ali.

627 The unsuccessful siege of Medina by combined force of Meccans and Bedouins (Battle of the Ditch).

628 The Treaty of Hudaybiyya gives Muslims the right to make the pilgrimage to Mecca. The Prophet sends envoys to the rulers of Egypt, Persia, Byzantium and the Yemen with an invitation to accept Islam.

629 The Prophet leads the pilgrimage to Mecca.

630 Mecca submits to the authority of the Prophet. General amnesty is declared and the Kaba is rededicated to the worship of God. The Battle of Hunayn. Tribal conversions throughout Arabia. The Prophet leads expedition to Tabuk.

632 The Prophet's final pilgrimage and the year of his death.

632–634 Caliphate of Abu Bakr. Expeditions against Syria and Iraq.

634 The Muslim army defeats Byzantines at Battle of Ajnadyan in Palestine. Umar becomes caliph on the death of Abu Bakr.

636 Byzantine forces defeated at the Battle of Yarmuk. Conquest of Syria.

637 The Persian Sassanian army defeated at the Battle of Qadisiyya (Iraq), Muslim authority extends over the Fertile Crescent.

638 Jerusalem comes under Muslim rule.

640 Invasion of Egypt. The Battle of Nihavand results in collapse of Sasanian rule in Egypt.

644–656 Uthman succeeds Umar as caliph.

656 The assassination of Uthman. Civil war breaks out. Battle of the Camel at Basra between Ali and Aisha, Talha, and Zubayr. Ali settles in Kufa. Uqba ibn Nafi founds Kairouan in North Africa.

656–660 Caliphate of Ali.

657–660 Muawiyah, governor of Syria, challenges the authority of Ali resulting in the Battle of Siffin. After arbitration fails, Muawiya rejects the authority of Ali and proclaims himself ruler. Group of Muslims called Khwarij secede from the rest of the community.

661 Assassination of Ali. With the forceful assumption of rule by Muawiyah, the period of the "rightly-guided caliphs" comes to an end.

661–750 The period of Umayyad dynastic rule based in Damascus.

680 Yazid succeeds Muawiya and suppresses attempts to restore authority to Husayn, son of Ali and grandson of the Prophet. Husayn and his followers are massacred at Karbala, intensifying opposition by supporters who are called Shia.

711 Tariq ibn Ziyad lands in Spain, initiating the period of Muslim control and influence. Muslim conquest of Sind in India under Muhammad ibn Qasim.

712 Muslims gain control of Transoxiana and conquer Central Asia (Samarkand, Balkh, Bukhara).

713 Death of the Shia Imam Ali Zayn al-Abidin, father of Zayd. Beginning of Zaydi Shia sect.

732 Charles Martel turns back Muslim advance at Tours and Poitiers.

742 Founding of the mosque of Xian in China.

749 Umayyad rule ends, Abbasid dynasty come to power.

750 Muslim presence on the East Coast of Africa.

762 Baghdad is founded by al-Mansur as capital of Abbasid Caliphate.

765 Death of sixth Shia Imam Jafar al-Sadiq results in Shia split over the imamate and emergence of two main groups: the Ithna Ashari and the Ismaili.

767 Death of Abu Hanifah, founder of Sunni Hanafi School of Law.

786–809 Caliphate of Harun al-Rashid, height of Abbasid and culture.

795 Death of Malik ibn Anas, founder of Sunni Maliki School of Law.

813–833 Caliphate of al-Mamun, son of Harun al-Rashid. Period of translation of classical works of Philosophy, Medicine, etc. into Arabic begins. Cultural flowering. Rise of the Mutazila.

820 Death of Muhammad ibn Idris al-Shafii, founder of Sunni Shafii School of Law.

855 Death of Ahmad ibn Hanbal, founder of Hanbali Sunni School of Law.

870 Death of al-Bukhari, scholar and compiler of hadith. Death of philosopher al-Kindi.

873 The eleventh Ithna Ashari Imam dies and his son becomes the "hidden imam."

877 Construction of Ibn Tulun mosque in Cairo.

909–972 Shia Ismaili Fatimids establish a state in North Africa.

929 Abd al-Rahman III takes the title of caliph in Cordova. Muslim world exists under three caliphates: Abbasids, Fatimids, and Spanish Umayyads. Death of mathematician and astronomer al-Battani.

969 Construction begins on al-Azhar in Cairo under the Fatimids as a center of science and learning, mosque and university.

996–1021 Fatimid caliphate of al-Hakim. Emergence of the Druze movement on the death of al-Hakim.

998–1030 Rule of Mahmud of Ghazna. Raids into India with expansion of power over Afghanistan, Punjab, Indus Valley, and Khurasan. The *Shahname* is completed by the Persian poet, Firdawsi.

1009 Emergence of a Muslim dynasty in Songhay, West Africa.

1037 Death of philosopher and physician Ibn Sina (Avicenna).

1038–1194 The Saljuq dynasty founded by Toghril Beg, who takes the title sultan.

1067 Founding of al-Nizamiyyah *madrasa* and college in Baghdad.

1071 Alp Arslan captures Byzantine Emperor Romanos Diogenes at Manzikert. Saljuqs control most of Asia Minor.

1095 At Council of Clermont Pope Urban II launches the First Crusade in reaction to the destruction of the Church of the Holy Sepulchre.

1099 Crusaders take Jerusalem. Christian kingdom of Jerusalem established under Baldwin.

1111 Death of theologian and scholar al-Ghazali.

1143 First major translation of Quran into Latin.

1166 Death of Sufi Abd al-Qadir al-Jilani, founder of the Qadiriyya order.

1171 Saladin establishes the Ayyubid dynasty in Egypt.

1175 Ahmed al-Rifai, founder of the Rifaiyya Sufi movement, dies.

1187 Saladin defeats Crusaders at the Battle of the Horn of Hattin and takes Jerusalem. Ghurids in eastern Afghanistan begin expansion into Khurasan and northern India.

1198 Death of physician and philosopher Ibn Rushd (Averroes).

1200 Arrival of Islam in southeast Asia.

1218 The fifth Crusade. Mongols invade Turkestan. Khwarazm-Shah Ala al-Din Muhammad kills envoys of Genghiz Khan as spies, provoking Mongol retaliation.

1227 Death of Genghiz Khan, Mongol ruler.

1254–1517 Mamluk dynasty established in Egypt.

1258 Hulagu Khan sacks Baghdad; establishes the Mongol Il-Khanid dynasty in Persia with capital at Tabriz.

1273 Death of Jalal al-Din Rumi, author of the *Mathnawi*.

1281–1328 Ottoman rule established in Bithynia under Osman I.

1300 Establishment of small Muslim states in Indonesia.

1301 Sufi Safavid order established in Azerbaijan.

1325–1353 Travels of Ibn Battuta through the world of Islam.

1328 Death of Hanbali jurist and theologian Ibn Taymiyya.

1333–1354 Construction of the Alhambra in Granada, Spain.

1361–1389 Rule of Ottoman Murad I, who takes title sultan. Expansion into Anatolia and Balkans.

1395–1400 Conquest of western Persia and Iraq by Timur (Tamerlane).

1396 Ottoman victory over Byzantines at Battle of Nicopolis.

1398–1399 Timur sacks Delhi, conquers north India. Delhi sultanate ends.

1450–1459 Muslim states established in Arakan in Burma (Myanamar).

1453 Ottoman conquest of Constantinople; city renamed Istanbul.

1458–1519 The Portuguese navy seizes ports in Morocco.

1479 Mosque of Demak is built in Indonesia.

1481 Establishment of the Inquisition in Spain.

1492 Ferdinand and Isabella end Muslim rule in Granada. Columbus sets out on his voyage, leading him to the New World.

1497 Babur, founder of the Moghul empire, captures Samarkand.

1498 The east African Arab Ibn Majid guides Vasco da Gama across the Indian Ocean to India.

1498–1509 The Portuguese gain trade supremacy in Indian Ocean, displacing Muslim control.

1500 Muhammad Shaybani, Khan of Siberian Mongol state, overcomes Timurids and establishes Ozbeg dynasty in Transoxiana and Khwarazm. Muslim sultanates replace Hindu rulers in Sumatra and Java.

1501–1524 Shah Ismail establishes the Safavid dynasty in Azerbaijan, Iran, and Mesopotamia. Shia Twelver School of thought and practice becomes dominant.

1506–1603 Ahmad Gran challenges Christian Ethiopia. Muslims conquer Nubia.

1520–1566 Rule of Sultan Suleyman the Magnificent. Height of Ottoman power.

1521 Belgrade falls to Ottomans.

1526 Babur establishes Mughal dynasty in India. Ottomans control Hungary.

1530 Islam spreads to Java, the Moluccas and Borneo. Beginning of the Muslim kingdom of Aceh in Sumatra.

1600–1850 Forced migration of hundreds of thousands of Africans as slaves to the Americas, including Mande and Wolof-speaking Muslims from West Africa.

1538 The Ottomans defeat the Holy League at the Battle of Preveza by taking naval control of Mediterranean.

1542 Francis Xavier, the Jesuit, arrives in India.

1556–1605 Mughal Emperor Akbar in Delhi; the flowering of Mughal culture.

1562 Spain seizes the Philippines, including Muslim principalities in Mindanao.

1568 Alpujarra uprising of the Moriscos in Spain.

1570–1619 King Idris Aloma makes Kanem-Bornu a power in the central Sahara. Songhai empire of Gao weakened by antipathy between Muslims and followers of traditional African religions.

1596 Shah Abbas establishes Isfahan as Safavid capital.

1613–1646 Sultan Agung controls most of Java from Mataram; Islamization of South East Asia continues.

1623–1654 Shah Jahan builds the Taj Mahal at Agra.

1633 The ruler of Muslim state in Java takes the title of Sultan.

1638 Murad IV retakes Baghdad from Safavids. Treaty of Qasr-i Shirin turns Caucasus and Azerbaijan over to Safavids. Boundaries are established between the two empires. New Moghal capital built at Delhi (Shahjahanabad).

1640 Death of Mulla Sadra (Sadr al-Din), Shia theologian and philosopher in Iran. Great age of Sufism in Aceh in Sumatra.

1641 The Dutch conquer Malacca in Southeast Asia.

1642 Chinese Muslim scholar Wang Tai-Yu publishes the *Cheng Chiao Chen Chuan* (*Veritable Explanation of True Religion*) expressing common ground between Muslim and Confucian belief.

1644 The Manchu dynasty alienates Chinese Muslims.

1680 The first Fulani war results in establishment of Islamic state in Bornu.

1684 The Holy Alliance (Austria, Poland, Venice, and Papacy) formed against Ottomans.

1694 The French gain concessions in North Africa.

1727 First Ottoman printing press.

1730–1740 Climax of campaign of conversion of Muslims to orthodox Christianity started under Peter the Great. Mosques and Quranic schools in Central Asia destroyed.

1739 Peace of Belgrade concludes Ottoman war with Austria and Russia; Ottomans receive northern Siberia and Belgrade and regain supremacy in Black Sea region.

1746 Beginning of Wahhabi reform movement in Arabia through alliance of Muhammad ibn Abd al-Wahhab and tribal chief Muhammad ibn Saud.

1747 Nadir Shah is murdered by Afshar and Qajar leaders. Ahmad Shah establishes autonomous rule in Afghanistan.

1750–1779 Muhammad Karim Khan Zand of Shiraz becomes ruler of Persia. England establishes trade with Persia.

1758–1760 Muslims rebel against Chinese Emperor. China dominates Tarim Basin in Northwest China.

1770 The Ottoman fleet is destroyed by Russians in Battle of Cheshme.

1776 The third Fulani war establishes Islam in Futa Toro.

1783 Catherine II imposes Russian rule over Crimean Tartars.

1791 Death of Ma (Muhammad) Ming-hsin, founder of the "New Sect" in China.

1794–1924 The Qajar dynasty in Shiraz replaces the Zand dynasty and extends rule throughout Persia.

1798–1801 The French enter Egypt under Napoleon Bonaparte. England and Russia forge alliance with Ottomans.

1799–1701 The French are forced out of Egypt by the Ottomans under Muhammad Ali.

1800 Fath Ali Shah signs treaty with British East India Company against France and Afghanistan. The Dutch control Islamic sultanates on Java and Sumatra.

1803 Delhi falls to the British. Wahhabis seize control of Mecca and Medina in Arabia.

1804 Usuman dan Fodio, supported by Fulani and Hausa, forms sultanate of Sokoto.

1805–1848 Muhammad Ali initiates struggle for Egyptian independence by seizing power and gaining Ottoman recognition as governor. Reform measures begin.

1818 British rule is established throughout India.

1821 First government printing press in Egypt. Muslims revolt in Xinkiang, China.

1823 Founding of Khartoum, capital of Sudan.

1830 France occupies Algeria.

1833 Muhammad Ali al-Sanusi founds Sanusiyya movement in Libya. Ottoman-Russian Treaty of Hunkar Iskelesi.

1839–1861 Period of reforms in Ottoman Empire.

1842 British are forced out of Afghanistan by Amir Dost Muhammad. Druze revolt in Lebanon.

1848–1850 The "Bab" Sayyid Ali Muhammad leads religious uprising in Persia until his execution by the government. Founding of the Babi sect, and the onset of the Bahai movement.

1853 The Tijaniyya Sufi tariqa spreads in West Africa.

1854 The Council of Tanzimat in Turkey. Ferdinand de Lesseps receives concession to build Suez Canal.

1856–1872 Ma T-hsin leads an independence movement among Chinese Muslims in Yunnan.

1857 The Indian Mutiny. Muslim rule ended by the onset of the British Raj.

1858 Construction of Suez Canal begins.

1861 First modern constitution enacted by a Muslim country is promulgated by Muhammad al-Sadiq in Tunisia. Creation of the Majlis-i ahkam-i adliyye, an Ottoman legislative body.

1863–1893 Tijani Muslim Empire from Niger to Senegal.

1864 The independent Muslim kingdom of Xinjiang established in Northwest China.

1867 Dar al-Ulum founded at Deoband in British India.

1869 Opening of the Suez Canal.

1870 The "Mahdi" appears in the Sudan and initiates resistance to British rule.

1871–1879 Jamal al-Din al-Afghani initiates reform activity in Cairo.

1873–1910 Aceh war in Sumatra opposing Dutch expansion in Indonesia.

1875 Rebellions in Bulgaria, Bosnia, and Herzegovina.

1876 Sultan Abd al-Aziz is deposed in Turkey. Brief sultanate of Murad V (also deposed). Serbia and Montenegro declare war against the empire. Russia intercedes and forces armistice after Ottomans occupy Serbia. Constitution based on parliamentary government is promulgated for the Ottoman Empire.

1878 Uganda becomes the scene of intense rivalry among Catholic and Protestant Christian missions and Muslims for control and conversion of the Kabaka and his people.

1881 France occupies Tunisia.

1884 Afghani publishes *Al-Urwa al-Wuthqa* with Muhammad Abduh in Paris, a journal of modern Muslim reform and political opinion.

1885 Muhammad al-Mahdi initiates a reform movement in the Sudan and captures Khartoum from the British. Sultan Muhammad Shah becomes forty-eight Imam of the Shia Ismailis.

1891 Mascat and Oman in the Persian Gulf become British protectorates.

1891–1892 Shia scholars join in tobacco revolts in Iran, resulting in cancellation of British concession.

1892–1905 Muhammad Abduh initiates reforms in Cairo and at al-Azhar.

1898 Lord Kitchener defeats Muslim resistance movement in Sudan. *Al-Manar* is published in Cairo, as a journal of reforming Muslim opinion.

1900 Britain colonizes Nigeria, including Sokoto, the Muslim kingdom in the North.

1900–1908 Construction of the Hijaz railway to Mecca.

1905–1906 Revolution in Iran. Parliamentary government with constitution is instituted. The Sinai peninsula in Egypt is ceded to Britain.

1906 Formation of the Muslim League in India to seek political rights for Muslims.

1907 Revolution in Iran fails and it is divided between Russian and British spheres of influence. The Ottoman Society for Freedom becomes active as a revolutionary movement.

1908 Shah Muhammad Ali dissolves parliament and executes opposition leaders. "Young Turks" lead rebellion. Turkish nationalism is advocated by Ziya Gokalp. Bulgaria declares independence. Austria annexes Bosnia and Herzegovina.

1908–1909 Civil war in Iran forces the Shah to flee to Russia.

1909 Deposition of Sultan Abd al-Hamid of Turkey.

1909 Discovery of oil in Iran leads to creation of the Anglo-Persian Oil Company.

1912 Formation of the Islamic League in Southeast Asia. Emergence of the Muhammadiyya reform movement in Indonesia.

1912–1913 First Balkan war. Ottomans lose Adrianople and Thessalonika. France and Spain form protectorates in Morocco.

1914–1918 First World War. Ottomans are allied with Germany and Austria. Egypt is made a British protectorate.

1916 Sykes-Picot delimits English and French interests in the Middle East. Osmania College established in Hyderabad, India.

1916–1918 Arabs under the Sharif of Mecca revolt against Ottoman rule.

1917 Balfour Declaration. Russians withdraw from Iran. Ottomans leave Iraq after defeat by the British. Russian revolution begins. Emir of Bukhara issues manifesto promising extensive reform and freedoms.

1918 T. E. Lawrence leads a Arab army against Ottoman rule. Damascus falls. Dismissal and flight of leader of the Young Turks, opens straits, leading to the occupation of Istanbul and parts of Anatolia by the Allies. Independence of the Yemen; constitution creates a kingdom.

1919 Sad Zaghlul, leader of the Wafd party for Egyptian independence is arrested by the British; popular rebellion is quashed by occupation troops.

1919–1922 After Greek invasion of Anatolia, gathering of nationalistic fighting forces under Mustafa Kemal (Ataturk); Turkish war of independence against the Allies.

1920 Conference of the League of Nations declares Syria and Lebanon a French mandate; France occupies Damascus and overthrows Faysal's government. Independence for Hijaz. Bolshevik's occupy Rasht in Iran. Emirate of Bukhara comes to an end. Peoples Republic of Bukhara declared. Soviet Republic of Gilan is proclaimed. Basmachi Muslim resistance group in Central Asia are driven by Russians into rural areas and eventually crushed.

1921 Iraq becomes a constitutional monarchy under Hashimite Faysal ibn Husayn. Abd Allah ibn Husayn is made King of Transjordan. Turks repel Greek invasion at battle on the Sakaarya. Turkish national assembly proclaims Constitution in Ankara. Coup d'etat in Iran by Reza Khan, officer of the Cossack Brigade.

1922 The Ottoman sultanate is abolished by Mustafa Kemal Ataturk. Independent Kingdom of Egypt is formed with Ahmad Fuad I as king under British control. Kurds revolt in Iraq.

1923 Proclamation of Egyptian constitution. Proclamation of the Turkish Republic with Mustafa Kemal Ataturk as President. Transjordan is recognized as autonomous state under British mandate. Reza Khan becomes prime minister in Iran.

1924 Ibn Saud conquers the Hijaz, forcing out Sharif Husayn and establishing a Wahhabi state. The caliphate is abolished in Turkey. Turkey adopts civil law. Four closely controlled republics created by the Soviet Union in Central Asia: Uzbekistan, Turkmenistan, Kazakhstan, and Kirghizia.

1925–1941 Reza Khan ends the Qajar dynasty in Iran, proclaiming himself shah and establishing the Pahlavi dynasty.

1926 Abd al-Aziz ibn Saud conquers Mecca and is proclaimed king of the Najd and Hijaz. The Republic of Lebanon is created under French mandate.

1927 Mawlana Muhammad Ilyas founds the Tablighi movement in India.

1928 Turkey becomes a secular state. The Latin alphabet replaces Arabic script. The Muslim Brotherhood is founded by Hasan al-Banna in Egypt.

1935 Iran becomes the official name of Persia. University of Tehran is founded. The Shah undertakes policies of modernization and limits authority of religious leaders.

1938 Formation of Partai Islam Indonesia.

1939–1945 World War II.

1941 Formal removal of British-French mandate and proclamation of the Republic of Syria. Reza Shah is forced to abdicate in favor of his son Muhammad Reza Shah. Abu Ala Mawdudi founds the Jamat-i-Islami in India.

1942–1945 Japanese occupation of Indonesia.

1945 The Arab League is founded. The Eastern Turkestan Republic free of Chinese control is proclaimed in Xinkiang. Proclamation of Indonesia independence. World War II ends.

1946 Jordan, Lebanon, and Syria become independent. The British and French troops withdraw. Establishment of the Kingdom of Jordan. Albania is declared a republic under a Communist government.

1947 Formation of the Muslim state of Pakistan after partition of British India. Violence mars independence as war breaks out between India and Pakistan.

1949 End of the British Palestine mandate; the United Nations sanctions partition of the country and establishment of the State of Israel. First Arab-Israeli war.

1949 Indonesia becomes independent. Assassination of Hasan al-Banna, founder of the Muslim Brotherhood. Communists triumph in China.

1951 The Kingdom of Libya becomes independent.

1952 Revolution in Egypt deposes King Faruq. Constitutional monarchy is established in Jordan.

1953 Egypt is declared a republic by Colonel Gamal Abdul Nasser after a military coup. A Western-led coup deposes Musaddeq in Iran and returns the Shah to power. Death of King Abd al-Aziz ibn Saud of Saudi Arabia.

1954 Tunisia wins autonomy from France. Algeria begins war of independence against France.

1955 The Xinjiang Uighur Autonomous region is created within the Peoples Republic of China.

1956 The Kingdom of Morocco becomes independent under Muhammad V. Tunisia becomes independent. Nasser nationalizes the Suez Canal.

1957 The Bey is deposed and Tunisia becomes a republic under President Bourguiba. Malaysia becomes independent. The Islamic Dawa Party is established in Iraq led by Ayatollah Muhammad Baqir al-Sadr. Karim Aga Khan becomes imam of the Ismailis.

1959 Abd al-Karim Qasim leads revolution in Iraq, toppling the monarchy and establishing a republic.

1958–1964 Strong anti-religious campaigns are inacted in the Soviet Union under Kruschev.

1962 Algeria wins independence under President Ben Bella. Morocco adopts constitution. Creation of the Yemen Arab Republic.

1963 Civil war in Cyprus.

1965 Assassination of Malcolm X in New York.

1966–1976 During the Cultural Revolution in China, mosques as well as other religious buildings, were defaced and practice of the faith diminished.

1967 Proclamation of the Peoples Republic of South Yemen. Second Arab-Israeli war results in Jerusalem coming under Israeli control. Mosques and churches are closed in Albania as all forms of public worship are banned by the Communist Party.

1969 Colonel Muammar al-Qadhafi leads a military coup in Libya; end of the monarchy of King Idris.

1971 Pakistani civil war results in secession of eastern half and the establishment of Bangladesh.

1973 King Zahir Shah of Afghanistan is overthrown. Third Arab-Israeli war. Israel continues to occupy the Sinai, the Golan Heights, and the West Bank.

1974 Turkish intervention in Cyprus leads to the emergence of an autonomous Turkish-Cypriot zone.

1975 Death of Elijah Muhammad. Wallace Warith Deen Muhammad becomes leader of the African American Muslim community. Civil war begins in Lebanon.

1977 Establishment of the Aga Khan Award for Architecture to foster and promote a better built environment in the Muslim world.

1978 Disappearance of Imam Musa Sadr, religious leader of Lebanese Shia and founder of Amal. Mosques in China are reopened as climate of religious tolerance returns.

1979 Iranian revolution deposes Shah Reza Pahlavi; proclamation of the Islamic Republic of Iran. Soviet invasion of Afghanistan. A Muslim resistance movement, the Mujahidin, is organized and thousands of Afghanis flee to Pakistan as refugees. The Grand Mosque of Mecca is captured and held for two weeks until the capture and execution of the dissidents. General reopening of places of worship, including many mosques in China.

1980–1988 Iran-Iraq War.

1981 Assassination of Egyptian President Anwar Sadat.

1983 Institute of Muslim Minority Affairs Incorporated in London. Founding of International Islamic University in Malaysia..

1985 Military coup in Sudan.

1987 The Muslim Brotherhood in Egypt forms a coalition known as the Islamic Alliance that wins several seats in Parliament.

1988 Military coup deposes Bourguiba in Tunisia. The Intifada movement begins among Palestinians. Publication of Salman Rushdie's *Satanic Verses* leads to violent protests. A fatwa is issued by the Ayatollah denouncing him as an apostate.

1989 Soviet troops withdraw from Afghanistan. Struggle for power among various groups begins. Death of Ayatollah Khomeini. Civil war begins in Somalia. The Front Islamique du Salut (FIS), also known as the Islamic Salvation Front, an Algerian Muslim movement is legalized.

1990–1991 Saddam Hussain, Iraqi dictator, annexes the Kingdom of Kuwait. Iraqi forces are forced out by a Muslim/Western coalition led by the United States. Continuing state of tension in Iraq between the government, the Shia community, and the Kurdish population, who are forced to become refugees.

1991 The collapse of Communist power and the dismantling of the Soviet Union leads to the emergence of independent Muslim republics in Central Asia which, however, remain linked to the newly established Commonwealth of Independent States. They are Azerbaijan, Kazakhstan, Kyrghiztan, Tajikistan, Turkemenistan and Uzbekistan.

1992 Kurds revolt in Iraq. Arab-Israeli peace talks begin. Constitutional government is suspended in Algeria because of the growing power of Muslim parties, which are all banned. Persecuted Muslims in Burma (Myanmar) flee to Bangladesh. Bosnia-Herzogivina, a newly created state in former Yugoslavia, declares its independence. Serbian forces surround and attack the capital Sarajevo and initiate a campaign of "ethnic cleansing" against the Muslims and Croats. Somalia and Sudan face severe draught and famine. Death of Ayatollah Khoi, considered senior juridical authority of majority of Twelver Shia Muslims. Restoration work on the Dome of the Rock in Jerusalem begins.

1993– War between Bosnia, Croatia and Serbia continues. International peace efforts have sporadic success and are continuously violated by Serbs who continue attacks on Sarajevo and other Bosnian Muslim enclaves, leading to a major refugee problem and ethnic cleansing. Peace accord signed in Washington between Israel and the Palestine Liberation Organization. Allies consisting of Western powers and several Middle Eastern and Gulf States launched an attack on Iraq to force withdrawal of Iraqi troops who had invaded Kuwait. Iraq eventually withdrew in the face of massive air and ground offensive. Benazir Bhutto returned as Prime Minister of Pakistan following her party's victory in national elections.

Presidential Elections in Nigeria were annulled and military rule was established by General Sami Abacha, drawing international criticism and vehement opposition from pro-democracy forces. Elections were held to Jordan's House of Representatives. New Lebanese Government was announced. A Consultative Council was established in Saudi Arabia. A cease fire and agreement was signed between the Philippine Government and the Muslim secessionist group, the Moro National Liberation Front.

1994 There was a continuing deterioration of the political and social situation in Algeria leading to increased violence under a military backed government. Most of the opposition led by "Islamist" groups went underground. Abdou Diouf was re-elected President of Senegal after election marked by sporadic violence. Senegal, Mali and Mauritania signed agreement to reduce border conflicts. In spite of continuing negotiations, no peace settlement could be reached among factions in Somalia, and the threat of famine continued to loom in parts of the country. Muslim citizens participated in the first all race democratic elections in South Africa which led to the election of Nelson Mandela to the Presidency at the head of the African National Congress. Fighting between North and South continued in the Sudan, and peace talks and efforts at reconciliation proved fruitless. Fighting erupted between North and South Yemen, but a cease fire took place and a new coalition government was formed. Israel and Jordan signed a joint declaration formally ending the State of was between them followed by the signing of a comprehensive peace treaty. United Nations Population Council Conference was held in Cairo. The Sultan Tuanku Abdul Rahman succeeded to the throne of Malaysia for a five-year period, continuing a tradition of symbolic rule. The controversial Bangla Deshi feminist author, Taslima Nasreen, left the country secretly for exile in Sweden. First-ever elections to a new Northern Areas Council in Pakistan took place. A new Department of Jammu and Kashmir Affairs was established by the Government of India to deal with ongoing sectarian problems which have become worse after the destruction of an important Muslim mausoleum in Kashmir.

Distribution of Muslim Populations by Nation-State

Afghanistan
Area: 250,001 sq. mi. (647,500 sq. km.)
Population: 16.4 million (1991 estimates)
Percent Muslim: 100% More than 75% are Sunnis, the remainder are Shia.
Official language: Pashtu and Dari
Capital: Kabul

Albania
Area: 11,100 sq. mi. (28,750 sq. km.)
Population: 2.5 million (1994 estimate)
Percent Muslim: 65%
Official language: Albanian
Capital: Tirana

Algeria
Area: 919,595 sq. mi. (2,381,740 sq. km.)
Population: 27.9 million (1994 estimate)
Percent Muslim: Over 99%
Official Language: Arabic
Capital: Algiers

Azerbaijan
Area: 33,436 sq. mi. (86,600 sq. km.)
Population: 7.4 million (1992 estimates)
Percent Muslim: 87%; 70% are Shia and the remainder are Sunnis.
Official language: Azerbaijani
Capital: Baku

Bahrain
Area: 239 sq. mi. (620 sq. km.)
Population: 508,000 (1991 census)
Percent Muslim: All indigenous Bahrainis are Muslims. Over 70% are Shia and approximately 30% are Sunnis.
Official language: Arabic
Capital: Manama

Bangladesh
Area: 55,599 sq. mi. (144,000 sq. km.)
Population: 112.8 million (1992 estimate)
Percent Muslim: 87% of Bengalis are Muslims, making Bangledesh the third largest Muslim country after Indonesia and Pakistan.
Official langauage: Bengali
Capital: Dhaka (formerly Dacca)

Benin
Area: 43,483 sq. mi. (112,620 sq. km.)
Population: 5.3 million (1994 estimate)
Percent Muslim: 13-15%
Official language: French
Capital: Porto-Novo

Bosnia-Herzegovina
Area: 19,781 sq. mi. (51,233 sq. km.)
Population: 4.6 million (1993 estimate)
Percent Muslim: 40%
Official language: Serbo-Croatian
Capital: Sarajevo

Brunei Darussalam
Area: 2,228 sq. mi. (5,770 sq. km.)
Population: 260,482 (1991 estimate)
Percent Muslim: 63%
Official language: Malay and English
Capital: Bandar Seri Begawan

Bulgaria
Area: 42,823 sq. mi. (110,901 sq. km.)
Population: 8.9 million (1994 estimate)
Percent Muslim: 9-13%
Official language: Bulgarian
Capital: Sofia

Burkina Faso
Area: 105,869 sq. mi. (274,200 sq. km.)
Population: 10.2 million (1994 estimate)
Percent Muslim: 25%
Official language: French (Indigenous language Moré spoken by 55% of the population)
Capital: Ougadougou

Cameroon
Area: 183,568 sq. mi. (475,440 sq. km.)
Population: 12.3 million (1994 estimate)
Percent Muslim: 25%
Official language: French and English
Capital: Yaoundé

Canada
Area: 3,851,808 sq. mi. (9,976,140 sq. km.)
Population: 28.5 million (1993 estimate)
Percent Muslim: Less than 3%
Official language: French and English
Capital: Ottawa

Central African Republic
Area: 240,535 sq. mi. (622,980 sq. km.)
Population: 3.1 million (1994 estimate)
Percent Muslim: 5%, primarily in the north.
Official language: French is the official language while Sango which is spoken by the majority is the national language.
Capital: Bangui

Chad
Area: 495,755 sq. mi. (1,284,000, sq. km.)
Population: 6.2 million (1993 census)
Percent Muslim: 44%
Official language: French and Arabic
Capital: N'Djamena (Formerly Fort-Lamy)

China
Area: 3,646,448 sq. mi. (9,444,292 sq. km.)
Population: 1.1 billion
Percent Muslim: 5% (1990 estimate)
Official language: Mandarin Chinese
Capital: Beijing

Comoros
Area: 838 sq. mi. (2,170 sq. km.)
Population: 530,000
Percent Muslim: Almost 100%
Official language: French and Arabic
Capital: Moroni

Cote d'Ivoire
Area: 124,502 sq. mi. (322,460 sq. km.)
Population: 14.5 million (1994 estimate)

Percent Muslim: 24%
Official language: French
Capital: Yamoussoukro

Cyprus
Area: 3,571 sq. mi. (9,250 sq. km.)
Population: 725,000 (1992 estimate)
Percent Muslim: 18.7%
Official language: Greek and Turkish
Capital: Nicosia

Djibouti
Area: 8,494 sq. mi. (22,000 sq. km.)
Population: 542,000 (1991 estimate)
Percent Muslim: 94% Primarily Sunni with a small Shia minority
Official language: French and English. Somali and Afar are widely spoken.
Capital: Djibouti

Egypt
Area: 386,662 sq. mi. (1,001,450 sq. km.)
Population: 58.2 million (1994 estimate)
Percent Muslim: 90%
Official language: Arabic
Capital: Cairo

Eritrea
Area: 46,842 sq. mi. (121,930 sq. km.)
Population: 2.6 million (1992 non-governmental estimate)
Percent Muslim: 50%
Official language: No official language has been designated. Arabic and Tigrinya are the working languages of the Eritrean government.
Capital: Asmara

Ethiopia
Area: 435,186 sq. mi. (1,127,127 sq. km.)
Population: 55 million (1994 estimate)
Percent Muslim: 45%
Official language: Amharic
Capital: Addis Ababa

France
Area: 211,209 sq. mi. (547,030 sq. km.
Population: 56.6 million (1990 census)
Percent Muslim: 1.2%
Official language: French
Capital: Paris

The Gambia
Area: 4,363 sq. mi. (11,300 sq. km.)
Population: 1.0 million (1993 census)

Percent Muslim: 85%
Official language: English; principal vernaculars are
   Wolof and Mandinka
Capital: Banjul (formerly Bathurst)

Georgia
Area: 26,911 sq. mi. (69,700 sq. km.)
Population: 5.4 million (1989 census)
Percent Muslim: 11%
Official language: Georgian
Capital: T'bilisi

Germany
Area: 137,804 sq. mi. (356,910 sq. km.)
Population: 80.2 million (1991 census)
Percent Muslim: 3%
Official language: German
Capital: Berlin

Ghana
Area: 92,100 sq. mi. (238,540 sq. km.)
Population: 17.1 million (1994 estimate)
Percent Muslim: 12%
Official language: English
Capital: Accra

Guinea
Area: 94,927 sq. mi. (245,860 sq. km.)
Population: 7.7 million (1995 estimate)
Percent Muslim: 90%
Official language: French
Capital: Conakry

Guinea-Bissau
Area: 13,946 sq. mi. (36,120 sq. km.)
Population: 1.1 million (1994 census)
Percent Muslim: 38%
Official language: Portugese is the official language.
   A Guinean "Crioulo" or Africanized version of
   Portugese is the lingua franca.
Capital: Bissau

Guyana
Area: 83,000 sq. mi. (214,970 sq. km.)
Population: 808,000 (1992 estimate)
Percent Muslim: 9%
Official language: English
Capital: Georgetown

India
Area: 1,269,345 sq. mi. (3,287,590 sq. km.)
Population: 919.1 million (1994 estimate)
Percent Muslim: 11%
Official language: Hindi and English
Capital: New Dehli

Indonesia
Area: 741,000 sq. mi. (1,919,440 sq. km.)
Population: 184.3 million (1992 estimate)
Percent Muslim: 87%
Official language: Bahasa Indonesia
Capital: Jakarta

Iran
Area: 636,296 sq. mi. (1,648,000 sq. km.)
Population: 59.8 million (1992 estimate)
Percent Muslim: 93.8%; Sunnis consitute about 6%.
Official language: Farsi
Capital: Tehran

Iraq
Area: 168,754 sq. mi. (437,072 sq. km.)
Population: 19.2 million (1992 estimate)
Percent Muslim: 95%; 60% Shia; 35% Sunni.
Official language: Arabic
Capital: Baghdad

Jordan
Area: 32,175 sq. mi. (83,335 sq. km.)
Population: 3.9 million (1992 estimate)
Percent Muslim: 92%
Official language: Arabic
Capital: Amman

Kazakhstan
Area: 1,049,155 sq. mi. (2,717,300 sq. km.)
Population: 17 million (1992 estimate)
Percent Muslim: 40%
Official language: Kazakh is the national language
   with Russian spoken widely by all ethnic groups.
Capital: Almaty

Kenya
Area: 224,962 sq. mi. (582,650 sq. km.)
Population: 27.8 million (1995 estimate)
Percent Muslim: 16%
Official language: Swahili and English
Capital: Nairobi

Kyrgystan
Area: 76,641 sq. mi. (198,500 sq. km.)
Population: 4.7 million (1995 estimate)
Percent Muslim: 52%
Official language: Kyrgyz
Capital: Bishkek

Kuwait
Area: 6,880 sq. mi. (17,820 sq. km.)
Population: 1.4 million (1994 census)
Percent Muslim: 90%; 63% Sunni and about 27% Shia.

Official language: Arabic
Capital: Kuwait City

Lebanon
Area: 4,015 sq. mi. (10,400 sq. km.)
Population: 2.8 million (1992 estimate)
Percent Muslim: 57% (including Druze)
Official language: Arabic; with French as a second
  language.
Capital: Beirut

Libya
Area: 679,362 sq. mi. (1,759,540 sq. km.)
Population: 4.7 million
Percent Muslim: 97%
Official language: Arabic
Capital: Tripoli

Madagascar
Area: 226,657 sq. mi. (587,040 sq. km.)
Population: 13.4 million (1994 estimate)
Percent Muslim: 1.7%
Official language: No official language is given.
  Principal languages are French and Malagasy.
Capital: Antananarivo

Malyasia
Area: 127,581 sq. mi. (329,750 sq. km.)
Population: 17.5 million (1991 estimate)
Percent Muslim: 53%
Official language: Bahasa Malaysia or Malay
Capital: Kuala Lumpur

Maldives
Area: 116 sq. mi. (300 sq. km.)
Population: 214,000 (1990 estimate)
Percent Muslim: 100%
Official language: Divehi
Capital: Malé

Mali
Area: 478,767 sq. mi. (1,240,000 sq. km.)
Population: 8.9 million (1994 estimate)
Percent Muslim: 80%
Official language: French
Capital: Bamako

Mauritania
Area: 397,955 sq. mi. (1,030,700 sq. km.)
Population: 2.1 million (1994 estimate)
Percent Muslim: 99%
Official language: Arabic, Wolof, Peular, Soninke are
  spoken in southern Mauritania and recognized as
  national languages.
Capital: Nouakchott

Mauritius
Area: 718 sq. mi. (1,860 sq. km.)
Population: 1.1 million (1994 census)
Percent Muslim: 17%
Official language: English
Capital: Port Louis

Mongolia
Area: 604,250 sq. mi. (1,565,000)
Population: 2.2 million (1992 estimate)
Percent Muslim: 4%
Official language: Khalka Mongolian
Capital: Ulaanbaatar

Morocco (including Western Sahara)
Area: 172,414 sq. mi. (446,550 sq. km.)
Population: 27.8 million (1994 estimate)
Percent Muslim: 99%
Official language: Arabic
Capital: Rabat

Myanmar (formerly Burma)
Area: 261,970 sq. mi. (678,500 sq. km.)
Population: 43.6 million (1992 estimate)
Percent Muslim: 4%; mostly of Pakistani extraction.
Official language: Burmese
Capital: Yangoon (formerly Rangoon)

Mozambique
Area: 309,496 sq. mi. (801,590 sq. km.)
Population: 16.3 million (1995 estimates)
Percent Muslim: 25%
Official language: Portuguese
Capital: Maputo (formerly Lauenco Marques)

Netherlands
Area: 14,413 sq. mi. (37,330 sq. km.)
Population: 15 million (1991 estimate)
Percent Muslim: 2%
Official language: Dutch
Capital: Constitutional *Capital:* Amsterdam
Seat of Government: The Hague

Niger
Area: 489,191 sq. mi. (1,267,000 sq. km.)
Population: 9 million (1994 estimates)
Percent Muslim: 88%
Official language: French; Hausa is also spoken all
  over the country as the language of trade.
Capital: Niamey

Nigeria
Area: 356,670 sq. mi. (923,770 sq. km.)
Population: 126 million (1995 census)

Percent Muslim: 48-50%
Official language: English, Hausa is spoken widely in the north and Yoruba in the south.
Capital: Abuja

Oman
Area: 82,031 sq. mi. (212,460 sq. km.)
Population: 2.0 million (1990 estimate)
Percent Muslim: 100%, Mostly Ibadi
Official language: Arabic
Capital: Muscat

Pakistan
Area: 310,403 sq. mi. (803,940 sq. km.)
Population: 125.2 million (1993 estimate)
Percent Muslim: 95%
Official language: Urdu
Capital: Islamabad

Philippines
Area: 115,831 sq. mi. (300,000 sq. km.)
Population: 60.5 million (1990 estimate)
Percent Muslim: 5%, primarily Sunni
Official language: Philipino; English
Capital: Manila

Qatar
Area: 4,247 sq. mi. (11,000 sq. km.)
Population: 486,000 (1990 estimate)
Percent Muslim: 99.9%
Official language: Arabic is the national language, but English is widely spoken and Farsi is used by smaller groups in Doha.
Capital: Doha

Russian Federation
Area: 6,592,771 sq. mi. (17,075,200 sq. km.)
Population: 148.6 million (1993 estimate)
Percent Muslim: 12%
Official language: Russian
Capital: Moscow

Saudi Arabia
Area: 756,985 sq. mi. (1,960,582 sq. km.)
Population: 16.9 million (1992 estimate)
Percent Muslim: 100%
Official language: Arabic
Capital: Riyadh

Senegal
Area: 75,749 sq. mi. (1,196,190 sq. km.)
Population: 8.3 million (1995 estimate)
Percent Muslim: 93%
Official language: French; Wolof is widely spoken.
Capital: Dakar

Sierra Leone
Area: 27,699 sq. mi. (71,740 sq. km.)
Population: 4.6 million (1994 estimate)
Percent Muslim: 40%
Official language: English; Krio, a creole language derived largely from English and African languages is the lingua franca.
Capital: Freetown

Singapore
Area: 244.2 sq. mi. (632.6 sq. km.)
Population: 2.8 million (1993 estimate)
Percent Muslim: 16%
Official language: Chinese (Mandarin dialect), Malay, English and Tamil.
Capital: Singapore

Somalia
Area: 246,202 sq. mi. (637,660, sq. km.)
Population: 7.4 million (1994 census)
Percent Muslim: 99%
Official language: Somali, Arabic and English
Capital: Mogadishu

Spain
Area: 194,885 sq. mi. (504,750 sq. km.)
Population: 39.4 million (1991 census)
Number of Muslims: Less than 1%
Official language: Spanish is the national language; Catalan, Basque, Galician, Bable and Valencian are also official in respective autonomous communities.
Capital: Madrid

Sudan
Area: 967,490 sq. mi. (2,505,810 sq. km.)
Population: 29.7 million (1994 estimate)
Percent Muslim: 70%
Official language: Arabic
Capital: Khartoum

Surinam
Area: 63,039 sq. mi. (163,270 sq. km.)
Population: 416,000 (1994 estimate)
Percent Muslim: 20-25%
Official language: Dutch; English is widely spoken.
Capital: Paramaribo

Syria
Area: 71,498 sq. mi. (185,180 sq. km.)
Population: 12.9 (1992 estimate)
Percent Muslim: 90%
Official language: Arabic
Capital: Damascus (Dimashq)

Tajikistan
Area: 55,251 sq. mi. (143,100 sq. km.)
Population: 6.1 million (1995 estimate)
Percent Muslim: 62%
Official language: Tajik (Persian)
Capital: Dushanbe

Tanzania (including Zanzibar)
Area: 364,901 sq. mi. (945,090 sq. km.)
Population: 29.7 million (1994 estimate)
Percent Muslim: 35%
Official language: Swahili (or Kiswahili) is the lingua
    franca. English and Swahili are the official languages.
Capital: Dar es Salaam

Thailand
Area: 198,456 sq. mi. (514,000 sq. km.)
Population: 56.3 million (1990 census)
Percent Muslim: 4%
Official language: Thai
Capital: Bangkok

Togo
Area: 21,927 sq. mi. (56,790 sq. km.)
Population: 4.2 million (1994 estimate)
Percent Muslim: 15%
Official language: French
Capital: Lome

Trinidad and Tobago
Area: 1,981 sq. mi. (5,130 sq. km.)
Population: 1.2 million (1990 census)
Percent Muslim: 6%
Official language: English
Capital: Port of Spain

Tunisia
Area: 63,170 sq. mi. (163,610 sq. km.)
Population: 8.7 million (1994 census)
Percent Muslim: 99%
Official language: Arabic
Capital: Tunis

Turkey
Area: 301,384 sq. mi. (780,580 sq. km.)
Population: 56.4 million (1990 census)
Percent Muslim: 99%; mostly Sunni, but substantial
    Shia minority exists.
Official language: Turkish
Capital: Ankara

Turkmenistan
Area: 188,456 sq. mi. (488,100 sq. km.)
Population: 4 million (1995 census)

Percent Muslim: 72%
Official language: Turkmen is Mandatory in schools.
    Russian continues in use in government and busi-
    ness.
Capital: Ashgabat

Uganda
Area: 91,136 sq. mi. (236,040 sq. km.)
Population: 20.8 million (1995 estimate)
Percent Muslim: 6%
Official language: English
Capital: Kampala

United Arab Emirates
Area: 29,182 sq. mi. (75,581 sq. km.)
Population: 1.9 million (1991 estimate)
Percent Muslim: 100%
Official language: Arabic; English is widely used in
    business.
Capital: Abu Dhabi

United Kingdom
Area: 94,526 sq. mi. (244,820 sq. km.)
Population: 97.9 million (1994 census)
Percent Muslim: 2%
Official language: English
Capital: London

United States
Area: 3,618,773 sq. mi. (9,372,607 sq. km.)
Population: 248.7 million (1990 estimate)
Percent Muslim: 3%
Official langauage: English
Capital: Washington, D.C.

Uzbekistan
Area: 172,742 sq. mi. (447,400 sq. km.)
Population: 23.0 million (1995 estimate)
Percent Muslim: 75%
Official language: Uzbek
Capital: Tashkent

Yemen
Area: 203,850 sq. mi. (527,970 sq. km.)
Population: 11.4 million (1995 estimate)
Percent Muslim: 100%, Zaydi Shia majority
Official language: Arabic
Capital: Sana

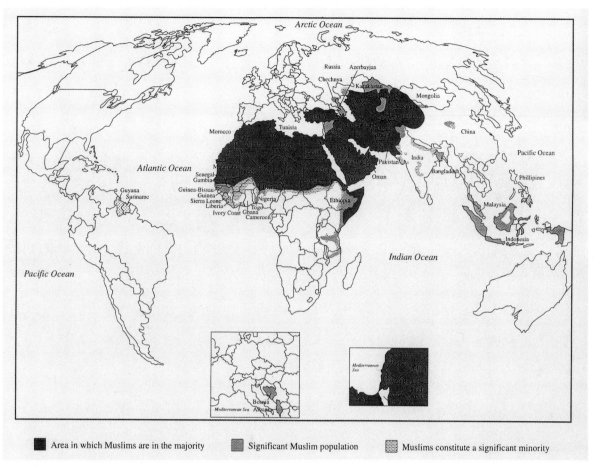

Muslim Population Distribution by Nation-State.

References

The Europa World Year Book. London, England: Europa Publications Ltd., 1994.

Shaykh, Farzana, ed. *Islam and Islamic Groups: A Worldwide Reference Guide.* Longman: Haslow (U.K.), 1992.

Worldmark Encyclopedia of the Nations. Detroit: Gale Research, 1995

Razia Jinha Nanji

Part I:

The Beginnings and Foundations of Islam

1

The Prophet, the Revelation, and the Founding of Islam

◆ The Founding of Islam ◆ The Quranic Revelation
◆ Foundational Concepts ◆ Practices of the Faith

The first Muslim community emerged in Arabia in the seventh century. This community arose in a region dominated by ancient civilizations and empires: to the east of Arabia, where the Tigris and the Euphrates Rivers flow, was the center of what had been the ancient Mesopotamian culture; the region of the Persian Gulf that bordered on Persia had been another major center of civilization; neighboring Egypt, separated from Arabia by the Red Sea, also had a long history of culture. In the seventh century, Byzantium (the Eastern Roman and Orthodox Christian Empire) and the Sassanian Kingdom (Iranian and Zoroastrian) dominated like two super-powers exerting their influence on the many small states and kingdoms in the region, exercising their influence and controlling trade while using the Arabian peninsula as a buffer in their conflict for power against each other.

◆ THE FOUNDING OF ISLAM

North and south of Arabia there had been a history of culture and local rule, a tradition of agriculture and trade and contact with the major civilizations and religions of the Mediterranean and the Near East. The Arab kingdom known as Hira had been a satellite state under Sassanian influence. In south Arabia, Byzantine influence had created the presence of Christian communities. The Byzantine army also recruited soldiers and militias from local groups to defend their frontier, the most well-known being an Arab group called the Ghassanids.

The Northwestern area of the Arabian Peninsula, known as the Hijaz, meaning the barrier, separates the north from the south and the low-lying region near the

Red Sea from the higher reaches of the interior. Its major center was the town of Mecca, a community made-up primarily of Bedouins, who depended on commerce and on the caravans that stopped there while traveling the great trade routes that connected the region with and to the outside world. A major source of prestige for Mecca during pre-Islamic times was the presence of the ancient shrine, the Kaba. A number of commemorative events, including fairs and festivals, took place in Mecca and made it a trading center. Mecca was also cultural nexus for the various Arab groups, the wealthiest of whom belonged to the family of the Quraysh who controlled affairs in the town and acted as custodians of the Kaba.

The Hijaz was by no means a complete backwater, surrounded as it was by regions rich in culture history and military tradition; however, it was not united. Although the people of the region perceived themselves to be a people with a common ancestral and ethnic tradition, bound up with strong loyalties to their land and their local histories, they were in constant conflict with each other.

Muhammad's Birth and Early Life

In Muslim tradition, the period before the coming of Islam, is referred to as *jahilliya*, the age of ignorance. The event that transformed it and gave it true historical significance was the life and prophetic mission of Muhammad, who according to Muslim historical sources was born around 570 in Mecca. This year is also known as the "Year of the Elephant," because an army led by a general riding an elephant attempted to invade Mecca and was driven away, according to tradition, by a miraculous natural catastrophe that saved the city. The year is thus considered doubly auspicious.

Quran scholar with assistant, Al Azhar University mosque.

Comparatively little is known about Muhammad's early years. He was an orphan, his father having died before he was born. His mother and grandfather, in whose house he was raised, both died before he had turned eight. His uncle, Abu Talib, became his guardian. He trained Muhammad in the family business, eventually taking him on trading missions along the caravan routes. As his experience grew he took on greater responsibility and earned a reputation for being an able businessman and a trustworthy and honest member of one of Mecca's leading families.

By the age of twenty-five, Muhammad was approached to manage the caravans and business of a widow, Khadija. Her trust and reliance in him grew into admiration and affection. They married, thus establishing Muhammad further as an important and integral member of the society and community of merchants in Mecca.

Muhammad, the Messenger

While he was a good husband and father to his children and an active member of the Meccan merchant community, Muhammad also was concerned about the moral and spiritual condition of his people. He occasionally sought moments of introspection and contemplation by retreating to a cave on Mount Hira; Arab society contained individuals, called *hanifs*, meaning pure ones, people of upright nature who rejected traditional practices, adhered to a belief in monotheism, and who often sought retreat from society to cultivate their own spiritual lives.

In the year 610, Muhammad's spiritual retreats culminated in a profound experience that included a vision and a voice. The message delivered to him was,

> Recite! In the name of your Lord who has created, created a human being from a clot of blood. Recite! For your Lord is generous, teaching by the pen, teaching humanity what it does not yet know. (Quran, sura 96)

He returned home to his wife, moved but troubled. She comforted him, believing in the truth of his experience. In time it became clear that Muhammad had experienced a deep and transforming awareness of God.

This event is believed to be the first revelation of Islam and marks the beginning of the process, culminating in the collected scripture, the Quran, twenty-two years later. Khadija was the first to believe in Muhammad and supported him as he struggled through those early periods of profound spiritual transformation. In time he came to recognize the role of this revelatory experience that summoned him to be a messenger, and to proclaim the revealed message to his people. He understood his own mission to be parallel to that of the ancient prophets, proclaiming the divine message and alerting his people to God's word.

Soon after these events, strengthened by Khadija's support, he conveyed the message to members of his immediate family, including his cousin Ali, the son of his uncle Abu Talib. Among others who were converted during this time were his adopted son Zayd (whom Muhammad had freed from slavery) and Abu Bakr, a future leader of the community.

He soon began to deliver his message, preaching publicly and reciting to the people the verses of the Quran revealed to him. He asked them to submit to One God, Allah, and to forsake their traditions of polytheism. He also urged them to be compassionate and caring, to share their wealth, and exercise good stewardship by paying attention to the poor and the disadvantaged, reminding them of the judgement to come after death. Most Meccans responded with some apprehension; they were astonished that a trusted and respected fellow citizen would turn on their long held beliefs and practices and claim to be the recipient of divine revelation. Some thought him to be affected with temporary madness or a possessed poet. However, Muhammad persisted, preaching openly, with increased fervor.

His message focussed on Allah's merciful nature:

We have sent you to a people, before whom many others have passed away so that you may transmit to them what We have revealed to you. Do they not believe in the Merciful God? Say to them: 'He is my Lord, there is no god but He, in Him do I trust and to Him do I turn.' (Quran 13:30)

Allah was described as the unique, singular, and majestic lord of the day of judgement. Idol worship and traditional Arab religious practices were denounced; people were urged to have faith, to pray, and to exercise justice and morality in human affairs. The earlier themes in Muhammad's message were a denunciation of the materialism and chauvinism prevalent in Meccan society and among the Bedouins of the desert. His call was for people to accept divine governance of all creation and of human history.

Muhammad also urged the people to use their reason to reflect on signs in the universe that they might understand that in addition to achieving material goals, human life also had a higher moral and spiritual purpose.

Meccan Opposition to Muhammad's Message

As Muhammad's public preaching increased in intensity and boldness, representatives of tradition and the local hierarchy began mount opposition. Since Muhammad belonged to the same tribe as the ruling merchants, the Quraysh, an attempt was made through his uncle, Abu Talib, to exert pressure on him to desist from preaching; they also attempted to bribe Muhammad by offering him a more important role in the affairs of the city. He did not relent. In fact, by this time, a small band of followers had grown around Muhammad, and they often met and prayed together. When efforts to stop Muhammad had failed, the Meccan leaders began to persecute him along with his followers. They incited people to ostracize them, to boycott those who had become Muslim and their families, and even to physically harm them. Muhammad became concerned about the safety of his followers and sent some of them by ship across the Red Sea to seek refuge at the court of the Christian king, the Negus, of Abyssinia. The Meccans sent envoys to the king to have the followers extradited but he refused, granting them his protection.

Muhammad remained in Mecca with some of his followers, continuing to preach in the face of hostile opposition. During this time he won an important convert, Umar al-Khattab, who was to become a future leader of Muslims. Provoked, the Quraysh now turned to a total boycott, hoping in this way to estrange Muhammad from his followers. Though it was not totally successful, the boycott caused great economic hardship to Muhammad, his family, and followers.

In the year 619, Muhammad lost two of his closest supporters, his wife Khadija and his uncle Abu Talib who both died. Khadija had been his confidant and main pillar of support, believing in him, supporting him, and standing by him during his period of struggle. Abu Talib, though he never formally converted, acted as an important buffer against the leaders of the Quraysh, shielding Muhammad from their anger and persecution. Having had little success in converting people from nearby towns and oasis, facing violent persecution, and with his staunchest allies lost, Muhammad drew solace from the voice of revelation at this time of growing desperation:

By the radiance of morning
and the hush of night,
your Lord has neither forsaken you
nor left you forlorn.
The end shall be better for you than the beginning.
Your Lord shall provide and you shall be satisfied.
Did he not find you an orphan and shelter you?

Did he not find you erring and guide you?
Did he not find you needy and enrich you?
As for the orphan, do not oppress him,
and as for the one in need, do not spurn him,
and as for your Lord's blessing, declare it without fear (Quran, sura 93)

He remained mindful of the teaching about other prophets that was revealed to him. These too had been beset by misfortune, each of whom, like Abraham, Joseph, Moses, and Jesus had been persecuted, tested, and challenged by their enemies. However, their ulti- mate success testified to divine providence. Sustained by his belief, Muhammad's small community drew to- gether, drawing courage from his example and leader- ship.

The *Hijra* and After

North of Mecca, some 300 miles away, lay an oasis town known as Yathrib. It was an agricultural settle- ment combining a predominantly Arab population with that of a Jewish community. Yathrib was beset with in- ternal conflicts and tension. Some of its leaders, who had heard of and were attracted by Muhammad and his message of peace and morality, decided to invite him to settle their affairs. They agreed to pledge support to Muhammad and his followers and to convert to the new faith. In the meantime, opposition in Mecca had turned violent, and the small community which until then had endured peacefully, was now forced to defend itself or leave. They arranged quickly to have their families moved to Yathrib, and at the opportune time Muhammad, accompanied by Abu Bakr, evaded Meccan guards who were posted to prevent him from leaving and set out for their new home. The year was 622 and in Muslim history the event became known as the *Hijra* (the migration) and Yathrib became known as Medina, the city of the Prophet. The year also marked the begin- ning of the new lunar Muslim calendar.

The fortunes of the community in Medina differed dramatically from those in Mecca. Here they were able to organize themselves without fear of persecution; they were free to practice their faith and build their community in an environment where the message of revelation could actually be translated into daily life and institutions. Moreover, at this time Muhammad was accepted as a Prophet of Allah and a leader by those who had migrated and those in Medina who had of- fered them friendship and assistance. Here Muhammad built a house, organized prayers in its courtyard, and set up a market place for trade and exchange of goods. He also established peace in Medina through a series of agreements, referred to as the "Constitution of Medina." Parts of this constitution have been preserved by Ibn Ishaq (died 767), an early Muslim historian:

In the Name of God, most Gracious, most Merciful. This is a document from Muhammad the Prophet (concerning the relations) between the believers, the Muslims of Mecca and Medina and those who followed them, formed with them and labored with them. They constitute an *Umma*, one community, excluding all others.

By the provisions listed in the contract everyone rec- ognized Muhammad's authority as Prophet of God, agreeing to his role as leader and judge, referring all disputes to him. They agreed to support each other against all enemies, committing not to fight or kill each other. The Jewish community was included in the pact and the Jews were considered free to practice their faith and maintain their institutions.

There were three major elements of institutional and community development that reinforced the *Umma's* (community) new identity. The first was the systematic organization of ritual activity, primarily the offering of daily, congregational prayers led by the Prophet. Initially, Muslims, in common with Jewish and Christian practice, faced in the direction of Jerusalem while pray- ing, however, in time the direction was changed to face the Kaba in Mecca. With prayer, the Prophet instituted the practice of wealth-sharing, both as a way of dedi- cating and purifying one's wealth and possessions and also as a way of implementing the values of compassion and caring for the disadvantaged, which he had preached in Mecca. In time additional acts of devotion and piety, including the practice of fasting, were estab- lished. The second factor in the development of com- munity identity was the ongoing translation and consolidation of the revelation to the Prophet into more specific ways in which the faith could be practiced and the community organized. These revelations continued to inspire the life of the growing community, who pre- served, remembered, and taught the revelation to each other and to new converts. The revelation widened the historical and religious identity of Muslims, linking them to previous revelations and messengers, conform- ing their new status as a community to whom God was speaking in their own language and through one of their own. The third aspect involved the organization of the community as a cohesive social and economic group. A number of pre-Islamic Arab social practices and cus- toms related to inheritance, marriage, the role of women, and the portion of orphans and slaves were an- nulled or changed. The particularly cruel custom of burying unwanted female infants was abolished; Muslims were encouraged to free slaves and the partic- ipation of women in public and religious activity be- came more pronounced. In economic life, the hoarding of wealth and the charging of usury was abolished, but people were encouraged to trade freely and ethically.

Meccan Hostility and Warfare

The Meccans were troubled by developments in Medina, which appeared to them to threaten their future hold on trade and political affairs in the region. Following a skirmish during a caravan raid, the Meccans prepared for a major military assault. In 624, the first major battle took place. It is known as the Battle of Badr. The smaller, less organized Muslim army was victorious; the triumph was seen as a sign of God's support and the justice of the Muslim cause. It reinforced their faith and consolidated their belief in Muhammad's divine mission and leadership. It strengthened the morale of the new community and readied it for defense against further acts of hostility. In the following year, a larger Meccan army prepared for an assault on Medina. The resulting battle, known as Uhud, almost led to a Muslim defeat, but the Meccans were unable to press home their advantage and a stand-off resulted. Some of the Jewish communities sought alliances with the Meccans. They were perceived to have broken their agreement by assisting the enemy, and because of their treachery they were punished with expulsion and some were executed.

Following success in other battles, Muhammad attempted to arrange a truce with the Quraysh, so that his followers could go to Mecca to perform a pilgrimage and to visit their families. An armistice was arranged and the Muslims were able to visit Mecca. A year later, Muhammad and his followers marched again to Mecca; the citizens and their leaders offered no opposition and the city came under Muslim control. This final victory was a peaceful one. To underline his ties to the city and his intentions to reunite his followers and their past enemies, Muhammad invited all to embrace Islam, to shun their past way of life, and to declare an end to hostility. The idols in the Kaba were destroyed and the sacred enclave was dedicated as the site of the annual Muslim pilgrimage, the *Hajj*.

In Muslim history, the struggle to defend the community and to exercise control over their own destiny, was seen as a *jihad*, (striving) in the way of God. It signified the military struggle to defend and consolidate the *Umma* and the task of spreading Islam through preaching and conversion.

The year 630 is known as the "Year of Delegations." Representatives of many tribes from all over Arabia came to the Prophet to pay him homage and to convert to the new faith. Muslim representatives had been sent also to Byzantium and Persia to invite their rulers to join the *Umma*. Muhammad clearly envisaged his message as not being limited to the Arabs, but to extend beyond the borders of Arabia. By now the fundamental characteristics of the new community had become well defined. Those who belonged to it were no longer, in theory, to be bound by the constraints of their former status, wealth, or privileges; they would be members of a community in which they were regarded as equal before God, free to pursue a life in alliance with fellow Muslims and others, and ultimately accountable before God and the community, only by the quality of their moral action and adherence to Quranic values.

In the year 632, Muhammad performed what has come to be known as the "Farewell Pilgrimage." The *Hajj*, as it was now called, linked the identity of Muslims to the history of the Kaba's founding by Abraham and extending its heritage even further by attributing it as a sacred enclave founded by Adam. In this new historical vision, it became a place of ritual fulfilling earlier revelations and messages. Later during that year Muhammad fell ill and, according to traditional sources, passed away on the twelfth day of Rabi al Awwal, the year 10 of the new Muslim era. He was sixty three years old.

The most accessible picture of Muhammad's life comes from the narratives preserved by the early Muslim community. His words and actions were preserved, collected, systematized, and verified by future scholars. These individual traditions merged to produce a *sira*, a life history, which reconstructs the major events in Muhammad's life and offers a powerful image of the significance of his mission. In time, world historians have come to agree that Muhammad was indeed one of the most influential persons who ever lived. Within the immediate Arab setting of his time, he provided an impetus to his followers which would lead them to spread the Islamic message, far and wide. His own mission encompassed several achievements. He created the basis of a society cemented by loyalty to Islam rather than ethnic heritage or land. He succeeded in linking his people to the monotheistic tradition of the worship of One Absolute Divine Being who had chosen to speak to them, as He had spoken earlier to others, through one of their own and in their language. He inaugurated a faith-community, providing a framework of beliefs, values, and institutions that would continue to inspire them to be a model, in the words of the Quran, "an Umma of the middle way, a witness to humanity as the Prophet had been a witness to them." (Quran 2:143)

The Prophet Muhammad's practice of prayer and devotion; his spirituality; the example of humility, compassion, and justice; his role as husband and parent; his acts of kindness to children, orphans, the disadvantaged, and animals and birds; and his commitment to the use of reason and the pursuit of knowledge all have served for Muslims as a model of ideal conduct. It is this picture of Muhammad as a teacher, exemplar, and friend of Allah that has given him a special place in the hearts of Muslims through the ages. In their daily prayers and whenever his name is mentioned, they invoke God's blessings on him and his descendants, as a continuing mark of remembrance and gratitude. His life has been recorded in all Muslim languages and folk traditions, celebrated in poetry, and commemorated on his birthday. Above all for Muslims he is the recipient of God's final revelation preserved in the Quran.

♦ THE QURANIC REVELATION

The revelations that came to Muhammad in the form of divine inspiration are believed by Muslims to be contained in the Quran. The word Quran literally means "recitation or reading," and it was in this recited form that he communicated it to his followers. Revelation came to Muhammad over a period of twenty-two years in the form of powerful, jolting experiences that often left him shaken and cold. The process of revelation involved vision as well as hearing. The medium of revelation is described as a "Spirit of Holiness" (Quran 16:102). The angel Gabriel acted as a mediator of revelation. The signs of Allah are described symbolically as a "figure on the clear horizon" (Quran 81:20) who revealed to Muhammad the message. The Quranic conception of revelation involves a "descent" (*tanzil*), a universal process by which all previous revelations also come to have their specific forms as a text or book (*kitab*). They all, including the Quran, have an original source, referred to as *Umm al-Kitab* (*The Mother of the Book*) (Quran 43:1–5). All revelations are thus rooted in one transcendent primary source, which through inspiration becomes articulated to humanity. The Quran in Arabic represents the culmination of this process, completing and fulfilling previous revelations. It was a cumulative process revealed at intervals and appropriate times. Muhammad communicated them to his followers who memorized it while scribes also put it in writing under his supervision. Certain individuals came to be noted for both their power of recitation and their ability to memorize the text. By the time of Muhammad's death, the Quran existed as an oral discourse, and in written form. After his death, a complete written text was compiled so that there would be no differences regarding its contents and no risk of having the sacred scripture violated. Muslims believe that the Quranic text has therefore been preserved unchanged, systematized, and arranged as a written text, based on Muhammad's instructions and contains the complete message revealed to Muhammad.

The Quran is divided into one-hundred-fourteen chapters or *sura*. The number of verses in each chapter varies greatly, each verse being referred to as an *ayah*. After a short opening *sura*, subsequent chapters came to be arranged more or less according to length. The chapter titles either indicate the main content or refer to a word or phrase from the text. All of the chapters, with the exception of sura nine, begin with the formula or *Bismillah*, "In the name of God, most Gracious, most Merciful." Chapters are also identified as having been revealed in Mecca or Medina or as having verses revealed in both places. Thus, Muslims also recognize a chronological order of revelation.

The aspect of recitation is the key to understanding the power and impact of the oral discourse of the Quran. The Quran is meant to be recited, to be heard, and to be experienced. The power of the "Word of God" for a Muslim lies not only in its impact on the mind, but also on the heart. Muslims have developed the art of recitation into an organized tradition. They often gather in groups and listen to practitioners of this art; today there is even an international competition held every year to find the best reciters of the Quran.

The language of the Quran pervades all walks of Muslim life, influencing even the mode of writing Arabic and other languages used by Muslims who adopted the Arabic script, such as Persian, Turkish, Urdu, Hausa, and Swahili. The art of calligraphy developed from the Quranic text represents much of the aesthetic impulse in Muslim art, and the written text is given the same devoted reverence as the art of recitation. Calligraphy, in all its elaborate forms, is the means of providing an experience for the eye, as is the recited word for the ear. The art of calligraphy, coupled with illumination and coloring, has produced copies of the Quran that represent some of the most skilled creations of decorative art in Islam, which has in turn influenced the decoration of places of worship and the tradition of the arts in the Muslim world.

A variety of Quranic formulae, such as "in the name of God" (*Bismillah*), "If God wills" (*Inshallah*), "Glory be to God" (*Subhanallah*), are an integral part of the daily life of Muslims. Even the physical presence of the Quran is considered a source of blessing. Verses are recited during moments of personal and family crises, occasions of celebration and joy, and the moments of birth and death; a copy of the Quran is given an honored place in the house, where it is generally placed at a level higher than other belongings and furnishings. Muslims often carry a text from the Quran on their persons in a small ornamental amulet.

The Quran is the starting point for the Muslim search for knowledge about self and the world. It provides a new language, a tool of inquiry, a new mode of expression, and a means to explore new vistas of knowledge. The effort to understand the Quranic message has given rise to the sciences related to linguistics and grammar, primarily of Arabic. Muslim scholars also devote themselves to clarifying and explaining the Quran through works of exegesis known as *tafsir*. The study of the Quran is thus at the heart of all Muslim scholar-

Page from an eleventh-century copy of the Quran.

ship and has given the intellectual and scientific endeavors of the Islamic world a great sense of unity in the quest for new knowledge.

♦ **FOUNDATIONAL CONCEPTS**

In the name of God, most Gracious, most
Merciful.
Say: 'He is God, One, the Ultimate.
He does not give birth, nor was he born (of anyone).

There, is none comparable to the One.' (Quran, sura 112)

The central concept in the Quran is that of *tawhid*, the unity or oneness of God. In denying plurality, the Quran rejects all forms of idolatry and association of any other divinities with God. Called Allah in Arabic, God is the sole reality on whom all existence depends.

God's majesty and power are expressed through the creative process. The whole of the cosmos, nature as well as humanity, and all that might lie beyond and is not yet perceived or become visible, are created and sustained by God. Reality in this sense has a visible and invisible dimension, a material as well as a spiritual aspect. God's unity encompasses it all, transcending any attempt to define or limit Him. The well-known "verse of the throne" in the Quran is often cited to illustrate divine majesty:

God, there is no god but Him,
the Living, the Eternal,
neither slumber nor sleep affects Him,
To Him belongs what is in the
heavens and on earth.
Who can intercede with Him,
except by His permission?
He is aware of what has passed
and what is to come but
people are unaware of His knowledge,
except that which He wills.
His throne strides the heavens and the earth
and He never tires of caring for them.
He is Sublime, Exalted (Quran 2:255)

Divine nature is alluded to through "the most beautiful attributes" (Quran 59:24) that capture Allah's transcendence and presence. That presence radiates like light making it possible to experience and to begin to draw near in love and devotion. Knowledge of Allah is best understood through the spiritual symbolism of *Nur*: "Radiant Light" in the famous Quranic "verse of light:"

Allah is the light of the heavens and of the earth.
The symbol of His light is a niche,
in which burns a lamp,
enclosed in a glass,
like a shining star
which is lit from a blessed tree—
an olive tree, neither of the East
nor of the West, whose
oil illuminates even though no
fire touches it—light upon light—
Allah guides to His light whom He pleases
and He strikes parables for humankind,
always Aware. (Quran 24:35)

His universality is total—"to Him belongs the East and the West: wherever you turn, there is His Face. He is all-present, all-knowing." (Quran 2:115)

Divine providence extends to all of creation. The universe as a whole, according to the Quran is a sign (*ayah*) of God. His creative power and the principle of unity thus pervades through the natural order, endowing all creation with qualities that enable them to function in equilibrium, affirming the divine presence: "The

seven heavens and the earth and everything in it, glorify God" (Quran 17:44).

The behavior of insects such as bees, for example is inspired by God:

Your Lord inspired the bee, saying: Make your hives in the hills and trees . . . there comes from bees a delicately colored drink, with the power to heal. It is a sign for those who reflect. (Quran 16:68–69)

This providence is extended to the dimension of human history, by providing a means of communication, through revelation or divinely inspired messengers, a process identified in the Quran as being universal: "to every people have we sent a messenger" (Quran 16:36).

All of these messengers come from the same, One God with the mission of mediating between God and their peoples. They established communities, transmitted revelation, and acted as a reminder of the continuing divine presence of God in a purposeful human history.

The Quran refers to many Biblical prophetic-figures and others, placing them in this scheme of a universal human history:

We have inspired you [Muhammad] as We inspired Noah and the prophets after him, as we inspired Abraham, Ishmael, Isaac, Jacob and the tribes; and Jesus, Job, Jonah, Aaron and Solomon; and we gave to David the Psalms. [These are] messengers of whom we have spoken to you and others that we have not mentioned. (Quran 4:163–164)

Muhammad is regarded as the "Seal of the Prophets" (Quran 33:40), through whom this process of communication is fulfilled and completed, encompassing previous histories of revelation and at the same time opening them up to new possibilities of interpretation and understanding.

One implication of this comprehensive and universal notion of revelation throughout human history is that the great prophetic voices are not seen separately, nor simply as reflections of a local history, but collectively as representing the diverse threads of the common destiny of humankind.

The Individual and the *Umma*: Islam as an Ethic of Personal and Community Life

Human beings have a special place within creation (Quran 95:4). In the Quranic retelling of the story of creation, Adam is distinguished from other creatures, such as angels. Adam is shaped from clay, enlivened by divine spirit and endowed with the capacity to "name things" (Quran 2:31). This combination suggests a layered multi-dimensional being, in whom material, spiritual, and intellectual orientations are fused. According to the Quran, God created humanity from one soul, then from it male and female (Quran 39:6), like all of creation, in binary fashion (Quran 36:36). So the origin of humankind involves male and female, gendering history from its beginnings. The couple lived in the "garden" (Quran 2:35), in proximity to Allah and were provided with all that they might need in this idyllic setting. God, however, presented them with a moral challenge, restricting them from approaching the symbolic tree of knowledge. They were tempted by the figure of Iblis (Satan) playing the role of seducer, who urged them to disobey. They succumbed and thereby lost their right to live in the garden, and were thrust upon a new stage, the earth, where they lived and created societies. This new human destiny of living on earth, presented an opportunity to create conditions that enabled life to be lived according to an ethical and moral purpose, so that one might rediscover and regain the spiritual quality of life of the "garden."

This is what gives meaning and purpose to human history. God will, however, provide guidance through messengers and revelations to facilitate the quest and provide criteria for moral conduct, to which human beings can respond with the creative faculty of reason. There is a chapter in the Quran, entitled, *al-Furqan* (the Criterion) (Sura 25) which cites examples of messengers who act as mediators and initiate faith communities. The beginning of all religions in this view of history are grounded in the divine command which provides a basis for establishing an intellectual and moral engagement with the totality of life. The story of creation exemplifies the choices that persons must make to transform their own condition by accepting and committing to God to discover the necessary equilibrium in personal and social life. It is in that wider sense that the word Islam, signifies acceptance and giving of oneself and a Muslim is one whose attitude and actions are based on such a commitment. All are, however, accountable for their action and will be judged accordingly. This concept of accountability relates also to the acceptance of a life hereafter. Each soul is accountable after death and all communities must face an ultimate "Day of Judgement." This signifies the important Quranic concept of justice and reward for good deeds and punishment for evil actions. In the hereafter, the reward is a life of bliss in heaven and punishment is the torment of hell.

The Quran articulates multiple acts of personal and community devotion.

When addressing the first Muslims, the Quran refers to them as a "community of the middle way, witnesses to humankind, just as the Messenger Muhammad is a witness for you" (Quran 2:143). However, in the development of humankind, there is also diversity and the Quran urges a positive approach to difference:

> O humankind! We have created you out of male and female and constituted you into different groups and societies, so that you may come to know each other . . . the best of you in the sight of Allah, are the truly committed. (Quran 49:11–13)

> And among His signs is the creation of the heavens and the earth and the diversity in your language and color. (Quran 30:22)

In describing other faith communities who possess their own history of revelation and scripture, the Quran refers to them as the "People of the Book" (*Ahl al Kitab*). With reference particularly to the Christian and Jewish communities among whom the early Muslims lived, the Quran regards them as *dhimmi*, (faiths and communities that have protected status through mutual agreement). Their properties, law, religious way of life and places are to be protected. They are required to pay taxes and not to engage in conflict with Muslims. While acknowledging the pre-eminent role of the *Umma*, the Quran encourages a respect for difference, pointing to common moral goals and encouraging peace, rather than division and antagonism: "For each Community, We have granted a Law and a code of conduct. If God had wished, He could have made you into one Community, but He wishes rather to test you through what has been granted to you. So vie with each other in the pursuit of goodness and moral excellence." (Quran 5:48)

The *Umma* or Muslim community is the context in which such ideals and values can be translated. Individuals are trustees of these values, accountable to God and community. The Quran affirms the material as well as spiritual dimensions of all life, but these are not in conflict, rather they are complementary. Human conduct and goals are relevant as acts of faith within the wider personal, cultural and social context. It is in this sense that the *Umma* can be said to embody a total way of life that addresses Muslims and others among whom Muslims live.

While revelation opens up this new space for the community to articulate its vision through society, it also brings about a new emphasis on the need to transform one's own inner being. This transformation is achieved through multiple acts of faith which in the Quran anchor the identity of the community through ritual action and practice of the faith.

Muslims at Friday Prayer.

◆ PRACTICES OF THE FAITH

Muslims profess their faith by way of the *shahada*, witnessing that: "There is no god but God and Muhammad is the messenger of God."

The *shahada* is the initial act of commitment as well as a statement of faith, encompassing the foundational belief in the absolute unity of God and relating this to the medium through which the Absolute manifests His will. The *shahada* links believers to God, revelation, and the Prophet Muhammad.

Salat, *Dhikr*, and *Dua*: Acts of Devotion

The Quran articulates multiple acts of personal and community devotion to Allah. These aspects of worship encompass the formal ritual prayer, the *salat*, acts of remembrance of God, *dhikr*, and prayers of supplication and praise, *dua*. Based on the experiences and example of the Prophet, they combine to represent the different forms of devotional expressions mentioned in the Quran.

The *salat* is the formal, ritual prayer. While Muslims may pray and remember God at any time, the evolution of the practice of the *salat*, has led to its practice at traditional times: dawn, noon, afternoon, sunset, and

Dua consists of prayers of supplication that can be said in times of crisis or to fulfil individual and community needs.

late evening. One may say the *salat* by oneself or preferably with others, particularly at mid-day on Friday, the day of congregational prayer. *Salat* is to be preceded by an act of ablution. The cleansing involves the hands, the arms, the mouth, the nostrils, and the feet. Where water may not be available for ablution, the act may be performed symbolically, using sand or stone. The act of ablution links purity of the body to prayer as a means of purifying one's inner self.

Muslims may pray in any clean space, at home, at work, or in a congregational space such as a mosque. The *salat* is preceded by a call to prayer, *adhan*, inviting believers to hasten to prayer. The *salat* is performed by facing in the direction of the Kaba, which serves as a point of orientation called the *qibla*. As the form of the *salat* evolved, based on the example of the Prophet and the early community, it developed a formal pattern. In congregation, it is performed behind a prayer-leader, called *imam* and consists of units, called *raka*. Every unit begins with the recitation of the opening chapter of the Quran, *al-Fatiha*:

In the name of God, most Gracious, most Merciful. All praise is due to God, the Sustainer of the worlds, most Gracious most Merciful, Lord of the Day of Judgement. You alone we worship and from You alone, we seek help. Guide us on the right path, the path of those on whom you have bestowed grace, not of those who give cause for condemnation nor those who choose to go astray. (Quran, sura 1)

Salat includes other verses and prayers from the Quran. Each unit of recitation and prayer is a rhythmic cycle of seven steps: (1) facing the *qibla*, invoking Allah's praise by saying *Allahu Akbar*, ("God is most Great") and readying one's attention by affirming within the intention to say the prayer; (2) Reciting of the *fatiha* and other verses, while standing; (3) bowing, while invoking God's praise; (4) prostrating as an act of humility and acceptance of divine majesty; (5) continuing praise of God and prayer while sitting; (6) a second act of prostration, and repetition of praise; (7) silent recitation of personal prayer after resuming a seating position, after which individuals turn their faces to the right and to the left to greet and offer a salutation of peace to each other and to the Prophet and his descendants, thus concluding the prayer. Where additional *rakas* are to be said, the first six steps are always repeated before concluding with the greeting of peace.

On Friday Muslims are enjoined by the Quran to take part in a congregational mid-day prayer, accompanied by a sermon. Muslims assembled for such Friday congregational prayers and at other times, in Medina, first in the courtyard of the Prophet's house and as the community grew, in spaces which the Quran refers to as *masjid*, a place of prostration (Quran 9:108). The Arabic term *masjid* is the basis for the word "mosque."

Dhikr, remembrance of God, is also referred to in the Quran as an act of devotion and love: "Within [your] hearts, the remembrance of God, brings peace and tranquility." (Quran 13:28). The example of the Prophet's early retreat and his acts of contemplation and personal meditation are seen as an important means to seek a loving relationship with God. Such remembrance can be practiced within, at any time and complements the performance of formal ritual prayer. *Dua* consists of prayers of supplication that can be said in times of crisis or to fulfil individual and community needs and requests. All of these forms of devotion, permit Muslims a means of communication with and a constant reminder of the presence of God in their lives.

Zakat: Compassion and Sharing

An important practice, almost invariably linked in the Quran to the act of prayer, is the sharing of one's wealth. The word *zakat*, means purification. By an act of sharing, one's possessions and property as well as oneself is purified: "Those who share their wealth in Allah's way may be compared to a grain which grows seven ears, each with a hundred grains." (Quran 2:261)

Such an act instills a social conscience and promotes a philanthropic instinct urging Muslims to share individual resources and to act as stewards on behalf of the less privileged. *Zakat* is meant for orphans, the poor, the homeless, the needy, and to free the enslaved. It also represents an extension of the concept of social justice in the Quran.

Devotion and Discipline Through Fasting

Fasting, one of the universal practices of most of the major religions of the world also has an important place among Quranic prescriptions. The Quran urges Muslims to fast during the month of Ramadan the ninth month of the Muslim calendar. It is prescribed for all able adults. The physical, moral, and spiritual discipline observed during the period of fasting reflects a more intensive commitment to practice the faith. The discipline involves abstinence during the hours between daybreak and sunset, from food, drink, and sexual activity, a heightening of one's spiritual consciousness through additional prayers and contemplation, and a greater sharing of one's time and re-

sources with the family and those in need. Ramadan is regarded as auspicious because the Quran was first revealed during the month. It also contains the *Laylat al Qadr*, the "Night of Power," described in the Quran (Sura 97), a time of heightened spirituality and peace, during which people stay awake, reading the Quran, contemplating and remembering God often. The end of the period of fasting is signalled by a celebration, called *Idd al Fitr*, a time of rejoicing, feasting, and sharing.

Hajj, the Pilgrimage

Each year, during the month of Dhul-Hijja, the Quran enjoins Muslims, who have the means and are able, to join in an act of pilgrimage to the Kaba in Mecca. When the Prophet reentered the city of his birth and took charge of its affairs in the year 630, he cleansed the Kaba of its pre-Islamic images and idols and rededicated it to the worship of One God. According to the Quran it is the noblest and the most ancient sanctuary, (Quran 2:125) where Abraham erected the place of worship. The *Hajj* thus links together, the monotheistic traditions. All pilgrims are to be in a purified state called *ihram*, by wearing a common dress, a simple garment of white and committed during the time of pilgrimage to avoid taking any life or commit acts of violence to others or to the environment. They are to practice abstinence by not displaying jewelry, grooming oneself by shaving, or having sexual relations.

The sequence of ritual actions performed by Muslims were based on revelation and the practice of the Prophet. Upon entering the precincts, pilgrims perform the "circling" of the Kaba, seven circuits counter clockwise. After acknowledging the "station of Abraham," marking the spot symbolizing the space of worship built in ancient times, the pilgrims cross to the hills of Safa and Marwa and run or walk briskly between the two spots. This ritual act signifies the running of Hagar, Abraham's second wife, as she sought water for their son Ishmael. According to Muslim tradition, Abraham had left Hagar and Ishmael there, while on his mission for God. As food and water ran out, Hagar ran between the two hilly spots, searching desperately for water in the blazing sun. Water miraculously sprang forth in a spot called *zam-zam*.

Next the pilgrims set out some distance away to a place called Mina where they spend the night. The following morning they proceed to the plains of Arafat and spend the whole day there in prayer, remembrance, and reading of the Quran. The ritual is called the "standing," since pilgrims remain standing throughout the day. At sunset they go next to Muzdalifa to spend the night. Before daybreak the next day, the pilgrims leave to return to Mina where they participate in the ritual stoning of three pillars, symbolizing the repudiation of evil by Abraham who rejected all temptation put be-

The Kaba.

fore him so that he might fulfill God's will by sacrificing his son. The theme is continued in the preparation of the festival that is to follow, which marks a formal end of each person's pilgrimage. The event is known as the *Idd al Adha* (the Holiday of Sacrifice) commemorating Abraham's willingness to sacrifice his son and the miraculous transformation of his son to a lamb.

After offering a sacrifice and sharing the food with the needy and the poor, the pilgrims complete another circling of the Kaba, thus completing the *Hajj*.

The pilgrimage is a dramatic re-enactment of the be-

ginnings of Islam. The rituals memorialize the ancient history of the Kaba and its founding as a sacred sanctuary by Abraham and its restoration by Muhammad. The state of *ihram*, underlines the equality of all Muslims before God and their identity as a new community of believers. The days of the Hajj also represent a way of reaffirming one's commitment and sense of belonging and an opportunity to renew one's faith in the largest gathering of Muslims, before returning to daily life. Participation in the *Hajj* becomes a way of sharing in the founding experiences of the *Umma*.

Stations of the *Hajj*.

This overview of the foundational period of Islam is meant to provide a framework for understanding through the Quran and the life of the Prophet, those principles and practices that have helped to shape subsequent Muslim thought and life. It also serves as a background for how later generations of Muslims developed diverse interpretations and expressions, inspired by these foundations, commonly acknowledged for their universal significance.

The Quran addresses personal as well as collective goals. A faith community however cannot be reduced simply to prescriptions and attributes, its vision must be enduring and transcendent. In connecting personal virtue and social integration the following verse sums up the spirit of the Quranic ideal:

It is not righteousness that you turn your faces to the East or the West. But righteousness means believing in God, the Final Day, Angels, the Revelation, and the Prophets. It is to give, out of love for Him, from your cherished possessions to your family, to orphans, and those in need, and the refugee, those who ask for help and for the freeing of slaves. It is those who pray and give *zakat*, honor their word and are steadfast and patient in the midst of adversity, hardship and peril. They are the people of moral excellence. (Quran 2:177)

Azim Nanji

References

Ahmed, K. *Islam: Its Meaning and Message*. Leicester: The Islamic Foundation, 1976.

Arkoun, M. *The Concept of Revelation: From Ahl al Kitab to Societies of the Book*. Claremont: Claremont Graduate School, 1988.

Armstrong, K. *Muhammad: A Biography of the Prophet*. San Francisco: Harper and Row, 1992.

Denny F. *An Introduction to Islam* (2nd edition). New York: Macmillan, 1994.

Esposito, J. *Islam: The Straight Path*. New York: Oxford University Press, 1991.

Graham, W. *Divine Word and Prophetic Word in Early Islam*. The Hague: Mouton, 1977.

Ibn Ishaq. *Life of Muhammad*. trans. by A. Guillaume. Oxford: Oxford University Press, 1955.

Izutsu, T. *Ethico-Religious Concepts in the Quran*. Montreal: McGill University Press, 1966.

The Koran Interpreted, trans. by A. J. Arberry. New York: Macmillan, 1964.

Lings, M. *Muhammad—His Life According to the Earliest Sources*. London: George Allen and University, 1983.

Mawdudi, S. A. *Towards Understanding Islam*. Indianapolis: Islamic Teaching Center, 1988.

The Meaning of the Glorious Koran, trans. by Mohammed Pickthall. New York: Mentor, 1953.

The Message of the Quran, trans. by Muhammad Asad. Gibraltar: Dar al Andalus, 1980.

Mottahedeh, R. *The Mantle of the Prophet*. New York: Simon and Schuster, 1986.

Nass, S. H. *Ideals and Realities in Islam*. New York: Praeger, 1966.

Nelson, K. *The Art of Reciting the Quran*. Houston: University of Texas Press, 1985.

Newby, G. *The Making of the Last Prophet: A Reconstruction of the Earliest Biography of Muhammad*. Columbia: University of South Carolina Press, 1989.

Peters, F. E. *Muhammad and the Origins of Islam*. Albany: State University of New York Press, 1994.

The Quran and Its Interpreters, vols. 1 and 2. Trans. with commentary by M. Ayoub. Albany: State University of New York Press, 1984.

Rahman, F. *Islam*. Chicago: University of Chicago Press, 1979.

———. *Major Themes in the Quran*. Minneapolis: Bibliothica Islamica, 1980.

Schimmel, A. *Islam: An Introduction*. Albany: State University of New York Press, 1992.

———. *And Muhammad is His Messenger*. Chapel Hill: University of North Carolina Press, 1986.

Schuon, F. *Understanding Islam*. Bloomington, Ind.: World Wisdom Books: 1994.

Smith, W. C. *On Understanding Islam: Selected Studies*. New York: Mouton, 1981.

Stowasser, B. *Women in the Quran, Traditions and Interpretations*. New York: Oxford University Press, 1994.

Tabari. *The History of al-Tabari* (vols. 6,7,9), trans. by W. M. Watt and M. V. Mcdonald. Albany: State University of New York Press, 1987.

2

The Quran in Muslim Life and Practice

♦ The Quran as Revelation ♦ The Quran as Recitation ♦ The Quran as Inspiration

Much has been said and written about the Quran—that it is sacred scripture, a forgery, a concoction of disparate ideas, great literature, or a confused piece dreamed by a primitive mind. While the Quran has been a source of bewilderment for Western understanding, it has been for Muslims a source of inspiration, solace, and salvation. Ultimately, it is not so much the Quran but its impact on Muslim society that has motivated Western readers to discover some of the Quran's power and beauty.

♦ THE QURAN AS REVELATION

In the Quran, a pious Muslim hears God's voice guiding and encouraging, consoling and reproaching, promising the righteous mercy and eternal bliss, while threatening the wicked with wrath and eternal torment. For Muslims the Quran is the word of God, which has entered human time to shape history. According to Muslim sources, the Angel Gabriel revealed himself to Muhammad in 610 while he was in prayerful retreat in a cave on Mount Hira outside Mecca. It is said that in this initial meeting, the Angel Gabriel pressed Muhammad so vehemently that he felt he was being choked. The Quran states that the angel then commanded:

Recite in the name of your Lord who created, created man from a blood clot. Recite, for your Lord is most magnanimous—who taught by the pen; taught man that which he did not know" (Quran 96:1—5).

Muslims claim that God, warned Muhammad: "We shall surely lay upon you weighty speech," and enjoined him to rise up through most of the night in prayer, and remember fervently what he was told to be, "the Lord of the east and the west" (Quran 73:5 and 73:8). For Muslims this "weighty speech" marked Muhammad as the last Messenger of God to humankind; this event was to have a great impact on the course of human history.

The Quran is said to have been communicated to the Prophet Muhammad in two ways. Muslims believe that it was communicated through the Angel Gabriel. These communications were revealed in small portions: single verses, groups of verses, and entire chapters or *suras* over a period of twenty to twenty-two years. The Quran for Muslims is not only words that can be uttered, heard, and recorded; it is also the heavenly archetype of which the recited and written Quran is only an earthly copy. The Quran in its heavenly archetypal form is for Muslims the source of divine revelation throughout human history and is eternally preserved by God. It is the covenant of God with humankind, which he established with the children of Adam when they were but ideas or essences in the divine realm. The Prophet Muhammad also professed to have experienced this heavenly Quran, in addition to having been the recipient of revelation. He would experience a profound spiritual state, shivering on a hot summer day or sweating on a cold winter day, hearing sounds like the ringing of a bell. These sounds transformed themselves in his consciousness into human words, which he memorized and had recorded.

Muslims also believe that the Quran was also sent down in part, to Muhammad's heart on the "night of determination" (Quran 44:3 and 97:1), a blessed night for all Muslims. This event sanctified his life and made Muhammed an example for Muslims to follow. In the Quran God asked: "Am I not your Lord?" and those who chose to worship God affirmed as Lord responded with

Calligraphy at al-Aqsa Jerusalem

the words, "Yes, we bear witness. . . ." (Quran 7:172). The Quran is the seal and testimony to this covenant; its message is for Muslims a powerful affirmation of divine lordship and Muslim commitment.

The Quran as an earthly text has been inextricably bound to Muslim history. It served as an answer to the problems of the Arab society in the Prophet Muhammad's time. The Quran was also a response to Muhammed's questions about the meaning of human life and the mystery of creation, and was closely linked to the history of the nascent Muslim community in Mecca and, later, in Medina. Many of the Quran verses are said to have been revealed in answer to specific questions or life situations. The answers given are seen by Muslims to be general principles, moral imperatives, or precepts applicable to all times and places. The family of the Prophet, which the Quran directly addressed (see Quran 33:32), is seen by Muslims to be a model for all families and all societies in the world.

Arrangement of the Quran

The Quran was subsequently written down and memorized by professing Muslim men and women. Yet, when the Prophet died in 632, ten years after the *Hijra*,

or Muhammad's migration from Mecca to Medina, the Quran as it is known today, did not exist. The verses and chapters, or *suras*, were at that time scattered fragments of the writings of Muhammad's scribes preserved on privately collected pieces of parchment, stone, palm leaf, and leather, in addition to words preserved in human memory. It was during the reign of the third Muslim caliph (or religious leader), Uthman, who governed the existing Muslim community several generations after Muhammad's death that the Quran was given its standard form, which remains unchanged to this day. The *suras* were arranged so that there would be progression from longest chapter to shortest. It is that arrangement that has been preserved as the authoritative version of the Quran.

It is essential for every pious Muslim to memorize as much of the Quran as possible. A Muslim prayer in the solitude of a room or in a congregation begins with the words of the Quran's opening *sura* ("*Al-Fatihah*"). Prayer is considered to be a way for Muslims to appropriate the word of Allah. This divine-human interchange is eloquently expressed in a *hadith qudsi*, a saying of the Prophet quoting God,

> I have divided the prayer (*salat*) between me and my servant, and my servant shall have whatever

An example of Kufic script.

An example of Arabic calligraphy.

he prays for. For when the servant says, All praise be to "God, the Lord of all beings," God says, "My servant has praised me." When the servant says, "The All-merciful, the Compassionate," God says, "My servant has glorified me . . . this is my portion and to him belongs what remains" (M. Ayoub, *The Quran and Its Interpreters*).

The *Fatiha*, the opening *sura* of the Quran, is considered by Muslims to be the perfect prayer. The first three and one-half of its seven verses is a prayer of praise. The rest of the *sura* is a prayer for divine guidance and grace. Not only the *Fatiha* but the entire Quran is a Muslim prayer. It is also a divine address to Muslims. Thus, in every prayer God is believed to reveal Himself and the Muslim believer is to receive the word of God. Muslim prayer is the human connection to God through the Quran.

♦ THE QURAN AS RECITATION

The Quran for Muslims is a source of divine blessing and merit, tranquility and guidance. With it, a child is greeted at birth, by it, he or she is guided through life's journey, and with it, sent to the final abode. This long journey through life with the Quran is to include a recitation of the entire Quran over a specific period of a week, a month, or longer in accordance with divisions of the sacred text for daily recitation. This process is known as *khatm al-Quran*, or completion of its recitation. On special occasions, such as the fasting month of Ramadan, the pious undertake to recite the entire Quran by dividing it up into thirty equal parts that correspond with the thirty nights of the Muslim sacred month. The Prophet Muhammed is said to have called such a person who journeys through the Quran "the sojourning traveler." This is because when the reciter comes to the end of his or her recitation, he or she must start over at the beginning again.

Muslims find the recitation, memorizing, copying, or possessing of a copy of the Quran in their homes a source of great blessing. Indeed, it is believed that on the day of resurrection, the status of a Muslim man or woman in paradise will be determined by the number of verses of the Quran that he or she has memorized during their earthly life. An even greater source of merit and blessing for Muslims is found in studying and understanding the principles and precepts of the Quran. The Prophet is said to have declared: "There are no people assembled in one of the houses of God to recite the Book of God and study it together but that the *sakinah* (divine tranquility) descends upon them." The term *sakinah* is possibly derived from the Hebrew term *sheckinah*, which means "to the glory of Jehovah." Such a derivation may have been the result of contact

On special occasions, such as the fasting month of Ramadan, the pious undertake to recite the entire Quran.

Muhammad had with both Jews and Christians prior to and during his revelations. "Mercy covers them, angels draw near to them, and God remembers them in the company of those who are with him." The reciters of the Quran, those who memorize its words and live by its precepts, are said to be heirs to the Prophet. The Quran is believed to sanctify the heart and home of the Muslim and make him or her a partaker of divine revelation. Its word inscribed on a building, a business, or, vehicle is believed to invoke a blessing or protection.

Above all, the Quran is "a book of guidance to the God-fearing" (Quran 2:1—5). Faithful are enjoined to ponder the Quran, study both the meaning and applications of its verses, and be guided by them in their daily conduct. The Quran is intended to be the basis of Muslim society.

The Quran regulates the filial relation of a child to parents and their responsibilities toward the child. It regulates the relations of a Muslim to fellow Muslims and non-Muslims, the relationship of a subject to the state and its ruling authorities, and the relationship of a human being to God. It regulates the life of society in times of war and peace, and even stipulates the reasons for and rules governing war. The Quran is, in short, a school for Muslims; it disciplines them physically, morally, and spiritually.

♦ THE QURAN AS INSPIRATION

The Quran is essentially a series of self-contained statements—parables, stories, injunctions, and prohibitions. However, Muslims believe that underlying this diverse grouping is a unity of purpose, message, idiom, and style. The Quran in Arabic has been rightly described by Muslims and non-Muslims alike as a symphony of words. Not only the teachings and ideas of the Quran but its words and phrases have permeated the lives and speech of Muslims, regardless of differences of language, race, and culture.

With the words of the Quran a Muslim expresses their satisfaction and gratitude to God for success when exclaiming: "*Tabarak Allah*" (blessed be God) or "*Alhamdu lil-lah*" (praise be to God). With the words of the Quran a Muslim also expresses sorrow and acceptance of God's will when losing a loved one or in encountering death by saying "To God do we belong, and to Him we shall return." With the words of the Quran, and especially with the pronouncement of its opening

chapter or *sura*, marriages are blessed, agreements are sealed, and fear and danger, believed to be averted.

The Quran has been regarded by Muslims as a miracle of speech. Its inimitable style, idioms, and perceived unity are seen to be proof of its divine origin for Muslims. Its interpretation (*tafsir*) has occupied some of the best minds of the Muslim community. The study of its grammar and language, eloquence, similes and metaphors, parables, stories, and precepts have evolved into a venerable science. Likewise, its recitation, whether in a simple chant (*tartil*) or highly developed artistic musical rendition (*tajwid*), has attracted the best voices and talents of Muslim society throughout Islamic history. It is in the recitation of the Quran that its power and beauty are felt by pious Muslims. Quran reciters have, therefore, occupied a special place of honor in the Muslim community.

The Quran has set the standard of excellence for Arabic literature. It has, moreover, permeated the literature of all other Islamic languages. Muslims greet each other with the words of the Quran, and with its words and ideas, they express their own feelings and ideas.

The Quran is believed to have been sent down to the Prophet Muhammad and through him to humankind "in clear Arabic speech" (Quran 16:103). Although the

Calligraphy at Bhong Mosque, Pakistan

Muslim children learning to write Quranic verses. Sierra Leone.

Quran has been translated into most of the major languages of the globe, it is recited in its original language. The Quran is translated and its meanings interpreted into other languages only for the purpose of studying and understanding its teachings. To know the Quran in all its dimensions it must be studied in its original language.

This goal has motivated many non-Arabic—speaking Muslim scholars to excel in the study of the language of the Quran. For centuries, Arabic was the international language of Islamic literature, philosophy, and science. The Quran has been the symbol, source, and framework of Muslim unity.

Islam has spread over a vast geographically and culturally diverse area of the world. It has been adapted to suit the needs of various peoples and cultures. In the process, however, it has assumed many and widely different characters and expressions. The Quran underlies this great diversity and provides a fundamental unity in worship practices, literary expression, and popular culture. This paradoxical unity and diversity of Islam and its grounding in the Quran is its perceived strength. The principle of unity of the human family is an important Quranic principle—"Humankind, fear your Lord who created you all from one soul, from it He created its partner, and from them both He scattereth many men and women" (Quran 4:1). The principle of diversity is also a Quranic principle. Difference of race, color, and creed are divinely preordained.

The Quran has been an inexhaustible source of inspiration for Muslims in every discipline of knowledge and human endeavor. Devout Muslims claim that it speaks to every situation in the life of Muslim societies as well as to the condition of every Muslim individual; Muslims have insisted that the Quran is applicable to all situations at all times. Yet, for it to be universal in its scope and meaning, the Quran is read and committed to heart by every Muslim as though it were sent down at that moment, and for him or her alone.

Mahmoud Ayoub

References

Ayoub, Mahmoud. *The Quran and Its Interpreters*. 2 vols. to date. New York: State University of New York Press, 1984.

Izutsu, T. *God and Man in the Koran*. Tokyo: Keio Institute of Cultural and Linguistic Studies, 1964.

Kassis, H.E. *A Concordance of the Quran*. Berkeley: University of California Press, 1983.

Lings, M. *The Quranic Art of Calligraphy and Illumination.* Boulder: Shawbhala, 1976.

Nelson, K. *The Art of Reciting the Quran.* Austin: University of Texas Press, 1985.

Safadgi, Y.H. *Islamic Calligraphy.* Boulder: Shambhala, 1978.

Tabari, al. *The Commentary on the Quran.* Vol. 1, New York: Oxford University Press, 1987.

Tabatabai, M.H. *The Quran in Islam: Its Impact and Influence on the Life of Muslims.* London: Muhammadi Trust, 1987.

Part II:
The History and Extension of Islam

❸

Islam In the Middle East

♦ Arabia before the Founding of Islam ♦ The Early Muslim Community ♦
♦ Modern Developments in the Middle East ♦ Reformism and Revivalism in the Middle East ♦
♦ Beyond Tradition and Modernity

It is tempting to consider the emergence of Islam only within the limits of the Arabian Peninsula, particularly the western region known as the Hijaz, which contains Mecca and Medina, the cities responsible for shaping so much of Muhammad's life. Yet this would be short-sighted, for it neglects to make adequate account, both of Islam's Near Eastern civilizational matrix and of the wider world that its adherents encountered when they moved to new lands outside the Peninsula. Although formulated as sacred historical narratives, the early Islamic texts themselves admit to broader temporal and cultural horizons, that include the ancient Egypt of the Pharaohs, the sojourns of Biblical patriarchs and the Israelites, and the affairs of the Christians of Byzantium, Ethiopia, and Yemen. They also describe the grandeur of the Persian royal court and reflect familiarity with Zoroastrianism, the chief religion of the Persians.

♦ ARABIA BEFORE THE FOUNDING OF ISLAM

Seventh-century Arabia stood on the southern outskirts of two rival empires, Byzantium and Sasanian Persia. Byzantium, the eastern half of the old Roman empire, controlled the Mediterranean basin, Asia Minor, and the Nile valley from its capital in Constantinople. Its head of the state, the emperor, took an active role in civil, cultural, and religious affairs, in addition to his military functions. Since the fourth century, Christianity had been the state religion, and the emperor, "crowned by God" and "Vicar of Christ," acted as supreme protector of the faith. Although he often could and did intervene in doctrinal matters, religious affairs were normally managed by priests, bishops, and patriarchal councils, who laid the foundations for what is now Eastern Orthodox Christianity.

The Sassanid empire, established in the third cen-

tury, administered a region that encompassed Mesopotamia and Persia from its capital Ctesiphon, located on the shores of the Tigris. The supreme head of state and religion was the *shah*, who embodied the "kingly majesty" of Ahura Mazda, the chief deity of the Zoroastrians. Indeed, as was the case with Byzantium, religion and government were interwoven, as reflected in a statement attributed to Ardashir, an early Sasanian king:

> Religion and kingship are brothers—one cannot do without the other. Religion is the foundation of kingship, kingship is its protector. That which has no foundation will fall, that which has no protector will perish. The rulers of Byzantium and Persia alike worked closely with their respective priesthoods to uphold the purity both of faith and worship.

These empires established defensive alliances with Arab tribes who occupied the frontier region that stood between them, the deserts of Syria and northern Arabia. This area had been a home for Arab peoples for centuries. The Nabateans (first century B.C.–first century A.D.) and Palmyrans (2d–3d century A.D.) were Arab kingdoms that controlled caravan trade between Mesopotamia, Arabia, the Nile valley, and the eastern Mediterranean coast, and they engaged in desert agriculture. During the sixth and early seventh centuries, the Banu Ghassan were the leaders of an Arab Bedouin tribal confederation that monitored the Syrian steppe as clients of Byzantium. Their counterparts on the Sasanian side were the Banu Lakhm, a dynasty of sedentary Arab rulers based in the town of Hira on the lower Euphrates. The ties of both groups with their patrons were considerably weakened in the early 600s, leaving the way open for a Persian invasion of Syria,

Palestine, Egypt, and Anatolia from 613 to 620 and for a Byzantine counteroffensive that ended with a short occupation of Ctesiphon and the execution of the *shah* in 628.

The religious profile of the Arabs at this time was quite complex. The Banu Ghassan and other pastoral Arabs in Syria belonged to local churches that held a Monophysite view of Christianity. This doctrine, which stressed Christ's divinity, was maintained in opposition to the Byzantine Diophysite doctrine that affirmed both the divine and human aspects of Jesus' person. The Banu Lakhm and a majority of other sedentary Arab tribes in Iraq, on the other hand, belonged to the Nestorian Christian community, which prospered under Sasanian rule. The Nestorians differed from both Monophysite and Diophysite Christians, in that they believed in a Christ who embodied two persons, divine and human, acting as one. They also contested the doctrine that Mary was the mother of God.

In the Arabian Peninsula itself, many Arabs worshipped gods and goddesses associated with natural phenomena and the power of destiny. The most important of these were worshipped at shrines such as the Kaba in Mecca. Arabs also recognized the existence of lesser spirits who could bring good luck and misfortune, or possess people. Some scholars maintain, on the basis of ancient Arab poetry, that a tribal humanism pervaded Arabian society. More a set of values than a formal religion, it extolled the virtues of the noble Arab warrior: bravery, honor, solidarity, and generosity. Christianity had also established roots in the peninsula; Nestorian influence extended into the al-Ahsa region on the Gulf coast and possibly into the Hejaz and the region that is now the Yemen, contained Monophysite Christians who were closely allied to the Ethiopian church. There is also evidence for Jewish communities in Yemen and the Hejaz, especially at Yathrib (Medina). Clearly, when the Quran related stories about the Hebrew patriarchs, the Jews, Jesus, and Mary, the seventh-century Arabic-speaking audience was already familiar with much of what they were hearing.

◆ THE EARLY MUSLIM COMMUNITY

Muhammad initiated a religious and social reform movement in Mecca that had developed into a distinct religious community by the time of his death twenty-three years after receiving the first Quranic revelations. The message he promulgated obliged his listeners to decide between the status quo and a challenging vision that redefined concepts of God, time, space, and existence. It attacked long-held Arab religious ideas, questioned the materialism of the privileged, urged compassion for the weak and the poor, and applied key elements of Jewish and Christian belief and practice.

The movement started with the involvement of Muhammad's wife Khadija, close relatives from the clans of his father and mother, including Ali ibn Abi Talib of the Banu Hashim and Abd al-Rahman ibn Awf of the Banu Zuhra, friends such as Abu Bakr of the Quraysh tribe, and people of marginal social status like Khabbab ibn al-Aratt, a client of the Zuhra, and Suhayb ibn Sinan, a freedman who had been a captive of the Byzantines. Muslim sources also indicate that there were a few non-Arab foreigners among the Prophet's early followers, including Bilal, a freedman from Ethiopia, and Salman, a freedman of Persian origin. Each subgroup within the movement seems to have complemented the others—a factor that may well have given it much needed strength and flexibility in the face of adversity, as well as a basis from which to recruit new members. For example, Umar ibn al-Khattab was said to have been strongly opposed to the movement. One day, he set forth to kill Muhammad because of the trouble he felt he was causing the Quraysh. He was swayed from doing so, however, after discovering his sister and her husband listening to Khabbab's recitation of a chapter of the Quran in his own home. They had converted to Islam. After violently rebuking his sister, Umar's mood changed, and he asked to read the Quran. His sister instructed him to purify himself, and when he read it, he exclaimed, "How beautiful and noble are these words!" Khabbab then intervened to direct him to Muhammad, before whom he converted. Umar's conversion gave the movement one of its strongest leaders and the support it needed to perform prayers openly at the Kaba. This narrative illustrates the way in which elements from the different subgroups in the movement—in this case a woman, Quraysh converts, and a client—interacted to overcome challenges and increase the number of converts.

The increasing hostility Muslims encountered in Mecca after the year 615 at the hands of the Quraysh obliged them to begin looking outward for support. This resulted in the dispatch of one or more small groups to Ethiopia, where they won the protection of the Negus, its Christian sovereign and a Byzantine ally. The decisive event, however, was the emigration (*Hijra*) of Muhammad and his Meccan followers to Yathrib (known as Medina after the *Hijra*) in 622. This came about as a result of a series of agreements between Muhammad and delegations from the chief tribes of that town who were seeking an arbiter for the bitter conflicts that had erupted among Arab and Jewish clans there. Muhammad agreed to arbitrate and the Yathrib Arabs accepted Islam and the Meccan Muslims. The *Hijra* signified both an enhancement in Muhammad's stature—he became a prophet with juridical and political authority—and a marked increase in the size of his movement. Indeed, so decisive was the

Al Aqsa Mosque, Jerusalem

Hijra in Islamic history that Muslims later used it to determine the inauguration of the Islamic era, just as Jews use the creation of the world and Christians the birth of Christ to determine the beginning of theirs. The reform movement was well on its way to becoming a viable religious community (*umma*).

The move to Medina required that new measures be taken to enhance the cohesion of the community. These included the promulgation of a series of agreements, known collectively as the "Constitution of Medina," that set forth the mutual rights and obligations of the emigrants and the various parties in Medina, including Jew and polytheists. It contained provisions that called upon disputing parties to turn to Allah and Muhammad for arbitration, and designated the town as a sanctuary. Solidarity was also achieved in the realm of religious practice. Muhammad's house became the center of community prayer, the prayer direction (*qibla*) was established—first towards Jerusalem, then towards Mecca—alms-giving and fasting were regularized, and dietary rules were proclaimed. In the realm of social life, the Medinan chapters of the Quran addressed questions pertaining to marriage, divorce, inheritance, crime and punishment, as well as commercial transactions. Muhammad

took the leading role in implementing this new communal order, but his project was greatly facilitated by the assistance he received from his "companions," loyal followers from among the emigrants and the Medina converts.

Rarely if ever in the history of religions does a religious polity come about without conflict. In the case of Islam, the net result of the conflicts in which its adherents participated was the establishment of an empire and civilization that extended from the Atlantic shores of Africa to the Indus River valley in less than a century after Muhammad's death. Without this series of conquests, the history and character of Islam would have taken a profoundly different shape. What were the conditions that precipitated them, and what factors contributed to their irrefutable success?

Conquest and Empire

By the year 712, just eighty years after the death of Muhammad, Muslim armies had begun to take control of the Iberian Peninsula in the west and the Indus River valley and Central Asia in the east. Islam was no longer the religion of a small Arabian community, but that of an incipient empire that encompassed many different ethnic and religious communities. This situation was brought about by several waves of armed conquest, the first of which began shortly after the Hijra. From his base in Medina, the Prophet had triumphed over his opponents in Mecca and the Hijaz, and extended his influence to Arab tribes throughout the Arabian Peninsula through a series of alliances. Those who did not convert from among Arab groups and continued to oppose and fight with Muslims, including Jews and Christians were expelled or defeated in battle. After Muhammad's death, the caliphs—"successors" to leadership in the Umma—and their representatives succeeded both in consolidating the religious identity of the community and harnessing tribal energies by authorizing raids into Syria and Iraq. These raids brought new wealth, as well as new allies and subjects. Soon thereafter Arab Muslim forces inflicted defeats on Byzantine and Persian armies, which had been weakened by years of warfare and political instability. This opened the way for the conquest of Syria, Mesopotamia, western Iran and Egypt between 634 and 644. From the ancient city of Damascus and the newly created garrison towns of Iraq (Basra and Kufa) and Egypt (Fustat), a third wave of conquests emanated that brought Arab Muslim armies into eastern Iran, Armenia, Libya and Tunisia by 670. The Sasanian empire was thus destroyed and the Byzantines were forced to retreat into Anatolia. The last wave of early conquests occurred only after order had been restored within the Muslim polity, which had suffered a civil war and internal revolts during the 680s and 90s.

Conquest of territories outside of the Arabian Peninsula did not immediately result in mass conversions to Islam, contrary to widely held belief. Rather, the evidence suggests that Islam remained a minority religion in these regions for more than two centuries after the conquests. One reason is that military campaigns targeted Byzantine and Persian armies so as to achieve strategic objectives and booty, not civilian populations for the purpose of religious conversion. Secondly, noncombatant populations were given a choice of either converting to Islam or paying tribute to their new rulers and accepting protected status. At first, most chose the latter option, which suited Arab rulers because it assured greater fiscal benefits. A tiered society based on religious and ethnic identities that lasted for more than a century evolved from this situation. The Arab Muslim minority formed an aristocracy who preferred to live in their own cantonments, near the communal mosque and the ruler's palace, and collect taxes from non-Muslim subjects. Offspring of Arab Muslim fathers and non-Arab, non-Muslim mothers when raised as Muslims held second class status. There were also non-Arab converts (mawali), many of whom had been captured as prisoners of war during

the conquests, then granted freedom upon conversion. The Arab Muslim aristocracy considered them to be their clients. The majority—mostly Christians, as well as Jews, Zoroastrians and others—were considered to be "People of the Book." They held "protected" (dhimmi) status, meaning that they were secure in their property, community, and worship as long as they paid taxes and remained loyal to Muslim authorities. Moreover, dhimmis with knowledge of Byzantine and Persian fiscal and administrative policies became functionaries for the new Arab empire. Islam in the newly conquered lands, as in Arabia, thus became largely an urban religion; the countryside, however, remained largely in the hands of non Muslim tributaries until they later became Islamized. Polytheistic beliefs and practices, so strongly condemned in the Quran, either disappeared, or persisted as features of popular religiosity and custom.

The only part of the region to which we refer today as the Middle East that remained unconquered was Anatolia. Byzantine forces there successfully repelled three attacks by Arab armies in 660, 668, and 717. Indeed, the Byzantines maintained control of the area until 1071, when the Emperor's army was routed by the Saljuq Turks at Manzikert. This opened the way for the immigration of Turkish Muslim nomadic populations from the east, the rise of Turkish principalities, and eventual conversion of much of the indigenous population. Under the leadership of the Ottoman dynasty, one of these principalities, located on the western frontier, extended its control across the Bosphorus into Europe, annexed other Turkish states in Anatolia, and conquered Constantinople in 1453. This brought an end to the Byzantine empire and marked the establishment of a new Islamic empire that would govern much of the Middle East and North Africa until the twentieth century. In accordance with precedents set during the early Islamic conquests, the Greek Orthodox Church was placed under the protection of the Ottoman state.

As noted earlier, leadership in the Muslim community after Muhammad's death was held by Caliphs, a series of rulers elected or designated from among Muslims of Arab Qurashi descent. They faced the challenging tasks of maintaining and extending the religious vision of the Prophet, ensuring community solidarity, security, and justice, and administering an empire composed of diverse and often competing interests. They were active in religious and mundane affairs alike. The first four—Abu Bakr, Umar, Uthman, and Ali—were remembered collectively in the Sunni tradition as the Rashidun "rightly guided" Caliphs. All were from the Quraysh of Mecca, early converts and emigrants to Medina, and close companions of the Prophet. Each was credited with having had a hand in the establishment of an official consonantal text of the

Quran—especially Uthman (reigned 644–656)—and each was considered a respected source of traditions (hadiths) about the Prophet and the early community. It was during Umar's reign (634–644) that Muslim armies won control over territories in Syria, Mesopotamia, and the Nile Valley. He was also credited with having established the Islamic calendar, based on the Hijra year.

With the violent and tragic deaths of Uthman in 656 and Ali in 661, the caliphate was claimed by Ali's rivals—the Banu Umayya, close kinsman of Uthman, and, ironically, former leaders of the opposition to Muhammad in Mecca. Ruling as an Arab monarchy from Damascus, the Umayyad dynasty achieved the greatest territorial expansion of the Muslim empire, the consolidation of Islam as the religion of state, and the adoption of Arabic as the official administrative language, a decision which eventually favored the Arabization and the Islamization of their subjects. They gave symbolic expression to the new order they endeavored to create by issuing coinage containing religious declarations in Arabic and sponsoring the construction of monumental mosques in Damascus, Jerusalem, Medina, as well as congregational mosques in outlying towns.

Weakened by dynastic conflicts, tribal rivalries, and local uprisings, the Umayyad dynasty was ended in 750 by a coalition of forces from Iraq and eastern Iran which sought to restore the Caliphate to the house of the Prophet. A surviving member of the dynasty, Abd al-Rahman, escaped to Spain via North Africa, where he established the western branch of the Umayyads in Cordoba. In the central Islamic lands, the Abbasids, claiming descent from an uncle of the Prophet, seized control of the empire in what some have called a revolution. They inaugurated an era of Caliphal rule with the founding of Baghdad on the banks of the Tigris River in Iraq, the adoption of elaborate Persian forms of courtly ceremonial, the organization of administrative bureaucracies, and the creation of private armies. Several Abbasid caliphs, beginning with Mamun (reigned 813–833), attempted to monopolize authority in religious affairs, but were unsuccessful. During this era the grip Arab Muslims had in the wielding of power and influence gave way to allow the predominance of Muslims from various backgrounds, as the majority of subjects converted to Islam. Above all, the Abbasids are remembered for having marshaled in a period of magnificent efflorescence in learning, science, literary production, and art that had lasting effects on subsequent generations in the Middle Eastern region and beyond. Abbasid civilization witnessed the systematization of Muslim doctrines and institutions, translation and elaboration of ancient Greek and Persian learning, development of sciences such as: astronomy, geography, mathematics, optics, and medicine, and the emergence of a rich and varied musical tradition.

In time the Abbasid state dissolved into a patchwork of kingdoms and principalities governed mostly by non-Arab Muslim military and tribal elites. This came about through the rise of new dynasties on the edges of the empire and the subordination of the caliph to non-Arab war lords at home. In North Africa, Shia Fatimids claiming descent from Ali and Fatima (the Prophet's daughter) established a rival caliphate and founded the royal city of Cairo as their capital with the backing of Berber troops. The rule of the Fatimid dynasty and the intellectual and cultural developments under its patronage, rivalled that of the Abbasids. Cairo became a center of learning, science and the arts. The Umayyad caliphate was revived for a short time in Spain (929-1031), followed by the Berber Almoravid and Almohad kingdoms, which encompassed territories both in North Africa and the Iberian Peninsula. Iraq, meanwhile, fell under the control first of the Shia Buyid shahs "kings" from Iran in the tenth century, then the Sunni Saljuq Sultans of Turkish origins in the eleventh. Other dynasties were to follow, such as the Kurdish Ayyubids and the Mamluk "slave" kings of Egypt and Syria who came from Turkish and Circassian origins. Both of these regimes combated the Crusaders for control of Syria, Palestine, and Egypt. The upshot of these developments is that after the tenth century the Caliphate came to function mainly as a symbol of legitimacy for new ruling elites in Iraq, Iran, Syria and Egypt. In 1258 the Mongols put an end to the Abbasid Caliphate of Baghdad. The Mamluks of Egypt were to keep an Abbasid caliph in their court and the Ottoman sultans revive the title much later, but the institution became little more than a souvenir of Sunni Muslim tradition. The region was not to experience the likes of an imperial order on the scale of the Umayyads, Abbasids and Fatimids, until the arrival of the Ottoman, Safavid and Mughal dynasties in the sixteenth century.

Classical Islamic Pathways

In the closing years of the eleventh century, before European Crusaders and Mongols appeared on the horizons, the son of a Persian wool spinner from Tus named Abu Hamid al-Ghazali (1058–1111) sojourned among the religious scholars of northeastern Iran studying the sciences of Quran and hadith, discursive theology (kalam), philosophy, and logic. Nizam al-Mulk, the Saljuq vizier, appointed him to the faculty of his newly founded religious college (madrassa) in Baghdad in 1091. After a meteoric rise to fame as a teacher, however, al-Ghazali experienced a life crisis that obliged him to abandon his family and position in search of spiritual alternatives to worldly success. His quest led him to holy sites in Damascus, Jerusalem, Mecca and Medina, where he met with Sufi adepts—seekers of mystical communion with God. After several years, he returned to his native land, where he founded a Sufi lodge (khanqa) and wrote The Revival of the Religious Sciences, one of the classic works of medieval Islamic learning.

Approximately two hundred and thirty years after al-Ghazali abandoned his position in Baghdad, Abu Abd Allah ibn Battuta (1304–1368), a twenty year-old Berber student of Islamic law, set out from Tangiers in Morocco on a pilgrimage to Mecca. En route he met with scholars, judges, Sufis and rulers in Tunisia, Egypt, Palestine and Syria. He usually took up lodging in mosques, madrasas, and Sufi hospices of the sort familiar to al-Ghazali, and which had by now proliferated throughout the region. After completing the Hajj in 1326, he set out to visit as many other lands as possible, including the Mongol-dominated regions of Iraq and Iran, East Africa, Saljuq Anatolia, Byzantium, Central Asia, India, the Maldives and Sri Lanka, Mali, and perhaps even China. Ibn Battuta used his legal training to obtain appointments as an Islamic judge (qadi) in several of the places he visited. He eventually ended his travels back in Morocco in 1355, where he spent his remaining years as judge. All told, he had traversed an estimated 73,000 miles in thirty years, sojourning mostly among fellow Muslims. He recorded his memoirs at the request of the Moroccan sultan, but his Rihla did not become widely known until European scholars discovered manuscripts of it during the nineteenth century.

These thumb-nail biographies tell us that despite the political fragmentation of the Muslim world after the ninth century, there was remarkable degree of coherence achieved in its religious and cultural life. Thus, although they each came from different homelands and ethnic backgrounds, and pursued different careers, both al-Ghazali and Ibn Battuta were fluent in Arabic, had knowledge of the Quran and hadith, and had varying degrees of expertise in Islamic law, mysticism, and theology. Arabic, the foremost language of religion and learning, had become a lingua franca that facilitated communication between teachers and students, Sufi masters and disciples, travelers and pilgrims—no matter what their ethnic backgrounds happened to be.

Since the early years of empire, Muslims had gradually formed a consensus concerning belief and practice, thanks to the efforts of religious men and women residing in the towns and capitals of the new empire. The promulgation of a canonical version of the Quran gave rise to traditions of commentary and exegetical methods; the transmission and collection of hadiths from throughout the empire resulted in the creation of canonical hadith books and a "hadith science" to prop-

erly distinguish between authentic and spurious traditions. The rise of both of these scriptural disciplines helped communicate Islamic knowledge to growing numbers of converts, and was essential to the systematic implementation of the Sharia, the law. By the tenth century, this consensus had crystallized as Sunni Islam, which takes its name from normative Muslim practice, or Sunna, based on authoritative hadiths about the Prophet and early community—including the first four caliphs. Although Sunni Islam has existed in various localized forms, it has come to be regarded by many as the mainstream Islamic tradition.

The new locus for organized Islamic learning in al-Ghazali's time was the mosque-madrasa, an Islamic college. Previously learning occurred in homes, mosques, and shops. The madrasa, however, was a residential building complex devoted specifically to religious study—staffed by religious scholars known as ulama and fuqaha—and was usually supported in perpetuity by private endowments from wealthy elites. Ibn Battuta found madrasas in cities throughout the Muslim world; in Cairo, he said, "They were too many for anyone to count." Madrasa education emphasized the study of sacred texts and fiqh, the legal discipline used for understanding and applying the Sharia. Each madrasa usually specialized in teaching one of the chief Sunni legal traditions: Hanafi (named after Abu Hanifa, d. 767), Maliki (named after Malik ibn Anas, d. 795), Shafii (named after Muhammad ibn Idris al-Shafii, d. 820), and Hanbali (named after Ahmad ibn Hanbal, d. 855) These schools agreed upon a common legal structure, but differed from each other in respect to whether and to what extent independent human reason (qiyas and ijtihad) could be used in Islamic jurisprudence, as well as on specific points of law. Al-Ghazali was educated in the Shafii school, which had been feuding with the Hanafis for dominance in eastern Iranian cities. Ibn Battuta was trained in the Maliki school, which had been established in Spain and the Maghreb with Almoravid support.

The history of Sufism paralleled that of the Islamic legal schools, evolving from the efforts first of individual ascetics (eighth-ninth centuries), particularly in Iraq and Iran, then of Sufi masters and disciples (tenth-eleventh centuries), then of formally instituted brotherhoods with their own doctrines and ritual practices (twelfth-fourteenth centuries). Mosques, homes, and madrasas served as centers for mystical pursuits, but the chief meeting places were known variously as khanqas, ribats, tekkes, and zawiyas. In these places Sufi shaykhs and disciples could live, study and worship together on a regular basis. Conservative ulama would intermittently attack Sufis who claimed that seekers can attain unity with God, or who endorsed saint veneration; and Sufis would criticize jurists for being too concerned with their reputations and the letter of the law. Nonetheless, a degree of consensus was reached by scholars and mystics, as reflected in the examples both of al-Ghazali and Ibn Battuta. Indeed, it became rather commonplace for jurists to be members of the brotherhoods.

Sufis considered Muhammad and several of his companions to be models for their mystical endeavors because of the closeness they had achieved to God through their detachment from worldly passions and pursuits. With the guidance of their teachers, Sufis hoped to obtain similar closeness or union with the divine. As the example of al-Ghazali suggests, the growth of Sufism was partly a reaction to the worldly orientation taken by the community in the wake of the conquests, to political instability and corruption. It is likely that with the growing number of converts mystical ideas and practices were introduced into the Islamic milieu from Judaism, Christianity, gnostic and South Asian religions. Sufis subsequently played a leading role in indigenizing Islam among the masses in lands governed by Muslim rulers, and carried Islam via trade routes into sub-Saharan Africa, South and Southeast Asia—where new conversions were accomplished. The leading orders, or "paths" (turuq), that appeared in the Middle Eastern region between the twelfth and fourteenth centuries were the Suhrawardis, Qadiris, Rifais, Kubrawis, Shadhilis, Mevlevis, Naqshbandis, and Bektashis.

The contribution of women to the development of Islam in the medieval era is obscured by the fact that men monopolized the production of written knowledge and controlled political and religious institutions. This situation was reinforced by a conservative ideology among elites that aimed at confining women to the roles of housekeeper and childbearer. The Maliki jurist Ibn al-Hajj (died 1337), for example, invoked ancient authorities to rule that, "A woman is permitted three exits: one to the house of the husband when she is married tom him, one when her parents die; and one when she is carried to her grave." Indeed, when a kingdom was faced with disaster, rulers occasionally blamed in on female visibility and licentiousness, and attempted to confine women to their homes. Recent research, however, has shown that women were in fact often autonomous agents who contributed to the Muslim religious life and were instrumental in fostering solidarity in local Muslim communities. Muslim sources inform us that this was the case during the Prophet's lifetime and the era of the early caliphs. Muhammad's widows, for example, were credited with being authoritative sources of hadith; as many as 2,210 traditions have been attributed to his wife Aisha, Abu Bakr's daughter. Another widow, Hafsa, Umar's daughter, reportedly took custody of the early copy of the Quran that was

IMPORTANT RULERS AND DYNASTIES IN THE MIDDLE EAST, 622–1700*

Muhammad ibn Abd Allah, the Prophet, 622–632
Rashidun Caliphs, 632–661
Umayyad Caliphs, 661–750
Abbasid Caliphs, 750–1258
Fatimid Caliphs, 909–1171, North Africa, Egypt, Syria, Iran, India, and the Mediterranean
Buyids, 932–1062, Iran, Iraq
Saljuqs, 1038–1194, Iran, Iraq; 1077–1307, Central and Eastern Anatolia
Almoravids, 1056–1147, North Africa, Spain
Crusader States, 1099–1291, Anatolia, Syria, Palestine
Almohads, 1130–1269, North Africa, Spain
Ayyubids, 1169–1260, Egypt, Syria
Mongol States, 1219–1508, Iran, Iraq
Mamluks, 1250–1517, Egypt, Syria
Ottomans, 1281–1922, Anatolia, Syria, Iraq, Egypt, Tunisia, Algeria
Safavids, 1501–1732, Iran

*Adapted from T. Mostyn (ed.), The Cambridge Encyclopedia of the Middle East and North Africa. (Cambridge: Cambridge University Press, 1988), p. 59; Ira M. Lapidus, A History of Islamic Societies. (Cambridge: Cambridge University Press, 1988), pp. 55, 134, 280.

used later to establish the canonical version. The conquest brought many women as slaves, concubines, and wives for the Arab rulers and soldiers, which increased the size of the half-and non-Arab portions of Muslim population, but we have little biographical information about these women. Not surprisingly, neither Ibn Battuta nor al-Ghazali paid very much attention to the accomplishments of Muslim females in their times, but information about prominent women was recorded in exhaustive medieval biographical encyclopedias and histories. From these documents we know of women in the elite who founded mosques, madrasas, and Sufi hospices. Although they were excluded from the madrasa, daughters and wives of scholars, such as Zaynab al-Tukhiyya (died 1398) mastered Arabic grammar and the disciplines of the Quran and hadith, as well as fiqh. Other women had opportunity to acquire Islamic learning from shaykhs at the mosque. Although they could not be judges, outstanding female scholars became teachers of both men and women, particularly in the hadith sciences and women's fiqh. Sufi texts show ambivalent attitudes towards women. Nonetheless, they record anecdotes about female mystics in Iran and Iraq, the foremost of whom was Rabia of Basra (died 801), who is credited with having advocated the mystical union of God and the seeker in a bond of selfless love. During the Mamluk era several khanqas were established for female Sufis, and from Ibn al-Hajj's jaundiced remarks, we know that women in Cairo formed their own Sufi groups, participated with men in Sufi ritual performances, and frequented the tombs of holy men and women weekly to gain solace, healing, and divine blessing.

Al-Ghazali and Ibn Battuta both mentioned Shiism, the leading alternative to Sunni Islam, in their writings. The Shia path developed from a dispute over leadership of the community that erupted in the wake of Uthman's assassination in 656 between Ali's factions (shia) and that of Uthman and his kinsmen, the Umayyads. For the Shia the legitimate heirs to leadership (imama) in the community had to be designated descendants of the Prophet via Ali and Fatima, the Prophet's daughter. Most considered these "Imams" to be legitimate authorities for interpreting the Quran and hadith—their own words were exemplary and preserved in hadith collections. On the other hand, all Sunni caliphs, with the exception of Ali, were held to have usurped legitimate authority. By the tenth century, the doctrine of Imama had evolved among some Shia, to include the belief that personal redemption could be achieved through commemorative observances of the martyrdom of Ali's son Husayn, the third Imam, who was killed by the Umayyads in 680 at Karbala, Iraq. This belief was conjoined with the messianic expectation that the last Imam would arise from a state of occultation at the end of time to establish the universal rule of Islam. Shia groups held differing views as to which of the Imams this was to be. One of the two leading subdivisions held that it was to be seventh Imam, son of Ismail (died 760), and hence became known as Ismailis. The other identified him as the twelfth, son of Hasan al-Askari (died 874), and thus became known as the Twelvers. Jafar al-Sadiq (died 765), the sixth Imam, is credited with establishing the Twelver school of fiqh, known as the Jafari, which resembles the Sunni schools in structure, but allows greater latitude for independent human reason and differs on a number of points of substantive law. Later, particularly with Safavid support, Shia ulama were to establish their own madrasas in Najaf, Karbala, Hilla, Qum, Isfahan, Shiraz, and Mashhad. Sufism also flourished among the Shia.

Al-Ghazali, a staunch proponent of Sunni doctrines, denounced the Shia for placing too much weight on the authority of the Imam. His interest in them was not purely doctrinal, however, because at that time Abbasid-Saljuq hegemony was being challenged by the Ismaili Fatimid dynasty in Egypt and its representatives in Iran, and Syria. By the time Ibn Battuta had arrived in Egypt in 1326, the Fatimid dynasty had long since been displaced by the Sunni dynasties of the Ayyubids and the Mamluks. When he traveled into Mongol-held Iraq, however, he encountered Twelver Shia—whom he called "dissenters" (rafidis) in keeping with Sunni custom—in Najaf and Karbala, the preeminent Shia cen-

ters. Other leading Twelver Shia centers had emerged by that time in Syria, Lebanon, Bahrain, and northern Iran. Shiism was not to become the Islam for the majority of Iranians, however, until after 1500, when the Safavid dynasty started to promote it as the state religion.

Both continuity and discontinuity characterize the history of Islam in the Middle East between the seventh and the sixteenth century. The era of al-Ghazali differed substantially from that of the Prophet and the early Caliphs as a result of the currents of internal religious and political dissidence and mass conversions that swept through the empire. Persian increasingly was becoming a high literary language among with Arabic, especially in the eastern areas. No longer did lack of Arab ancestry limit one's chances for attaining high position in religion or government. Islamic learning and law were crystallizing into formal disciplines, and alternative Sufi and Shia movements had begun to organize their own doctrines, ritual practices, and institutions. Ibn Battuta's world in turn differed from that of al-Ghazali. The Abbasid empire had been penetrated by European Crusader armies, then finally destroyed by the Mongols in 1258. Turkish rulers governed Egypt, Syria, and Anatolia. Muslims in the west were obliged to contend with the loss of Iberian lands to European Christian armies. Elites in both the eastern and western edges of the Islamic world consequently sought refuge among coreligionists in North Africa, Egypt, Syria, and Anatolia, where they gave new impetus to religious and cultural life. For example, Jalal al-din Rumi (1207–1273), the inspired author of Sufi poetry and eponymous founder of the Mevlevi order, was among the Persians who retreated to Saljuq Anatolia at the advance of the Mongol onslaught into Iran. The famous historian Ibn Khaldun (1332–1406) came from a family that had fled Spain and settled in Tunis. The Black Death had caused losses in both his and Ibn Battuta's families as it decimated the populations of Asia, North Africa, and Europe during the fourteenth century. Finally, a second wave of Mongol warriors under the leadership of Tamerlane swept through eastern Islamic lands and parts of Anatolia between 1394 and 1405.

The Quran, Sunna, and Arabic language, however, provided a fabric of continuity that withstood centuries of natural calamity and profound social, political and cultural change, thanks to the concerted efforts of Muslim men and women through the generations. During the sixteenth century, which Western historians associate with the beginning of the modern era, Islamic history entered into its second millennium. Middle Eastern Muslim populations began to face new challenges and experience discontinuities that would be at least as profound as those they had encountered previously.

◆ MODERN DEVELOPMENTS IN THE MIDDLE EAST

Modernity and Islam are often regarded as being in confrontation with each other. The first is understood to be Western, dynamic, rational, secular, individualistic, based in an industrial economy, and usually democratic. Islam, on the other hand, is characterized as being Oriental, static, irrational, sacerdotal, collective, based in a pastoral or agricultural economy, and inclined toward authoritarianism. This perception of difference has become embedded in specific policies devised by Western powers with respect to Muslim polities, and in Western scholarship about Islamic culture and religion. This perception, which Edward W. Said has described as "Orientalism," first emerged into full view in the nineteenth century. Furthermore, it has since become "re-embedded" or "indigenized" within Muslim cultures themselves such that they use it to effect their own transformation or to assert their difference from the West. In fact, this perception of polarities has become so pervasive that in recent years there has been renewed discussion concerning the likelihood of a clash between Western and Islamic civilizations in the aftermath of the Cold War.

Such polarities rely on cultural stereotypes and accentuate what appear to be insurmountable differences between Muslims and non-Muslims. A more fruitful way to begin to approach the subject of the history of Islam in the Middle East during the last few centuries is to think of modernity as being first of all an awareness of rupture with the past coupled with the conviction that human agents can act rationally to improve the conditions of their own existence. In the Middle Eastern region, as in other regions of the globe, the forms that modernity has taken have been governed by the interplay of three historical forces: reformism and revivalism, imperialism, and nationalism. Each of these has been decisive in the shaping of Muslim identities; together they have generated a variety of ideas, practices, and institutions which make what is "Islamic" today distinctly modern.

◆ REFORMISM AND REVIVALISM IN THE MIDDLE EAST

The eighteenth century witnessed the emergence of a new spirit of revival and reform that swept Muslim lands from Africa to Asia. It was characterized by consciousness that Muslims had strayed from the essential principles of their religion, and it advocated renewed attentiveness to the Quran, emulation of the Prophet in daily conduct, and strict adherence to the *sharia*. Reformers frowned upon what they saw as a corruption of Islamic ideals by foreign influences and popular ignorance as manifested in the veneration of saints and other forms of worship not explicitly endorsed by the

Many reformers have based their ideas on reviving the role of the *Sharia*. Pictured Iman Shafii's mausoleum in Cairo. He is regarded as the founder of one school of Sunni law.

Quran and the *sunna*. Moreover, their reform program emphasized the use of *ijtihad* (independent human judgment) by qualified individuals to eradicate the encrustations that traditionally-minded jurists had allowed to accumulate in the body of Islamic law.

In seeking to explain this phenomenon, some scholars point to a reformist impulse or style inherent in Islam that periodically manifests itself in history. By itself, this is an unsatisfactory explanation for the emergence of modern Islamic reform movements, unless it can be linked to empirically verifiable evidence. Not only must we inquire about the content of the reform message, but we also must identify which Muslim organizations and individuals promoted reform. Where did it develop and spread? How? Why? What makes call to reform acceptable to the wider community at some moments and not others? What has been its impact, and how has it in turn been affected by he accidents of history?

Modern Sunni Islamic reformism was nurtured among *hadith* scholars and Sufi organizations, then transmitted via their international networks from bases in India, Mecca and Medina, Damascus, and

Cairo. Two Sufi orders played an especially active role in this: the Naqshbandis and the Khalwatis. The Naqshbandis—based in India under the leadership of Ahmad Sirhindi (1564–1624), the "Renewer of the Second (Islamic) Millennium," and Shah Wali Allah(1703–1762)—spread their reformist ideas throughout Asia and the Ottoman lands during the seventeenth and eighteenth centuries. Among the leading Naqshbandi teachers in the Middle Eastern region were Taj al-Din ibn Zakariya (died 1640) in Mecca, Murad al-Bukhari (died 1720) and Abd al-Ghani al-Nablusi (died 1731) in the eastern Mediterranean and Syria, and Khalid al-Baghdadi (died 1827) in Kurdistan and among Ottoman religious and political authorities. The introduction of the Khalwati brand of reformism was initiated by Mustafa al-Bakri (died 1748), a student of al-Nablusi, and his leading disciple in Egypt, Muhammad al-Hifnawi (died 1767). It was well received by many of the religious scholars (*ulama*) and Sufis, and together with Naqshbandi ideas, gave rise to new Sufi orders in Algeria, Tunisia, Sudan, and the Arabian Peninsula.

The earliest, most remarkable result of Islamic renewal and reform in the Middle East was the *Muwahhidun* "Unitarian," or Wahhabi movement that sprang forth from the Najd in the Arabian peninsula's interior. Its founder Muhammad ibn Abd al-Wahhab (1703–1791), the son of a Hanbali judge, preached pure monotheism (*tawhid*) and enforcement of the *sharia*, based on a narrow reading of the Quran and the traditions, along with limited use of *ijtihad*. He viciously attacked the popular practice of saint veneration, Shia devotion to the *imams*, and any other forms of religious belief and practice he considered not to be explicitly sanctioned by the scriptural canon. In his eyes, Muslims who entertained such beliefs should be denounced as infidels and killed. The Wahhabi message was not well received in many quarters, but around 1746 Ibn Abd al-Wahhab joined in an alliance with the chieftain of a prominent Najdi tribe, Muhammad ibn Saud. By 1803, with the capture of Mecca, the Wahhabi/Saudi alliance had become the dominant religio-political force on the peninsula. This new tribal state was short-lived—the army of Mehmet Ali, the Ottoman governor of Egypt, put an end to it in 1818. Eventually, however, a new Saudi state would be built on its foundations slightly more than a century later under the leadership of Abd al-Aziz ibn Saud (1876–1953), in alliance with a new generation of enthusiastic Wahhabi proponents, the *Ikhwan* (brotherhood).

Among the Twelver Shia of Iran and southern Iraq there were also significant developments, but they involved different configurations of reform and renewal. Two opposing schools of jurisprudence, the Akhbaris

and the Usulis arose among *ulama* there after the establishment of the Safavid empire in 1501. With its demise in 1722, and with the incursions of the Portuguese from Europe and the Omanis from the gulf, competition between the two groups increased. The Akhbaris ruled that valid legal judgments could only be based on the Quran and explicit knowledge obtained from the traditions (*akhbar*) of the Prophet and the *imams*. The Usulis argued that the only valid ruling was one made by a living jurist who had to reach his decisions by way of reason (*aql*) and *ijtihad*. On this basis, any action that is not explicitly forbidden by scripture is permissible. The Akhbaris rejected *ijtihad* and urged caution in regard to actions that were not explicitly authorized by scripture. For them, all Muslims were obliged to imitate the *imams*. For the Usulis, Muslims were to be divided into two groups: those qualified to practice *ijtihad* (the *mujtahids*) and those who imitated them. The Akhbari school, with its conservative approach to tradition, prevailed in the shrine cities of Karbala, Najaf, Samarra, and Kazimayn in Iraq for much of the eighteenth century. It gave way, however, to the Usulis, thanks to an influx of Usuli *ulama* refugees from Iran and the efforts of jurists like Muhammad Baqir Bihbihani (died 1791), remembered in Shia circles as "Renewer of the Thirteenth (Islamic) Century." With the enhanced authority gained from their triumph, their more flexible approach to law, and the independence gained from having the right to extract annual contributions from their supporters. Usuli scholars established the basis from which they were to take active roles in the politics of Iraq and Iran for at least the next two centuries. Their efforts contributed decisively to the conversion of Arab tribes of southern Iraq to Shiism in the nineteenth century, and to the success of the Iranian Revolution of 1977–1979.

Although neither the early modern Sunni nor the Shia expressions of revival and reform were initially "popular," their influence spread widely, thanks in no small part to the annual *Hajj* and pilgrimage to Shia shrines. The *Hajj* brought Muslims from many regions into contact with reformist teachers and Sufi orders in Cairo and the holy cities of Mecca and Medina. Some then carried their new visions of Islam back to their homelands where they actively sought to implement them. Pilgrimage to Shia shrine towns gave jurists living there a regular source of student recruits and revenue, and it helped the Persians among them stay in touch with associates back home. The political disintegration occurring in the Ottoman and Mughal empires, as well as the turbulence that swept Iran in the decades following the collapse of the Safavid empire probably enhanced receptivity to reform ideas among the peoples living in this regions.

Imperialism in the Middle East

The expansion of European control and influence in the Middle East during modern times has had far-ranging effects on its cultures, political structures, and economies. The region, of course, has witnessed the rise and fall of numerous empires through the centuries, including Islamic ones. Several characteristics distinguish the modern European form of imperialism from earlier Middle Eastern ones: they have been conducted through the agency of competing nation-states; they have been structured largely in accordance with the principles of secularized rationality; they possessed superior technology; and the economic system has been based on the acquisition of raw materials and cheap human labor to sustain industrial production at home and ready markets for finished products abroad. No single set of religious communities experienced the effects of modern European imperialism more extensively than the Islamic one, and in few regions in the Eastern Hemisphere was its impact more immediate and heterogeneous than in the Middle East. Muslims there had to find ways to contend with superordinate foreign powers who could not be as easily contained as the Crusaders, nor as readily absorbed as the Mongols.

The bridgeheads for European involvement in Muslim lands were first established when Europeans discovered that they could intervene in the Indian Ocean spice trade by navigating around the Cape of Good Hope at the end of the fifteenth century, and when the Ottomans suffered a series of costly defeats on battlefields in southeastern Europe, beginning towards the end of the seventeenth century. Access to the spice trade led to establishment of coastal footholds in South Asia from which the Portuguese, Dutch, and eventually the British extended influence into the Persian Gulf region. The Ottoman losses in Europe led to the involvement of competing European powers in the political and economic affairs of the empire, Russian invasions into Ottoman lands around the Black Sea (1774–1829), as well as French invasions of Egypt (1798) and Algeria (1830). By the eve of World War I the Caspian region and Muslim lands in inner Asia had been incorporated into the Russian empire and northern Iran had entered its sphere of influence. France had won control of Algeria and Tunisia and partitioned Morocco with Spain (1912). Britain, meanwhile had converted the Persian Gulf into a "British lake," created a sphere of influence in southern Iran, and won control of Egypt, Sudan, and coastal regions of southern Arabia as protectorates. Italy, one of the newest European nation-states, began colonizing Libya in 1912.

The entry of the Ottoman empire into World War I, on the side of the Central Powers, brought about its destruction and greater European entanglement in the political affairs of Middle Eastern peoples. The British, in particular, sent their troops into Iraq, expanded their military presence in Iran, and supported an "Arab Revolt" against the Ottomans as part of their war effort. In the post-war settlement, the territories of Palestine, Transjordan, and Iraq became British mandates, while Lebanon and Syria became French ones. Concomitantly, British diplomats heeded the call of the Zionist Organization for a Jewish homeland in Palestine without due regard for growing Arab national aspirations, thus setting the stage for a long series of nationalist conflicts between Arabs and Jews. The only sizable areas in the Middle East-North African region, to have escaped some form of European imperial control by 1920, were most of Anatolia and the Arabian Peninsula, but even the remotest regions experienced its effects nonetheless.

Responses of indigenous populations in the region, including Muslims, to modern imperialism were by no means uniform. They ranged from various forms of acceptance and adaptation to rejection and armed opposition. Among ruling elites in Istanbul, Cairo, and Tehran, it became apparent that the best way to check European expansion was to modernize their armies. This meant importing European experts and technologies, which were accompanied by Western ideas and values. Modernizing regimes began to produce Turkish, Arabic, and Persian translations of European manuals and books using newly imported printing presses. They opened new, secularized educational institutions in their capital cities and sent missions to Europe to study, train, and observe. A new, disciplinary authoritarianism prevailed in the Westernizing regimes as governmental, the military, transportation, and communication became more centralized and efficient. Concomitantly, enlightenment concepts of individual liberty and equality were also appropriated. Constitutionalist movements arose in Tunisia, the Ottoman empire, Egypt, and Iran. Before the end of the nineteenth century western-educated Muslim elites who knew European languages were assuming prominent roles in government, while Middle Eastern Jews and Christians continued to be active in international commerce—increasingly so with the Europeans.

For many Muslims, the sea change caused by imperialism did not bring about immediately discernible changes in their religious outlook and ritual activities. Religious scholars continued to write and teach about the traditional Islamic sciences. In Sunni lands especially they became subordinated to the new secular, centralized states. The performance of prayer, alms-giving, fasting and *Hajj* continued much as it had during the preceding centuries. Saint veneration and Sufi orders continued to be viable forms of religious belief and action for many communities.

From within the Ottoman sphere itself there arose a renewed consciousness of Muslim solidarity to which Europeans referred as Pan-Islamism. Sultan Abdulhamid II (reigned 1876–1909) promoted it as state policy to solidify Ottoman control over its lands and to unify Muslims against further European penetration. While modernizing law, education, and communications, he concomitantly revived the title of caliph in an attempt to win spiritual and temporal control over Muslim subjects, and for the first time, over Muslims living in lands controlled by non-Muslims. As a countermeasure to European involvement with his Christian subjects, Abdulhamid gave preferred treatment to Muslims, and sought to strengthen the Ottoman hold on the holy cities in the Hejaz by building of a railway from Damascus to Medina. Even though these efforts were short-lived, a panislamic spirit has continued to reappear during the twentieth century in the form of international Islamic organizations and Pan-Islamic writings.

Outside the Ottoman court, there were a number of instances of armed Muslim resistance and opposition to imperial expansion. Between 1830 and 1847, Abd al-Qadir (1808–1883), a Qadiri Sufi *shaykh* inspired in part by Naqshbandi reformist ideas, led a *jihad* of Algerian tribes against the French. Similar forms of resistance, continued after Abd al-Qadir's deportation, culminating in the great Algerian revolt of 1871, which ended with a strengthening of French colonial control. A Sammaniya Sufi *shaykh* named Muhammad Ahmad (1848–1885), proclaimed to be the *Mahdi* (a messianic figure), led a coalition of tribal forces against Ottoman-Egyptian troops and established a *Mahdist* state in northern Sudan in 1885. British forces put an end to it in 1898, but *Mahdist* loyalists have continued to play prominent role in Sudanese religious and political affairs ever since. Another reform-minded Sufi order, the Sanusiyya, established a network of lodges throughout much of Libya and central Sahara during the nineteenth century. From 1901 to 1914 they led unsuccessful resistance campaigns against French expansion in Chad, then against the Italians in Libya from 1911 to 1932. Despite the involvement of Sufi orders in such movements, modernists came to hold Sufi ideas and practices to blame for making the *Umma* vulnerable to foreign domination.

The oppositional disposition of Shia *ulama* has been exaggerated because of the pivotal role they played in the Iranian revolution of 1977–1979. They have taken the lead, however, in anti-imperial actions several times in the last two centuries. Between 1812 and 1828 they joined with the reforming Qajar crown prince Abbas Mirza (died 1833) to declare a *jihad* and mobilize the people against Russian troops in Azerbaijan. The results were disastrous for the Iranians, however. When the Qajar Shah Nasir al-Din (died 1896) granted a British consortium monopolistic control over domestic tobacco production and sale in 1890, the *ulama* led popular demonstrations, and the chief jurist at the time, Mirza Hasan Shirazi (died 1895), issued a legal decree endorsing a boycott which was widely observed. The concession was canceled. Political activism among Shia *ulama* resurfaced in the context of the Iranian Constitutional Revolution (1905–1911), which sought to check royal absolutism and concessions to foreign powers with a constitutional democracy. The jurists were divided on this issue, but leading *mujtahids* in Najaf, such as Muhammad Husayn Naini (died 1936), came out strongly in favor of constitutionalism. Later, Naini and other jurists incited an unsuccessful uprising (1920–1923) against the British occupation of Iraq.

The *Salafiyya*, or Islamic modernist movement, embodied another kind of response on the part of the *ulama* and intellectuals to the extraordinary changes occurring in the region. Initiated by Jamal al-Din al-Afghani (1837–97), a Persian, and his Egyptian student Muhammad Abduh (1849–1905), this movement sought to define a middle path for Islam between assertion that it had been surpassed by Western scientific learning, on the one hand, and that it must reject Western science in favor of sacred tradition on the other. They posited that pristine Islam—founded on a belief in a single transcendent God as expressed in the Quran and the lives of the first pious Muslims (*al-salaf al-salih*)—was in conformity with reason, science, and progress. Over time, however, it had ossified in the hands of *ulama* who adhered blindly to traditional schools of doctrine and practice. Islam's survival in the modern era, therefore, required uncovering its original essence as conveyed by the Quran and the *sunna* and implementing it. Exercise of the human intellect (*ijtihad*) was encouraged in areas not specifically addressed by sacred texts. The upshot of this was the that in theory reason and revelation were one, and Western learning could be synthesized with Islam. Indeed, Salafis proudly asserted that the West had actually derived its sciences from the Muslims at an early stage of its history. The *Salafiyya* drew inspiration from earlier reform movements, and during the twentieth century stimulated modernist reform programs in Islamic law and education from North Africa to Indonesia. During the 1920s and 1930s the movement produced two offshoots, one which led to secularism among educated elites and another which led to urban-based Islamic activism.

Nationalism in the Middle East

Imperialism produced centralized colonial states with artificially imposed borders throughout much of the Middle East during the twentieth century. It also

Women's Library and Information Center, Istanbul, Turkey.

manipulated religious and ethnic identities among indigenous peoples to facilitate access and control, thus putting the complex intergroup networks and intercultural ties that had been constructed during the foregoing centuries under great stress. Moreover, intensified contact with Europe and the establishment of educational institutions, modeled after those of Europe, made it possible for people in the region to become familiar with nationalist ideas and writings, to begin to appropriate them both to gain some measure of autonomy as Ottoman and Qajar power declined, and to check further interference on the part of European powers.

From this interplay of foreign and native forces, nationalist formulations of religious, ethnic, and territorial identities began to crystallize between the 1870s and 1920s among the Muslim urban elite in Iranian, Turkish and Arab communities. Iranian nationalism—based on a distinctly Persian heritage, language, and Shia Islam—was instigated by resistance to foreign penetration and the Constitutional Revolution. In Ottoman lands, along with state-sponsored modernization and centralization, came intermittent efforts to create a common identity for its subjects based on loyalty to the sultanate, Pan-Islamism, and Pan-Turkism. With the

collapse of the empire after World War I and the establishment of the Republic of Turkey in 1923, Anatolian-based Turkish nationalism, personified by Mustafa Kemal Ataturk (1881–1938), proved to be the most viable collective identity for the country.

Armenian Christians in eastern Ottoman lands were among the first minorities to develop an active nationalist movement, for which they suffered dearly at the hands of Ottoman forces during this era. Kurdish Muslims, chief antagonists of the Armenians, also began to experience nationalist impulses. By contrast, in Syrian towns, Christians worked with Sunni Muslims to forge a shared national identity based on their common Arabic language and heritage. Coptic and Muslim leaders in Egypt, meanwhile, promoted the uniqueness of their Egyptian identity, which was based on their attachment to the land and a legacy consisting of Pharaonic, Christian, and Arab Muslim components. Although scholars have maintained that such nationalism was produced by indigenous Westernized elite, the new middle class, and emigres, there is also evidence for the development of *populist* national sentiments that could erupt into mass demonstrations and rebellions. Renewed attention to native languages and rapid adaptation of new modes of communication and cul-

At the beginning of the twentieth century, the Arab world had a population of about thirty-five million; now it is more than two hundred million.

tural expression, such as newspapers, printed books, and plays—followed by radio and recorded music, greatly facilitated the propagation of national sentiments across a wide social spectrum.

Two World Wars and respect for the principle of national self-determination contributed to a slackening of the European grip on Middle Eastern political affairs and the creation of modernizing nation-states in the region. These new political entities on the whole have had secular orientations, with government, law, and education patterned after Western models. Islam was subordinated to the nation-state in varying degrees, but never completely divorced from it. Turkey, where the caliphate was abolished, *madrasas* closed, Sufi orders banned, the *sharia* replaced by a Swiss civil code, and the Gregorian calendar adopted between 1924 and 1926, is regarded by many as the most secularized country in the region. Yet even there a modernist vision of Islam is used by the state to mobilize its citizens in the service of national interests. Other countries such as Egypt, Syria, Iran under the Pahlavis (1925–1979), and Tunisia have emulated Turkey in many respects. In most, however, when it comes to matters such as worship and personal status laws, the *sharia* continues to

be largely respected. Even in Iraq, where the government since 1968 has been in the hands of Sunni Arabs adhering to a Bath Arab socialist ideology, Islam is conceived to be the purest expression of the Arab spirit. Under Saddam Husayn, the government has learned to co-opt Sunni and Shia symbols, while violently suppressing Kurdish and Shia opposition. When it invaded Kuwait in August 1990, it added the phrase *Allah akbar* "God is greater" to its national flag.

Several states have identified themselves more closely with Islam, such as the Kingdom of Saudi Arabia (founded in 1932), where the Quran is claimed to be the constitution and the Saudi rulers derive much of their legitimacy from patronage of the *ulama*, the Hajj, and religious institutions at home and abroad. On the opposite shore of the Persian Gulf, since the revolution of 1979, Iran considers itself to be an "Islamic republic," with a constitution that grants supreme executive authority to the chief Shia *mujtahid* and a religious Council of Guardians who govern in the absence of the hidden imam. Moreover, both Saudi Arabia and Iran have competed against each other for leadership in regional and Islamic affairs. Thus even in two neighboring countries where

Islam is the official state ideology, it is articulated very differently in contrasting political and cultural milieus.

The Status of Women in the Middle East

Modernity has been credited with an improvement in the status of women in the region. As a result of new educational and career opportunities available to people there, especially in the upper and middle classes, a significant minority of women have been enabled to pursue careers in public education, business, medicine, engineering, and government. They have taken visible roles in national life, participating in anti-colonial demonstrations and revolutions, publishing magazines, writing books, poetry and newspaper columns, and managing private charitable organizations, clinics, and hospitals. With the incorporation of the region into the global economic system and rapid urbanization, women have also become active agents in agricultural, commercial, industrial, as well as domestic production.

Muslim traditions have been articulated differently in relation to such changes in female identity and social activity. Much attention has been given to conservative religious authorities who invoke sacred tradition to constrain the sphere of female activity to the home and protect male privilege. Indeed, Islam together with other social and cultural factors have been invoked by conservative forces to block reforming the *sharia* in regard to marriage, divorce, child custody, and inheritance—areas of law where males usually have the upper hand. In doing so, they have helped make women a focal point in the heated contest between Islamization and secularization.

However, it is incorrect to conclude that Islam is only a reactionary force in relation to issues of gender in contemporary societies. Feminist movements have emerged in all countries of the region, starting in the first decades of this century in Iran, Turkey, and, above all, Egypt. Huda Sharawi (1879–1947), the French-tutored daughter of a wealthy landowner in Minya, was the founder and leader of the Egyptian feminist movement for decades. Drawing upon Islamic modernist ideas, she promoted the improvement of education and medical services for women, took an active role in nationalist politics, and, in 1923, joined with other women activists to establish the Egyptian Feminist Union, dedicated to helping women achieve greater parity with men.

Another extraordinary Egyptian woman—one very different from Sharawi—was Umm Kulthoum (1904–1975), the premier vocalist of the Arab world from the 1920s to the 1970s. The daughter of a poor village Quran reciter, she started as a singer of religious songs together with her father and brother at saints festivals and weddings in the Nile delta, then rose to stardom after moving to Cairo, thanks to the assistance of that city's leading musicians and the pioneering work of other female performers. Taking advantage of the opportunities offered by the proliferation of western-style music halls and the nascent commercial recording industry, she shifted from a classical Islamic music repertoire to one that consisted of more modern compositions with passionate love lyrics and nationalistic themes. Umm Kulthoum's vocal artistry, conservative bearing, and ambition won her widespread respect in the music world and among the Egyptian public at large. Not only did she commission her own music and dictate the terms of her recording and performance contracts, but was elected president of the musicians union seven times between 1945 and 1952, performed benefit concerts for her country, and established centers to aid 1967 war refugees. Throughout her life, moreover, she remained mindful of her Muslim identity, incorporating religious themes in several of her songs and movies and fulfilling personal religious obligations. When she died, millions attended her funeral—reportedly more than attended that of Abd al-Nasir, Egypt's charismatic president during the 1950s and 60s.

♦ BEYOND TRADITION AND MODERNITY

In the contemporary era, Islam is often associated by outsiders with the misnomer "fundamentalism," a Western term which usually implies that Muslims are uniformly backward-looking, anti-science, fanatical or conservative, and tied to a literalist interpretation of scripture. It is clear, however, that widespread reformism, encounters with imperialism, and the establishment of nation-states, individually and together, have shaped Islam in many subtle and complex ways, both in and outside the Middle East. Now, as never before, Islam is being construed by Muslims who not only have an awareness of other religions, but who also know of and have direct experience with secular ideologies such as capitalism, democracy, communism, socialism, nationalism, and feminism. Some Muslims have tried to reject these ideologies, but many have either embraced them or transformed them to fit into Islamic milieus. In many respects, therefore, there is no "going back"—even rejectionists couch their ideas in very modern idioms, and use the latest electronic and print media to convey them.

"Political Islam," or "Islamism," the controversial formulation of Islam to which the term "fundamentalism" is often applied, appeared in the Middle East during the second half of the twentieth century. Seeking to replace colonial and secular nationalist regimes with explicitly Islamic ones, and to substitute Western-inspired laws with the Sharia, its ideologies, structures,

Children in a park, Cairo, Egypt.

and strategies were shaped by the events and transformations that have occurred during the modern era. Much of the discontent upon which Islamists have drawn can be attributed to rapid demographic shifts in the region and the shortcomings of the newly formed nation-states.

It is estimated that in 1800 the population of the Middle East region was thirty million, 80 percent of whom lived in Ottoman lands. At the beginning of the twentieth century, the Arab world had a population of about thirty-five million; now it is more than two hundred million. Egypt and Iran's populations have each grown from ten million to fifty-nine million and sixty-two million respectively between 1900 and 1993. Cities, which have long existed in a symbiotic relationship with the countryside, now dominate nearly all aspects of life in the region. Nomadic pastoralism has virtually disappeared. Concomitantly, urban populations have grown from less than 20 percent of the total to 50 percent or more in the 1980s–1990s, thanks to the forced settlement of nomads, voluntary rural migration to industrializing regions, and increasing refugee populations, in addition to high population growth rates. Urbanization has been particularly pronounced in the Arab Gulf countries, where from 80 percent to 90 per-

cent of the population now lives in cities. In Turkey the percentage of the urban population increased from 23 percent to 59 percent between 1965 and 1993. During the same period in Iran it grew from 37 percent to 54 percent. Besides becoming more urbanized, these populations are growing increasingly younger. Perhaps as much as 45 percent of the population in Arab countries is now under the age of fifteen, compared to 35.5 percent in Turkey and 47 percent in Iran. Since the 1950s oil revenues have stimulated these changes and helped assuage the socio-economic strains caused by them, but they have not always been evenly or efficiently distributed. Moreover, national governments have diverted valuable resources to the military or lost them to corruption, such that they are unable to provide the educational, employment, housing, and health care opportunities that they had led their citizens to expect.

Leftist movements have arisen in connection with these developments, but it is the Islamic ones that prevail at the end of the century. An Islamist agenda was first set forth by the Muslim Brotherhood, founded in 1928 by Hasan al-Banna (1906–1949). It gained a wide following in Egypt, where it still plays an active role in national affairs, then established branches in Palestine, Jordan, Syria, Lebanon, Iraq, Yemen, and Sudan during the next forty years. It has also had some appeal in North Africa. The Sudanese branch, known as the National Islamic Front, joined with the army to seize the government in 1989 under the leadership of Hasan al-Turabi, a Western-educated lawyer. After the shattering defeat the Arab nationalist cause suffered at the hands of the Israelis in 1967, radical Islamic opposition groups were spawned by the Muslim Brotherhood, such as the Muslims Group and al-Jihad in Egypt, and the Islamic Jihad Movement and Hamas (Islamic Resistant Movement) in Gaza and the West Bank.

Islamist movements have emerged elsewhere in the Middle East that were not offshoots of the Muslim Brotherhood. The most noteworthy of these is the one led by Ayatollah Ruhallah Khomeini (1902–1989) and other Shia *ulama*, who helped provoke the popular revolution against the Shah of Iran in 1978–1979, then succeeded in transforming the country from a pro-Western monarchy into an Islamic republic. Lebanese Shia authorities founded AMAL (Lebanese Resistance Battalions) and Hizbullah (Party of God) to protect their communities during the years of civil war and invasion suffered by that country, starting in 1975. Shia *ulama* have also attempted to organize opposition to Saddam Husayn's regime in Iraq, with little success. In Algeria, where the majority of citizens are Sunni Muslims, the leading Islamist organization is the Islamic Salvation Front (FIS), which was outlawed by the government after winning national elections in 1991, thus igniting a conflict that has since caused more than thirty thousand fatalities. Lastly, unlike the Islamist movements of Egypt, Sudan, Iran, Lebanon, and Algeria, the leading agent of religious activism in Turkey at present is the reformist Naqshabandi Sufi order. Although it has clashed with the republican government of Turkey in the past, it has more recently integrated itself into national politics on behalf of preserving Islamic values, national solidarity, and middle class economic interests. Restoration of the *sharia* is not one of its goals, in contrast to other Islamist organizations. It has been closely associated with the Motherland Party, which emerged in the 1980s to become the leading party in the country under Turgut Ozal, who served as prime minister than president 1983 and 1993.

Islam in the contemporary Middle East has developed into a variety of specific forms—traditional, popular, reformist, nationalist, modernist, secularist, and Islamist—each of which is itself affected by an interplay of local cultural geographies, historical events, and global processes. In general, Muslims in the region remain profoundly attentive to their past, yet they are also aware of the dramatic changes they have both made and experienced during the modern era. As a result, there have been strong currents of anti-Westernism. It is unlikely that these currents will produce a clash of civilizations as has been predicted in some quarters because they are countered by others that are more accommodational, or are based on constructions of identity that are more national or ethnic in character than religious. For the foreseeable future, Islam is likely to become an even more important component in national ideologies and in the everyday lives of people in the region—but it is also likely to do so in ways that cannot yet be anticipated, just as the changes that occurred there during this century were largely unanticipated at the end of the last.

Juan E. Campo

References

Ahmed, Leila. *Women and Gender in Islam.* New Haven: Yale University Press, 1992.

Bulliet, Richard W. *Islam: The View From the Edge.* New York: Columbia University Press, 1994.

Campo, Juan. *The Other Side of Paradise: Explorations into the Religious Meaning of Domestic Space in Islam.* Columbia: University of South Carolina Press, 1991.

Hourani, Albert. *A History of the Arab Peoples.* Cambridge: Harvard University Press, 1991.

Humphreys, R. Stephen. *Islamic History: A Framework For Inquiry.* Princeton: Princeton University Press, 1991.

Keddie, Nikki R., and Beth Baron. *Women in Middle Eastern History.* New Haven: Yale University Press, 1991.

Kennedy, Hugh. *The Prophet and the Age of the Caliphates.* London: Longman, 1986.

Lapidus, Ira M. *A History of Islamic Societies.* Cambridge: Cambridge University Press, 1988.

Lewis, Bernard. *The Shaping of the Modern Middle East.* New York: Oxford University Press, 1994.

Nakash, Yitzhak. *The Shiis of Iraq.* Princeton: Princeton University Press, 1994.

The Oxford Encyclopedia of the Modern Islamic World, 4 vols. Edited by John Esposito. Oxford: Oxford University Press, 1995.

Peters, F. E. *Muhammad and the Origins of Islam.* Albany: State University of New York Press, 1994.

Voll, John Obert. *Islam: Continuity and Change in the Modern World.* Boulder, Colo.: Westview Press, 1982.

4

Islam in Sub-Saharan Africa

♦ Early Muslim Contact with Sub-Saharan Africa ♦ Islam in the Horn of Africa
♦ Islam in the Sudan Region ♦ Islam in West Africa ♦ Islam in Southern Africa
♦ The Great *Jihads* ♦ The Emergence of the Swahili Culture
♦ Muslim Revivalism and European Rule ♦ Modern Trends in Africa South of the Sahara

Islam came to Africa very early in its history. When its followers in Arabia began to face serious persecution from the Meccan aristocracy, the Prophet Muhammad advised his harassed followers to seek refuge in Abyssinia (modern day Ethiopia) in the year 615. This event, which is known as the first hijra (migration), played an important role in the development of the movement. The Muslim refugees returned to Arabia only after the Muslims had triumphed over their enemies in Mecca. They came to be known as the "People of the Ship," and represent the first phase in the contact of Islam with Africa. In due course the presence of Muslims in Africa would grow and extend as Muslim scholars and merchants exchanged their material and intellectual wares with African peoples. Following the establishment of Muslim influence and rule in North Africa, Islam's first extension into sub-Saharan Africa was by way of conquest, trade and commerce in West Africa and through immigration and trade along the East African coast.

♦ EARLY MUSLIM CONTACT WITH SUB-SAHARAN AFRICA

In West Africa, the arrival of Islam dates to the tenth century. The earliest contacts were made with African kingdoms such as Tekrur and ancient Ghana. These initial contacts were largely inspired by trade and commercial considerations, but the rise of dynasties such as the Almoravids (1056–1147) and the Almohads (1145–1269), eventually paved the way for the extension of Islam through the Berber people, who came from the Sahel region. The participation of these groups in the trans-Saharan trade, dating back to pre-Islamic times, helped diffuse Islam to their southern neighbors.

In East Africa, recent archaeological work suggests that the coming of Islam to the coast followed the long-established trade patterns in the Indian Ocean between the west coast of Asia, the Gulf, and the East African coast. This archaeological evidence indicates the presence of Muslims on the coast as early as the eighth century.

In very broad terms, the diffusion and growth of Islam in Africa is generally seen as occurring in five phases: (1) The conquest of Egypt and North Africa in the seventh century and the eventual Islamization and Arabization of the region. (2) The movement of Muslims in the northern part of Africa to the Sudan and the Sahel, through trade, and the steady conversion of West African peoples to Islam; the diffusion of Islam through trade and settlement in East Africa. This phase lasted through the thirteenth century. (3) The permeation of Islam through the conversion of rulers of major West African kingdoms and peoples from the fourteenth century onwards. In this phase, several Muslim states developed in West and East Africa and there was an increasing use of Arabic and other cultural influences resulting from interaction with many Muslim regions. (4)The consolidation of Muslim influence in all these regions and its extension to other African peoples. In this phase, which can be dated to the nineteenth century, the networks of commerce and Sufi *tariqas* predominated and Muslim institutions and practices and the use of Arabic became widespread. (5) The modern and contemporary phase which coincides with *jihad*-movements to spread Islam and to resist European rule. This phase also coincides with eventual colonization, loss and retrieval of power, and emergence of independent nation-states. During this phase diverse patterns emerge. Although loss of power and control of trade to Europeans are evident in all regions, one sees the continuing growth of Islam in the interior

Archaeological evidence indicates the presence of Muslims on the east coast of Africa as early as the eighth century.

regions of West and East Africa, reaching as far as Uganda and Zaire.

A simple reading of these phases might ignore the long term and enduring influences generated by institution building, the establishment of legal systems and the synthesis of spirituality between Islam and various African traditions. The entry of Islam into African space is not marked simply by displacement but by a long and elaborate exchange between ideas, institutions, and persons. It is this ongoing exchange that in spite of moments of tension and conflict, led also to convergence and helped create and build the enduring presence of a diverse and cosmopolitan Muslim heritage in sub-Saharan Africa, a process that is still ongoing.

◆ ISLAM IN THE HORN OF AFRICA

Muslim influence followed a southward course, along the Nile and also across from the Red Sea. It was consolidated by contacts developed along trading routes. The Christian dynasties that ruled Ethiopia and Eritrea participated in a flourishing trade with Muslim rulers to the north during the tenth and eleventh centuries. Muslim immigrants established communities, particularly along the coast. Traditional Somali history,

which has been presented orally, gives an account of how Muslim and Somali culture came together through trade and intermarriage. By the year 1100 the influence of Islam stretched along the Somali coast as far south as the island of Madagascar. Muslim travellers in the region provided description of various communities and their religious and commercial activities. In Ethiopia, Muslim influence led to the establishment of a kingdom in the Shoan plateau and anticipated the ongoing rivalry between various kingdoms over the next several centuries. By the year 1300 many of the peoples in the Horn of Africa had embraced Islam and the communities were linked by trade to other Muslim communities along the coast and indeed with other Muslims in Asia and the Middle East.

During the second half of the fourteenth century, there were a number of Muslim kingdoms in Ethiopia as well. When Ibn Battuta, the great Muslim traveller, visited the Horn of Africa in 1331, Muslim institutions had already become well-established in the region.

◆ ISLAM IN THE SUDAN REGION

In ancient times, this region, south of Egypt, encompassed most of the modern state of the Sudan and extended along the Nile River. It was geographically distinct from the more arid regions of the Sahara and the Sahel.

Before the coming of Islam, there existed two major kingdoms in the northern part of this region: the Nubian Christian state and the kingdom of Axum along the Red Sea coast. Muslims arrived in these regions by way of the Red Sea and Egypt. In time a blend of populations occurred and Muslim influence and control was established by a group known as the Banu Kanz, a people whose roots lay in the cosmopolitan heritage of Nubia and Arabia. By the year 1500, most of the region had come under Muslim control.

In the southern parts of the area, the population consisted of peoples who were pastoral, living along the Nile River and in interior regions of the savannah. Some of them converted to Islam but many remained close to their ancient, traditional roots.

By the sixteenth century, Ottoman influence had extended to both Egypt and the Sudan, and the region was linked to the vast trade, commercial, and cultural network of the Ottoman Empire. Sufi *tariqas* became well established in the Sudan. European influence increased in the nineteenth century as they became involved in the existing ivory and slave trade and sought control of these resources.

The Muslims of the Sudan sought autonomy in the face of foreign influence and trade. In 1881 they revolted under the leadership of a Sufi teacher, Muhammad bin Abdullah, who became known as the *mahdi* and who attempted to set up a new state based on the perceived model of the early Muslim community. However, the British were able to put down the revolt and established colonial rule until Sudan's independence in 1956.

♦ ISLAM IN WEST AFRICA

Islam in West Africa followed the ancient trading routes that linked Egypt to the West African empire of Ghana which flourished from the eighth century onwards. The western Sudan had also forged a trade, including gold, with West Africa since the ninth century. Muslim traders and scholars thus became the early transmitters of Islamic culture and faith to the region.

In the tenth and eleventh centuries, the trading relationships between the empire of Ghana and Muslims from North Africa, had already resulted in the presence of Muslim advisors and converts in the court. The Almoravid dynasty of North Africa consolidated this relationship and under its influence the region came increasingly under Muslim influence. Smaller states

The Great Mosque of Niono, West Africa.

The central mosque at Porto Novo, Benin, in West Africa.

emerged under the rule of African Muslim leaders such as the Diafure state of the Muslim Soninkes.

In the middle of the thirteenth century another major state emerged in the region once controlled by the empire of Ghana. This was the Muslim state of Mali, founded by the legendary *Sunjata Kaita*. His successors became the new rulers of the state and were known by the title, *mansa*. They developed further links with regions to the north such as Egypt and undertook pilgrimages with their followers to Mecca. The most famous of these rulers was Mansa Musa, whose pilgrimage in 1324 became a major event exemplifying his acceptance as a leading Muslim ruler in West Africa at the time. Under him the Mali kingdom expanded to include much of the Sudan and the Sahel. Mansa Musa died in 1337, the head of an extensive and wealthy state, noted for its institutions of learning, law and government.

Another major state that emerged in the region was the Kingdom of Songhay which in the fifteenth century was ruled by Sonni Ali. During his rule, the city of Timbuktu attained fame as a center for learning and a flourishing trade. It was regarded as the most important metropolis of Muslim West Africa at the time. Following the death of Sonni Ali in 1492, the Songhay

empire came to be ruled by Askiyya Muhammad, who established a dynasty named after him. He extended his rule through a *jihad* to the Hausa region (today northern Nigeria); the Songhay empire continued to be ruled by various successors after Askiya Muhammad's death in 1528. By the end of the century a Moroccan dynasty had defeated the army of the Songhay kingdom and bought the state under their control.

Islam spread to parts of modern day Nigeria through trading routes by land and water. The regions known as Kanem and Bornu had been in contact with Muslims in North Africa since at least the ninth century. Major conversions of the local groups in the area to Islam probably took place gradually over the next four hundred to five hundred years. Muslim dynasties led by rulers known as *mai*, had come to be established by the thirteenth and fourteenth centuries and Sufi communities were well-known in the region during the fifteenth century.

Other centers of the spread of Islam in West Africa were Senegambia where the Wolof and Tukolor peoples accepted Islam, probably as early as the eleventh century.

The trade in gold also caused migration and contacts of Muslim from parts of Hausaland to present-day

Nigeria and in time the Hausa language and culture would become an important medium for the expression of Muslim culture and learning in that region. In fact it has become the lingua franca of a very large population in West Africa.

During this period of the spread of Islam in West Africa, the region became part of the larger cosmopolitan world of Muslim culture and civilization in North Africa and the Mediterranean, linked by trade and faith. Ibn Battuta, who travelled in the region, visiting Mali in 1352, noted the presence of mosques, institutions of learning, and the widespread tradition of Muslim practices and education, among the majority of the inhabitants he encountered. During his visit to Timbuktu he noted the presence of centers of learning, including the well-known Mosque-University of Sankore. The reputation of its scholars had spread far and wide and the institution was recognized for its scholarship as well as its intellectual pluralism in the study of various branches of law and theology.

By the seventeenth century, major Sufi *tariqas* from the north had also begun to establish themselves in West Africa. The most important of these were the Qadiriyya and Tijaniyya, who to this day, remain among the largest Sufi communities in the region.

◆ ISLAM IN SOUTHERN AFRICA

While the number of Muslims in Southern Africa has always remained small, the region reflects the overall pattern of migration that characterized Muslim history in Africa as a whole.

During the period of the Dutch Cape Colony in the seventeenth century, the Dutch sent several Muslim leaders from Indonesia (which was also a Dutch colony) into forced exile in the Cape region. These exiles constituted a Muslim community which increased by way of intermarriage. In the later part of the nineteenth century Asian Muslim immigrants from British-ruled India also migrated and settled in South Africa.

◆ THE GREAT *JIHADS*

Though the major currents of Muslim practice and culture had become well established in West Africa by the eighteenth century, political divisions and internal tensions between Muslim and non-Muslim peoples, would give rise to a period of conflict, known as the era of the great *jihads*, in several West African states. The situation would become further complicated as European encroachment and commercial and military activity began to emerge in a significant way in the nineteenth century. This period of tension and conflict took place between 1785 and 1900, marking the end of Muslim control over many parts of the region and the beginning of European colonialism in the area.

The first of the major *jihads* took place in the Gobir around 1785. Led by a charismatic preacher and scholar, Uthman Dan Fodio, several Muslim activists began to preach reform against what they regarded as the moral laxity of the ruling family and the insufficient efforts to build a framework for Muslim society. This "*jihad* by word" was opposed by the ruler who recognized the broad scope of revivalism and reform implied in the demands. This opposition crystallized the emergence of a more activist stance that led Uthman Dan Fodio to attempt broad reforms in social practice and organization. He insisted on more formal adherence to Islamic law, a greater commitment to the observance of the practices of the faith and the institutionalization of a system of governance based on the model of the early Muslim Community. His supporters regarded Uthman Dan Fodio as a *mujaddid*, a renewer of faith. The *jihad* was successful and a sultanate was established in Sokoto.

In Masina, a *jihad* was led by Ahmad ibn Muhammad in 1818, who succeeded in creating a centralized state based in a city he founded in the region called Hamdallahi.

By the middle of the nineteenth century French influence had become established in the Senegambia region. Under the leadership of al-Hajj umar al-Futi, the followers of the Tijani Sufi *tariqa* were able to harness forces and organize military resistance to French rule and to the loss of Muslim control in the region. By 1862, the military *jihad* had succeeded in gaining control of a large territory but ensuing conflicts with other Muslims, who combatted al-Hajj Umar's expansion, led to internal conflicts and he was killed in battle. His son succeeded to the role and was able to sustain the new Muslim state until the French were finally able to exercise their authority over the region in 1891.

A number of other *jihad* movements arose in other parts of West Africa; these major movements led to a significant reorientation of Muslim societies. There

Interior of a Swahili house. The Swahili culture developed in cities along Africa's east coast.

was greater centralization of authority, an increase in the influence of Muslim legal, educational, and social institutions and practices, and an increase in contacts with other regions of the Muslim world where the spirit of reform and change was active. The *jihad* movement also marked the prelude to the rise of European colonial influence and power that displaced Muslim authority but left intact a well-established frame of Muslim life and sense of allegiance, which would act as a cushion against being overwhelmed by respective colonial cultural influences.

♦ THE EMERGENCE OF THE SWAHILI CULTURE

In East Africa, a less militant pattern of development led to a synthesis generally referred to as Muslim Swahili culture in the coastal cities and areas. Earlier African traditions interacted with the culture and traditions of Muslim immigrants from across the Indian Ocean, to evolve into a well-developed civilization called Swahili from the Arabic word *sawahil*, referring to coastal peoples. On this Muslim frontier, African and transoceanic Muslim cultures merged to create a corridor along the coast (from Somalia to Mozambique) that consisted of a new heterogeneous people, sharing a common language, mercantile economy, architecture, and common adherence to Islam. This new synthesis cannot be defined in simplistic racial or ethnic terms but represents the multiple elements that came to constitute a cosmopolitan Muslim society that is still very much in evidence in East Africa today.

♦ MUSLIM REVIVALISM AND EUROPEAN RULE

The West African Experience

Most of the revivalist ideas underlying the *jihads* in West Africa were inspired by common ideas; their links to Sufi orders played a part in the process of dissemination. For example, the influence of Shaykh al-Mukhtar al-Kunti (1729–1811) was felt widely in the western Sudan. His interpretation of the concept of *mujadid* (the renewer) affected the course of Muslim activism in the region. The idea that the *mujadid* does not have to be a single person living in a single area at a given time lends support to the concept of a multiplicity of such renewers. Another point that deserves our attention is al-Kunti's understanding that the renewer had different roles. He can appear in the form of a scholar-*jihadist* or a scholar-missionary.

What is interesting is that the shaykh enjoyed a great deal of influence among the African followers of the *Qadriyya tariqa*. They did not only own some of the salt mines on the path of the trans-Saharan trade, but they also established a series of *zawiyas* (Sufi centers)

which connected their members all over the region. Given the existence of such an organizational framework, European colonists were unable to contain the growth of Islam. By ushering into African Muslim societies changes that were neither expected nor desired, the colonizing powers from Europe unintentionally created African Muslim resistance. It should be pointed out that this African Muslim resistance was occasioned by the fear of cultural contamination and political domination. However, what is not always noted by historians is the fact that conversion to Islam, especially among the members of a *tariqa* provided a tremendous sense of identity and belonging. African Muslims understood and asserted who they were and what their role in human society was to be. By internalizing the teachings of the faith, the more learned African Muslims felt secure and perhaps even superior in the presence of alien traditions.

It was indeed this manner of thinking and acting that led to the decision by Muslim minorities in the Sahel region to challenge the political authority of the traditional African rulers. But while stating this fact, it must also be noted that for the greater part of the history of Muslim and non-Muslim relations, a spirit of tolerance existed.

Muslims reacted to the coming of European colonial rule in much the same way. After having lived as minorities within predominantly traditional societies, Muslims found it unacceptable to be ruled by those that they perceived as European Christians. The migration of many people from the Senegambia region into modern day Mali and beyond was to a large extent occasioned by such considerations. Colonialism affected the history and development of Islam in West Africa in six important ways.

First, in the Senegambian region, where the Muslims were beginning to establish states under al-Hajj Umar, Muhammad Lamin, and Maba Jahu Ba, the decision of the French authorities to build a French African empire was a major setback. Trade with the north was not only threatened but most significantly Muslims engaged in such trade were caught in the turmoil in the region. But if the French, for example, were successful in implanting French imperial rule in the Senegambian region, they failed to redirect trade routes in the Sahel hinterland until much later. In these parts trade with the north continued right into the early decades of the twentieth century.

Second, besides the redirection of trade there was also the dismantling of Muslim state power in the region, particularly by the French. They colonized Algeria, Tunisia, Morocco, Mauritania, Senegambia, Mali, Niger, Muslim Upper Volta, Muslim Guinea, and the Muslim areas around the Lake Chad region. In talking about factors and forces responsible for Muslim resistance in the western Sudan, one must take note of this historical development. The French authorities were mindful of this fact. They succeeded in their campaign against Muslims through the centralization of colonial power and the co-optation of those Muslim elements who proved to be pliable under colonial rule. It is on account of the French approach to colonial rule that some of the commentators on colonialism have made distinctions between British colonialism and French colonialism. Those who entertained the notion that the British were more responsive to African institutional arrangements, traditional or Islamic, argue that the concept of indirect rule allow some degree of autonomy to the continued existence of Muslim and traditional African customs. The Muslims of northern Nigeria opposed the British, but their efforts were tempered by the deference to their institutions by the British. However, even the most liberal colonial policies were inadequate substitutes for Muslim self-rule. One can now argue that colonialism did create a sense of alienation among Nigerian Muslims and gave rise to effects that would later affect the nature of political relationships in independent Nigeria.

The third development during the colonial period was the implantation of western cultural values. The process of cultural implantation was carried out by two institutions: the missionary school and the colonial bureaucracy. The first acted as the intellectual and cultural arm of the evangelical groups from Europe and later America in their search for souls and converts in the "Dark Continent." Convinced that Africa being outside pale of Christianity needed to be saved, these missionaries set about building missionary stations and schools to provide Africans with the Roman alphabet so that they too could travel mentally in the realm of Christian understanding. Since European languages were the road maps in these realms of religious instruction, it soon became necessary for African converts to adopt the language of the missionary. This association of the language of the "conqueror" with the "message of Christ" was destined to affect Muslim attitude towards Western languages. Indeed, in retrospect, one can now argue that the late adoption of modern skills and knowledge in Muslim Africa was largely occasioned by their suspicion and fear of the missionary. English and French were associated with Westernization and de-Islamization; hence the early Muslim developed an aversion to European schools and forms of learning in the period before the efforts at modernization and reinterpretation in the late nineteenth and early twentieth centuries.

The fourth development which affected the Muslims of Africa and created the prospects for Islamic revivalism in the colonial and post colonial periods was the secularization of human life under colonial rule.

Together with mission schools, an important role was played by the colonial administration.

The fifth development which affected Muslim society and continues to be an issue was the influence and to a certain extent adoption of a materialistic philosophy of life and society. Western technology and forms of education did not only introduce new ways of looking at the world, they also ushered in an era of new economics and goods in the context of a web of international mercantile systems. As a result of this development Muslim Africans whose trade routes were gradually appropriated and controlled by the colonial powers, namely France and Britain, began to import European manufactures which were certainly not designed to be adapted readily into their culture or existing networks. In time, as economic values and principles went through a transformation in Europe, heralding the rise of communist and socialist perspectives, African Muslims were occasionally driven to regard economic and material imperatives as being of primary importance to the exclusion of other cultural and religious values.

The sixth and last development which colonial rule ushered into Muslim society was the separation of the established African Muslim networks and contacts from other Muslims elsewhere in *Dar al Islam* (the abode of Islam). The process of separation was made possible by the loss of Muslim political power and the redirection of Muslim trade routes from the Sahara to the coastal zones controlled by the European powers. Having lost their steady supply of goods and services from the Muslim heartlands and caught within the orbit of western hegemony, the African Muslims soon found themselves without leaders who were, as in the past, in direct and constant contact with Muslim intellectual and cultural centers. If one is to understand contemporary revivalism in its broader context, this sense of separation constitutes an important reason. Although one can argue that the bonds were not completely severed during the colonial period, the fact still remains that the contact was closely monitored by the colonial powers and no expression of solidarity which could be construed as detrimental to British or French interest was permitted. The most visible context of communication was the pilgrimage, but if one examines the available data on this major gathering of pilgrims, one finds that in the colonial era contact was relatively limited. Not many African Muslims were able to travel to Mecca.

Taken together, these developments change the nature and direction of both African and African Muslim society.

This period of colonialism in the African experience with the West transformed the nature of society from what it was in the early nineteenth century. Among the visible signs of change was the monetization of the

African economy. By introducing their own currencies the European powers soon created their economic spheres of influence and as a result African Muslims under different colonial rulers had to trade in different currencies, accentuating economic and commercial separation. The Wolof Muslims of Gambia, for example, no longer used the *pagne* as a medium of exchange; rather they used francs when visiting Senegalese relatives and the Senegalese had to accept the use of the British pound sterling whenever they crossed the frontier between The Gambia and Senegal. This demarcation lines which resulted from the colonial period would also constitute formidable barriers to any movements projecting Muslim unity. For instance, the efforts of the Muslim leader, Maba Jah, to overcome such boundaries was not acceptable to the colonial power.

During the colonial period, as we have already seen, the colonial power feared the Muslim groups. It employed two strategies in its relationship with the Muslim leadership, namely, co-optation and coercion. Where the Muslim leaders were suspected of plotting the doom of the colonial power, force was employed. On the other hand, where the Muslim leadership expressed willingness to collaborate, the masters used the carrot instead of the stick. This was most evident in the relationship between the French colonial powers in Senegal and the leader/founder of the Muridiyya movement in that country. At the beginning of the movement the French feared the leader, Shaykh Ahmad Bamba. So afraid were the French officers in Senegal that they decided to banish him to faraway Gabon and then later to Mauretania. He returned to Senegal only after it became clear that it was no longer a threat to French colonial interest in this part of Africa.

◆ MODERN TRENDS IN AFRICA SOUTH OF THE SAHARA

The alienation of the Muslims created under colonial rule, generated the conditions which could be effectively harnessed for the development of resistance against European rule. Towards the end of colonial rule in French West Africa many young graduates from al-Azhar University in Cairo, Egypt developed what were perceived by French officials as "radical Islamic ideas." These young men, who were known in West Africa as Wahhabis, had embraced reformist ideas current in the Middle East and tried to create the necessary vehicles to educate and inform fellow Muslims in West Africa. Though they did not advocate the use of violence to im-

Worshippers outside a mosque in Sierra Leone.

plement their brand of Islam, the French authorities put the leaders under constant surveillance.

The source of inspiration for such Muslim reform came from the writings of reformers such as Shaykh Muhammad Abouh in Egypt, Shaykh Uthman Dan Fodio, and other leaders of the *jihad* tradition in West Africa. The ideas for reform and transformation of the Muslim community were carried around the Sahelian zone and below largely by the *julas* (traders). Committed to trade and commerce, and following a long tradition of education and culture dating back to ancient Mali, many of these Muslim merchants found the teachings of the young graduates from Egypt appealing and useful. As a result they made it a point to carry reformist ideas along with their wares.

Some of these reformers differed from established Muslim groups in Africa south of the Sahara, because of their reformist or puritanical zeal. To achieve their objectives the fundamentalists preached in the urban centers of West Africa an "Islam" which they claimed was neither "colonial" nor "maraboutic." Colonial Islam, in their view, was an instrument of oppression in the hands of the French colonial official. Maraboutic Islam (the practice of the Sufi tariqas), on the other hand, was perceived to be the ideology of the African Muslim who was willing to collaborate with the French or other European power ruling and exploiting Muslims. This reformist brand, however, was short-lived.

Founded by King Faisal and his advisers in response to the propagandistic vituperations of the Nasserites, the Muslim World League soon grouped together some of the most prominent Muslim ulama around the world. Among the prominent Africans from areas south of the Sahara were Shaykh Ibrahima Niasse, Sir Ahmadou Bello, Sarduna of Sokoto and Mufti Gummi of Nigeria.

Arab organizations established links with almost all African Muslim groups of significance. The Egyptians sent out Arabic teachers to work with members of the reformist groups discussed in the previous section. Where such arrangements were impractical or unacceptable to the colonial powers, scholarships were quietly given to deserving students who would cross the colonial borders and journeyed to Cairo. The number of African students increased dramatically after independence.

While turbulence and events in many parts of the Muslim world, affect the consciousness of African Muslims, the evidence seems to point to a widespread continuity with African Muslim identity, characterized by the spirit always manifested through their cultural and spiritual development in African contexts.

Sulayman Nyang

References

Abun-Nasr, Jamil M. *A History of the Maghrib in the Islamic Period. Cambridge: Cambridge University Press, 1987.*

Ahed, J.M. *The Intellectual Origins of Egyptian Nationalism.* New York: Oxford University Press, 1960.

Brenner, Louis, ed. *Muslim Identity and Social Change in Sub-Saharan Africa.* London: C. Hurst & Co., 1993.

Burgat, Francios. *The Islamic Movement in North Africa.* Austin: Center for Middle Eastern Studies, University of Texas at Austin, 1993.

Christelow, A. "The Tatsine Distrubances in Kano—A Search for Perspective," *The Muslim World,* Vol. LXXV.

Clarke, Peter B. *West Africa and Islam.* London: Edward Arnold Publishers, Ltd., 1982.

Flint, John E. ed. *The Cambridge History of Africa* Vol. 5. Cambridge, England: Cambridge University Press, 1976.

Gibb, H. A. R. *Ibn Batttuta: Travels in Asia and Africa 1325–1354.* Cambridge, England: Hakluyt Society, Cambridge University Press, 1958.

Hiskett, Mervyn. *The Course of Islam in Africa.* Edinburgh, Scotland: Edinburgh University Press, 1994.

———. *The Sword of Truth: The Life and Times of the Shehu Usuman Dan Fodio.* New York: Oxford University Press, 1973.

———. *The Development of Islam in West Africa.* London and New York: Longman, 1984.

Hunwick, John C. *Sharia in Songhay. The Replies of al-Maghili to the Questions of Askia al-Hajj Muhammad.* New York: Oxford University Press, 1985.

Kaba, L. *West Africa.* Evanston, Illinois: Northwestern University Press, 1974.

Knappert, J. *Traditional Swahili Poetry: an Investigation Into the Concepts of East African Islam.* Leiden: E. J. Brill, 1967.

Kritzeck, James and William H. Lewis eds. *Islam in Africa.* New York: Van Nostrand-Reinhold Co., 1969.

Moreau, R. L. *Africains Musulmans.* Paris, France: Presence Africaines, 1982.

Nurse, Derek and Thomas Spear. *The Swahili: Reconstructing the History and Language of an African Society 800–1500.* Philadelphia: University of Pennsylvania, 1985.

Nyang, S. "Islam and Politics in West Africa," *Issue.* Vol. 13.

———. "Saudi Arabia's Foreign Policy Towards Africa," *Horn of Africa.* Vol. 5.

———. *Islam, Christianity and African Identity.* Brattleboro, Vermont: Amana Books, 1984.

O'Brien, Donal Cruise. *The Mourides of Senegal.* New York: Oxford University Press, 1971.

Peel, J. D. Y. and C. C. Stewart. *Popular Islam South of the Sahara.* Manchester: Manchester University Press in association with *Africa, Journal of the International African Institute,* 1987.

Pouwels, Randall Lee. *Horn and Crescent: Cultural Change and Traditional Islam on the East African Coast, 800–1900.* New York: Cambridge University Press, 1987.

Samura, M O'Bai. *The Libyan Revolution. Its Lessons for Africa.* Washington, D.C.: Inernational Institute for Policy and Development Studies, 1986.

Trimmingham, J. S. *Islam in Ethiopia.* London: F. Cass, 1965.

Vatikiotis, P. J. *The Modern History of Egypt.* New York: Praeger, 1969.

Willis, J. R. "Jihad fi Sabil Allah: Its Doctrine Bases in Islam and Some Aspects of Its Evolution in Nineteenth Century West Africa," *Journal of African History.* Vol. 8, No. 3, 1967.

————. *Studies in West African Islamic History.* Vol. 1 *Cultivators of Islam.* London: Frank Cass, 1979.

————. *Religion and Change in African Societies.* Edinburgh: University of Edinburgh Press, 1979.

5

Islam in South Asia

♦ The Establishment of Muslim Rule ♦ Political Power, the Community, and the Issue of Conversion
♦ Spiritual and Mystical Life ♦ "Separatism" and "Syncretism" in Medieval India
♦ The Eighteenth Century: A "Dark" Century? ♦ The Intelligentsia and the New Realities
♦ Educational System: The Eighteenth Century

On August 14, 1947, a new country named Pakistan was created. This country, contemplated as a separate home for Indian Muslims, could be viewed as: a geographic manifestation of the politics of Indian Muslims as a minority group in a pluralistic Indian society; an expression of a community with a firm belief in a separate social order with its own political power base; and a sovereign state embodying the legacy of Islamic culture, which had developed in India for about eight hundred years. The two Muslim states in South Asia, Pakistan and Bangladesh (the eastern wing of Pakistan in 1947, and a sovereign state since 1971), and the Muslim presence in modern-day India signify the long history of Islamization of India from the north to Bengal in the east.

In comparison with other parts of the Islamic world, the development of Muslim life and culture in south Asia represents some unique features. Today, this region has the largest concentration of Muslims (approximately three-hundred-sixty million). It was here that in 1988, a woman, Benazir Bhutto, was elected (reelected in 1993) as the prime minister of Pakistan, the first woman in the modern Muslim world to lead a government. The second instance was in the same region when, in March 1991, Khaleda Zia was elected as prime minister of Bangladesh. The regional historical legacy for women leaders goes back 755 years when Sultan Iltutmish (reigned 1211–36) nominated his daughter, Raziya, to succeed him. She ruled for four years.

This chapter traces the political, social, religious, and cultural history of Islam in South Asia in two parts. The first covers the period from 711 to 1757, and the second, from 1757 to the present. Specific topics include: the formation of the Muslim community; the process of conversion and Islamization; religious and intellectual contributions; and developments during the colonialist British Raj government, reflected in the dilemmas of modernity and its impact on the area after the independence in 1947.

♦ THE ESTABLISHMENT OF MUSLIM RULE

The First Phase (711–1186)

The year 711 marks the initial contact of Muslims with India under the leadership of seventeen-year-old Commander Muhammad ibn Qasim who arrived in Sind, the first cradle of Islam in the India. This was to be the only area in India where Muslim rule would persist for three hundred years.

Three hundred years later, Sultan Mahmud of Ghazna (died 1030), a Turkish-born son of a former slave, invaded India seventeen times. Mahmud did not establish an infrastructure to administer and control his conquered areas. Instead of incorporating the Indian territories in his empire, he used the wealth from India for beautifying his capital, Ghazni, and solidifying his empire in Afghanistan and Khurasan. Mahmud's descendants, however, introduced and nurtured Muslim cultural traditions in the city of Lahore after the death of Mahmud in 1030. These descendants were eventually forced out of Mahmud's Ghaznavid empire and had to move their capital to the city of Lahore. From the death of Mahmud until the end of the Ghaznavid rule in India in 1186, scholars, poets, and mystics from cities in Central Asia, Iran, and the Arab world, such as Samarqand, Bukhara, Kashghar, Nishapur, and Baghdad, were attracted to Lahore.

The Sultanate Period (1192–1525)

In 1192 Muizuddin Ghori (a governor of Turkish Muslim origin from Ghazni) initiated a major invasion

Agra Fort, India.

of India. He extended the territory held by the later Ghaznavids in the northwest and captured the cities of Delhi and Ajmer. Ghori's lieutenant, Bakhtiar Muhammad Khalji, captured Bihar and established Muslim rule in Bengal in 1204. Unlike Mahmud of Ghazna, the purpose of Ghori's invasion was not plunder and military glory, but the establishment of political control over northern India. The period from Ghori's successors, known as the "slave" sultans, until the advent of the Mughals in 1526 is known as the Sultanate period. During this time a total of seventeen sultans ruled over various parts of India. One of the sultans, Ala al-Din Khalji (1296–1316), extended Muslim control to central and parts of southern India. Muhammad ibn Tughluq (1325–1351) conquered territory in the deep south of India and moved his capital to Devagiri (renamed Daulatabad).

Successor independent states emerged in different parts of India and played a crucial role in Islamizing the regions they controlled. The process of Islamization was accelerated by the state's emphasis on the translation of Arabic and Persian religious texts into local vernaculars. By 1500 Islamic culture and faith had become integrated into Indian society. With the exception of the Hindu kingdom in the extreme south at Vijayanagar, Muslim rulers exercised control and put down various rebellions. The Persian language and the administrative apparatus of the Muslim rulers came to be adapted and implemented in all regions under Muslim control.

The Muslims of South Asia built on a legacy of Irano-Turkish culture and further developed and spread this culture in their dominion. Though they were of Turkish origin, the language of high culture and administration was Persian. Although Turkish hegemony was weakened by later dynasties such as the Khaljis (1290–1320) and the Tughluqs (1320–1413) when indigenous

Badshahi Mosque, Lahore, Pakistan.

Muslims and non-Muslims were incorporated into the ruling polity, Persian remained the language of administration. The flow of ideas from the rest of the Islamic world to medieval South Asia was through the movement of people as well as through the travel of south Asian Muslim thinkers to the Hijaz for the purpose of undertaking *Hajj*, the Muslim pilgrimage, and for trade. If we were to look for specific examples of such influences, the case of Muhammad ibn Tughluq provides an illustration. This sultan was deeply influenced by one of the most dynamic Muslim reformist thinkers of the post-Mongol period, Ibn Taimiyya (1263–1327). Based on this influence, the sultan opposed and initiated the withdrawal from state service of mystically inclined Muslims, enforced the more strict *sharia* laws on the Muslim population, and propagated his respect for the *sunna* of the Prophet and of the institution of the caliphate for the Islamic world.

The Mughals (1526–1748)

The Mughals were heirs to the Sultanate period's Indo-Islamic tradition and built a magnificent empire based on well-established and enduring institutions. The founder of the Mughal rule, Muhammad Zahir al-Din Babur (reigned 1526–1530) encountered the two concentrations of power in India: the Muslim Afghan ruler, Ibrahim Lodi, and the Rajput Hindu leader, Rana Sanga in 1526 and 1527 respectively. Having defeated both of them, he laid the foundations of a dynastic rule, which inaugurated the most glorious period in the history of south Asian Islam. Babur and his descendants were born leaders of men, connoisseurs of art and literature, and the builders of the most magnificent monuments on the Indian landscape. Babur's son, Humayun, could not consolidate the areas he inherited from his father. In 1539 he was ousted and replaced by a capable Afghan leader, Sher Khan Sur, whom even the defeated Humayun called, "the master of rulers." As one of the most efficient Muslim rulers in India, Sher Khan left a brilliant record of his administrative reforms in a very short period of his leadership (1539–1545). Humayun, after spending fifteen years in Iran as a fugitive, recovered his throne in India in 1555 only to die in 1556.

Humayun's son, Jalal al-Din Muhammad Akbar (1556–1605), is remembered in Indo-Islamic history as the builder of the Mughal empire and the most capable ruler of the dynasty. He initiated territorial expansion, centralized administration, inaugurated an effective fiscal policy, and, above all, assimilated and united the heterogeneous ruling—polity of Persians, Turks, Uzbeks, Afghans, Indian Muslims, and the Rajputs by imbuing a common identity of their spiritual and political bond to the person of the emperor. His successors, Jahangir (1605–1627), Shahjahan (1628–1658), and

Awrangzeb (1658–1707), successfully implemented his policies with some changes. The frontiers of the empire expanded, and the architectural, artistic, and literary activities thrived. Through the dynamism of the rulers, an efficient administrative structure, a proverbial sense of justice, and an extremely loyal nobility, the Mughals were able to unify India. Imperial demands for revenue stimulated the economy to bring famed prosperity. The Mughal culture and presence left a deep imprint on the fabric of the society, and hardly any religious and ethnic community was left untouched. However, wars of succession, an inefficient bureaucracy, and weakened

The Qutb Minar, Delhi, India.

leadership caused the decline and collapse of the centralized imperial system. The East India Company's representative, Lord Clive, defeated the Muslim forces in the battle of Plassey in 1757, and Lord Lake took over the administration of Delhi in 1803. However, the successor states, the former provinces of the Mughal empire, namely Sind, Awadh, and Deccan, carried the Mughal cultural traditions until 1857 when the colonization of India by the British was completed and an English colonial political, social, and economic order came to be enforced over India.

The Coming of British Rule

By the time of the great Mutiny of 1857 in which an attempt was made to resist the growing military power and presence of the British, Muslim power in India had largely ceased to exist except in a few provincial pockets.

The British East India Company had in fact been engaged in trade with India since the year 1600. In 1772, Warren Hastings was appointed as British Governor of Bengal and consolidated existing British commercial interests and allied them with his administration bringing trade and colonial rule under one umbrella. British power came to be extended over various regions formerly under Muslim control. Eventually the token recognition of Mughal rule and Muslim sovereignty gave way to the rise of the British Empire in the Subcontinent. With it begins a new chapter in the history of Muslims in South Asia.

◆ POLITICAL POWER, THE COMMUNITY, AND THE ISSUE OF CONVERSION

The history of Muslims in India is very much tied to their control of political power. As a minority group that ruled over the majority, the Muslims needed the anchor of state for their survival and stability. Muslim thinkers unequivocally agreed that state control was a prerequisite for the community's growth and well-being. "It was the might of a sultan's arms which ensured the implementation of *sharia*," wrote Fakhr-i Mudabbir. "Power not personal piety, represented the most effective way to implement laws of *sharia*," reiterated Barani a century later. Various Muslim historians in India during the medieval period believed that it was necessary for Muslims to exercise temporal power. Muslim rulers, in turn, were aware of this dimension of their responsibilities and took it seriously. Both the sultans and the emperors, for example, maintained cordial relations with the custodians (*sharifs*) of the Holy Cities, partly to ensure the safety and comfort of the pilgrims leaving India. The Bahmani sultans of Deccan and the sultans of Bengal and Gujarat sent gifts for the

sharifs, charity for the poor, constructed lodging houses for the poor and travelers, and built colleges. The bounties and largesses of the Mughals for the poor at the Holy Places dazzled their contemporaries. In 1581 the Mughal emperor, Akbar, reorganized the *Hajj* voyage by creating a position of *Mir Hajj* (the leader of the pilgrimage) to lead the *Hajj* caravan and look after the pilgrims. The historical chronicles also record that the expenses of the pilgrims were covered by the imperial treasury, and the emperors ensured the safety of the pilgrims' voyage to the Hijaz.

The rulers also constructed mosques, founded cities (Mansura, built by Muhammad bin Qasim in Sind), minted coins bearing Islamic symbols and messages, and established institutions for higher learning (*madrasas*) and Sufi hospices (*khanqas*).

The numerical growth of the Muslim community in India over the centuries brings up the controversial subject of the conversion of the indigenous population to Islam. Unlike the Muslim experience elsewhere in Asia and Africa, the existing civilization and culture of India retained its distinct, dominant, and established character. Islam and Hinduism, two distinct belief systems and worldviews, coexisted and influenced one another, with neither being able to fully absorb the other.

Street scene, Pakistan

The issues of forcible mass conversion, the relationship between the communities, and the status of non-Muslims under the Muslim rule have been debated by modern historians of India belonging to various schools of thought—British, Hindu Nationalists, and Muslims (the Indian Muslims and the Pakistanis after 1947). The subjective and sometimes distorted views of the orientalists and the nationalistic and modernistic interpretations have created confusion. Against the backdrop of Western concepts of "liberalism," democracy, and human rights, sweeping judgments, by all parties, have been passed on the basis of meager textual evidence. The purpose here is not to choose sides in the debate but to suggest that historical sources, when analyzed in their respective socio-political contexts, reveal that rulers of the Sultanate and Mughal periods were aware of their responsibility to different communities living in their dominion. There was a conscious effort of grouping Muslims and non-Muslims together for the purpose of running the state administration and economy. In the political culture, religious identities played only a minor role. Despite the polemical discussions in the nineteenth and the first five decades of this century, the current scholarly consensus is that there were no forcible mass conversions.

Bhong Mosque.

A review of religious and military policies of early Muslim rulers shows that religious considerations did not determine Muhammad bin Qasim's administration. In the mainly Hindu and Buddhist Indus Valley, the socioreligious patterns of Damascus, the center of power at the time, were not imposed. The Buddhists, urbanized and involved in mercantile activity, did not survive as a community after the occupation. They converted to Islam, Hinduism, or migrated to Buddhist-dominated areas. The Hindus, on the other hand, survived as a vital group. Their stronghold in rural Sind was largely unaffected by the new domination. In 1911 (marking twelve hundred years of the Muslim invasion) the province of Sind under British rule was about one-quarter Hindu. Hindus had been given the status of *ahl al-kitab* (people of the Book) and *ahl al-dhimma* (the protected subjects) as had been done for Zoroastrians, Christians, and Jews in Iran, Syria, and Egypt.

There are four proposed factors leading to conversion: immigration, conquest, political patronage, and egalitarianism of Islam. All these theories have proven to be inconclusive. However, the four factors are useful demarcations for understanding the process of Islamization and acculturation.

The Sufis are also given credit for promulgation and adoption of the Muslim identity by the non-Muslim population primarily in rural areas. Sufi *khanqas* were open to all, where a Sufi master would offer spiritual guidance and psychological support. The Sufi shrines, sources of blessings because of the deceased masters' spiritual attainment, and the annual celebrations to commemorate their deaths provided forums for the convergence of different ethnic and religious backgrounds from all strata of society. Over generations, as a result of this phenomenon of acculturation, many populations adopted Muslim identity. Thus, Islamization in the Indian context has to be viewed as a result of multiple influences, social acculturation, and religious motivation. The conversion to Islam of the indigenous population did not represent a sudden and abrupt break from their cultural and social traditions. It is the combination of these factors that gives Muslim life and culture in India its special features.

Muslim rulers, intellectuals, and writers in South Asia were part of a broad Muslim cultural zone rooted in Iran and Turkey. At the time of Mahmud's repeated invasions on India, he patronized the cosmopolitan culture of Baghdad, a combination of Arabo-Persian-Turkish traditions, in his court in Ghazna. This cultural tradition was transplanted in the northwestern part of India by his descendants, was enriched and enhanced with the help of the influx of intellectuals from the different Muslim cultural zones, and was nurtured by influences from aspects of Indian culture.

Statements such as "knowledge is power and learning is worship," "ink of a scholar will supersede the blood of a martyr on the Day of Judgment," and "the scholars (*ulama*) are heirs to the Prophet Muhammad because they expound and transmit his message" abound in the religious texts produced in India over the centuries. These statements are universal in the world of Islam, and transcend regional, linguistic, and ethnic frontiers. Similarly, the system of education in medieval India was the same as in any other Islamic country. The emigres in the region realized the significance of learning as an integral part of the Islamic heritage. Like their predecessors, the later Ghaznavids built schools and libraries attached to the mosques. The mosque-schools trained individuals to fulfill the elementary educational needs of the masses in teaching them the fundamentals of Islam. The children of the elite were privately tutored. There were noteworthy luminaries belonging to this period who left an imprint on future trends in educational and literary spheres. Shaykh Muhammad Ismail Bukhari (died 1056), in the tradition of the Sindhi traditionalists, propagated and popularized the study of *hadith* in the northwestern part of India. The accomplished poets, Abul Farj Runi and Masud Sad Salman (died 1121 or 1122), spent most of their lives in Lahore. Salman's literary works entitled him to be considered one of the ten greatest poets of the Persian language.

The state and the ruling order also established institutions for higher learning called *madrasas*, providing financial support for the teaching staff and students in these institutions. The graduates of these institutions became experts in various branches of Islamic learning and served the community as well as the state as teachers, jurists, and judges. Books written outside India were considered to be authoritative only when scholars of Delhi approved of them. The influx of scholars from the heartlands of the Islamic world did enrich the intellectual and literary life in Delhi. However, scholars could not bring their libraries with them, which explains the absence of strong scholarship at that time. Although Delhi could not compete with Baghdad and Cordova's scholarly achievements, a respectable tradition in jurisprudence, theology, exegesis of the Quran, and *hadith* was established. Apart from the religious subjects, Persian language and literature, historical writings, linguistics sciences, ethics, and Greco-Arab medicine also flourished.

Official patronage and the level of scholarship and instruction of certain disciplines were closely interconnected. In Deccan, the able Bahmani ruler, Firuz (1397–1422), popularized such subjects as botany, geometry, and logic. He also initiated the construction of an observatory in Daulatabad because of his interest in astronomy. Rational and philosophical trends gained popularity during the reign of Muhammad ibn Tughluq

because of his personal interest and sound knowledge in those areas. Scholarship gained a renewed impetus during the reign of Sultan Sikandar Lodi (1489–1517), reaching new heights in the Mughal era. Muhammad ibn Tughluq's cousin and successor, Firuz Shah Tughluq (1351–1388), was a scholar of theology, and two major works on jurisprudence were compiled under his patronage. He constructed numerous *madrasas* and allocated generous endowments to run them.

Toward the end of the Sultanate period, a trend of establishing nonreligious schools emerged. Sultan Sikandar Lodi took two administrative steps: insistence on a certain minimum level of education for all his civil and military officers, and substitution of Persian for Hindi as a language of lower administration. To fulfill these requirements, special schools were established independently of mosques.

The Mughals further refined and systematized the educational and cultural traditions they inherited. Along with the mosque-based Islamic schools and *madrasas*, they built nonreligious schools with a diverse curriculum. Persian language training was offered at elementary and secondary levels, and sciences (mathematics, geometry, astronomy, and physics), natural philosophy, ethics, logic, scholastic theology, and history were offered at higher levels. The Mughal emperors, empresses, nobles, princes, and princesses all contributed to the construction of magnificent *madrasas* befitting their positions in the social and political order, resulting in a vast expansion of educational institutions. The provincial cities of Ahmadabad, Burhanpur, Lahore, and Sialkot became centers of Islamic scholarship. The standardization of curriculum in Islamic sciences took place in the eighteenth century at a prominent *madrasa* at Farangi Mahall in Lucknow, and also at Madrasa-i Rahimiyya in Delhi. The greatest contribution of Awrangzeb's period was the officially commissioned monumental work on Islamic jurisprudence titled *Fatawa-i Alamgiri*, a collection of legal rulings made during the Mughal Empire.

The patronage of the sophisticated and cultured Mughal ruling elite resulted in solid scholarship in Islamic sciences. This era is remembered for introducing new forms of historical writing and a richness in historiographical literature. There was an unprecedented refinement in Persian language and literature with a new style that was introduced as *sabk-i Hindi*. Miniature painting and music attained new heights in elegant and refined styles. Above all, the Indo-Islamic style of architecture reached its apogee.

◆ SPIRITUAL AND MYSTICAL LIFE

There is yet another rich spiritual-intellectual tradition that greatly contributed to the Indo-Islamic culture and religion. Unlike the mosque and *madrasa*-based scholarly heritage, the *khanqa*-based mystical tradition was independent of the sultans' and emperors' patronage. However, the establishment of the Sufi *tariqas* (orders) in India (originally from Iran and Central Asia) coincided with the rising political power of Muslims. The founder of the Chishtiyya order, Muin al-Din Chishti, for example, died in 1236, and Baha al-Din Zakariya, founder of the Suhrawardiyya order, died in 1267. Forty years later, the founder of the Firdawsiyya (a minor order), Badr al-Din Samarqandi, died in 1316. In the sixteenth century, two more *tariqas*, the Qadiriyya and the Naqshbandiyya, were introduced in India. They flourished during the Mughal period. The Qadariyya rose to prominence with Muhammad Mir (known as Miyan Mir, died 1635). The Naqshbandiyya was firmly established by Khwaja Baqi-billah (died 1603). The founder of the Mughal dynasty, Babur, was already initiated in this *tariqa* before his arrival in India. This order remained popular among the ruling power throughout the Mughal period.

Of these orders, the Chishtiyya is known for its other-worldliness and pride in poverty. In contrast, the Suhrawardiyya and the Naqshbandiyya are characterized by their involvement in social and political issues and for interacting with the ruling elite. The Naqshbandiyya is distinct from other orders on the basis of the solid scholarship of its membership. Its contributions in the renewal and reform of Islamic practices date from the seventeenth century to the present. The Mujaddidiyya branch, established by Khwaja Baqi-billah's disciple, Shaykh Ahmad Sirhindi (died 1624), had widespread influence beyond the frontiers of the Central Asia, Turkey, the European territories of the former Ottoman Turkey, and Indonesia. The Qadiriyya is known for its liberalism, tolerance of non-Muslims, and syncretic elements.

Modern scholarship tends to divide the religious elite into two distinct groups: the *ulama* (the scholars) and the Sufis (the mystics), with clearly identifiable orientations. The *ulama* are exclusive, *sharia*-oriented, and orthodox, and the Sufis are inclusive, accommodating, and receptive to local non-Muslim norms and traditions. It is hard to accept such a clear-cut demarcation. There is enough evidence in the historical chronicles and biographical dictionaries of the medieval period to support the conclusion that the compilers of these dictionaries did not make such hard and fast distinctions.

By the time the *tariqas* gained a foothold in India, the Sufi tradition with its organizations, institutions, and specific practices was already embedded in Muslim life throughout the Islamic world. Nevertheless, belief in and practice of the *sharia* was the bedrock of all *tariqas*. The initiates were expected to have good understanding of the fundamentals of Islam. They were expected to complete their education in the mosque-based Islamic schools, and many had graduated from the *madrasas* before their initiation in a particular *tariqa*. The Sufi masters usually had profound understanding of the Quran, *hadith*, and jurisprudence; the two fountainheads of Sufism, after all, were the Quran and the Prophet Muhammad, his life, sayings, and examples.

In India, as elsewhere in the Islamic world, the mystical approach to Islam was not a replacement of knowledge transmitted through mosques and *madrasas*. Rather mysticism was built upon the foundations of the mosque-schools and the *madrasas*. Its spiritual orientation was meant to refine consciousness of the divine, to intensify piety, and to inculcate a humanistic attitude. Life in a Sufi center or *khanqa* was very different from a *madrasa*, with the emphasis on the close relations between the master and the disciple. The disciple was initiated into the mystical path under the guidance of his master. In order to attain higher levels of spiritualism and self-understanding, the foci of a disciple were the master, his personality, his discourses, and, his spiritual capacity. The master's legitimacy and authority were not based on his written scholarly writings but on his understanding of Islamic sciences, spiritual attainments, historical and spiritual genealogy linking him to the Prophet and Ali, and also (in some *tariqas*) on his ability to perform miracles. The disciples in this relationship were not expending their energies on deciphering the complexities of the language, grammar, and syntax of the Quranic text. Rather they were pursuing the mystical and allegorical message of the scripture. The discussions were not on the chain of the transmitters of *hadith* and its authenticity, but on the personality of the Prophet and other Muslim models of spirituality.

The mystical literature represents a different current of concerns than do jurisprudential and theological works. Mystical literature produced in South Asia over the centuries may be divided into three broad categories: hagiographical, discourses of the master, and letters of the master. Letters answered a disciple's questions on mystical, theological, and scriptural issues and also addressed the mundane problems of employment, state officials, physical ailments, and concerns regarding spiritual ailments. There are also manuals for disciples that broadly outlined a code of conduct. It may be noted here that the first such manual written in India was by Ali ibn Uthman al-Hujwiri (died 1071). He came from the Ghazni area, settled in Lahore, and wrote in Persian *Kashf al-Mahjub* (*Revealing the Secrets*), one of the most important and oldest extant works on the theory and practice of mysticism. Mystical literature, on the whole, is an indispensable source for the religious and social history of Muslims in India over the course of centuries.

♦ "SEPARATISM" AND "SYNCRETISM" IN MEDIEVAL INDIA

Modern historians in their search for the antecedents of communalism and separatism, a distinct feature of Indian politics in the nineteenth and twentieth centuries, labeled and categorized individuals and movements within the medieval period as exclusive and inclusive. A discussion of intellectual and cultural contributions of Muslims would not be complete without making a reference to some thinkers and rulers who have been consistently placed in these two categories. Modern historians have been disappointed that medieval Muslim thinkers showed little interest in understanding the belief system and rites and rituals of the Hindu majority surrounding them. Abu Raihan al-Biruni (died 1048?) was the first Muslim thinker who showed an interest in Indian religion, culture, and customs. His pioneering work, *al-Kitab al-Hind* (originally written in Arabic, translated into English as *Alberuni's India*), has been lauded in modern times by Western historians and specialists of comparative religions to a greater extent than by al-Biruni's contemporaries and subsequent generations of thinkers in premodern India. It took another six-hundred years for the next book to be written in India by a Muslim on comparative religion. It was titled *Dabistan-i Mazahib* (*School of Religions*) and attributed to Fani Kashmiri (poet and prose writer who lived in the mid-seventeenth century). One possible reason for the paucity of literature on Hinduism and other religions could be that comparative religious studies as a discipline was never part of the curriculum at any of the Islamic educational institutions.

Modern historians are quick to label those medieval thinkers as bigots and communalists who in their writings used vernacular idioms to describe minorities and religious matters, which would not be considered appropriate today. Barani, for example, writing during the Sultanate period, is a communalist because he was critical of Hindus. His contemporary, the most accomplished, versatile, and prolific poet and innovative music composer, Amir Khusrau (died 1325), is categorized as a patriotic Indian because of his pride in his Indian heritage. He is also categorized as a liberal because of his sympathetic approach to Hinduism. The Mughals inherited an accommodating and tolerant religious climate because of the popular syncretic movement known as the Bhakti movement, which was pervasive in the Hindu community, and also because of the existing mysticism among the Muslims.

Akbar's steps, such as establishing a translation bu-

reau and ordering a systematic translation of Hindu religious classics from Sanskrit into Persian, made the Hindu religious heritage accessible to the Muslim thinkers. Furthermore, Akbar's evolving of a new concept of loyalty to the person of the emperor transcending religious, ethnic, and linguistic identities makes Akbar, in the eyes of a modern historian, the most liberal, secular and nationalist emperor in the Mughal dynasty. Akbar's image-maker was the accomplished historian, Abul Fazl. Abul Fazl's contemporary, Abd al-Qadir Badauni (died 1605), an erudite scholar and historian critical of Akbar's policies and of Abul Fazl and his family's influence on Akbar, was accused by the royal court of being a "bigot" and "reactionary." Historians are keen to trace the legacy of Akbar's "liberalism" or, conversely, the reversal of his policies by the succeeding Mughal rulers. Jahangir, for example, is erroneously characterized as a "bigot" and a "fanatic" because of the misinterpretation of two incidents: the executions of Arjun (the tenth guru of the Sikh community) and Nur-Allah Shushtari (a revered Shia theologian) who emigrated from Iran and served in the department of justice in Jahangir's administration. It is Jahangir's grandson, Sufi and scholar prince Dara Shukoh (1615–1659), whom the modern historians laud for his religious syncretism. Dara translated the Hindu sacred text of Upanishads into Persian and considered it the forerunner of other scriptures. Dara could not succeed his father, Shahjahan (the builder of the Taj Mahal). Instead, Dara's younger brother, Awrangzeb, the last powerful ruler of the Mughal dynasty, occupied the throne. Awrangzeb is the most controversial ruler of the dynasty because of his personality and policies. He is viewed by some a narrow-minded, *sharia*-oriented puritan and anti-Hindu emperor, and by others the reviver and upholder of Islamic traditions. He is held responsible by some for the decline of the empire because of such policies as the imposition of *jizya* (poll tax) on non-Muslim minorities. Much has been written for and against Awrangzeb, primarily because of the colonization of India and the subsequent political developments. It suffices to comment here that Awrangzeb continued the Mughal administrative traditions by recruiting the most resourceful individuals, irrespective of their creed and race. It is known that minorities, as such, were not persecuted in the name of Islam during his period.

The mystical tradition has been usually identified with syncretism and the spirit of coexistence. Modern historians attribute this situation to factors such as the use of local vernaculars for mystical poetry and religious literature, the relaxed interaction between the masses belonging to different religious communities, the charismatic personalities of Sufi masters, and, interaction and dialogue of debates between Sufi and

The Taj Mahal, tomb and mosque in Agra, India.

Hindu ascetics. As noted above, major Sufi orders observed the sanctity of *sharia* in their practices, and thus had the unwavering conviction of the superiority of Islam over other religions, and especially over the polytheistic Hindu tradition. They were, however, not extremist in their views. The tendency of projecting twentieth-century concepts, ideologies, and preoccupations in their study of mystical literature of medieval times remains a problem in scholarship on Sufism in South Asia.

Before concluding this section, a few words should be written on the diplomatic, intellectual, and commercial relations of the three contemporaneous Muslim empires, the Ottomans, Safavids, and Mughals. The Ottoman influence in the Deccan and western coastal states predates the advent of the Mughals in India. Ottoman Muslims held prominent administrative positions in the Gujarat state. Their influence is discernible particularly in the use of weapons and the art of warfare. The diplomatic relations between the Mughals and the Ottomans were lukewarm at best. The exchange of diplomatic missions was infrequent with the exception of Shahjahan's reign when the number of the exchange of ambassadors increased. The possible reasons for the indifferent relations were: the Ottomans'

claim for the universal caliphate for their being the supreme power in the world of Islam, and the Mughals' self-image of their being equal to the Ottomans in their political and economic power; the Mughals' assertion for their being the legitimate heirs of Amir Timur and rightful claimants of the territories held by the Amir; the Ottoman officials' mistreatment of the members of Mughal royal family while they were in the Holy Places for *Hajj;* and geographical distance.

Conversely, the relations with the Safavids, the immediate neighboring state, were much more cordial. Despite the fact that the control of the city of Qandhar was a contentious issue, the armies of both states fighting each other to seize its control, the diplomatic relations remained strong. In cultural and artistic spheres as well, the Iranian imprint was much more pronounced. The emigration of capable Iranian "men of the sword" and "men of the pen" enriched the political and cultural life. The literary tradition of Persian poetry, the art of historiography, the epistle, and the norms of the transmission of traditional Islam as well as mystical Islam were the manifestations of the persistent affinity of the Indo-Islamic culture with the Turko-Persian cultural sphere. The Persian language remained the language of administration well into the nineteenth century. The language of courts in British India, for example, was changed from Persian to English in 1837.

◆ THE EIGHTEENTH CENTURY: A "DARK" CENTURY?

The eighteenth century is a bridge between the medieval and modern times, a transition from the old to the new order and a shift from Muslim to European control of India. Trade provided the first basis of contact between the growing empire of Britain and the Muslim rulers of India. The British East India Company's purpose of acquiring control of parts of India, at least in the eighteenth century, was primarily economic. The symbols of power for the conquering Muslims were victory towers (Qutb Minar in Delhi, built during the beginning of the thirteenth century and Chhota Pandua, built during the late thirteenth century in Bengal), mosques, *madrasas*, palaces, and founding new urban centers. The symbols of control for the British were massive forts (to protect themselves from attack and from the indigenous population) and government houses.

In 1707 the death of Awrangzeb signaled the collapse of the centralized Mughal government. The former provinces of the Mughal empire became successor states, notably Awadh, Bengal, Haiderabad (Deccan), and Sind. In 1739 Delhi was sacked by the Iranian ruler, Nadir Shah Afshar. The Hindu Maratha attempt to gain power received a setback when they were defeated in 1761 by the Afghan ruler, Ahmad Shah Abdali. British and French trading companies had appeared by this time in Bengal and Deccan. However, it was not until 1748 when the ruler of Haiderabad, Nizam al-Mulk, died that Muslims began to become aware of the new threats to their authority. Deccan was the only region where the French and the British fought against each other by supporting two contenders of succession to Nizam al-Mulk. With the success of their candidate, the British East India Company officials became the general administrators and the tax collectors in the region. However, the most important power base of the East India Company was in Bengal where the British gradually gained influence with the support of the Hindu mercantile class. In 1757, in the skirmish of Plassey, the East India Company's forces, with the help of their local allies, defeated the governor of Bengal and installed a puppet governor. The company was solidly entrenched in the region when they defeated the local allied forces, including the Mughals in 1764. They then forced the Mughal ruler, Shah Alam II (died 1806), to hand over the civil governments of Bengal, Bihar, and Orissa to the company. Through their strategy of playing one group against the other, the company gradually gained control over other regions of India, including

Delhi in 1803, the Punjab in 1842, Sind in 1843, and Awadh by 1856.

◆ THE INTELLIGENTSIA AND THE NEW REALITIES

This section focuses on the intellectual and cultural reactions of Muslims to British rule and dominion. The responses of the intelligentsia were varied. The religious scholars and the Sufis sought to remedy the ills of society through a religious revival; the poets and writers encouraged the use of Urdu rather than Persian as a medium of self-expression and assertion of their Indian Muslim cultural identity; the poets satirized the ruling elite and popularized a genre of poetry lamenting social and political chaos; and the historians criticized the Muslim regime and held the ruling elite responsible for the destruction of the administrative institutions. In the nineteenth century, two trends emerged. One group of intellectuals turned increasingly toward Western civilization for inspiration and became more critical of their own tradition. The other group continued the reform movement of the eighteenth century.

Even though northern India was in a period of political turmoil, economic strife, and social disorder, these conditions did not inhibit the richness and creativity of intellectual endeavors. Before the eighteenth century, writers and artists were integrated into the social structures in which they worked, devoting themselves to creative pursuits under imperial patronage. With the disintegration of the sociopolitical structure, intellectuals could no longer count on the favors of the imperial court. They had to develop a more independent stance and assume a new role in society under changed circumstances. The understanding of this change is crucial to a proper evaluation of the social, political, and religious developments that followed.

With the virtual collapse of the Mughal power, the Muslim community in India was without the protection and support of the state. No longer able to count on the patronage of the Mughal imperial court, the intelligentsia gradually emerged as an independent force, increasingly aware of its position in the changing society. Important elements of this intellectual elite, the *ulama* and the Sufis played a crucial role in the educational, social, and religious life of the Muslim community. They served as teachers, opinion makers, interpreters of law, and guides to the community. In their efforts to understand and deal with chaotic conditions around them and to guide their community, the *ulama* utilized their expertise in religion to initiate intellectual reform. The reform or renewal movement in northern India during this century was not so much a reaction to the threat of British domination as it was the fear of survival as a minority in the absence of Muslim political supremacy. The religious elite of the period were responding to the challenges of the time by turning inward in their search for their Muslim identity and by trying to find solutions and remedies from within their own tradition.

♦ EDUCATIONAL SYSTEM: THE EIGHTEENTH CENTURY

The examples of two *madrasas*, the Madrasa-i Rahimiyya and Farangi Mahall, provide differing approaches to change. Shah Wali-Allah (1703–1762) as head of the Madrasa-i Rahimiyya was an heir to the Indo-Islamic intellectual and theological heritage as well as that of Arabia where he also studied. He claimed for himself the title of *mujaddid* (religious renewer) of his time. In his monumental work, *Hujjat Allah al-Baligha* (*Great Divine Proof*), he attempted to integrate the spiritual and material domains of human life. His emphasis on reinterpretation of the sources of Islamic law, the devaluing of differences among the four schools of Sunni law, the benefits of making the Quranic text available through translation to the community, and his belief in the power of the prophetic tradition to reform communal behavior and morals made him the forerunner of nineteenth-century modernists. Shah Wali-Allah devised a much simpler syllabus for his *madrasa* with a focus on the core sciences of Islamic law, theology, the *hadith*, and the sole study of Quranic text to the exclusion of Quranic commentaries. Shah Wali-Allah's mission of teaching and guiding was carried on by his sons and grandsons.

At the Farangi Mahall, a school established for Muslim education, the emphasis was on philosophy and rational sciences. The curriculum, developed by Mulla Nizam al-Din (died 1748), remained popular in the Indo-Pakistan subcontinent until 1969 when the doors of Farangi Mahall were officially closed. Just like the heirs of the Wali-Allah intellectual tradition which drew its inspiration from the work of the Shah Wali-Allah, the scholars covered most aspects of Islamic learning, particularly law and logic. They venerated deceased Sufi masters as well as their shrines.

In the eighteenth century, the Naqshbandiyya stand out among Sufi groups for their reform activities and scholarship. In their centers or *khanqas* in Sirhind, Delhi, Panjab, and Sind, they expended their energies in popularizing the prophetic tradition, in detailing the proper application of Muslim law, and in reconstructing the religio-moral behavior of their disciples. Their influence extended to areas outside the frontier of South Asia.

Muslims and the British Raj: 1757–1857

Muslim religious leadership continued to evolve in the face of overwhelming British control in political,

economic and social spheres. Whereas the Wali-Allahi generation tried to revive dynamism in the community through religio-moral reconstruction, subsequent generations showed sensitivity to political, economic and social developments. This change is reflected in the activities of the Faraidis in Bengal and the Mujahidins in the Northwestern part of India. The founder of the Faraidi movement, Haji Shariat-Allah (1781–1840), while focusing on the proper practice of the obligatory duties of Islam, also sensitized Bengali Muslims to the economic inequities they were experiencing. The movement maintained its puritanical stance but became more political and aggressive under the leadership of Shariat-Allah's son, Muhsin al-Din Ahmad, known as Dudu Miyan. The Faraidis clashed with the landlords, indigo planters and the police, and refused to pay the taxes the majority of which they considered illegal.

The other contemporary religio-political movement in Uttar Pardesh, Bihar, and the north western part of India is known as the Mujahididn movement. The leaders of this movement, Sayyid Ahmad Shahid (1786–1831)and Shah Muhammad Ismail (1781–1831) were greatly influenced by the Wali-Allahi tradition. These leaders, however, disagreed with Wali-Allah's conciliatory approach in resolving differences among various schools of thought. They adopted aggressive means to implement their ideology which resulted in dividing the Muslim community instead of uniting them. They unsuccessfully tried to rejuvenate the Muslim community in India by fusing Tariqa-i Muhammadiyya (the Sufi order led by Sayyid Ahmad) with Wahhabism (puritanical Islamic movement started by Muhammd bin Abd al-Wahhab in the Arabian Hijaz in late eighteenth century).

Both movements were influenced by the Wahhabi movement; both had social, economic, and political concerns; and, most importantly, both lacked an institutional base. The Faraidi movement was more effective in reforming the Bengali Muslims than the Mujahidins. The Pathans in the Northwestern Frontier province rebelled against the leaders of the Mujahidin movement. A sense of communal identity became more pronounced among the Bengali Muslims as a result of the Faraidi movement and its subsequent off-shoots. The followers of the Mujahidins split into various schools of thought such as the Ahl-i Hadith (People of the *Hadith*), the Barelwis and the Deobandis.

The Religious Thinkers Vis-a-Vis the New Political Order

The Muslim religious elite was not unanimous in its reactions to the British political and economic control. Haji Shariat-Allah, for example, declared Bengal to be a non-Islamic region and a land of war (*dar al-harb*), encouraging his followers to wage war against their non-Muslim rulers. He suspended Friday and *Id* congregational prayers. His followers also refused to pay certain taxes and cesses which they regarded as non-Islamic. Shah Abd al-Aziz's juridical ruling that India had become *dar al-harb* under the British rule was little more than a theoretical statement. Unlike Shariat-Allah, Abd al-Aziz did not urge the Muslims to take up arms against the British, nor did he suspend congregational prayers in Delhi. Indeed, he supported the Mujahidin movement which was directed against the Sikhs, not the British. He maintained cordial relations with the British officials and was not opposed to the Muslims' seeking employment with the East India Company. Shah Abd al-Aziz's contemporary, the Naqshbandiyya Sufi master, Shah Ghulam Ali (died 1824), was, on the other hand, very much opposed to the British administration, and discouraged his disciples from working for the British. His counterparts, the Chishtiyya masters, Shah Niaz Ahmad of Barailly (died 1834) and Shah Muhammad Sulayman of Taunsa (died 1850), remained aloof of the political developments and continued to concentrate on the spiritual and religious well-being of their disciples in small towns and villages across north and Northwestern provinces. The Farangi Mahallis who had a history of working closely with the rulers, did not extend this practice to the British after their takeover of Awadh in 1856. They rejected government employment and any honors the government tried to confer upon them in recognition of their scholarship.

From a Quest For Rapprochement To Seeking Independence (1857–1947)

The subject of the uprising of 1857—an armed conflict between local groups (primarily Hindus and Muslims) and the British—has intrigued generations of historians since its occurrence. It has been viewed by the majority as a watershed in India's history—the end of a medieval social and political order and the ushering of a modern era. It has been viewed by some Hindu and Muslim historians to be the first "war of independence," and by others a revolt against the agrarian and fiscal policies of the British.

In religious and cultural spheres, however, this event did not bring about an abrupt end to the previous trends. Nevertheless, leadership of the community in political, cultural as well as religious matters shifted from religious scholars to the descendants of Mughal nobility. This new group of intellectuals, called the "modernists," were not a product of traditional education. They had been exposed to the British system of education which had been introduced in India earlier,

and had also worked for the British. Noteworthy among them were Sayyid Ahmad Khan, also called Sir Sayyid Ahmad (1817–1898), Sayyid Ameer Ali (1849–1928), and Shibli Numani (1857–1914). Sayyid Ahmad, grandson of a Mughal noble, was raised in the Mughal capital of Delhi with traditional liberal arts education. Sayyid Ameer Ali—the descendant, of an Iranian noble who came to India in 1738 with Nadir Shah and did not return to Iran—was educated in Bengal in an English school with some traditional Islamic education along with Persian language and literature; he later went to England to study law. Shibli belonged to the landed and educated aristocracy and preferred traditional Islamic education to his siblings who received modern education.

The main preoccupation of these modernists was the uplift of Muslims as a group by defending their position as former rulers. Through their writings they defended the Muslims' religious and cultural heritage in the face of British imperialism. The criticism and devaluing of Islam by Christian missionaries of the early period and by British intellectuals resulted in attempts by Muslim intellectuals to defend their heritage. British rule had a major impact on the traditional educational system. The introduction of modern educational system and the need to learn English language for employment gradually marginalized traditional education. The loss of state patronage and of an economic base caused a sharp decline in their prestige. This led the modernists to establish modern educational institutions for helping Muslims acquire necessary skills to function within the new British intellectual, political and moral imperial order imposed upon them. The models of educational institutions provided by the new masters were limited and inadequate. In 1781 Warren Hastings, British governor of Eastern India, established a Muslim institution in Calcutta, to produce staff trained in classical traditional Islamic curriculum to serve the East India Company's administration in the region. Another center in Delhi, was established in 1792 to introduce students to modern sciences and English language along with classical Islamic and Indian languages and traditional education.

Sayyid Ahmad Khan played an important role in developing an awareness of social, political and religious issues among Muslims. He presented Islam as a rational and natural religion fully capable of accommodating historical and and socio-political changes. In 1875, with the support of the British, he established the Muhammadan Anglo-Oriental College which later became a university known as Aligarh Muslim University. His dream to synthesize traditional Islam with modernity at M.A.O. College, however, remained unfulfilled.

Shibli, an historian and literary critic with expertise in philosophy of religion and theology, also envisioned a modern Islam with traditional roots. He taught at Aligarh for sixteen years and was deeply influenced by Sir Sayyid Ahmad's thinking. Shibli, frustrated with the lack of depth in the training of students at Aligarh, took keen interest in an institution, known as Nadwat al-Ulama. Founded by Muhammad Ali Mongheri in Lucknow in 1894 for training future *ulama*, it was masterful in traditional Islamic and modern sciences and capable of producing scholarship of a high calibre. However, like Sayyid Ahmad, Shibli's dreams were also not realized— the Nadwa turned into a conservative Islamic institution with research focusing on Islamic history.

Although Sayyid Ameer Ali did not establish any educational or research institution, he responded to the missionaries' adverse criticism of the life and mission of the Prophet and the history of the Arabs. He wrote extensively on a wide range of historical, religious, legal, social and political issues. Sayyid Ahmad and Shibli used Urdu as their medium of expression while Sayyid Ameer Ali adopted English to reach his western and westernized audience.

The next generation of intellectual, political and social leadership was provided by men who were journalists and poets in their early careers, namely, Muhammad Ali (1878–1931), Muhammad Iqbal (1876–1938), Abul Kalam Azad (1888–1958), and Sayyid Abul Ala Maududi (1903–1979). Because of their training in modern education, the *ulama* did not let these intellectuals claim religious authority. However, they were in the forefront of political movements in mobilizing their community to seek social and political gains. Unlike the earlier generation, they were not descendants of former Mughal nobility. Of the four intellectuals mentioned above, only Muhammad Ali came from a petty land-owning family. The family was allotted land not by the Mughals but by the British in recognition of the family's support to the British during the 1857 disturbances.

Muhammad Ali was educated at an English school and was the first graduate from the Oxford University returning to his home-state, Rampur (150 miles east of Delhi). He majored in history and adopted journalism as his profession by starting the journal *Comrade* in 1911. This journal became an effective vehicle for expression of the discontent and anger of the Muslim intelligentsia. He is known for his successful mobilization of the masses during the Khilafat movement. In 1920, at the height of Indian opposition to the British, and the short-term unity of the Hindus and Muslims in the cause of saving the position of Ottoman caliph, Muhammad Ali founded Jamia Millia, an educational institution in Delhi in 1920, rivalling Aligarh College. Unlike Aligarh College and Nadwa, its underlying goal was to encourage opposition to the British and promote loyalty and commitment to the Hindu

leader, Mohandas K. Gandhi (died 1948), and to Indian nationalism.

Muhammad Iqbal, "the most daring intellectual modernist, the Muslim World has produced," in the words of the late scholar of Islam Fazlur Rahman, was the son of a tailor and grandson of a shawl peddlar in Sialkot, a small town in West Punjab. Like other modernists, he studied in Western institutions—studied philosophy at Cambridge and Law at London's Lincoln Inn; and received a doctorate from Munich University by writing Ph.D. dissertation on Persian metaphysics. Like Shibli, Iqbal had a solid background in Arabic, Persian and Islamic philosophy prior to his exposure to Western thought. He was a recognized poet at the age of 22. His Urdu and Persian poetry— reflecting his ideas on movement and change, dynamism of human spirit, love, search for truth, and significance of independent reasoning—served as the main vehicle for mobilizing and energizing Muslims. The most enduring legacy of Iqbal, however, is not his reconstruction of Islamic thought but his idea of an autonomous homeland for Indian Muslims which was realized in 1947 with the establishment of Pakistan.

Azad and Maududi could be considered together because of similarities in their backgrounds and activities. Both had taken on many different roles during the colonial and post-independence periods. Each had traditional Islamic education, did not attend English schools, chose journalism as a profession, and was involved in Islamic religious reinterpretation. Azad founded a serious journal *al-Hilal* in 1912. Twenty years later, Maududi started his *Tarjuman al-Quran*. Both used their journals as their main instrument for expounding their views on religious, state, law, and socio-political issues. Azad's *al-Hilal* was an immediate success. However, the British government in India did not like his extensive coverage of injustices to Muslims in Turkey, his advocacy of the independence of India from the British rule through the joint struggle of Hindus and Muslims, and his preaching of "true" Islam. His journal had a short span of only over two years. Maududi's *Tarjuman* outlived him and is still in circulation with a large readership. In 1913, Azad founded a party called *Hizbullah* (Party of God) to establish a system of government for social welfare in accordance with Divine injunctions. Due to lack of the *ulama* 's support, this party did not take off very well. Maududi also founded *Jamaat-i Islami* (Islamic Party), an organization of his own, to counter the drive for a homeland for Muslims under the secular leadership of Muhammad Ali Jinnah (1876–1948) as well as of the Muslim League—a political party founded in 1906 to represent the interests of Muslims. The *Jamaat* became an active political party only after independence in 1947. Azad vigorously participated in politics in the

1920s and 1930s by allowing himself to be elected the President of Indian National Congress which was founded in 1885 to represent Indian interests. Conversely, Maududi was preoccupied with writing about the Muslim community and an ideal Islamic state. In March, 1938, upon the request of Iqbal, Maududi moved from Hyderabad, Deccan, to Gurdaspur, Punjab, to build a training center called *Dar al-Islam* (House of Islam) for the select graduates of traditional and modern educational systems and train them for moral and intellectual leadership. However, this venture lasted only until December of that year. Both Azad and Maududi wrote commentaries on the Quran in Urdu (*Tarjuman al-Quran* and *Tafhim al-Quran* respectively) for the purpose of religious reform of Indian Muslims by providing them direct access to the Quranic text in Urdu. Azad translated and commented on the first eighteen of the thirty chapters of the Quran and Maududi's exegesis covered the entire Quranic text. Maududi's major writings, including the *Tafhim* have been translated into English and several languages whereas Azad's writings are accessible only to an Urdu readership. Maududi remained at the center stage with his involvement in Pakistan's constitutional debates, and in politics of the country through his party, while still maintaining his prolific writing career until his death in 1979.

Pan-Islamism, Separatism and Composite Nationalism

In the early 1920s, many Indian Muslims joined in launching the Khilafat movement (1919–1924). The goal of this movement was to pressure the British government to preserve the Ottoman Turkish territories as they were in 1914, and to safeguard the centrality of the spiritual and temporal position of the Ottoman sultan as a caliph of the Islamic world. This movement was an anomaly because it was not an Indian problem and had little support in Turkey itself, and the Arab world was against it. But its uniqueness rested in the fact that it became a pan-Indian movement. On March 1, 1924, the National Assembly of Turkey voted to depose the Ottoman Sultan and abolish the institution of caliphate. The imprint of this movement on subsequent political developments in India was, however, deep. Both Hindu and Muslim leadership learned the techniques of manipulating symbols and mobilizing popular support. It also accentuated the divisions between Hindus and Muslims, as well as differences among Muslim ranks.

A heightened sense of identity and separateness among Muslims in modern period is linked with British policies in India which defined various communities on the basis of their religion and race and gave them political representation accordingly. The issue of Muslim separateness is closely associated with Sir Sayyid Ahmad. He is generally mentioned as the first champion of Muslim distinctiveness which later set a trend in political thinking and culminated in the creation of a separate homeland for Indian Muslims. Muhammad Ali Jinnah (1876–1948) was a lawyer trained in London's Lincoln Inn, who stood for Hindu-Muslim unity for most of his life, successfully led the Muslims to secure their own country. The politics of Hindu majority had disillusioned Jinnah causing a shift in his thinking. On the other hand, Abul Kalam Azad and other notables including Mawdudi, along with a segment of Muslim intellectuals stood for a united India. They became known as composite nationalists. Both groups of Muslims had intellectual and religious reasons for their position. The weak theoretical base of the composite nationalists' argument and the dubious role played by the Indian National Congress (established in 1885 to represent Indian interests) contributed to the separatists' success. Unlike the *ulama*, the Naqshbandiyyas in the Punjab, led by Jamaat Ali (died 1951), supported the Pakistan movement. Factors such as the enthusiastic support of the able elite from the U.P., effective use of religious symbols, the intensified consciousness of Muslim identity, and political participation of Muslim masses, contributed to the success of Jinnah and the Muslim League (a political party established in 1906 to represent Muslim interests), in achieving a homeland for Muslims. During their spirited campaign for a sovereign state for Muslims, the acronym, Pakistan (the Abode of the Pure), was coined. After much arguments on the territories to be part of the new state, the British created two independent and often hostile states, India and Pakistan. Pakistan, divided into two wings—East and West Pakistan with approximately 1000 miles of Indian territory between them—emerged on the world map. East Pakistan included the former East Bengal and the Sylhet district of Assam, Bengali-speaking Muslims with numerical majority. It seceded from Pakistan in 1971 and became a sovereign state of Bangladesh). The Western part comprised four provinces, Punjab, Sind, Baluchistan, and Northwestern Frontier province with four regional languages. The partition of India took a heavy toll on human life. Hundreds of thousands of people died and millions were displaced. It left the Muslims in India as a much smaller minority when millions of their brethren migrated to Pakistan. The inexperienced leadership of the newly-born state of Pakistan—the most underdeveloped region of the Subcontinent—was confronted with the settlement of a huge influx of Muslims who migrated from India, and more importantly, was hard-pressed to learn quickly the tasks of nation-building.

Continuity and Change: 1947 and Beyond

After independence, an obvious and major change occurred in the intelligentsia's role in shaping the destiny of Muslims in Pakistan and India. Unlike the developments in British India, the initiative in social, religious and political reform was expected to come from the political leadership and not from religious and social reformers. The issues confronting the Muslims in the two countries were different. In Pakistan, the shape of the social order and the role of religion in politics were to become concerns of both political leadership and the intelligentsia. In India, having become a small and powerless minority, the Muslims had to cope with and adjust to the changed reality of living in a "secular" India. The intellectuals continued to provide leadership to the community and serve as spokespersons of their community.

The Political Leadership and Islam

Muhammad Ali Jinnah, the founder of Pakistan, fondly called by his people, Quaid-i Azam (the Great Leader), spoke to the Constituent assembly on August 11, 1947:

You are free; you may go to your temples, you are free to to go to your mosques or to any other place to worship in this State of Pakistan . . . You may belong to any religion or caste or creed—that has nothing to do with the business of the State . . . We are starting in the days when there is no discrimination, no distinction between one community and another, no discrimination between one caste or creed and another.

Contrary to the vision of the founder, the subject of Islam and its place in this newly-born fledgling state and its affairs became an important element of political discourse. The ideological polarization of the community between the *ulama* and the modernists which had divided the community before 1947 continued after 1947 and shaped and nurtured the ideological cross-currents in Pakistan. Its first manifestation was in the constitutional debates. The constitutions of 1956, 1962 and 1973 reflect the fusion of secular and modernistic Islamic elements. The constitution of 1962 promulgated during the military rule of General Ayub Khan's mirrored his vision of a modern state. He was the product of Aligarh as well as the British army tradition. Ayub abrogated the constitution of 1956 when he imposed the first martial law on the pretext of preventing political decay. During his eleven years military rule (1958–1969), he precluded the participation of *ulama* in the government's policy making process. In scores of commissions and committees which he set up to re-view all aspects of Pakistani society, the subject of Islamization was never raised. In his policies and decisions, whether concerning family law reforms or education, elements of modernism were very present. In his constitution of 1962, Ayub even removed the word "Islamic" from the Islamic Republic of Pakistan, the name of the country agreed upon in the constitution of 1956.

After the dismemberment of Pakistan in 1971 and creation of Bangladesh, Pakistanis experienced an identity crisis. In search of a new source of unity among the four remaining provinces with different languages and cultural norms, Islam provided a viable ideology to unite them as a nation. It was Prime Minister, Zulfiqar Ali Bhutto (1971–1977), a moving force in the dismemberment of Pakistan and the most secular of Pakistan's heads of state gave visible recognition to the *ulama* by officially involving them in the Islamization process. He also succumbed to the pressures of the religious groups in September 1974 in declaring a movement known as Ahmadiyya, non-Muslim. His attempts to bring Pakistan closer to the Arab and Iranian world may have been designed to distance Pakistan from South Asian cultural and political orbit. In retrospect, however, these moves did not bring about any real change in the government's administrative structure which remained secular.

General Zia ul-Haq (1977–1988) deposed Bhutto in July 1977 in the name of restoring law and order. In his quest for legitimation as an a non-elected head of state, he made Islamization of the social and political order of the country the cornerstone of his government. He received the support of religious scholars to the extent that a group of them turned against elections and parliamentary democracy and favored vesting all powers in the individual who seized power. Islamization in their view was more important than the efficiency of government. Thus, Zia introduced a comprehensive Islamization plan covering religious institutions, educational system, economy and law. These measures, in the short term, brought confusion and chaos; nor did they contribute to improved law and order. With the sudden death of Zia in an airline accident in 1988, democracy was restored. In November 1988, Benazir Bhutto was elected as Prime Minister, the first woman in the modern Muslim world to become the head of state. She was reelected in 1993. The advent of democracy did not bring stability and order to the country. The socio-political decline, sectarian violence and regional conflicts have added to the confusion and made the country difficult to govern.

In East Pakistan, during the secession movement, there was an upsurge of Benagli nationalism and secularism. After the creation of a sovereign state of Bangladesh, the government headed by Mujibur

Rahman—the founder of the nation (killed in 1975)—and intellectuals, denounced important elements of their religious and cultural heritage. Subsequently all Islamic parties were banned. During Mujibur Rahman's time in office (1971–1975), the government and intellectuals could not resolve the divisive forces of nationalism, secularism and Islam. After Mujib's death and General Ziaur Rahman's takeover, secularism lost its central position in body politics and Muslim parties were allowed to function again. Ziaur Rahman established a division of Religious Affairs, encouraged Islamic research, and proposed an Islamic University. His successor, General H.M. Ershad (1982–91) continued the policy of Islamization. But his actions were limited in comparison with Bhutto's and Zia ul-Haq's policies in Pakistan. In 1988, Bangladesh's National Assembly amended the constitution and declared Islam as the state religion. With the lifting of ban on Islamic parties, Jamaat-i Islami was revived and actively participated in politics. In 1991 elections, it won 18 of the 300 National Assembly seats, renewing its demand for an Islamic state.

Modernism and Traditionalism: An Overview

As noted above, Pakistan's ruling elite and governmental policies have remained secular since independence. The modernist religious thinking failed to dominate the intellectual landscape. Among the post-independence modernists in Pakistan, the most noteworthy is Dr. Fazlur Rahman (1919–1988), a Cambridge University graduate with a solid background in traditional Islam. He made a substantial contribution to the modernization of Pakistani laws. During Ayub Khan's era, he worked as a Visiting Professor for two years (1961–63) at the Pakistan's Central Institute of Islamic Research. He was appointed the director of the Institute in 1963 and held that position until 1968. Dr. Fazlur Rahman drew inspiration from earlier modernists such as Shibli and Iqbal. He left his imprint on the Family Laws Ordinance (1961) which has survived despite the recent trend toward conservatism. The women's rights groups deserve much credit for protecting the family laws reforms enacted under the Ordinance. Fazlur Rahman's bold criticism of traditional approach to Islam and the study of the Quran, and radical reinterpretation of Islamic laws drew the wrath of Jamaat-i Islami. During public protests against Ayub Khan in 1968–69, Rahman had to resign from his position of Director of the research institute. He left Pakistan and in the fall of 1969, took up a Professorship in Islamic Thought at the University of Chicago and taught there until his death in 1988. His departure from Pakistan was a major setback to the modernists. No other modernist has carried his legacy in as meaningful a manner as of yet in Pakistan. Despite Bhutto's and

Zia-ul Haq's drive for Islamization, the basic character of the government remains secular.

Traditional Islam is a major force in Pakistan. The Deobandis, Ahl-i Hadith, and the Barelawis each with a large following are serious rivals and engage in debates on theological issues. These religious groups have also formed themselves into political parties. Jamaat-i Islami's influence is by far the most widespread because of its large membership. Only a small number of its members are *madrasa* graduates. The rest represent all strata of society—educated laypersons, professional and non-professionals, coming from lower and middle classes. Jamaat's educated membership has played a prominent role at both social and political levels throughout the history of Pakistan. It has also gained a foothold in the younger population of colleges and universities. This younger group is an active participant in politics and mobilizing masses to take part in protests and demonstrations against the government. It has remained persistent in its demand for the establishment of an Islamic state. This is a reformist group who wishes to bring about social change through peaceful means. Nevertheless, the Pakistanis have not shown much trust in the Jamaat at the ballot box. The Jamaat's performance has remained consistently poor in all general elections held so far.

Tablighi Jamaat is a grass-root level organization which has affected millions of Muslims in South and Southeast Asia, the Middle East, Africa, Europe and North America. It is an apolitical organization founded by Maulana Ilyas (a graduate of Deoband) in 1926 in Mewat, near Delhi. Its mission is to reach out to masses in rural areas as well as in cities and to teach them the basics of Islam in order to help them become better Muslims and human beings. The message is transmitted by simple preaching of the fundamentals of Islam, not through pamphlets and books.

The *madrasas*, centers of traditional education in Pakistan, are growing rapidly in number with or without the government support. At the time of independence, there were 137 *madrasas* in West Pakistan; and according to a survey of 1986, their number was over 2200 during that year. These *madrasas* are playing a major role in increasing literacy in rural areas, in developing Muslim consciousness, and in providing guidance to the masses through teaching and through their interpretation of Islamic law by writing *fatwas* (opinions on points of law). Through their newsletters and magazines, they also disseminate their views on religious, social and political matters. The Sufi shrines and *khanqas* are other forums of religious and spiritual activities. The Naqshbandiyyas and the Chishtiyyas have the largest following in Pakistan. The Nashbandiyya are maintaining their scholarly tradition by writing on social and political issues. It should also be noted that

Islamic Studies is taught as a required subject from elementary to high school and is an elective subject at college and university levels both in Pakistan and Bangladesh.

In Bangladesh, the *Jamaat-i Islami* was rejuvenated after a major set back during the secession movement. Now it is an important player in politics. Khaleda Zia, the first female Prime Minister of Bangladesh, could initially form her government in 1991 only with the support of the *Jamaat.* Tablighi Jamaat has also become very active in Bangladesh. Among nineteenth century reformist groups, the *Ahl-i Hadith* was a small, but a vibrant group. The leadership of the group is held by highly educated individuals such as Professor Muhammad Abdul Bari, a recognized scholar of Islamic studies. Parallel to the trend in Pakistan, the number of religious schools and mosques is growing rapidly in Bangladesh. According to the *1991 Statistical Year Book of Bangladesh*, there are more than 131,641 mosques, 5,766 *madrasas* and 58,126 *maktabs* (elementary schools) across about 65,000 villages.@PP:In the Republic of India, the *ulama* do not have opportunities to play a central role as their counterparts in Pakistan and Bangladesh do. Traditional institutions such as Deoband and Nadwa have full freedom to run their *madrasas* as they did before independence. The *Farangi Mahall* closed down in 1969, as indicated earlier. After independence, the *Jamaat-i Islami* of India was organized as a separate organization. The needs of the community and the pressures of its milieu have affected the mandate of the Jamaat in India. The demand for an Islamic state is not relevant there. They are in agreement with their Pakistani counterpart that secularism as a philosophy is antithetical to religion. However, the Indian Jamaat supports India as a secular state. Nadwat al-Ulama is engaged in teaching and research with a traditional outlook. In research, Mawlana Abul Hasan Nadwi is maintaining the tradition of historical writings. Dar al-Ulum Deoband is serving the needs of the community by producing teachers and scholars who teach in *madrasas* across India. They guide the masses by giving opinions on legal issues which are written as *fatwas.* They, like other *madrasas*, have resisted changes in the Muslim personal and family laws.

The traditions of modernism and composite nationalism established by Muhammad Ali at *Jamia Millia Islamia* have been kept alive after partition by individuals such as Muhammad Mujeeb, Zakir Hussain and Abid Hussain, Mushirul Haq and Z.A. Faruqi. They provided leadership on topics ranging from secularism to Indo-Islamic heritage and the place of Muslims as a minority in the Republic of India. Aligarh Muslim University has made a solid contribution to research and writing in the area of medieval Indo-Islamic history but not to religious thought and Islamic modernism. Sufi centers and shrines remain central to providing guidance in spiritual and religious matters to Muslims. The Nashbandiyya Dargah-i Shah Abul Khayr in Old Delhi, for example, still maintains its scholarly tradition under the leadership of Abul Hasan Zaid Faruqi along with its other functions.

In sum, Islam is a vibrant and dynamic force in South Asia today. Muslims in the region have diverse linguistic, cultural and ethnic identities. Mappila Muslims living in Kerala, descendants of the earliest Arab settlers in the coastal cities, are very different from the descendants of the Arab conquerors of Sind, the first region brought under Muslim control. The Pathans of Northwest too stand apart in their cultural traditions and ethnicity from the Begladeshis—their former Pakistani countrymen. The common bond they all share is their Muslim identity. Muslims in Pakistan and India feel the anguish of fellow Muslims elsewhere in the Subcontinent, whether it be over the demolition of the Babri mosque in Ayodhia, India, or in the Government of India's military response to Kashmir (a state with a Muslim majority). Indian Muslims feel a need to defend their minority rights as Hindu nationalism becomes more forcefully expressed. Bangladesh, the youngest sovereign state in the region, is still going through a period of consolidation and institution building. The tradition of leftist and liberal thinking is still being sustained by the intelligentsia of this country. The violent reaction by an extremist group in 1994 against the feminist writings of Dr. Tasleema Nasreen does not reflect the collective tolerant thinking of the Bangladeshi intelligentsia. In Pakistan, the successive military regimes which interrupted the democratic process, the Russian invasion of Afghanistan in 1979, and subsequent influx of refugees and weapons, and drug-trafficking, have contributed to social and political unrest in the country. With the collapse of Soviet Union and independence of Muslim Republics in Central Asia, Pakistan has the opportunity to renew its historical contacts with these states and reinvigorate its cosmopolitan heritage. Overall, the Muslims in South Asia are going through a period of rapid social, political and economic transformation. Disillusioned with socialism, modernism, secularism, and westernization, they, like Muslims around the world, are going back to their roots in search of solutions for their problems.

Sajida S. Alvi

References

Ahmad, Aziz. *An Intellectual History of Islam in India.* Edinburgh: Edinburgh University Press, 1969.

————. *Islamic Culture in the Indian Environment.* London: Oxford University Press, 1964.

————. *Islamic Modernism in India and Pakistan, 1857–1964.* London: Oxford University Press, 1967.

Ahmad, I. *Caste and Social Stratification Among Muslims in India.* 2d rev. ed. Columbia, Mo.: South Asia Books, 1978.

————. *Ritual and Religion Among Muslims in India.* Columbia, Mo.: South Asia Books, 1982.

Alvi, Sajida S. *Advice on the Art of Governance: An Indo-Islamic Mirror For Princes: Mauijah-i Jahangiri of Muhammad Baqir Najim-i Sami.* Albany: State University of New York Press, 1989.

Amin, Mohammad. *Islamization of Laws in Pakistan.* Lahore: Sang-e-Meal Publications, 1989.

Baljon, J.M.S. *Religion and Thought of Shah Wali Allah Dihlawi, 1703–1762.* Leiden: E. J. Brill, 1986

Bosworth, C.E. *The Later Ghaznavids. Splendour and Decay: The Dynasty in Afghanistan and Northern India, 1040–1186.* Edinburgh, 1977.

Dale, S. *Islamic Society on the South Asian Frontier: The Mappilas of Malabar, 1498–1922.* Oxford, 1980.

Eaton, R.M. *Sufis of Bijapur.* Princeton: Princeton University Press, 1978.

————. Eaton, R.M. *The Rise of Islam and the Bengal Frontier.* Berkeley: University of California Press, 1993.

Friedmann, Y. *Shaykh Ahmad Sirhindi: An Outline of His Thought and a Study of His Image in the Eyes of Posterity.* Montreal: McGill University Press, 1971.

Fyzee, Asaf Ali Asghar. "Bohoras," *EI* 2, I, 1960.

————. *Cases in the Muhammadan Law of India and Pakistan.* Oxford: Clarendon Press, 1965.

Gandhi, Rajimohan. *Eight Lives: A Study of the Hindu Muslim Encounter.* Albany: State University of New York Press, 1986.

Habibullah, A.W. *The Foundation of Muslim Rule in India.* 2d rev. ed. Allahabad: Central Book Depot, 1961.

Hardy, Peter. *Historians of Medieval India.* London: Luzac and Co., 1960.

————. *The Muslims of British India.* Cambridge: Cambridge University Press, 1972.

Haroon, Mohammed. *Muslims of India: Their Literature on Education, History, Politics, Religion, Socio-Economic, and Communal Problems.* Delhi, 1991. (A comprehensive bibliography)

Hollister, J. *The Shia of India.* London: Luzac, 1953.

Ikram, S.M. *Muslim Civilization in India.* New York: Columbia University Press, 1993.

Inden, R. *Marriage and Rank in Bengali Culture: A History of Caste and Clan in Middle Period Bengal.* Berkeley: University of California Press, 1976.

Koch. *Mughal Architecture: An Outline of Its History and Development (1526–1858)*

Lelyveld, David. *Aligarh's First Generation: Muslim Solidarity in British India.* Princeton: Princeton University Press, 1978.

MacLean, Derryl N. *Religion and Society in Arab Sind.* Leiden: B.J. Brill, 1989.

Metcalf, B. *Islamic Revival in British India: Deoband, 1860–1900.* Princeton, Princeton University Press, 1982.

Misra, S.C. *Muslim Communities in Gujarat.* London: Asia Publishing House, 1964.

Mujeeb, M. *The Indian Muslims.* Montreal: McGill University Press, 1967.

Nasr, Seyyed Vali Reza. *The Vanguard of the Islamic Revolution.* Berkeley and Los Angeles: University of California Press, 1994.

Nizami, K.A. *Some Aspects of Religion and Politics in India in the Thirteenth Century.* Aligargh: Department of History, Muslim University, 1961.

Nizami, K.A. and M. Habib, eds. *A Comprehensive History of India, The Delhi Sultanate.* Vol. 5. Bombay: Peoples Publishing House, 1970.

Pearson, M.N. *Merchants and Rulers in Gujarat: The Response to the Portuguese in the Sixteenth Century.* Berkeley: University of California Press, 1976.

Phillips, C.H., ed. *Historians of India, Pakistan and Ceylon.* London: Oxford University Press, 1961.

Powell, Avril Ann. *Muslims and Missionaries In Pre-Mutiny India.*

Surrey, 1993.

Rahman, Razlur. *Islam and Modernity, Transformation of an Intellectual Tradition.* Chicago: The University of Chicago Press, 1982.

Richards, John F. *The Mughal Empire. The New Cambridge History of India.* New York: Cambridge University Press, 1993.

Rizvi, S.A.A. *A Socio-Intellectual History of the Isna Ashari Shiis in India.* 2 vols. New Delhi, 1986.

Roy, Asim. *The Islamic Syncretistic Tradition in Bengal.* Princeton: Princeton University Press, 1984.

Russell. *The Pursuit of Urdu Literature: A Select History.* London: Zed Book Ltd.

Sachau, E.C. *Alberuni's India.* New Delhi: S. Chand, 1983.

Schimmel, A. *Islam in the Indian Subcontinent.* Leiden: E. J. Brill, 1980.

————. *Mystical Dimensions of Islam.* Chapel Hill: University of North Carolina Press, 1975.

Shaikh, Fanzana. *Community and Consensus in Islam: Muslim Representation in Colonial India, 1860–1947.* Cambridge: Cambridge University Press, 1989.

Smith, W.C. *Modern Islam in India.* rev. ed. New York: Russell and Russell, 1972.

Troll, C. *Sayyid Ahmad Khan: A Reinterpretation of Muslim Theology.* New Delhi: Vikas Publishing House, 1978.

Veer, P. Van Der. *Religious Nationalism: Hindus and Muslims in India.* Berkeley: University of California Press, 1994.

Wolpert, Stanley. Jinnah of Pakistan. Oxford: Oxford University Press, 1984.

6

Islam in Southeast Asia

♦ Islam in Indonesia ♦ The Spread of Islam ♦ Islam in Malaysia

Indonesia is a very large country, extending from Sabang, the western-most tip of the country, all the way to Merauke, the eastern-most tip, a distance comparable to that from London, England to Teheran, Iran and covering the whole of eastern and western Europe and the Near East; a fact that even Indonesians themselves are sometimes not aware of, not to mention most non-Indonesians. Indonesia is also the largest archipelago on earth, consisting of about seventeen-thousand islands, large and small, inhabited and uninhabited. The magnitude of this country and the complexity its physical features are reflected in the ethnic, linguistic, and cultural plurality and diversity of the Indonesian population.

♦ ISLAM IN INDONESIA

Indonesia is the largest Muslim nation in the world. Approximately 90 percent of its population of more than 180 million is Muslim. At the same time, it is the least culturally and linguistically Arabized. Although a major proportion of Muslims here, as everywhere else in the Muslim world, read the Quran in Arabic, they read it as part of their ritual practice. Arabic is a foreign language and the Arabic script is not used to write the national and vernacular language; this is due in part because the region had been under Dutch colonial rule for 350 years. As a result, the use of Arabic script is limited, primarily reserved for use in traditional Islamic schools or *pesantrens.*

Islam in Indonesia has been viewed as being different from Islam in such regions as India and the Middle East. Historically speaking, Islam in Indonesia is a relatively new phenomenon. The relative newness of Islam in this area may be illustrated by the fact that the most magnificent Buddhist monument in Indonesia is Borobudur, a temple that was erected between 778 and 850, within a hundred or so years after the erection of the Dome of the Rock in 690. When the Indus valley

was conquered by a Muslim army in the eighth century, Indonesia was still undergoing the process of being introduced to Buddhism. By the time of the flourishing Delhi sultanate in thirteenth century in India, Indonesia was witnessing the ascendance of the mighty Hindu empire of Majapahit.

Historical evidence shows that the Arabs first arrived in Indonesia as far back as the fourth century, long before the birth of Prophet Muhammad, to take part in the trade between India and China. Despite some evidence that shows Islam began to be present here as early as the tenth century, it is not until the fourteenth century that the religion consolidated its hold from Gujarat in India and began to expand through commercial contacts. This marked the beginning of the "Islamic period" in the islands.

Islam was established first in far northern Sumatra notably Aceh, and then spread to Java. The capture of Melaka by the Portuguese in 1511 resulted in a scattering of Muslim merchants all over the archipelago, who took their faith with them. However, Islam found Indonesian soil had already been very thickly populated with all branches of the Indic tradition of Hinduism and Buddhism. Indonesia was a fertile land for Hinduism, and this flourished into a full fledged civilization from the eighth to the fifteenth centuries.

As a result, Islam took hold most solidly in those areas of Indonesia which had been least affected by the Hindu civilizations: the north-central Java coast, Banten in West Java, and the Aceh and Minangkabau regions of North and West Sumatra. The Hindu princes of Java were probably first converted to Islam by a desire for trade, wealth, and power. Principalities on the north Java coast employed a skillful Muslim harbormaster to merchandise for them and to run shipping warehouses. The king was converted first, then the people accepted Islam as a group.

The converted rulers adjusted to indigenous sentiment by permitting monarchs to be worshipped as

Islam in Indonesia was established first in northern Sumatra. Pictured is the mosque near Padaug, Sumatra.

saints after death. Pre-Islamic signal towers became Muslim minarets and the native Indonesian meeting hall was transformed into a mosque. Rulers placed their royal *gamelans* in the mosques and people came to listen, and stayed to be converted to the new religion. Demak in Java was the first important city to convert to Islam (in 1477), followed by Cirebon (in 1480). In 1487, a coalition of Muslim princes attacked what was left of the Hindu Majapahit empire. By the end of the fifteenth century there were twenty Muslim kingdoms over the entire archipelago.

Pancasila

Such a historical background would imply that ideologically Indonesia does not perceive itself to be an "Islamic state." The official constitutional view of the state is embodied in Five Principals called *Pancasila*; belief in One Supreme God (Monotheism); just and civilized humanism; the unity of Indonesia; democracy; and social justice. Sukarno, (1901–1970) the first president of the republic is commonly credited as the inventor of *Pancasila*. He proposed the five principles as a *modus vivendi* between secular nationalism advocated by nationalists and the idea of a state demanded by Islamically-oriented politicians. As a national ideology,

Pancasila was accepted only after long and tedious deliberations, and after having some of the principles Islamized further in one way or another. Thus monotheism as the first *sila* (principle) is the Islamization of Sukarno's original concept of a more generalized "belief in God" (which may include polytheism). While Sukarno proposed it to be the fourth principle, the Muslims wanted it to be the first and the most important one. "Unity of Indonesia," the third principle, was originally entitled "nationalism," and was changed to the more neutral but dynamic term as a solution to the objection expressed by Muslims, since nationalism, narrowly conceived, goes against Islamic universalism and reminded Indonesians of the chauvinistic nationalism found in Germany and Japan during the Second World War. "Democracy," the fourth principle, is short for a longer formulation, "democracy under the guidance of wisdom through deliberation of the people's representatives." ("Wisdom through deliberation" is a paraphrase of a saying ascribed to the Prophet Muhammad.) Muhammad Hatta (who would be the first vice president of the republic), Haji Agus Salim (a prominent Muslim intellectual of the revolutionary Indonesia), Ki Bagus Hadikusumo (head of the Muhammadiyah Islamic modernist movement), and

Abdul-Wahid Hashim (head of the *Nahdat al-Ulama*, an Islamic traditionalist movement), were most credited with the Islamization of *Pancasila* which eventually made it acceptable to most Muslims.

An interruption in the otherwise smooth acceptance of *Pancasila* happened when in 1955, as part of the Indonesian experimentation with democracy and following a general election, the door was opened to all political parties to discuss again the philosophical basis of the republic. In the Constituent Assembly, the politicians were divided into the adherents of three main ideologies: nationalism, communism/socialism, and Islamism. The nationalists wanted to keep the *Pancasila* as the philosophical basis of the state, the communists aspired for a Marxist state modeled upon the example of Soviet Union, and the Islamists returned to the idea of an Islamic state. The deliberations in the assembly came to a deadlock and Sukarno, the president, backed by the military, decreed the return of the republic to the "1945 Constitution" with its *Pancasila* as the permanent philosophical basis for the nation. In a gesture to accommodate Muslims aspiration for a state imbued with Islamic values, Sukarno declared that the 1945 Constitution and *Pancasila* should be seen as the historical continuation of the Jakarta Charter (a document drafted originally as the would-be Indonesian Declaration of Independence in which a provision was made that observation of the *sharia* would be obligatory upon Muslims).

Muslims were not very enthusiastic in accepting the presidential decree, and another unfavorable development of *Pancasila* occurred when the Communists, with the support of Sukarno, dominated the political arena of the republic shortly after the presidential decree of 1959. The situation led to a political debacle in 1965 when the Communists tried unsuccessfully to seize power by force. General Suharto's intervention ended the crisis, and having learned the lesson of the dangerous ideological uncertainty in previous years, he made efforts through heavy-handed persuasion to ensure that *Pancasila* would be accepted as the sole ideological basis for "Indonesia as a nation, a state, and a society." *Pancasila* was to be the one and only framework guiding the Indonesian people in their activities at the national, political, and societal levels, but individually they could and were even encouraged to profess their personal world-outlook. This is very close to saying that adherence to a religion is a matter of individual conscience, and yet, put in the Indonesian context, it is also recognition that religions are, as Indonesian leaders like to say, very important elements of nation-building.

Five religious traditions in Indonesia are given official recognition: Islam, Protestantism, Catholicism, Hinduism, and Buddhism. Each of them has its own offices in the Department of Religious Affairs, in the form of general directorates, commensurate with their respective social and religious scope of activities.

♦ THE SPREAD OF ISLAM

What was the attraction of Islam to Indonesia? Indonesia is one of the few countries where Islam did not supplant the existing religion through conquest; its appeal was first and foremost psychological. Radically egalitarian and possessing a spiritual and intellectual spirit, Islam appeared as a forceful concept that freed people from feudal bondage. Indonesians had lived in a land where the king, an absolute monarch, was in total charge of the land and other belongings. The Muslim message of equality before God and the strong sense of community, without the intermediaries of priests and initiation, was very persuasive. It permitted a direct and personal relationship between man and God. Though Muhammad was a Prophet, he was also a mortal human being.

Islam also had great political appeal. It was adopted by coastal princes to counter the threat of Portuguese and Dutch Christianity and as a rallying point of identity. Islam first gained prominence in the early sixteenth century as a force against Portuguese colonial domination, then one hundred years later as a force against the Dutch.

It appeared to be ideally suited to an island nation, a trader's religion which stresses the virtues of prosperity and hard work. It allowed for individual initiative and freedom of movement in order to take advantage of trade opportunities everywhere in the Muslim network. The religion was not tied to a locality, God could be worshipped anywhere, not necessarily just in a mosque. In short, Islam exerted a modernizing, civilizing influence over the peoples of the archipelago.

The Muslim Calendar in Indonesia

The Javanese calendar maintains its Hindu origin as a Shaka calendar but was changed from solar to lunar system, using the Arabic names of the twelve months with some adjustment to Javanism: (1) *Suro* (the Javanese translation of the Arabic *ashura*) for *Muharram*; (2) *Sapar,* for *Safar;* (3) *Malud* (translated from the Arabic *Mawlid,* the Prophet's Birthday festival), for *Rabi al-Awwal;* (4) *Bakdo Malud* (translated from the Arabic, *bad-a l-mawlid* meaning "after mawlid"), for *Rabi al-Thani;* (5) *Jumadilawal,* for *Jumada al-ula* ; (6) *Jumadilakhir,* for *Jumada al-Thaniyah;* (7) *Rejeb,* for *Rajab;* (8) *Ruwah* (translated from the Arabic *arwah* —"meaning the souls"—due to the popular belief that in the eighth month of the calendar the souls of the dead are awakened from their graves to welcome the arrival of the holy month of

Ramadan), for *Shaban*; (9) *Poso* (that Javanese word meaning "fasting"), for *Ramadan*; (10) *Sawal*, for *Shawwal*, (11) *Selo* (a Javense word meaning "in between," that is, in between two festivals of *Id al-Fitr* in *Shawwal* and *Id al-Adha* in *Dhu l-Hijjah*) for *Dhu l-Qadah*; and finally, (12) *Besar* (a Javenese word meaning "great," that is, the month of the great festival of *Id al-Adha*), for *Dhu l-Hijjah*. The Javanese Islamic calendar in 1955, corresponds to the Jananese 1924 (instead of 1413 used in traditional Muslim calendars). The importance of the Javanese Islamic calendar cannot be exaggerated. President Suharto considers a birthday commemoration in Javanese Islamic calendar to be more important and spiritually more meaningful than when it is celebrated according to the western calendar. Thus he commemorated his *"Tumbuk Besar"* (Great Event) of reaching sixty-four years of age in Javanese Islamic calendar, on the first of *Sawal*, 1915, which coincided with the thirteenth of July 1983.

Muslim Culture in Indonesia

The development of Muslim culture in Indonesia is very much the result of dialogue between the cultural characteristics of the archipelago. According to Clifford Geertz, the well-known American anthropologist, there are three variants of Islam in Java in particular and in Indonesia in general, the variants of *Priyayi*, *Santri*, and *Abangan*. All three variants may be conceived as Islamic in so far as they involve verbally confessing to be Muslim. In his judgement, only the *Santri* variant, with its heavy orientation toward the Middle Eastern cultural pattern, is the "real Islam," and is numerically rather small among the population. The *Priyayi* variant is for him too Indic in its outlook, and the *Abangan* seems too indigenous and even animistic. This view suggests that the great majority of Javanese or Indonesians are Muslim and Islam in actuality is the religion of only a small fraction of the population. However, the late Marshall Hodgson, in his critique of this position, argued that it suffered from a colonial bias which defined Islam from a limited perspective. In reviewing this thesis, he stated:

> The most important study of Islam in Malaysia (i.e., Malay archipelago) is Clifford Geertz' *Religion of Java* (Glencoe, 1960); it deals with the twentieth century, and with inner Java in particular, but much in it throws light on what happened earlier and is relevant to other parts of the archipelago. Unfortunately, its general high excellence is marred by a major systematic error; influenced by the polemics of a certain school of modern Sharia-minded Muslims, Geertz identifies "Islam" only with what that school of modernists happens to approve, and ascribes everything else to an aboriginal or a Hindu-Buddhist background, gratuitously labeling much of the Muslim religious life in Java "Hindu." He identifies a long series of phenomena, virtually universal to Islam and sometimes found even in the Quran itself, as un-Islamic; and hence his interpretation of the Islamic past as well as of some recent anti-Islamic reactions is highly misleading.

(M. Hodgson, *Venture of Islam*)

Other research supports Hodgson's view with findings that show that even among such populations as the Hindu Tenggerese enclave found in some mountainous areas of East Java, Muslim features are quite obvious. The Javanese court of Yogyakarta according to such research was not so much Indic in the overall cultural orientation as it was Muslim. All of this leads to a conclusion that Islam has in fact become one of the foundational layers of Indonesian culture. This is particularly true after the establishment of the Malay language of the Riau province to the status of a national and official language of the republic. Much more cosmopolitan than Javanese, Malay is the language of the Muslim culture of Southeast Asia and is more or less comparable to the position of Arabic in the Arab world and of Persian in Iran, Afghanistan, and Central Asia. As a national language for the Indonesian state—which is then called Indonesian language or Bahasa Indonesia—Malay contributes greatly to the Muslim coloring of Indonesian modern political culture, as the nomenclature is vested with the Malay adaptation of Arabic words. Examples of such include the words *rakyat* (*raiyya*) for people or subjects; *majelis* (*majlis*) for House of representatives; *dewan* (*diwan*) for council; *musyawarah* (*mushawara*) for deliberation; *mufakat* (*muwafaqa*) for consensus; *wajib* (*wajib*) for duty; *bina* (*bina*) for building or development; *hukum* (*hukm*) for law; *hakim* (*hakim*) for judge; *wujud* (*wujud*) for existence or creation; *amal* (*amal*) for work or implementation; *mahkama* (*mahkama*) for judicial court; *adil* (*adl*) for justice; *aman* (*aman*) for security; *tertib* (*tartib*) for order; *makmur* (*mamur*) for prosperous; *wakil* (*wakil*) for representative; *daerah* (*daira*) for region or province; *wilaya* (*wilaya*) for territory; *amar* (*amr*) for legal decision or verdict; *maklumat* (*malumat*) for political announcement; *resmi* (*rasmi*) for official, and so on. Thus, a very common phrase to describe the concept of Indonesian politics could be translated from Malay as: "the people's representatives in the House and in the Council have the duty of carrying out deliberation leading to consensus to promote order, security and law for the sake of developing the just and prosperous society with the blessing of God the Almighty." The phrase is syntactically

Indonesian but all of the main words, except for prepositions and conjunctions, are Arabic. Modern Indonesian is influenced by this interaction with Muslim concepts.

Arabic is not the only source of Indonesian culture; Sanskrit, through Javanese culture, is also very important. However, most Indonesians having adopted Islam, regard Arabic as the necessary source of values for political legitimacy. Thus, *Pancasila* represents from a Quranic perspective, a mediating concept between different religious traditions.

Javanese Islam

In terms of sheer numbers the peoples of Java are the most potent force in Indonesia. In its early years, Javanese Islam was a merger of Sufism and local tradition, rather than of Islam and Hinduism proper. For centuries Javanese feudalism formed the main tradition, not the law of the Quran. Only in the nineteenth and twentieth centuries did Islam penetrate rural Java deeply enough to upset the traditional patterns of authority. *Agama Jawa* (religion of Java) has evolved into a totality of religious beliefs and practices, and as a result is an incredible blending of doctrines. In the Javanese story of creation, all the world's major religions have been taken into account.

At the historical site of Sendangduwur, along the north coast of East Java near Tuban, some two hundred kilometers from Surabaya, for example, we find an early Islamic cemetery, mosque, gateways with wings, and a wooden building containing the tomb of legendary *wali*. This could be Java's oldest mosque, built on what may have been a pre-Islamic temple ground, with early Muslim art which is very similar to Balinese art, both having been derived from the late Hindu-Javanese style.

At Gresik which is also considered among the oldest Muslim settlements in Java, dating back to the thirteenth century, there is Sunan Giri Hill, a venerated cemetery compound guarded by two Hindu mythological creatures. The artistically Hindu-inspired gate of the mosque is now the trade mark of the famous Gresik Portland Cement Company in Indonesia.

Demak, twenty-five kilometers from Semarang on road to Surabaya, was the first Muslim kingdom in Java to come to power between 1500 and 1546. In 1478 the ruler built Demak's wooden mosque, the oldest mosque in Java and a prime example of the joint architectural influences of the Java-Hindu and Muslim cultures. It is interesting to note that on the wall in front of the mihrab there is representation of a turtle to commemorate the dating of the erection of the building, despite the assumed iconoclasm of Islam.

At Kudus, not far from Demak, is a sixteenth century high red brick minaret which looks like a Javanese

The minaret at the Sunan Kudus Mosque.

Hindu temple. The structure combines Hindu and Muslim architecture. This minaret is so different from the traditional minaret in the Middle East or India that it is believed to be a modified *kulkul* tower (watch-tower) which was added to the fortified temples during Hindu times to warn rice farmers of impending catastrophe.

Another medium of the artistic expression of Islam in Indonesia is the art of *batik*. Java produces the finest *batik* in Indonesia. *Batik*, a traditional method of decorating cloth, is an art of great antiquity. The word is derived from a Javanese word meaning "fine point" but in everyday usage is means "wax painting" or "wax-resist painting." Indonesia has been trading in *batik* since the days of the Arab and Indian merchant fleets of the early sixteenth century. The craft was probably introduced into Indonesia during the twelfth century; no one knows from where exactly, however, it possibly originated in Turkey or Egypt. Most *batik* can be traced back to Javanese influence and some believe that it evolved in Java and Madura out of an ancient way of painting on textiles.

Still, another medium of artistic expression in Indonesia is *wayang*, a theatrical performance of living actors, puppets, or of shadow images held before a lighted screen from behind. This art dates from before the ninth century. *Wayang* came before Indian influences, the present day heroes having evolved from ancestral spirits. During the time of significant Hindu influence (eighth to fifteenth centuries), Hindu teachers used the *wayang* medium to propagate and popularize their religion. Indian epic heroes and gods, demons and giants, supplanted the Javanese ancestor figures. These *wayang* performances had a strong influence on sculpture; thirteenth century bas-reliefs show figures similar to those of the *wayang* puppets of the time, portraying all the same persons and events as the characters do today.

With the coming of Islam in the thirteenth century, Indonesians appropriated the heroic figures of the Muslim tradition into *wayangs*. Shadow plays were used by sultans to flatter themselves and their courts and to glorify and perpetuate the feudalistic court ritual of the Javanese royalty. *Wayang*, by reinforcing hierarchy, had always kept everyone exactly in their place. Since Islam banned the reproduction of the human form, both good and evil puppets were made ugly and grotesque so that they would not resemble living beings, and the puppets' faces, coloring, hairdo, clothes, and jewelry are to this day so strongly stylized that they are more symbols than actual representations of humans. *Wayang* figures are the only figural representations left over from the graphic arts of the early Islamic period in Indonesia.

◆ ISLAMIZATION IN THE MODERN AGE

Many motifs and styles of the previous Hindu-Javanese culture permeate Indonesian art. In Java there are gates leading to the mosques and cemeteries of the Sufi saints or (*walis*) constructed in Hindu style. As indicated by many scholars on Indonesian culture, Indian epic poems have been adapted into living Indonesian theater, and their heroes dominate the plot. Pallawa scripts persisted until Indonesia was latinized by the Dutch in the twentieth century, and Sanskrit words still abound in many Indonesian languages. Indonesia's present state motto, "Behinneka Tunggal Ika," is a Sanskrit phrase, and the national emblem of the Indonesian Republic is the mythical bird Garuda.

However, at the same time, the process of Islamization of the country. From its foundation in 1945, the republic has been invested with value orientations that draw on Islam. The concepts of people or populism (*rakyat*), council (*dewan*), deliberation (*musyawarah*), peoples's representation (*wakil rakyat*), law (*hukum*), court (*mahkamah*), justice (*adil*), agreement or consensus (*mufakat*, from the Arabic *muwafaqah*), orderliness (*tertib*), security (*aman*), society (*masyarakat*, from the Arabic

Musyarakah), prosperity (*makmur*), and so on, are words and phrases conceptually grounded in Muslim tradition.

Even more symbolic of this process of Islamization are the mosques built by the "Amal Bakti Muslim Pancasila" Foundation. These mosques are an attempt to revive and recreate the historical Demak Mosque, with its famous roofs of three tiers representing three stages of spiritual development reflected in the concepts of *sharia*, *tariqa*, and *marifa* (practice, quest, and wisdom). Such example shows that the process of Islamization continues.

Nurcholish Madjid

◆ ISLAM IN MALAYSIA

Islam Comes To The Malay World

Islam had been an integral part of Malay ethnic and cultural identity since long before the British ruled Malaya from the late nineteenth to the mid-twentieth century. Although pre-Islamic and many Muslim Arabs traded in the Malay regions for centuries, historical sources reveal that Islam was planted there definitively by Middle Eastern and especially by South Asian Muslims through trade, intermarriage, and preaching from the twelfth century on. The religion became solidly established by the fifteenth century in such places as the seaport of Melaka, the northern and eastern coastal regions of Sumatra, and ports on the north coast of Java, especially between Demak and Surabaya.

Possibly the first substantial Muslim population was at Pasai in north Sumatra, where in the thirteenth century a sultan reigned over Muslim subjects, as Marco Polo reported. It is not known what the ethnic composition of that Islamic regime was, but evidence suggests strong South Indian influence. Melaka was later a major center of Islamic power and influence from its founding around 1400 until its conquest by the Portuguese in 1511. Its strategic location on the straits between Sumatra and the Malay peninsula made it a world crossroads between the Indian Ocean and the South China Sea. After Melaka's conquest the center of Muslim royal power in the region was at Johore, just north of Singapore. Other important Muslim regions of the traditional Malay world include the communities in what is now southern Thailand, such as Pattani, which share an ancient heritage as gateways of Islamization in Southeast Asia, and the southern Philippines and Sulu Sea Muslim communities.

Reasons for Islam's successful development in the Malay regions include its titles and protocols that were appealing to royalty; its close ties between trade, commerce, and government; its egalitarianism; and its profound spirituality that supported a moral vision compatible with traditional Malay values of human dignity, community loyalty, and moderation. Royalty found reasons to adopt Muslim court styles imported from South Asia, but the Islamization of Malay society was a far more complex process rooted in habits of the heart. Many of the bearers of Islam to the Malay world were Sufi mystics, some of whom emphasized the ultimate unity of reality in ways that appealed to peoples who already were well versed in Hindu and Buddhist as well as indigenous forms of contemplative life and discipline.

Malay Language And Literature

The Malay language, which possibly originated on Sumatra, can be traced in inscriptions to the seventh century. Malay eventually became the common language of trade, government, and Islamic religion throughout the peninsula and island Southeast Asia, regardless of what local languages or dialects were spoken. Malay is the basis of Indonesian, which because of the great population of that Republic, makes it sixth in the world in numbers of speakers. Malay occurs in numerous variants and has greatly influenced other languages in the region. A classical Malay literature arose in Islamic times—beginning in the sixteenth century Sultanate of Aceh in northern Sumatra—using the Arabic alphabet, known as *jawi* script (from Java). Several genres of literature developed, including chronicle (*sejarah*), history (*hikayat*), fiction, romance, and various divisions of the Islamic religious sciences (theology, Quranic commentary, law, *hadith*, prophetic biography, mystical texts, etc.), and poetry.

Some of the earliest Islamic literature in the Malay language is concerned with Islamic mystical philosophy and theology, for example the writings and controversies centering in the monistically inclined Sufi thinkers Hamzah Fansuri (d. ca. 1600) and Shams al-Din al-Pasai (d. 1630), both from northern Sumatra, and their orthodox antagonist, the Indian scholar and polemicist Nur al-Din al-Raniri (d. 1658), who spent many years in the Malay world and reached a high level of proficiency in the language. The medieval Sufi theosophy of the Andalusian thinker Ibn al-Arabi (d. 1240) and its further elaboration by the Iraqi Sufi Abd al-Karim al-Jili (d. 1417), whose treatise on "The Perfect Man" (*Al-Insan al-Kamil*) had a great impact on Muslim Southeast Asia, has continued to be discussed in modern times.

The classical Malay poem, a much beloved legacy along with Malay proverbs, is typically composed of four-line stanzas called pantun. The following example is from the religious verse of the mystic Hamzah Fansuri, introduced above:

He [i.e. Allah], the Beloved, is utterly manifest/To those who are wise to it/If truly you have eyes to see/Then behold your beloved is everywhere. . . . . He is in permanent hiding /Concealing Himself in the seeker/For more often   than not the trick of the Beloved/Is to hide in the full light (Poems, pp. 93-94).

These lines, probably composed in   the late 1500's, are, in the original, an harmonious, idiomatic and at points utterly arresting blending of Malay and Arabic words and idioms, showing a literary maturity   that suggests   a considerable   prior   development of Islamic   expression in Malay.

Malay history and chronicle are represented by many works, the most famous of which is the so-called Malay Annals (*Sejarah Melayu*), which as a court document recounts the histories and genealogies of the Muslim rulers of Melaka before the Portuguese conquest. The Annals, available in English, make for entertaining reading, with adventure, romance, noble themes, and humor, as when depicting Muslim teachers and officials.

Islam In Malaysia

European colonial powers ruled parts of the Malay-Indonesian world for centuries, with the British and Dutch being the last before independence in Malaya (1957) and Indonesia (1949), respectively. Malaysia was founded in 1963 comprising the former Malaya (the peninsula), Singapore, Sabah in northwest Borneo, and Sarawak in north Borneo. Singapore withdrew in 1965 and established itself as a sovereign nation, because of its majority Chinese population that did not want to be under Malay rule. Throughout its history, Malaysia has experienced ethnic and communal tensions between its majority Malay population (approximately 59%), its Chinese (approximately 32%), and its Indians (approximately 9%). Although the Malays are not the original people of the peninsula, they have been dominant for many centuries and see themselves as the "sons of the soil" (*bumiputera*).

Malaysia has a federal parliamentary democracy with a prime minister. There is also a constitutional monarch elected every five years from among the sultans of several of the traditional states of peninsular Malaysia. Islam is the state religion and Muslims comprise around 58% of the population of around 18 million. Other religions, which are protected by law, include Buddhism, Confucianism, Taoism, Christianity, and Hinduism, as well as indigenous traditions. Although Malays are the ruling class, they have since the nineteenth century been somewhat marginalized in the economic sphere by the growing Chinese and Indian populations that were imported by the British for labor.

Most of the commercial, technological and entrepreneurial vitality of Malaysia is on the peninsula's west coast, where in its thriving urban centers Chinese dominate. The peninsula's east coast, with sandy, palm lined beaches and picturesque villages is the homeland of classical Malay life, with strong traditional Muslim beliefs and customs, agriculture, and fishing.

The majority of Malaysia's agricultural workers and poorer, deprived citizens have been Malay, with educational levels, wages and living conditions significantly lower than other ethnic groups. The government of Malaysia has, in recent decades, provided affirmative action style incentives and benefits to ethnic Malays in order to help them improve their educational, economic, and occupational status. Large numbers of Malays have received resources to study for advanced degrees in Europe, North America, and Australia, where they have, at times, been one of the largest national foreign student groups. They return to their homeland to take up responsible and often important positions in education, government, the civil service, business, and the professions. In the process large numbers of ethnic Malays have become urbanized and, in many cases, secularized. There is sometimes a tension between Islamic expectations and development of modern independent lifestyles, especially when young Malay adults see non-Muslim Chinese and Indian Malaysians enjoying social and personal freedoms more in line with the West than with traditional Malay society. For example, single Muslim men and women are forbidden to be alone together under the law of "suspicious (i.e. sexual) proximity" (*khalwat*), which is enforced by the police. Yet non-Muslim unmarried men and women can be together in private and go to discos and other entertainments.

There is strong Malay ethnicity in the majority population's continuing control of government and cultural matters, but there is also considerable Islamic motivation. Malays, as a whole, occupied a marginal position during the British occupation. In rural areas, where they dominated, life proceeded in traditional ways as a mixture of Islamic and local beliefs, customs, and values. Children were educated in traditional Islamic schools known as *pondoks*, where the Quran and traditional Islamic texts served as the core curriculum. But the twentieth century brought, in Malaysia as well as in neighboring Indonesia, a reforming and revitalizing mentality influenced by modernist reformers like the Egyptian theologian and educator Muhammad Abduh (d. 1905). New educational institutions and methods were created and influential publications were launched.

Malaysian Muslims generally are careful observers of the canonical Islamic beliefs and practices of the Sunni majority of the worldwide *Umma*. The dominant legal school is Shafiite, although as anywhere law reflects the local and regional customs and practices as well as the precepts of the Quran and *Sunna*. Malaysian Muslims energetically enforce Islamic teachings such as those concerning the social mixing of the sexes and the observance of the Ramadan fast. There are numerous regional cultural rites associated with Islam, including marriage festivities, circumcision observances, funerary practices, and magical shamanistic rites for various occasions (which transcend Muslim boundaries and can be traced to the pre-Islamic past).

After independence and the establishment of the nation-state of Malaysia, came a renewed sense of Malays being members of the global Islamic *Umma*. In the 1970's the *dawa* (Islamic missionary activity) movement arose, with Malay youth being particularly active and influential through their organizations (such as ABIM, the Muslim Youth Movement of Malaysia). The government had been favoring a secularist approach to administration and rule, but the activities of the *dawa* oriented Malays and other strongly Islamist factions, like PAS (the Pan-Malayan Islamic Party), demanded change along Islamic lines. PAS, which is based in the Islamically very pious state of Kelantan, has steadily favored establishing an Islamic ethos in Malaysia, with rule according to the *Sharia* (though it has not called for an Islamic state as such and pledges to protect the rights and freedoms of non-Muslims).

In 1981 Dr. Mahathir Mohamed, a strongly pro-Malay physician of Indian background, became prime minister and continues to hold that position today. Dr. Mahathir has done much to respond to the calls from various Muslim sectors for Islamization of government and society in Malaysia, but he does not support the creation of an Islamic state. He attracted one of the youth movement's most persuasive *dawa* oriented leaders, Anwar Ibrahim, to his government in 1982. Since then, the government has greatly increased Islamic consciousness in government and administrative life, established an Islamic Bank, founded the International Islamic University—which attracts Muslim students from many foreign countries—and improved the Islamic court system in the country, among other things. Prime Minister Mahathir is a strong, shrewd and principled leader who understands that Malaysia's continued economic, social, and moral progress requires the creative contributions of all its citizens. He respects the multicultural and religiously pluralistic diversity of Malaysia and at the same time supports unity among the diverse Muslim factions in the country. Malaysia is a beautiful, richly endowed, prosperous, well ordered nation without an overpopulation problem and with great promise to become an industrial power, a goal it hopes to achieve in the coming century through its long range "Vision 2020" program.

Malaysia's Muslims are proud to be Malay, as most of them are (although there are many Indian and some Chinese Muslims, too), and staunchly dedicated as well to supporting the global *Umma*, in all its racial and cultural diversity. Malaysian Muslims, whether Malay or other, are generally more theologically conservative and cautious than Indonesia's Muslims—who constitute the largest national Muslim community in the world—although they share with them important linguistic, social, cultural, emotional, aesthetic and temperamental traditions and characteristics.

Frederick M. Denny

References: Indonesia

Bowen, John. *Muslims through Discourse: Religion and Ritual in Gayo Society.* Princeton: Princeton University Press, 1993.

Deliar Noer. *The Modernist Muslim Movement in Indonesia 1900-1942.* Kuala Lumpur: Oxford University Press, 1973.

Geertz, C. *The Religion of Java.* Glenco Ill.: Free Press, 1960.

Heffner, R. *Hindu Javanese: Tengger Tradition and Islam.* Princeton: Princeton University Press, 1985.

Hodgson, M.G.S. *The Venture of Islam,* 3 vols. Chicago: The University of Chicago Press, 1974.

Hooker, M.B., ed. *Islam in Southeast Asia.* Leiden: E. J. Brill, 1988.

Modern Malay Literary Culture: A Historical Perspective. Singapore, 1987.

Naguib al-Attas, Syed Muhammad. *The Mysticism of Hamzah Fansuri.* Kuala Lumpur: University of Malaya Press, 1970.

———. *Preliminary Statement of a General Theory of the Islamization of the Malay-Indonesian Archipelago.* Kuala Lumpur: University of Malaya Press, 1969.

Roff, W. R. *The Origins of Malay Nationalism.* New Haven: Yale University Press, 1967.

Sweeney A. *A Full Hearing: Orality and Literacy in the Malay World.* Berkeley: University of California Press, 1987.

Taufik, Abdullah and Sharon Siddique, eds. *Islam and Society in Southeast Asia.* Singapore: Oxford University Press, 1986.

Woodward Mark R. *Islam in Java.* Tucson: Arizona University Press: 1989.

References: Malaysia

Al-Attas, Syed Muhammad Naguib. *The Mysticism of Hamzah Fansuri.* Kuala Lumpur: University of Malaya Press, 1970.

Andaya, B. W. and V. Matheson. "Islamic Thought and Malay Tradition." In A. Reid and D. Marr (eds.), *Perceptions of the Past in Southeast Asia.* Singapore: Heinemann, 1976.

Drewes, G.W.J. and L. F. Brakel. *The Poems of Hamzah Fansuri.* Dordrecht, Holland: Foris Publications, 1986.

Fatimi, S.Q. *Islam Comes to Malaysia.* Singapore: Malaysian Sociological Research Institute, 1963.

Hasan, M. Kamal. "Malaysia." *The Oxford Encyclopedia of the Modern Islamic World.* John L. Esposito (ed.). New York and Oxford: Oxford University Press, 1995, vol. 3.

Hooker, M.B. (ed.). *Islam in Southeast Asia.* Leiden: E.J. Brill, 1983.

Johns, A.J. "Islam in Southeast Asia." *The Encyclopedia of Religion.* Mircea Eliade (ed.). New York: Macmillan, 1987, vol. 7.

Kessler, Clive S. *Islam and Politics in a Malay State: Kelantan 1838-1969.* Ithaca, NY: Cornell University Press, 1978.

Kim, Khoo Kay. *Malay Society: Transformation and Democratization.* Petaling Jaya, Malaysia: Pelanduk Publications, 1991.

Mutalib, Hussin. *Islam and Ethnicity in Malay Politics.* Singapore: Oxford University Press, 1990.

Nagata, Judith. *The Reflowering of Malaysian Islam: Modern Religious Radicals and their Roots.* Vancouver: University of British Columbia Press, 1984.

Sandhu, Kernial Singh and Paul Wheatley. *Melaka: The Transformation of a Malay Capital c. 1400–1980.* 2 volumes. Kuala Lumpur: Oxford University Press, 1983.

Sejarah Melayu (Malay Annals). Kuala Lumpur and Singapore: Oxford University Press, 1970.

Sweeney, Amin. *A Full Hearing: Orality and Literacy in the Malay World.* Berkeley: University of California Press, 1987.

Winstedt, Richard. *A History of Classical Malay Literature.* Revised, edited and introduced by Y.A. Talib. Petaling Jaya, Malaysia: M.B.R.A.S. Reprint, 1989.

Winstedt, Richard. *The Malays: A Cultural History.* 6th edition. London: Routledge and Kegan Paul, 1961.

Islam in Central Asia and the Caucasus

♦ Muslims in Twentieth Century Politics ♦ Russification of Muslims in the Soviet Union
♦ Muslims in Modern Russia

Islam arrived in the Caucasus region at an early date during the caliphate of Uthman (reigned 644–56). The Caucasus was at that time, as now, a highly fragmented region, both ethnically and politically, and Islam had to compete with such faiths as Christianity, Zoroastrianism, and various forms of animism. For some three centuries, the advance of Islam was blocked by such Christian peoples as the Georgians and Alans or Ossetes in the Caucasus itself, and to the north of the mountain barrier in what later became the south Russian steppes, by the Turkish Khazars.

Within the Khazar kingdom, the three great Near Eastern monotheistic faiths all had footholds among the ruling classes, however, the basic belief of the peoples of the inner Eurasian steppelands and forests was a form of shamanism or primitive spiritualism. This belief slowly declined in the face of Islamic evangelization northwards through the Caucasus and through Central Asia. In Siberia, Russian Orthodox Christianity brought by the princes of Muscovy also served to eradicate the local belief systems. Across the Urals in the steppes and the *taigha* or forest zone, these Christians eventually reached eastern Siberia and the shores of the Pacific Ocean, founding Yakutsk and the fort of Okhotsk by the mid-seventeenth century. Although the Khazar state began to disintegrate in the eleventh century, the Kuban steppes north of the Caucasus and the south Russian steppes were becoming Muslim due to the Turkish invasions. The whole area became known as the Qipchaq Steppe, named after one of the prominent Turks there.

When the Moroccan traveller Ibn Battuta visited the lands of the Mongols of the Golden Horde in south Russia during the 1330s, he visited the city of Machar

on the Kuma River north of the Caucasus and found it a great center of Turkish Muslim life and culture. While in Machar he stayed at the *zawiya* or hospice of a local *skaykh* of the Rifaiyya Sufi order. It can be surmised that here, and in Central Asia in general, missionary and educational work by dervish *skaykhs* and other religious devotees must have been important factors in Islamization.

The mountainous and inaccessible heartland of the Caucasus was most resistant to Islamization. The Georgian people of the Laz in Mingrelia on the Black Sea coast only gradually became Muslim after the Ottoman Turkish annexation of the Greek empire of Trebizond in the later fifteenth century, and it was only around this time, too, that Roman Catholic and Eastern Christianity disappeared from Daghistan in the northeastern Caucasus.

In the wake of advancing Arab armies, Islam also first appeared further east, in Central Asia in the region called Transoxania or "the land beyond the river Oxus" (the modern Uzbekistan, Tadjikistan, and western Kirghizstan). The Oxus River was first crossed in the mid-seventh century, but the overrunning of Transoxania and of Khwarazm, the adjacent land on the lower reaches of the Oxus (classical Chorasmia, now divided between Uzbekistan and Turkmenistan) did not come until later. In Central Asia at this time, as far as the borders of China, older faiths like Zoroastrianism, Buddhism, Christianity, and Manicheism were firmly established. The local Iranian and Turkish princes sought help from the Chinese emperors who claimed a vague suzerainty over the whole region of Inner Asia; hence the adoption of Islam proceeded slowly. In the early eighth century, a governor in Bukhara had to pay the local populace to attend the newly-built mosque. However, the new faith of Islam did eventually become firmly rooted there, encouraged by such local dynasties as the Samanids (819–1005), who lavishly patronized the Islamic religious classes and built many fine mosques, colleges, and mausoleums. From the ninth century onwards, Khurasan (eastern Persia), Transoxania, and Khwarazm became strongholds of Sunni Islam and of the Hanafi law school, producing a disproportionately large number of theological and legal scholars. Most of the compilers of the great collections of traditions or sayings of the Prophet Muhammad, al-Bukhari, al-Nasai, al-Tirmidhi being just a few, came from these far northeastern fringes of the Islamic world.

The northern fringes of Transoxania and Khwarazm bordered on the pagan Turkish steppes, and it was from fortresses and *ribats* (outposts for religious devotion and expansion) that military expeditions were undertaken into the steppes. Islam, however, prevailed, not through conquest, but by the more peaceful work of Sufis and other enthusiasts of the faith. Certain Turkish tribes of the steppes were converted in the late tenth and early eleventh centuries. The Yasawiyya order was formed around a Turkish Sufi *shaykh* named Ahmad Yasawi (died 1166) and was very influential among the Turks of Central Asia. The Order's ritual beliefs were drawn from the Turks' pre-Islamic shamanist past and incorporated an indigenous component. In later times, Ahmad's tomb at Yasi in central Syr Darya (in modern southwestern Kazakhstan) drew Turkish and Tatar pilgrims from as far away as the central Volga lands, eager to receive the saint's *baraka* or blessing.

Trade was also a means for the transmission of Islam. It is known that caravans regularly travelled from Khwarazm northwards to the Emba and Ural rivers and eventually to the Volga. In the tenth century the Turkish Bulghars founded a state at the Volga's confluence with the Kama, subduing the Finno-Ugrian peoples of the forest lands who lived there. Islam, in the Sunni Hanafi form, was then introduced, almost certainly by the Muslims from Transoxania. In 922 the envoy of the caliph, Ibn Fadlan found mosques there and the king was a Muslim. It seems that it was from this center in Bulghar that the Islamization of such nomadic Turkish peoples as the Pechenegs and Qipchaq began. Bulghar marked the northernmost outpost of Islam. The long nights and short days of winter and the short nights and long days of summer, posed problems for ritual observances, especially the performance of the five daily prayers, *salats*, and for fasting in the month of Ramadan. An extensive legal literature grew up around such questions passed among the scholars of Kazan some centuries later. The rise of nearby Kazan, originally called New Bulghar, eventually eclipsed Bulghar. This region continued to be a center

for Islam among local Turkish or Tatar peoples, the nucleus of the modern Volga Tatars. During the fifteenth and sixteenth centuries Kazan became the capital of a Mongol Khanate until it fell into anarchy and became an easy target for the Russian conquest under Tsar Ivan IV in 1552.

The progress of Islam in Central Asia and in the inner Asian steppes was not a smooth one. The movement of the Buddhist Qara Khitay from northern China into Transoxania in the mid-twelfth century served as a major setback for Islam. These peoples displayed a traditional tolerance for all faiths. However, in the following century, a more widespread and disruptive invasions of the Mongols from southern Siberian took place. Their lightning advances into Syria, Turkey, and the Caucasus resulted in the subjugation of the Muslim populations there. The expansion of the Mongols was of particular significance for the Central Asian and Eurasian steppe lands. These areas became *ulus* or patrimonies for the descendants of Chingiz Khan. Chingiz's grandson Batu Khan came to rule over the so-called Blue Horde in south Russia and the adjacent steppes extending southeastward to Khwarazm, the Qipchaq steppe; this was the core of the later Golden Horde. Another grandson of Chingiz, Orda, founded the White Horde in western Siberia. Chingiz's second son Chaghatay received the lands stretching eastward from Transoxania into what later became Chinese Turkestan or Sin-kiang (the modern Uyghur Autonomous Region of the Chinese People's Republic), forming the Chaghatayid Khanate.

The consequences for Islam were for a while serious, though not lasting. For nearly a century Islam was patronized by the minority in this area. It was not until almost the fourteenth century that the provincial or Il-Khans controlling Persia and Transoxania became predominantly Muslim. It was well into the fourteenth century that the Khans of the Golden Horde and the Chaghatayids were converted, those Chaghatayids in eastern Turkestan being especially resistant to conversion.

The Golden Horde, with its capital at Saray on the lower Volga, held power for some two centuries before splitting up into various regional khanates, such as those of Astrakhan at the Volga mouth, Kazan and the Crimea. Although Kasimov, to the southeast of Moscow, became Christian, the end of the Golden Horde was not due to expanding Christian powers like the kingdom of Poland-Lithuania and the princedom of Moscow, but because of the efforts of the Crimean Tatar Khan (1502). Being essentially a nomadic, military ruling minority in south Russia, the Golden Horde minimally affected the lives and the faith of Russian Orthodox Christian subjects. Only in the middle Volga region and in the Crimea were there substantial concentrations of Turkish or Tatar Muslims. The Volga Tatars of Kazan were the first Muslims to come under Russian control and contrived to retain their faith and their national consciousness for more than four centuries. The Crimean Tatars did not come under imperial Russian rule until 1781 and remained a substantial population in the Crimea until World War II.

The consolidation of Muscovy and its expansion to form a European Russian imperial power entailed expansion eastward across the Ural mountains. This was partly the result of private commercial activity centered around the avid desire for furs. By 1552 Ivan the Terrible was "Emperor of Siberia." During the mid-sixteenth century, Kuchum became the Muslim Khan of Sibir, later called Tobolsk, near the east of the Urals to the confluence of the Irtysh and Tobol rivers in the wooded steppe lands. By the end of the sixteenth century, the Russians controlled the khanate's lands, although bitter warfare continued along this frontier until the 1670s. The consequence was a permanent check to the expansion of Islam in western and central Siberia. This area remained firmly within the imperial Russian orbit.

By the eighteenth century, the cattle-breeding Kazakhs to the south of this region formed three hordes, stretching from the southern Urals to the Semirechye or "Land of the Seven Rivers" (to the northeast of modern Kirghizstan and the extreme southeast of Kazakhstan adjacent to the Tien-shan mountains which form the border with China). These hordes were the first Turkish people of southern Siberia to confront imperial Russia when the Tsars' ambitions began to be directed southward as well as westward across Siberia. Peter the Great (reigned 1682–1725) had plans for the development of Russian trade with the khanates of Turkestan and then with India, although he does not seem to have had in mind the conquest of the whole region. By 1730, however, a line of Russian fortified posts was being pushed forward, with the aim of incorporating the unwilling Kazakhs into the empire, so that Russian influence increased within the Kazakh steppe as far as the Aral Sea-Orenburg-Irtysh River line.

The three khanates of western Turkestan—Bukhara, Khiva, and Khokand—remained almost totally untouched by outside influences until the third quarter of the nineteenth century. They were characterized socially by a large, mainly Persian captive, slave class. Rulers employed unbridled cruelty. A class of orthodox *mullas* and Sufi *shaykhs* strenuously resisted any enforced changes, and Khokand was eventually suppressed by 1876. A governorate-general of Turkestan was set up in 1866 at the strategically-important center of Tashkent. Bukhara lost Samarkand to Russia in 1868, and Khiva had to submit to a similar state of vassalage in 1873. The region was opened up to capitalist ven-

tures, especially after the construction of the Trans-Caspian Railway which reached Samarkand in 1888 and Tashkent in 1899. Intensive cotton production began, leading to decreased production of foodstuffs, which then had to be imported. Paradoxically, the Russian drive into Turkestan increased the amir of Bukhara's power and prestige. No Russian army ever entered Bukhara, and the city remained the inviolate religious capital of Central Asia. The protection of Russian power enabled the Amirs, or Muslim political leaders, to increase their central authority over the outlying parts of their realm; the Amirs' prestige seemed to reflect the strength of traditional Islam. The Amirs claimed to be *Sayyids*, descendants of the Prophet, and the last Amir, Mir Muhammad Alim Khan (reigned 1911–20), even added the title of Caliph to his existing one.

During this period, Sufism continued to be the primary vehicle for the expression of Islam in Turkistan. The Naqshbandiyya, the most numerous of all the orders there, was centered in Samarqand and Bukhara; the Qadiriyya, were strong in Ferghana; the Kubrawiyya, in Khiva; and the Khwajagan in Bukhara. Among the nomads, the Yasawiyya were influential, and among shamanist diviners and healers remained a perceptible element. Occasionally there was a syncretism of shamanistic rites with the more established Sufi orders.

Despite the distance of Central Asia from the heartlands of the Islamic Middle East or India, it was not impervious to the new strains of Islamic reform manifest in those regions promulgated by such figures as Jamal al-din al-Afghani, Muhammad Abduh, Sir Sayyid Ahmad Khan, and Amir Ali. Nor was it unaffected by imperial Russia's colonial policies in the Caucasus and Central Asia, or to pan-Turkism, the union of all Turkish peoples, an idea which rose to prominence when other movements like pan-Islamism and pan-Ottomanism had clearly lost their appeal by the early twentieth century. Hence, there appeared among the Muslims of the Russian empire *Jadidis* (partisans of novelty or new ideas) or reformers who, while for the most part remained fervent Muslims attached to the moral and ethical values of Islam, worked for an extension of education and the reduction of clerical influence. They hoped thereby to make Russian and Central Asian Islam more able to withstand the cultural, religious, and political impact of imperial Russia with its Orthodox Christianity and secularism. Their ranks included such tireless reformers as Ismail Bey Gaspirali or Gasprinsky (1851–1914), a Crimean Tatar from Baghche Seray, whose newspaper *Tarjuman* (*The Interpreter*) was influential from 1883 onwards in the cause of pan-Turkism; and Abd al-Rauf Fitrat (circa 1937) of Bukhara, who opposed the dominant, reactionary forms of Islam in the khanate and especially the Sufi orders, whom he regarded as inculcators of political passivity.

Meanwhile, within the Kuban steppes north of the Caucasus and then in Caucasia proper, imperial Russia was extending her direct military and political authority during the early nineteenth century. The Russian advance into the northwestern Caucasus sent a stream of Muslim refugees from Circassia and Kabardia into Ottoman Turkey, so that the Cherkes or Circassians remain to this day a significant ethnic element in both Turkey and those Arab lands which were once part of the Ottoman empire. According to one Ottoman report, six-hundred thousand Circassians emigrated thence to Turkey between 1856 and 1864 alone. In Daghistan, the mountainous region between the northeastern spurs of the Caucasus and the Caspian Sea (now the Daghistan Republic), resistance to the incoming Russians was particularly fierce, with opposition spearheaded by *shaykhs* of the *Naqshbandi* order. For twenty-five years, Shaykh Shamil (circa 1798–1871) established in Daghistan, a regime based on the *sharia* (Islamic religious law) and led his *murids* (followers) in campaigns against the Russians until he finally surrendered to them in 1859.

♦ MUSLIMS IN TWENTIETH CENTURY POLITICS

The Asiatic power of Japan which defeated the Russian empire in 1904 and the 1905 Revolution within Russia had electrifying effects for the Muslims of Russia, as these events aroused dreams of the independence for the Tatar-Turkish peoples and the full recovery of their national consciousness. The short-lived First and Second Dumas (the indirectly elected parliamentary assemblies) of 1906 and 1907 contained Muslim deputies of the group known as *Ittifaq al-Muslimin* (Concord of the Muslims), which were allied in practice to the Constitutional Democrats. The idea of popular representation thus appeared. There grew up a lively newspaper press in Tashkent to supplement the existing Muslim ones of St. Petersburg, Kazan, Baku, and other places, until it was suppressed in 1908. Secret societies for the promotion of non-clerical education then appeared. Yet the strength of the backward-looking, traditional Islam of the *Qadimis* (those attached to the past) continued to be strong in a khanate like Bukhara, and the Amir himself, fearful of the attrition of his despotic powers, finally threw his weight on the side of the status quo and even of reaction.

It required the Bolshevik Revolution of 1917 and the subsequent years of civil war to dissolve the surviving Islamic local regimes and institutions. Reform-minded Muslims, at first, greeted the revolution as a liberating

movement and were delighted to see the end of Tsarist autocracy. When a North Caucasus Emirate was set up in 1918–20, Chechen-Ingush forces headed by a Naqshbandi Cossack cooperated with the Red Army in clearing the White Russian forces of General Denikin from the Don-Terek-Kuban steppelands. However, the Muslims of the Caucasus and Central Asia soon found out that the Bolshevik Soviets of an industrial center like Baku or of the Russian industrial and railway towns in Turkestan were, of all the Russian political groups of the time, the most inimical to the aspirations of the Muslims. Russian Party of Muslim Communists was formed in 1918 under a Kazan Tatar, Mulla Nur Vakhitov, former head of the 1917 Kazan Socialist Committee (the Kazan Tatars supplied the overwhelming majority of Muslim national Communists in Russia), but this was speedily dissolved and the functions of its Central Committee taken over by the Central Bureau of Organizations of the Peoples of the East of the Russian Communist Party. Muslim resistance to the Communist Party's attempts to impose its ideology had shown that a separate Muslim Communist Party was unlikely to ensure the adherence of Muslims to the Communist state. Resistance to Communism and to what turned out to be simply a new manifestation of Russian colonial power in the Muslim regions took the form of devastating civil warfare as the Muslim peoples of Bashkiria, Transcaucasia, and Turkestan unsuccessfully strove to set up and make viable their own independent or federated states. The *khanate* of Bukhara collapsed in 1920, but the shortlived non-Communist People's Republics of Bukhara and Khiva were never allowed by the Bolsheviks to develop their own democratic institutions. Rather a much reduced role for the Muslim scholars and official was envisaged. Resistance to the imposition of a Communist regime by the Turkish Muslim national movement continued until 1924 and thereafter, especially among the peasants, in the form of the activities in Turkestan of the Basmachis (Uzbek Turkish "bandits") or guerrillas until 1930 and after.

♦ RUSSIFICATION OF MUSLIMS IN THE SOVIET UNION

The Soviets thus came to rule over one of the major concentrations of Muslims in the world, between forty-five and fifty million in the 1979 official census. These Muslims were the largest religious group living in the the then Union of Soviet Socialist Republics after the Russian Orthodox Christians. Central Asia was home to 75 percent of the Muslims, while the rest were spread over the middle Volga region, Crimea, the Caucasus, and Azerbaijan (the latter being the only substantial Shia group amidst the Sunni majority).

With the consolidation of Bolshevism, Islam was dethroned from its position of primacy in education and culture within the Muslim parts of the USSR. The All-Russia Bolshevik Party Congress of 1919 called for the elimination of all religious influence from schools and the use of vernacular languages instead of Arabic. These vernacular languages, whether the Caucasian ones, the varieties of Turkish, or the Iranian Tajik of Tajikistan, very soon received the so-called Unified Latin alphabet (in 1929 onwards) and then the Cyrillic alphabet (in the late 1930s and early 1940s), thereby causing a break with the past religious culture. Muslim *waqf*, lands and property used as charitable and educational endowments, were taken over by the Soviet state in 1925 (in the nineteenth-century khanate of Bukhara, these *waqfs* had amounted to 24 percent of all land). The poor-tax contributions or *zakat* were now collected by the state and distributed only to those considered ideologically sound and not to "kulaks" and "religious reactionaries." The public meetings, at least of the dervish orders, were no longer allowed; the customary law (*adat*) and Islamic law (*shariat*) courts were abolished in 1925; and many mosques and *madrasas* or colleges were allowed to fall into disrepair or taken over for secular purposes. With the introduction of compulsory primary education in 1930, the last Muslim schools, deprived of much of their financial backing by the sequestration of the *waqf* disappeared. Russification in education and culture went hand-in-hand with an influx of ethnic Russian settlers in southern Siberia and Kazakhstan, Turkestan, the Crimea, and elsewhere, leading to the present situation in which there are substantial numbers of Russians and Ukrainians in most of the present-day new republics of Central Asia and the Caucasus, with especial concentrations in Kazakhstan, in industrial regions around Baku and Tashkent, and in the Crimea.

It is difficult, in the absence of relevant and dispassionate Soviet statistics and the paucity of informed cultural and social studies, to assess the position of Islam under Communism. In a sense, the Basmachi movement in Turkestan of the 1920s had a certain success in that Moscow realized that the Muslim population could not be bulldozed into submission and that some material concessions and a semblance of local autonomy had to be conceded. During this period, republics of the Soviet Union were set up in Azerbaijan, Turkmenistan, Uzbekistan, Tajikistan, Kirghizstan, and Kazakhstan. Autonomous republics included those of the Tatar, Bashkir, Chechen-Ingush, Kabardin-Balkar and Daghistan. After 1957 the Karachay-Cherkess Autonomous *Oblast* (district) was reconstituted. The Soviet policy of establishing such local units was part of a general policy of divide and rule and of promoting the idea of separate nations and nationalities amongst the Muslims, thus reducing the universality of Islam in the minds of its adherents, for such universalist claims made Islam more dangerous in the eyes of Soviet officialdom than, for instance, the state-dominated Russian Orthodox Church. The boundaries of these Muslim republics were often arbitrarily drawn. Only a minority of the Tatars living on the middle Volga were included in the Tatar Republic when these Tatars actually formed the majority of the population. The ethnic and cultural consciousness aroused were to have an increasing effect during the Communist period and can be seen today in the political and cultural rivalries of Turkish Uzbeks and Iranian Tajiks in Turkestan.

Specific anti-Islamic measures by the state were at their most stringent in the period up to 1941. The number of mosques allowed to remain open shrank dramatically, leaving only a few hundred. The *Hajj*, or pilgrimage to Mecca and Medina, was in effect banned, with the number of pilgrims allowed annually reduced to a tiny trickle. All Islamic *madrasas* or colleges and all religious schools were officially closed. Those *mullas*, religious teachers, who remained after extensive purges in the 1930s functioned entirely unofficially and often clandestinely, supported financially only by the contributions of the faithful. There was no normative Islamic teaching available for Muslims in the USSR such as was available in the major cities of India and of the Arab and Persian lands of the Middle East. Even the less fundamental aspects of Islam were attacked outright: the veiling of women, pilgrimages to saints' tombs and shrines, celebrations of festivals, and practices such as male circumcision. The hope was that, in the face of officially-promulgated atheistic propaganda and the universality of secular, Communist-inspired education, religion would gradually wither away. This never happened to the Muslims. When Nazi Germany attacked the USSR in 1941 anti-Islamic and atheistic propaganda was temporarily played down, and the support of Islam and other religions was enlisted in the cause of national struggle. The Mufti Abd al-Rahman Rasul or Rasulaev, the puppet leader of Soviet Muslims, issued a manifesto urging Muslims to rise in defense of the fatherland and the Islamic faith, and in 1943 the Soviet authorities allowed the restoration of the *muftiyat*, the spiritual directorate of the Muslim peoples, in Tashkent perhaps as an appeasement strategy.

Nevertheless, sporadic local revolts against Soviet and Russian domination continued in Turkestan and the Caucasus during the 1920s and 1930s. Within European Russia, Muslim soldiers of various Muslim nationalities defected to the invading German army, while Muslim communities welcomed the Germans as liberators. The ensuing climate of fear among the Soviets led to mass deportations of Muslims and others from the Crimea, the Volga Tatar region and northern Caucasus to Siberia and Central Asia, ostensibly to forestall collaboration with the Germans. The struggle in the post-war period for the rehabilitation of such Muslim groups and their return to their homelands has been a protracted one and, for some peoples, has still not been achieved half-a-century later. While the Chechens and the Ingushes were allowed to return from Siberia and Kazakhaslan to the lowland areas of central Caucasian homeland after 1957, the Crimean Tartars were less fortunate. A grudgingly-issued Soviet decree of 1967 withdrew the indiscriminate accusation that all Crimean Tatars had collaborated with the Germans, but gave no promise of a return of these Tatars from Uzbekistan and elsewhere where they had been forcibly resettled. It was not until 1988 that the official prohibition of returning to the Crimea was lifted. Attempts at returning to the Crimea where, among others, displaced Ukrainians from the Polish lands of Galicia had been planted after 1945, have been resisted, both under the Soviet regime and under the post-Communist governments of the Ukrainian Republic which presently controls the Crimea and of Russia which would like to recover the Crimea for itself. Nevertheless, by the end of 1991, 166,000 Crimean Tatars had returned to their homeland, though many are compelled to live in tents or dug-out dwellings. They have formed their own *milli mejlis* or national assembly. As of 1994 the Ukrainian government has shown more understanding towards these Tatars.

♦ MUSLIMS IN MODERN RUSSIA

During the post-war period, after 1945, there was a slight alleviation of official Soviet hostility towards Islam. The Miri Arab *madrasa* at Bukhara was allowed to re-open in 1945, and the Baraq Khan *madrasa* was opened at Tashkent in 1956 as a secondary-level college. In 1971 it was upgraded to become an institution for training clergy and it was renamed the al-Bukhari Islamic Institute. The costs of restoration of the buildings, running expenses, and salaries of lecturers were all borne by the Muslim community. By 1982 there were eighty-six students in residence at the Mir-i Arab *madrasas* and by 1986, forty-five students at the al-Bukhari Institute, all of whom had previously studied at the college in Bukhara. Although these two schools were the only colleges that offered Muslim theological training in the entire USSR, authorities did not readily allow their Muslim subjects to study outside the Soviet Union. On the completion of studies, graduates of the two colleges were placed either in the larger mosques in the main cities of the USSR or in one of the four "spiritual directorates" set up by the Soviet government in 1943, directly subordinate to the state-controlled Council for the Affairs of Religious Cults.

Central Asia and Kazakhstan, centered in Tashkent used Uzbek as its official language. European Russia and Siberia, centered in Ufa in the Bashkir ASSR used Volga Tatar. Daghistan and North Caucasus, in recent years centered in Makhach-Kala in the Daghistan ASSR used Classical Arabic. Transcaucasia, centered in Baku and covering not only the Shia Azeris and Transcaucasian Sunnis, but also all other Shia communities of the USSR, used Azeri Turkish. Even so, Soviet policy towards Islam remained, on the whole, severely discriminatory during these decades. At the unofficial, local level, the attachment of ordinary Muslims to their faith clearly remained strong during these years. (By "ordinary" Muslims it is meant those not enrolled within the Soviet administrative and cultural hierarchy.)

Mikhail Gorbachev's policies of *glasnost* (openness) and *perestroika* (reconstruction) from the mid 1980s onwards augured a more relaxed policy of the Communist regime towards its Muslim populations. After 1989 many more mosques were opened, Qurans became more readily available and new *madrasas* were opened. To take one area as an illustration, in 1990 in the Chechen-Ingush ASSR Islam was almost completely legalized. Mosques were reopened or new ones built, Quran and Arabic classes were allowed, restrictions on the *Hajj* were lifted, and the Sufi orders permitted to play a part in society once more. The emphasis has been on national rather than Islamic ideology in the new, secularly-oriented political parties which have emerged there. In such a mountainous region as this, where the Soviets had always had difficulty in asserting their authority, Islam could reemerge at the popular level because the informal Islam of the Sufi orders had continued to exist clandestinely. Contrastingly in the western Caucasus, the orders had been destroyed together with the formal organization of Islamic institutions, and there was very little left to salvage.

By 1990, the Central Asian and other republics of the USSR had made declarations of sovereignty, but these declarations were largely symbolic. In 1991 in the aftermath of the August 1991 attempt by the hardline Communist left in Moscow to unseat Gorbachev, the Central Asian republics made formal declarations of independence. And when the USSR ceased to exist in December 1991, the Central Asian republics and Azerbaijan acquired their independence and suddenly and unpreparedly emerged as separate sovereign states, while those units still within the Russian Federation, such as the Chechen-Ingush ASSR and Daghistan, acquired varying degrees of autonomy tempered by continuing economic and financial dependence on Moscow.

Events in the post-1992 period are too close to the present for a realistic evaluation of trends. Recent events in Chechnya, however, suggest that past Russian inclinations of brutal repression of full sovereignty by regions seeking autonomy is likely to continue, provoking ongoing conflict and violence against local peoples. In contrast, the Turkish-speaking republics feel attracted culturally to Turkey, as the ideal of pan-Turkism which was current a century or so ago now is in some measure attainable on the cultural level. The official attitude towards Islam in the Turkey of Ataturk and his successors was in accord with the role envisaged for Islam by the ruling elites of the new republics. These elites which virtually without exception were the same as those who were in power under Communism. Within the new Turcophone republics, the new *mufis* elected in Alma Ata and Tashkent are moderates, and fundamentalist religio-political parties have been banned, for instance, in Uzbekistan. Only in Tajikistan has an unstable political and ideological situation developed with the preindependence elite still tenuously in control but with destablizing influences coming from the neighboring Islamic Republic of Iran and Islamic fundamentalist elements in post-Communist Afghanistan and Pakistan. It is clear that the powers, just mentioned and also Wahhabi Saudi Arabia would like to exert influence within Central Asia but the groups and classes at present in control would, however, prefer to work out their own conflicts without outside interference.

C. E. Bosworth

References

Akiner, Shirin. *The Islamic Peoples of the Soviet Union.* London: n.p., 1983.

Allworth, Edward A. *The Modern Uzbeks, from the 14th Century to the Present.* Stanford, Calif.: Hoover Institution Press, 1990.

Central Asia, 120 years of Russian Rule. Durham, N.C.: Duke University Press, 1989.

The Nationality Question in Soviet Central Asia. New York: Praeger, 1973.

Bacon, Elizabeth E. *Central Asia under Russian Rule. A Study in Cultural Change.* Ithaca, N.Y.: Cornell University Press, 1980.

Barthold, W. *Turkestan Down to the Mongol Invasion,* 2nd ed. London: Luzac, 1928.

Bennigsen, Alexandre, and S. E. Wimbush, *Mystics and Commissars: Suffism in the Soviet Union.* London: C. Hurst, 1985.

Boxup, Marie Bennigsen. *The North Caucasus Barrier: Russia's Advance Towards the Muslim World.* London: C. Hurst, 1992.

Carrere d'Encausse, Helene. *Islam and the Russian Empire, Reform and Revolution in Central Asia.* London: I.B. Tauris, 1988.

Curzon, The Hon. G. N. *Russia in Central Asia in 1889, and the Anglo-Russian Question.* London: Longmans, Green, 1889.

Eickelman, Dale F., ed. *Russia's Muslim Frontiers: New Directions in Cross-Cultural Analysis.* Bloomington: Indiana University Press, 1993.

Fisher, Alan W. *The Crimean Tatars.* Stanford, Calif.: Hoover Institution Press, 1978.

Forsythe, James A. *A History of the Peoples of Siberia: Russia's North Asian Colony 1581–1990.* Cambridge: Cambridge University Press, 1992.

Gibb, H. A. R. *The Arab Conquests in Central Asia.* London: Royal Asiatic Society, 1923.

Gross, Jo-Ann, ed. *Muslims in Central Asia: Expression of Identity and Change,* Durham, N.C.: Duke University Press, 1992.

Grousset, Rene. *The Empire of the Steppes: A History of Central Asia.* Brunswick, N.J.: Rutgers University Press, 1970.

Hambly, Gavin, ed. *Central Asia.* London: Weidenfeld and Nicolson, 1969.

Rashid, A. *The Resurgence of Central Asia: Islam or Nationalism?* London: Zed Books, 1994.

Rorlich, Azade-Ayse. *The Volga Tatars: A Profile in National Resistance.* Stanford, Calif.: Hoover Institution Press, 1986.

Sinor, Denis, ed. *The Cambridge History of Early Inner Asia.* Cambridge: Cambridge University Press, 1990.

Skrine, F. H. and E. D. Ross. *The Heart of Asia: A History of Russian Turkestan and the Central Asian Khanates from the Earliest Times.* London: Methuen, 1899.

Thrower, James. "Notes on Muslim Theological Education in the USSR in the 1980s." In *Political and Economic Trends in Central Asia.* Edited by S. Akiner, London: British Academic Press, 1994: 175–80.

Wheeler, Geoffrey, *The Modern History of Soviet Central Asia.* London: Weidenfeld and Nicolson, 1964.

8

Islam in China

◆ Muslim Ethnic Groups and Population Figures ◆ Geographical Distribution of Muslims in China
◆ Religious Observance ◆ Language and Muslim Communities
◆ Muslim Communities in China and the Economic Reform Program
◆ Muslim Communities in China and International Relations ◆ China's Islamic Gamble

The existence of important Muslim communities in China has been recognized since the early period of Islamic history. Closer to our time, they were the object of much interest in the first decade of the twentieth century to European travelers and missionaries. They felt that residents of China, who already had a monotheistic belief system, might be more easily converted to Christianity than the Han Chinese majority. Even less attention has been paid to the fate of China's long-standing Muslim communities since the establishment of the People's Republic of China in 1949.

These communities suffered along with other ethnic and religious minorities, such as the Tibetans and Mongols, from the Chinese Communist Party's (CCP) desire to impose uniformity and superimpose an overarching ethonym *Zhongguo ren* ("Chinese" in the sense of citizen of the PRC) over all existing identities. The hostility of the CCP to religion also meant that, not only were religious groups suppressed, but no reliable figures are available for the number of Muslims or other believers in China.

The situation has changed radically since the end of the Cultural Revolution and the death of Mao Zedong in 1976, and in the decade since 1979, there has been a remarkable resurgence of Muslim communities and Islamic religious activity. This is attributed by the government press to the influence of *gaige kaifang*, the reform and opening up policies of Deng Xiaoping. With the rebuilding of mosques demolished during the Cultural Revolution, the publication of books, journals, and newspapers specifically for Muslims in China and the realization that China had to be able to convince the Muslim world with which it wished to trade and establish political alliances that Islam could be practiced freely in China. As a result, China's Muslims have been allowed something of a renaissance.

According to statistics published in official news and academic publications, since 1979 more than 20,000 mosques have been opened for Muslims, or, more accurately, reopened, as most were closed and not destroyed during the Cultural Revolution. Furthermore, 800,000 copies of the Quran and nine other religious texts have been printed and distributed. *Muslims in China (Zhonnguo Musilin)*, the magazine of the government-controlled Islamic Association of China formed in 1953, has been published in the Chinese and Uyghur languages. It was estimated in the 1980's that each year 2,000 Muslims visit Mecca from China on the state-supervised *Hajj*. The official New China News Agency reported the departure in 1988 of a group of over five hundred Chinese Muslims from Xinjiang who left on pilgrimage for Mecca via Pakistan. According to statistics released by religious authorities in Xinjiang, 6,500 people of different Muslim ethnic groups made the pilgrimage to Mecca from 1980 to 1987. The figures are somewhat confusing, but it is known that at least 2,000 Muslims from China undertook the *Hajj* in 1993, and this is expected to increase to well over 6,000 in 1995.

This article will begin by examining the size and distribution of the Muslim population of contemporary China. Two of the most important Muslim communities, the Hui (also known as the Chinese Muslims or Dungans) and the Uyghurs of Xinjiang, will be examined in more detail. A brief historical background and special consideration will be given to religious practices, education, and language which are key issues for Muslims in China as in other regions of Islam.

With the collapse of the Soviet Union and the reemergence on the borders of China of independent Central Asian republics, which have Islamic histories and traditions, the role of China's Muslims, many of

Since 1979 more than 20,000 mosques in China have been reopened. Pictured, Xian Mosque.

whom share ethnic and linguistic as well as religious ties with their neighbors, is likely to become more significant. At the time of writing, the role of Islam in the former Soviet Central Asia hangs in the balance with tensions between secular nationalist and Muslim movements and the competition for influence in the region between Iran and Turkey.

♦ MUSLIM ETHNIC GROUPS AND POPULATION FIGURES

It is very difficult to arrive at a precise figure for the number of Muslim people in China today for a variety of historical reasons. The term Muslim is used to include all those who belong to communities, which by tradition, have been Muslim for centuries. This generalization is unavoidable because the government of the People's Republic of China has never collected statistics on religious adherence. The only figures available are those for the populations of ethnic minority groups which are traditionally Muslim, and who identify themselves closely with their ethnic communities and with the Islamic culture of those communities.

The Chinese authorities recognize ten ethnic groups as Muslim: the Hui, Uyghur, Kazakh, Uzbek, Tajik,

Tartar Khalkhas, Dongxiang, Salar, and Baoan. The total number of Muslims within the borders of China today has been officially estimated at about 14 million, but many scholars consider this to be a considerable underestimate as there are still villages and other communities petitioning to be recognized as Hui or as belonging to other ethnic groups. Estimates of the Muslim population of China before the Second World War often used a round figure of 50 million, giving rise to the suggestion of genocide. The problem with this figure is that there was no reliable census in China before 1953, and it is far from clear on which statistics, if any, this was based. The 1990 census statistics suggest a Muslim population of over 17 million, and a round figure for the 1990s of 20 million Muslims in China could well be a reasonable working estimate.

In addition, there are between 20,000 and 50,000 Muslims in Taiwan as well as a thriving minority Muslim community in Hong Kong, which is quite cosmopolitan. The lower figure represents those who fled China in the 1946–49 Civil War and describes those who are active Muslims. The higher figure includes those who migrated to the island in the seventeenth century and are now largely assimilated to the Han population.

Broadly speaking, the Muslims of China can be divided into two groups. The first group includes all of the communities which are grouped together and designated as the Hui, often assumed to be Han Chinese who converted to Islam, but descended from Central Asian, Arab, and Persian Muslims who intermarried with the Han Chinese. Their spoken language has been primarily Chinese since the Ming dynasty (1368–1644), but has retained significant elements of Arabic and Persian vocabulary. The Hui also have an attachment to the Arabic script for cultural, symbolic and decorative purposes, and it can be found in mosques, on *halal* restaurant signs and as decoration on books and pottery. Hui people live in most countries and cities in China, with the largest concentrations in the Ningxia Hui Autonomous Region, Gansu, and Qinghai in northwest China. There are also significant populations in Henan, Hebei, Shandong, Yunnan and the Xinjiang Uyghur Autonomous Region.

It is difficult to generalize about the Hui because of this wide dispersion throughout China and the variety

Populations of Main Ethnic Groups (From Chinese Government Sources)

	1990	1982
Hui	8,602,978	7,227,022
Uyghur	7,214,978	5,962,814
Kazakh	1,111,718	908,414
Kyrgryz	141,549	113,999
Tajik	33,538	26,503

There are between 20,000 and 50,000 Muslims in Taiwan as well as a thriving minority Muslim community in Hong Kong. Pictured, the Mosque of Hong Kong.

of Hui experience both historically and in contemporary China. The lives of Hui people in major cities such as Beijing, Xian, Guangzhou, Tianjin and Shanghai are very different from those of rural Hui living in the mountainous south of Ningxia or Yunnan. The Hui of Changzhou Quanzhou, and Guangzhou have had a very different history. Given this diversity, the usefulness of treating the Hui as a single separate ethnic group or nationality has been questioned, notably by Dru C. Gladney. Gladney has also drawn attention to a related question, the identity of the Uyghurs, and is equally skeptical about treating them as a single ethnic group, arguing that the term Uyghur, as it is used at present, probably dates back only to Soviet advisers in Xinjiang in the 1930s. There is no evidence to suggest that the term Hui is also a recent revival, but studies under Communist Party auspices, beginning with *The Question of the Huihui Nationality*, first published in Yanan in 1941, have reinforced the idea of the Hui as a single and separate ethnic group. Within the Hui, two categories can be identified, practicing Muslims attending mosque and avoiding *haram* products, and those claiming genealogical descent from identified Muslim forbears, although no longer professing Islam.

The second group live mainly in Xinjiang. In their ethnic origin and status, they are quite clearly not Chinese. They embrace all the ethnic groups named above apart from the Hui and are marked out from the Han Chinese by language and culture. All, apart from the Tajiks (whose language belongs to the Persian family) and the Mongolian-speaking Dongxiang and Baoan, speak a Turkic language, and all are related to communities outside China, mainly in the former Soviet Union but with some branches in Afghanistan. In Xinjiang where ethnic and linguistic ties with Central Asia are strong, ethnic consciousness and ethnic allegiance are usually considered to be more important than religious consciousness and allegiance. Conversely, in Gansu, Ningxia and Qinghai, ethnic consciousness takes second place to religion. This is usually explained by geographical and social differences. Nomads in particular have found it more difficult or less necessary to bother about the niceties of ritual than the settled Hui or Uyghur, although they are no less sensitive to attacks on their beliefs. Muslims in both groups are Sunni and follow the Hanafi school of law, the only exception being the Tajiks in Xinjiang who are followers of Shia Islam.

♦ GEOGRAPHICAL DISTRIBUTION OF MUSLIMS IN CHINA

The distinction between the two groups is reinforced by the pattern of their distribution within China. The Hui live throughout the country with scattered communities in every province, and there is hardly a major town or city, including Beijing, that does not have its Hui community and mosques. There are concentrations along the southeastern seaboard reflecting the influence of Arab and Persian maritime traders from the Tang dynasty (618–907 A.D.) onwards. Significant communities also exist in Guangzhou, Shanghai and throughout Henan and Yunnan provinces.

Two examples will show the diversity of Hui experience. The first is Tianmu, a Hui village in the northern suburbs of Tianjin, one of north China's largest port cities. Tianmu is on the western side of the Beijing-Tianjin road in the northern suburbs of the city. The Hui comprise 14,500 of a total village population of 24,400. Tradition has it that the origins of the village date from the arrival of Mu Chonghe, bodyguard of the Ming emperor Zhu Di, who stayed in the village after he came with troops sent there to wipe out bandits in 1404. His descendants built a hamlet, Mujiazhuang, which was merged with Tianqimiao in 1951 to form Tianmu. Over the centuries, Hui and Han mixed through intermarriage, and villagers claim that even Hans in the village do not eat pork and are known as "Huis by custom." The village has two mosques, the northern dating from the fifteenth century and the southern built in 1854. Both were damaged in the Second World War and were repaired in the 1950s. When the southern mosque was rebuilt in 1989 after the depredations of the Cultural Revolution, the inauguration ceremony was attended by Politburo member Li Ruihuan and Ilyas Shen Xiaxi, president of the China Islamic Association. Specialist Muslim trades in Tianmu include meat production and baking, and there is an Islamic Perfumed Soap Factory which sells its products in Xinjiang and other Muslim areas.

There is also an important Hui community in Hunan, Mao Zedong's home province. The origin of this community has been traced back to the first year of the Hongwu reign of the Ming dynasty, 1368, when Muslim troops came into Hunan with the military units of the new dynasty, many of them settling in the area. Later, with the development of commerce and trade, a section of Hui traders moved from the southeastern coast and the market towns of the lower Yangzi and entered Hunan via the Dongting lake and the rivers Xiang, Zi, Yuan and Li. Most of the Muslim military came from Nanjing and Beijing and settled in the strategic towns of Shaoyang and Changde, which later became the major centers of Hui settlement in Hunan.

However, by far the largest Hui population is in northwest of China in the provinces of Gansu and Qinghai (part of old Tibet) and in Ningxia, designated a Hui Autonomous Region in 1958. In the northwest, the Hui areas overlap with areas where the second group of Muslims live. Although individual Uyghurs, Kazakhs, and others can be found throughout China, communities of these ethnic groups are found only in what the Han Chinese refer to as the Xinjiang Uyghur Autonomous Region, but this area is also known as East Turkestan (*Sharqi Turkistan*) in the Turkic languages and is regarded by the Uyghurs as their homeland.

Hui History

There have been Muslims in China from the earliest years of the existence of Islam, traders who came to the southeastern ports of Guangzhou, Quanzhou and Changzhou as part of the Indian Ocean trade, but contemporary scholarship in China emphasizes the distinctive nature of Hui history from the Yuan dynasty (1271–1368), as the Mongols designated their conquering dynasty in China.

The term Huihui or Hui, which later came to be the usual name for Muslims in China, was rarely seen in Chinese historical records before the Mongol conquests, but there is a record in the basic annals of the reign of the Liao emperor Tianzuo (reigned 1101–19) in which Yelu Dashi, the founder of the Qarakhitai Western Liao dynasty, on his epic journey west accepted the surrender of the king of the Huihui. The *Liaoshi* also includes a Huihui tribe in its list of tribes encountered by Yelu Dashi on his expedition and it is clear from these sources that they lived in the region of Samarkand in the eastern part of Persian-speaking Central Asia. Sources from Iranian history support this. In the thirteenth century the Mongols subjugated Central Asian Muslim peoples, many of whom migrated east as the fighting subsided. These numbers included conscripted soldiers, artisans, captured women, children, scholars and aristocrats. As communications between China and Central Asia opened up, many traders also went east voluntarily. In Yuan official documents all of these people were referred to as Huihui and classified as one group of the *semu* (colored eyes). As many as two or three million conscripts from Muslim areas of Central Asia may have been used by the Mongols in their conquest of China. It is likely that craftsmen were the first Muslims that nomad Mongols found useful, but, as the empire grew, all classes entered into its service, and Muslims spread throughout China. By the Yuan dynasty there were already mosques in Guangzhou, Quanzhou, Hangzhou, Xian and Kunming. The Mongol rule of China provided highly favorable conditions for the Hui merchants to

develop their businesses. In particular, the close relationship between Hui merchants and the ruling
Mongols was established at an early stage. The political
status of the Hui was higher than that of the Han, and
there were fewer legal restrictions on trade for the Hui
than for Han or southerners. Muslims also received
preferential treatment in imperial examinations, official appointments, limitations on punishment, and in
matters regarding the possession of troops and horses.
Individual Hui had real power in the court and in local
government which helped the official-trader relationships. Muslim traders migrated throughout Yuan China
following the conquering armies. Hui merchants enlivened the cities of Yuan dynasty China, especially the
capital Dadu and the southeastern port cities, specializing in perfumes and spices, pearls and precious
goods. They became known as "Hui traders who know
treasures." Muslim soldier-settlers gravitated to cul-
tivable or reclaimable land, such as the area between
Liupanshan and the Yellow River in the present-day
Ningxia Hui Autonomous Region.

During the Ming dynasty, the Hui began to emerge as
a nationality, and the Hui population of Shaanxi and
Gansu, already large, increased substantially. Hui people were dispersed around China, mostly in areas
where they were greatly outnumbered by the Han population, but they countered this by establishing Hui villages or urban Hui streets wherever they settled.
Intermarriage increased the population. Han wives of
Hui men and Han men marrying Hui women became
Hui. This dilution of the original community had the effect of reducing the influence of the Arabic and Persian
languages as Chinese became the general medium of
communication. As early as 1536 there were complaints that the Hui people could no longer understand
the Quran. During the Ming dynasty major Islamic texts
were written in classical Chinese, such as the works on
religious practice and doctrine by the well known
Chinese Muslim scholar Wang Daiyu. Many present-day
Hui communities trace their origins back to a Ming ancestor, including those of Hunan and Tianjin referred to
above.

The history of the Hui during the Qing dynasty
(1644–1911) is usually defined in terms of their conflicts with the Han majority, including the rebellions of
the early Qing, the major and well-documented risings
of the 1860s, and the lesser documented ones of 1895
when China was more preoccupied with its war with
Japan. One of the problems in analyzing these out-
breaks of violence is that it is difficult to discern where
intra-Hui factional conflict and Hui rebellion against
the Han began.

In the early part of the Qing dynasty the imperial
government initially lifted restrictions on foreign trade
but later confined it to Guangzhou. From 1644 to 1655

the Ming restrictions on foreign trade were continued,
but from 1655 to 1684 strict prohibition was enforced
to deal with the resistance to the Qing conquest. After
1684, when Taiwan was occupied and the power base
of Zheng Chenggong destroyed, the prohibition disappeared and the decision was made to open up China to
overseas trade. This made it possible for more and
more Muslims to go to Mecca on the *Hajj* which, in
turn, gave a boost to Islam within China. In addition,
the travels of Chinese pilgrims in the Muslim world
brought them into contact with Sufi beliefs and practices which they brought back with them to China.

The Hui of Ningxia

The Ningxia Hui Autonomous Region is the provin-
cial-level administrative unit of China with the highest
population of Hui and the largest concentrated Hui residential area. At the end of 1985 the total Hui population of the autonomous region was 1,337,561, which
was 32.3 percent of the total population of the province
and 18 percent of the total Hui population of China.
Although the Hui are distributed throughout the region,
there are two main areas of concentration: one is in the
southern mountainous area which includes the almost
purely Hui country of Jinghai where the Hui occupy
96.9 percent of the total population as well as the
Tongxin, Haiyuan and Xiji countries; the other is in the
Wuzhong and Lingfu countries in the Yinchuan area in
the north of the region where the Hui populations are
respectively 55.2 and 48.0 percent of the total population.

Ningxia is on the upper and middle reaches of the
Yellow River and is approximately 66,000 square kilometers in area. It has water and mineral resources including gypsum and ranks fifth in China for coal stocks.
Irrigation and canals on the Yinchuan plain date back
to the Qin dynasty (221–207 B.C.) and were further developed during Han, Tang, and Xixia rule. The Ningxia
plain is known locally as "the Jiangnan on the Wall."
Agriculture in the region includes wheat and, surprisingly for such a northerly location, paddy rice (irrigation from the Yellow River is important for both),
hemp, oil-bearing crops, melons and other fruit. The
grasslands are a fur- and skin-producing area including
Tibetan lambskins. Sheep are particularly important
livestock resource in the foothills of the Helan mountains where tree planting has been both an end in itself
and a barrier to the drift of the desert.

To the Han officials who control the region, Ningxia
is relatively unproductive and backward in commerce,
education, culture, science and technology. They com-
plain of fast population growth and ignorance on the
part of the population of the concept of a commodity
economy. The cities on the bend of the Yellow River
and surrounding rural areas have developed much

more quickly than the mountainous areas of southern Ningxia. Southern Ningxia has 59 percent of the area and 43 percent of the population of the autonomous region, but the gross value of industrial and agricultural output was only 9.6 percent of the regional total in 1987.

The importance attached to the promotion of a Muslim region can be seen in Ningxia's thirtieth anniversary celebration on October 25, 1988. The People's Bank of China announced the issue of a commemorative one *yuan* copper-nickel coin which depicts the great mosque in Yinchuan on one side and two young Hui women on the other. This coin was intended mainly for use in the region. Celebratory speeches inevitably praised nationality, solidarity and unity, claiming that disputes between the Hui and Han nationalities have all but vanished. It was pointed out that Hui officials occupy most senior posts in the autonomous region and its cities, but at a meeting with cadres on September 27 in the regional capital, Yinchuan, senior CCP figure Wang Zhen, former commander of Chinese military units in Xinjiang, called for measures to increase the number of cadres from minority nationalities and train them properly. It was revealed that, in spite of the fact that Hui people account for 32.5 percent of the total

population of the region, they constitute only 14.5 percent of the cadres although most of the leading posts at all levels are occupied by Hui-origin cadres.

The Uyghurs of Xinjiang

The Xinjiang Uyghur Autonomous Region is on the northwest frontier of China. It stretches 2,000 kilometers east to west and 1,650 kilometers north to south, has an area of over 1,600,000 square kilometers, and is the largest administrative unit in the PRC. Bordering Mongolia, Afghanistan, Pakistan, and India and three Central Asian states, Kazakhstan, Kyrgyzstan and Tajikistan, it is close to Uzbekistan and Turkmenistan. Its nearest neighbors within China are Gansu and Ningxia, both of which have substantial Muslim communities: Tibet, which constitutes Beijing's main separatist problem; Qinghai, part of old Tibet; and Tibetan Buddhist and Muslim communities.

The original Turkic inhabitants of Xinjiang were migrants from Mongolia from whom the Uyghurs claim descent. The ethnic make-up of the Turkic peoples is complex, and names have changed throughout history, the ethonym Uyghur being one of the most problematic. Chinese influence in the region was consolidated

The Islamic Institute of Xinjiang.

in the eighteenth century, and the name Xinjiang (New Dominion or New Frontier) was used first in 1768. The Qing dynasty's military administration encountered constant nationalist and religious resistance, allied to Islamic forces in neighboring Khokand, but in 1831, the first Han immigrants from China were allowed to move into southwestern Xinjiang to cultivate reclaimable land. A Muslim insurrection under Yakub Beg created an independent *khanate* based on Kashgar until it was overthrown by Qing forces in 1878. Xinjiang was formally incorporated into the Chinese empire as a province in 1884 at a time of intense British and Russian imperial rivalry in Central Asia.

After the 1911 Revolution, which overthrew the Manchu Qing dynasty and brought to an end the Chinese empire, Xinjiang suffered civil wars and armed risings involving Turkic-speaking Muslims, the Hui and the Han Chinese until the warlord Sheng Shicai took power, ruling from 1933 to 1944 with support from the USSR for part of that period. Turkic Muslims rose against Sheng in southern Xinjiang in 1933 and 1937, and an independent Kazakh and Uyghur East Turkestan Republic controlled the northwestern Ili region from 1944 to 1946.

In 1949, troops of the CCP's People's Liberation Army took control of Xinjiang, and a Han immigration program was announced in 1950. The campaign against counter-revolutionaries and land reform, which included the confiscation and redistribution of mosque-owned *waqf* land, was used to break down the traditional social structure and political and religious authority. On October 1, 1955 the Xinjiang Uyghur Autonomous Region was created with autonomous Mongol, Kyrgyz, Kazakh and Hui countries. Burhan Shahidi, a Tatar, and Seypidin Aziz (Saifudin), an Uyghur, headed the regional government. Real power rested with Wang Zhen, commander of the PLA units which took control in 1949, and the regional Communist Party Secretary, Wang Enmao, both ethnic Hans. The quasi-military Xinjiang Production and Construction Corps, a predominantly Han organization of demobilized PLA men, former Guomindang soldiers and resettled Han people, was central in establishing control.

The 1958 Great Leap Forward radical policies, which were less sensitive to local feelings, replaced the cautious approach of the early 1950s. "Local nationalism" and Han and Muslim leaders sympathetic to the USSR were systematically criticized and bazaars and Islamic organizations closed down. Wang Enmao moderated policies in 1962 after the exodus of 60,000 Kazakhs to Kazakhstan, but the 1966 Cultural Revolution, during which he was dismissed, caused chaos until the imposition of direct military control in 1971.

The CCP leadership was divided on policy towards Xinjiang in the early 1980s. After a visit to Tibet in May 1980, Hu Yaobang, shortly to become CCP Secretary General, proposed a reform program which recommended genuine autonomy, economic policies suited to local needs, investment in agriculture and animal husbandry, the revival of cultural, educational, and scientific projects, and the phased transfer to the interior of Han officials. In a modified form these proposals were adopted for use in Xinjiang by the CCP Central Committee Secretariat. Hu considered that Xinjiang was less of a problem than Tibet as there were no religious leaders or governments in exile comparable to the Dalai Lama in Dharamsala and no independence movement with sufficient overseas support to pose a real threat. At that time Isa Alptekin's Eastern Turkestan Liberation Movement appeared to be isolated and impotent.

These reformist policies were abandoned after conflict in the central leadership between Wang Zhen, the former Xinjiang military commander, and Hu Yaobang, who was purged in 1987. A Han official in Xinjiang sympathetic to Wang Zhen, agreed that, if they were given autonomy, they would create an Eastern Turkestan. Hence the only way to stabilize Xinjiang was to send in hard-liners like Wang Zhen.

Tomur Dawamat, the Chairman of the Xinjiang Regional Government, urged ethnic groups in 1988 in Xinjiang to practice family planning for their own benefit. He went on to say that unplanned population growth among Xinjiang's ethnic minorities, who made up over 60 per cent of the population, had not only laid a heavy financial burden on each family but also brought about social difficulties in education, medical treatment, transportation, goods supply, and employment. He called on religious leaders to support the policy or at least to refrain from obstructing the work. Many Muslims, especially in Xinjiang, along with members of other ethnic minority groups, continue to perceive the one-child policy as designed to reduce their numbers and overwhelm them with Han immigrants.

The issue that has provoked the greatest hostility in Xinjiang is the encouragement of Han Chinese immigrants, seen as a way of diluting local culture and ensuring Beijing's control. Migration increased after the suppression of the Yakub Beg regime in 1878, but the government of the PRC has consciously and effectively used it to control Xinjiang. The proportion of Hans in Xinjiang rose from 5.5 percent in 1949 to about 40 percent in 1970. The Han population is made up of five groups: a small group of the descendants of early settlers; troops of the Guomindang garrison who defected to the Communist General Wang Zhen in 1949 and their descendants, many of whom serve in the Xinjiang Production and Construction Corps; administrative, professional, and technical personnel assigned to key government jobs; young people transferred to Xinjiang in the 1960s and 1970s during the Cultural Revolution; and prisoners from the Labor Reform and Labor Education camps that are spread throughout Kinjiang, together with released prisoners who have been found work placements in the region. Local non-Han people find the policy of turning Xinjiang into a vast prison camp particularly offensive.

Beijing has been peculiarly insensitive to the feelings of the non-Han people on matters of immigration. It is official policy to attract qualified professional and technical staff from other parts of China, most of whom would be Han. Kashgar announced in December 1992 that it would be prepared to resettle up to 100,000 people, all Han, who will be displaced by the Three Gorges Dam project on the Yangzi River. A national and international outcry over these proposals, came at the same time as the visit of a delegation from the Muslim CIS states, the signing of an agreement of troop reduction on the border, and President Yeltsin's December visit to China. The Beijing authorities were ultimately forced to back down.

The opening of the borders with former Soviet Central Asia and the increase in cross-border trade in the early 1990s created another outcry. Kazakh newspapers began to report fears in Kazakhstan and in Almaty (Alma Ata) over a massive influx of Chinese, many of whom had come to trade but then decided to settle.

◆ RELIGIOUS OBSERVANCE

Religious observance was stifled during the Cultural Revolution (approximately 1966 to 1976). Many mosques were completely destroyed, and others lost much of their land and buildings. For Muslims in China, the most important feature of the reform program associated with Deng Xiaoping has been the possibility of rebuilding or reopening mosques. There are probably no accurate figures for the loss of these mosques, but some examples will illustrate the point.

The Nanguan (South Bar) Mosque is the largest in Yinchuan, the capital of the Ningxia Hui Autonomous Region. In the courtyard is a shop where the Quran and various devotional materials are on sale. On the wall of the shop is a display of photographs depicting the destruction of the mosque in the mid-1960s, the makeshift prayer hall made up of mats and tables which the congregation used on the site, and the reconstruction of the mosque in a Middle Eastern style in the mid-1980s. In March 1991 the Mosque was fully active with a *madrasa* or school. Also in Yinchuan, the Xiguan Mosque was rebuilt in 1981 in a Middle Eastern style. According to the Ahong, it dates back to the 1880s. One such Ahong had taken part in the *Hajj* in 1987 and an-

other Ahong had also been to Mecca. His congregation was approximately one hundred on regular days but over three hundred on Fridays. In Yinchuan there are twelve or so mosques. Most were destroyed in the Cultural Revolution, and rebuilding commenced in the 1980s. Construction of mosques continues in Yinchuan and a new mosque, the Xincheng Nanmen (New Town South Gate) on Mancheng Street South, was being built in September 1992.

The Wuzhong Mosque in Wuzhong, a busy market town south of Yinchuan, was built in 1778 and extended twice during the late nineteenth century. After severe damage during the Cultural Revolution, it was re-established in 1979, and further repairs were carried out in 1987. However, the present-day mosque occupies far less land than the original.

The Najiahu Mosque in Najiahu village near Wuzhong was badly damaged during the Cultural Revolution, but the prayer hall, reflecting a mixture of Chinese and Muslim architectural patterns remained untouched.

The Great Mosque in Tongxin, a predominantly Hui town in central Ningxia, was a Buddhist temple during the Mongol conquest and has that appearance. It was rededicated as a mosque when it was taken over by local Muslims after the expulsion of the Mongols. It was not damaged at all during the Cultural Revolution and the congregation is proud of their role in defending it. According to the Ahong, the daily congregation consists of a few dozen, but hundreds attend on a Friday.

Islamic literature is on sale in Muslim centers in China but with restrictions. *Zhongguo Musilin* (Chinese Muslim) is published nationally in Chinese and Uyghur. The Quran in Chinese and Arabic, commentaries and other classic devotional literature such as the writings of the Ming-dynasty Muslim scholar Wang Daiyu are published openly and on sale in the main state bookshops in Ningxia and Gansu as well as in Beijing. Religious publications are also available in Urumqi bookshops. In Kasghar, there are no Islamic books at all in the New China bookshop, the main state outlet, apart from a Chinese-language book, *Stories from the Quran*. In the Kashghar bazaar religious works in Arabic and Chinese can be brought from street stalls, and in Linxia, the main Hui area of south western Gansu and Guanghe, a nearby country town, new and second-hand books on religious topics and Arabic language courses are on sale from barrows or stalls on the main streets. There is also a widespread network of underground or unofficial Islamic publishing with the Ahongs publishing and distributing their own books, but these are difficult for outsiders to obtain.

Chinese Islam reflects the theological and historical diversity found in the rest of the Muslim world. The os-

The Great Mosque in Tongxin, Ningxia.

tensible reasons for division were either doctrinal or connected with the interpretation of religious practice, but a detailed examination of the emergence of groups within Chinese Islam reveals a complex interplay of religious, personal, and social causes. Almost all Chinese Muslims are considered to be mainstream Sunnis who follow the Hanafi school of law. There are Shia members among the mountain Tajiks of Xinjiary, mostly Ismailis. Although Shiism has few followers outside this small group, it has been influential in creating the culture of Chinese Islam because of the role played by the Persian language in its transmission.

By convention, there are four major groupings within Chinese Islam, although some contemporary Chinese official sources say six. The oldest is the Gedimu (Arabic *al-qadim*), meaning the ancient. The Yihewani is the Chinese group corresponding to the Ikhwan al-Muslimin or Muslim Brotherhood of Egypt. The Xidaotang or Hall of the Western Pathway developed within China. The fourth group is made up of branches of Sufi orders, most of which can be traced to origins outside China, primarily in the Arabia peninsula and Central Asia.

The scholarly inquiry into the operation of Sufi networks in China is a recent phenomenon. During the late nineteenth and early twentieth centuries, they were grouped together with other sects which were not Gedimu and termed the *xinjiao* or New Teachings, to contrast them with the Old Teaching Gedimu. However, Sufism has a long history in China and has played an important role in sustaining Islam through centuries of repression.

Sufi orders or brotherhoods in China, and particularly in Gansu, Ningxia and Qinghai where they are strongest, are usually known as *menhuan*. This term, its origins and its Chinese etymology are still imperfectly understood but it corresponds to the Arabic *tariqa* or path. In Xinjiang, the same orders are called *yichan*, from the Persian, but the differences are in name only.

There are four main groups of Sufi orders in China: the Khufiyya *Hufuye*, the Jahriyya *Zheherenye* or *Zhehelinye* (which has been the most influential of all the orders in China), the Qadiriyya *Gadelinye*, and the Kubrawiyya *Kuburenye*. The Sufi groups in Xinjiang mainly belong to the Naqshbandiyya, which is also the most influential order in Gansu.

Chinese officials treat the above Muslim groups as if they were political factions. There are considered to be six Muslim factions in Ningxia: the Gedimu, Ihewani,

Hufuye, Zhehelinye, Gadelinye and Sailaifeiye. In the view of CCP officials, the 1.4 million Islamic Hui people in Ningxia belong to six factions, all Sunni, the largest faction having 33,000 members and the smallest 1,000. Government policy is to treat factions equally with each faction having its own representatives in People's Congresses and the local committees of the Chinese Peoples's Political Consultative Conference, an organization designed to integrate non-Communists into the Chinese polity.

Among the newly reopened girls' school is the Tongxin Girls' Hui Middle School, a boarding school in Tongxin. The school is spacious, modern, and well equipped by the standards of northwest China. All the girls board as they are from the Hui villages around Tongxin. Before the school was opened, many parents refused to allow their daughters to attend mixed schools, and Hui village girls missed out on an education. Other rural Hui children attend the Tongxin Number 2 Hui Middle School which had 1,100 pupils, only ten percent of them girls because of the success of the Girls' Schools. Pupils here also board, go home on Saturday afternoons, and return to the school on Sunday evening. Children who live in the town attend the Tongxin Number 1 Hui Middle School. The effect of mixed schools on Hui girls is illustrated by the school attendance and literacy figures for Guyuan prefecture in southern Ningxia. It is an overwhelmingly Hui region, but only 4.7 percent of school pupils were Hui girls in 1986. Half the Hui women are illiterate, whereas, the illiteracy rate for women as a whole in the region is 34.4 percent.

As part of the resurgence of Islam in China, eight Islamic academies for the training of scholars were opened. By 1988 four hundred students had been enrolled in four- to five-year courses which include the Quran, Islamic culture and management. The aim of the academies is to train researchers, teachers, and high-ranking personnel engaged in international Islamic academic exchanges. Many of the students are Ahongs who have been in post for some time, but were unable to obtain formal theological training because of restrictions on religion during the Cultural Revolution.

The Ningxia Islamic Academy (*Ningxia Yisilanjiao jingxueyuan*), situated in the western suburbs of Yinchuan, occupies 40.5 mu of land. Construction has been made possible by funding provided by the Islamic Development Bank. The government of the Autonomous Region also authorized a bridging loan of 2.3 million *renminbi* to enable construction to take place. Further technical support was provided by visits from a Saudi engineer in February 1986 and October 1988.

Since the opening of the Academy, it has recruited seventy-six students, among them the twenty-six members of the class of 1985 who graduated ahead of schedule. In 1989 there were said to be fifty still studying in the academy and thirty-one on the teaching and administrative staff. In March 1991 the Academy was completed; the library was well stocked with books in Arabic and Chinese. However, there were no staff or students to be seen possibly because it was the beginning of Ramadan. In September 1992, the building still looked unused and, although there were a few staff on duty, there was no sign of the hundred students reported to have been enrolled by then.

The Tongxin Arabic Language School in Tongxin, central Ningxia, was founded in 1985, also with the aid of the Islamic Development Bank, to promote economic and cultural exchange between China and Islamic countries of the Middle East. The design of the building is very similar to the Islamic Academy in Yinchuan, but, unlike the academies, its role is almost entirely secular. It is designated a "secondary vocational school" specializing in training translators and interpreters at elementary and intermediate level, although the students are of university age. It is the only state-run specialist Arabic school in China. There are privately run ones in Shaanxi province and elsewhere. The three years of study include Arabic language, history, Islamic general knowledge, nationality theory and policies, and students graduating are said to have a satisfactory knowledge of spoken and written Arabic. Some have already been employed by organizations dealing with the Middle East.

By 1988 student numbers had grown to ninety-eight, mostly Hui, and there was a staff of twenty-nine. In 1992 the 260 students were all Hui, and three of its graduates were working in the Ministry of Foreign Affairs as Arabic translators. Although many of the students are from Ningxia, there are some from Xian and northeast China. Teachers at the school have studied in Kuwait, Egypt, Syria, and Saudi Arabia. Teaching materials are provided by the Foreign Languages College in Beijing, supplemented by newspapers and other materials from the Arab world.

◆ LANGUAGE AND MUSLIM COMMUNITIES

There is great confusion in China about the language spoken by the Hui and about the role of written and spoken Arabic in their lives. According to a guidebook for tourists to Lanzhou published in English entitled *Discover China's Cities* (1989), the Hui speak the Han language or Mandarin outside their own communities and speak Arabic among themselves. Arabic is certainly extremely important to the Hui in China today. A Hui woman making the four-day rail journey from Nanjing to Urumqi on business assured me that Arabic is still considered by the Hui to be one of their lan-

Arabic often is used for liturgical purposes, for calligraphic decoration of mosques, and as a foreign language to be studied in Islamic academics for religious purposes. Pictured the Chinese-Arabic Girls School in Larzhon.

guages. The Stars and Moon Restaurant at 113 Beiyuan Gate, Xian, which specializes in *yangrou paomo*, a lamb hotpot poured over broken nan bread considered to be the finest Hui food in the city, has the phrase *matam al Muslimin* in Arabic in green print on its business and menu card. The phrase appears in the same form on the signs of *halal* restaurants and food stalls throughout China, making them instantly recognizable. Arabic is used for liturgical purposes, for calligraphic decoration of mosques, and as a foreign language to be studied in Islamic academics for religious purposes. In private schools and at the Tongxin Arabic School, it is used for secular reasons.

The academic consensus in China concerning the spoken language of the Hui is that, because of a long history of contact and coexistence with the Han, Hui people have completely mastered the Han spoken language and script, and that, apart from using the Chinese dialect of the area in which they live, they also preserve a special social dialect which employs some Arabic and Persian words. During the initial stage of their eastward exodus, the Hui used the Arab, Persian

and Han languages. However, in the course of their long years living with the Hans, and especially due to the increasing number of Hans joining their ranks, they gradually began to speak only the Han language, maintaining only certain Arab and Persian phrases. The extent to which there is a separate Hui language or *Huihui hua* is not entirely clear. Arabic words are used in connection with religious observance and, as the Quran is read and studied in Arabic, this is not surprising. More interesting is the persistence of Persian vocabulary which has social and historical rather than religious connotations. According to Huang Tinghui, an ethnic Hui and a leading historian of the Hui minority, when Huis are talking among themselves, as much as 20 to 30 percent of their vocabulary is of foreign origin, and much of their conversation would be unintelligible to non-Hui. The existence of a special Hui language is widespread. In the Hui community in Hunan, for example, the most common greeting is *seliamu* for al-Salamu alaykum. The *se* and *mu* are written with the characters used to write *semu* or blue-eyed foreigners in the Yuan dynasty. The expounding of doctrine by an Ahong from the Persian word Akhund is called *waersi;* Muslim co-religionists are addressed as *dositi; dost* is used in Persian, Turkish, Uyghur, and Urdu, but its use by the Hui is probably of Persian origin). Malevolent spirits are referred to as *yibulisi* (Arabic *iblis* meaning satan or devil) and non-Muslims are known as *kafeile* (Arabic *kafir*, infidel).

The relaxation of restrictions on religious activity in the 1980s and a general desire to open up China led to a revival of interest in Arabic. The Hui area of Tianjin is one example. As an article in *Beijing Review* put it,

Muslims in Tianmu village have used Chinese for a long time, but they still speak old Arabic in the mosque. Since the implementation of reform and open policy of 1978, the residents of Tianmu have met Muslims from Arab countries and found a great difference between modern and old Arabic. Gao Yaokuan suggested that the villagers learn modern Arabic and his idea received support. In November 1986, some teachers of Tianjin Foreign Languages Institute were invited to teach an Arabic class in the village. After three years of effort, many people can now read the Koran and more than ten people can converse in Arabic. Four young people are now studying Arabic at the Oriental Languages and Literature Department of Beijing University.

As referred to earlier, Tongxin, in Ningxia, one of the major centers of Islam, has an Arabic-language school.

China under the Mongol Yuan dynasty was a multicultural and multilingual society. In terms of the num-

Gate at the Ginghai Hui mosque in Urumqi, Xinjiang shows the use of both "Chinese" and Arabic.

bers of speakers, the two most important languages were Chinese, in all its regional varieties, and the Mongol of the conquerors, but other languages were important for trade, commerce, and local usage. Arabic and Turkic languages were spoken by foreign residents in China, but by far the most important was Persian, spoken by many of the conscripted artisans and soldiers from Central Asia and traders. In the documentary evidence that has come down from the Yuan period there is some confusion about the language which is sometimes referred to as *Huihuihua*. Like

many names used in connection with the Muslims to the west of China, including the name Hui or Huihui itself, there is evidence that the meanings have changed over time. Some writers used the term *Huihuihua* to mean both Arabic and Persian, reflecting the similarity of the writing to outsiders, who did not appreciate that the spoken languages were quite dissimilar. Other writers clearly used the term to refer to Arabic, implemented by all Muslims for religious purposes. In the majority of cases Huihuiha refers to Persian, the common written language of the eastern part of the Islamic world from the tenth century onwards and the dominant language of the region conquered by the Mongols.

In his seminal work on Islam in China, Dabry de Thiersant, French Consul and Charge d'Affaires, noted the emergence of the term *Huihui shu* to refer to the script or rather to the language of the former Huihui or the inhabitants of the kingdom of Huihui. This has been equated with the Persian of Bukhara on the basis of research carried out on a volume of Persian documents. Thiersant's work was part of a series of sixteen volumes published on the orders of the Kangxi emperor and was based on the memorials of a number of young scholars sent by him to study the languages, mores and polities of various regions.

Evidence for the persistent influence of Persian in the northwest of China was uncovered by the D'Ollone mission of 1911 which retrieved eleven Persian manuscripts from Gansu and donated them to the Bibliotheque Nationale in Paris.

The documents analyzed included: a fragment of a history of the prophets in Persian with many extracts from the Quran in Naskhi handwriting without a date, but probably copied in Gansu at the beginning of the nineteenth century and bound with pages from a Tibetan book; a commentary in Persian on the *Lawaih* of Nur al-din Abd al-Rahman al Jami (898 AH); a collection of Sufi sayings paraphrased in Persian by Jami, one of the most celebrated scholars of Persian Sufism; and lastly Naskhi handwriting copied in Gansu, probably in the early part of the nineteenth century; a Persian treatise on prayer also in Naskhi script copied by one Ahmad ibn Ahmad with no date, perhaps in the seventeenth century.

The Uyghur language, the most important among Xinjiang's Muslims, belongs to the eastern or Altay branch of the Turkic family and is related to Kazakh, Krygyz, Turkmen, Turkish, and, most closely, to Uzbek. The Uyghur language gave the Uyghurs a means of communication with their counterparts in Central Asia but not with the Chinese. Fluency in Standard Chinese (Mandarin, *putonghua*) is essential for Uyghur officials or teachers, but the standard of spoken Chinese among Uyghur and Kazakh academics is surprisingly poor. Traders and small shopkeepers in the bazaars know little Chinese, and few Han Chinese can communicate effectively in Uyghur although the language is taught in schools and at Xinjiang University. The result of all this is a serious language barrier between the communities.

Uyghur was written in the Arabic script after the adoption of Islam in the fifteenth and sixteenth centuries, but unlike Turkish it did not change to the Latin script in 1928. As part of China's language reform program, a new script based on a modified Latin alphabet was created in June 1958, replacing an experimental Cyrillic script which effected the influence of Russian in the region. The new script was seen as a Han imposition. The "old script" reappeared in 1978 and was authorized in 1980 for both the Uyghur and Kazakh languages. The current version is a modified Perso-Arabic script with diacritical marks and additional letters for the complex vowel system. All books and newspapers now appear in the old script.

The re-emergence of the old script helps Uyghurs to identify with the rest of the Muslim world. Religious observance and cultural features associated with Islam, including distinctive colored hats for men, head coverings for women in Kashgar and the Altishahr or head scarves in Urumqi and Turpan, reinforce this identity. Uyghur folk and popular music can be distinguished immediately from Chinese music and is constantly played in bazaars, restaurants and at wedding parties as a statement of cultural assertion. Some Uyghurs, particularly emigres, have expressed concern at the sinicization of the Uyghur language, which has absorbed Chinese loan words in the same way that it absorbed Russian in the past.

♦ MUSLIM COMMUNITIES IN CHINA AND THE ECONOMIC REFORM PROGRAM

Mosques in Ningxia have benefited from the move towards a market-orientated economy by developing business interests which have helped to finance their religious activities. The Nanguan Mosque in Yinchuan, for example, has an allocation from public funds but needs at least four times that amount. In August 1986 the Nanguan Mosque set up a Muslim services company. It manages a hotel with sixty to seventy beds, a canteen, grocery, shop and clinic, and by 1988, it had made a profit of over 100,000 yuan. The regional government gives preferential treatment to mosques involved in business, including tax exemption for the first three to five years. The mosque employs thirty-six local people, and the poor, the young and the elderly receive free medical treatment in the clinic. Plans for developing the business interests of the mosque include the creation of an Islamic bazaar in Yinchuan supported by foreign investment.

The situation further west in Xinjiang is very similar and mosques in Urumqi have begun to develop commercial interests. Of the seventy-five mosques in the city, nearly two-thirds have opened shops, hotels, or barber shops within the grounds of the mosque. Small shopkeepers rent space in the main hall of the largest mosque, attracting thousands of buyers, while the upper floor is reserved for prayer. The Xiheba Mosque does not have to collect money from its congregation for water, electricity and upkeep as it did in the past because it makes enough profit from its commercial interests. It is even able to make a donation to the local education department for developing education for ethnic minority students.

Hui Muslims in Qinghai have opened their own Islamic bank, the Muslim savings deposit center, run by the Xining City Bank of Industry and Commerce. The bank took 150,000 *renminbi* in deposits in its first month. Some Muslims were wary of the new bank, but the provincial party secretary Yin Kesheng attempted to reassure them.

The Hui people have a tradition of involvement in trade and finance and are likely to prosper in the more open financial environment created by the reform program.

♦ MUSLIM COMMUNITIES IN CHINA AND INTERNATIONAL RELATIONS

The Muslim community has acquired a new significance as relations with the Islamic world become more important to China. The possibility of developing Muslim special economic zones to encourage investment from Muslim countries, particularly oil-rich ones, is being considered. China is developing relations with major powers in the Middle East. A Chinese Muslim regional delegation visited Turkey after a visit to Hungary, a probe the possibility of increasing trade. The delegation called on the Governor of the Istanbul province.

China has also established diplomatic relations with Saudi Arabia. This was announced in July 1990 as Foreign Minister Qian Qichen left Beijing for a surprise visit to Saudi Arabia which still has full diplomatic relations with Taiwan and is a major source of its oil imports. Saudi Arabia opened a trade mission in Beijing in August of 1989. The Saudi rulers are known to want stronger links with China's Muslim population.

China's relations with Iran have also become crucial. In the field of nuclear co-operation, China has sold Iran equipment capable of producing fissile material.

In 1992, President Rafsanjani, who had been taking part in a Non-Aligned Movement conference in Jakarta, returned home via Beijing for a three-day official visit to discuss nuclear, financial, and military co-operation. Iranian and Chinese news agencies and Xinjiang television in its Chinese- and Uyghur-language services reported his visit to Beijing and the meetings he held in Urumqi, the capital of Xinjiang, and his departure for Tehran. In Urumqi he met Tomur Dawamat, the regional government chairman, for discussions on economic, commercial, scientific, technological, and cultural exchanges, including talks on joint Xinjiang-Iran projects, rail links via Kyrgyzstan and Tajikistan, and a new air route. His visit to Kashgar, and the fact that he led the Friday prayers at the Etgar mosque, was not mentioned by the Chinese media.

♦ CHINA'S ISLAMIC GAMBLE

Since the mid-1980s, and particularly since the suppression of the democracy movement in Beijing in June of 1989 and the consequent condemnation by Western countries, China has attempted to make its relationship with Muslim states, especially Iran, Saudi Arabia, and Pakistan, and with international Islamic organizations, such as the Islamic Development Bank, even closer. This policy may be a massive gamble. If it is to succeed, the Chinese government must convince the Islamic world that Muslims in China are free to worship and to live as Muslims, and there is therefore pressure to grant a degree of real autonomy to Muslim communities in China. So far, this public relations exercise has had some success. A visiting delegation of the Muslim World League in 1984 pronounced itself well satisfied with the piety of Chinese Muslims and their freedom to worship, and diplomats from Muslim countries are regular attendees at Beijing's mosques.

The problem for the Chinese authorities is their ambivalence about the loyalty of Muslims to China. Muslim communities within the boundaries of present-day China, especially the Uyghurs, have a history of secessionist movements. Any suggestion of secession is anathema to the leadership in Zhongnanhai, China's Kremlin, which regards the integrity of Chinese territory defined by the limits established in the eighteenth century as inviolable. Tibetan demands for autonomy are the best-known example of what Beijing terms "ethnic separatism," but it is also a major political concern in Xinjiang.

For China's leadership there is particular danger in encouraging or permitting the expansion of Islam among Turkic-speaking ethnic groups such as the Uyghurs, Kazakhs and Kyrgyz. Islam is an essential component of their ethnic identity and distinguishes them from the majority Han Chinese population. Links with other members of the same ethnic groups in former Soviet Central Asia and in Afghanistan are likely to encourage ethnic and national consciousness.

The other group of Muslims, the Hui, are considered to be more loyal to China than Turkic-speaking Muslims and less likely to attempt to secede. This may be wishful thinking as the Hui rose in the 1860s and 1930s against Han Chinese domination and have played a leading role in demonstrations against the Han in Xinjiang. Religious activity is discouraged less in Gansu and Ningxia than in Xinjiang because the Chinese authorities are less concerned about possible Hui secessionist activity.

Northwest China is aggressively marketing itself abroad in an attempt to bridge the immense gap between the standard of living of the interior and that of the coastal regions. People in Ningxia, Gansu, Qinghai,

Xinjiang, and, to a lesser extent, in Shaanxi, are conscious of being remote from the centers of power and the decision-making process and of the lack of opportunities for travel, academic exchange, and trading opportunities compared with their counterparts in what they term the "coastal regions." Because it is less easy to attract European, Japanese, or American investment to the region than to the now prospering southeast, the five northwestern provincial governments are looking directly to both the Middle East and the Central Asian republics for trade and investment. There has been a move to have Ningxia, the Hui heartland, declared an Islamic Special Economic Zone, and several books published within the last few years have promoted the development of economic relations with mainland Asia to the west. One of them, published in Urumqi, has the title *Head for the Middle East*.

Xinjiang has a pivotal role to play in this development, if only because of its geographical location on China's north west frontier. Border trade is now at an unprecedentedly high level. Urumqi has a trading area used exclusively by Russian traders, and thousands of Chinese entrepreneurs are moving into former Soviet Central Asia in search of business opportunities.

The question, that must be in the minds of China's leaders, is how far they can exploit Islamic sentiment for trade and investment without encouraging Uyghur and Hui identity to the point where they may have to concede genuine political autonomy. Beijing has already had to concede a degree of economic autonomy to the powerhouse Shenzhen Special Economic Zone in Guangdong province. With unrest in Tajikistan and some other Central Asian republics threatening to spill over into Xinjiang, and emigre and internal independence movements looking for political opportunities to promote their causes, the authorities in Zhongnanhai will be hoping that speedy economic growth and new prosperity for the northwestern regions will buy off demands for independence or autonomy. The history of

the region suggests that religious and political activity is likely to follow the new trade routes. The Muslim revivalist movements and Sufism came to China by this route. Beijing may then be faced with new political challenges from its Muslim subjects with no obvious way of responding without risking the perceived integrity of China.

Michael Dillion

References

Broomhall, Marshall. *Islam in China: A Neglected Problem*. London: Darf, 1910.

China's Minority Nationalities. Edited by Ma Yin. Beijing: Foreign Languages Press, 1989.

Chu, Wen-djang. *The Moslem Rebellion in Northwest China 1862–1878*. The Hague, Netherlands: Mouton, 1966.

The Crescent in the East: Islam in Asia Major. Edited by Raphael Israeli. London: Curzon, 1982.

Dreyer, June Teufel. *China's Forty Millions: Minority Nationalities and National Integration in the People's Republic of China*. Cambridge: Harvard University Press, 1976.

Forbes, Andrew D.W. *Warlords and Muslims in Chinese Central Asia*. Cambridge: Cambridge University Press, 1986.

Gladney, Dru C. *Muslim Chinese: Ethnic Nationalism in the People's Republic*. Cambridge: Council on East Asian Studies, Harvard University Press, 1991.

Israeli, Raphael. *Muslims in China: A Study in Cultural Confrontation*. London: Curzon, 1980.

Pillsbury, Barbara L.K. "The Muslim Population of China: Clarifying the Questions of Size and Ethnicity." *Journal of the Institute of Muslim Minority Affairs* 3:2 (1981), 35–58.

———. "Muslim Population in China According to the 1982 Census." *Journal of the Institute of Muslim Minority Affairs* 5:1 (1983), 231–233.

———. "Muslim History in China: a 1300–Year Chronology." *Journal of the Institute of Muslim Minority Affairs* 3:2 (1981), 10-29.

9

Islam in Spain and Western Europe

♦ Muslims in Early Spain ♦ The Tayfa Period ♦ The *Murabitun*
♦ Christian conquest of Muslim Spain ♦ Intellectual and Cultural Life in al-Andalus

Though there have been other areas of what is now western Europe which were under Islamic rule for lengthy periods in the Middle Ages (such as Sicily), al-Andalus, the Arabic name for Islamic Spain, was by far the most important such area. Significant portions of the Iberian Peninsula were ruled by Muslims for nearly 800 years. During those many centuries, a strikingly creative and remarkably diverse civilization flourished in Islamic Spain. Yet, al-Andalus was unique among the regions of the Islamic world conquered in the first dramatic century of the expansion of Islam, for it was the only such area which was eventually lost to Islamic rule and settlement. Ironically, the very ethnic and religious diversity of al-Andalus which contributed in no small measure to its cultural creativity weakened al-Andalus politically, making it unable to defend itself against the expanding Europe of the High and Later Middle Ages.

♦ MUSLIMS IN EARLY SPAIN

On the eve of the Muslims conquest of the Iberian Peninsula in the early eighth century, that land was suffering under the unstable rule of a series of Christian kings. Having never adopted the principle of hereditary succession, the Visigothic nobility that had ruled over the largely Roman population since their invasion of the peninsula in late Antiquity, quarreled endlessly among themselves over who should be king. These divisions among the nobility, together with the disaffection of the peninsula's large Jewish, population whom the Visigoths had persecuted through harshly restrictive anti-Jewish legislation, rendered the peninsula helpless before the Muslim invasion. When the Berber Muslim governor of Tangier, Tariq ibn Ziyad, crossed

the Straits of Gibraltar in 711 with 7000 men, therefore, he was able to defeat the last embattled King of Visigothic Spain in short order near present-day Medina Sidonia. Soon after, he conquered other key Iberian cities: Cordoba, Guadalajara, and Toledo. In the following year, Taiq's superior, Musa ibn Nusayr, the Umayyad governor of North Africa, took direct control of these military operations in Spain, entering the peninsula at the head of 18,000 Arab and Berber soldiers. He, and his son after him, went on to conquer virtually all the rest of the Iberian peninsula by 716. Al-Andalus (the term referred from then on only to the portions of Spain under Islamic rule) was governed from that year until 756 by a lengthy series of Arab governors theoretically appointed by the Umayyad caliphs in Damascus. In reality the previous quarrels between Visigothic nobles now gave way to similar quarrels between Arab tribes over who would assume this governorship.

Thorough political unity came to al-Andalus only after the one of the few surviving members of the ousted Umayyad caliphal family, Abd al-Rahman ibn Muawiyah (died 788) fled to Spain, overthrew the previous governor, and established himself as the independent governor of al-Andalus in 756, insuring thereby that the peninsula never came under direct Abbaaid control. He and his Umayyad successors would rule Spain until 1031, the first four members of this dynasty alone ruling for nearly one hundred years. Abd al-Rahman energetically solidified Umayyad control of al-Andalus, dividing it into provinces each headed by a hand-picked governor. He likewise established a standing professional army staffed largely, like many armies elsewhere in the Islamic world, by slaves recruited from non-Muslim Europe and raised as Muslims and eventually manumitted to serve in military and government.

This mercenary army played a crucial role in the relative success of the first Umayyads in imposing unity on the heavily divided society of al-Andalus. The divisive tribal rivalries of the pre-Umayyad period now gave way before conflicts between the original Arab invaders and later immigrants, especially the Syrian warriors who settled in al-Andalus and were granted fiefs in the 740s. The thousands of mercenary slaves (known in al-Andalus as *Saqalib*, or Slavs, since many were of Slavic origin) eventually evolved into a distinct ethnic group which, especially later, would also threaten the unity of al-Andalus. The much larger population of Berber Muslims, who took up an agricultural life upon settling in Spain, and the ever-increasing number of native Christian and Jewish converts to Islam (known as the *muwalladun*), both frequently clashed with the other Muslim groups. All the while, there remained a large, but slowly shrinking population of Christians and Jews. Though scholars still do not agree on the rate of conversion of the Christian population of al-Andalus to Islam, it is very likely that, just as in some other areas of the Islamic world, as many as two centuries may have passed before the majority of the population of the peninsula were Muslims. This very large community of Christians, like the sizable minority of Jews, had been granted the same protected religious minority (*dhimmi*) status as Christians and Jews elsewhere in Islamic lands. As "People of the Book," they were allowed a substantial amount of autonomy, the Christians in their local communities governing their affairs with their own judges according to a compilation of Visigothic law, the Jews being subject to the Rabbical law of the Talmud. The head of each Christian and Jewish community (usually given the Latin title of comes, or count) was responsible to the Muslim rulers for paying the special taxes owed by those of the *dhimmi* status, and for preserving order within the community.

Though Abd al-Rahman and his immediate Umayyad successors had to fight off a variety of external enemies—the Carolingian Franks in northeastern Iberia, independent Christian rulers in tiny enclaves in north-central Iberia, and raiding Norsemen who extended their attacks on ninth-century Christian Europe to contemporary Muslim al-Andalus—domestic uprisings emerging out of this ethnic diversity of al-Andalus most seriously threatened their rule of the peninsula. The Muslim governors of the regions bordering on the Christian north (usually known as Marches in English, but referred to in Arabic as *al-thughur*, "the teeth") were regularly granted more autonomy by the Umayyad governors so as to be ale to effectively and quickly defend al-Andalus from Christian invaders or raiders. But very often their limited autonomy developed into practical independence, and the Umayyad rulers were forced to put down rebellions fomented by them. More serious still were rebellions lead by largely independent local leaders in the heartlands of al-Andalus. The most dangerous of these was Umar ibn Hafsun, a warlord based in Bobastro in the mountains of southeastern Spain. Between 879 and 928 he and his sons battled regularly and often very successfully against the Umayyad rulers, at one point nearly conquering Cordoba, the Umayyad capital. Ibn Hafsun's rebellious movement reflected the ethnic and religious cleavages of the peninsula in a complicated way. As a *muwallad*, he originally seems to have had considerable support from the sizeable *muwallad* community of al-Andalus as well as from the unconverted Christians of the peninsula. He and his movement, therefore, may represent the same sort of *shuubite*, or non-Arab Muslim unrest, as developed in areas such as Persia. Moreover, Ibn Hafsun is thought to have converted to Christianity in 900, his movement metamorphosing into a more purely native-Christian rebellion against Muslim rule.

These internal and external threats gravely weakened Umayyad control in the latter part of the ninth century, and were only nullified by the military and political leadership of Abd al-Rahman III (912–961), perhaps the greatest Umayyad ruler of al-Andalus. Having stamped out the last embers of the long-smoldering rebellion of Ibn Hafsun and his followers, he once again subjected the Marches to obedience to the Umayyads by about 940. At the same time he managed to halt the frequent raids into Islamic territory by the rulers of the tiny independent Christian principalities to the north, and then to subject them to tributary status by 960. He and his immediate successors also successfully held in check the expansionist designs of the Fatimid rulers based in the early tenth century in Tunisia. Internally, Abd al-Rahman III directed his attention to developing an efficient and highly centralized administration with himself at the center ruling as an autocrat from Cordoba. As governor (and later caliph), he was directly responsible for governing al-Andalus, and was commander-in-chief of the army, and he possessed the power of life or death at his will. Beneath him was a fairly complex administrative machine headed by an official called the *hajib* (chamberlain) who, as a sort of chief minister to the governor, directed the central military and political administration. Beneath the *hajib* were a varying number of *wazirs* in charge of specific administrative departments. A similar administrative structure developed in each province (*kurah*) under a provincial governor (*wali*) appointed directly by the Umayyad ruler.

Having achieved peace and stability domestically,

and having successfully beat back the various enemies of al-Andalus, Abd al-Rahman III proclaimed himself caliph in 929 and assumed the title of Commander of the Faithful, thereby asserting the full independence of al-Andalus from the Abbasid caliphs in Baghdad and the newly independent Fatimid caliphs in Egypt. From then until 1031, therefore, he and his descendents ruled a wholly independent Umayyad caliphate in al-Andalus.

♦ THE TAYFA PERIOD

But the rule of the Umayyads of the late part of the tenth century was not as effective as Abd al-Rahman III's. During the reign of Hisham II (976–1013), who became caliph at the age of eleven, a series of *hajibs* usurped most of the authority and dignity of the caliph, leaving Hisham II in power largely as a figure-head. The most famous of these usurping *hajibs*, a man of old ancestory known as al-Mansur, governed al-Andalus from 978–1002. As a particular energetic general, he managed to perpetuate and even extend the dominance of al-Andalus over the Northern Christian kingdoms. But after his period of rule and that of his son which ended in 1008, al-Andalus plunged into a time of dismaying chaos, as one military strong man after another usurped governing authority. Eventually in 1031, the caliphate was officially abolished after a series of powerless caliphs had been dragged in and out of office in the years since 1008. Not surprisingly, as the central government collapsed, regional leaders in al-Andalus began to assert their independence from Cordoba, and after the abolition of the caliphate, they emerged as fully independent principalities, usually known as the Tayfah Kingdoms (*tayfa* means 'party' or 'faction' in Arabic). There were some twenty of these kingdoms in existence at various times, and they fought endlessly with each other. In general they were ruled by families drawn from one of the three important Muslim ethnic groups of this period: Berber dynasties tended to flourish in the south, especially in Malaga and Granada; Andalus families (Muslims of mixed Arab and *muwallad* stock) dominated the Tayfa kingdoms in central al-Andalus, especially in Seville and Cordoba; Slav dynasties took control of many cities along the east coast of Spain. Each Tayfa kingdom had its own court in its own capital. These courts generally were miniature versions of the former Umayyad court in Cordoba, each with its own administrative structure, palaces, and army. As would be expected, this collapse of centralized rule into a collection of rival principalities representative of the continuing ethnic divisions of al-Andalus presented the Christian kingdoms in the north with a splendid opportunity to expand their own realms. They quickly began forcing Tayfa kingdoms to pay tribute, and then began to conquer the weakest of

them: Toledo, the ancient capital of Visigothic Spain and capital of one of the Tayfahs, fell to Alfonso VI of Castile in 1085; the city of Valencia fell to the Christian warrior and adventurer El Cid Rodrigo Diaz de Vivar in 1081.

♦ THE *MURABITUN*

The so-called Tayfah period, which began in 1031 with the abolition of the caliphate, endured for almost sixty years, until soon after the fall of Toledo, when various Tayfa kings turned to a growing North African power to help defend themselves from the attacks of the Christian rulers. Since the middle of the century a political-religious movement known in Arabic as the *Murabitun*, and in English as the Almoravids, had been gradually emerging as the dominant force in western North Africa. This movement, which stressed both careful adherence to Islamic law and reform of society along Islamic lines, had conquered much of western North Africa by the 1070s. At the request of the beleaguered rulers of al-Andalus, they crossed the straits of Gibraltar into al-Andalus for the first time in 1086 and established themselves as the rulers of a reunified al-Andalus by the early 1090s, Islamic Spain becoming, therefore, an appendage of their North African empire. By the turn of the century, they had reconquered many areas, such as Valencia, which had fallen to Christian rule during the Tayfa Period. Toledo, however, remained under the control of the kings of Castile. Though the Almoravids had the support particularly of the religious leadership of al-Andalus, they were not able to create a very stable government in the Iberian peninsula. By the second decade of the twelfth century, centralized Almoravid rule in al-Andalus began in its turn to break down, and Almoravid generals ceased to be able to defend Islamic lands from renewed attacks from the north. The king of Christian Aragon, Alfonso I, conquered Saragossa in 1118, for example, and both he and other Christian leaders launched extensive raids into al-Andalus in the following decades. By about 1145, Almoravid rule in al-Andalus had virtually ceased, and Islamic Spain fractured once again into what is sometimes referred to as a second Tayfa period.

By this time, however, the Almoravid empire in North Africa had likewise collapsed in the face of another political-religious movement founded by a North African visionary named Ibn Tumart (died 1130). This movement was known in Arabic as the *Muwahhidun* (the believers in God's absolute unity) and is normally referred to in English as the Almohads. As the name suggests, this movement particularly stressed the thorough monotheism, so central to Islam, but did so in a way that involved an intriguing mixture of philosophical rationalism and religious legalism. By the late

1140s, they had destroyed Almoravid power in North Africa, and went on to gain complete control of al-Andalus in stages by 1172. They were able to effectively rule al-Andalus longer than the Almoravids. In a stunning defeat of the army of the king of Castile in 1195, the Almohads even indicated that they were on the point of reversing the twelfth-century Christian advances. For whatever reason, however, this great victory was never followed up, allowing the Christian rulers to rebuild and fight another day. That day came in July 1212 when the combined armies of the Christian kingdoms of Leon, Castile, Navarre, and Aragon destroyed the Almohad armies and drastically weakened al-Andalus.

♦ CHRISTIAN CONQUEST OF MUSLIM SPAIN

In the four following decades, the Christian rulers of Portugal, Castile, and Aragon—kingdoms that had once been insignificant Christian enclaves on the borders of Islamic al-Andalus—were able to conquer all that remained of Islamic Spain except a small principality in the southeastern corner of the peninsula called Granada. Here an Andalusi Muslim leader named Muhammad ibn Yusuf ibn Nasr, established himself as

king in 1235 and installed his family as the ruling Nasrid dynasty. Partly because he had previously become a vassal of the king of Castile in order to save himself—thereby making his Kingdom of Granada a vassal state, and not technically an enemy, of Castile—partly because of Granada's naturally defensible mountain borders, and partly because of Castile's preoccupation with other foreign-policy concerns, Granada was able to endure a Muslim kingdom in a now thoroughly Christian-ruled peninsula until 1492. In that year, however, Ferninand and Isabella, the king and queen respectively of Aragon and Castile, whose marriage united the peninsula into the Spain of the modern world, conquered Granada and integrated it into their realms.

Al-Andalus thereby ceased to exist, as the peninsula, after more than 700 years, ceased to be ruled even in part by Muslims. This did not, however, mean that Muslims no longer inhabited the land that had once been one of the jewels of the Islamic world. Ever since the Christian kingdoms had first begun making substantial conquests of Muslim territories in the late eleventh century, ever larger numbers of Arabic-speaking Muslims had become subjects of Christian kings, who normally encouraged these Muslims to submit to their rule and contribute to the economic stability of

Zafra House, Granada, Spain. A restored Andalusian Building.

their realms. In some areas of Christian Spain such as Valencia, such Muslims, usually known as *mudejars* (apparently from the Arabic *mudajjan*, 'one allowed to remain behind'), formed by far the majority of the population long after the Christian conquest of these areas. Typically the wealthy and learned Muslims chose to immigrate to Muslim-ruled areas such as North Africa, so that the large *Mudejar* communities were often deprived of their natural leaders. Nevertheless, even as late as the fifteenth century, Muslim scholars of a modest degree of religious learning could be found providing guidance and continuity to the lives of Muslim subjects of the king of Aragon. These Muslims lived within the Spanish Christian kingdoms under a set of regulations that in many ways resembled the *dhimmah* system which governed how Christians and Jews lived within Islamic countries: the *Mudejars* were allowed to continue practicing their Islamic religion; they were allowed to govern the internal affairs of their communities on the basis of Islamic law; they were forbidden to proselytize among the Christians, but were often encouraged to convert themselves; Muslim men were forbidden from marrying (or having any sexual relations with) Christian women, though Christian men could marry (and carry on affairs with) Muslim women; *Mudejars* were subject to special and often specially burdensome taxes; they were theoretically (though rarely burdensome in actuality) required to wear distinctive clothing to indicate their infidelity.

In the early sixteenth century, however, after having expelled the very large Jewish population of the peninsula, the kings of Spain forcibly converted their still large *Mudejar* population to Christianity, though the great majority only converted outwardly, continuing to practice their Islamic religion in private. This enormous group of nominal Christians came to be known as *Moriscos*, and they formed a still highly Islamic sector of Spanish society for about another one hundred years. Though they were generally very productive agricultural laborers or skilled craftsmen, they too became troublesome to the rulers of Spain because of their unwillingness to completely assimilate, and in 1609 and 1620, they, like the Jews before them, were expelled from Spain. Some 275,000 Moriscos left their home of nearly nine centuries and settled en masse in North Africa. Though many Spaniards of Muslim ancestory remained on Christian soil, the expulsion of the Moriscos in the early seventeenth century represents the end of any sort of truly Islamic presence in the peninsula until the current century.

♦ INTELLECTUAL AND CULTURAL LIFE IN AL-ANDALUS

The Islamic civilization of al-Andalus, as might be expected of such a peripheral region, tended originally to be heavily reliant on the models provided by thinkers, writers, artists, and musicians from the heartlands of Islam. Nevertheless, al-Andalus—and especially its great cities of Cordoba and Seville—eventually became the center of a great civilization, a civilization that was particularly fructified by non-Arab, non-Muslim influences. Therefore, though in the early Middle ages Andalusi scholars had typically travelled to the East to finish their education by studying with the great Egyptian, Arabian, and Iraqi masters, by the Tayfah period and later, we find great Andalusi figures such as Ibn Arabi and Moses Maimonides, exercising a profound influence on the rest of the Arab-Islamic world.

Al-Andalus was thoroughly Sunni in its religious beliefs, though certain Shia ideas played an important role particularly in the Almohad movement (Ibn Tumart proclaimed himself to be the Mahdi). Like North Africa, al-Andalus was intellectually dominated by a nearly universal adherence to only one of the four so-called orthodox schools of Islamic law, in this case, the Maliki rite, which reflected the religious practices of the early Muslims of Medina. This overwhelmingly Maliki cast to Andalusi civilization meant that originally scholarly activities in the peninsula focused on the interpretation of the elaborate Maliki legal commentaries, more than on the other typically Islamic religious disciplines such as Quranic exigesis, Hadith criticism, or speculative theology. Nevertheless, the political decentralization of al-Andalus in the Tayfa period, together with the importation of certain extra-peninsular ideas in the Almoravid and Almohad periods led to a diversification of the Andalusi intellectual milieu. *Kalam*, or Islamic speculative theology, for example, gained a new and important prominence in twelfth-century al-Andalus in part because of the Almohad domination of the peninsula politically: Ibn Tumart's eclectic religious thought was heavily influenced by the *Kalam* and his regime tended to foster it. Likewise the study of pure philosophy, which had been only a minor pursuit in the earlier period, reached a level of considerable prominence in the Tayfa period and after, when such Andalusi thinkers such as Ibn Tufayl (died 1185) and Ibn Rushd (died 1198) wrote some of the greatest philosophical works of Islamic history, the latter exercising an immense influence in medieval Christendom through the medium of Latin translations of his commentaries on the works of Aristotle.

Despite its nearly universal adherence to Sunni Islam as interpreted by Maliki legal scholars, the greatest minds of al-Andalus were very often unusually original in their view and approaches. The two philosophers just mentioned qualify here, but perhaps even more notable are the great Cordoban polymath

Ibn Hazm (994–1064) and the brilliant speculative mystic Ibn al-Arabi (1165–1240). A man of both great intellectual originality and unbending conviction, Ibn Hazm was a rare partisan of the Zahiri school of legal jurisprudence, which insisted that the only sources of Islamic law were the Quran and *hadith* interpreted with extreme literalness. But in the hands of Ibn Hazm, these Zahiri doctrines did not just have legal application; he expanded these literalist ideas into a universal theory of language that informed all his thought, and his thought was wide-ranging indeed. In dozens of volumes he wrote not only on Islamic law in the strict sense, but also on logic, the origins of law, theology, religious psychology, and ethics. His two most famous works reflect his great range particularly well. His *Dove's Necklace* is an anthology of love poems heavily influenced by Platonic ideas and exemplifying well his psychological insight; his massive polemical encyclopedia of religions, *The Definitive Study on Sects, Hetereodoxies, and Religious Groups* describes and refutes at great length, and with considerable accuracy and erudition, all the religious persuasions known to him—he spends hundreds of pages in analyzing and refuting the Jewish and Christian scriptures alone. Ibn al-Arabi similarly embraced the Zahiri rite in legal matters, and therefore showed himself to be well outside the main stream of the Andalusi intellectual milieu. But his originality did not end there, for his great contribution was in mystical thought where he was the culmination of a long line of great Andalusi mystics. He developed a vast and complicated system of esoteric interpretation of scripture (a striking counterpoise to his professed Zahirism) and theosophy, rooted in a monistic view of creation, and emphasizing knowledge of God's Beautiful Names as a means of spiritual ascent. Like Ibn Hazm, Ibn al-Arabi's output was massive, and his works have been read widely ever since his death throughout the Islamic world by both partisans of his exotic ideas and countless opponents concerned to stamp out what they saw as his corrosive influence.

The same early reliance on eastern models followed by bold innovatativeness characterizes Andalusi poetry and literature. Ibn Zaydun (1003–70), generally reckoned the greatest of Andalusi poets, wrote masterfully within the well-established conventions of Arabic poetry. But during his lifetime, there emerged an anonymous Andalusi poetic form, the *muwashshah*. In its most typical form, the *muwashshah* consisted of five or more stanzas with an initial and usually repeated couplet. A repeated final couplet, called a *kharja* was normally added to the end of the poem, this last element usually written in the vernacular and very often in a Romance dialect (most Andalusis, Muslim or otherwise, spoke a Romance dialect as well as Arabic), and placed generally in the mouth of a woman. Andalusi po-

Alhambra Column, Spain

ets also eventually developed a completely vernacular variety of the *muwashshah* known as the *zajal*, and another of the great poets of al-Andalus, Ibn Quzman (died 1160 or 1169), won himself considerable renown for his compositions in this vernacular form. Likewise Andalusi prose writers began imitating the *maqamas*, or short stories, of eastern writers during the course of the eleventh century, but eventually they began to take this form in new directions. Abu-Amir ibn Shuhayd (died 1035), for example, composed an amusing and unique account of a journey into the supernatural world where he meets the *jinn* who inspire poets. Later Andalusi men of letters, such as Lisan al-Din ibn al-Khatib (1313-74), while generally reckoned less innovative, continued to write with great mastery in both the *muwashshah* (which eventually became popular outside al-Andalus) and the *maqama* as well as other Arabic poetic and prose forms.

From the very beginning, the art and architecture of al-Andalus were in many ways an intriguing combination of western and eastern themes and motifs. The tenth-century Great Mosque of Cordoba, for example, was modeled in part on eastern, Umayyad architecture, but its characteristically Andalusi horse-shoe arch was borrowed from Visigothic architecture. This hybrid tradition continued throughout the history of al-Andalus, and was even exported to North Africa during the Almoravid period.

The fact that Ibn Hazm was the descendent of converted Christians, that both Muslims and non-Muslims composed in the *muwashshah* form with its frequently Romance concluding couplet, and that Andalusi architecture adopted and adapted the Visigothic horse-shoe arch is indicative of the synthesis of non-Muslim, non-Arab influences in Andalusi civilization. However, the cultural significance of the ethnic and religious pluralism of al-Andalus—the very feature that helped weaken it in the face of Christian expansion-deserves still further comment. For the civilization of al-Andalus, just as that of contemporaneous Egypt, Syria, and Iraq, was not by any means exclusively Muslim. Jewish poets produced some of the greatest Hebrew poetry of all times in al-Andalus, some of it in the *muwashshah* formed borrowed from Arabic. Jehuda ha-Levi (1075–1141), for example, produced poems revered to this day in both Hebrew and Arabic, but was also a philosopher of considerable note, remembered especially for his defense of Judaism against the dangers of Aristotelian philosophy. Like ha-Levi, the Talmudist and philosopher Moses Maimonides (1135–1204), who was born in Cordoba and died in Egypt, wrote in both Hebrew and Arabic; his great philosophical summa, *The Guide for the Perplexed*, is considered one of the greatest works of the Arabic-Aristotelian tradition. This cultural prominence of Jews in the civilization of al-Andalus was accompanied by a surprising Jewish prominence in the political affairs of that land. Hasdai ibn Shaprut (915 circa 970) acted as court physician, administrator, and diplomat for Abd al-Rahman III; Samuel ibn Naghrila (circa 993–1056) was the chief minister and general of the armies of the Tayfah kingdom of Granada, in addition to being a fine Hebrew and Arabic poet. Surprisingly, the Christians of Islamic Spain, who by the ninth century at least had become Arabic–speakers, played a much less important role than the Jews, though the Jewish population was undoubtedly smaller. Nevertheless, the Christian Hafs ibn Albar (flourished circa 890) translated Latin psalms into a standard Arabic poetic form, while later Arabicized Christians studied Arabic philosophy and developed a Christianized form of Arabic speculative theology based on Islamic models.

While the political rulers of al-Andalus never fully overcame the ethnic and religious pluralism of the peninsula, this very multiculturalism contributed to the civilization of al-Andalus much of what is most distinctive about it. Moreover, just as Muslims lived on in Spain after Muslim rule had come to an end, so also the culture of al-Andalus lived on in various ways in Spain

and the Americas after al-Andalus was no more. The so-called Mudejar architecture, a hybrid style produced by both Mudejar and Andalusi-influenced Christian artisans, became the standard secular and ecclesiastical architecture of many parts of later medieval Spain, especially Castile. The *Mudejars* and *Moriscos* living within Christian Spain produced a distinctively Islamic literature in the Romance dialect but written in Arabic characters (the so-called *Aljamiado* literature). The Romance dialects of Spain borrowed thousands of Arabic words which live on to this day on the tongues of Spanish speakers. Indeed, the contemporary Spanish-speaker, wherever he lives, reflects the great influence of Andalusi civilization on Spanish culture every time he or she utters a wish. In the Spanish idiom, such a statement begins with the word *Ojalá*, which is merely the Castilian corruption of the familiar Arabic phrase which still roles easily off the Arabic tongue: *In shaa Allah*, "If God wills . . ."

Thomas Burman

References

Ashtor, E. *The Jews of Moslem Spain*. 2 vols., trans. A. Klein and J. Macholowitz Klein. Philadelphia: Jewish Publication Society of America, 1973-79.

Boswell, J. *The Royal Treasure: Muslim Communities under the Crown of Aragon in the Fourteenth Century*. New Haven: Yale University Press, 1977.

Burman, T. *Religious Polemic and the Intellectual History of the Mozarabs, 1050–1200*. Leiden: E.J. Brill, 1994.

Burns, R. *Islam Under the Crusaders: Colonial Survival in the Thirteenth-Century Kingdom of Aragon*. Princeton: Princeton University Press, 1973.

Crusader Kingdom of Valencia: Reconstruction of a Thirteenth-Century Frontier, Cambridge, MA: Harvard University Press, 1967.

Chejne, A. *Muslim Spain*. Minneapolis: University of Minnesota Press, 1974.

Colbert, E. *The Martyrs of Cordoba (850–59): A Study of the Sources*. Washington, D.C.: Catholic University of America Press, 1962.

Collins, R. *Early Medieval Spain: Unity in Diversity, 400–1000*. New York: St. Martins Press, 1983.

id. *The Arab conquest of Spain, 710–797*. Oxford: B. Blackwell, 1989.

Glick, Thomas. *Islamic and Christian Spain in the Early Middle Ages: Comparative Perspective on Social and Cultural Formation*. Princeton: Princeton University Press, 1979.

Jayyusi, S. *The Legacy of Muslim Spain*. Leiden: E. J. Brill, 1992.

Menocal, M. *The Arabic Role in Medieval Literary History: A Forgotten Heritage*. Philadelphia: University of Pennsylvania Press, 1987.

Monroe, J. *Hispano-Arabic Poetry: A Student Anthology*. Berkely: University of California Press, 1974.

Meyerson, M. *The Muslims of Valencia in the Age of Fernando and Isabel.* Berkeley: University of California Press, 1991.

O'Callaghan, J.F. *A History of Medieval Spain.* Ithaca: Cornell University Press, 1975.

Wasserstein, D. *The Rise and Fall of the Party-Kings: Politics and Society in Islamic Spain, 1002–1086.* Princeton: Princeton University Press, 1985.

Watt, W. M. *A History of Islamic Spain.* Edinburgh: Edinburgh University Press, 1965.

Wolf, K. *Christian Martyrs in Muslim Spain.* Cambridge: Cambridge University Press, 1988.

10

Islam in North Africa and the Mediterranean

♦ Islamization and the Berber Population ♦ Political Fragmentation—Ibn Khaldun's Maghrib
♦ Foreign Incursions and Sharifian Resurgence ♦ Ottoman Power and Local Autonomy
♦ Alawid Dynasty in Morocco ♦ Islam and the West in the Modern Age
♦ Nationalism, Independence, and Resurgent Islam

♦ ISLAMIZATION AND THE BERBER POPULATION

Muslim expansion into North Africa and the Mediterranean basin dates from the first decades of Islam. In 640 the armies crossed the Suez into Egypt, and between 642 and 643 Cyrenaica (eastern Libya) and Tripoli were conquered. Raids continued westward, and over the next few decades the Maghrib (literally, place of sunset) was conquered. These military raids were led by Uqba ibn Nafi who founded the town of Qayrawan in Ifriqiyya (today's Tunisia) in 670. Qayrawan grew to be a major center of the Islamic Maghrib, and the eighth-century Uqba ibn Nafi mosque still stands today as a symbol of the early Muslim conquest.

The Arab conquest of North Africa, although relatively rapid, met with resistance by the indigenous population, the Berbers, the name used to refer to the inhabitants stretching from western Egypt to Morocco since ancient times. Little evidence exists concerning this resistance, but legends about the fierce fighting of Berber chiefs remain. In western Algeria and Morocco a Berber chief named Kusayla led a confederation of allegedly Christianized tribesmen against the invading armies. In the Aurès Mountains of Algeria, stories of the Berber Jewish "priestess" al-Kahina, the leader of the resistance in eastern Algeria, have been part of the folklore since medieval times.

While the historicity of these legends and the religious adherence of al-Kahina and her followers remain shrouded in mystery, the preservation of these traditions underlines the continued importance of Berber identity in the Maghrib. Of obscure origins, the Berbers seem to have originally migrated across North Africa from Asia. The linguistic origins of the Berber language, divided into a number of regional dialects, also is unknown. The Berbers believe that they belong to three major tribes: the Sanhaja, Zanata, and Masmuda. In the first centuries after the rise of Christianity, under the successive rule of Romans, Vandals, and Byzantines, the Maghrib witnessed intense missionary activity. Judaism and Christianity seem to have made some inroads into Berber society, but, with the Arab expansion, Islam predominated. Many Berber tribesmen joined in the conquests, benefiting from their participation in the Arab victories. The Berbers were probably the predominant element in the conquest of Spain, which began in 711, led by Tariq ibn Ziyad. It was advantageous for the Berbers to join the religion of the Muslim rulers and to avoid having a minority status. Berbers were regarded as pagans and therefore not entitled to the status of "protected person" (*dhimmi*) as were Christians and Jews. Perhaps the most important reason for the Islamization of the indigenous population was the compatibility of Islam with the Berber society. Among the pre-Islamic Berber tribes, an important role was played by holy men through their tribal lineages. Islam served to consolidate their roles as intercessors in a society that in many regions remained mainly nomadic.

Islamization of the Maghrib, however, did not simply mean the replacement of local with Arab Muslim customs. For many centuries, most Berbers retained their language and culture. Pre-Islamic customs were absorbed and infused with Islamic meaning. After be-

A mosque in North Africa.

fifteenth centuries, migrations of Arab tribes from the Arabian peninsula, known as the Banu Hilal, Banu Sulaym, and Maqil, further Arabized the Maghrib. The extent of the destruction that these marauding Arab nomads wrought, especially the Banu Hilal, has been debated (historians often refer to these raids as the "Hilalian invasion"), but the enduring effect was the further Arabization of the countryside. This was especially apparent in Ifriqiya, evidenced by the fact that today only a very minute percentage of the population is Berber-speaking (for example, on the island of Jerba to the south). In Morocco, at least until relatively recently, nearly half the population has been Berber-speaking, with three principal dialects: Tashelhit in the High Atlas and Sous valleys, Tamazight in the Middle Atlas, and Rif Berber in the mountains to the north. In Algeria Berbers are still dominant in the western Kabylia (a French term derived from the Arabic *qabil*, meaning tribe), the Aurès Mountains in eastern Algeria, and in Libya in the Jebel Nefusa. Although the Maghrib today is considered part of the Arab world, it has been the enduring influence of the Berber population that gave the Maghrib a cultural identity distinct from the Islamic lands to the east, the *Mashriq* (place of sunrise).

After Islam became well entrenched, the Maghrib

coming Muslims, the Berbers gradually began to reject the political domination of the ruling class that settled predominantly in the cites of the Maghrib. In the eighth century a separatist tendency emerged that repudiated the dynastic claims of both Sunni and Shia rulers, inspired by the idea that a Berber could become a caliph. As the caliphate became politically fragmented with the fall of the Umayyad dynasty of Damascus and the rise of the Abbasids in 750, a number of Kharijite states emerged in the Maghrib, most importantly the Rustimid dynasty centered in Algeria (776–910). Spain also broke away from the Abbasids and established an Umayyad state from a surviving member of the dynasty in 756. At the beginning of the ninth century, the Aghlabid dynasty was founded in Tunisia. In the ninth century Morocco established the Idrisid dynasty, founded by an Alawi *sharif* (a descendant of Ali from the Prophet Muhammad's family, regarded to be endowed with special honor). The Idrisids moved against the Kharijites, though not wholly successfully. The city of Fez dates from this period, and though the city and its surroundings became predominantly Arab, most of Morocco was still mainly Berber.

Gradually the Maghrib became more Arabized with the influx of Arab settlers. From the tenth through the

Kairouan Okra Mosque, Tunisia.

gave birth to a number of empires. In the beginning of the tenth century, the most powerful dynasty outside of the Abbasid caliphate arose in Tunisia ruled by the Fatimids. Of Shia Ismaili origin, the dynasty began in Mahdiyya in Tunisia, but then moved its capital to Egypt in 969 where the Fatimids remained for two centuries as one of the most flourishing states of the Islamic world.

In Morocco, the far west (*al-Maghrib al-Aqsa*) of North Africa, a Berber dynasty from the Sanhaja, known in Europe as the Almoravids (*al-Murabitun*), arose out of the southern Moroccan Sahara, established its capital in Marrakesh, and created a large empire. Literally, the name of the dynasty meant the "men of the *ribat* "(being the place where the faithful "bind themselves" together for the purpose of *jihad.*) Led by Yusuf ibn Tashfin, the Almoravids were responsible for further spreading Islamic teachings to the Berber inhabitants and consolidating the Malikite school of jurisprudence (*madhhab*) in Morocco. From the center of Islamic learning in Qayrawan, the Malikite school of Sunni Muslim law (more rigorous than in the Mashriq), had already become dominant in the Maghrib out of the four major schools in Sunnite Islam. Sponsored by the Almoravid dynasty, the Malikite jurisconsults (*fuqaha*) sought to combat both the heterodox doctrines of the

Kharijites and the speculative thinking of Muslim scholasticism prevalent in the Islamic world at that time. The Almoravids built an extensive empire in the western Sahara, Maghrib, and Spain. They also expanded their influence to the south, contributing to the further Islamization of West Africa, south of the Sahara.

The Almoravids were followed at the end of the twelfth century by the Almohads from the Masmuda Berbers who arose in the High Atlas Mountains and again made their capital in Marrakesh. Led by Ibn Tumart, who assumed the millenarian title of *mahdi* (the guided one), the Almohads further spread Islamic teachings through instruction in Masmuda Berber. The Almohads (from al-Muwahidun, "those who unify," from the doctrine of *tawhid*, the transcendent unity of Allah) espoused a puritanical reformism and rejected the authority of the Malikite scholars. In the areas under their control, all practices deemed immoral or inconsistent with their view of fundamental Islamic teachings were fanatically purged. Against the Quranic injunction that conversion should come only by persuasion, they forced Jews to convert to Islam (though the Jews survived the ordeal, which was apparently of short duration, and were, as was their right by Muslim belief and prophetic tradition, able to practice Judaism during all subsequent periods). The Almohads ex-

Sidi Bou Said, Tunisia.

tended their dynasty even further than the Almoravids, encompassing Spain to the North and Tunisia to the east, even reaching as far as Tripoli. They were unable, however, to maintain political control over a unified state, and in the mid-thirteenth century the Almohad empire collapsed. The reformist Almohad agenda did not survive, nor did Malikite influence diminish. But the Almohads were nonetheless significant in furthering the Islamization of the Maghrib as a whole.

♦ POLITICAL FRAGMENTATION—IBN KHALDUN'S MAGHRIB

Following the disintegration of the Almohad empire, three major dynasties arose in the Maghrib. The Hafsid dynasty in Tunisia claimed to be the successors to the Almohads. In Morocco, the Marinid dynasty arose out of a movement of Zanata Berbers. The Marinids based their capital in Fez, which they greatly beautified. In Algeria, wedged between the Hafsids and the Marinids, were the Zayyanids.

The fourteenth century was a period of political fragmentation, witnessed incisively by the great fourteenth-century historian Ibn Khaldun, born in Tunis in 1332 from an Arab Andalusian family. Ibn Khaldun became a courtier of the Hafsids and therefore had firsthand experience in government. He became embroiled in various court intrigues and, during his long career in government and later as a Malikite *qadi*, fell in and out of favor with a number of his royal protectors. For a period of time he served the Marinids in Fez, witnessing the declining power of this Moroccan dynasty. Later, he returned to the service of a Hafsid ruler and, ultimately, wound up in Egypt. He was sponsored by the Mamluk ruler Barquq and pursued a successful career in teaching, becoming the chief Malikite *qadi* for a period of time. He died in Egypt in 1406.

During a period of withdrawal from public life, Ibn Khaldun settled down in Qalat in the province of Oran. There he wrote his history of the world, completing his famous first book, or "Introduction" (*Muqaddimah*), in 1377. The *Muqaddimah* was intended to establish principles of history for all times but is most valuable as a political and sociological analysis of North African politics and society during this period. Ibn Khaldun lived at a time when he believed he was witness to the disintegration of civilization. He developed a cyclical notion of history, which seemed to correspond to the rise and fall of the Almoravids and Almohads. In Ibn Khaldun's cycle, dynasties, like people, have a life span ideally three generations or about 120 years. Ibn Khaldun considered these dynasties initially strong because their founders came from the purity of Bedouin life and the strength of the tribal group solidarity (*asabiya*). The tribes aspired for royal authority, and through the force

of religion, they were able to transform and establish dynastic rule. With the transition to sedentary culture and the growing wealth and prosperity of the dynasty came luxuries, more diverse professions, crafts, monuments, and other attributes of civilization. Although this initially brought strength to the dynasties, they were corrupted by luxuries and lost the purity of the desert life and its group solidarity that originally brought them to power. Consequently, a new dynasty invigorated by the purity and solidarity of the nonsedentary, tribal life established itself.

According to Ibn Khaldun, the dynasties of the Maghrib of the late fourteenth century must have seemed to be reaching their last, decadent stages, according to his paradigm. Political fragmentation, disputes between the different dynasties, reliance on foreign mercenaries, and the growing threat of European intervention threatened to undermine sovereignty in the Maghribi states. Already in the late thirteenth century, the Europeans were launching forays on the North African ports. In 1260 the Castillians attacked Salé, the Sicilians occupied Jerba from 1286 to 1335 and also Mahdiya, the Genoese attacked Ceuta, and in 1355, Tripoli. Aragon and Castille continued to harass the North African coast in the fourteenth century, and in 1401 Tetuan was sacked by the Castilians. In 1415 Ceuta was taken by the Portuguese. The town is still held by Spain today, a remaining vestige of the period of aggressive Iberian expansion against Islam.

♦ FOREIGN INCURSIONS AND SHARIFIAN RESURGENCE

As control of the Mediterranean was being contested between Islam and Christendom, the Maghrib increasingly appeared as a Spanish and Portuguese sphere of influence. The conflict over the Maghrib was also seen as a kind of religious war, especially following the conquest of Constantinople in 1453 by the Ottoman Turks. In Spain, the advance of the Christian Reconquista was invigorated by the marriage of Isabella of Castille with Ferdinand of Aragon in 1479 and the union of the two Christian kingdoms. Spain achieved victory over the last remaining Muslim state of Grenada in 1492. The Marinids, who previously had been able to successfully launch military campaigns in Spain, were henceforth in retreat. In contrast to the Iberians, the Maghribi states were slower to advance their military technology.

In the fifteenth century a branch of the Marinids, the Wattasids, emerged in eastern Morocco. Though they ruled in the name of the Marinids, they were effectively in control of the kingdom of Fez from 1430 to 1457. Until the demise of the Marinids, power was contested between Wattasid pretenders and the Marinids. State power was further eroded by the continued incursions of the Spanish and Portuguese along the Moroccan coastline. The Portuguese established themselves mainly along the Atlantic coast: Mazagan (El Jadida) in 1502, Santa Cruz (Agadir) in 1505, Safi in 1507, and Azemour in 1513. From the fortified coastal strongholds, the Portuguese led forays into the interior of Morocco, engaged in trade, and forged alliances with dissident leaders. The legacy of the Portuguese presence has left an indelible impression in the Moroccan historical consciousness, for yet today Moroccans in the interior and mountainous Atlas regions often refer to all ruins as "Portuguese." The Spanish also extended their presence along the Mediterranean coastline of the Maghrib, establishing themselves in Melilla (the other North African enclave still held by Spain today), Mars al-Kabir, Oran, Bougie, Tripoli, and Algiers. Like the Portuguese, the Spanish established fortified bastions, called *presidios*, from where they sometimes launched forays into the interior.

In Morocco, one of the results of these foreign incursions was the effort to find an alternative leadership to the reigning dynasty as well as to the traditional tribal leadership. The call for *jihad* strengthened the authority of some of the *shaykhs*, or leaders, of the Sufi orders. The Sufi *shaykhs* were often also *shurafa* (plural of *sharif*), descendants from the family of the Prophet through Ali and his progeny, and around these personalities, local divisions were often transcended. Sufi orders found in urban and rural areas often spread through the confraternities of the different orders. The actual lodge of the confraternity was called a *zawiya* (retreat), and the same term was used to refer to the Sufi order (*tariqa*, or way) as a whole. Political decentralization also helped spread Sufism, aided by the network of *zawiyas* located throughout the country. Though this type of mystical religion was an integral part of Sunni Islam, it also drew from ancient local customs, such as seasonal agrarian rituals. The common people were tied together in the community through the different activities associated to the *zawiya* and through pilgrimages to holy shrines (*ziyaras*), often during seasonal fairs (*mawsims*), where gifts were brought by the people for services rendered.

Some of the sufi *shaykhs* were also considered to be endowed with saintly qualities and were thought to be *marabouts* (the French rendition of the Arabic, singular *murabit*). The political and social disintegration of the late Marinid period and the growing Portuguese incursions along the Moroccan coastline contributed to the emergence of a number of new religious movements with *marabouts* as their leaders. An important dimension of these new popular movements was the *jihad* against the Portuguese. Along the Atlantic coast still lie the tombs of the venerated *mujahidun*, martyrs for Islam who allegedly died in the struggle against the

Christians. Along the coast, fortified centers of religious and military activities (*ribats*) were established, centering around charismatic *maraboutic* leaders.

Of great political importance in the fifteenth century was the growth of the *shurafa* (descendants of the Prophet). The belief in the power of the *shurafa* was an ideology that transcended local and tribal loyalties. Families aspiring for positions of power would claim descent from the Prophet. Sharifian status was enhanced by the privileges of tax exemption and the support of religious endowments (*hubus*). The most important *shurafa* were the Idrisids, going back to the ninth-century dynasty. In the fifteenth century, the tomb of Mawlay Idris II, the founder of Fez, was "discovered." Symbolically important was the belief that he had an Arab father and Berber mother, consolidating the growing status and legitimacy of the *shurafa* in society, especially because of the ability of the Sharifian ideology to transcend local particularisms.

It was the *shurafa* of Bani Zaydan from the Dra valley that gave birth to the Sadian dynasty. The founder of the Sadians, Abu Abdallah al-Qaim, though neither a *marabout* nor head of a Sufi order, became closely identified with one of the popular *zawiyas*, the Jazuliyya, and adopted the doctrine of this order during his rule. In the 1520s and 1530s the Sadians consolidated their control of the south under the leadership of Muhammad ash-Shaykh, and later took control of Fez, and in 1549 won acceptance of the *ulama*.

◆ OTTOMAN POWER AND LOCAL AUTONOMY

Political change in other regions of the Maghrib in the sixteenth century was due mainly to the rise of the Ottomans. In the second decade of the sixteenth century under Sultan Selim I, most of the Middle East was taken over by the Ottoman Turks. The Ottomans became the main contenders for control of the Mediterranean. The Maghribi dynasties of the Hafsids and Zayanids were not able to prevent Ottoman expansion. From the beginning of the sixteenth century, the Maghrib was contested by both the Spaniards and the Ottomans. The North African coast came within Ottoman orbit by the Barbarossa brothers: Aruj and Khayr ad-Din. The two brothers attacked Spanish ships from Gouletta in Tunisia, allowing the Hafsids to share in the profits of their spoils. They also operated out of the island of Jerba. Aruj then established a more or less independent principality in Djidjelli, in the Gulf of Bougie, and from there moved to Algiers. Aruj encountered opposition from the local Zayyanid *amir* who joined with the Spanish from Oran and killed Aruj. The Ottoman Sultan Selim then appointed Khayr ad-Din, Aruj's brother, as *beylerbey* (or head pasha), furnishing him with both men and weapons. From 1525 Algiers became his base of operations, and from there he set out to conquer other parts of the Maghrib. Due to his great success, he was put in charge of the Ottoman fleet. His policies helped consolidate Ottoman power along the North African coast.

During the course of the sixteenth century, Ottoman hegemony over the North African coast caused the disintegration of the Hafsid and Zayyanid dynasties, and the Regencies of Tunis, Algiers, and Tripolitania were established. Tripoli was captured in 1551 and, subsequently, Tripolitania was brought under Ottoman authority. Over the next two decades, the Spaniards and Turks struggled for the control of Algiers, Tunis, and Tlemcen. The Western victory of Lepanto in 1571, during which the Ottoman navy was defeated, has often been seen as a great turning point. The Spaniards again took Tunis. However, the Ottomans were able to restore their power to the east of Morocco.

Morocco under the Sadians was able to maintain its independence, build up its army, and embellish its southern capital of Marrakesh. A tripartite balance of power emerged between the Sadians, Ottomans, and Iberians and, consequently, prevented Ottoman expansion westward. This balance was challenged in the famous "Battle of the Three Kings" in 1578. The Ottomans

had favored one Sadian prince, Abd al-Malik, who usurped power from his nephew in power, al-Mutawakkil. The Moroccan state was reduced to a kind of Turkish dependency no longer in control of its own army. This caused the concern of the Portuguese, and King Sebastian of Portugal led an expedition in northern Morocco, together with al-Mutawakkil. The three rulers were killed in battle, but the conflict prevented the Sadians from becoming a Turkish dependency.

Al-Mutawakkil's brother, Ahmad al-Mansur, became sultan, and under him the Sadians reached the full extent of their power, expanding trade relations with Elizabethan England and launching a major military expedition to West Africa in 1591, leading to the collapse of the Songhay state. Descendants of the Moroccan expeditionary force later were to establish the Arma dynasty in Timbuktu, and this dynasty maintained control of Timbuktu and its surroundings until the French invaded the area in 1893.

Power in Algiers was centered in the hands of the Turkish military elite. The head pasha, the *beylerbey*, was appointed by the sultan to represent Ottoman interests in the western Mediterranean. By the end of the sixteenth century, though nominally invested in power by the Ottoman sultan in Istanbul, the *beylerbey* oper-

Military Hammam Marrakesh, Morocco

ated locally with no real help from the Ottoman capital. Control of Algiers was in the hands of the Ottoman troops, known as the *ujak*. Of growing importance throughout the empire was a new kind of infantry recruited primarily in Anatolia, the Jannisaries. Egalitarian in ranks, they elected a commander, the *agha*, and a council, the *diwan*. The *agha* of the Janissaries, as head of the *diwan*, became the chief center of power locally, and was responsible for collecting taxes. Of growing importance also was the *rais* (or head) of the navy. The exploits at sea and the dependency on the activities of the corsairs gave the seamen increasing prestige at home. Consequently, they began operating independently of the Janissaries. By 1671 the chief authority in Algiers was in the hands of the *dey* (local governor), who was chosen by the *rais*, rather than the pasha sent by Istanbul. The *dey* of Algiers remained the chief authority of the country until the French occupation began in 1830.

Many from the Turkish military elite married locally, and their offspring were called *kulughli*, though they were generally not admitted to the militia. The city of Algiers grew under the Turks with a pluralistic population of Turks, renegades, Andalusians, slaves, and Jews. This urban development also attracted the indigenous population of Arabs and Berbers to the town. The Turks, however, did not transform society as a whole, tending to govern through the local and still largely autonomous groups, especially in the interior regions. Although the Turks followed the Hanafite school of jurisprudence, they respected the Malikite rite. There was also little interference with the local urban notables, and the indigenous population was generally responsible for the urban administration.

Government in Tunis was similar to that of Algiers, at first with a *beylerbey* appointed by the Porte and control in the hands of Janissaries. By the end of the sixteenth century, the Janissaries began protesting the control of the Port, and the *deys* (in Tunisia, officers commanding units of one hundred men), eventually were able to consolidate their control, ruling through the *diwan* that selected the new *deys*. They began to extend their control of the interior, operating as independent sovereigns. In the seventeenth century, the *beys* began to supplant the *deys* as the chief authorities in the country. The *beys* were the heads of the expedition sent out from the capital to collect taxes and tribute. By gaining support of the local notables as well as the sedentary population by their suppression of dissident nomads, the authority of the *beys* was enhanced. A local dynasty of *beys*, founded by Murad and extended by his son, Hammuda Bey 1631–1666) emerged. The *beys* built a residence at Bardo, outside Tunis, symbolically linking themselves to the country. Their position was strengthened by their links to notables in

Great Mosque, Kairouan, Tunisia.

Tunis, and the indigenous, tribal elite. In 1705 a new dynasty of Husaynid *beys* was established and, although still nominally a part of the Ottoman empire, the Husaynids became virtually an independent local dynasty. Increasingly, the local administration became Arabized as growing numbers of natives were incorporated into the military.

Until 1711 the Ottomans remained in direct control of Tripoli, a city that had been controlled by successive foreign rulers: Spanish, Sicilians, and the Knights of St. John from Malta. While Tripolitania came under Ottoman control, little is known about the administration of Cyrenaica. Libya remained predominantly a tribal, pastoral society and, for the most part, the tribes remained autonomous. In Tripoli, the center of Ottoman administration, the power of the *kulughlis* grew, and they began to contest Turkish control. After 1711 when a *kulughli*, Yusuf Qaramanli, seized power, Libya came under the control of the hereditary Qaramanli dynasty, only nominally a part of the Ottoman empire. In 1835 the Turks again asserted their authority and Libya came under direct Ottoman administration.

Tinghir Miner's Township, Quarzazate, Morocco.

♦ ALAWID DYNASTY IN MOROCCO

After the death of Ahmad al-Mansur in 1603, Morocco was contested by three dynastic pretenders to the Sadian throne. The power of the dynasty was further weakened by the emergence of regional centers of power, struggling for control of the country. From the citadel of Iligh in Tazarwalt, the *marabout* Abu Hasun al-Samlali built up an autonomous principality in the Sous, extending his hegemony over much of the south from 1626. Another important center of power was the Bu Ragrag republic, based in Salé, which established a kind of ministate in 1627. Its power was enhanced when it became aligned to a religious and tribal leader, al-Ayashi, noted as a *mujahid* for his attacks against the various Spanish Atlantic settlements. From 1641 to 1660, another group supplanted the Bu Ragrag republic and al-Ayashi and attempted to establish a new dynasty, the Dila, Middle Atlas Berbers who established a *zawiya* in 1612. The Dila, however, were not regarded as *shurafa*, and the movement did not have the legitimacy to sustain its power. The way was paved for the success of the movement of the Alawi *shurafa* of the Tafilalt. Under Mawlay ar-Rashid, the power of both the Dila and Bu

Hasun of Iligh were destroyed, enabling the Alawids to secure control of the country.

The Alawids became one of the longest-lasting Islamic dynasties of history and are still reigning today despite the period of French and Spanish occupation in the twentieth century. Following the consolidation of political power in Fez by Mawlay ar-Rashid, the Alawid state reached its peak of power under Mawlay Ismail (1672–1727) who took twenty-four years of his reign to bring Morocco firmly under his control, such that it was said by the noted nineteenth-century historian, al-Nasiri, that "a Jew or a woman could go from Oujda to Wad Nun without anyone asking where she came from or where she was going." Mawlay Ismail constructed an elaborate palace complex in the town of Meknes, which became his preferred capital city, in an effort to separate himself from the entrenched elite groups of power in Fez. The consolidation of centralized power by Mawlay Ismail was not achieved without protesting against the sultan's despotism, and this is especially memorialized by the epistle of the famous seventeenth-century scholar, Abu al-Hasan al-Yusi. The sultan also encountered considerable opposition from the *ulama* of Fez against the sultan's recruitment of a powerful army of black slaves and nontribal blacks for his army.

The *ulama* were opposed to what they saw as the enslavement of Muslims, but the sultan was determined to build up an independent and loyal military force (which grew to about fifty-thousand at its height), and severely repressed his opponents in the process.

The army of Mawlay Ismail became the source of disorder after the sultan's death, and the commanders were able to install or eliminate a sultan at their will. Nevertheless, the legitimacy of the Alawid dynasty and its survival were assured by the widespread submission to the principle of Sharifian authority represented by the Filali sultans. No other dynastic force emerged that was able to supplant this legitimacy on a broad regional basis. This, however, did not guarantee political stability, and it was not until the 1750s that some order was restored in the country, especially under the sultan Sidi Muhammad ibn Abdallah (1757–1790) who was able to suppress the rebel leader and dissident tribes, consolidating his power in the southern capital of Marrakesh. The sultan concluded numerous treaties with the European powers and, to firmly maintain control of foreign trade, built the town of Essaouira (Mogador) to the west of Marrakesh as a royal port. At the same time, the sultan pursued the duties of *jihad* incumbent on the Muslim ruler and successfully captured the town of Mazagan (henceforth El Jadida) from the Portuguese in 1769.

♦ ISLAM AND THE WEST IN THE MODERN AGE

A new age of aggressive European expansion was initiated by Napoleon's invasion of Egypt in 1798, and the Islamic world generally saw itself under attack. Morocco during the Napoleonic wars entered into a period of more limited commercial intercourse with Europe. The Moroccan sultan Sulayman turned his attention to the Wahabbi movement that came to predominate in Arabia. Though not openly adopting Wahabbism because of the strength of the religious establishment, the sultan's reform was a result of his opposition to some of the popular Sufi movements and their religious practices such as *dhikr* (the repetitive chanting of the name of Allah or certain words in praise of Allah) and the celebration of seasonal fairs where sacrifice and visitation to the tombs of pious figures take place.

However, the Maghrib in the nineteenth century was no longer able to repel foreign penetration and domination. Western powers had pursued a course of military confrontation with the states of the Maghrib over piracy, and by the first decades of the nineteenth century, the corsair trade had all but ceased. Government in Algiers was particularly weak, with the *deys* becoming virtual prisoners of military figures who readily overthrew and chose new *deys*. Many of the regions of the interior were autonomous, and Algiers, though nominally a part of the Ottoman empire with the chief religious authority, the *mufti* appointed from Istanbul, was mostly independent of any real Turkish control. The French invaded Algeria in 1830 following the rupture of relations a few years previously. The diplomatic break followed a dispute over some debts owed by France in which the *dey* allegedly swatted the insolent French consul with a fly whisk.

What was proclaimed to be a punitive expedition turned into a full-fledged occupation of the country. The French encountered considerable resistance and it took several decades before they were able to secure the hinterland. The first major resistance movement was led by Hajj Ahmad Bey from Constantine who attempted to maintain national independence by reconstituting a government and state type of apparatus. By 1837 Constantine was captured. The most important resistance movement was then led by a *maraboutic* leader, Abd al-Qadir of the Qadiriyya *zawiya*. Assuming the title of *amir al-muminin* (commander of the faithful), Abd al-Qadir was able to take control of about two-thirds of Algeria, building an Islamic state that rallied diverse elements of the population around the cause of *jihad*. The French had to deploy over one-hundred thousand troops before Abd al-Qadir finally surrendered in 1847. The legacy of Abd al-Qadir later became an important symbol for Algerian nationalism.

With most of Algeria controlled by the military, the colonization of the country by French settlers intensified. Millenarian-type resistance movements, with the goal of restoring Islamic rule, continued into the 1870s. The French responded with repressive measures and wide-scale expropriation of land. Numerous peasants were uprooted, becoming wage earners in the countryside and joining the ranks of a growing urban proletariat in the cities. Muslim religious institutions were also undermined by the efforts of the French authorities to impose controls on the *sharia* courts. The French introduced new state-run schools, and suppressed Islamic institutions such as *zawiyas*, devotional spaces, and mosques. Algeria was formally annexed to France, and French settlers from the three created Algerian provinces elected six representatives to the Chamber of Deputies. The indigenous Muslim population as a whole, however, did not receive rights as French citizens. The Algerian Jewish population was naturalized en masse in 1870 by the so-called Crémieux Decree. The consequence of these changes was that Algerian Muslims became subordinate to the settler population and the colonial economy with little control over their own lives.

In the decades preceding the French occupation of Tunisia in 1881, the Husaynid government embarked on a program of reform, following somewhat the Ottoman pattern. Efforts were first made to modernize the army, and then under considerable pressure from the British and French, constitutional reforms were implemented along the lines of the Tanzimat reform movement, with the establishment of the "Fundamental Pact" in 1857 and the constitution of 1861. These reforms established a general capitation tax for all "Tunisians" to replace various other tribute taxes, declared rights for minorities, and created mixed courts for litigation between Muslims and non-Muslims. The rebellion of Ali al-Ghadhahim in 1864, which rapidly spread throughout the country, came as a response to the government's efforts to impose the new order and the non-Islamic taxes. The revolt was brutally suppressed, but nonetheless led the Husaynid government to suspend the constitution.

Also mirroring the experience of Egypt and the Ottoman Porte, the Husaynid government fell increasingly in debt as European loans were contracted in the 1860s to pay for the growing expenses of the state. In 1869 the government was declared bankrupt, unable to negotiate a new loan. An international commission to administer the Tunisian debt, consisting of Britain, France, and Italy, was established. Recognizing the growing dangers of foreign intervention and dependency, some Tunisians began advocating the idea of liberal reform. Most notably among them was Khayr al-Din, the president of the financial commission and later prime minister. Khayr al-Din also was responsible for the establishment of a modernist Islamic institution, the Saddiqi school, and was the author of a noted political treatise (published in 1867). Although, in theory, not abandoning the conventional formulation of the Islamic polity, misgovernment and arbitrary rule were attributed to decline, while the virtues of constitutional government, the cause for European advance, were acclaimed.

Reformist ideas, however, were insufficient to prevent the occupation of Tunisia. Tunisia's fate was sealed in the Congress of Berlin in 1878, where the European powers divided up their spheres of influence in Africa. The pretext for French military intervention came when a border tribe near Algeria became involved in some skirmishes, and the French landed near Tunis in 1881. Within a year, the occupation of Tunisia was complete, and a "protectorate" was established. The French took over the debt and controlled taxes and most administrative and judicial functions. The position of *bey* was maintained but with few powers, and most all internal and foreign affairs were in the hands of the French administration.

It was the Ottomans that put an end to the virtually independent Qaramanli dynasty in 1835. Tripolitania came under the direct rule of the Ottoman government, and the various administrative and legal reforms of the Tanzimat were implemented. But Ottoman efforts at centralization encountered considerable resistance for about twenty years, especially in the western mountains (Al-Jabal al-Gharbi).

Centralized control was much less felt in Cyrenaica where the Sanusiyya were more firmly in control. The Sanusi brotherhood, founded in 1843 by Muhammad ibn Ali al-Sanusi, combined Sufism with a strict orthodoxy. They were opposed to saint worship and advocated a return to the fundamentals of Islam. The Sanusiyya can be seen as a kind of militant reaction to the dislocation of Muslim society, stemming in part from the growing confrontation with the West. Politics also was an important factor, with the founder of the movement having lived and studied in Egypt, Algeria, and sub-Saharan Africa. The movement established an extensive network of *zawiyas* (over one hundred by 1911), which became an important symbolic countermeasure to the growing European presence.

Casting its eyes on what it believed to be its "fourth shore," and invoking the heritage of the ancient Roman Empire, Italy focussed its attention on Libya as an outlet to the country's emigration problem. Italian penetration of Libya accelerated toward the end of the nineteenth and the beginning of the twentieth century. With the other European powers already accepting the idea of an eventual Italian occupation of Tripoli and Cyrenaica, the Italians announced their annexation of Libya in 1911. The Ottomans refused to cede Libya to the Italians, but unable to maintain their forces in Libya, declared the Libyan province autonomous with the right to appoint officials to represent Ottoman interests. World War I brought an end to the Ottoman empire, and in Tripolitania a republican government was declared (*al-jumhuriyya at-tarablusiyya*) by a loose coalition of leaders that was never recognized by the Italians who increased their grip on the country. The Sanusis remained the major opposition and engaged the Italians in a long war from 1923–1932 until their movement and independence were crushed.

Foreign influence in Morocco accelerated after the French invasion of Algeria in 1830. The French reacted to Moroccan support for the Algerian resistance led by Abd al-Qadir by sending a punitive expedition, which defeated a Moroccan force at Wad Isly near the Algerian border, and the French fleet bombarded the ports of Essaouira and Tangier. This attack underlined Morocco's military weakness, and as in the Ottoman empire and Egypt, caused the sultan, Abd al-Rahman, to embark on a program of military and administrative reforms, though less far-reaching than in the Middle East.

Pressures increased on Morocco to open the country to unrestricted foreign trade, and in 1856 a commercial treaty was signed with Great Britain that gave privileges to British trade in Morocco. This treaty became the model for other foreign countries, and, consequently, Morocco increasingly was brought into the European circuit of trade and intervention. A Spanish expedition against northern Morocco in 1860 led to an occupation centered in Tetuan. The Spanish occupation ended in 1862 after Morocco agreed to pay massive indemnities that bankrupted the Makhzan (the name of the central administration and government). Further reforms by Sultan Muhammad IV to strengthen the state failed to stem the tide of growing foreign intervention. One of the principal means by which the foreign powers were able to gain a foothold in Morocco, not only in the coastal towns but in the interior as well, was through the system of protection. Like the capitulations of the Ottoman empire, consular protection enabled foreign governments to issue patents of protection to native subjects of the sultan that granted them extraterritorial rights, exempting them from taxes and removing them from the jurisdiction of the sultan and the *sharia* courts. Among the beneficiaries of protection were Jews who were enabled to escape their *dhimmi* status defined by the Islamic state. This move caused the growing consternation of the *ulama*. The abuse of protection undermined the ability of the Moroccan government to rule the country, but owing to the rivalries between the foreign powers, an international conference was held in Madrid in 1880 that sought to regulate the problem. While the Madrid Convention sought to regulate the abuse of protection, such as eliminating the tax-exempt status of foreigners and their protégés, it still maintained the principle of consular protection, and the intended reforms remained a dead letter as abuse of the system continued.

Sultan Hasan I (1873–1894) was the last vigorous ruler who was able to preserve the territorial integrity of Morocco and embark on important reforms prior to the loss of Moroccan independence in 1912. Military, fiscal, and administrative reforms helped create a more centralized state but also led to growing unrest among the population and discontent among the *ulama*. Among the sultan's reforms was the establishment of a tax for all residents, *tartib*, stemming from the Madrid Convention. The tax-exempt status of *zawiyas*, *marabouts*, and *shurafa*, in addition to foreigners, was to be abolished. A new *tartib* was implemented in 1901 by Sultan Mawlay Abd al-Aziz as a kind of uniform tax on agriculture and livestock, doing away with the canonical Islamic taxes (*ashar* and *zakat*). This measure was ineffective and caused increasing opposition to government reforms on Islamic grounds. The sultan was unable to rule effectively, and the country fell increasingly into debt. He brought in Western advisors to introduce modernizing reforms as he increased expenses for Western amenities.

Foreign interference and influence in Morocco caused a reaction comparable to other Muslim countries on the eve of foreign occupation. Though some of the *ulama* supported the reforms, many were staunchly opposed and invoked the call for *jihad*. The growing influence of the Salafiyya reformist movement, calling for the return to the fundamentals of the early period of Islam (articulated in Morocco by the new Kataniyya order), shaped the ideas of a new generation of Moroccan *ulama*. Internal divisions in Morocco also led to a dynastic struggle between Abd al-Aziz and Abd al-Hafiz. Rural rebellion also became prevalent in the years leading up to foreign occupation. A dissident leader, Bu Himara ("man with the she donkey"), proclaiming himself as the precursor of the *mahdi*, launched a *jihad* in northeastern Morocco. Although the Makhzan was able to reassert its control, he again emerged in 1908, to be subdued in 1909. In 1907 French troops intervened in Casablanca and Oujda, and supporters of Abd al-Hafiz called for *jihad* to recover the weakening state under Abd al-Aziz. Abd al-Hafiz was declared sultan, and under pressure of the mob, the *ulama* declared their loyalty (*baya*). A major uprising in the south in 1912, led by al-Hiba, took on the appearance of a *jihad;* Marrakesh was captured, but retaken by French troops. Territorial encroachments by the French and Spanish had already begun well before the French and Spanish protectorates were established. The protectorate began in 1912, with the French zone including most of the country. The Spanish zone was predominantly in the north, and Tangier became an international city.

◆ NATIONALISM, INDEPENDENCE, AND RESURGENT ISLAM

Colonialism in North Africa produced a variety of reactions among the indigenous population. The demarcation of boundaries and the separate French administrations in Morocco, Algeria, and Tunisia, the Spanish protectorate in Morocco, and the Italian administration in Libya engendered the emergence of distinctive regional nationalist movements in each country. In the three countries under French rule, a small group of Western-educated North Africans (referred to as *evolués*) began pressing for liberal, democratic reforms. These groups, somewhat modeling themselves after the Young Turks who led a secular revolution in Turkey in the waning days of the Ottoman empire, fashioned themselves in Algeria and Tunisia as "Young Algerians" and "Young Tunisians." Later, these movements gave way to the first political parties that demanded reforms of the French administration. In Algeria the dominant figure was Ferhat Abbas, a pharmacist by training, who became a leading nationalist figure in the interwar years. The Young Tunisians formed the *Parti Evolutionniste* in 1907, and despite the modest demands for greater native participation in the political process, the party was suppressed by the French.

The demands for reform especially began to accelerate after World War I. Numerous North Africans served in the French Army but were disillusioned upon returning to the Maghrib when they discovered that the colonial power had no intention of extending to them further rights. Failure to achieve more than the slightest electoral reforms led the westernized, liberal politicians to demand full independence, and these nationalist movements accelerated after World War II.

The nationalist movement in Tunisia was first led by the *Destour* (constitutional party), founded in 1920 and advocated the right of Tunisians for self-government. A younger generation of Tunisians, led by Habib Bourguiba, and critical of the *Destour's* conservative ties with Muslim religious leaders, formed the *Neo-Destour* as a mass party that led Tunisia to independence. A political party calling for a separate Algeria began to emerge after World War I, the *Etoile Nord-Africain*, led by Messali al-Hajj, who combined socialism with pan-Islamic ideals. The *Etoile* was dissolved, was reconstituted as the *Parti du Peuple Algérien* during the Popular Front government in France, and banned in 1939.

Parallel to these movements, a reformist *ulama* began to play an increasingly important role in shaping the cultural and national identity of the countries of the Maghrib. The way in which reformist Islam and national identity merged is perhaps best expressed in an often-quoted saying of the leader of the Algerian Association of Reformist Ulama, Shaykh Abd al-Hamid Ben Badis: "Islam is my religion, Arabic is my language, Algeria is my fatherland." In Algeria the reformist *ulama* did not explicitly espouse political aims at first but later helped shape the cultural identity of the revolution. In Libya, it was the reformist Sanusiyya movement that led the resistance to Italian colonialism until its brutal suppression in 1935, but it was the Sanusi leader Idris that led Libya into independence after World War II.

Reformist Islam also shaped the nationalist movement in Morocco but with a more explicitly political agenda than in Algeria. Staunch resistance to the expansion of Spanish rule in northern Morocco was led by Abd al-Karim al-Khattabi in the Rif Mountains from 1921–1926. With Salafiyyist notions and the call for religious reform, Abd al-Karim established the "Confederated Republic of the Tribes of the Rif," refusing to recognize the protectorate, which he considered a violation of Moroccan sovereignty. His plan to create

Sidi El Aloui School, Tunis, Tunisia.

an independent state in the Rif was destroyed under the joint assault of Spanish and French troops. His resistance to colonialism became an important symbol for the Moroccan nationalist movement. It was in the cities that a nationalist elite began to form in the period after the demise of Abd al-Karim's republic. Especially important for fostering the development of Moroccan nationalism was the free school movement, a system of schools outside the control of the colonial state. These schools, influenced by Salafiyyist doctrines, emphasized a reformist Islam, an Arab culture, and a Moroccan nation. What served as a catalyst for the nationalist movement was the issuing of the so-called Berber Dahir in 1930. In an effort to separate the Berbers juridically from the Arabs and Islam, the French gave the Berber councils (*jamaas*) control in civil and penal matters according to French law. This measure, which backfired, invoked calls for Muslim unity between Arabs and Berbers, and was eventually abandoned.

The leading figure in the nationalist movement to emerge was Allal al-Fassi who led the first political party, the *Comité d'Action Marocaine*, and during World War II, the *Istiqlal* (Independence), which helped lead Morocco to independence. Morocco never really had the secular and liberal nationalist tendency that was so important in Tunisia and Algeria. But the focus on reformist Islam and Salafiyyist doctrines did not exclude the incorporation of modernist, Western ideals such as the notion of equality of men and women, liberation from the bourgeoisie, or the use of liberal vehicles to agitate for change (i.e., the press and political parties). A distinctive feature of Moroccan nationalism was the link between the nationalist movement and the Sharifian Sultan Sidi Mohamed Ben Youssef who, despite his subservience to the colonial authorities, became a national symbol and provided an important link between the nationalist movement and the population as a whole. After World War II, the Sultan took the lead in the struggle for independence, provoking the French to depose him. But it was the sultan who negotiated Morocco's independence with the French, and he returned to power in 1956 to lead an independent country with the title of King Mohamed V.

Although the French protectorate in Tunisia superficially maintained the facade of beylical authority, unlike in Morocco the *bey* had no popular legitimacy nor did he represent an Islamic symbol around which the population could rally. The largely secular orientation of the *Neo-Destour* shaped the policy of President Bourguiba after Tunisian independence in 1956. The *bey* was deposed, and a republican constitution gave Bourguiba almost complete dominance of the affairs of the state, which he used to bring under his control the often militant trade union movement. In the 1960s Bourguiba launched a program of state control of the economy with a socialist platform, changing the name of the *Neo-Destour* to the *Parti Socialiste Destourien*. Bourguiba advocated modern secularism and took steps to undermine the power of religious institutions by integrating the *sharia* courts into the secular judicial system, nationalizing the lands belonging to the *hubus* (religious endowments), and bringing Muslim educational institutions, such as the Zitouna school, under the control of the Ministry of Education. Particularly offensive to a large sector of the Tunisian population was his ultimately unsuccessful effort to suppress adherence to fasting on Ramadan from 1959 to 1961. A result of these secular efforts was the polarization between the state and Islam, a major factor in the emergence of the modern Islamic activist group in 1981, the *Mouvement de Tendance Islamique*, which was repressed by President Bourguiba. Bourguiba's successor, General Zine al Abidine Ben Ali, who took power in 1987, promised political liberalization, and the Islamic movement was revived as the *Nahda* (Renaissance) Party. The Islamic revivalist groups fared no better under Ben Ali who has regarded them as a major threat

to the secular aims of the state, and the *Nahda* party has been subjected to repression.

The group that was to emerge and to lead Algeria to independence did not come from the westernized *evolués*. Taking the preeminent position in the nationalist movement after the war was the Front de Libération Nationale (FLN), which led a protracted revolutionary struggle against French rule. Independence was achieved in 1962. It was the FLN, with its popular democratic revolution, an ideology combining socialism with Islam, that dominated Algerian politics after independence under the leadership of President Ben Bella until his removal from power by Boumedienne in 1965. The policy of Arabization led to clashes with the Berber population who saw French as their avenue to advancement. Islam became the state religion, and Islamic institutions were incorporated into the state bureaucracy. The state's total monopolization of power, however, did not prevent a grass-roots Islamic revivalist movement from growing. This movement was and is committed to the notion of establishing an Islamic state in Algeria. In 1991, after Colonel Chedli Benjedid called for general elections, the *Front Islamique du Salut* (FIS) won the majority of votes in the first round of the elections. Fearing the formation of an Islamic state, the government then suspended the electoral process and began a repressive campaign against the leaders of the FIS. A general breakdown in order ensued, with retaliatory actions by various Islamic revivalist groups against both foreigners and those perceived to be westernized secularists in Algeria.

While Islam was used in Algeria to legitimize the largely secular preoccupations of the state, such as industrialization and agrarian reform, the leaders themselves did not have the same measure of Islamic legitimacy as did the monarch, Mohamed V, of Morocco. As a *sharif* and member of the Alawid dynasty that has ruled Morocco since the seventeenth century, Mohamed V was considered to be God's shadow on earth. But independent Morocco was, in theory, to have developed a constitutional monarchy based on the principles of participatory democracy. The king was to have allowed for the existence of political parties, but was to be "above" politics himself, thus able to serve as the arbiter in the interests of the people. Following the death of Mohamed V in 1961, King Hasan II sought to further legitimize his position through elections, political parties, and the promulgation of a constitution. However, the king made it clear that the legislature had no real authority, nor could he be subject to criticism. When confronted with challenges from the political parties, such as the *Union National des Forces Populaires*, King Hasan pursued a policy of political repression. Not inconsequential in the 1980s and early 1990s has been the emergence of

Muslim revivalist groups, advocating the idea of establishing an Islamic state and hostile to the ideas of Western democracy. These groups, however, have been weaker than in either Algeria or Tunisia because they also have had to compete with the monarchy's claims to Islamic legitimacy. The politicized Islam of the revivalist groups, while appealing to students and some of the disenfranchised urban youth, appears divergent from the Muslim practices and beliefs of much of the population.

Monarchial rule in Libya was much more precarious than in Morocco, largely because of the fragility of the state structure. King Idris of Libya was unable to maintain power and was overthrown in 1969 by Colonel Muammar Qaddafi. The proclaimed principles that were to guide the new regime were Nasserism, Arab Unity, anti-imperialism, Arab socialism, and Islam. Qaddafi's emphasis on Islam also served to legitimize the regime that had deposed the Sanusi leader. The strict adherence to Islam and exclusive use of Arabic as the official language also underlined the ideological repudiation of the West. From 1973 on, Qaddafi embarked on a "popular" or "cultural" revolution, advocating the need for mass participation. Qaddafi's "third universal theory," promulgated in his green book, is opposed to both capitalism and communism. The people themselves were to have authority, unencumbered by the administration of the state. All governing bodies were seen as tools used for the exploitation of the people. Libya was to become a *jamahariyya*, a term coined by Qaddafi that implied a "state of the masses."

Qaddafi's ideology, in many respects, supported an Islamicist agenda with his Quranic code of punishment, the green flag, and his efforts to suppress aspects of Western culture. Moreover, it represented a fundamentalism of the state with radical new interpretations that conflicted with the *ulama*. In the late 1980s members of a Muslim revivalist group, the "Party of God," were executed by the regime. It is doubtful if Qaddafi's Islamic innovations will survive his passing.

The four states of the Maghrib have all taken somewhat different paths following independence, depending on the particular characteristics of their pre colonial and colonial histories. Yet a common thread that runs through all four of the countries today is that of authoritarian and sometimes despotic regimes and the failings of these regimes in their programs of modernization to bring great benefits to an ever-increasing Muslim population, many of whom are seeking a new type of identity. Cultural authenticity, many believe, is not to be found in the promises of Western culture but in visions of the uncorrupted early days of Islam. Through a perceived return to these values, the contemporary life of Muslims, transformed by the detachment from their tribal and rural origins and localized expressions of popular Islam, could be immeasurably ameliorated.

Daniel J. Schroeter

References

Abun-Nasr, Jamil M. *A History of the Maghrib in the Islamic Period.* Cambridge: Cambridge University Press, 1987.

Ahmida, Ali Abdullatif. *The Making of Modern Libya: State Formation, Colonization and Resistance, 1830–1932.* Albany, N.Y.: State University of New York Press, 1994.

Brett, Michael (ed.). *Northern Africa: Islam and Modernization.* London: F. Cass, 1973.

Burgat, François & Dowell, William. *The Islamic Movement in North Africa.* Austin: University of Texas Press, 1993.

Burke, Edmund. *Prelude to Protectorate in Morocco: Precolonial Protest and Resistance, 1860–1912.* Chicago: University of Chicago Press, 1976.

El Mansour, Mohamed. *Morocco in the Reign of Mawlay Sulayman.* Cambridgeshire, England: Middle East and North African Studies Press, 1990.

Evans-Pritchard, E. E. *The Sanusi of Cyrenaica.* Oxford: Oxford University Press, 1949.

Geertz, Clifford. *Islam Observed: Religious Development in Morocco and Indonesia.* New Haven: Yale University Press, 1968.

Green, Arnold H. *The Tunisian Ulama, 1873–1915: Social Structure and Response to Ideological Currents.* Leiden: E. J. Brill, 1978.

Hess, Andrew C. *The Forgotten Frontier: A History of the Sixteenth-Century Ibero-African Frontier.* Chicago: University of Chicago Press, 1978.

Ibn Khaldun. *The Muqaddimah.* Translated by F. Rosenthal. 3 vols. New York: Pantheon Books, 1958.

Julien, Charles-André. *History of North Africa: Tunisia, Algeria Morocco; from the Arab Conquest to 1830.* New York: Praeger, 1970.

Khayr al-Din al-Tunisi. *The Surest Path.* [*Aqwam al-masalik fi marifat ahwal al-mamalik*]. Translated by L. C. Brown. Cambridge, Mass., 1967.

Laroui, Abdallah. *The History of the Maghrib: An Interpretive Essay.* Princeton: Princeton University Press, 1977.

Le Tourneau, Roger. *The Almohad Movement in North Africa in the Twelfth and Thirteenth Century.* Princeton: Princeton University Press, 1969.

———. *Fez in the Age of the Marinids.* Norman: University of Oklahoma Press, 1962.

Montagne, Robert. *The Berbers: Their Social and Political Organization.* Translated and introduction by David Seddon. London: Cass, 1973.

Munson, Henry. *Religion and Power in Morocco.* New Haven: Yale University Press, 1993.

al-Qadiri, Muhammad. *Muhammad al-Qadiri's Nashr Al Mathani: The Chronicles.* Translated and edited by N. Cigar. London, 1981.

Reudy, John. *Modern Algeria: The Origins and Development of a Nation.* Bloomington: Indiana University Press, 1992.

as-Saffar, Muhammad. *Disorienting Encounters: Travels of a Moroccan Scholar in France in 1845–1846.* Translated and edited by S. G. Miller. Berkeley: University of California Press, 1992.

Valensi, Lucette. *On the Eve of Colonialism: North Africa Before the French Conquest, 1790–1830.* New York: Africana Publishing, 1977.

———. *Tunisian Peasants in the Eighteenth and Nineteenth Centuries.* Cambridge: Cambridge University Press, 1985.

Islam in Contemporary Europe

♦ Muslim Immigration ♦ Public Life ♦ Educational Issues ♦ Religious Observances
♦ Muslim and Mixed Marriages ♦ Muslim Identity

Islam in Europe is both an old and a new phenomenon. It has been in existence for about four-hundred years in sections of southeastern Europe (i.e., Bulgaria and sections of former Yugoslavia) where Muslims settled under Ottoman rule and continued living after the political takeover of the area by non-Muslims. The establishment of Islamic communities in western and northern Europe is a recent development due to immigration during the second half of the twentieth century.

♦ MUSLIM IMMIGRATION

Muslim immigration was, and still is, primarily the result of three factors. First, colonization and decolonization brought Muslims from the Indo-Pakistani world to Great Britain, from Indonesia and Surinam to the Netherlands, from North and West African countries to France, and Muslims of Indian origin from Portuguese Africa to Portugal. Second, a labor migration resulted in the immigration of other Muslims, in particular Turks, to European Free Trade Association (EFTA) and European Economic Community (EEC) countries (especially Germany, Belgium, France, and the Netherlands). Moroccan, Algerian, and Tunisian Muslims migrated first to France and, more recently, to neighboring Spain and Italy. Third, political as well as religious persecution in some Arab countries, in Turkey and Iran, as well as other parts of the Muslim world, led large numbers of Muslims to seek asylum in western European countries. The number of non-European Muslims settling in Europe as students, merchants, or businesspeople has been insignificant so far as the number of European converts to Islam is concerned.

Initially, host European societies saw in these Muslim residents (temporary and permanent) individuals of different backgrounds who did not appear representative of their perception of traditional Muslim backgrounds. Consequently, they expected full assimilation by these Muslims to the culture and customs of the countries. Only gradually did the European societies become aware of problems of integration.

Unlike Muslim residents in less-developed countries of southeastern Europe, Muslim workers and their families found it necessary in EFTA and EEC countries to adjust to a modern industrial lifestyle with high technological standards and cultural customs and habits alien to those of their home countries. Many, obviously, adapted to Western ways. Others tried to keep their distance and thus developed an identity of their own while maintaining some openness to Western society. The establishment of Muslim communities was and is an indication of the increasing need for an expression of Muslim identity and a result, in part, of the growing acceptance in EEC countries of a multicultural or multifaith society. It is permitting, if not encouraging, religious freedom for foreign residents, opening the door for increased religious and political influence of the home countries on these communities.

Muslims in Western Europe

	Population: 1989	Estimates: 1995
FRANCE	2.7 million	5 million
GERMANY	1.8 million	2 million
UNITED KINGDOM	1 million	1 million
NETHERLANDS	408,000	0.5 million
BELGIUM	250,000	0.3 million
SCANDINAVIA	180,000	0.2 million
SWITZERLAND	100,000	100,000
ITALY	500,000	0.7 million

The 1989 statistics are based on data compiled in J. S. Nielsen, Muslims in Western Europe. *Edinburgh: Edinburgh University Press, 1992. The more recent estimates are based on Farzana Shaikh,* Islam and Islamic Groups: A Worldwide Reference Guide, *London, Longman, 1992 and statistics summarized in* The New York Times, *May 5, 1995.*

Mahmudia Mosque, Constanta, Romania.

◆ PUBLIC LIFE

Public life has proved to be problematic for Muslims in western and northern Europe due to the difference in attitudes. They are reflected in modes of attire, the separation of the sexes, dietary prescriptions, holidays, funeral rites and cemeteries, religious and mixed marriages, mosque-schools, the building of mosques, Christian-Muslim dialogue, and politics with special regard to democracy and secularization. Many immigrant families believe that special precautionary measures need to be taken. For example, some immigrant par-

ents insist that their daughters wear headscarves in school and in the streets as a sign of their adherence to Islam. Thus, the headscarf carries a symbolic value that goes far beyond similar traditional dress customs known in eastern and southeastern Europe. The decision for or against headscarves is the visible expression of a deliberate plea for Muslims to adopt Western standards. Europeans often see the headscarf as a symbol of an outdated value system that oppresses women or, as in the "foulard" (i.e., headscarf) affair of France, an attack against the secular principle of the French public school system. At the same time, Muslims argue that it helps to protect the dignity of Muslim women in their desire not to be like European women. The headscarf has become symbolic of the larger field of issues concerning the behavior of women in society.

◆ EDUCATIONAL ISSUES

Traditional Muslim education defines separate and distinct roles for men and women, while modern European educational values try to make these roles, to a large extent, interchangeable, and education of boys and girls in the same classroom is seen as a means to achieve this goal. Although coeducation in western and northern Europe is a recent phenomenon, it has become a vital element of modern society. Coeducation is perceived by some Muslim immigrants as an attempt to undermine the traditional relationship between men and women in their society. Muslim insistence on the establishment of separate schools for boys and girls is perceived to contradict the achievements of modernization and provokes a negative reaction from many Europeans. Coeducation in many sporting activities, swimming courses, and the teaching of biology is seen by many Muslims as an attack on values of honor and modesty. An increasing number of Muslim girls who choose not to attend such classes are bringing their cases to the attention of legal authorities. Some Muslims defend the girls nonparticipation in the name of their religion, while school authorities argue against it in terms of modern educational principles.

As a solution to this dilemma, a number of Muslims in EEC countries such as Great Britain, Belgium, and the Netherlands are demanding the establishment of "Islamic" schools run in accordance with the principles of their tradition; similar efforts are also being made in France. The only such program established so far is in Germany; the Islam-Kolleg Berlin E.V. was founded in 1989 as an elementary school with coeducational classes introduced as an experiment by Berlin's Senator of Education. It is not known whether the students will continue to be permitted to attend coeducational classes once they reach puberty. If so, there will undoubtedly arise, as is the case in all other coeducational institutions, a myriad of problems resulting from social contacts between teenagers of the opposite sex.

Mosque-schools must be distinguished from Islamic schools. The objective of mosque-schools is the teaching of the Quran and Islamic principles to Muslim children, who in most cases also attend state school

The Institut du Monde Arabe, Paris.

programs as well. Strong criticism has been levied against these mosque-schools in Germany where they have been accused of giving too much work to the children, utilizing old-fashioned teaching methods, which include corporal punishment, and teaching anti-Western propaganda. Since most of these schools operate illegally, it is difficult to judge their value or quality.

The antagonism of differing values is not only a problem between Muslims and non-Muslims; it is the cause of division among Muslims themselves. Second and third generation immigrants are faced with exposure to two different worlds: a modern lifestyle at school and traditional values at home. It is noteworthy that the antagonism between the two is very much felt among working-class immigrants. It seems to be less noticeable among professionals and intellectuals.

♦ RELIGIOUS OBSERVANCES

Islamic dietary rules, such as those prohibiting the consumption of pork and alcohol, as well as religious

Public life has proved to be problematic for Muslims in western and northern Europe due to the different attitudes they may have regarding education, modes of attire, and rites and cemeteries.

Sherefudin's White Mosque, Visoko, Bosnia.

regulations concerning the slaughter of animals have created many difficulties for Muslims in Europe. This is not so much the case with regard to cooking at home, because more and more Muslim merchants have opened shops (in particular, butcher shops found in most big cities of EFTA and EEC countries) to assure that Muslims are able to buy food in accordance with their religious needs. Difficulties arise when Muslims are forced to rely on food that is not especially prepared for them (i.e., in schools and restaurants catering to students, and in hospitals, the military, and prisons). Although there is a desire on the part of European communities to be sensitive to the needs of Muslims in most countries, the manifestation of the concern is not always apparent. The culinary traditions of individual countries often include ingredients that may be taboo for orthodox Muslims. In Germany, for instance, the consumption of pork sausages and ham is very common. Most German soup is cooked with pork bouillon. In France, on the other hand, the consumption of wine is nearly compulsory while eating.

Particular problems exist for Muslims during the fasting month of Ramadan where eating, drinking, and smoking are strictly forbidden during the daytime. This impacts Muslim contact with non-Muslims. Many Muslims feel uncomfortable justifying their obedience to rules, or do so with religious zeal to rationalize what might appear to a non-Muslim as unusual behavior.

Holiday Observances

Islamic holidays are another area of difficulty for Muslims in predominantly non-Muslim European societies. Complaints are often made because Muslim workers are forbidden to leave work to attend noon prayers on Fridays or are forced to take vacation days in order to celebrate Islamic holidays, whereas non-Muslim or Christian workers are not required to use their vacations to celebrate their religious holidays. Consequently many Muslims feel their treatment in EFTA and EEC countries is inequitable.

Funeral Rites

Issues relating to funeral rites and cemeteries must be added to the list of other problems that Muslims in western and northern Europe must deal with. Originally, only the first generation of Muslim Turkish workers tried to transport their deceased to the homeland for burial. However, more recently there has been a steady increase in funerals being held in host countries because more Muslims have begun to consider these countries their home, in spite of foreign citizenship. As a result, they would prefer to have funeral rites performed in an acceptable manner in their new homeland.

Muslim burials have presented some conflicts. In the Netherlands, for example, local authorities accept Islamic funeral rituals and reserve special sections of cemeteries for Muslims in accordance with requirements that the bodies be buried facing the correct direction—toward Mecca. Many European officials request a waiting period of at least thirty-six hours after death before burial. This legal observation is in direct conflict with the traditional Muslim practice of holding funerals as soon as possible after death.

Mosques

The building of mosques is also somewhat controversial in most European countries, although congregational centers operating as mosques can be found everywhere. In nearly all cases, the non-Muslim neighborhoods, due to fears that Islam will become established in their neighborhood, make every attempt to hinder Muslims from building mosques. In any case, bans against the five times daily call to prayer from the minaret exist nearly everywhere and are, if ever, only lifted for special purposes.

A Christian-Muslim dialogue has been established in many countries. Such dialogue has been encouraged by the Roman Catholic Church as well as by the Anglican and most Protestant churches—although many Christians reject compromise with Muslims as a betrayal of Christianity. Those institutions in favor of dialogue seek a common basis for theological and religious exchange. Muslim intellectuals are open to dialogue, while most working-class Muslims are not and, therefore, are often unwilling to participate. Those Muslims who do choose to seek an exchange look for answers to problems concerning everyday life situations and attempt to work toward juridical as well as practical support and cooperation in resolving their difficulties. Tensions can arise when specific Muslim sects seek to use dialogue as a forum to garner support for their particular doctrinal belief.

♦ MUSLIM AND MIXED MARRIAGES

The issue of marriages pose a difficult situation in most countries of western and northern Europe. Although Muslim law allows men to have more than one wife, most European governments refuse to recognize polygamous marriages. Consequently, a man from a Muslim country in which polygamy is more common may only be able to bring one wife to the host country. Moreover, he is not allowed to contract another mar-

riage while in the host country. Some cases are known where a civil marriage took place in the host country while a religious marriage was held in the home country on the grounds that the husband could not be accused of being a polygamist by either government. There are also problems if a marriage that has taken place in the home country is dissolved by official divorce in the host country.

There has been an increase in the number of mar-

The building of mosques is somewhat controversial in most European countries, although congregational centers operating as mosques can be found everywhere.

riages between Christian women and Muslim men and, more rarely, Christian men with Muslim women. Muslim women are strictly forbidden to marry non-Muslim men under traditional Muslim law unless the husband is ready to convert to Islam. Christian churches have published directives and encouraged their clergymen to explain the difficulties that people in such marriages encounter.

♦ MUSLIM IDENTITY

Politically divergent views among Muslims are significant with regard to the issues of democracy and secularization. Since the 1980s the mass media in Europe has speculated that Muslims are unwilling and unable to accept democracy and secularization and that they work instead for the destruction of modern, pluralistic societies. However, surveys show that most Muslims in contemporary Europe are in favor of democracy and secularization as modern principles.

M. S. Abdullah's survey in Germany (1993) indicates that only a small number of Muslims are organized into political communities, that these communities have very close ties with the Islamic world and that they are not very encouraging of the younger generation and their aspirations. Similar observations have also been made in other European countries. P. S. Van Koningsveld (1993) sees in the Muslim European community a specific phenomenon of Islam that has no parallel in the Islamic world. These communities are often used as political instruments by the homelands. For example, Turkey, through DITIB, a semistatal Islamic representation, keeps the majority of Turkish Islamic communities under its command. In Morocco the king's plea that Muslims be exempt from Dutch local elections for foreign councils shows how influential outside forces can be in such situations.

Close ties between activists in the Muslim world and European Muslims occasionally make European Muslim communities strongholds of political influence. This seems to hinder some Muslims from becoming politically acculturated by contemporary European standards. However, free from the censorship practiced in their homelands, many European Muslims are being exposed to and are accepting a variety of Western views and opinions.

Islam in contemporary Europe is multifaceted and perhaps more diverse than Islam as practiced in the traditional Islamic world, and is worthy of study for this very reason. Historical affiliation with the Sunni or Shia sects, and/or belonging to one of the four traditional schools of law within Sunnism, is less foundational for European Islamic identity today than political preference. Muslims in Europe are in the forefront, attempting to formulate answers for the younger

generation. Abdullah's inquiry results show that of all the Turkish Muslims in Germany under the age of sixteen, fifty-eight percent declared their lack of engagement with Muslim practice, 22 percent said that they practice their religion because of respect for parents or under their pressure, and only twelve percent were prepared and willing to preserve their religious traditions in Germany. This study, done in Germany, parallels other European countries. The general public perception is that Islamic culture is an obstacle to the integration of peoples from non-European Muslim countries into European societies. However, traditional Muslim life is no longer representative for a majority of the second and third generations who no longer identify fully with their parents' heritage and wish to reinterpret their tradition. The question is which interpretation of Islam will prove attractive to the next generation that has grown up in societies where there has been a great amount of: personal freedom, exposure to secular values and popular Western culture, and perceived benefits from democratic institutions, education, and professional opportunities.

Peter Antes

♦ MUSLIMS IN BRITAIN

Arrival in Britain and Growth of Muslim Communities

The first records of Muslims in Britain date back at least 300 years when Muslim sailors were found in the ships of the East India Company. When they arrived in ports like London they sometimes remained to build a new life. During the nineteenth century, there were small but active groups of Muslims in Britain. These tended to fall into two divisions: those who had converted to Islam through the influence of sufism, and those who arrived here from the former Empire as students, diplomats or businessmen. The first mosque was built in Woking in 1889. There was a 150-strong Muslim community in Liverpool in 1887 with its own weekly journal. The leader of this community, a British lawyer, was named *Shaykh al-Islam* for Britain by the Ottoman sultan.

After World War I, there were around 11,000 Muslims in Britain with 1,000 of them being British converts. These numbers were boosted by Arab seamen, especially from Yemen, who settled in the ports of Cardiff and South Shields. By far the biggest waves of immigration occurred in the years following World War II when Britain called on Commonwealth citizens to come and rebuild "the mother country." During the 1950s, about 10,000 men per year came to Britain from the Indian subcontinent. Many of these were unskilled laborers who had been dispossessed by the division of India or through development projects in part of the subcontinent. Primary immigration was stopped in 1962 but families were allowed to reassemble in Britain which brought the influx of many wives and children which changed the nature of the Muslim communities. By 1971 there were around 170,000 Pakistanis in Britain. Many of these Muslims came to work in specific industries and often they followed a member of their family in what was called "chain migration." In this way certain towns in Britain have a direct link with a particular region in the original country and many of the Muslims living in such town are inter-related.

Data on Population, Settlement, Backgrounds

Any statistics on Muslim population are bound to be estimates as the national census does not contain a question on religious affiliation. The best estimate for the Muslim population of Britain is around 1.5 million. They are concentrated in Greater London, the Midlands and the former textiles towns around Manchester and in Yorkshire, with Bradford a particular example. Of these, approximately 55 percent belong to families which originate in the Indian subcontinent. The remainder of the Muslim population is made up of people from Algeria, Egypt, Iran, Iraq, Libya, Malaysia, Morocco, Nigeria, Somalia, Tunisia, Turkey (Cyprus) and Yemen with smaller contingents from many countries in Africa, the Middle East and the Far East. It is thought that there might be around 10,000 British converts to Islam. The usual distribution of Sunni/Shia is found with most of the subcontinent Muslims being attached to the Barelvi or Deobandi schools.

The age distribution of Muslims is important with only around 1.5 percent being over 65 years old (compared to 17 percent in the population as a whole) and 60 percent being aged under 25 (compared to 32 percent). This suggests that the population may well double before reaching demographic stability. Muslim young people are over-represented in colleges where many are using further education as a way of improving their prospects in employment. Unemployment is generally up to twice as high amongst 16-24 year-olds as in the general population.

Institution Building, Organizations, Mosques

There are some 600 mosques formally registered with the authorities in Britain and, in addition, perhaps another 400 unregistered mosques. Whilst the majority of these mosques are converted buildings (often rows of houses, shops, factories, public buildings), the trend in the 1990s has been to build large new mosques in prominent positions as a sign to people that Muslims are part of the community. Most of the registered mosques have permission to conduct civilly recognized marriages on the premises. The position of the

imam has developed away from the tradition of being a prayer leader into a function modelled on the role of the Christian pastor with an emphasis on counselling, community leadership and official representation to the authorities.

Every Muslim community has a variety of organizations attached to it. These include specialized organizations for education, welfare work, youth support, concern for the elderly, women's groups and racial equality awareness. In general, there is little interaction between these groups and no real national structure to bind then into a common voice. There are several groups which claim to be nationally representative, the largest being the Union of Muslim Organizations, but none of these are inclusive.

Key Issues

The single most important issue for Muslims in Britain is education. Britain permits public funding for religious schools, which is open to Muslims, but at present there are only Christian and Jewish schools thus provided. Some Muslims want to establish such separate Muslim schools, others want their children to be educated alongside other communities to assist in breaking down barriers. All want educational standards raised and for Muslim children to be allowed to observe their religion in every aspect of school life. English is becoming the most important and universal language with children having enough of their community language to talk to grandparents. Whilst community relations are generally good, there is a growing fear of racism with the growth of right-wing political groups.

Future Directions

Three important issues are facing Muslims in Britain. Firstly, how to educate a new generation of religious leaders who have a sound knowledge of English, British culture and the Islamic sciences. Secondly, how to re-interpret the essence of Islam so that it can thrive in a minority western society. Thirdly, how to maintain community strength and identity in a time when families will have to move away from the dense concentrations of the inner city areas they currently occupy.

Chris Hewer

References

Abadan-Unat N., ed. *Turkish Workers in Europe 1960–1975*. Leiden: E. J. Brill, 1976.

Akhtar, S. *Be Careful With Muhammad: The Salman Rushdie Affair*. London: Bellow, 1989.

Ally, M. M. *History of Muslims in Britain*. (MA thesis, University of Birmingham, 1981).

Anwar, M. *Young Muslims in a Multicultural Society*. Leicester: The Islamic Foundation, 1982.

Butt, W. M. *The Life of Pakistanis in the Netherlands*. Amsterdam: University of Amsterdam, 1990.

Castles, S. *Here For Good: Western Europe's New Ethnic Minorities*. London: Pluto Press, 1984.

Crespi, Gabriele. *The Arabs in Europe*. New York: Rizzoli, 1986, 1979.

Djait, H. *Europe and Islam: Cultures and Modernity*. Berkeley: University of California Press, 1985.

Engelbrektson, U. B. *The Force of Tradition: Turkish Migrants at Home and Abroad*. Gothenburg: Gothenburg Studies in Social Anthropology, 1978.

Gerholm, T., and Y. G. Lithman, eds. *The New Islamic Presence in Europe*. London and New York: Mansell, 1988.

Joly, D., and J. S. Nielsen. *Muslims in Britain: An Annotated Bibliography 1960–84*. Coventry: University of Warwick, Center for Research in Ethnic Relations, 1985.

Kettani, A. *Muslim Minorities in the World Today*. London and New York: Mansell, 1986.

Koningsveld, P. S., and W. Shadid (eds). *The Integration of Muslim and Hindus in Western Europe*. Kampen: Kok Pharos, 1991.

Lewis, Bernard. *Muslims in Europe*. St. Martin's Press, 1994.

Murad, K. *Muslim Youth in the West*. Leicester: The Islamic Foundation, 1986.

Nadwi, S. A. H. A. *Muslims in the West*. Leicester: The Islamic Foundation, 1983.

Nielsen, Jorgen S. *Muslims in Western Europe*. Edinburgh: Edinburgh University Press, 1992.

Poulter, S.M. *English Law and Ethnic Minority Customs*. London: Butterworth, 1986.

Robinson, F. *Varieties of South Asian Islam*. Coventry: University of Warwick, Center for Research in Ethnic Relations, 1988.

Sachs, L. *Evil Eye or Bacteria: Turkish Migrant Women and Swedish Health Care*. Stockholm: Stockholm Studies in Social Anthropology, 1983.

Speelman, G. *Muslims and Christians in Europe: Breaking New Ground*. Kampen: Kok, 1993.

Wahab, I. *Muslims in Britain: Profile of a Community*. London: Runnymede Trust, 1989.

Islam in the Americas

♦ Ethnicity and Population Statistics ♦ Large-Scale Muslim Organizations in North America
♦ Local Muslim Congregations ♦ Muslim Women in North America ♦ Sufism in North America
♦ Muslims in American Corrections ♦ African American Muslims

Muslims started arriving in North America as free immigrants during the last third of the nineteenth century. Before that time, sizable numbers of Muslim Africans had reached the New World as slaves between the seventeenth and eighteenth centuries. Perhaps 15 to 20 percent of the total number were brought over in such condition. They came from various locations, mostly in western Africa. There are records showing that some had knowledge of Arabic and the Quran and attempted to maintain ritual, dietary, and other Islamic practices. The cultivation of authentic Islamic life—which, in addition to the free exercise of devotional practices, requires a support community, including a strong family structure—was not permitted. Thus, the Islamic beliefs and practices of virtually all African Muslim slaves in America gradually perished. Nevertheless, the collective awareness of their Muslim past has made many contemporary African Americans proud of their own conversions to Islam. They view the growing Muslim African American community as, in part, a return to spiritual roots.

♦ ETHNICITY AND POPULATION STATISTICS

Muslims in North America constitute what one scholarly specialist has aptly called a "special cluster of ethnic groups, unified in their religious faith and present nationhood with common concerns, attempting to achieve a unique understanding among themselves" (Husaini, 15). The first wave of voluntary Muslim immigration to the United States in the late nineteenth century was largely of ethnic Arab origin, mostly from Syria, Lebanon, Jordan, and Palestine. At the same time, Canada also began to receive Muslim immigrants, the majority of whom were of Turkish origin, the rest Arabs. Whether in Canada or the United States, people

from those countries did not come as part of religious migrations but for economic betterment in the earlier periods and later, increasingly, for education and political and social freedom.

Today, Muslim Arabs are the third largest ethnic component in the American Islamic community (20 percent), after African Americans (29 percent) and south Asians (29 percent). Other Muslim ethnic groups in the United States include Albanians, Bosnians, Iranians, Turks, Africans, Southeast Asians, Euro-Americans, Eastern Europeans, and others. These estimates are based on the as yet unpublished questionnaire-based research of Dr. Ihsan Bagby of Shaw University, Raleigh, North Carolina. Another recent estimate of the American Muslim population—at five million, but based on different criteria in computing—is that of Fareed H. Numan, *The Muslim Population of the United States: A Brief Statement.* A much lower estimate of the size of the American Muslim population is that of Barry A. Kosmin and Jeffrey Scheckner at no more than one million.

In Canada, also, Muslims of south Asian origin are the largest Muslim ethnic group (35.1 percent), with Muslims of Arab origin next. The Muslim populations of the two countries are difficult to estimate accurately, but a conservative estimate is four to five million for the United States and three-hundred thousand for Canada. Those numbers do not convey the relative proportions of Muslims as percentages of the total populations of the two countries. Canada has a total population of between twenty-seven to twenty-eight million, so that Muslims comprise about 1 percent there. Muslims in the United States may now approach 2 percent of the population of about two-hundred-sixty million. A satisfactory instrument for accurately measuring the American Muslim population has yet to be achieved, whereas in Canada the official census in-

The mosque complex of the Shia Ithna Ashari community in Toronto.

cludes a mandatory question on religious affiliation. In the United States the question is optional.

All told, ethnic origins of Muslims in the United States, whether indigenous or from other countries, show an overwhelming preponderance of persons of color. In Canada the situation is similar, although, unlike in the United States, the number of Muslims of African background is small. And most of the immigrants or refugees from Africa to Canada in recent times have been either from Arab North Africa and Egypt or from the ethnic south Asian populations of eastern Africa (Kenya, Uganda, and Tanzania) and South Africa. Muslims of African as well as Asian heritage have migrated in significant numbers from Somalia and the Caribbean to Canada in recent years. The number of Euro-North American Muslims is also small, probably under 2 percent, whether in Canada or the United States. Thus, the Muslim population of North America shares in the general trend toward increasing percentages of people of color largely because of immigration and regardless of religious affiliation. Islam is by no means the only major new religion being transplanted in significant numbers to North America in these times. In both Canada and the United States

sizable Buddhist, Hindu, and Confucian communities are also developing. But Islam is a special case because of its theological and ethical affinities with Judaism and Christianity, as well as the three religions' relations with one another in European, Middle Eastern, and Mediterranean history.

In public discourse in Canada and the United States, Muslims are increasingly recognized as belonging to the monotheistic religious and moral heritage that Christians and Jews share. Already the Muslim populations of both countries are approaching the size of their Jewish populations (about three-hundred thousand in Canada and about five million in the United States), whereas the nominal Christian populations of North America are numerically dominant (83.4 percent in Canada and 90 percent in the United States). It is significant that in the media one increasingly hears references to such terms as mosque (*masjid*) and imam.

Although all urban areas of North America have Muslim congregations and Islamic centers, the greatest concentrations are in New York, California, Illinois, Ontario, Michigan, Ohio, Quebec, Texas, New Jersey, and Alberta. Most urban regions also have quite diverse Muslim populations from the standpoints of ethnicity, language, and culture. The Islamic Center of Greater Toledo, for example, has a formal paid membership of some three-hundred families (about fifteen-hundred individuals) representing more than thirty different national and ethnic backgrounds.

It is of the greatest interest and significance that the Muslim *Umma*, or community, of North America is as nearly a microcosm of the global *Umma* as has ever occurred since Islam became a major religion of the Middle East, Africa, and Asia. Of particular importance is that Muslims in North America live in two similar pluralistic, secular political systems where freedom of religion and expression are protected by law. It is, in a way, an irony of history that the greatly diverse Muslim communities that are forming in North America should be doing so in a context where Muslim law and tradition do not hold sway.

The subcommunities of Muslims in North America represent a wide range of opinions, temperaments, historical experiences, preferences, and convictions. Yet there is, as is traditionally the case with Muslims through the ages, a transcending consensus about the basic doctrines and duties of Islam, as well as the social and moral boundaries of acceptable behavior. That is not to say that all Muslims in North America agree about such things as social relations between the sexes, women's dress, the extent to which Islamic law can and should govern Muslim behavior, how (and whether) to associate with non-Muslims, roles of husband and wife, and political participation in the larger society, among many other issues.

A mosque in New Mexico.

Muslim communities in North America do not yet have a common organizational structure, like many Christian and Jewish denominations, by which they can realize large-scale goals and economies of scale in missions (known in Arabic as *dawa*), education, publishing, and social and medical services. Muslims are in the process of creating and adapting the kinds of institutions and polities that will serve them effectively in the North American setting, where anything that gets done for the betterment of Muslim community-building has to be done by the participants themselves.

This is in contrast to the institutional, social, and cultural traditions and structures that many immigrants knew in their Muslim majority countries of origin such as Egypt, Saudi Arabia, Iraq, Iran, Pakistan, Bangladesh, Turkey, and Indonesia. For example, in Egypt a physical infrastructure of *masjids* (mosque buildings), ablution facilities, religious schools, and so forth is long established with custodial institutions dedicated to their maintenance and funding. Parishes in the Western Christian sense do not exist. Muslims simply attend a nearby *masjid* for worship or go where they please in a religious society that is not differentiated by denominational boundaries. There are privately endowed *masjids*, schools, and other institutions in Muslim countries, but they fit into a long-established system of Muslim life and do not have to be invented or adapted to a non-Muslim, however otherwise tolerant, environment.

♦ LARGE-SCALE MUSLIM ORGANIZATIONS IN NORTH AMERICA

Muslims in North America are attempting to develop large-scale associations, but in ways that will not deprive them of local community independence. The largest "umbrella" group for predominately Sunni Muslims in Canada and the United States is the Islamic Society of North America (ISNA), with headquarters in Plainfield, Indiana, a suburb of Indianapolis. ISNA, whose origins were with the Muslim Student Association, is not like a Christian or Jewish denomination; rather it is an attempt to provide a means of bringing Muslims together for common purposes in education, exchange of ideas, mutual support, developing a jurisprudence appropriate to the North American context, financing new mosque building, and other things.

ISNA has a tradition of highly successful annual meetings, where several thousand members gather for a long weekend, beginning with Friday congregational prayer and followed by panels, speeches, workshops, common meals, exhibits, and socialization. Most of the people associated with ISNA are immigrant Muslims and their children, with south Asians and Arabs dominating. A fair degree of nostalgia for the "old country" is experienced by immigrants in North America, so ISNA functions, in part, as a gathering for cultural reunion and celebration.

But more important are ISNA's purposes. Convention attendees enjoy, for a few days, a strong sense of Muslim community solidarity in a country where daily life at work or school possesses little that is reassuring and familiar to Muslims. Members observe the regular daily prayers together, youth have discussions on how to grow up with Islamic values while coping with American and Canadian secular life, and friendships are renewed. There is a marriage bureau that operates a computerized database for matching potential spouses, a task that is as important for authentic Islamic life as it is often difficult to achieve in Western countries where suitable candidates may be hard to locate. This is especially the case for Euro-American women converts to Islam in North America who do not usually have the network of kinship relations where a spouse might be found. On the other hand, eligible Muslim men from immigrant back-

grounds often find suitable wives in their families' homeland. This is particularly true of south Asian Muslims who tend to be group endogamous. However, Arabs, Iranians, and Turks, for example, also often find spouses from their own ethnic communities.

♦ LOCAL MUSLIM CONGREGATIONS

Although the growth of large-scale Muslim associations in North America is an important development, the local context is where Muslims strive to live life Islamically, both as individuals and in community with their brothers and sisters in the faith. Although Muslims share a much more cohesive system of doctrine and worship across their "great tradition" than do Christian or Jewish denominations, their polity is essentially congregational, residing in the authority of the local community as it interprets and tries to follow the principles and practices found in the Quran, the Prophet's *sunna*, and the mainstream traditions of Islamic doctrinal and legal discourse.

Local congregations number more than one-thousand in North America and range from little storefront *masjids* to major Islamic centers with schools, publications, huge Friday worship attendance, and salaried staffs. In the United States there are about four-hundred Islamic schools (more than one-hundred fulltime), over four-hundred Muslim associations, as many as two-hundred-thousand Muslim-owned and operated businesses, and over eighty Islamic publications (Numan, "Islam in America," 1994, p. 26). Canada is proportionally no less richly endowed with *masjids*, schools, centers, organizations and other Islamically based initiatives.

In addition to the long-standing Toledo, Ohio, Muslim community mentioned above, there are other substantial congregations that possess the human and financial resources to serve as major hubs of Islamic life in their locales. Such large organizations may be less inclined toward actively promoting large-scale associations like ISNA and ICNA than are smaller *masjids* and individual Muslims. This is not to suggest that such large centers are not dedicated to cooperating with fellow Muslims at the national and North American levels to promote Islam; it is rather to recognize that such promotion may be better sustained by means of strong local congregations attuned to the needs of their immediate constituencies. "Think globally, act locally" would appear to be the byword for such operations.

An example of a large urban Islamic center is the Islamic Center of Southern California in Los Angeles. This large, professionally staffed center is led by two Egyptian-born brothers, one a physician and the other a businessman, plus a professional staff. The physical

ISNA Mosque of Indiana.

plant houses a sizable *masjid*, a media center for the production of Islamic videos and audio-cassettes, an Islamic school, a publishing operation, and meeting rooms. Friday noon prayer attracts from one-thousand to fifteen-hundred worshippers, and other programs bring people to the center at other times in the week. The community is ethnically very diverse and includes a wide range of religious perspectives, from traditional and strict to liberal. Periodic retreats are sponsored for youth, couples, adults, and families where urgent and sometimes controversial issues are openly discussed, for example, drug and alcohol problems, marriage and divorce, relations with non-Muslims, coping with negative stereotyping in the popular media, teen problems, and so forth. The center's leadership is unabashedly devoted to helping its members as well as Muslims anywhere in the country to adapt successfully to the majority culture in ways that do not violate Islamic principles. Like the Toledo community, the Islamic Center of Southern California is decidedly on the liberal side and does not fear some kind of harmonious assimilation into American society in the belief that such domestication is necessary to ensure the future of Muslims as equal and respected participants in the national life. In the process, it is believed that Muslims

will be able to contribute positively to the life of the larger society while maintaining their Islamic ideals and practices.

Some Muslim communities in North America are essentially conservative and disinclined to favor any kind of assimilation into non-Islamic life. One occasionally hears Muslims debating whether assimilation and integration, on the one hand, or strict separation in an "Amish" style should be the way for Muslims to go in North America. There are risks in following either path, but we discern a trend toward some kind of integration as not only pragmatically preferable but also inevitable as new generations as well as new converts accept the challenge to develop the North American *Umma* in the future.

The congregational polity of local Muslim communities has both advantages and problems. Occasionally, a group of members—for example, recently arrived immigrants—disapprove of what they consider to be "unIslamic" practices such as coeducational religious classes, mixed congregations during worship (even if, as they always are, females are in the back or in a separate space altogether), using the *masjid* for social and cultural purposes, not criticizing members for building homes with interest-bearing mortgages, and owning or operating liquor stores and bars. A strongly motivated "fundamentalist" or other faction can (and sometimes does) take over a *masjid* and install its own agenda in a manner not unlike what sometimes happens in Christian communities (e.g. Baptist,) that have congregational polities. Bitter relations result, caused in part by the new group's effective confiscation of funds and physical assets that perhaps took a generation or more for the charter community, now usually successfully assimilated into American life, to acquire.

Shia Muslims in North America

Most Muslims in North America are members of the Sunni branch of Islam, as are most in the world at large. However, there are significant numbers of Shia Muslims in both Canada and the United States, with one knowledgeable estimate as high as 30 percent in all of North America (Sachedina, 6). One of the largest Islamic centers in Toronto, for example, has a congregation composed principally of Twelver (also known as *Imami*) Shias. The Jaffari Islamic Center, as it is known, occupies a beautiful, commodious building on a well-landscaped parcel of land in a mostly residential section. The center's activities are varied and popular. Friday noon prayer draws a very large congregation, including many Sunnis. The special observance of events commemorating the martyrdom of Imam Husain (died 680) are also performed at these centers during the Muslim month of Muharra.

Although exclusively Shia and Sunni congregations predominate in North America, there is, nevertheless, a certain amount of crossing over and joining together, especially at Friday noon worship and during the celebration of major festivals such as the two Idd festivals and the *mawlid al-nabi*, the birthday of the Prophet Muhammad. The Islamic Center of Toledo has Shia members who also participate readily in other larger Islamic centers throughout North America where they are welcome.

The Nizari Ismaili branch of Shia continues to maintain its identity through its emphasis on spirituality and ethics and the disciplined hierarchical structure of worldwide governance under its imam (spiritual "leader") who at present is Agha Khan IV. It has retained a strong social identity as a minority sect that has endured through the centuries under persecution and threat. Canada has a substantial Nizari Ismaili community, probably the single, most organized Muslim group in the country, drawn principally from south Asian Muslims who had been longtime residents in eastern African nations but who, beginning with the expulsions of south Asians from Uganda in 1972, have migrated in large numbers to North America where their present population is about seventy-five-thousand.

They have been joined recently by immigrants from Afghanistan. Their places of gathering and congregational activity are known as *jamat khana*.

Most Ismailis in North America tend to be well-educated professionals, businessmen, and entrepreneurs who readily assimilate, in clothing and bearing, to the dignified, moderate lifestyles of their peers in Canadian and United States society. They identify strongly with other Muslims and the many countries in which they live, through a global development network, which undertakes development and philanthropic activity on a nonsectarian basis. They do possess a distinctive identity, but they are also devoted to the development of a strong Muslim community in North America and are contributing to that, as are other Shia communities, through conspicuously excellent educational, cultural, and philanthropic activities.

♦ MUSLIM WOMEN IN NORTH AMERICA

Muslim women in North America are playing important roles in defining and articulating Islamic life through their families, workplaces, professions, and networking and formal organizations. Women are conspicuous by their presence and participation at gatherings of Muslims, such as the annual meetings of ISNA, ICNA, and other organizations. There are ongoing discussions as well as debates in these organizations about the proper role(s) of Muslim women in the West. Whereas many Muslims view women's roles in traditional perspective, (i.e., centered in domestic activities and refraining from any social mixing with the opposite sex), a growing number of Muslims agree that women have the freedom to define their own lives as Muslims in relation to the social, religious, and cultural realities of the North American context. Opinions are divided over such issues as veiling and proper dress, social and professional relations outside the family, leadership in the mosque community, and so forth, but the very diversity among Muslims with respect to these matters is an indicator of the vitality of Islam.

There are several important Muslim women's organizations that are serving to focus on urgent issues, develop educational opportunities for Islamic growth, help people network across a wide range of perspectives, raise consciousness about and resources for persecuted and suffering Muslims (e.g., in Bosnia and Kashmir), and generally share experiences and views. One of these is the North American Council for Muslim Women, with headquarters in northern Virginia. A leading Canadian organization is the long-established Canadian Council of Muslim Women based in Toronto. A recent survey, still in process, indicates that Muslim women are active par-

Muslim women in North America are playing important roles in defining and articulating Islamic life through their families, workplaces, professions, and networking and formal organizations.

ticipants in virtually every level of professional and business life in North America.

♦ SUFISM IN NORTH AMERICA

Sufism is the mystical dimension of Islam and dates from the early history of the tradition. Sufis seek a "closer walk with Allah" and emphasize intimate, loving union with him. Sufism is not a single, organized movement but rather a wide range of spiritual paths. In North America Sufism has enjoyed wide interest from both spiritual and intellectual seekers. Many people who study Sufism are not themselves Muslims, although authentic Sufism is Islamic to the core. Indeed, for many, it is the "heartbeat" of Islam.

There are not large numbers of Sufis in North America, even though there is considerable interest in the Sufi path. One scholarly specialist has divided North American Sufis into two main types, using the gardening metaphor of "hybrids" and "perennials." The hybrids are:

> those movements which identify more closely with an Islamic source and content. . . . In

America these hybrid Sufi groups generally are founded and led by persons who were born and raised in Muslim societies, in other words led by immigrants to the West. . . . "The perennials" of the garden are those movements in which the specifically Islamic identification and content of the movement have been de-emphasized in favor of a "perennialist" outlook . . . [which holds] that there is a universal, eternal truth which underlies all religions.

The most disciplined of the Sufi movements, at least in the traditional sense, are the "hybrids," while many attracted to the "perennial" type tend to believe that "spiritual practices from various religious traditions may be combined since they all emerge from the same true source which is, in fact, primarily gnostic, rather than religious" (Hermansen, 1–2).

Sufis in North America often stand aloof from mainstream Muslim life, fearing the criticism of the orthodox for what are often considered by them to be deviant doctrines and practices. But there are also many Muslims for whom some sort of Sufi discipline is a higher calling but based solidly on orthodox doctrine and devotional practices. One finds this diversity in attitudes in many parts of the Muslim world, too, so it is not surprising that it should carry over to North America. It is true that in America, like traditional Muslim societies, Sufism may be tolerated (most), condemned (e.g., Saudi Arabia), or enthusiastically embraced (e.g., Egypt). In North America Sufism has a potential for attracting new converts to Islam by virtue of its openness, tolerance, appreciation of personal religious experience, friendliness, and accessibility to outsiders.

♦ MUSLIMS IN AMERICAN CORRECTIONS

A unique dimension of Islam in North America is primarily a United States phenomenon. That is the role that the criminal justice system plays in fostering conversions to Islam among incarcerated inmates. A disproportionate number of American minorities—African Americans, Hispanics, and Native Americans— are serving sentences in jails and prisons. One estimate has nearly 25 percent of all African American males between the ages of twenty to twenty-nine involved in the criminal justice system on any given day. A remarkable dynamic in American prisons is the high percentage of inmates who convert to Islam behind bars, perhaps because of the conversion of Malcolm X to the Nation of Islam while in prison. Large numbers of African Americans have been positively influenced by Malcolm X's radical reorientation of his life and subsequent success as a great religious leader.

The large numbers of conversions that occur in prison show no sign of letting up. In the process, many people find new lives and start out on the path of discipline, moral development, cultivating a work ethic, and learning social as well as political skills that serve them well after release. The recidivism rate among former inmates who have converted to Islam, while not low, is lower than the average. And the numbers of new Muslims who sustain their newfound Islamic lifestyle after release are large enough to add substantially to the American Muslim community as a whole. Increasingly, corrections authorities are recognizing the beneficial effects of Islam in the prison environment, where many Muslim teachers and missionaries do difficult but important work, mostly as volunteers. Prison chaplaincies are increasingly hiring trained Muslim imams who work alongside Christian and Jewish clergy in the facilities. As this trend grows, it is likely that Islam in prisons will become more orthodox, meaning in most cases Sunni, whereas at present there is a variety of sectarian forms of Islam existing alongside Sunnism.

The needs of incarcerated Muslims are great. Jurisdictions have greatly improved their policies and practices in the area of inmates' religious rights—to have *halal* (religiously acceptable) food, to meet for Friday noon worship, to grow facial hair, and to use perfumed oils, but pre- and postrelease programs are still rare, and the needs of released inmates are not being met very effectively by fellow Muslims. More and more *masjids* and Islamic organizations are taking note of the plight of new Muslims in and out of prison. This awareness is leading to initiatives to provide resources and programs for former as well as current Muslim inmates according to traditional Islamic principles of mutual support and social justice within the *Umma*.

Frederick M. Denny

♦ AFRICAN AMERICAN MUSLIMS

Muslims in the Slave Era

The presence of Muslim slaves has been ignored by most historians who have tended to focus upon the conversion of Africans to Christianity or upon the attempts to preserve aspects of traditional African religions. Yet the presence of Muslim slaves have been attested to by narrative and documentary accounts, some of which were written in Arabic. Yarrow Mamout, Job Ben Solomon, and Lamine Jay arrived in colonial Maryland in the 1730s. Abdul Rahaman, Mohammed Kaba, Bilali, Salih Bilali, and "Benjamin Cochrane" were enslaved in the late eighteenth century. Omar ibn Said, Kebe, and Abu Bakr were brought to southern plantations in the early 1800s, while two others, Mahommah Baquaqua and Mohammed Ali bin Said, came to the United States as freedmen about 1850. Abdul Rahaman was a Muslim prince of the Fula people in Timbo. Futa Jallon became a slave for close to twenty years in Natchez, Mississippi, before he was finally freed and eventually made his way back to Africa through the aid of abolitionist groups.

Court records in South Carolina spoke of African slaves who prayed to Allah and refused to eat pork. Missionaries in Georgia and South Carolina observed that some Muslim slaves attempted to blend Islam and Christianity by identifying God with Allah and Muhammad with Jesus. A conservative estimate is that there were close to thirty-thousand Muslim slaves who came from Islamic-dominated ethnic groups such as Mandigos, Fulas, Gambians, Senegambians, Senegalese, Cape Verdeans, and Sierra Leoneans in West Africa. However, in spite of the much larger presence of African Muslims in North America than previously thought, the Islamic influence did not survive the impact of the slave period. Except for the documents left by the Muslims named above, only scattered traces and family memories of Islam remained among African

Americans like Alex Haley's ancestral Muslim character, Kunta Kinte of the Senegambia, in his novel *Roots*.

By the late nineteenth century, black Christian churches had become so dominant in the religious and social life of black communities that only a few African American leaders who had traveled to Africa knew anything about Islam. Contacts between immigrant Arab groups and African Americans were almost nonexistent at this time. After touring Liberia and South Africa, Bishop Henry McNeil Turner (1834–1915) of the African Methodist Episcopal Church recognized the "dignity, majesty, and consciousness of [the] word of Muslims" (Austin, 1984). However, it was Edward Wilmot Blyden (1832–1912), the West Indian educator, Christian missionary, and minister for the government of Liberia who became the most enthusiastic supporter of Islam for African Americans. Blyden, who began teaching Arabic in Liberia in 1867, wrote *Christianity, Islam and the Negro Race* and concluded that Islam had a much better record of racial equality than Christianity, especially after comparing the racial attitudes of Christian and Muslim missionaries whom he had encountered in Africa. Islam, he felt, could also be a positive force in improving the life conditions for African Americans in the United States. Although he lectured extensively, Blyden did not become a leader of a social movement that established Islam effectively in America at that time. This task awaited the forceful personalities of the black urban migrations in the twentieth century.

The Proto-Islamic Movements of the Twentieth Century: Noble Drew Ali and the Moorish Holy Temple of Science

The massive rural and urban migrations by more than four million African Americans during the first decades of the twentieth century provided the conditions for the rise of a number of black militant and separatist movements, including a few which had a tangential relationship to Islam. These "proto-Islamic" movements combined the religious trappings of Islam, a few rituals, symbols, or dress with a core message of black nationalism. In 1913 Timothy Drew (1886-1929), a black delivery man and street corner preacher from North Carolina, founded the first Moorish Holy Temple of Science in Newark, New Jersey. Rejecting Christianity as the white man's religion, Drew took advantage of the widespread discontent among the newly arrived black migrants and rapidly established temples in Detroit, Harlem, Chicago, Pittsburgh, and in cities across the South. Calling himself Prophet Noble Drew Ali, he forged a message aimed at the confusion about names, national origins, and the self-identity of black people. Black people were not "Negroes" but "Asiatics," "Moors," or "Moorish Americans." Their

true home was Morocco and their true religion was Moorish Science, whose doctrines were elaborated in a sixty-page book written by Ali called the Holy Koran (which should not be confused with the Quran). Nobel Ali issued "Nationality and Identification Cards" stamped with the Islamic symbol of the star and crescent. There was a belief that these identity cards would prevent harm from the white man or European who was, in any case, soon to be destroyed or ultimately controlled by "Asiatics." As the movement spread from the East Coast to the Midwest, Ali's followers in Chicago practiced "bumping days": Aggressive male members would accost whites on the sidewalks and surreptitiously bump them out of the way, a practice that reversed the Jim Crow custom of southern whites forcing blacks off the sidewalks. After numerous complaints to the police, Noble Drew Ali ordered a halt to the disorders and urged his followers to exercise restraint. "Stop flashing your cards before Europeans," he said, "as this only causes confusion. We did not come to cause confusion; our work is to uplift the nation." The headquarters of the movement was moved to Chicago in 1925.

The growth of the Moorish Science movement was accelerated during the post–World War I years by the recruitment of better-educated but less-dedicated members who quickly assumed leadership positions. These new leaders began to grow rich by exploiting the less-educated membership of the movement and selling them herbs, magical charms, potions, and literature. When Ali intervened to prevent further exploitation, he was pushed aside, and his interference eventually led to his mysterious death in 1929. Noble Drew Ali died of a beating; whether it was done by the police when he was in their custody or by dissident members in the movement is not known. After his death, the movement split into numerous smaller contending factions with different rival leaders who claimed to be "reincarnations" of Noble Drew Ali.

The Moorish Science Temple movement has survived with active temples in Chicago, Detroit, New York, and a few other cities. In present-day Moorish temples, membership is restricted to "Asiatics" or non-Caucasians who have rejected their former identities as "colored" or "Negro." The terms *el* or *bey* are attached to the name of each member as a sign of their Asiatic status and inward transformation. Friday is the Sabbath for the Moors, and they have adopted a mixture of Islamic and Christian rituals in worship. They face Mecca when they pray three times a day, but they have also incorporated Jesus and the singing of transposed hymns in their services. The Moorish Science Temple movement was the first proto-Islamic group of African-Americans who helped to pave the way for more orthodox Islamic practices and beliefs. Many

Moors were among the earliest converts to the Nation of Islam or Black Muslim movement.

The Ahmadiyyah and the Growth of African American Sunni Islamic Movements

While the Moors became the first to introduce aspects of Islam to black communities, sometime around 1920 the Ahmadiyyah movement sent missionaries to the United States who began to proselytize among African Americans. Founded in India in 1889 by Mizra Ghulam Ahmad, a self-proclaimed Mahdi or Muslim messiah, the Ahmadiyyah were a controversial group that was concerned with interpretations of the Christian gospel, including the Second Coming. The Ahmadiyyah also emphasized some of the subtle criticisms of Christianity that were found in the Quran such as the view that Jesus did not really die on the cross (Quran 4: 157–59).

As an energetic missionary movement, the Ahmadiyyah first sent missionaries to West Africa, then later to the diaspora in the United States. Although it was relatively unknown and unnoticed, the Ahmadiyyah mission movement is significant in that it provided one of the first contacts for African Americans with a worldwide sectarian Islamic group whose traditions were more orthodox than the proto-Islamic black nationalist movements.

Shaykh Deen of the Ahmadiyyah mission was influential in converting Walter Gregg. Gregg became one of the first African American converts to Islam and changed his name to Wali Akram. After a period of studying the Quran and Arabic with the *shaykh*, Akram founded the First Cleveland Mosque in 1933. Although he eventually became independent of the Ahmadiyyah movement, Wali Akram continued to use teaching materials published by the Ahmadiyyah. He taught Islam to several generations of midwesterners, including many African Americans. An accomplished mechanical engineer and inventor, Akram designed the Gregg coupling to link railroad cars and he also ran a print shop in his mosque. Akram served as the president of the Uniting Islamic Societies of America from 1943 to 1944, one of the first of many attempts to unite African American Sunni Muslim groups in the United States. He also developed the "Muslim Ten-Year Plan," adapted from the Ahmadiyyah, which called on Muslims to contribute financially to the economic development of Muslim communities: buying land, creating businesses and schools, and developing a Muslim environment in neighborhoods. The membership of the First Cleveland Mosque ranged from fifty to two-hundred families, and it is presently being led by Wali Akram's grandson, Imam Abbas Ahmed.

About the same time that the Ahmadiyyah move-ment began its missionary work in the United States, another small group of Muslims, led by a West Indian named Shaykh Dawud Hamed Faisel, established the Islamic Mission to America in 1923 on State Street in Brooklyn. At the State Street Mosque, Shaykh Dawud taught a more authentic version of Islam than the Ahmadiyyahs because he followed the *sunna* (practices) of the Prophet Muhammad. While the Ahmadiyyahs believed that Mizra Ghulam Ahmad was the Mahdi, Dawud belonged to the tradition of Sunni Islam that did not identify the Mahdi with a historical person. The Shaykh welcomed black Americans to mingle with immigrant Muslims. He taught Arabic, the Quran, the *sunna-hadith* tradition, *sharia*, or Islamic law and emphasized the five "pillars" of Islam—the credo (*shahada*) of Islam that emphasizes belief in the One God of Islam and Muhammad as the Messenger of Allah; prayer (*salat*) five times a day facing Mecca; charity tax (*zakat*); fasting (*sawm*) during the month of Ramadan; and pilgrimage to Mecca (*Hajj*) if it is possible. Shaykh Dawud's work was concentrated mainly in New York and New England. He became responsible for converting a number of African American Muslims.

A smaller group and third source of African American Sunni Muslims was the community of Buffalo, New York, that was taught Sunni Islam and Arabic by an African American Muslim, Professor Muhammad EzalDeen in 1933. EzalDeen was a former member of the Moorish Science Temple in the 1920s. In 1926 Noble Drew Ali sent EzalDeen and several other Moors to Turkey as part of an international delegation to a conference. While he was abroad, EzalDeen became interested in Sunni Islam and went to the University of Al-Azhar in Cairo to study Arabic and the Islamic religion. After several years of study, he returned to Newark, New Jersey, to inform Noble Drew Ali of his new Islamic perspective and left the Moorish Science movement. While he was teaching Islam and Arabic in New York City, EzalDeen received an invitation from a small group of African Americans in Buffalo who had been learning some rudimentary Arabic and desired to learn more about Islam. In 1933 Professor EzalDeen and his wife moved to Buffalo and lived there for about ten years.

In 1938 he convinced the members in Buffalo to buy three-hundred acres of land in the rural area of West Valley, New York, and to establish a new community of Muslims. Jabal Arabiyya, or the Arab Mountain, became the official name of the small community of African American Muslims who built houses on the land, farmed it, and continue to live there. EzalDeen formed several organizations, including a national one called Uniting Islamic Societies of America in the early 1940s. This organization elected Imam Wali Akram as the president. EzalDeen traveled continuously between various Sunni Muslim groups that were formed in black communities in Cleveland, Pittsburgh, Philadelphia, New York City, and Buffalo. After an internal dispute with members of the Buffalo community in the mid-1940s, EzalDeen returned to Newark and established another rural community of Muslims in southern New Jersey, which took the name EzalDeen Village. More than twenty families built houses on land purchased by the community. They built their own *masjid* (mosque) and established a Muslim neighborhood along a road called EzalDeen Village.

The work of the Ahmadiyyah movement, Shaykh Dawud's Islamic Mission to America and the State Street Mosque in New York City, Imam Wali Akram of the First Cleveland Mosque of Cleveland, Ohio, and Professor EzalDeen's rural Muslim communities, Jabul Arabiyya and EzalDeen Village, were important in establishing a beachhead for a more orthodox and universal Sunni Islam in African American communities.

During the turmoil of the 1960s young African Americans were exposed more and more to authentic Sunni Islam through international travel and Muslim reformist and revivalist movements such as the Tablighi Jamaat in Pakistan or the Ikhwan in Egypt. Others were influenced by the life and death of Malcolm X, who converted to Sunni Islam from his black nationalist teachings in the Nation of Islam. Three African American Muslim movements emerged in the 1960s: the Mosque of Islamic Brotherhood, the Darul Islam movement, and the Islamic Party.

The Mosque of Islamic Brotherhood The Mosque of Islamic Brotherhood in Harlem was conceived in 1964 by Shaykh Khalid Ahmad Tawfiq who was then a student at the Al-Azhar University in Cairo, Egypt. Tawfiq was his father's name, given to him after he and several relatives joined the Moorish Science Temple. Khalid Ahmad Tawfiq attended the DeWitt Clinton High School in New York City. However, Tawfiq was greatly influenced by Minister Malcolm X and became a member of Malcolm's Muslim Mosque Inc. where he made his profession of faith or *shahada* at age seventeen. Although he admired the black nationalism of the Nation of Islam, he never submitted to the distortions of the authentic Islamic message or to the racial doctrines propagated by the Nation. During his international travels in early 1964, Malcolm made arrangements for Tawfiq, one of his youngest members of the Muslim Mosque Inc., to study at Al-Azhar University on a scholarship. Malcolm X fondly referred to Tawfiq as the "samurai" because of Tawfiq's expertise in the martial arts. From 1964 to 1967, Tawfiq, after becoming a shaykh, or religious leader, founded the American Muslim Students Association at Al-Azhar. He also played his French horn with various musical groups, including the Cairo symphony orchestra. When

Malcolm X was assassinated in 1965, Tawfiq led a large campus demonstration. He also participated in student protests in 1966 as President Nasser's policies became more repressive. During the 1967 War, Tawfiq and Akbar Muhammad, the youngest of Elijah Muhammad's six sons, were arrested, imprisoned, and transferred out of Egypt.

The Mosque of the Islamic Brotherhood (MIB) was officially founded in Harlem in 1967 upon Shaykh Tawfiq's return to the United States. Among African American Sunni Muslim groups, the MIB was unique because it melded known Islamic teachings with common concerns of African Americans. He felt that African nationhood was a common thread. Tawfiq taught his followers that they could properly identify with their African heritage—as Moors, Nubians, Ethiopians, tribe of Shabazz, and so on—and still be authentically Islamic, as long as they did not reject people of other races. He called his followers "Cushites," the first builders of civilization. Although he was training his members for nationhood, they would hold dual citizenship as Cushites and Americans. Shaykh Tawfiq's vision of nationhood was deeply influenced by Marcus Garvey's United Negro Improvement Association and Hassan al-Banna's Muslim Brotherhood of Egypt. Following Garvey, the MIB developed its own unique red, black, and green flag showing a crescent and star and a curved sword with acknowledgements to Allah written in the Arabic script. In 1971 he published the first issue of *Western Sunrise*, the newspaper of the MIB. In 1986 Shaykh Tawfiq was diagnosed with Parkinson's disease and he died in December 1988. Presently led by Imam Talib Abdur Rashid, the MIB has established its own school for children and communal living quarters for members in several buildings in central Harlem.

The Darul Islam Movement The Darul Islam movement began in 1962 among dissatisfied African American members of Shaykh Dawud's State Street Mosque in Brooklyn. Tajab Mahoud, Yahya Abdul Karim, Ishaqq A. Shaheed, and a few other dedicated African American Muslims met for Friday prayer at State Street. They organized gradually and were eventually led by the charismatic Yahya Abdul Karim, who was chosen as the imam in 1968 when the group left the State Street Mosque and established their own permanent center at 240 Sumpter Street in Brooklyn. Sensing the dissatisfaction with the lack of indigenous African American leadership, organization, and community programs at State Street, Imam Karim instituted the Darul Islam, the call to establish the kingdom of Allah on earth where the *sharia* or Islamic law according to the Quran and *sunna-hadith* tradition would be established as the governing legislation. Each member had to take a *bayah* or pledge to the imam/amir to work and struggle to establish this kingdom of Allah on earth. Members also worked to keep the *masjid* open twenty-four hours a day for the five *salats* (prayers). The deeply faithful and trustworthy members were those who showed up daily at the *masjid* for the *fajr* (early morning) and *isha* (evening) prayers. The *musalla* also held classes in Arabic and the fundamentals of Islam and developed programs for community service. The movement spread to Cleveland, Baltimore, Philadelphia, and Washington, D.C. A network of over forty mosques was developed between 1968 and 1982.

By 1970 the attendance at the center on Sumpter Street had outgrown its space, and a move to a bigger place at 52 Herkimer Street was made; the Yasin Mosque was established there. The period of the 1970s was a period of greater internal organization and development of different departments and services (i.e., a ministry of information, a ministry of *dawa* or proselytization, ministries of education, culture, health and welfare, etc.). During the 1970s and early 1980s, an organized and disciplined paramilitary group called the Rad (named after the thunder mentioned in the thirteenth *sura* of the Quran) was established. The Rad was the training ground to produce the well-rounded Muslim worker for Islam. All members learned the martial arts and also how to fight, shoot, and handle weapons. They had to learn military as well as spiritual tasks such as giving a *khutba* (religious sermon), leading prayers, and reading the Quran in Arabic. It was a heady time, filled with the fervor and enthusiasm of being part of a new and serious religious movement. In 1979 a Sufi teacher, Shaykh Mubarik Ali Jilani Hasmi from Pakistan, influenced Imam Yahya Karim and became part of the *Dar* (house). The movement split in 1982 with some core members choosing to follow Shaykh Jilani's teachings, which emphasized *jihad* (translated directly as "holy war" but with greater spiritual implications) and Sufism. This core group took on the name Al-Fuqara. Other members left the movement because many felt that they could not follow a Muslim leader who was not African American; this was one of the key principles for founding the *Dar*.

After the schism in 1982, the Darul Islam movement declined in influence, but it is presently being revived under the charismatic leadership of Imam Jamil Al-Amin (the former H. Rap Brown of the Student Nonviolent Coordinating Committee) in Atlanta. Imam Jamil has been able to gather about twenty communities who have pledged to follow his leadership. He has refused to use the name Darul Islam, but he still identifies with the need to establish the kingdom of Allah in the United States. He has a small *masjid* located in a house as well as a grocery store/social center across the street. Jamil has emphasized establishing the *salat* five times a day and keeping the *masjid* open on a twenty-four-hour basis. In keeping with the vision of the former Darul Islam movement, establishing the prayer is viewed as a religious and organizing strategy. His local efforts have been directed toward establishing a Muslim neighborhood in Atlanta by cleaning out the neighborhood park of drug dealers and encouraging Muslims to move in. While his national efforts are directed toward rebuilding a movement of Sunni communities, all of the communities must take a pledge to follow his leadership. Jamil al-Amin has written a book, *Revolution by the Book*, published in 1993, which contains some of his views on Islamic teachings and activism.

The Islamic Party The Islamic Party was established in December 1971 by Muzzafruddin Hamid as an outgrowth of Masjid al-Umma, which was founded earlier in 1969 in Washington, D.C. Muzzafruddin was a jazz musician from Atlanta, Georgia, who played the trumpet with Dakota Staton's group in New York City until he took his *shahadah*. He had heard Malcolm X speak after his break from the Nation of Islam. When his musical career did not take off, Muzzafruddin decided to travel to Muslim countries and to educate himself about Islam. The founding of the Islamic Party was the major result from Muzzafruddin's growing knowledge both of Sunni Islam and some of the Islamic ideological movements especially the Ikhwan (Islamic Brotherhood movement) in Egypt and Shaykh Maulana Mawdudi's teachings in Pakistan. He is reported to have stayed in Mawdudi's home for a while. Upon his return to the United States, Muzzafruddin became dissatisfied with the lack of community outreach of the Islamic Center of Washington, D.C., and the fact that the majority of the immigrant Arabs did not give *dawa* (propagation to spread Islam) to the large community of African Americans who were showing an increased interest in Islam. With some close Muslim friends, especially Zaid Ahmad and Hakim Qawi, Muzzafruddin formed Masjid al-Umma or the Community Mosque in 1969. Two years later, the Islamic Party was established on 101 S Street in Washington, D.C. In ensuing years branches were formed in other places like Chicago, Akron, Pittsburgh, New York City, and later in Houston and New Orleans.

In 1974 the headquarters of the Party was moved to a larger structure on 77 Park Road near Howard University. Students from Howard were given *dawa* and many joined the Party, which quickly reached its activist peak. It was a period of dramatic growth and enabled the Islamic Party to establish a twenty-four-hour restaurant, Islamic bookstore, culture center, and taxi cab business of seven cars. In the mid-1970s there was an atmosphere of fervor and enthusiasm among the members who often put in long hours doing *dawa*, community service, or working for the Party. The Civil

Rights movement had faded from the scene after the death of Dr. Martin Luther King Jr., and for many young, dissatisfied African Americans, the new movement of Islam replaced it. Islam was the answer because it embodied a total way of life where religion, politics, economics, and social relations were melded in an orderly fashion. Islam was the means of liberating an oppressed people from their oppression. "Movement Islam," with its ideological teachings from Egypt and Pakistan, stressed *jihad* or struggle both internally and externally. Internal *jihad* meant a continual struggle with one's knowledge of and practice of Islam. External *jihad* emphasized a struggle with the problems of society from an Islamic point of view. For many, *jihad* had a revolutionary meaning: to challenge mainstream American society by any means possible. The Party's newspaper was called *Faithful Struggle*. In 1975 Muzzafruddin was also influenced by the teachings of Colonel Qadaffi of Libya, from whom the Islamic Party received an interest-free loan of $100,000.

In 1977, a fateful decision was made to begin moving Islamic Party members and their families, and eventually the headquarters, to Connally, Georgia, where the Party had bought some rural farmland. The decision caused the movement to split and fissure into different factions. The Chicago contingent left and the offices in Houston, Pittsburgh, and Akron were closed. By 1979 the movement had declined precipitously so the Party sold its buildings in Washington, D.C. Muzzafruddin and some close associates decided to move to Trinidad where they had acquired a large building. After two years in Trinidad, another split occurred, and the main faction led by Muzzafruddin moved to Guyana then to Dominica. The major reason for the move to the Caribbean was to use armed struggle to take over an island or country and to establish an Islamic government and way of life. However, the Dominican government had them deported. In 1983 some followers went to St. Croix while Muzzafruddin moved back to the United States. A rural village called "New Medina" was established in Taste, Georgia. Muzzafruddin and some others lived there before he died of an illness in 1989. After Muzzafruddin was buried in New Medina, some of his followers became Shia, inspired by the Iranian revolution of 1979 and the teachings of Ayatollah Khomeini.

Ironically, the greatest impact and influence of Islam among black people was exerted by another proto-Islamic movement called the Nation of Islam.

The Nation of Islam

In midsummer of 1930, a friendly but mysterious peddler appeared among rural southern migrants in a Detroit neighborhood known as "Paradise Valley" selling raincoats, silks, and sundries, but he also began to give advice to the poor residents about their health and spiritual development. He told them about their "true religion," not Christianity, but the "religion of the Black Men" of Asia and Africa. Using both the teachings of the Bible and the Quran in his messages, he taught at first in the private homes of his followers, then later rented a hall that was called the Temple of Islam. This mysterious stranger often referred to himself as Mr. Farrad Mohammed, or sometimes as Mr. Wali Farrad, Wallace D. Fard, W. D. Fard, or Professor Fard.

Master Fard, as he was called, taught his followers about a period of temporary domination and persecution by white, "blue-eyed devils" who had achieved their power by brutality, murder, and trickery. But as a prerequisite for black liberation, he stressed the importance of attaining "knowledge of self." He told his followers that they were not Americans and therefore owed no allegiance to the American flag. He wrote two manuals for the movement, *The Secret Ritual of the Nation of Islam*, which is transmitted orally to members, and *Teaching for the Lost-Found Nation of Islam in a Mathematical Way*, which is written in symbolic language and requires special interpretation. Fard established several organizations: the University of Islam to propagate his teachings; the Muslim Girls Training to teach home economics to female members and methods in how to be a proper Muslim woman; the Fruit of Islam, consisting of select male members, to provide security for Muslim leaders and to enforce the disciplinary rules.

One of the earliest officers of the movement and Fard's most trusted lieutenant was Robert Poole (1897–1975), also known as Elijah Poole, who was given the Muslim name Elijah Muhammad. As the son of a rural Baptist minister and sharecropper from Sandersville, Georgia, Poole had migrated with his family to Detroit in 1923, and he and several of his brothers joined the Nation of Islam in 1931. Although he only had a third-grade education, Elijah Muhammad's shrewd native intelligence and hard work enabled him to rise through the ranks rapidly, and he was chosen by

Elijah Muhammad

Fard as the chief minister of Islam to preside over the daily affairs of the organization.

Fard's mysterious disappearance in 1934 led to an internal struggle for the leadership of the Nation of Islam among several contending factions. As a result of this strife, Elijah Muhammad eventually moved his family and close followers to the south side of Chicago in 1936 where they established Temple of Islam No. 2, which eventually became the national headquarters of the movement. Throughout the decade of the 1940s Elijah Muhammad reshaped the Nation and gave it his own imprint. He firmly established the doctrine that Master Fard was "Allah" and that he, Elijah Muhammad, knew Allah personally and was anointed the "Messenger" of Allah.

Under Muhammad's guidance, the Nation developed a two-pronged attack on the problems of the black masses: a stress upon the development of economic independence and an emphasis upon the recovery of an acceptable identity. "Do for Self" became the rallying cry of the movement, which encouraged economic self-reliance for black individuals and the black community. The economic ethic of the Black Muslims was a kind of "Black Puritanism"— hard work, frugality, the avoidance of debt, self-improvement, and a conservative lifestyle. During the forty-one-year period of his leadership, Elijah Muhammad and his followers established more than one hundred temples nationwide, innumerable grocery stores, restaurants, and bakeries. The Nation of Islam also became known for its famous bean pies and whiting fish, which were peddled in black communities to improve the nutrition and physical health of African Americans. It strictly forbade alcohol, drugs, pork, and an unhealthy diet. Elijah Muhammad was prescient in his advice to his followers on nutrition: "You are what you eat," he often said.

In his "Message to the Black Man" (1965), Muhammad diagnosed the vulnerabilities of the black psyche as stemming from a confusion of identity and self-hatred caused by white racism. The cure he prescribed was radical surgery through the formation of a separate black nation. Muhammad's 120 "degrees," or lessons, and the major doctrines and beliefs of the Nation of Islam elaborated on aspects of this central message. The white man was portrayed as a "devil by nature," unable to respect anyone who is not white, and he was represented as the historic and persistent source of harm and injury to black people. The central theological myth of the Nation tells of Yakub, a black mad scientist who rebelled against Allah by creating the white race, a weak hybrid people who were permitted temporary dominance of the world. But according to the apocalyptic beliefs of the Black Muslims, there will be a future clash between the forces of good (blacks) and the forces of evil (whites) in the not-too-distant future, a Battle of Armageddon where black people will emerge victorious and re-create their original hegemony under Allah throughout the world.

All of these myths and doctrines have functioned as a theodicy for the Black Muslims, as an explanation and rationalization for the pain and suffering inflicted upon black people in America. For example, Malcolm Little (1925–1965) described the powerful, jarring impact that the revelation of the religious truth of the Nation of Islam had upon him in the Norfolk state prison in Massachusetts after his brother Reginald told him, "The white man is the Devil." The doctrines of the Nation deeply affected his thinking; the chaos of the world behind prison bars became a cosmos, an ordered reality. Malcolm finally had an explanation for the extreme poverty and tragedies his family suffered and for all of the years he spent hustling and pimping on the streets of Roxbury and Harlem as "Detroit Red." The conversion and total transformation of Malcolm Little into Malcolm X in prison in 1947 is a story of the effectiveness of Elijah Muhammad's message, which has been repeated many thousands of times over during the forty-one-year history of the Nation of Islam under Mr. Muhammad's leadership. Dropping one's surname and taking on an X, standard practice in the movement, was an outward symbol of inward change: It meant ex-Christian, ex-Negro, and ex-slave.

The years between Malcolm's release from prison and his assassination, 1952 to 1965, mark the period of the greatest growth and influence of the Nation of Islam. After meeting Elijah Muhammad in 1952, he began organizing Muslim temples in New York, Philadelphia, Boston, in the South, and on the West Coast as well. Malcolm founded the Nation's newspaper, *Muhammad Speaks*, in the basement of his home, and he initiated the practice of requiring every male Muslim to sell an assigned quota of newspapers on the street as a recruiting and fund-raising device. He rose

The influence of the Nation of Islam refracted through the public charisma of Malcolm X.

rapidly through the ranks to become minister of Boston Temple No. 11 and was later rewarded with the post of minister of Temple No. 7 in Harlem, the largest and most prestigious temple in the Nation of Islam after the Chicago headquarters. Elijah Muhammad recognized his organizational talents and his enormous charismatic appeal and forensic abilities by naming Malcolm his national representative of the Nation of Islam, second in rank to the Messenger himself. Under his lieutenancy, the Nation of Islam achieved a membership estimated at five-hundred thousand. But like the other movements of this kind, the numbers involved were quite fluid, and the influence of the Nation of Islam refracted through the public charisma of Malcolm X greatly exceeded its actual numbers.

Malcolm's keen intellect, incisive wit, and ardent radicalism made him a formidable critic of American society, including the Civil Rights movement. As a favorite media personality, he challenged Dr. Martin Luther King's central notions of integration and nonviolence. Malcolm felt that what was at stake at a deeper level than the civil right to sit in a restaurant or even to vote was the integrity of black selfhood and its independence. His biting critique of the "so-called Negro" and his emphasis upon the recovery of black self-identity and independence provided the intellectual foundations for the Black Power and black consciousness movements of the late 1960s and 1970s in American society. In contrast to King's nonviolence, Malcolm urged his followers to defend themselves "by any means possible." He also articulated the pent-up anger, frustration, bitterness, and rage felt by the dispossessed black masses, the "grass roots."

After making the *Hajj*, or the pilgrimage to Mecca, and realizing that traditional Islam is not a religion of racism, hatred, and separation, Malcolm left the Nation of Islam in March 1964 in order to form his own organizations, the Muslim Mosque Inc. and the Organization for Afro-American Unity. He took the Muslim name El-

Louis Farrakhan

Hajj Malik el-Shabazz, the result of converting to orthodox Sunni Islam. Malcolm was assassinated on February 21, 1965 while he was delivering a lecture at the Audubon Ballroom in Harlem.

From 1965 until Elijah Muhammad's death in February 1975, the Nation of Islam prospered economically but its membership never surged again. Minister Louis X of Boston, also called Louis Abdul Farrakhan, replaced Malcolm as the national representative and the head minister of Temple No. 7 in New York. During this period, the Nation acquired an ultramodern printing press, cattle farms in Georgia and Alabama, and a bank in Chicago.

After a bout of illness, Mr. Muhammad died in Chicago, and one of his six sons, Wallace Dean Muhammad (later Imam Warith Deen Mohammad), was named supreme minister of the Nation of Islam. However, two months later Wallace shocked everyone by announcing an end to the racial doctrines and black nationalist teachings. He disbanded the Fruit of Islam and the Muslim Girls Training, the elite internal organizations, and gradually moved his followers toward orthodox Sunni Islam. Wallace's moves led to a number of schisms, which produced several competing black nationalist groups: Minister Louis Farrakhan's resurrected Nation of Islam in Chicago, the largest and most well known of the groups; Silas Muhammad's Nation of Islam in Atlanta; and a brother of Elijah Muhammad, John Muhammad's Nation of Islam in Detroit.

Imam Warith Deen Mohammed's Sunni Muslim Movement

In the evolution of his movement, Wallace took the Muslim title and name Imam Warith Deen Muhammad (in 1991 the spelling of the surname was changed to the British usage of Mohammed). The movement's name and the name of its newspaper also changed several times: from the *World Community of Al-Islam in the West* (*Bilalian News*) in 1976 to the *American Muslim Mission* (*American Muslim Mission Journal*) in 1980; then in 1985 Warith decentralized the movement into independent *masjids*. With several hundred thousand predominantly African American followers who identify with his teachings, Imam Warith Deen Mohammed has continued to deepen their knowledge of the Arabic language, the Quran, and the *sunna*, or practices of the Prophet. Immigrant Muslims from Africa, Pakistan, and other Middle Eastern countries also participate in the Friday prayer services.

Although they adhere to the basic tenets of Sunni Islam, the movement has not yet settled on a particular school of theological thought to follow. Since every significant culture in Islamic history has produced its own school of thought, it is Mohammed's conviction that eventually an American school of Islamic thought will emerge in the United States, comprised of the views of African American and immigrant Muslims. Imam Warith Deen Mohammed has been accepted by the World Muslim Council as a representative of Muslims in the United States, and he has been given the responsibility of certifying Americans who desire to make the pilgrimage to Mecca. The African American Sunni Muslims who follow Imam Warith Deen Mohammed constitute the largest movement of Muslims in the black community, estimated at about three-hundred-thousand. His *masjids* are also active in their communities, providing family and religious counseling services, antidrug and antialcohol patrols, and a wide variety of social services.

As Muslims who follow the Quran and the *sunna*, they have been open in working with other Christian and Jewish religious groups to solve community problems. Imam Mohammed's movement is identified with the weekly newspaper they publish, the *Muslim Journal*. A Muslim Teacher's College has been established in Sedalia, North Carolina, to provide training for those who want to teach in the thirty-eight Sister Clara Muhammad Schools across the country and for training imams and other religious leaders.

Minister Louis Farrakhan's Nation of Islam

The changes introduced by Imam Warith Deen Mohammad led to a splintering of the movement, especially among the hard-core black nationalist followers. From 1975 to 1978, Minister Louis Farrakhan, the former Louis Eugene Walcott of Boston who had expected that he would be chosen as Elijah's successor, kept silent in public and traveled extensively in Muslim countries, where he found a need to recover the focus upon race and black nationalism that the Nation had emphasized earlier. Farrakhan's Nation, which is based in Chicago, retains the black nationalist and separatist beliefs and doctrines that were central to the teachings of Elijah Muhammad. Minister Farrakhan displays much of the charisma and candor of Malcolm X, and his message of black nationalism is again directed to those mired in the underclass as well as to disillusioned intellectuals via the Nation's *Final Call* newspaper. There were other disaffected leaders and followers who formed splinter Nation of Islam groups: Silas Muhammad in Atlanta, John Muhammad in Detroit, and Caliph in Baltimore. Among splinter groups, Farrakhan's Nation of Islam is the largest and most dynamic.

Minister Farrakhan became known to the American public via a series of controversies that stirred when he first supported the Reverend Jesse Jackson's 1984 presidential campaign. His Fruit of Islam guards provided security for Reverend Jackson. He exacerbated the "Hymietown" controversy of the Jackson campaign by threatening to censure *Washington Post* reporter Milton Coleman in the black community. Minister Farrakhan has also become embroiled in a continuing controversy with the American Jewish community by making allegedly anti-Semitic statements. Claiming that his statements were taken out of context, Farrakhan has denied being anti-Semitic. Furthermore, he contends that a distorted media focus on this issue has not adequately covered the achievements of his movement.

Farrakhan's Nation of Islam has been successful in eliminating drug dealers in a number of public housing projects and private apartment buildings. In addition, a national private security agency for hire, manned by the Fruit of Islam, has been established. The Nation has been at the forefront of organizing a peace pact between gang members in Los Angeles and several other cities. They have established a clinic for treatment of AIDS patients in Washington, D.C. A cosmetics company, Clean and Fresh, has marketed its products in the black community. Moreover, they have continued to reach out to reform black people with the Nation's traditional dual focus: self-identity, to know yourself and economic independence, and to "do for self." Under Minister Louis Farrakhan's leadership, the Nation has allowed its members to participate in electoral politics and to run for office, actions which were forbidden under Elijah Muhammad. He has also allowed women to become ministers and public leaders in the Nation, which places his group ahead of all of the orthodox Muslim groups in giving women equality. Although the core of Farrakhan's Nation of Islam continues to be about twenty-thousand members, his influence is much greater. He attracts crowds of forty-thousand or more in speeches across the country. His group is the fastest growing of the various Muslim movements, aided by the support of such rap performers as Public Enemy and Prince Akeem. International branches of the nation have been formed in Ghana, London, and the Caribbean islands.

Minister Louis Farrakhan and his wife Khadijah have eleven children, several of whom serve in the Nation's leadership hierarchy.

For more than sixty years, the Nation of Islam in its various forms has become the longest lasting and most enduring of the black militant and separatist movements that have appeared in the history of black people in the United States. Besides its crucial role in the development of the black consciousness movement, the Nation is important for having introduced Islam as a fourth major alternative religious tradition in American society, alongside Protestantism, Catholicism, and Judaism. It is important to note that traditional Muslims see African American Muslims and the Nation of Islam as two different religions.

Lawrence H. Mamiya

References: Islam in the Americas

Haddad, Yvonne Yazbeck, ed., *The Muslims of America* (New York: Oxford University Press, 1991)

Haddad, Yvonne Yazbeck and Adair T. Lummis, *Islamic Values in the United States: A Comparative Study.* New York: Oxford University Press, 1987.

Haddad, Yvonne Yazbeck and Jane Idleman Smith, eds., *Muslim Communities in North America.* Albany: State University of New York Press, 1994.

Hermansen, Marcia. "In the Garden of America Sufi Movements: Hybrids and Perennials." To be published in *New Islamic Movements*, edited by Peter Clarke. London: Curzon Press, forthcoming. Quoted with author's permission.

Husaini, Zohra. *Muslims in the Canadian Mosaic: Socio-Cultural and Economic Links with their Countries of Origin.* Edmonton, Alberta: Muslim Research Foundation, 1990.

Kosmin, Barry A. and Jeffery Scheckner. "Estimating the Muslim Population of the United States in 1990." New York: City University of New York, April, 1991.

Koszegi, Michael A. and J. Gordon Melton, eds., *Islam in North America: A Sourcebook.* New York and London: Garland, 1992.

Numan, Farid H. *The Muslim Population of the United States: "A Brief Statement."* Washington, D.C.: The American Muslim Council, 1992.

———. "Islam in America." *The American Muslim*, vol. II, nos. 11-12 (July-December, Summer-Fall 1994).

Poston, Larry. *Islamic Dawah in the West.* New York: Oxford University Pres, 1992.

Sachedina, Abdulaziz A. "A Minority Within a Minority: The Case of the Shia Community in North America," in Haddad and Smith, *Muslim Communities in North America*, op. cit., p. 6.

Waugh, Earle H., Baha Abu-Laban, and Regula B. Qureshi, eds., *The Muslim Community in North America.* Edmonton, ALTA: The University of Alberta Press, 1983.

Waugh, Earle H., Sharon McIrvin Abu-Laban, and Regula Burckhardt Qureshi, eds., *Muslim Families in North America.* Edmonton: University of Alberta Press, 1991.

References: African American Muslims

Austin, Allen. *African Muslim Slaves in Anti-Bellum America.* New York, 1984.

Blyden, Edward Wilmot. *Christianity, Islam and the Negro Race.* Edinburgh: Edinburgh University Press, 1967 repr.

Breitman, George, ed. *Malcolm X Speaks.* New York: Merit Publishers, 1965.

Essien-Udom, E.U. Black Nationalism: A Search for identity in America. Chicago: University of Chicago Press, 1962.

Farrakhan, Louis. *Torchlight for America.* Final Call Press, 1993.

———. *Seven Speeches.* Chicago, 1974.

Haddad, Yvonne, ed. *The Muslims of America.* New York: Oxford University Press, 1991.

Hill, Robert A., ed. *The Marcus Garvey and the Universal Improvement Association Papers.* Los Angeles: University of California Press, 3 volumes (1983–1984).

Lincoln, C. Eric. *The Black Muslims in America.* Boston: Beacon Press, 1960.

Malcolm X, and Alex Haley. *The Autobiography of Malcolm X.* New York: Grove Press, 1965.

Mamiya, Lawrence H. "The Nation of Islam"; "Islam"; and "Minister Louis Farrakhan" in *Encyclopedia of African American Culture and History.* Macmillan, 1994.

———. "From Black Muslim to Bilalian: The Evolution of A Movement," *Journal for the Scientific Study of Religion* 21, two (June 1982): 138-52. Reprinted in *Islam in North America: A Sourcebook*, edited by Michael A. Koszegi and J. Gordon Melton. New York: Garland Publishing, 1992.

Mamiya, Lawrence H., and C. Eric Lincoln. "Black Militant and Separatist Movements," in *Encyclopedia of Religion in America*, edited by Charles H. Lippy and Peter W. Williams. vol. II, New York: Charles Scribner's Sons, 1988. 755-71.

Muhammad, Elijah. *Message to the Black Man in America.* Chicago, 1965.

Muhammad, Warith Deen. *As the Light Shineeth from the East.* Chicago, 1980.

Perry, Bruce. *Malcolm: The Life of a Man Who Changed Black America.* Barrytown, NY: Staten Hill Press, 1991.

Turner, Richard B. *Islam in the United States in the 1920's: The Quest for a New Vision in Afro-American Religion.* Ph.D. diss., Princeton University, 1986.

Waugh, Earle H., Baha Abu-Laban, and Regula B. Qureshi, eds. *The Muslim Community in North America.* Edmonton: University of Alberta Press, 1983.

Part III:

Diversity in Islam

🔞

Diversity in Islam: Communities of Interpretation

♦ Diversity in Early Islam ♦ The Emergence of Communities of Interpretation

It was during a short ten-year period, stretching from his emigration (hijra) from Mecca in September 622 (which marks the initiation of the Islamic era) until his death in the year 632, that the Prophet Muhammad laid the foundations of a newly revealed religion, a religion portrayed by Muslims as the seal of the great monotheistic religions of the Abrahamic tradition. Islam from early on recognized the followers of Judaism and Christianity as the People of the Book (ahl al-kitab). Meanwhile, Muhammad had founded a community and state of considerable importance according to the standards then prevailing in Arabia. During those earliest years of Islamic history, most of the desert-dwelling Bedouin tribes of Arabia had accepted the new religion and pledged their allegiance to Muhammad, the Messenger of God (rasul Allah). The ground was prepared for the subsequent expansion of Islam beyond the Arabian peninsula.

♦ DIVERSITY IN EARLY ISLAM

The death of the Prophet Muhammad after a brief illness confronted the nascent Islamic community (*umma*) with its first major crisis, the crisis of succession to the Prophet. As a result, the hitherto unified Muslim community was soon split into its two major divisions or distinct communities of interpretation, designated subsequently as Sunnism and Shiism. In time, the Sunni and Shias themselves were subdivided into a number of smaller communities and groupings with particular theological and legal doctrines that evolved gradually over several centuries. In addition to the Sunnis and the Shia, other communities of interpretation in the form of religio-political movements or schools of thought began to appear among the early

Muslims during this formative period. Most of these early communities proved short-lived although several of them left lasting influences on the teachings of the surviving communities and shaped important aspects of Islamic thought. The Kharijis (or Khawarij), a religio-political community of the first Islamic century who were opposed to both the Shia and the Sunnis, have survived to the present times, and as such they are generally considered as Islam's third major division. Other important movements of the early Islamic times, such as the Murjia who originated in response to the harsh stances of the Khawarij and who adopted a more compromising position regarding other Muslim communities, did not survive long under their own names. There were also famous contemporary theological schools such as the Mutazila and Maturidism, which disappeared in medieval times after leaving permanent imprints on aspects of Shia and Sunni theology.

Modern scholarship indicates that the early Muslims lived, especially during the first three centuries of their history, in an intellectually dynamic milieu characterized by a multiplicity of communities, schools of thought, and stances on major religio-political issues of the time. On a political level, which remained closely linked to religious perspectives and theological considerations, the diversity in early Islam ranged widely from the viewpoints of those (later designated as Sunnis) who endorsed the historical caliphate to the various oppositional groups (notably the Shia and the Khawarij) who aspired toward the establishment of new orders. In this fluid and intellectually effervescent atmosphere in which ordinary individuals as well as scholars and theorists often moved freely among different communities, Muslims engaged in lively discourses revolving around a host of issues that were of vital significance to the emerging Muslim *umma*. At the time, the Muslims were confronted by many gaps in their religious knowledge and teachings related to issues such as the attributes of God, the source and nature of authority, and the definitions of true believers and sinners. It was under such circumstances that different religious communities and schools of thought formulated their doctrines in stages and acquired their own identities as well as designations that often encapsulated central aspects of their beliefs and practices.

The Sunni Muslims of medieval times, or, more specifically, their religious scholars (*ulama*), painted a picture of early Islam that is at variance with the findings of modern scholarship on the subject. According to the Sunnis, who have always regarded themselves as the "true" custodians and interpreters of the "Islamic truth," Islam from early on represented a monolithic community with a well-established doctrinal basis from which various groups then deviated and went astray. Sunni Islam was portrayed by its adherents as the "true Islam," while all non-Sunni communities of the Muslims, especially the Shia among them who had allegedly deviated from the right path, were accused of "heresy" (*ilhad*) or even irreligiosity. It is interesting to note that the same highly distorted perceptions and biased classifications came to be adopted in the nineteenth century by the European Orientalists who had then begun their "scientific" study of Islam on the basis of Muslim sources of different genres produced mainly by Sunni authors. Consequently, they, too, endorsed the normativeness of Sunnism and distinguished it from Shiism, or any non-Sunni interpretation of Islam, with the use of terms such as "orthodoxy" and "heterodoxy," terms grounded in the Christian experience and inappropriate in an Islamic context. The Shia, too, have had their own idealized model of "true Islam" based on a particular interpretation of early Islamic history and a distinctive conception of religious authority vested in the Prophet's family (*ahl al-bayt*). The Shia, whose medieval scholars (like the Sunni ones) did not generally allow for doctrinal evolution, have also disagreed among themselves regarding the identity of the rightful imams or spiritual leaders of the community. As a result, the Shias have in the course of their history subdivided into a number of major communities and minor groupings, each possessing an idealized self-image and rationalizing its own legitimacy to the exclusion of other communities.

In short, almost every Muslim community, major or minor in terms of the size of its membership, has developed its own self-image and retrospective perceptions of its earlier history. In such a milieu, characterized by diversity and competing communal interpretations, "true Islam" (or "orthodoxy") defied a universally acceptable definition, although the designation of "heresy" was utilized more readily in reference

to certain groups. Such definitions were usually adopted by the religious scholars of particular states, scholars who performed the important function of legitimizing the established regimes and, refuted their political opponents in return for enjoying privileged social positions among the elite of the society. This is why the perception of "true Islam" depicted as "official Islam" and the "law of the land" has varied so widely over time and space and manifested itself in Sunnism of the Abbasid caliphate, Kharijism of the North African states, Ismaili Shiism of the Fatimid caliphate, Nizari Ismaili Shiism of the Alamut state, Mustalian Ismaili Shiism of the Sulayhid state in Yemen, Zaydi Shiism of the territorial states of the Zaydi dynasties of Yemen and northern Iran, and the Ithnaashari or Twelver Shiism of Safawid and post-Safawid Iran. Several versions of the so-called "true Islam" existed concurrently in different regions of the Muslim world when for about two centuries the Shia Fatimids and the Sunni Abbasids, each ruling over vast territories, were diligently competing with one another for winning the allegiance of the Muslims at large. Under such circumstances, different communities qualified in different states for the status of "heterodoxy" or "heresy" depending on the religious toleration of the various regimes as well as the religio-political strengths and prospects of the communities not associated with the ruling regime and its legitimizing *ulama* in the particular state.

It is important to emphasize at this juncture that many of the fundamental disagreements between Sunnis, Shias, and other Muslims, as well as the less pronounced differences among the factions of any particular Muslim community, will probably never be satisfactorily explained by modern scholarship because of a lack of reliable sources, especially those dating from early Islam. As is well known, extensive written records dealing with these issues among Muslims have not survived from the first two centuries of Islam, while the later writings produced by historians, theologians, and others display their own "sectarian" bias. Any critical study of the formative period of Islam and its tradition of diversity would be severely hampered by important gaps in knowledge of early Islam and the biases of the available literature produced later by different Muslim communities.

Diversity in Islam is abundantly attested to in the dissenting or heresiographical literature of the Muslims. The authors of such heresiographies, which were supposedly written to explain the internal divisions of Islam, had one major preoccupation: to prove the legitimacy of the particular community to which the author of any such work belonged, refuting and condemning other communities as heretical. However, the heresiographers used the term *firqa* (plural *firaq*),

Many of the fundamental disagreements between Sunnis, Shias, and other Muslims will never be satisfactorily explained by modern scholarship.

meaning sect, rather loosely and indiscriminately in reference to a major community, a smaller independent group, a subgroup, a school of thought, or even a minor doctrinal position. As a result, heresiographers, who in a sense gave wide currency to "sectarianism," exaggerated the number of Islamic "sects" in their writings. This may have partly resulted from their misinterpretation of a *hadith* reported from the Prophet. According to this *hadith*, the Prophet had said that "the Jews are divided into 71 sects, and the Christians are divided into 72 sects; and, my people will be divided into 73 sects, all of them are destined to hell fire except one, and these are the true believers." This *hadith*, as first pointed out by the famous Orientalist I. Goldziher (1850–1921), had evidently come into existence as a result of a misunderstanding of a somewhat similar tradition, which is included in the major compendia of the Prophetic traditions. Ultimately, most heresiographers have arranged their accounts of the Muslim sects so as to adhere to a scheme of some 72 heretical sects, with the author's community depicted as the "saved sect." At any rate, the famous Muslim heresiographers of the medieval times, such as al-Ashari (died 935–6), al-

Baghdadi (died 1037), and Ibn Hazm (died 1064), who were devout Sunnis, and al-Shahrastani (died 1153), the Ashari theologian who may have been an Ismaili, as well as the earliest Shia heresiographers al-Nawbakhti (died circa 912-3) and al-Qummi (died 913–4), were much better informed about the teachings of different Muslim communities, which they aimed to refute. As a result, despite their shortcomings and distortions, these heresiographies continue to provide an important source of information for the study of diversity in medieval Islam. It is within such a frame of reference that we shall now present an overview of the major Muslim communities, especially during the formative period of Islam.

♦ THE EMERGENCE OF COMMUNITIES OF INTERPRETATION

The origins of Sunnism and Shiism may be traced to the crisis of succession in the Islamic community, then centered in Medina, following the death of the Prophet Muhammad. According to the message of Islam, Muhammad was the Seal of the Prophets (*khatim al-anbiya*), and he could not be succeeded by another prophet. However, a successor was needed to assume Muhammad's functions as leader of the Islamic community and state, ensuring the continued unity of the Muslims under a single leader. The Prophet had not designated a successor, and so this important appointment had to be made. After some heated debate among the leading Muslim groups, including the Companions of the Prophet from among the Meccan Emigrants (*Muhajirun*) and his Medinese Helpers (*Ansar*), the communal choice fell upon Abu Bakr, who became *khalifat rasul Allah*, successor to the Messenger of Allah. This title was soon simplified to *khalifa*, from which the word *caliph* in Western languages originates. By electing the first successor to the Prophet, the Muslims had founded the unique Islamic institution of the caliphate. The precise nature of the authority of Abu Bakr and his immediate successors during the earliest decades of Islamic history remains obscure, and modern scholarship is just beginning to take a more analytical look at the nature of caliphal authority in early Islam. It is clear, however, that from its inception the historical caliphate embodied not only aspects of the political but also of the religious leadership of the community while different groups gradually formulated various conceptions of the caliphal religio-political authority, and the caliph's moral responsibility toward the community.

Abu Bakr led the Muslims for just over two years (632–634,); and the next two heads of the Muslim community, Umar (634–644) and Uthman (644–656), were also installed to the caliphate by various elective procedures. These three early caliphs all belonged to the influential Meccan tribe of Quraysh and they were also among the early converts to Islam and the Companions of the Prophet who had accompanied Muhammad on his historic journey from Mecca to Medina in 622. Only the fourth caliph, Ali ibn Ali Talib (656–661), who occupies a unique position in the annals of Shiism, belonged to the Banu Hashim, part of the Prophet's own clan of Quraysh. Ali ibn Ali Talib was also closely related to the Prophet, being his cousin and son-in-law, and bound by marriage to the Prophet's daughter Fatima.

The Early Shia

Upon the death of the Prophet there appeared a small group in Medina who believed that Ali was better qualified than any other candidate to succeed the Prophet. This minority group, originally comprised of some of Ali's friends and supporters, in time expanded and came to be generally designated as the *Shiat Ali,* Party of Ali, or simply as the Shia. It is the fundamental belief of the Shia, including the major communities of Ithnaashariyya, Ismailiyya, and Zaydiyya, that the Prophet had designated a successor or an imam as the Shia have preferred to call the leader of the Muslim community. On the basis of specific Quranic verses and certain *hadiths,* the Shia have maintained that the Prophet designated Ali as his successor; a designation or *nass* that had been instituted through divine revelation. Thus, from early on the Shia believed that the succession to the Prophet was the legitimate right of Ali. This contention was, however, not accepted by the Muslim majority who supported the caliphate of Abu Bakr and refused to concede that the Prophet had designated a successor. In fact, they had chosen to refer the decision of the caliphate to the *ijma* or consensus of community. Ali's partisans were obliged to protest against the act of choosing the Prophet's successor through elective methods. According to the Shia, it was this very protest that separated them from the rest of the Muslims.

Indeed, the Shia came to hold a particular conception of religious authority, a conception that was eventually developed in terms of the central Shia doctrine of the imamate. According to the Shia sources, the partisans of Ali believed that the most important issue facing the Muslim community after the death of the Prophet was the elucidation of Islamic teachings. This was because they were aware that the Quran and the revealed law of Islam (*sharia*) had emanated from sources beyond the comprehension of ordinary men. Hence, they believed the Islamic message contained inner truths that could not be understood directly through human reason. In order to understand the true meaning of the Islamic revelation, the Shia had recog-

nized the need for a religiously authoritative teacher and guide, the imam. According to this view, the possibility of a Shia interpretation existed within the very message of Islam, and this possibility was merely actualized in Shiism.

The Shia, then, adhered to their own distinctive conception of authority and leadership in the community. While the majority who endorsed the historical caliphate came to consider the caliph as the administrator and guardian of the *sharia* and leader of the community, the Shia, in addition, saw in the succession to the Prophet an important spiritual function. As a result, the successor also had to possess legitimate authority for elucidating the teachings of Islam and for providing spiritual guidance for the Muslims. According to the Shia, a person with such qualifications could belong only to the *ahl al-bayt,* eventually defined to include only certain members of the Prophet's immediate family, notably Ali and Fatima and their progeny. At any rate, it seems that Ali was from the beginning considered by his devoted partisans as the most prominent member of the Prophet's family, and as such, he was believed to have inherited a true understanding of the Prophet's teachings and religious knowledge or *ilm.* According to the Shia, Ali's unique qualifications as successor to the Prophet held another dimension in that he was believed to have been designated by divine command. This meant that Ali was also divinely inspired and immune from error and sin (*masum*), making him infallible both in his knowledge and as an authoritative teacher or imam after the Prophet. In sum, it was the Shia view that the two ends of governing the community and exercising religious authority could be discharged only by Ali.

This Shia point of view on the origins of Shiism contains distinctive doctrinal elements that cannot be entirely attributed to the early Shia, especially the original partisans of Ali. At any rate, emphasizing hereditary attributes of the individuals and the imam's kinship to the Prophet as a prerequisite for possessing the required religious knowledge, the Shia later also held that after Ali, the leadership of the Muslim community was the exclusive right of certain descendants of Ali, the Alids, who belonged to the *ahl al-bayt* and possessed religious authority. The earliest Shia currents of thought developed gradually, finding their full formulation and consolidation in the doctrine of the imamate, expounded in its fundamental form at the time of the imam Jafar al-Sadiq (died 765).

Pro-Alid sentiments and Shiism remained in a dormant state during the earliest Islamic decades. But Shia aspirations were revived during the caliphate of Uthman, initiating a period of strife and civil war in the community. Diverse grievances against Uthman's policies finally erupted into open rebellion, culminating in the murder of the caliph in Medina in 656 at the hands of rebel contingents from the provinces. In the aftermath of this murder, the Islamic community became divided over the question of Uthman's behavior as a basis for justification of the rebels' action, and soon the disagreements found expression in terms of broad theoretical discussions revolving around the question of the rightful leadership, caliphate or imamate, in the Muslim community. Matters came to a head in the caliphate of Ali, who had succeeded Uthman. Ali's caliphal authority was challenged by Muawiya, the powerful governor of Syria and leader of a pro-Uthman party. As a member of the influential Banu Umayya and a relative of Uthman, Muawiya found the call for avenging the slain caliph a suitable pretext for establishing Umayyad rule.

It was under such circumstances that the forces of Ali and Muawiya met at Siffin on the upper Euphrates in the spring of 657. The events of Siffin, the most controversial battle in early Islam, was followed by a Syrian arbitration proposal. Ali's acceptance of it and the resulting arbitration verdict issued sometime later, all had critical consequences for the early Muslim community. It was also during this prolonged conflict that different groups seceded from Ali's forces, the seceders being subsequently designated as the Khawarij or Kharijis. During the last two years of the civil war, Ali rapidly lost ground to Muawiya. Soon after Ali's murder, at the hand of a Khariji in 661, Muawiya was recognized as the new de facto caliph by the majority of the Muslims except the Shia and the Khawarij. Muawiya also succeeded in founding the Umayyad caliphate that ruled the Islamic state on a dynastic basis for nearly a century (661–750).

The Muslims emerged from their first civil war severely tested and split into factions or parties that differed in their interpretation of the rightful leadership of the community and the caliph's moral responsibility. These factions, which began to acquire definite shape in the aftermath of the murder of Uthman and the battle of Siffin, gradually developed their doctrinal positions and acquired distinct identities as separate communities of interpretation. They also continued to confront each other in theological discourses as well as on the battlefield throughout the Umayyad dynasty and later times. These parties acquired denominations that revealed their personal loyalties.

The upholders of Uthman as a just caliph, commonly designated as Uthmaniyya, had accepted the verdict of the arbitrators appointed at Siffin and held that Uthman had been murdered unjustly. Consequently, they repudiated the rebellion against Uthman and the resulting caliphate of Ali. In addition to the partisans of Muawiya, the Uthmaniyya included the upholders of the principles of the early caliphate, namely the rights of the non-Hashimid early Companions of the Prophet

to the caliphate. The partisans of Ali, the *Shiat Ali*, who now also referred to themselves as the *Shiat ahl al-bayt* or its equivalent *Shiat al Muhammad* (Party of the Prophet's Household), upheld the justice of the rebellion against Uthman, who, according to them, had invalidated his rule by his unjust acts. Repudiating the claims of Muawiya to leadership as the avenger of Uthman, they now aimed to reestablish rightful leadership or imamate in the community through the Hashimids, members of the Prophet's clan of Banu Hashim, and notably through Ali's sons. However, the support of the *ahl al-bayt* by the Shia at this time did not as yet imply a repudiation of the first two caliphs.

The Khawarij

The Khawarij, who originally seceded in different waves from Ali's Kufan army in opposition to his arbitration agreement with Muawiya after the battle of Siffin, shared the view of the Shia concerning Uthman and the rebellion against him. They upheld the initial legitimacy of Ali's caliphate but repudiated him from the time of his agreeing to the arbitration of his conflict with Muawiya. They also repudiated Muawiya for having rebelled against Ali when his caliphate was still legitimate. The Khawarij were strictly uncompromising in their application of the theocratic principle of Islam expressed in their slogan "judgment belongs to God alone." Even caliphs, according to them, were to submit unconditionally to this principle as embodied in the Quran. If caliphs failed to observe this rule, then they were to repent or be removed from the caliphate by force despite any valuable services they might have rendered to Islam. This is why they equally condemned Uthman and Ali and also dissociated themselves from Muawiya who had unjustly challenged Ali's initially legitimate caliphate.

The Khawarij posed fundamental questions concerning the definitions of a true believer, the Muslim community, its rightful leader, and the basis for the leader's authority. As a result, they contributed significantly to doctrinal disputations in the Muslim community. The Khawarij adhered to strict Islamic egalitarianism, maintaining that every meritorious Muslim of any ethnic origin, Arab or non-Arab, could be chosen through popular election as the legitimate leader or imam of the community. They aimed to establish a form of "Islamic democracy" in which leadership and authority could not be based on tribal and hereditary considerations or on any other attributes of individuals other than religious piety. They also had a strong communal spirit, regarding their community as the only "saved community." However, it was not mere membership in the Khariji community but strict adherence to religious tenets and conduct, covering both faith and works, that defined the status of a believer and guaranteed his salvation. Rejecting the doctrine of justification by faith without works propounded later by other communities of interpretation, the Khawarij professed a form of radical puritanism or moral austerity and readily considered anyone, even the caliph, as an apostate, if in their view he had slightly deviated from the right conduct. By committing a minor sin, a believer could thus become irrevocably an unbeliever deserving of dissociation. The Khariji insistence on right conduct, and the lack of any institutional form of authority among them, proved highly detrimental to the unity of their movement, characterized from early on by extreme factionalism. Heresiographers name a multitude of Khariji "sects," most of which were continuously engaged in insurrectional activities especially in the eastern provinces of Islam where they controlled extensive territories in Iran for long periods.

The Azariqa represented the most radical community among the Khawarij. They considered as polytheists (*mushrikun*) and infidels (*kuffar*) all non-Kharijis and even those Kharijis who had not joined their camp. They held the killing of these sinners, who could never reenter the faith, along with their wives and children, licit. The Azariqa established several communities in different parts of Iran. Later, Ibn Ajarrad, who may have been from Balkh, founded the Ajarida branch of Kharijism. Heresiographers name some fifteen groups of the Ajarida who were specific to eastern Iran and were more moderate in their views and policies than the Azariqa. The most moderate Khariji community was represented by the Ibadiyya, today the sole survivors of the Khawarij. The Ibadis considered the non-Ibadi Muslims, as well as the sinners of their own community, not as polytheists but merely as "infidels by ingratitude," and, as such, it was forbidden to kill or capture them in peacetime. In general, the Ibadis were more reluctant than other Kharijis to take up arms against other Muslims. In contrast, they were deeply engaged in the study of religious sciences and made important early contributions to the elaboration of legal and theological doctrines in Islam.

Development of the Shia Community

The early Shia, a small and zealous opposition party centered in Kufa in southern Iraq, survived Ali's murder and numerous subsequent tragic events during the Umayyad period. Upon Ali's death, the Shia recognized his eldest son Hasan as their new imam. Meanwhile, Hasan had also been acclaimed as caliph in succession to Ali, in Kufa, Ali's former capital. However, Muawiya speedily succeeded in inducing Hasan's abdication from the caliphate. Shiism remained subdued under Hasan who refrained from any political activity. On Hasan's death in 669, the Shia revived their aspirations for restoring the caliphate to the Alids, now headed by

Sayyidna al-Husayn Mosque, Cairo, Egypt.

their next imam, Husayn, the second son of Ali and Fatima. The Shia persistently invited Husayn to their midst in Kufa to launch a rebellion against the Umayyads. The tragic martyrdom of the Prophet's grandson, Husayn, and his small band of relatives and companions at Karbala, near Kufa, where they were brutally massacred by an Umayyad army in 680, played an important role in the consolidation of the Shia ethos, leading to the formation of radical trends among the partisans of Ali and the *ahl al-bayt*. The earliest of such radical trends, which left lasting marks on Shiism, became manifest a few years later in the movement of al-Mukhtar.

Al-Mukhtar organized his own Shia movement, with a general call for avenging Husayn's murder in the name of Muhammad ibn al-Hanafiyya, Ali's third son and Husayn's half-brother. Of much greater significance was al-Mukhtar's proclamation of this Muhammad as the Mahdi, "the divinely guided one," the messianic savior imam and the restorer of Islam who would establish justice on earth and deliver the oppressed from tyranny. This new eschatological concept of the imam-Mahdi was a very important doctrinal innovation, proving particularly appealing to the *mawali*, the non-Arab converts to Islam who, under the Umayyads, represented a large intermediary class between the Arab Muslims and the non-Muslim subjects of the Islamic state. The *mawali*, comprised of Aramean, Persian, and other non-Arab Muslims, represented second-class citizens in comparison to Arab Muslims. As a large and underprivileged social class concentrated in urban milieus and aspiring for the establishment of a state and society that would observe the egalitarian teachings of Islam, the *mawali* provided a valuable recruiting ground for any movement opposed to the exclusively Arab hegemony of the Umayyads. The *mawali* did, in fact, join the Khawarij and participated in many Khariji revolts. Above all, they became involved in Shiism, starting with the movement of al-Mukhtar. By attempting to remove their grievances and through the appeal of the idea of the Mahdi, al-Mukhtar easily succeeded in drawing the *mawali* to his movement. They now began to call themselves the *Shiat al-Mahdi* (Party of the Mahdi). Al-Mukhtar speedily won control of Kufa in an open revolt in 685. The success of al-Mukhtar proved short-lived, but his movement survived his demise in 687 and Muhammad ibn al-Hanafiyya's death in 700, and it continued under the general name of Kaysaniyya. This name, like many other community names, was coined by heresiographers.

The Kaysaniyya elaborated some of the doctrines that came to distinguish the radical wing of Shiism. For instance, they condemned the first three caliphs before Ali as illegitimate usurpers and also held that the community had gone astray by accepting their rule. They considered Ali and his three sons, Hasan, Husayn, and Muhammad, as their four imams, successors to the Prophet, who had been divinely appointed and were endowed with supernatural attributes. Many such ideas, first developed by different Kaysani groups, were subsequently adopted by other Shia communities. This explains why most Shia groups in time came to accuse the majority of the early companions of the Prophet of apostasy, which also led to the general Shia vilification (*sabb*) of the first three caliphs. Meanwhile, the

Uthmaniyya had adopted their own anti-Shia policies, such as the cursing of Ali from the pulpits after Friday prayers, a policy instituted by Muawiya. Many of the Alids and their partisans from different Shia groups were also continuously persecuted on the orders of the Umayyads and their officials in Iraq and elsewhere.

It was in the aftermath of the Shia revolt of al-Mukhtar that the religio-political movement known as Murjia appeared in Kufa, advocating a return to unity among the Muslims by refuting all extreme partisan views concerning the caliphate. The early Murjia held that judgment of the conduct of Uthman and Ali should be deferred (*irja*) to Allah, while the caliphates of Abu Bakr and Umar deserved praise and emulation. The early Murjia thus distanced themselves from the radical Shias, who now repudiated the first three caliphs, from the Khawarij who condemned both Uthman and Ali, and from the Uthmaniyya who condemned Ali. In general, the Murjia held that Muslims should not fight one another except in self-defense. The sources name Muhammad ibn Hanafiyya's son Hasan as the original author of the doctrine of *irja*, a Quranic term meaning "to defer judgment." The movement of the Murjia soon spread to Khurasan and Transoxania, where it became particularly identified with the cause of the *mawali*. The Murjia campaigned for the equality of the Arab and non-Arab Muslims, and the exemption from paying the special poll tax (*jizya*) levied on non-Muslim subjects of the Muslim state. In that context, the Murjia advocated the identity of faith (*iman*) with belief and confession of Islam to the exclusion of acts, namely the performance of the ritual and legal obligations of Islam. This meant that the legal status of a Muslim and of a true believer could not be denied to those new, non-Arab converts on the pretext that they ignored or failed to perform some of the essential duties of the Muslims. In time, the Murjia, too, split into several groups, some developing close relations with certain Sunni schools of law and theology.

From the time of al-Mukhtar's movement, different Shia communities and groups, consisting of Arabs and *mawali*, had come to coexist, each one having its own imam and developing its own teachings, and individuals moved rather freely from one Shia community to another. Furthermore, the Shia imams now issued not only from the three major branches of the extended Alid family—the Husaynids (descendants of Husayn ibn Ali), the Hanafids (descendants of Muhammad ibn al-Hanafiyya), and, later, the Hasanids (descendants of Hasan ibn Ali)—but also from other branches of the Prophet's clan of Banu Hashim. This was because the Prophet's family, whose sanctity was supreme for the Shia, was then still defined broadly in its old tribal sense. It was later, after the accession of the Abbasids, that the Shia began to define the *ahl al-bayt* more restrictively to include only the descendants of the Prophet through Fatima and Ali, known as the Fatimids (covering both the Hasanid and the Husaynid Alids), while the bulk of the non-Zaydi Shias came to acknowledge a particular Husaynid line of imams. At any rate, during this second phase in the formative period of Shiism, the Shias did not accord general recognition to any single line of imams, from which various dissident groups would diverge in favor of alternative claimants to the imamate.

In this fluid and confusing setting, Shiism developed in terms of two main branches or trends. Later, another Alid movement led to the formation of yet another Shia community known as the Zaydiyya. A radical branch, in terms of both doctrine and policy, evolved out of al-Mukhtar's movement and accounted for the allegiance of the bulk of the Shias until shortly after the Abbasid revolution. This branch, breaking away from the religiously moderate attitudes of the early Kufan Shia and generally designated as the Kaysaniyya by the heresiographers, was comprised of a number of interrelated groups recognizing various Hanafid Alids and other Hashimids as their imams. By the end of the Umayyad period, the majority body of the Kaysaniyya, namely the Hashimiyya, transferred their allegiance to the Abbasid family. With this transference, the Abbasids also inherited the party and the missionary or *dawa* organization, which became the main instruments for the eventual success of the Abbasid revolution.

The various Kaysani communities drew mainly on the support of the superficially Islamicized *mawali* in southern Iraq and elsewhere. The *mawali*, drawing on diverse pre-Islamic traditions, played an important part in transforming Shiism from an Arab party of limited size and doctrinal basis to a dynamic movement. The Kaysani Shias elaborated some of the beliefs that came to characterize the radical branch of Shiism. Many of the Kaysani doctrines were propounded by the *ghulat*, "exaggerators," who were accused by the more moderate Shias of later times of exaggeration (*ghuluww*) in religious matters. In addition to their condemnation of the early caliphs preceding Ali, the most common feature of the earliest ideas propagated by the Shia *ghulat* was the attribution of superhuman qualities to the imams. The early *ghulat* speculated rather freely on a host of issues and were responsible for many doctrinal innovations, including the spiritual interpretations of the Day of Judgment, Resurrection, Paradise, and Hell. They also held a cyclical view of the religious history of mankind in terms of eras initiated by different prophets. The Shia *ghulat* also speculated on the nature of Allah, often with tendencies toward anthropomorphism (*tashbih*). Many of them believed in the independence of the soul from the body, allowing for *tanasukh* or the transmigration of the soul from one body to another.

The Shia *ghulat*, like other contemporary Muslims, also concerned themselves with the status of the true believer. Emphasizing the acknowledgment of and the obedience to the rightful Shia imam of the time as the most essential religious obligation of the true believer, the role of the developing *sharia* became less important for these radical Shias. These Kaysani Shias seem to have regarded the particular details and the ritual prescriptions of the sacred law of Islam, such as prayer and fasting, as not binding on those who knew and were devoted to the true imam from the *ahl al-bayt*. Consequently, they were often accused of advocating that faith alone was necessary for salvation, and of tolerating libertinism. Much of the intellectual heritage of the Kaysaniyya was later absorbed into the teachings of the main Shia communities of the early Abbasid times. Politically, too, the Kaysaniyya pursued an activist policy, condemning Abu Bakr, Umar, and Uthman as well as the Umayyads as usurpers of the rights of Ali and his descendants, aiming to restore the caliphate to the Alids. As a result, several Kaysani groups, led by their various *ghulat* theorists, engaged in revolutionary activities against the Umayyad regime, especially in or around Kufa, the cradle of Shiism. However, as all these Shia revolts were poorly organized and their scenes were too close to the centers of caliphal power, they proved abortive.

In the meantime, there had appeared a second major branch or wing of Shiism, later designated as the Imamiyya. This branch, with its limited initial following, remained completely removed from any antiregime political activity. The Imami Shias, who, like other Shias of the time were centered in Kufa, recognized a line of Alid imams after Ali, Hasan, and Husayn, tracing the imamate through Husayn's sole surviving son Ali ibn al-Husayn, who received the honorific epithet of Zayn al-Abidin, "the Ornament of the Pious." It was through Zayn al-Abidin's son and successor as imam, Muhammad al-Baqir, that the Husaynid imams and Imami community began to acquire their particular identity and prominence within Shiism. Al-Baqir refrained from any political activity and concerned himself solely with the religious aspects of his authority, developing the rudiments of some of the ideas that were to become the legitimist principles of the Imamiyya. Above all, he seems to have concerned himself with explaining the functions and attributes of the imams. During the final Umayyad decades, with the rise of different theological and legal schools upholding conflicting views, many Shia sought the guidance of their imam as an authoritative teacher. Al-Baqir was the first imam of the Husaynid line to perform this role, and he acquired an increasing number of partisans who regarded him as the sole legitimate religious authority of the time. In line with his quiescent policy, al-Baqir is also credited with introducing the important Shia principle of *taqiyya*, precautionary disguising of one's true religious belief in the face of danger. This principle was later adopted by the Ithnaashari and Ismaili Shia communities, and it particularly served to save the Ismailis from much persecution throughout their history.

It may be pointed out at this juncture that al-Baqir's imamate also coincided with the initial stages of the Islamic science of law (*ilm al-fiqh*). It was, however, in the final decades of the second Islamic century that the old Arabian concept of *sunna*, the normative custom of the community that had reasserted itself under Islam, came to be explicitly identified with the *sunna* of the Prophet. This identification necessitated the collection of those *hadiths* or traditions, claimed reports of the sayings and actions of the Prophet, transmitted orally through an uninterrupted chain of trustworthy authorities. The activity of collecting and studying *hadith* for citing the authority of the Prophet to determine proper legal practices soon became a major field of Islamic learning, complementing the science of Islamic jurisprudence. In this formative period of the Islamic religious sciences, al-Baqir has been mentioned as a reporter of *hadith*, particularly of those supporting the Shia cause and derived from Ali. However, the imams al-Baqir and his successor Jafar al-Sadiq interpreted the law mostly on their own authority without much recourse to *hadith* from earlier authorities. It should be added that in Shiism, *hadith* is reported on the authority of the imams and it includes their sayings in addition to the Prophetic Traditions. Having laid the foundations of the Imami branch of Shiism, the common heritage of the great Shia communities of Ithnaashariyya and Ismailiyya, the imam Muhammad al-Baqir died around 732, a century after the death of the Prophet. It was during the long imamate of al-Baqir's son and successor Jafar al-Sadiq that the Shia movement of his uncle Zayd ibn Ali unfolded, leading eventually to the separate Zaydi community of Shiism.

The Zaydis and Imamis

Few details are available on the ideas propagated by Zayd and his original associates. Similar to the Khawarij, Zayd seems to have emphasized the need for a just imam and the community's obligation to remove an unjust leader. He also paid particular attention to the Islamic principle of "commanding the good and prohibiting the evil" (*al-amr bilmaruf walnahy an al-munkar*). He is also reported to have taught that if an imam wanted to be recognized, he had to assert his rights publicly with sword in hand, if required. In other words, Zayd did not attach any significance to hereditary succession to the imamate, nor was he prepared to accept the eschatological idea of the occultation

(*ghayba*) and return (*raja*) of an imam-Mahdi, an idea propagated by different Kaysani and, later, Imami groups. Thus, the Zaydis originally maintained that the imamate might legitimately be held by any member of the *ahl al-bayt*, though later restricted it only to the Hasanid and Husaynid Alids. They did not consider the imams as divinely protected from error and sin either. The claimant to the imamate had to possess the required religious learning. He would also have to be capable of launching an uprising, as Zayd himself was to do, against the illegitimate ruler of the time. Accordingly, there could be long periods without a legitimate Zaydi imam.

Zayd also realized that in order to achieve success in combating the Umayyads, he would need the support of a main body of the Muslims. It was to this end, and reflecting the moderate stances of the early Kufan Shia, that Zayd made an important doctrinal compromise. He asserted that although Ali was the most excellent (*al-afdal*) person for succeeding the Prophet, the allegiance given by the early Muslims to Abu Bakr and Umar who were less excellent (*al-mafdul*) was, nevertheless, valid. This view was, however, repudiated by the later Zaydis. Zayd's recognition of the rule of the first two caliphs won him the general sympathy of all those Muslims upholding the unity of the Muslim community. At any rate, Zayd's movement survived his abortive Kufan revolt of 740. Henceforth, the Zaydis retained their moderate views in the doctrinal field. Not only did they adopt conservative stances in elaborating the religious status of their imams, but they also continued to refrain from condemning the early caliphs before Ali and the rest of the Muslim community for having failed to support the legitimate rights of Ali and his descendants. Politically, the Zaydis maintained their militant position, advocating insurrections against the illegitimate rulers of the time. Led by different Alid imams after Zayd, the Zaydis succeeded by the second half of the ninth century to establish two territorial states, one in Yemen and another one in the Caspian region of northern Iran. In time, the Zaydis were subdivided into several communities.

The Imamiyya expanded significantly and became an important religious community during the long and eventful imamate of al-Baqir's son and successor Jafar al-Sadiq, the foremost scholar and teacher among the Husaynid imams. This happened particularly after the victory of the Abbasids who had preached their religio-political propaganda or *dawa* in the name of the *ahl al-bayt* largely on a Shia basis, but, after supplanting the Umayyads in 750, they installed their own dynasty to the caliphate to the great disappointment of the Shias who had all along expected the Alids to accede to the leadership of the Muslim community. Shia disillusionment was further felt when the Abbasids, soon after their victory, adopted persecutionary measures against the Alids and their Shia supporters. In the meantime, the Kaysani Shiism of the Umayyad times had largely aborted in the Abbasid cause. It was under such circumstances that Jafar al-Sadiq emerged as the main rallying point for the allegiance of the Shias.

Maintaining the Imami tradition of remaining aloof from any revolutionary activity, Jafar al-Sadiq had gradually acquired a widespread reputation as a religious scholar and teacher, and, besides his own partisans, large numbers of Muslims studied or consulted with him including Abu Hanifa al-Numan (died 767) and Malik ibn Anas (died 795), the famous jurists and eponymous founders of the Hanafi and Maliki schools of law. In time, al-Sadiq also acquired a noteworthy circle of Imami thinkers and associates that included some of the most learned scholars and theologians of the time, such as Hisham ibn al-Hakam (died 795), the foremost representative of Imami *kalam* or scholastic theology. As a result of the intense intellectual activities of the imam al-Sadiq and his associates, the Imamiyya now came to possess a distinctive legal school together with a body of ritual and theological thought.

The central doctrine of Imami thought, however, has been the doctrine of the imamate, which was formulated in al-Sadiq's time. This doctrine, essentially retained by the later Ithnaashari and Ismaili Shias, was based on the belief in the permanent need of mankind for a divinely guided, sinless, and infallible (*masum*) leader or imam who, after the Prophet Muhammad, would act as the authoritative teacher and guide of men in all their religious and spiritual affairs. The imam can practice *taqiyya*, and although he is entitled to temporal leadership as much as to religious authority, his mandate does not depend on his actual rule or any attempt at gaining it. It was further maintained that the Prophet himself had designated Ali ibn Abi Talib as his *wasi* (successor) by an explicit designation (*nass*), under divine command. However, the majority of the Companions of the Prophet had apostatized by ignoring this testament. After Ali, the imamate was to be transmitted from father to son by *nass*, among the descendants of Ali and Fatima, and after al-Husayn, in the Husaynid line until the end of time. This imam is also endowed by God with special knowledge or *ilm*, and has perfect understanding of the exoteric (*zahir*) and esoteric (*batin*) aspects and meanings of the Quran and the message of Islam. Indeed, the world could not exist for a moment without such an imam, the proof of Allah (*hujjat Allah*) on earth. Even if only two men were left upon the face of the earth, one of them would be the imam as there can only be a single imam at any one time. The recognition of the true imam and obedience to him were made the absolute duty of every be-

liever, while the ignorance or rejection of such an imam would be tantamount to infidelity. Having consolidated Shiism and laid a solid foundation for its subsequent doctrinal development, Jafar al-Sadiq, the last imam recognized by both the Ithnaasharis and Ismailis, died in 765. The dispute over his succession led to permanent divisions in the Imami Shia community.

The Ithnaashari Imami Shia

On Jafar al-Sadiq's death, the Imami Shia split into several groups. A large number recognized al-Sadiq's eldest surviving son Abd Allah al-Aftah. These Shia, known as Fathiyya, maintained some prominence until the tenth century. When Abd Allah died shortly after his father, however, the bulk of his supporters went over to his half-brother Musa ibn Jafar al-Kazim who had already been acknowledged as his father's successor by a faction of the Imamiyya. Musa, later counted as the seventh imam of the Ithnaasharis, refrained from all political activity, an Imami tradition retained by his successors. On Musa's death in 799, one group of his partisans acknowledged the imamate of his eldest son Ali ibn Musa al-Rida, later becoming the heir apparent of the Abbasid caliph al-Mamun who had attempted a temporary rapprochement with the Alids. When Ali al-Rida died in 818, most of his followers traced the imamate through four more imams, while others followed different Alid imams. At any rate, it was this subgroup of the Imamiyya that eventually became known as the Ithnaashariyya, or the Twelvers. This title refers to all those Imami Shias who recognized a line of twelve imams, starting with Ali ibn Abi Talib and ending with Muhammad ibn al-Hasan whose emergence as Mahdi has been awaited since 873. Twelver Shiism has remained the "official" religion of Iran since 1501.

The Shia Ismailis

In the meantime, two other groups from the Imami Shias supporting Ismail ibn Jafar, the original designated successor of the imam al-Sadiq, on al-Sadiq's death. These Kufan-based groups represented the earliest Ismailis who were soon organized into a rapidly expanding, revolutionary movement representing the most politically active wing of Shiism. By the middle of the ninth century, the Ismaili *dawa* or religio-political propaganda had begun to appear in many regions of the Muslim world. The Shia message of this *dawa*, based on an anti-Abbasid campaign and the promise of justice under the rule of the Ismaili imam, was successfully preached by numerous *dais* or missionaries in Iraq, Yemen, Iran, Central Asia, and elsewhere, appealing to different strata of the society.

By 899, the Ismaili imams, who had hitherto led the movement secretly from different headquarters, emerged from their underground existence. It was around that same time that a faction of the Ismaili community, later designated as Qarmati, disagreed with the central leadership of the movement over certain doctrinal issues and seceded. The Qarmati dissidents, who soon founded a powerful state of their own in Bahrayn, eastern Arabia, engaged in prolonged devastating activities against the loyal Ismailis and other Muslims. The ravaging activities of the Qarmatis, culminating in their attack on Mecca in 930, were capitalized on by the Muslim enemies of the Ismailis in order to discredit the entire Ismaili movement.

The success of the early Ismaili *dawa* was crowned in 909 by the establishment of the Fatimid caliphate (909–1171) in North Africa, under the direct leadership of the Ismaili imams who traced their ancestry to Ali and the Prophet's daughter Fatima. The Fatimid caliph-imams, who had successfully challenged the legitimacy of the Abbasids, now became ready targets for the polemical attacks of the Abbasids and their legitimizing *ulama*. In later times, the Ismailis themselves became subdivided into a number of major communities and minor groupings. A particular state centered at the mountain fortress of Alamut with territories in Iran and Syria was founded in the 1090s by the leaders of the Nizari branch of Ismailism. Currently, the bulk of the Isamilis of the world, who belong to the majority Nizari branch, recognize as their forty-ninth present and living imam, His Highness Karim Aga Khan.

The Mutazila

Meanwhile, by the late Umayyad decades, yet another religious movement had gained prominence in the Muslim community. This was the movement of the Mutazila, the defenders of human rationality, that arose in Basra with the aim of reuniting the Muslims on a compromise solution of the disputes among the various religio-political parties. The early Mutazilis were, however, mainly theologians who focused their attention on theological principles with a side interest in the issues related to the rightful leadership in the community.

In agreement with the Khariji position, the Mutazilis also emphasized the need for a just imam and the community's obligation to remove an unjust one. They were, however, opposed to the Khariju condemnation of Uthman and Ali and their partisans as infidels. In fact, they preferred to suspend the ultimate judgment on all the parties involved in these conflicts. They supported some of the Umayyad and early Abbasid caliphs while refuting others. Indeed, for several decades until 848, Mutazilism was the official doctrine of the Abbasid court. However, by the latter decades of the ninth century, Mutazilism had become increasingly pro-Alid, and it left permanent influences on Zaydi and Imami Shiism.

Emphasizing rationalism, in the sense that a certain awareness is accessible to man by means of his intelligence alone in the absence of any revelation, the early Mutazilis became known for five principles on which they had reached a consensus of opinion. These principles, with a number of related theological issues, included the unity of God (*tawhid*) and the divine attributes, the justice of God (*adl*), and the theory of an intermediate state (*al-manzila bayn al-manzilatayn*), according to which the same sinful Muslim cannot be classified either as a believer (*mumin*) or an infidel (*kafir*) but belongs to a separate intermediate category. Acknowledged as a major school of theology in early Islam, Mutazilism began to lose its prominence during the tenth century to other theological schools, notably Asharism and Maturidism.

The Community of the Ahl al-Sunna (Sunnis)

By the early Abbasid times, as noted, there had also appeared distinctive schools of law, such as the Hanafi and Maliki, named after their jurist-founders at the same time that Shia and Khariji communities were developing their own legal doctrines. It is beyond the scope of this chapter to investigate the evolution of these legal schools and the early history of the various theological movements of the Abbasid times, including particularly the two most important schools of Sunni *kalam* founded by Abu l-Hasan al-Ashari (died 935–6) and Abu Mansur al-Maturidi (died 944). We have also refrained from considering the organized Sufi orders that later developed their own mystical interpretations of Islam and the spiritual path (*tariqa*) to "truth," transcending Sunni-Shia-Khariji divisions. Nor have we dealt with the inquiries of the *falasifa*, the Muslim philosophers who formulated highly complex metaphysical systems drawing on different Hellenistic traditions and the teachings of Islam. Nonetheless, our survey attests sufficiently to the prevalence of pluralism in early Islam, which was characterized by a diversity of communities, movements, and schools of interpretation, none having had any monopoly over the sole interpretation of the Islamic message.

Within this perspective, it is also important to bear in mind that by the second Islamic century, there was no single community representing even what eventually became the Sunni interpretation of Islam. It was over the course of Muslim history that the majority of Muslims thought of themselves as the *ahl al-sunna* (People of the *sunna*), or simply as the Sunnis. This designation was used not because the majority were more attached than others to the *sunna* of the Prophet, but because they claimed to be the adherents to the correct Prophetic Traditions, also upholding the unity of the community. Different currents of what later became identified as Sunni Islam were elaborated gradually, as in the case of Shiism and other interpretations of Islam. For instance, Sunni doctrine on the imamate drew on the ideas of the earlier Uthmaniyya and the Murjia, aiming to defend the historical caliphate against the threats posed by the claims of the opposition movements. However, Sunnis, too, differed among themselves on theological and legal doctrines. For instance, on the matter of defining faith, there developed two opposing views in the Sunni camp. One group, associated with the Hanafi school of law and supported by the Maturidi school of theology, essentially defined faith as knowledge to the exclusion of acts. According to another view, upheld by the Hanbali school of law and Ashari theology and also reflected in the cannonical collections of Sunni *hadith*, faith would also require the inclusion of acts. This latter view has also become known as Sunni traditionalism. In contrast, the Shafii school of law, unlike Hanafism and Hanbalism, was essentially a legal school without strong interests in theological doctrines. In fact, the bulk of the early Shafiis were opposed to speculative reasoning used by the Muslim theologians. There were numerous other disagreements within every legal or theological school of thought associated with Sunni Islam. However, Maturidism, which became prevalent in Sunni Islam after the disappearance of Mutazilism, in broad terms provided the common theology of the Hanafis while Asharism eventually became the dominant theology of the Shafiis and Malikis.

While it is difficult to speak of "orthodoxy" even within Sunnism, the emergence of a powerful class of religious scholars (*ulama*) in the Abbasid state from around the middle of the ninth century led to a consolidated Sunni group as elaborated by the same "Sunni" *ulama* who had now come to possess religious authority under the aegis of the state.

One aspect of the definition of Muslim belief undertaken by Sunni scholars was the articulation of statements that constituted a creed. Abu Hanifa (died 767), the founder of the Hanafi school of Sunni law, and other major figures such as al-Ashari (died 935), al-Shafii (died 820) and al-Ghazali (died 1111) further elaborated and consolidated this process of systematizing belief. Some of the key elements of these creeds emphasized particular perspectives on understanding the foundational beliefs common to all Muslims. Al-Ashari, for example, emphasized belief in the Quran as Allah's uncreated word (in contrast to the beliefs of the Mutazila); he acknowledged the preeminent status of the Companions of the Prophet, without discriminating among them, but giving priority to the role of the first four caliphs; he emphasized the idea of *sunna* (tradition), authenticated on the basis of authoritative claims of transmission related from acknowledged transmitters and constituting a consensus of Sunni scholars; and lastly, he decried innovation in matters of belief and practice.

Such creedal statements, combined with the role of the Sunni scholars and jurists as custodians and interpreters of the faith, developed into a broad synthesis to which the composite term, Sunni, came to be applied. The major Sunni schools of law agreed on the principle that Muslim tradition and practice were best preserved through a legal and theological methodology founded on the collective consensus and interpretation of the learned scholars and jurists of the earlier period. The authoritative role and shared sense of purpose was integrated into the larger workings of the state so that the major ruling dynasties incorporated them into the structure of the state, endowing them with a role and a status in matters of governance and daily life. Sunni scholars and institutions of learning thus played a major role in mediating political authority and the role of the *sharia* in Muslim society.

Islamic diversity and pluralism continues down to our own times. The linking of specific Muslim interpretations to an ideological basis, however, is still pertinent to understanding how political hegemony determines the validity of any one particular interpretation of Islam, and whether the historical acceptance of the diversity of communities of interpretation might not be a more important umbrella for understanding the worldwide *umma*. This may be particularly crucial at a time when historical diversity needs to be reconciled with the existence of a plurality of Muslim communities in the majority of the Muslim nation-states of today.

Farhad Daftary

References

Bosworth, C. Edmund. *The Islamic Dynasties.* 2d ed. Edinburgh, Scotland: Edinburgh University Press, 1980.

Corbin, Henry. *History of Islamic Philosophy.* Translated by L. Sherrard. London: Kegan Paul, 1993.

Crone, Patricia, and Martin Hinds. *God's Caliph: Religious Authority in the First Centuries of Islam.* Cambridge: Cambridge University Press, 1986.

Debashi, Hamid. *Authority in Islam: From the Rise of Muhammad to the Establishment of the Umayyads.* New Brunswick, N.J.: Transaction Publishers, 1989.

Daftary, Farhad. *The Ismailis: Their History and Doctrines.* Cambridge: Cambridge University Press, 1990.

———. *The Assassin Legends: Myths of the Ismailis.* London: I. B. Tauris, 1994.

Halm, Heinz. *Shiism.* Translated by J. Watson. Edinburgh, Scotland: Edinburgh University Press, 1991.

Hodgson, Marshall G. S. *The Venture of Islam: The Classical Age of Islam,* vol. 1. Chicago: Chicago University Press, 1974.

Jafri, S. Husain M. *Origins and Early Development of Shia Islam*. London: Longman's, 1979.

Kohlberg, Etan. *Belief and Law in Imami Shiism*. London: Variorum, 1991.

Lapidus, Ira M. *A History of Islamic Societies*. Cambridge: Cambridge University Press, 1988.

Leaman, Oliver. *An Introduction to Medieval Islamic Philosophy*. Cambridge: Cambridge University Press, 1985.

Madelung, Wilferd. *Religious Schools and Sects in Medieval Islam*. London: Variorum, 1985.

———. *Religious Trends in Early Islamic Iran*. Albany, NY: State University of New York Press, 1988.

Momen, Moojan. *An Introduction to Shii Islam*. New Haven, Conn.: Yale University Press, 1985.

al-Mufid, Abu- Abd Allah Muhammad Muhammad. *Kitab al-Irshad: The Book of Guidance*, Translated by I. K. A. Howard. London: Muhammadi Trust, 1981.

Nasr, S. Hossein. *Ideals and Realities of Islam*. Boston: Beacon Press, 1967.

———, ed. *Islamic Spirituality: Foundations*. London: n.p., 1987.

Schimmel, Annemarie. *Mystical Dimensions of Islam*. Chapel Hill, N.C.: University of North Carolina Press, 1975.

Serjeant, R. B. "The Zaydis," *Religion in the Middle East*, vol. 2. Edited by A.J. Arberry. Cambridge: Cambridge University Press, 1969.

Shaban, M.A. *Islamic History: A New Interpretation*. Cambridge: Cambridge University Press, 1971–76.

al-Shahrastani, Abul-Fath Muhammad b. Abd al-Karim. *Kitab al-milal wal-nihal*, Partial English translation by A.K. Kazi and J.G. Flynn, *Muslim Sects and Divisions*. London: Kegan Paul International, 1984.

Stern, Samuel M. *Studies in Early Ismailism*. Jerusalem-Leiden: E. J. Brill, 1983.

Tabatabai, S. Muhammad Husayn. *Shiate Islam*, Edited and translated by S. H. Nasr. London: G. Allen and Unwin, 1973..

Wansbrough, John. *The Sectarian Milieu: Content and Composition of Islamic Salvation History*. Oxford: Oxford University Press, 1978.

Watt, W. Montgomery. "Kharijite Thought in the Umayyad Period." *Der Islam*, 36 (1961): 215–231.

———. *Islamic Philosophy and Theology*. Edinburgh: Edinburg University Press, 1962.

———. *The Formative Period of Islamic Thought*. Edinburgh: Edinburg University Press, 1973.

Young, M. J. L. et al., ed. *The Cambridge History of Arabic Literature: Religion, Learning and Science in the Abbasid Period*. Cambridge: Cambridge University Press, 1990.

Part IV:

The Intellectual Tradition in Islam

⓮

Intellectual Life in Islam

◆ The Academic Study of Muslim Intellectual Life ◆ The Genesis
◆ The Formative Period ◆ The Heritage of Previous Civilizations
◆ The Age of Islamic Classics ◆ Ottoman Safavi Mugul

The rich intellectual life of Muslims, beginning with Islam's seventh-century foundation continuing into the twenty-first (Christian era) century, and spanning the entire globe, is naturally difficult to encompass in a short chapter. In addition, the scope of a phrase like "intellectual life" is very broad. Through the centuries, Muslims developed elaborate linguistic sciences of grammar, lexicography, rhetoric, and poetics, and in the natural sciences chemistry, mathematics, astronomy, and medicine. In this chapter we will focus on the religious sciences—theology and law—and the "sciences of the ancients" that influenced, and in some ways, threatened those two fields of endeavor. Though Islamic history is complex, several trends stand out.

Muslims, from the very beginning of Islam, have sought to understand their religious history and the implications of the revelation that Muhammad vouchsafed and embodied in the Quran. Muslims inherited the intellectual treasures of the Greeks, Christians, and Jews, and from among these chose ideas and techniques that would enhance their own religious life. Though the discipline of theology began vigorously, Muslims increasingly distrusted it as an enterprise because of its tendency to divide rather than unify Muslims. And so, despite Muslims' flirtation with theology, it was law—the science of right activity in all domains of human life that became the dominant Islamic discipline.

◆ THE ACADEMIC STUDY OF MUSLIM INTELLECTUAL LIFE

The history of Muslim intellectual life has in the past been understood in two ways. The first and oldest view was shaped by European scholars' notion of their own history. Europeans saw themselves as heirs to the Greeks and Romans, saw the history of the West as pivoting around its contact with classical thought. Surely Muslims, whose history they studied partly to learn how classical thought had been transmitted to the West, also had been changed decisively by this encounter. Though it was believed that Muslims had been inspired by contact with Greek thought, there was at the same time some sense that Muslims had not quite profited from it as Western Europeans had. Some nineteenth-century scholars attributed this "failure" to "the Semitic mind"; others blamed Islamic religious rigidity or Arab literalness. Whatever the case, by the early twentieth century a scholarly consensus had determined that the Golden Age of Islam had been the period of most direct contact with Greek thought. This period was brought to a close, it was believed, by the mystic theologian Muhammad A-Ghaza l 's attack on philosophy, his famous *Incoherence of Philosophy*, or by the fall of Baghdad to the Mongols.

Partly in reaction to this Greco-centric view of Islamic intellectual history, other scholars, particularly French scholars such as Louis Massignon and Henri Laoust, emphasized the rootedness of Islamic thought in the conceptual world of the Quran and the anecdotes professing to be about the Prophet Muhammad (the *hadith*). These scholars perceived a nativist struggle between authentic Muslim ideas and foreign influence, as Muslim traditionalism grounded in scriptural sources of unchanging and unchangeable content and significance made war upon alien heresies. In this struggle, the authentic, primal, "traditionist" Islam won out against the "rationalist" and exogenous alternatives; or so they believed.

A more sophisticated point of view sees Muslims' intellectual history as akin to others' history, a movement grounded in certain historical moments (such as the revelation of the Quran to Muhammad) and the sources

177

that reflect those moments. Like others, Muslims have been receptive to the environment in which they found themselves, and converts brought with them their intellectual dowry and used it to reflect upon and try to understand the significance of those formative religious ideas. As this tradition was elaborated, it was in dialogue with itself. Its intellectual successes led to increasing self-sufficiency and a disinclination to look abroad for significant knowledge. Islamic intellectual life was never, we know now, utterly stagnant, but its intellectual resources seemed perfectly adequate until, like those of other Near Eastern traditions, they came up against modernity.

♦ THE GENESIS

A gradual consensus is emerging among scholars that Muslim intellectual life began during Islam's genesis. While this might seem obvious, some had argued that it was seventy or one-hundred or even more years after Muhammad's death until Muslims began reflecting upon their religion in a self-conscious way. As the Quran is the foundation of Islam, so too it can be seen as the cornerstone of Islamic intellectual life.

The Quran itself is filled with the material for what would become the Muslim religious sciences, and particularly with injunctions to reflect upon the world and to make sense of it. For instance, over fifty times the Quran enjoins Muslims to think, be reasonable, use commonsense:

Lo! in the creation of the heavens and the earth and the alternation of night and day and the ships that run on the sea with profit to men and the water Allah sends down from heaven therewith reviving the earth after it is dead and His scattering abroad in it all manner of crawling thing and the turning about of the winds and the clouds compelled between heaven and earth—surely there are signs for a people who use common sense/who have understanding. (Quran 2:164, translated by Arberry/Pickthall)

This passage and many more like it became the grounds for the characteristic method of Islamic knowledge, which is induction from the particular to the general. The jurist al-Shafii finds the implicit command to make sense of the world in the Quranic passage: "From whatsoever place you come forth, turn your face toward the Inviolable Mosque; and wherever you may be, turn your faces toward it" [when you worship] . . . (Quran) 2:150. As Al-Shafii says, "Thus He, glorified be His praise, guided [humankind] . . . by common sense (*aql*) (which he has implanted in humankind and which discriminates between things and

their opposites) and the landmarks (which [He] set up for them) when the inviolable mosque . . . is out of sight" (Al-Shafii's *Risala*, trans. by Khadduri). The entire edifice of Islamic intellectual activity then is built upon this injunction to figure out, from signs already given by God, in both nature and revelation what it is that God requires humans to do.

In addition, the Quran often alludes to stories that its listeners know, to notions of God, or to norms of practice that the Quran's first audience took for granted but which cried out to later Muslims for amplification. All the Islamic sciences proceed from the openness, the allusiveness of the Quran, which is a document of starts and stops, of stories or injunctions begun, interrupted, and then resumed again. For example, within a single *sura* the Quran offers theology: "We have not send down the Quran upon you . . . as a reminder to him who fears, a revelation from Him who created the earth, and the high heavens, the All-compassionate, sitting on a throne; to Him belongs all that is in the heavens and the earth"; anthropology: "and if you speak aloud yet He knows the secret and that yet more hidden"; mysterious allusion: "To Him belong the names most beautiful"; the story of Moses; eschatology: "The Hour is coming; I will conceal it that every soul may be rewarded for that which it endeavors"; the story of the child Moses in the river; the encounter with Pharaoh; and a catechetical injunction: "Whoever comes unto his Lord a sinner, for him awaits Gehenna wherein he shall neither die nor live. And whoever comes to Him faithful, having done deeds of righteousness, those, for them wait the most sublime stations, gardens, righteousness, those, for them wait the most sublime stations, gardens of Eden under which rivers flow. . . . " (Quran, sura 20).

Each of these revelational topics invites or demands interpretation, elaboration, and explanation, which led to the science of interpretation, at first lexical and grammatical for the difficult passages, then explanatory (e.g., description of who Moses was, a harmonization of disparate Quranic accounts, and further stories about him passed on by Christian and Jewish converts), then esoteric (e.g., explanations of the hidden significance of the names most beautiful).

As part of the attempt to understand the implications of the Quran and to amplify the knowledge it presented, Muslims turned to stories about the Prophet and his Companions. The stories of these founding figures enhanced the Quran and helped to fill in the gaps by explaining the circumstances of a particular revelation or the meaning of a difficult word. Moreover, because of the old Arabian notion of *sunna* —the idea of authority embodied in the normative acts of one's predecessors these stories of Muhammad and his Companions had an intrinsic importance of their own.

Script and ornamentation from Bhong Mosque.

♦ THE FORMATIVE PERIOD

The period from the 690s until the mid-800s of the Christian era might be called the formative period of Islamic intellectual life. During this period the general concerns and much of the argumentation of the Muslim intellectual life developed. Which parts of that heritage could be considered legitimately Islamic was contested in the late seventh and eighth centuries when the Islamic world was in the midst of political and ideological turmoil and all sides invoked their vision of Islam as justification for their actions.

By the late 600s or so the allusive openness of the Quran was recognized and nascent attempts to explain and understand it were underway. As part of that process, but also as part of an independent movement, the normative acts of the first generation of Muslims were circulating and being collected as well. Even in the pre-Islamic period the notion of *sunna*, the normative acts of important persons, was well-established. The first generation of Muslims and particularly Muhammad were without doubt figures whose importance meant that their sayings and deeds would be recalled and treated as significant. These accounts (*hadith*) of the normative acts and sayings (*sunna*) should be under-

sto as another form of Quranic commentary and a response to its limitations and its openness.

As part of the controversies during the late 600s, the statements attributed to the Prophet became an issue. The foremost technique of verification, used thereafter for all historical narrative, was the *isnad,* or "transmission." The names of all narrators of a specific account or quotation was given. A good *isnad* relaying a saying from the Prophet would begin with a contemporary person saying, "I heard from person A, who heard from person B, who heard from person C" and so on back to a person quoted who said, " I heard the Prophet say, "Seek knowledge, even if it be in China." Verification of the *isnad* would consist of checking to see that person A could have heard what he said heard from person B, that he or she was alive and of an age to pay attention when person B was actively relating information; that A and B had been in the same place at some time; that both A and B were known to have good memories and could accurately relate what they heard. Then the relation between B and C, and their character would be checked and so on, back to the narrator who had contact with the Prophet.

The sciences spawned by these concerns, those of

history, biography, and above all the science of Prophetic *hadith* became the cornerstones of religious knowledge from the middle 700s onward. The prodigious number of *hadith* of the Prophet, many of them recognized and rejected by specialists as forgeries, became what amounted to the second Scripture of Islam supplementary to the Quran. In fact, the body of the *hadith* served not just as commentary but often as the lens through which the Quran was read.

At roughly the same time that the science of *hadith* was being born, certain issues that we recognize as theological emerged as well. The first of these issues concerned the human capacity (*qadar*) to determine one's fate and affect the determination of life's course and its end (*qada*). This issue, often referred to in shorthand fashion as the "predestination" argument, involved not merely theological but also political issues since critics of the ruling Umayyad family argued that other alternatives to their rule and rules could have taken place, perhaps should have taken place, and might still come to be. The Umayyads asserted that things could not have been other than they were, and that this present situation amounted to a kind of divine motion of confidence in the order of things as it existed. Yet the more far-reaching aspect was not the political but the theological since the *qadar* controversy raised questions of human power, of the relation of God to Creation, of divine justice and many more issues besides.

The earliest theological text of likely authenticity we have discusses just this issue. In it al-Hasan al-Basri (died 728) asserts that there is a contract between God and humankind. In return for the benefaction of life and the world, humans have an obligation to proclaim God's generosity through obedience and devotion. Humans are free to default on the contract, and if they do so, they are justly punished. In his letter, sent to the Umayyad caliph, he argues that the punishment is, however, the result of humans freely failing. Failure cannot be predetermined by God, or else he would not be a just God, but an oppressor:

God does not alter his benefactions which He has conveyed upon a fold until they alter [i.e., corrupt] what is in themselves. (Quran 8:55)

God initiated [the relationship of benefactor to benefacted]; the change is on the part of the bondsmen, because they turn their backs on what He has ordered them to do. As God said, "Have you not seen those who gave up the benefaction of Allah ungratefully, and led their people down to the Abode of Loss, Hell?" (Quran 14:28–29).

The benefaction was from God most high, and the bondsmen reneged.... Were rejection (*kufr*)

what God decreed (*al-qada*) and determined (*al-qadar*), then He would have been pleased with it, as something He occasioned. God does not decree something and then be displeased with it; neither are injustice or oppression any [part] of the decree of God: but His command to do the virtuous and justice and go deeds and to be agreeable to one's kin *is* His decree. And He has forbidden abominations and the repudiated and the outrage. He said, "Your Lord has decreed (*qada*) that you worship none save Him; and show kindness to your parents" (Quran 17:23).

Al-Hasan's arguments were important in the development of Muslim theology, and in Basra, Iraq, a school of pious theologically-oriented scholars devoted themselves to polemical and missionary work with non-Muslims. Though they were very interested in the development of the discipline of formal religious thought, they abstained from the political squabbles of the time and withdrew (*itazala*) from them. They were consequently known as "the withdrawers" (Mutazila), but by their opponents they were called "the ones who assign capacity (*qadar*) to humans," the Qadariyyah. Eventually, the Mutazilah came to affirm five principles: (1) God's unity which meant that there could be no attribution of attributes like eternality to anything or anyone other than he; (2) God's justice, which meant that God could not predestine human action since he punished and rewarded humans for their deeds; if he punished humans for acts predestined, then he would not be just; (3) the threat and the promise, which meant that God indeed was obliged to punish the corrupt and reward the virtuous, as he had promised in the Quran; (4) the intermediate position of the status of the Muslim sinner who remained part of the Muslim community despite his sin, but was nonetheless to be distinguished from the virtuous within the community; and (5) commanding the right and forbidding the wrong, which evidently affirmed the role of the community leader in enforcing the practical and perhaps theological norms of Islam.

Early Mutazilism was initially important because, after the Abbasid revolution (750), the state viewed Mutazili doctrines as a compromise that would unify the religiously fractious polity of the empire. While Mutazilism affirmed that the Shia and the Khwarij were Muslims, it also recognized an important role for the imam or leader as a religious authority. It seems also that Mutazilism with its deductive hermeneutic, that is, its method of understanding the Quran and *hadith* through a series of first principles, offered great scope for authoritative religious determination by the organs of the state. It is not surprising then that the Caliph al-Mamun (died 833) embraced Mutazilism as the state doctrine, and at the beginning of the early 800s of the Christian era enforced a "test" (*mihnah*) upon holders of office and public religious figures. Specifically, they were required to affirm the "createdness of the Quran." That is, as his speech, the Quran could not be said to be coeternal with God; for the Mutazilah, that amounted to a compromise of God's unity and implied that something other than he was, like God, without beginning. To affirm the createdness of the Quran, moreover, was to affirm the Mutazili hermeneutic since it meant affirming that Quranic descriptions of Allah such as seeing, speaking, hearing, and the like were metaphoric and of a different order of truth than saying he was one, or powerful. All of the Quran, for the Mutazila, was to be read through the five principles.

Alongside the development of Mutazili theology, with its deductive hermeneutic, a different science, that of "law," also was developing, but this science was characterized by an inductive hermeneutic, that is, instead of reading Quran and *hadith* through certain first principles and deducing particulars from these generalities, the science of legal understanding (*fiqh*) sought to induce generalities from the particular and detailed injunctions of the two scriptural sources.

From its inception, Islam was a religion of practice. The core of membership was defined early on as proclaiming publicly the singularity of Allah and, messengerhood of Muhammad, the performance of the five times daily worship, fasting during the month of Ramadan, paying the welfare tax, and pilgrimage to Mecca and performance of the *hajj* rites at least once in one's lifetime if financially able (the so-called "five pillars of Islam"). Likewise, Muslims sought to obey the injunctions in the Quran (which lays down rules for inheritance, divorce, the welfare tax, as well as ritual requirements) and the normative conduct (*sunna*) of the early community and the Prophet. Rules of practice, then, are the heart of Islam.

However, new situations and the uncertainty of some prophetic and Quranic stipulations led Muslims to seek a method to interpret scripture and expand its scope so that there could be uniform agreement among believers. Various alternatives were tried. Malik ibn Anas (died 796) argued implicitly for continuity of local practice, saying in effect, "This is how we've always done it; we wouldn't have done it this way if it wasn't right." This argument was somewhat persuasive, particularly for Malik's native Medina, the Prophet's city, which might indeed have preserved otherwise unrecorded prophetic norms, and might also have extended them in ways consistent with Muhammad's practice.

Another approach was associated with Abu Hanifa (died 767) and his school in the newly Muslim Iraq. The Hanafis, like the Mutazila theologians, implicitly used a deductive approach to find the norms of Islamic conduct. First, they affirmed the value of maxims such as "the child belongs to the marriage bed" as general principles to determine the rulings in particular cases such as disputed paternity. They also argued for the applicability of such principles as "general welfare," a kind of utilitarian method of legal interpretation that said that the best ruling was the one that had the best consequences. To many Muslims these two Hanafi techniques seemed slippery and subjective, insufficiently certain and insufficiently grounded in Islamic sources. It remained to al-Shafii (died 820) to articulate an inductive method of legal interpretation that would allow unlimited application of Islamic norms to new circumstances while at the same time grounding that application more or less firmly in Islamic scriptural sources.

Al-Shafii stressed that Quran and *hadith* were not unified wholes from which general principles of practice could be inferred, but rather both contained virtually unlimited numbers of rules, guidelines, and modifications of rules. To understand God's intent properly, it was necessary to contextualize any given ruling within all other possibly relevant rulings, each of which potentially explained some aspect of the action in question. So for even straightforward dicta, such as "He hath forbidden you carrion (Quran 2:173), every related verse of Quran and *hadith* of the Prophet (al-Shafii denied the value of local practice or of anyone's *sunna* besides the Prophet's) had to be marshaled alongside to determine whether the rule was general (for all Muslims) or restricted (to some subgroup of Muslims), whether it had been abrogated by a later Quranic Revelation or some *hadith*, and so on. Only in this fashion could scripture be properly understood and applied. In cases in which there was no scriptural rule, one could refer to the consensus of the community (on the basis that such universally observed practices might preserve otherwise forgotten prophetic norms). Failing that, one could extend a rule for a similar case to the new case by finding some underlying link between the known case and the new case.

Though most of the details of this process were not worked out for more than two centuries, al-Shafii, with his inductive methology and stipulation of the "thick" rule based on all possibly relevant sources of knowledge, effectively founded the science of Islamic jurisprudence. Many of the rules of Islamic conduct were in place by the time he wrote his text on method, but for the rest of Islamic history his techniques were applied by all Muslims in the search for God's position on every detail of human conduct. Already in the eighth century elaborate books of practical law attempted to provide detailed Islamic guidance on every aspect of human conduct. With the acceptance of *hadith* as a source for knowledge of the Prophet's *sunna* and the

Mosaic from al-Aqsa Mosque, Jerusalem.

method of al-Shafii in place, Islamic law expanded its scope rapidly in the ninth and tenth centuries.

Although Islamic intellectual life grew out of characteristically Muslim concerns, Muslims were not isolated from the culture of the world around them, and in the late antique period the dominant intellectual culture was Hellenistic. As background, it must be remembered that Muslims in this period witnessed the transformation of Islam from the ethnic religion of provincial merchants and transport laborers to the civilization force linking an empire that stretched from China to France. Muslims in the seventh, eighth, and ninth centuries were heirs to all of human culture except the east Asian and the American, and among all its offerings they picked and chose those intellectual techniques and that knowledge that could enhance their lives as Muslims. Yet, these instruments remained subordinate to the Muslim heritage.

♦ THE HERITAGE OF PREVIOUS CIVILIZATIONS

Like Christians and Jews, Muslims were constantly in dialogue with Hellenistic knowledge. This Greek knowledge was often transmitted to them through Arabic's cognate language, Syriac, for by the seventh

Christian century most of the surviving Greek heritage—in philosophy, the natural sciences and law—had been translated by Christians into Syriac. With the rise of Arab Muslim patronage in the Umayyid period (661–750), a first wave of commissioned translations, from Syriac and also directly from the Greek, affected the content of Muslim thought. The translated works were at first primarily medical, but translators also brought some philosophical materials into the lingua franca of Muslim culture, that is, into Arabic. With the establishment of the Abbasid empire (750–1258) a second wave of translation under Caliph al-Mamun began, and talented polyglots, many of them Christian, labored to transmit and comment upon the Hellenistic culture of philosophy and the sciences. In this period, too, though in less systematic and institutional ways, Sanskrit and ancient Persian materials found their way into Arabic, as did Hellenistic romances, wisdom literature, and probably other literary works. These were followed by hermetic and religious literature, particularly what we call Neoplatonic texts. These latter were attributed, however, to Aristotle, so that the difference in perspective between Plato and Aristotle, so dialectically fruitful for European philosophical debate, was imperceptible to Muslim philosophers.

All of these intellectual disciplines had a significant impact on Islamic religious thought since Muslim controversialists and non-Muslim polemicists deployed these materials and techniques in argument, and Muslims of all stripes learned quickly to adapt these ideas for their own ends. By the ninth century, original Arabic philosophical texts were being written in Arabic, notably by al-Kindi (died a. 866), the so called "philosopher of the Arabs." Throughout the ninth, tenth, and eleventh centuries, a class of Muslim intellectuals called by the foreign term *faylasuf* (philosophers) indigenized this Hellenistic heritage and sought to reshape it to the irreducible doctrines of Islam, such as the createdness of the world. Mainstream Muslim theologians and other intellectuals were particularly influenced by the straightforward philosophical, though undoubtedly religious, works of *faylasufs* like Ibn Sina (Avicenna) (died 1037) in the East and Ibn Rushd (Averroes) (died 1204) in Spain. In addition, various non-Muslims, including Maimonides, were influential through the medium of philosophy, the nearest thing to a nondenominational intellectual science in the premodern period. Nonetheless, *falsafa* (philosophy) as an independent entity more or less disappeared after the thirteenth century.

Falsafa had three foci: cosmology, practical ethics, and logic. All three had important effects on Islamic intellectual life. It was the Ismaili Shia movement that perhaps most effectively made philosophical (which in this case means Neoplatonic) cosmology an Islamic undertaking. The Ismailis affirmed a cyclical history in which revelations and prophets succeeded each other throughout time, each revelation ushering in a new era. As the correlate of this, a group of Ismailis called the Brethren of Purity (*ikhwan al-safa*) as well as other Ismailis affirmed a theory of emanation that, on the one hand, portrayed God as utterly other and indescribable. On the other hand, they depicted God creating the material world through a series of "overflowings" so that the dualism of God and the world was eliminated. After the ebbing of Ismailism in the thirteenth century, this cosmology remained very important for Sufis who had adopted it to their purposes already by the tenth century.

The practical ethics of Hellenism passed into "Mirrors for Princes" literature of Islamdom—manuals of statecraft—and also into secretarial anthologies where they had important influence on the norms of rulership and general views of political conduct. Into this genre, too, passed a number of Persian and probably Indian notions of rulership. Though often cynical, these manuals tried to unify the ethical norms of Islam with the instrumentalist guidelines of rulership.

Finally, the logic that formed the first part of the Greek syllabus, *or Organon*, became for nearly all Islamic sciences the preliminary to pursuit of advanced knowledge. Various versions of the *Isogage*, a Hellenistic introduction to logic, became standard textbooks. Later works in religious disciplines often begin with an affirmation of the value of logic and sometimes with a lengthy introduction to formal logic, the syllogism, and the rules of induction and deduction.

Though the "foreign sciences" or "sciences of the ancients" had an important impact on Muslims and their intellectual life, academic scholars have in the past tended both to exaggerate the significance of these outside influences during the ninth through the thirteenth centuries and to neglect the continuing effect of the Greek sciences in subsequent time, up to and in some cases including the modern era. Logic remains a part of the curriculum at *madrasas*, and philosophy is still taught in Iranian religious schools.

◆ THE AGE OF ISLAMIC CLASSICS

In the tenth through the thirteenth centuries, Muslim scholars consolidated the work of previous centuries and made definitive choices among the options avail-

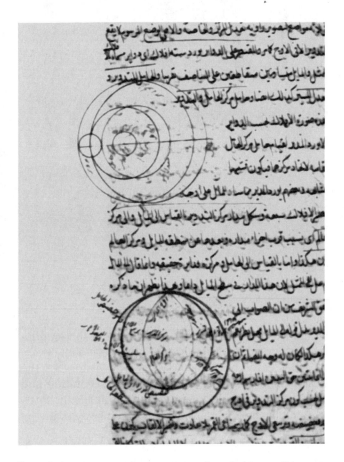

Page from a commentary on cosmology by the well-known thirteenth-century theologian and philosopher Nasir-al-Din Tusi.

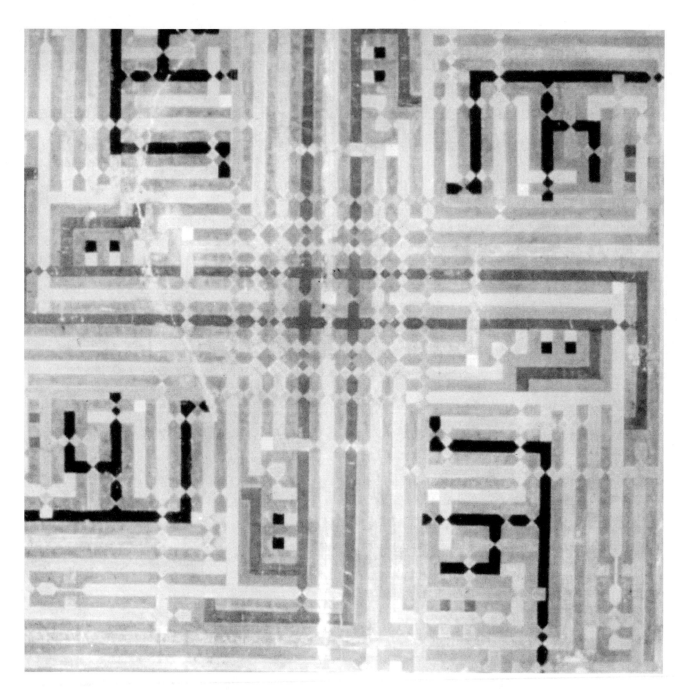

Fifteenth-century calligraphy.

able. In this period scholars wrote works that continued to be used throughout the middle period and even, in some cases, into the present. The history of the Islamic sciences after their period of elaboration and development can be summed up thus: All Islamic intellectual life came increasingly under the sway of the legal sciences.

Theology, a controversial science from the eighth through the tenth centuries, faded thereafter into formulaic catechisms and scholastic discussions of language and causality. The *mihnah* and the subsequent turmoil over theological doctrines made theology a suspect science in a religious climate antipathetic to schism and disunity. In this period three non-Mutazili movements developed in theology, two of them explicitly devised to refute the Mutazilah. The first was an inchoate movement, a cluster of popular literalists, *hadith* scholars, and conservative jurists. Ahmad ibn Hanbal (died 855) is remembered as the embodiment of this resistance. Those affiliated with him, called Hanbalis, were initially opposed to speculative reasoning of any sort, and argued for a theology limited to the language of scripture, the Quran and *hadith*. This "strict constructionist" approach focused upon law and praxis as the true Islamic sciences, and at first viewed the entire enterprise of theology as a blameworthy innovation. Gradually, however, under the pressure of polemics and public debate, Hanbalis were forced to articulate a theological method. After many diverse approaches were tried, Hanbalis settled on a method that might be described as catechetical, that is, theologically aware but in principle hostile to (particularly the "less-qualified") Muslims participating in the debates of theologians.

For the Hanbalis, God's characteristics were enumerated in the word of God and in sound *hadith*, and neither other techniques (such as formal logic) nor speculative inquiries (such as whether God's speech was part of his essence or not) were appropriate. The technique can be seen in the so-called Qadiri creed promulgated by Caliph al-Qadirbillah (died 1018), which is persuasive, not because of its logic, but because of its largely unarguable paraphrases or quotations from the Quran:

> Every human being must know that God, the mighty and the powerful, is unique and has no associate; He has not begotten nor been begotten and there is no one equal to him. (Quran 112);

> He has taken no [female] companion and no son and there has never been a partner to him in dominion (Quran 72:3);

> He is the First, who never ceased to be, and the Last, who never shall cease to be; omnipotent in everything, impotent in nothing: If He wishes a thing to be, He says of it be and it is (Quran 36:82);

> "Free of want," he has no need of anything. There is no god but Allah, He is the Living, the Self-subsistent, slumber seizes Him not, nor sleep (Quran 2:255);

> He feeds [others] but does not eat (Quran 6:14).

This approach reached its height with the genius of Ibn Taymiyya (died 1328), who in masterly fashion attacked Greek logic while declining to propose an alternative. As he says, "I have always known that Greek logic is neither needed by the intelligent nor of any use to the dullard. . . . All the communities of scholars, advocates of religious doctrines, craftsmen, and professionals know the things they need to know, and verify what they encounter . . . without speaking of [formal] definitions." This "plain man's Islam" proved popular

and gratifying particularly to less-educated Muslims, and its aversion to the "foreign" made it particularly important as part of the reconstruction of Islam from the eighteenth century through the present.

More sophisticated, though less enduring, were the two other major approaches to theology, that of Abu al-Hasan al-Ashari (died 935) and that attributed to Abu Mansur al-Maturidi (died 944) and found among followers of the Hanafi school of law. Al-Ashari had been a Mutazili before he rejected its doctrines as incompatible with God's absolute sovereignty and sole status as Creator. By the end of his life he affirmed a modified predestinarianism, and also, in ethics, what George Hourani called theological subjectivism, that is, that no category of act is intrinsically good or evil, and that God indeed could have commended lying, and had he done so, it would therefore be go, and obligatory. Both ideas were anathema to the Mutazila. The heirs of al-Ashari, such as al-Baqillani (died 403) and Ibn al-Furuk (died 406), developed from al-Ashari's ideas a sophisticated and devastating critique of the Mutazila that effectively constituted orthodoxy in the Arab lands and Iran by the early twelfth century. The Maturidis affirmed a somewhat more intrinsically rational universe but argued that revelation made human attempts at moral understanding irrelevant because they were unreliable. The following quotation from a creed of the Maturidi Najmaddin Umar al-Nasafi (died 1142) contrasts with the "amateurism" of the Qadiri creed quoted above.

> God exalted be He, is the creator of all human actions, whether of infidelity or of faith, whether of obedience or of disobedience. They are all of them by His desire and His will, by His judgment, His decreeing and His predetermining. Humans may perform actions by choice for which they are rewarded and punished, those of them that are good being by the good-pleasure of God exalted be He and those of them that are bad not by His good-pleasure. Ability [to perform action] comes along with the action and is the real power by which the action is performed. This word [ability] refers to the unimpaired functioning of the causes, the instruments, the bodily members [concerned in the performance of actions], and the validity of [the assignment of] legal responsibility is dependent on this ability, for no creature is held responsible for what is not within his capability.

In any case, all three anti-Mutazilite schools can be said to have succeeded, and by the twelfth Christian century, theology, once referred to as "disputatious words" (*kalam*), was now usually called by the more staid "principles of religion" (*usul al-din*). It was practiced with scholastic abandon by figures such as al-Taftazani (died 1389), and existential concerns became the province of Sufism.

As theology moved to the sidelines, law became more and more the sovereign realm of Muslim intellectual endeavor. Law evolved into two connected disciplines: the science of law (*fiqh*) and the principles of law (*usul al-fiqh*). *Fiqh* (which literally means "insight") referred to the rules for human conduct both in the realms of ritual (*ibadat*) and in the domain of human affairs (*muamilat*). *Usul al-fiqh* ("principles of discernment" or "principles of law") were increasingly systematic descriptions of how those rules should be inferred from the four sources of law identified by al-Shafii. The tenth century inherited a series of works that had unsystematically developed rules for the guidance of Muslims in these two domains of life and ritual. Their task in that and subsequent centuries was to articulate an implicit system to facilitate an ordered response to new problems. In other words, they had to define rules so that jurists confronted with new situations could use *ijtihad* (judgment based on the *usul-al-fiqh*) in a reliable Islamic way.

This the scholars of the tenth, eleventh, and twelfth centuries proceeded to do. Essentially, *usul al-fiqh* turned into the hermeneutic science of Islam through which the Quran and *hadith* were understood and applied. To this end, grammar, lexicography, the sciences of Quran commentary, *hadith* criticism, theology, and logic were all harnessed to the task of finding what it was God wanted Muslims to do in a particular situation. Yet the enterprise was always informed by a humility and sense of the limitations of human knowledge: Sunni scholars, together with the Zaydis among the Shia, argued that the knowledge obtained by the *usul al-fiqh* methology was at best suppositional knowledge, but Muslims were required by Allah to act on the basis of this supposition. (The Imami Shias and Ismailis believed that certain knowledge in legal matters could be obtained, only because of the additional guidance of the Imam.) In matters of morality and conduct, then, the legal sciences became the Islamic science par excellence, occupying a position of eminence and attaining a degree of sophistication and refinement similar to theology in Christianity.

This primacy of law was reflected in the institutions that developed for the propagation of Islam, the *madrasas*, which, according to George Makdisi, were the models for the later development of colleges in Christendom. These *madrasas* were endowed schools consisting of buildings, endowments for professors, and endowed scholarships for students. In nearly all cases, however, the endowed curriculum of the school was law, sometimes augmented with professorships of *hadith*, Arabic grammar, or Quranic exegesis.

(Theology was, for the most part, not offered in these *madrasas*, so the earlier theory that they developed to teach "orthodox theology" is clearly untenable.) The program of these schools, then, excluded the natural sciences, vernacular languages, Sufism, theology, and philosophy. Consequently, these sciences were marginalized or withered away in subsequent Islamic history.

♦ OTTOMAN SAFAVI MUGAL

As Islam spread to its growing frontiers, *madrasas* and the culture of the *ulama* (religious scholars) followed, and gradually, through the fourteenth, fifteenth, and sixteenth centuries, the intellectual labor of interpreting and transmitting Islamic knowledge passed into Anatolia, Eastern Europe, Central Asia, and India. With the rise of the "Gunpowder Empires" of the Ottomans in the eastern and central Mediterranean, the Safavis in Iran, and the Mughals in India, matrices passed into state control. Particularly in the Ottoman Empire, Islamic intellectual effort became an enterprise of the center and a further means by which the state worked its will upon the periphery. Recent work has shown, however, that Hanafi law was applied strictly throughout much of Ottoman history, and that Islamic scholars—judges and *muftis*—had precedence over state officials such as governors and military commanders. However, some *ulama* safeguarded their independence and were able to oppose state-sponsored interpretations of Islamic law and effect reform through polemical writing, sermons, and mobilization of the Muslim populace. Throughout Islamdom, legal scholars wrote treatises on new problems in *fiqh* as they arose, and refined and systematized the works of earlier scholars of the law.

Although it used to be believed that Islamic intellectual life waned with the passing of the "Golden Age of Baghdad," current scholarship recognizes the undiminished vitality of Muslim thought in some fields, particularly law, throughout the whole of Islamic history. The legacy of these labors remains an important part of contemporary Islamic life, and many Muslim scholars labor even now with the conviction that these sciences will be particularly germane to the religious and social life of Muslims in the next century.

A. Kevin Reinhart

References

Coulson, N. J. *A History of Islamic Law.* Islamic Surveys no. 2 Edinburgh, Scotland: Edinburgh University Press, 1978 [1964].

Doi, Abdur Rahman I. *Sharia: The Islamic Law.* London: Ta Ha Publishers, 1984.

Hodgson, Marshall G. S. *The Venture of Islam: Conscience and History in a World Civilization.* Chicago: University of Chicago Press, 1974.

Fakhry, Majid. *A History of Islamic Philosophy.* 2nd ed. New York: Columbia University Press, 1983.

Kraemer, Joel L. *Humanism in the Renaissance of Islam: The Cultural Revival during the Buyid Age,* Studies in Islamic Culture and History, v. 7. Leiden, Netherlands: E. J. Brill, 1986.

Lapidus, Ira M. A *History of Islamic Societies.* Cambridge: Cambridge University Press, 1988.

Ormsby, Eric L. *Theodicy in Islamic Thought: The Dispute over al-Ghazali's "Best of All Possible Worlds."* Princeton, NJ: Princeton University Press, 1984.

Schacht, Joseph. *An Intruction to Islamic Law.* Oxford: Clarendon Press, 1964.

Watt, W. Montgomery. *The Formative Philosophy of Islamic Thought.* Edinburgh, Scotland: Edinburgh University Press, 1973.

———. *Islamic Philosophy and Theology: An Extended Survey.* 2nd ed. Edinburgh, Scotland: Edinburgh University Press, 1985.

15

Muslim Philosophy and the Sciences

♦ The Search for Knowledge ♦ Philosophy ♦ The Sciences
♦ Educating Europe: The Arabo-Latin Translation Movement

The pursuit of knowledge is central to the Islamic message. The goal of knowledge is not mere contemplation but the discovery of action that leads to ultimate felicity. In the intellectually fertile, diverse, multifaith, multiethnic, and stimulating environment of medieval Islamic civilization, an intense debate existed among competing intellectual disciplines. This debate, which endured across continents and centuries even as these disciplines evolved, focused on the issues of the identity and foundations of "real" knowledge that one ought to acquire and make the basis for action.

♦ THE SEARCH FOR KNOWLEDGE

For many, such knowledge was to be found in Islamic law, which is derived from the religious sources of the Quran and the Prophetic Tradition. Salvation, then, required living a life in conformity with the law. For others, real knowledge was esoteric and mystical, and hence the path to salvation lay in seeking the right teacher and being initiated into devotional practices leading to union with God. Still others thought real knowledge consisted of a rational understanding of God's nature and attributes, his creation of the world, its dependency on him, and his bounty and mercy to the creatures of this world as manifested in prophecy. For them, salvation lay in the practices instituted by prophets, provided that the performance of these practices was grounded in rational knowledge. Still others regarded real knowledge to be the philosophical wisdom of the ancients as found in the Neoplatonized Aristotelian view of the world. Salvation, they held, was living in conformity with the ethical principles of this system, namely intellectual self-improvement and virtuous living, which allowed the soul to achieve immortality through the active intellect.

A naive analysis of these formulations would pit the "foreign" or secular sciences derived from the ancients (in particular, the Greeks) against the "religious" or revealed sciences, echoing the erroneous, but nonetheless prevalent, paradigmatic view of the incompatibility between reason and religion. In the medieval Islamic context, the interaction between secular and religious sciences had profound consequences, for this interaction was the process by which knowledge whose origins were non-Islamic was appropriated and then naturalized into a civilization with a different ethos. Within this interaction, both secular and religious sciences adopted methods and doctrines from each other in the course of centuries of critical, dialogical, and sometimes acrimonious, debate. Islamic philosophy was a product of this cosmopolitan civilization and one of its great intellectual achievements. Three philosophical movements can be broadly identified within the historical evolution of this interaction: religious or theological philosophy (*kalam*), Islamic Hellenistic philosophy (*falsafa*), and mystical philosophy or theosophy. The scientific tradition in Islamic civilization was primarily allied to the second of these, namely Islamic Hellenistic philosophy.

The geography of the early Islamic empire was fundamental to the emergence of the intellectual disciplines of medieval Islamic civilization. The Arabian peninsula, home to the Prophet Muhammad, was at the periphery of the centers of learning of late antiquity. Within a few decades after Muhammad's death, Muslim armies had gained control of a vast region from the Atlantic to the borders of India. As a result, such Hellenistic centers of learning as Alexandria and Antioch where Aristotelian, Neoplatonic, Platonic, and other texts had been studied over centuries, as well as the centers of Manichean, Bardaisanite, Buddhist,

Page from a fifteenth-century astronomical treatise.

Jewish, and Christian learning, now belonged to a nominally single empire, where, in time, Arabic became the language of intellectual discourse. Language was just one of the elements uniting this vast and diverse empire. Other elements include a measure of cultural uniformity, aesthetic sensibility, patronage, the struggle to find meaning and discover norms of practice and behavior in the Islamic message, and, most importantly, an attitude of reverence toward knowledge derived from the Quran. Material factors also played a role, in particular, the availability of paper. The discovery of its manufacture originated in China but spread across the Islamic empire in the eighth century. Since books could now be produced cheaply, the pace of the dissemination of knowledge accelerated. A flourishing book trade ensued, indicative of a desire for knowledge, which, in turn, fueled further intellectual activity.

◆ PHILOSOPHY

Religious Philosophy

Religious or theological philosophy (*kalam*) has no counterpart in the Western tradition. Although its orientation is theological, much of its subject matter is philosophical since it encompasses epistemology, analysis, cosmology, and metaphysics. Furthermore, its approach is rationalist and, as such, its method is philosophical. The epistemological foundation and role of religious philosophy in medieval Islamic civilization thus differ from and are somewhat opposed to those of medieval Christian theology.

Religious philosophy emerged within a hundred years after the death of the Prophet Muhammad in a milieu where Muslims were preoccupied with questions about their identity and thus engaged in a wide-ranging debate over beliefs, concepts, values, practices, and, in general, worldviews. This debate was conducted among Muslims and also with their non-Muslim neighbors. Several factors contributed to the urgency of such questions and related issues of correct practice, belief, and doctrine. Some non-Muslim subjects desired to convert to the new religion and better understand the work of the first two generations of Muslims who had laid the groundwork of knowledge about issues of the faith. In this diverse and steadily growing Muslim community, several approaches to the Islamic message were debated and developed, which, in due course, were embodied in the emerging intellectual disciplines. The problems of free will and predestination, God's nature and attributes, prophecy, revelation, God's relation to the created world, the attributes and properties of things, the nature of human beings, and causality were subjects that fell within the domain of religious philosophy. Given the multifaith milieu, the discussion of these problems included proponents of other faiths, primarily Christians and Manicheans, as well as proponents of epistemological and cosmological positions, for example, skepticism, relativism, natural causation, and the eternity of the world.

The writings of early Muslim religious philosophers have not survived. Fragments preserved in later works indicate an open-minded, yet critical, attitude. The multitude of individual and opposed views to a broad range of questions reflect the religious philosophers' engagement in the contemporary issues of those times, some of which derive from the epistemological and cosmological inquiries of late antiquity. For example, regarding the problem of attributes and properties of things, Hisham ibn al-Hakam (died circa 795) and his followers held that all objects besides God are corporeal, regardless of whether they are bodies or qualities (like color or taste). Therefore, perceptible bodies consist of a bundle of corporeal attributes (a similar position was taken on this by the Stoics). Dirar ibn Amr (died circa 815) and others held the opposite view that created objects are all incorporeal qualities, and that corporeal bodies arise when these qualities combine together. This was also the position of Gregory of Nyssa. Abu al-Hudhayl (died 841), Muammar (died 830), Bishr ibn Mutamir (died circa 825–840), and their followers held that created objects are corporeal atoms or incorporeal qualities, and that bodies are constituted out of their combination. This was that of some Dualists; the position of the Greek Atomists was also somewhat similar.

During the later half of the ninth century, as a result of the effort of Abu Ali al-Jubbai (died 915), his son Abu Hashim (died 933), and their followers, a coherent system emerged that characterized classical Mutazili religious philosophy. The Mutazili were one group of Muslim thinkers who had emerged as a distinctive school of thought by this time. In outline, they hold that objects either exist, are possible, or are impossible. Existent objects comprise the eternal God and the created world of space-occupying atoms and their inherent qualities. Qualities are either perceptible such as color, taste, and sound; nonperceptible such as force and motion; psychological states of animate beings such as knowledge, preception, and willingness; or are abilities such as being alive and capable of autonomous action. Atoms and qualities combine to form inanimate bodies, as well as compound animate beings. Simple objects have essential attributes that make them the kind of objects they are (God is eternal, alive, knowing, and possesses the power of autonomous action; atoms are space-occupying) and may have additional attributes (God's speech, an atom's being white). Causal agency belongs exclusively to volitional beings, for only they possess the power of autonomous action. Therefore, "nature" or "natural" agency is nonexistent. God's causal activity is unlimited, for the power of autonomous action is one of His essential attributes. The human power of action, however, is nonessential and human activity is limited. Causal agents may act directly, as in creating an atom or a person picking up a stone, or they may act indirectly through secondary causes, as when someone directly creates upward force in a stone, which engenders motion at another instance. God directly created the world. His creative activity is continuous and encompasses everything besides human actions.

Human knowledge is of two kinds: immediate knowledge of *a priori* truths, ethical principles, objects of perception, and man's internal states; and acquired knowledge deriving from reflection on argument, revelation, tradition, and so on. Because of self-interest, human beings desire to avoid harm and achieve benefit. They must therefore think, for in the important matter of achieving ultimate felicity and avoiding eternal harm, they would be foolish to blindly imitate someone claiming to have knowledge. They must seek rational and secure knowledge of God and recognize His bounty, in particular, his gracious act of sending prophets to guide humankind. They must pursue ethically sound actions to earn the reward promised by God. Reflection enables them to determine that the moral soundness of action for ethical principles is objective and immediately known to mature persons who are thus accountable to God. Intellectual reflection also leads to general religious truths. However, specific religious practices like forms of prayer and pilgrimage are established and instituted by prophets. Hence, while reason is primary, revelation is necessary for the establishment of religion and creates a social and political order conducive to its practice.

The role of logic, epistemology, cosmology, ethics, and politics in the Mutazili system is obvious as is its theological orientation. But the emphasis on reason and, above all, the method of argument and objection is philosophical. Moreover, apart from secondary causation, this system is nondeterministic, where agents are free to perform or withhold actions. Not surprisingly, the Mutazilis were challenged by traditionalist religious scholars and Islamic Hellenistic philosophers. The Mutazili view that God's speech, namely revelation, is nonessential and therefore created was rejected by traditionalists. Since, in the early ninth century, the Mutazilis were politically powerful, they imposed the doctrine of createdness of revelation upon governmental officials, including religious judges. The resulting inquisition led to the imprisonment of prominent traditionalists such as the well-known scholar Ahmad ibn Hanbal (died 855). The inquisition and Mutazili political ascendancy came to an end during the reign of Caliph Al-Mutawakkil (reigned 847–861).

In 912–913, one of al-Jubbai's most brilliant pupils, Abu al-Hasan al-Ashari (died 935), broke away to found Ashari *kalam*, which was sympathetic to the traditionalists. Over the course of the next three centuries, Ashari religious philosophy gradually became the predominant and "orthodox" *kalam* school. To a large degree, the subject matter—analytic structure, epistemology, and cosmology of the Mutazilis—was retained. The significant departure was over the nature of God and human beings. Whereas Mutazilis had emphasized God's justice, believing it absolutely impossible for God to commit unjust acts (for man and God are beholden to the same objective ethical principles), the Asharis emphasized God's absolute power and independence. Hence, they denied the objectivity of ethical principles. In their view, ethical principles were within God's determination, and human beings cannot gain access to them except through revelation. The primacy of revelation over reason was thus upheld. Furthermore, God's absolute power entails denying causal agency to persons. They may only metaphorically be said to be causal agents, for they "acquire" actions actually performed by God. Not surprisingly, the Asharis also denied secondary causation. Their system is therefore occasionalist, one in which every action in the world is directly caused by God. Consequently, attributing a causal relationship between a uniformly observed set of prior and posterior events (e.g., fire in contact with cotton followed by burning) is erroneous, for the uniformity reflects only God's habitual action that he may arbitrarily choose to alter. Finally, the Asharis rejected the Mutazili distinction between God's essence and attributes, and hence the createdness of God's speech.

The Ashari position was elucidated and defended from the critique of the Mutazilis, Islamic Hellenistic philosophers, and traditionalists by Al-Ashari's followers, notably Al-Baqillani (died 1013), Ibn Furak (died 1015), al-Juwayni (died 1085), and Abu al-Hamid al-Ghazali (died 1111), the author of *The Destruction of the Hellenistic Philosophers*. In this work, al-Ghazali defended the Ashari view of God's absolute freedom and causal determination, attacking the philosophers' doctrine of the eternity of the world; their doctrine of emanation, which denied God's causal activity and knowledge of particulars in the world but instead attributed intelligence and causal efficacy to celestial entities; their denial of bodily resurrection and their theory of natural causation. Al-Ghazali's thorough familiarity with Islamic Hellenistic philosophy is evident in *The Destruction*'s embrace of its conceptual language (his preliminary study, *The Aims of the Philosophers*, is a succinct summary of Islamic Hellenistic Philosophy which, along with *The Destruction*, was translated into Latin).

Religious philosophy enters a new phase with Al-Ghazali as he appropriated the conceptual language and logic of Hellenistic philosophy without compromising the premise of God's absolute freedom and determination. The historian Ibn Khaldun (died 1382) thus complained that al-Ghazali and his followers muddled religious philosophy with Islamic Hellenistic philosophy. Notable religious philosophers after Al-Ghazali include Fakhr al-din al-Razi (died 1209) and Adud al-din al-Iji (died 1355). Al-Iji's classic text, *The Stations of Religious Philosophy*, became the standard text and was the subject of many commentaries. Four of the six sections of the book are devoted to philosophical subjects of epistemology, ontology, qualities, and bodies, while the remaining two cover the properly theological topics of God and prophecy. Moreover, al-Iji and his commentators discuss the diversity of opinions on these subjects, including those of the Islamic Hellenistic philosophers.

This account of religious philosophy applies to Sunni *kalam*. Regarding the Shia, the Zaydis adapted Mutazili *kalam*, and so, initially, did the Ithna Ashari. The Ismailis adapted Hellenistic philosophy within their own intellectual framework. However, in the thirteenth century, the philosopher and scientist Nasir al-din al-Tusi (died 1274) reformulated Twelver Shia *kalam* within the conceptual language and system of the philosophers.

The influence of religious philosophy also extended into Judaism. The Karaites, including Yusuf al-Basir (died 942), were influenced by Mutazili religious philosophy. Consequently, the debate between religious philosophy and Islamic Hellenistic philosophy is also found among Jewish intellectuals of Islamic lands. In his *Guide to the Perplexed*, Maimonides (died 1204) presents an account of religious philosophy that he then refutes.

Islamic Hellenistic Philosophy

Islamic philosophy or *falsafa* is Hellenistic in inspiration and outlook. Its characterization as "Islamic" designates the milieu of Islamic civilization and not its conformity, or lack thereof, with what was understood to be the normative traditionalist understanding of Islam. Furthermore, not all its practitioners were

Muslims. Some were Christians and others Jews. The impetus for Islamic Hellenistic philosophy originated in the transmission of Greek texts into Arabic. In due course, the philosophy of these texts was developed further and naturalized by a milieu with its own problems and competing philosophies.

The impetus to appropriate and then naturalize ancient knowledge arose out of the Muslim ethic of reverence for knowledge. In one of the most significant premodern transfers of knowledge, almost the entire scientific and philosophical legacy of the ancient world was translated into Arabic. Some evidence suggests that translation into Arabic may have begun in the early eighth century, but its pace accelerated under the patronage of the Abbasid caliphs. Translation activity was deliberate, emphasizing classic scientific and philosophical texts yet leaving aside literary texts. The importance of translation is evident in the dispatch of official emissaries to Byzantium to procure manuscripts. Translation was facilitated by the ongoing activity of religious philosophers who had begun to forge philosophical terms in Arabic. Patronage also played a key role. The Abbasid caliph Al-Mansur (reigned 754–775) commissioned the translation of Sanskrit astronomical and medical texts. His successors, Harun al-Rashid (reigned 786–809) and Al-Mamun (reigned 813–833), went further, commissioning the translation of Greek texts and establishing the endowed institution of the House of Wisdom (*Bayt al-Hikma*) to supervise translation and engage in scientific activity. Other patrons of translation included wealthy government officials, princes, and individuals. Accordingly, by the tenth century, much of the Hellenistic intellectual legacy as well as material from ancient Iran and India were available in Arabic. Since the philosophical perspective of late antiquity dominated this legacy, Islamic Hellenistic philosophers approached Hellenistic philosophy from a Neoplatonic framework.

Most translators were Syriac-speaking Nestorian Christians or Sabians from Harran. The Nestorians were familiar with Hellenistic philosophy for their theological writings, particularly regarding the Trinity, and utilized its conceptual language. The Sabians were star-worshippers and knowledgeable about Greek mathematics and astronomy. Some Greek texts were thus available in Syriac before the Arab conquests. But Arabic translations, whether directly from the Greek or through the intermediary of Syriac, went further with regard to their quantity and quality. Among the translators, the Nestorians Hunayn ibn Ishaq (died 873) and his son Ishaq ibn Hunayn (died 910) were renowned. They authored scientific and philosophical treatises. The Sabian Thabit ibn Qurra (died 901) was also renowned as an astronomer and translator of scientific works.

Al-Kindi

Abu Yaqub al-Kindi (died 870) is regarded as the first Muslim philosopher or, according to the medieval biographers, the "Philosopher of the Arabs." He enjoyed the patronage of Caliphs Al-Mamun and Al-Mutasim (reigned 833–842). His interest in acquiring the knowledge of the ancients is remarkable and indicative of the stimulating milieu. He even commissioned an Arabic translation of Aristotle's *Metaphysics*. Conscious of the task of introducing Hellenistic learning, he said: "We ought not to be ashamed of appreciating truth and of acquiring it wherever it comes from, even if it comes from races distant and nations different from us." Al-Kindi wrote several introductory works in philosophy and science to acquaint readers with the Hellenistic legacy. His philosophy is notable in two aspects. First, he was alone among the Muslim philosophers to argue for the temporal creation of the world. Second, Al-Kindi's *Treatise on Intellect* introduced Neoplatonic epistemology, which became the hallmark of Muslim philosophy, purporting that intellect has a potential capacity for knowledge and that its transition to become actually knowledgeable is caused by active intellect. Aristotle had very briefly mentioned the active intellect, which is separate and immortal in his work *On the Soul*. This entity was identified with the emanated intellect governing the sphere of the moon by the Neoplatonist philosophers of late antiquity.

Al-Farabi

Al-Kindi had few students, and his influence was thus limited. However, the continuing tradition of Hellenistic philosophy among Nestorian Christians attracted Abu Nasr al-Farabi (died 950). Al-Farabi's role in the naturalization of the Hellenistic legacy earned him the epithet "The Second Teacher" (Aristotle being the first). Al-Farabi considered himself a member of the philosophical school of Alexandria. As he informs us, this school had spread from Alexandria to Antioch and then from Marw and Harran to Baghdad. In the tradition of the school, Al-Farabi wrote technical and philosophical commentaries that were influential among later philosophers. But Al-Farabi surpassed his Nestorian teachers who, for theological reasons, were forbidden to study logic beyond Aristotle's *Prior Analytics*. The eager student, however, read more advanced works, particularly the *Posterior Analytics*. Al-Farabi's achievement lies in his reinvigoration of philosophy by rejecting constraints that were stifling philosophy and, in his activist vision of philosophy, engaging in the critical problems of the day, analyzing prophetic religion, extending political philosophy to include religious states, and developing the relationship of language to logic.

Al-Farabi, like other philosophers, held that real knowledge is demonstrative knowledge and is accessible only to the elite who have the natural disposition and leisure to pursue philosophy. The multitude can only aspire to persuasive knowledge by means of images. Founders of religions or prophets for al-Farabi are philosophers insofar as their knowledge is demonstrative. Their achievement lies in their ability to fashion images appropriate for the multitude so that the multitude (and the elite) will pursue actions leading to happiness for all. Religion, then, is an imitation of philosophy, and the best ruler is a philosopher-king. The cosmological source of the knowledge of philosophers and prophets is the same. Islam, properly understood, and philosophy were, therefore, not in opposition to each other.

Al-Farabi's emanationist cosmology is innovative. According to Neoplatonism, the First Being or God is such that creation must originate from Him by continuous emanation. These emanations then give rise to other emanations. Al-Farabi limits emanations to ten intellects and their spheres. The first intellect has no sphere; the other nine intellects with celestial spheres: the outermost sphere, the sphere of the fixed stars, and the spheres of the seven planets (Saturn, Jupiter, Mars, Sun, Mercury, Venus, and the Moon). The tenth intellect, governing the sphere of the Moon, is the active intellect and the point of contact for the human intellect with celestial intellects. The active intellect is the cause of the transition of the human intellect from potentially knowing to actually knowing. Prophetic genius derives from the virtual union of the prophetic soul with the active intellect and God's granting of revelation through the active intellect.

Al-Farabi's account of religion and prophecy, which was mostly adopted by his followers, differed from the views of the religious philosophers. Al-Farabi's perspective (and of other Islamic Hellenistic philosophers) was that the religious philosophers' views were not demonstrative but dialectical and do not represent real knowledge. Other points of contention were Al-Farabi's espousal of emanationism, its corresponding determinism, and his belief in the eternity of the world.

Al-Razi

Al-Farabi's views contrast sharply with those of Abu Bakr al- Razi (died 925) who is regarded as a philosopher, although his accomplishments in medicine are more significant. Al-Razi was opposed to authority. His philosophy is egalitarian, anti-Aristotelian, and antireligion. His egalitarianism denied the special role accorded by Al-Farabi to philosophers and even the special role of prophets and religious leaders. He regarded religion to be the cause of conflict and revelation to be mythical. He opposed the hierarchical cosmology of the Hellenistic philosophers and instead espoused a version of Democritean atomism, which is unlike that of the religious philosophers. He upheld the eternal existence of God, soul, matter, time, and space. He subscribed to the idea that the ignorant soul desiring matter and God, and wishing to alleviate its misery, created the world, but also endowed soul with reason. The world will dissolve when the soul is enlightened.

That Al-Razi, despite his radical views, was tolerated is indicative of the tolerant milieu of medieval Islamic civilization. Not surprisingly, Al-Razi did not have any followers, while Al-Farabi's philosophical synthesis became the dominant paradigm of Muslim philosophy. Elements of this philosophy were adopted by the literati and belles lettrists and by intellectually inclined Muslim movements among the Shia, like Ismailism.

Ibn Sina

The naturalization of Hellenistic philosophy reached its apogee with Abu Ali ibn Sina (died 1037). In a fascinating autobiography, Ibn Sina (Avicenna in Latin) discusses his education, travels, court intrigues, study habits, and writings. He was a child prodigy, born to a family with Ismaili sympathies. He was educated in traditional Islamic subjects and the sciences, where he surpassed his teachers, progressing to a personal study of advanced scientific texts and Islamic Hellenistic philosophy. He found Aristotle's *Metaphysics* incomprehensible until he read Al-Farabi's *On the Goals of Aristotle's Metaphysics*, which he purchased in the booksellers' market cheaply for three silver coins. Already famous as a physician, the seventeen-year-old Ibn Sina was invited to attend to the Samanid ruler Nuh ibn Mansur (reigned 976–997) who had fallen ill. Obtaining permission to examine the royal library, Ibn Sina entered a building with many rooms, each containing piles of books on a single subject. He looked through the catalog of works by ancients and found works that he never encountered again. Ibn Sina assiduously studied them all. As he tells us, by the age of eighteen he had thoroughly exhausted his studies, and as he recalled later, he did not subsequently learn anything further. Ibn Sina's account is revealing. It shows that Hellenistic philosophy had penetrated into provincial centers like Bukhara, it illustrates the demand for and trade in philosophical works, and it verifies the existence of rich collections in private libraries.

Unlike Al-Farabi, Ibn Sina's philosophy is not dominated by political philosophy despite his service as minister to many rulers. His accomplishment lies in his writings, which surpassed those of his predeccesors and became the point of reference for later philosophy in the Islamic world. Particularly significant are his *The Cure* (a multivolume encyclopedia of the philosophical sciences), *The Salvation*, and *Pointers and Reminders*. Ibn Sina's specific contributions are numerous, but within the context of his Islamic milieu, his arguments for the existence of God, the existence of the immortal human soul, and his analysis of mysticism are very significant.

The existence of God, Ibn Sina maintained, is a subject for metaphysics, which investigates being in general, and is not a subject for physics, which investigates corporeal beings (but where Aristotle's cosmological argument for a First Mover is found). Ibn Sina's argument for God's existence derives from the distinction between essence and existence: Things either exist, may exist, or are impossible (like unicorns). Essence, namely that which makes a thing what it is (for example, the essence of a triangle is "a surface enclosed by three straight lines"; the essence of human beings is "mortal, rational, animal"), does not entail existence of a thing. Rather, existence requires a cause. This leads to infinite regression, and therefore a being, whose existence is part of its essence, must exist. This is the necessarily existent being, or God. Everything else is contingent because its existence derives from another. This view of God, while compatible with Islamic revelation, was not in accord with the view of the God of the writers of *kalam* or traditionalists.

In psychology, Ibn Sina devised the "Floating Human Argument," an argument for the existence of the human soul that resembles Descartes's "I think therefore I exist" argument. A fully formed human being devoid of any sensation or perception is created floating in the air. Even though he cannot sense his body and has no previous knowledge whatsoever, he must affirm his own existence. This entails the existence of the human soul as an entity distinct from the body although cocreated with it. This soul is the governor of the body and uses the body as an instrument to accomplish its objectives. It does not perish with the body but is immortal and is rewarded or punished for its earthly deeds.

Ibn Sina mentions that he had frankly expressed his own philosophical views in his text *Eastern Philosophy*. This book is elusive. It is not extant in its entirety, and may not have been available in its entirety in the medieval period (perhaps it was never completed). Nevertheless, it has been and remains the subject of speculation and controversy. The designation "Eastern" reflects antipathy to the views of the Christian Hellenistic philosophers of Baghdad who, in Ibn Sina's view, were inept. A major point of disagreement with them was his belief in the immortality of the human soul. The subject of the soul is also associated with mysticism. One of Ibn Sina's achievements is to treat the Sufi mystics, their practices, and states as subjects of philosophical discourse. In this treatment, Ibn Sina makes reference to his allegorical writings. These were extremely influential and interpreted widely, playing a significant role in the formation of mystical philosophy.

Other Philosophers

Philosophers were also active in the western Islamic world, notably twelfth-century Spain. Abu Bakr ibn Bajja (died 1139) was a commentator of Al-Farabi's logical works and interested in physics and psychology. His rejection of the Aristotelian relationship between motive force, resistance of the medium, and velocity of the object was influential in discussions of motion in the Latin West. He was pessimistic about the philosopher's political role in society as outlined by Al-Farabi. In his *The Regimen of the Solitary*, he believes that, in imperfect states, philosophers must, as far as possible, detach themselves from society and instead seek felicity in union with the active intellect. In this union, the individual intellect loses its particular characteristics. Ibn Bajja, therefore, rejects Ibn Sina's view of the immortality of the soul as baseless, for the soul dies with the body.

Ibn Bajja's student, Abu Bakr ibn Tufayl (died 1185–1186) was physician to the Almohad ruler Abu Yaqub Yusuf (reigned 1163–1184) and the author of the philosophical tale *Hayy ibn Yaqzan* (*Living, Son of Awake*), the model for Daniel Defoe's *Robinson Crusoe*. This work is named after one of Ibn Sina's allegorical works and is even framed as an unfolding of the secrets of Ibn Sina's Eastern philosophy. In his introduction, Ibn Tufayl is critical of Ibn Bajja's idea of felicity through union with the active intellect, endorsing instead Ibn Sina's sanction of mysticism. He acknowledges the role of rational truths and methods but holds that they are surpassed by mystical experience. He employs several Sufi concepts, including "direct vision," "mystical experience," and "sainthood." The tale describes the self-education of Hayy who lands on (or was spontaneously generated on) a tropical island and is raised by a doe, a female deer. As he grows up, he is able, by reflection, to deduce philosophical truths and derive actions that lead to ultimate felicity. His ascetic practices, reminiscent of Sufism, lead him to direct vision and then spiritual annihilation in God. Hayy then comes into contact with two men, first Absal who comes to the island in search of solitude, then Salaman (both characters in another allegorical work by Ibn Sina) from a nearby island whose inhabitants follow a prophetic religion. Absal inclines toward mysticism and allegorical interpretation of revelation, while his friend Salaman is a literalist. Hayy and Absal go to the nearby island now ruled by Salaman, and Hayy tries to teach his wisdom to its inhabitants. His attempt fails and he recognizes that mystical and philosophical truths are not meant for all and that literalist religion suffices for the majority. Ibn Tufayl thus seems to accept Ibn Bajja's pessimism of the political role of the philosopher while rejecting his disdain of mysticism.

Ibn Tufayl was responsible for introducing the young Abu al- Walid Ibn Rushd (died 1198) to the ruler Abu Yaqub. Ibn Rushd, known to the West as Averroes, hailed from a family of jurists. He was a jurist of note and the author of a work on Maliki law. Impressed by the young philosopher, Abu Yaqub commissioned him to write commentaries on Aristotle's works. Ibn Rushd continued in the service of this ruler, and his son, Yaqub ibn Mansur (reigned 1184–1199), was appointed judge of Seville, then physician to the ruler, and, later, chief judge of Cordoba. Toward the end of his life, he fell into disfavor and was exiled, probably because of Yaqub's political difficulties, but was recalled just before his death. His commentaries were soon translated and transmitted to the Latin West where they were extremely influential, earning him the title of "The Commentator" par excellence. Ibn Rushd revered Aristotle and considered him to be infallible. Thus, in his commentaries, Ibn Rushd is usually a literalist seeking to recover Aristotle from Ibn Sina's and, to a limited extent, Al-Farabi's accretions. Not surprisingly, Ibn Rushd does not uphold Ibn Sina's view of the immortality of the soul. The influence of Ibn Rushd's commentaries in the Islamic world was minor, but his *On the Harmony between Religion and Philosophy* and as his reply to al-Ghazali titled *Destruction of the Philosophers* were significant. In the latter work he responds point by point to Al-Ghazali's *Destruction of the Philosophers* and defends Islamic Hellenistic philosophy. *On the Harmony* examines the legal status of the pursuit of Hellenistic philosophy in the Islamic world. Ibn Rushd argues ingeniously that philosophy studies the world and reflects on the signs of its Creator. Such reflection is commanded by revelation and must therefore be conducted in the best manner, namely by philosophy, which is a demonstrative science. However, not everyone is qualified to undertake philosophy and achieve demonstrative knowledge of God and creation. Rather, Islam allows for rhetorical, dialectical, or demonstrative knowledge of these matters. Demonstrative knowledge does not conflict with revelation. But since revelation addresses all people regardless of their intellectual capacity, its apparent meaning may seem contradictory. Such apparent difference is to be resolved by allegorical interpretation of revelation by those who are well grounded in science (i.e., the Islamic Hellenistic philosophers). They must permit the allegorical interpretation only to those who are qualified to understand its true significance. Conflicts have arisen when allegorical interpretations have been misguidedly given by the religious philosophers to the multitude.

Some Muslim groups, notably the Ismailis, adapted Islamic Hellenistic philosophy in their doctrinal systems. This is evident in the *Epistles* of the anonymous Brethren of Purity (circa tenth century), which were widely circulated and read and in the works of Fatimid Ismaili thinkers (tenth and eleventh centuries). Notably, however, the First Being or Intellect is the result of God's command and is not an emanated being. Moreover, subscribing to the doctrine of the correspondence between macrocosm and microcosm, the Ismailis held that the cosmic hierarchy of intellects, souls, and spheres is reflected in the religio-political hierarchy of the imam and his representatives in society. Such an approach to the role of reason as complementing that of revelation was institutionalized in the curriculum of al-Azhar University, founded by the Fatimids in Cairo in 970, where the intellectual sciences were taught and further developed into various disciplines.

Mystical Philosophy

Ibn Sina's philosophy represents the culmination of philosophy in the eastern Islamic world. Its influence on subsequent Muslim intellectual history was, and continues to be, profound. One illustration, albeit a significant one, is that Al-Ghazali's understanding of philosophy derives from Ibn Sina, and hence his critique is a critique of Ibn Sina's philosophy. Yet Al-Ghazali not only adopted the methodology and terminology of Ibn Sina for his critique but, perhaps unwittingly, initiated its appropriation into religious philosophy. Some modern interpreters believe that Al-Ghazali was thus not able to escape the determinism of his opponents. Thus, the conceptual language of religious philosophy after Al-Ghazali is replete with Ibn Sina's concepts and terms. Al-Ghazali also incorporated the logic of Ibn Sina into Sunni jurisprudence, claiming that was a neutral tool. However, Al-Ghazali finally turned to Sufi mysticism as the path to real knowledge and ultimate felicity.

Shihab al-din al-Suhrawardi (died 1191), the founder of "Illuminationist" (*ishraqi*) philosophy, was also a critic of Ibn Sina's philosophy, which he characterized as "peripatetic." On the other hand, he characterizes Illuminationist philosophy as deriving from those who were travelers on the path to God, namely Plato, and before him, Hermes, "the father of sages," Empedocles, Pythagoras, Agathadaimon, and others, as well as the ancient Persian sages Jamasp, Farshadshur, Buzarjumihr, and so on, (but not the impious Magians, nor Mani and other polytheists), and also his own immediate Sufi predecessors like Abu Yazid al-Bastami, Mansur al-Hallaj, and others. Illuminationist philosophy attempts to appropriate and naturalize Gnostic, Hermetic, Zoroastrian, and Sufi learning into Islamic Hellenistic philosophy.

Illuminationist philosophy is based both on discursive reason (thus, Peripatetic philosophy is essential), mystical experience, and vision. It utilizes symbols, particularly the symbols of light and darkness. Illuminationist cosmology is a metaphysics of light; its beings are characterized by whether their light is self-subsistent or accidental and the degree of their darkness (or absence) of light. God is the self-subsistent "light of lights" that illuminates and gives existence to all other beings. An indefinite number of luminous angels with self-subsistent lights are intermediate between the light of lights and the shadows of the material world. Unlike the ten intellects of Islamic Hellenistic philosophy, Illuminationist philosophy does not restrict the number of luminous intermediaries. Ultimate felicity lies in ascending from the material world to the luminous world through mystical exercises. Souls that are unable to reach the luminous world remain suspended in the "world of images" where they undergo "visions" of paradise and hell.

Suhrawardi believed that the world can never be without an illuminationist teacher. This view is analogous to Shia views of the necessity of a religious guide (imam). This fact, in addition to the Persian orientation of his work, both conceptually as well as linguistically (a significant number of Suhrawardi's works are written in Persian), accounts for the continuation of Illuminationist philosophy in Shia Iran and its absence in other parts of the Islamic world.

A mystical philosophy of a different kind was proposed by the Sufi Muhyi al-din Ibn al-Arabi (died 1240) and his disciples, particularly Sadr al-din al-Qunawi (died 1274). An account of Ibn al-Arabi belongs to the study of the mystical tradition in Islam. However, his views played a significant role in later Islamic philosophy, in particular, his doctrine of the "unity of being." This doctrine holds there is only one Being, God, and everything else is in perpetual flux, existing only through God. Some aspects of the doctrine of perpetual flux derive from the occasionalism of the Ashari religious philosophers.

In 1501 the Safawid state was established in Iran, and Twelver Shiism was subsequently declared the official doctrine of the state. A cultural and intellectual renaissance followed, and within this broad movement, the study of philosophy was reinvigorated by the philosophers of the "School of Isfahan," primarily Mir Damad (died 1630) and Mulla Sadra (died 1640). The tradition that they established has continued and is studied today in Iran. The sources of this philosophy are religious philosophy as interpreted in the Shia tradition of Nasir al-din al-Tusi, the philosophy of Ibn Sina, the Illuminationist philosophy of Suhrawardi, and the doctrine of "unity of being" of Ibn al-Arabi.

Mulla Sadra is regarded as the most original philosopher of this school, in part for his innovative theories of the primacy of existence and substantial motion. His teacher, Mir Damad, had held the Illuminationist view of the primacy of essences (that which makes a thing what it is) for, in the Illuminationist view, essences define the mode and rank of being. In contrast, Sadra argued that essences are mental abstractions and therefore fictions, and only existence is real. This entails that mental comprehension, which is necessarily of essences, is not representative of real existing things, and therefore true knowledge, which is of existence, has another epistemological source, namely mystical experience. Mulla Sadra's theory of substantial motion augments the Aristotelian theory of motion accepted by Muslim philosophers, who held that change is either qualitative (i.e., color), quantitative (i.e., size), or spatial (i.e., motion), and that the substrate (or substance) undergoing change remains constant. He asserted to the contrary that substrates do indeed change, for beings are always in the process of evolving toward more perfection. Metamorphosis is constant and characteristic of the true nature of being. Thus, simple elements move on to more complex inanimate forms and thence to animate forms, from which they then move on to other higher forms of being, culminating in a return to the spiritual world from which being originates.

◆ THE SCIENCES

Like philosophy, the study of science in Islamic civilization was inspired by the love of learning, which had initiated the translation of texts from Greek and Syriac, as well as texts from other languages, primarily Sanskrit and Pahlavi. In its heyday, individuals from almost every ethnic and religious persuasion were engaged in the scientific enterprise, and then, in all of the disciplines of science: the mathematical sciences, the physical sciences, the life sciences including medicine, and the pseudo sciences of alchemy, astrology and so on. This enterprise may be broadly characterized as broadening scientific knowledge by investigating and solving puzzles and problems. This does not mean that science was static or lacking in originality. The critical attitude, which pervades all medieval Islamic learning, entailed an examination of the fundamental premises of scientific theories. Whenever necessary, theoretical and methodological innovations were proposed, even going as far as to found new disciplines or to transform received scientific procedures. Furthermore, the milieu of Islamic civilization suggested its own problems, which engaged the minds of its scientists. Material factors also contributed to the scientific enterprise: the establishment of endowed institutions, primarily academies (for example, the above-mentioned House of Wisdom), libraries, hospitals, observatories, and patronage, which flourished even with the disintegration of the unitary empire and the establishment of local dynasties and principalities. Most patrons employed scientists as astrologers or physicians. The interconnectedness of disciplines was such that, for example, an astrologer needed to know astronomy, and one could not know astronomy without being versed in mathematics and natural philosophy, which, in turn, required familiarity with the cosmology of Islamic Hellenistic philosophy. With the passage of time, a new scientific role arose, that of the timekeeper who was responsible for calculating prayer times as well as determining the start of the months of the Islamic lunar calendar.

The scientific contributions of Islamic civilization are enormous. Yet, at this stage of our knowledge of the scientific enterprise of Islamic civilization, with the continuing discovery of new manuscripts and the incomplete analysis of known works, remarks about the achievements of scientists or about the general character of science must, to some degree, remain tentative. This is true for all of the intellectual disciplines practiced in medieval Islam. The following survey of the sciences in the world of medieval Islam must therefore be regarded as a preliminary attempt. Moreover, it is illustrative rather than exhaustive.

Mathematical Sciences

An inkling of the contribution of medieval Islamic science to mathematics survives in the continuing use of the terms "Arabic numerals," "algorithm," and "algebra." They illustrate the study of number theory, methods of calculation, and the establishment of algebra as an independent mathematical subject. But beyond this, Muslim mathematicians were engaged in plane and spherical geometry, trigonometry, as well as the solution of higher orders of equations.

The significance of Arabic numerals for mathematics cannot be overemphasized. These numerals actually were derived from India, and in the Islamic world they were called Hindu numerals. They constituted the decimal system that we use today, consisting of nine numerals (from one to nine) and zero (the etymology of "zero" is derived through French and Italian from the Arabic term *sifr*, meaning zero). These numbers are used in conjunction with a place value notation, such that the number 1367 is equal to $1x10^3 +3x10^2 +6x10^1 +7x10^0$ (i.e., the place of each digit in the number indicates its value in powers of ten). These numerals were probably introduced to Islamic civilization with the translation of Sanskrit astronomical works. Prior to this, Hellenistic mathematics had used a cumbersome system similar to Roman numerals side by side with a sexagesimal system whose origins are Babylonian—in this system, numbers were represented in base sixty, similar to our continuing use of degrees, minutes, and

seconds (sixty minutes one degree, sixty seconds one minute, etc.). The sexagesimal system was primarily used in astronomy. The prospect of performing arithmetical operations of addition and subtraction in such a system, to say nothing of multiplication and division, is daunting indeed.

The first systematic discussion of the decimal value system was made by Muhammad al-Khawarizmi (died after 847). Al-Khawarizmi was active in mathematics and in astronomy and was a member of the House of Wisdom. In his *Treatise on Calculations with Hindu Numerals*, he deals with the basic arithmetical operations of addition, subtraction, multiplication, division, sexagesimal fractions, and the extraction of square roots. Later mathematicians like Abu al-Wafa al-Buzjani (died 997–8), Abu Rayhan al-Biruni (died after 1050), and Umar al-Khayyam (died circa 1131), who is better known as a poet, worked out methods to extract higher roots. A significant advance in the decimal system was made by Abu al-Hasan al-Uqlidisi's invention of decimal fractions in 952–953. Interestingly, this invention seems to have subsequently been lost until reinvented by Ghiyath al-din al-Kashi (died 1429), who added a sign indicating the decimal point. Al-Uqlidisi also adapted calculation methods for ink and paper in place of the dust-board. His contemporary Al-Buzjani further popularized the decimal system with his arithmetical textbook for bureaucrats.

Al-Khawarizmi was also a famous algebraist and coined the Arabic phrase *al-jabr wa al-muqabala* (restoration and balancing), which is the origin of the term "algebra." Arithmetical and geometrical methods for discovering unknown quantities had already been worked out in Babylonian, Hindu, and Greek mathematics. Al-Khawarizmi's innovation was to combine these together and create algebra. The process of "restoration" refers to the removal of negative quantities. Thus, in the equation 2x+4 = 9-3x, the step to get 5x+4 = 9 is restoration. The subsequent step of "balancing" reduces positive quantities on both sides of the equation and results in 5x = 5. Al-Khawarizmi discussed methods for solving equations of the second order (quadratic equations). He pointed out the practical applications of his method in solving problems of surveying as well as inheritance shares (which are quite complex under Islamic law). Later mathematicians like Abu Bakr al-Karaji (flourished circa 1000), Al-Samawal ben Yehuda al-Maghribi (died 1180), and Umar al-Khayyam devised methods for the solution of higher order equations.

The most advanced mathematics is found in astronomy. Here we find significant advances in geometry (particularly, spherical geometry), trigonometry, and methods of calculation. The preeminent text of Greek astronomy is Ptolemy's *Almagest*, which is de-

Page from Nasir al-Din al-Tusi's treatise on cosmography.

the beginning of the tenth century, the modern trigonometric functions of sine, cosine, tangent, cotangent, secant, and cosecant were established, as were the additional theorem of sines and the sine law. Trigonometry came into its own with the astronomer Nasir al-din al-Tusi's (died 1273) discussion of this subject without reference to astronomy. Apart from the discovery of these functions, Muslim mathematicians labored diligently to produce tables to greater degrees of accuracy, culminating in the sine table produced by the fifteenth-century astronomers at the Samarkand observatory, which has values for each minute and is accurate to the order of one to seven hundred million.

In addition to astronomical problems, mathematicians applied spherical trigonometry to solve the problems of finding the direction of prayer (*qibla*), Mecca from any point on the earth, and determining times of prayer. The former had already been solved by several mathematicians in the ninth century. The mathematician Ibn Yunus (died 1009), a member of the House of Science in Cairo, is thought to have been the first to systematically solve the latter, for which he compiled tables for the latitude of Cairo. The fourteenth-century mathematician Muhammad al-Khalili, who was employed as a timekeeper at the Umayyad mosque in Damascus, went much further in his tables for these and other problems. Significantly, his *qibla* tables are for every possible degree of latitude and longitude, while his prayer timetables are for the latitude of Damascus.

Physical Sciences

In the physical sciences, Muslim scientists were engaged in problems of natural philosophy, optics, and astronomy. The discussion of natural philosophy (the structure of matter, space, time, and motion) took place among the various philosophers. The *kalam* thinkers subscribed to atomism and the existence of the vacuum. In addition, they were proponents of an impetus theory of motion. Such views were in sharp opposition to Aristotelian natural philosophy. Those Muslim philosophers who subscribed to the Aristotelian position engaged in refutation of the "other" system. Nevertheless, the religious philosophers' theory of motion may have played a role in Ibn Sina's formulation of his non-Aristotelian theory of "forced" and "natural" motion. Furthermore, Abu al-Barakat al-Baghdadi (died after 1165) rejected the Aristotelian theory of time and place and also believed that a vacuum was possible under certain circumstances. Finally, as has been noted above, Ibn Bajja rejected Aristotle's equation of the relationship between force, resistance, and velocity.

For the Muslim scientists, optics was a mathemati-

voted largely to predicting positions of the planets. Ptolemy uses spherical geometry as well as a trigonometric function called the chord, (a straight line joining two points on a curve), for which he provides a table. However, the use of this function is cumbersome. Indian astronomers, on the other hand, used the well-known sine function (where in a right angle the sine of an acute angle is equal to the length of the opposite side divided by the length of the hypotenuse). In the Islamic milieu, once again, the Greek and Indian heritage was combined so that by cal examination of light rays as they were transmitted through or reflected by various media, including lenses and mirrors of various shapes. This examination drew upon the works of Euclid and Ptolemy and advocated a theory of vision in which a cone of "visual rays" streamed from the eye to the visual object. A different account of vision was formulated by the Aristotelian natural philosophers (including Ibn Sina and Ibn Rushd) in their discussion of perception. For them, vision is the reception of the "form" of the visual object by the eye. A third account of vision formulated by such medical writers as Galen and his followers (including the translator Hunayn ibn Ishaq) held that, as visual rays emerged from the eyes, the air was transformed into an instrument of vision. Therefore, the act of vision was the result of the contact of the "instrument" with the visual object. In the eleventh century, mathematician-scientist Al-Hasan ibn al-Haytham (died 1040) criticized the theories of his predecessors and revolutionized mathematical optics in his work entitled *Optics*. He maintained that optical inquiry requires a combination of the natural and mathematical sciences. Furthermore, Ibn al-Haytham recognized that any account of optics must include an account of vision and must therefore discuss the psychology of visual perception.

Methodologically, Ibn al-Haytham's work is significant for its clear concept and use of experiment to confirm the specific properties of light by setting up a controlled situation where certain parameters may be varied. With regard to vision, he rejects the visual ray hypothesis (rays stream from the eye to the visual object) in favor of the natural philosophers intromission hypothesis (vision is the reception of the form of the visual object in the eye). Ibn al-Haytham's achievement was to reverse the direction of the visual rays of the mathematicians and hence mathematicize the forms of the natural philosophers. Surprisingly, *Optics* does not seem to have made an impact in the Islamic world until the thirteenth century, and then only in a commentary by Kamal al-din al-Farisi (died circa 1320). In this work, Al-Farisi formulated an explanation of the shape and colors of the primary and secondary rainbow on the basis of refraction and reflection in raindrops. Quite independently, a similar formulation was almost simultaneously arrived at by Theoderic of Freiberg (died circa 1310).

Ibn al-Haytham's critical outlook also extended to astronomy where he was again critical of mathematical models of planetary motion and their lack of correspondence with physics. Astronomy was a technical mathematical science based primarily on Ptolemy's *Almagest*, although Sanskrit astronomical works had been translated into Arabic in the eighth century. The subsequent history of astronomy in medieval Islamic civilization consists of both observation as well as theory. Observations were not only made by individual astronomers but also were conducted within the institution of the astronomical observatory; this institution is one of the contributions of Islamic civilization to science. It was first founded by the Caliph Al-Mamun in the ninth century in Baghdad. The Baghdad observatory was staffed by several astronomers who were charged with revising Ptolemy's tables on the basis of fresh observations. The result was compiled into the *Tested Astronomical Tables*. The Baghdad observatory is but one of several observatories founded in medieval Islam. Others include the famous Maragha observatory of the thirteenth century and the fifteenth-century observatory of Ulugh Beg in Samarkand, both of which compiled astronomical tables. The precision reached by these observatories was such that one modern author exclaimed that the astronomer Tycho Brahe could have easily been a Turk! The influence of Arabic observational astronomy survives in star names in use today, many of which are derived from Arabic, as are such common astronomical terms as "nadir," "azimuth," and "zenith."

Astronomical measurements required innovation in measuring instruments. Here, too, Muslim astronomers surpassed their predecessors by designing new instruments, revising older ones, and sometimes building extremely large instruments to increase accuracy. The astrolabe is an example of an astronomical instrument that was derived from the Greeks but was improved by Islamic astronomers. Primarily used for determining the position of celestial bodies, it was combined with a number of movable plates and arcs to graphically solve complex trigonometrical functions and thereby determine direction or time of prayer.

Theoretical innovation in astronomy was initiated by Ibn al-Haytham's critical remarks about Ptolemy's planetary models. According to the then prevalent Aristotelian natural philosophy, celestial bodies could only move in geocentric circles around the stationary earth. While Ptolemy had acknowledged this principle in his *Almagest*, he had to abandon it in his planetary models to account for observed positions of planets. Ibn al-Haytham objected to this practice in his *Doubts against Ptolemy*. This initiated a research project that culminated in the formulation of a new method of devising planetary models by Nasir al-din al-Tusi in the thirteenth century. Significantly, the same objections underlie Nicolaus Copernicus's objections to Ptolemaic astronomy. Moreover, his earlier work on the motion of the moon resembles the discussion of Al-Tusi, raising speculation of a possible Muslim influence on the astronomer who revolutionized astronomy with his heliocentric system.

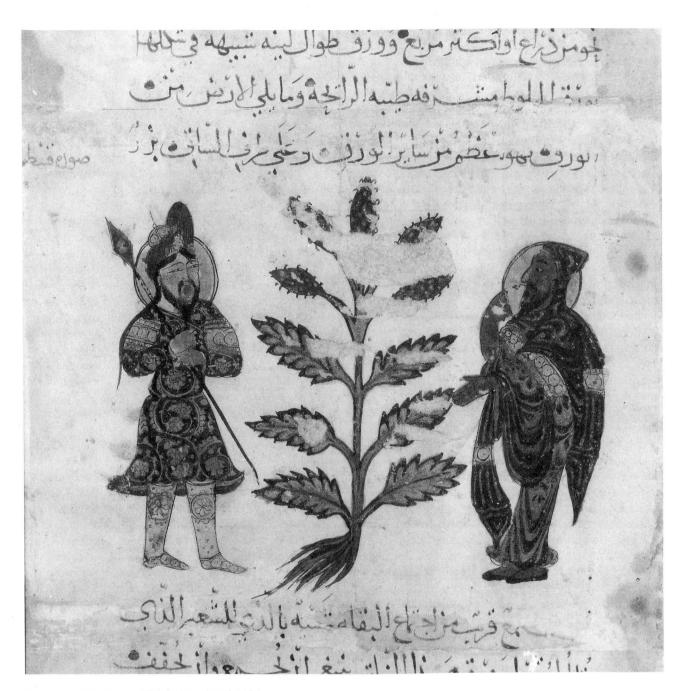

Painting of Warrior and Physician, dated 1224.

Medicine

The medicine of medieval Islam civilization was built primarily on Greek medicine, in particular, the writings of Hippocrates and Galen. Some of the translators of these texts had been trained at the medical center of Jundishapur, including the translator Hunayn ibn Ishaq. The physicians to the Abbasid caliphs during the eighth and ninth centuries, from the Christian medical family of Jurjis ibn Bukhtishu, were also affiliated with Jundishapur. Most physicians of this period were Syriac Christians. The most significant contribution of Islamic civilization to medicine was the establishment of the hospital as an institution for the treatment of patients and training of physicians. Hospices for the sick, poor, travelers, and orphans had existed in Byzantium and were the model for the Umayyad caliph Walid's (reigned 705–715) charitable institution for the care of lepers, the blind, and the infirm. The first real hospital (*bimaristan*), however, was built in Baghdad by Harun al-Rashid (reigned 786–809) and was modeled after

Jundishapur. This was soon followed by several other hospitals all over the Islamic world from Spain to India. Hospitals were built by caliphs, court officials, and wealthy individuals. Hospital revenue, derived from endowments under the control of a board of trustees, provided for the salaries of the medical staff as well as provisions for the patients. Endowments were religiously motivated, for charitable acts are greatly emphasized in the Quran. Hospitals were institutions where medical care was available to all regardless of their religious affiliations; hospitals also were centers of medical education, although in later periods, medicine was sometimes taught in mosques and *madrasas* (schools).

The Adudi hospital in Baghdad, for example, was founded by the ruler Adud al-Dawla in 982. It had twenty-four physicians, and its specialists included ophthalmologists, surgeons, and orthopedists. When the traveler Abu al-Husayn ibn Jubayr (died 1217) visited Baghdad two hundred years later, the hospital was still functioning. He tells us that it was as large as a castle and had its own water supply from the Tigris River. Another great hospital was the Nasiri hospital of Cairo completed in 1284. It had an annual endowment of one million dirhams in local currency. Formerly a palace with accommodation for eight thousand persons, it had separate wards for fever, ophthalmia, surgical cases, dysentery, a pharmacy, dispensary, storeroom, mosque, and a library. It also had a large administrative staff, attendants of both sexes, and lecture halls.

Muslim physicians, while respectful toward their Hellenist predecessors, were not content simply with the preservation of past medical knowledge. This is exemplified in the work *Doubts against Galen* by the famous physician and philosopher Abu Bakr al-Razi. Al-Razi believed in the progress of knowledge, which was to be achieved by adopting a critical attitude toward authorities. Al-Razi is the author of numerous medical works, including the twenty-three volume *Kitab al-Hawi*, which contains many personal observations and interesting case histories, and a small treatise *On Smallpox and the Measles*, which contains the first clear account of these two diseases. Al-Razi's works were influential but unsuitable as introductory texts as they omitted discussion of the general principles of medical science. Recognizing this deficiency, Ali ibn al-Abbas al-Majusi (died ca. circa 982) wrote his *Kitab al-Malaki* in which the subject matter is treated in a clear and concise, although sometimes dry, manner. This medical text was very soon surpassed by the philosopher Ibn Sina's *Canon of Medicine (al-Qanun fi l-Tibb)*, which became the medical textbook of the Islamic world. It even became the medical textbook in the Latin West and was printed thirty-six times in the fifteenth and sixteenth centuries. However, in keeping with the critical attitude toward knowledge, the *Canon* had its own critics. One of them, not surprisingly, was the Andalusian philosopher Ibn Rushd (who, as we have seen above, disagreed with Ibn Sina's philosophical doctrines) and his younger contemporary Abu al-Ala ibn Zuhr (died 1131). The latter not only rejected the *Canon* for his library, but used its paper for writing prescriptions! In the East, the reception of the *Canon* was more favorable, and it attracted several commentators. One of these was Ali al-Qurashi, also known as Ibn al-Nafis (died 1288), the director of the Nasiri hospital. Ibn al-Nafis argued for the first time for the existence of pulmonary circulation, claiming that blood pumped by the right ventricle is sent to the lungs where it mixes with air and then returns to the left ventricle. His discovery was not made on the basis of anatomical dissection but by logical argument. There is a strong likelihood that the European Renaissance author Michael Servetus (died 1553) was directly influenced by the discovery of Ibn al-Nafis, and that William Harvey's discovery of the circulation of the blood depends on the work of Servetus.

A widespread myth holds that science and philosophy were marginal to the civilization of Islam and that, for the most part, the scientific and philosophical enterprise in Islam was stagnant, preserving Hellenistic knowledge until Europe shook off the slumber of the Dark Ages and ushered in a renaissance of learning, culminating in the Scientific Revolution of the seventeenth century. Nothing could be further from the truth. Scientific and philosophical activity in Islamic civilization, as has been illustrated above, was vigorous. It was engaged in both the preservation and advancement of knowledge; it posed foundational questions; it was critical of past authorities; it made methodological contributions to science; and it formulated new discoveries and theories.

◆ EDUCATING EUROPE: THE ARABO-LATIN TRANSLATION MOVEMENT

The twelfth and thirteenth centuries witnessed yet another transfer of knowledge, this time from Arabic into Latin. As a result, a significant portion of Islamic philosophical and scientific learning of preceding centuries was made available to medieval European scholars. Most of this translation activity was performed in Spain, especially in Toledo where Jews, Christians, and Muslims lived side by side, and also in Sicily. Some translators were Jews who translated Arabic works into Hebrew, or translated/collaborated with others to translate Hebrew works into Latin. The family of Judah ibn Tibbon, based in Languedoc in southern, France is famous for the translation into Hebrew of several works by Jews who had written in Arabic, including Saadiah Gaon (died 942), Judah Halevi (died 1141), Solomon ibn Gabirol (died 1058), and Moses Maimonides (died 1204), as well as several philosophical works by Ibn Rushd. Other translators were Christians, including Constantine the African (flourished 1065–1085), Adelard of Bath (flourished 1116–1142), Robert of Chester (flourished 1141–1150), Gerard of Cremona (circa 1114–1187), and others. Translations were made not only of originally Greek works that had been translated into Arabic (for example, Euclid's *Elements*, Ptolemy's *Almagest*, and the Aristotelian corpus), but also of works by Islamic scientists and philosophers. The latter were now known through their Latinized names of Avicenna (Ibn Sina), Averroes (Ibn Rushd), Avempace (Ibn Bajja), Abubacer (Abu Bakr ibn Tufayl), Algazel (Al-Ghazali), Alhazen (Ibn al-Haytham), Rhazes (Al-Razi), Haly Abbas (Ali ibn Abbas al-Majusi), and so on.

It is impossible to satisfactorily discuss the influence of Muslim mathematicians and scientists on Europe in this short survey. Suffice it to say, their works and theories were known and studied and led to further advances. A few illustrations follow. Avicenna's *Canon* was the medical textbook for European medical schools; Alhazen's *Optics* was the foundation upon which Kepler built the modern science of optics in the sixteenth century; Copernicus's work refers to the views of Muslim astronomers; Al-Khawarizmi's work was responsible for the introduction of the decimal place value system and the Indo-Arab numerals; and the works of Muslim mathematicians introduced Europe to algebra and trigonometry.

In philosophy and theology, the views of Avicenna, Averroes, and Algazel and their readings of Aristotle are discernable in the works of Latin scholastics like Albertus Magnus (died 1280) and his student, Thomas Aquinas (died 1274). Whereas Albertus Magnus, Aquinas, and others accepted a limited role for reason within the overall context of faith, the writings of Averroes were seen to champion unaided reason. The Muslim philosophers' views on the active intellect, the eternity of the world, the nature of God, and so on were also considered to be contrary to Christian teachings. Some Latin writers like Siger of Brabant became proponents of these views and "founded" the movement characterized as Latin Averroism. Theological writers like Albertus Magnus and Aquinas wrote polemical works against the Latin Averroists, but the movement seems to have continued growing. In 1277 Etienne Templar, the Bishop of Paris, issued a condemnation of two-hundred-nineteen propositions linked with the naturalism advocated by the Latin Averroists, including some held by Thomas Aquinas. While the condemnation influenced the course of Latin natural philosophy, it did not hinder the study of the views of Muslim philosophers.

The fact that the influence of scientists and philosophers from the Muslim world pervaded medieval and even Renaissance European philosophy, theology, and science is incontestable and apparent to anyone who is familiar with the intellectual activity of these periods. But the influence went beyond these historical periods. The assertion that the paradigm-shattering scientific and philosophical revolutions of seventeenth-century Europe are inconceivable without the contributions of these Muslim scholars may be regarded in some circles as far-fetched, but it is nonetheless an accurate reflection of historical developments. Discomfort with the notion of the profound impact of non-Western contributions to Western intellectual history derives from the assumption that rationality, critical philosophy, and science are unique features of Western civilization. Assertions of the influence of the intellectual legacy of ancient Greek learning on these revolutions is acceptable. Even the assertion of the continuing influence of the Greek intellectual legacy on contemporary Western civilization garners considerable support. But such a depiction of exclusive Western ownership of rationality, philosophy, and science is essentialist as well as antihistorical as is evident from the practice of philosophy and science in the cosmopolitan civilization of medieval Islam.

Alnoor Dhanani

References

al-Ashari. *The Theology of al-Ashari.* Tr. Richard McCarthy, Beirut, 1953.

Averroes. *On the Harmony of Religions and Philosophy.* Tr. George Hourani. London: Luzac, 1967.

———. *The Incoherence of the Incoherence.* Tr. Simon van den Bergh. London: Luzac, 1978.

Avicenna. *The Life of Ibn Sina.* Ed. and tr. William Gohlman. New York: Suny Press, 1974.

———. *Avicenna's Psychology.* Tr. Fazlur Rahman. London: Oxford University Press, 1952.

Berggren, J. *Episodes in the Mathematics of Medieval Islam.* New York: Springer Verlag, 1986.

Chittick, William. *Ibn al-Arabi's Metaphysics of Imagination: The Sufi Path to Knowledge.* Albany: State University of New York Press, 1989.

Dhanani, Alnoor. *The Physical Theory of Kalam.* Leiden: Brill, 1994.

Dols, Michael W. *Medieval Islamic Medicine.* Berkeley: University of California Press, 1984.

Fakhry, Majid. *A History of Islamic Philosophy.* 2nd edition. New York: Columbia University Press, 1983.

———. *Ethical Theories in Islam.* Leiden: Brill, 1991.

Farabi. *On the Perfect State.* Ed. and tr. Richard Walzer. Oxford: Clarendon, 1985.

Frank, Richard. *Al-Ghazali and the Asharite School.* Durham, N.C.: Duke University Press, 1994.

Ghazali. *Freedom and Fulfillment: An Annotated Translation of al-Ghazali's al-Munqidh min al-dalal and Other Relevant Works of al-Ghazali.* Tr. Richard McCarthy. Boston: Twayne, 1980.

Gibb H. et al. ed. *The Encyclopedia of Islam.* New ed. 7 vols. Leiden: Brill, 1960.

Gillespie C. et al. ed. *Dictionary of Scientific Biography.* 18 vols. New York: Scribner's, 1972–80.

Goodman, Lenn E. *Avicenna.* London and New York: Routledge, 1992.

Gutas, Dimitri. *Avicenna and the Aristotelean Tradition.* Leiden: Brill, 1988.

Hyman, Arthur and James Walsh. *Philosophy in the Middle Ages: The Christian, Islamic, and Jewish Traditions.* New York: Harper and Row, 1967.

Ibn al-Haytham. *Ibn al-Haytham's Optics.* 2 vols. to date. Tr. A.I. Sabra. London: The Warburgh Institute, 1989.

Ibn Tufayl. *Ibn Tufayl's Hayy ibn Yaqzan: A Philosophical Tale.* Tr. Lenn E. Goodman, New York: Twayne, 1972.

Kennedy, E.S. *Studies in the Islamic Exact Sciences.* Beirut: American University of Berut Press, 1983.

al-Khuwarizmi, Muhammad. *The Algebra of Muhammed ben Musa.* Tr. F. Rosen. London: 1831.

King, David. *Islamic Mathematical Astronomy.* London: Variorum, 1986.

———. *Astronomy in the Service of Islam.* Aldershot, Hampshire, Great Britain: Brookfield, Vt.: Variorum, 1993.

Leaman, Oliver. *An Introduction to Medieval Islamic Philosophy.* Cambridge: Cambridge University Press, 1985.

———. *Averroes and His Philosophy.* Oxford: Clarendon Press, 1988.

Lerner, Ralph and Muhsin Mahdi, eds. *Medieval Political Philosophy: A Sourcebook.* Ithaca: Cornell University Press, 1972.

Lindberg, David (ed). *Science in the Middle Ages.* Chicago and London: University of Chicago Press, 1978.

Mulla Sadra. *The Wisdom of the Throne.* Tr. James W. Morris. Princeton: Princeton University Press, 1981.

Nasr, Seyyed Hossein. *Three Muslim Sages: Avicenna, Suhrawardi, Ibn Arabi.* Cambridge: Harvard University Press, 1964.

———. *Islamic Science: An Illustrated Study.* London: World of Islam Festival, 1976.

Pines, Shlomo. "What was original in Arabic Science" in *Scientific Change* ed. A.C. Crombie. New York: Basic Books, 1963.

Rosenthal, Franz. *Knowledge Triumphant.* Leiden: Brill, 1970.

———. *The Classical Heritage in Islam.* Berkeley and Los Angeles: University of California Press, 1975.

Sabra, A.I. *Optics, Astronomy, and Logic: Studies in Arabic Science and Philosophy.* Aldershot, Hampshire, Great Britain; Brookfield, Vt.: Variorum, 1993.

———. "Philosophy and Science in Medieval Islamic Theology: The Evidence of the Fourteenth Century." *Zeitschrift fur Geschichte der Arabisch-Islamischen Wissenschaften.* 1995.

Sayili, Aydin. *The Observatory in Islam.* Ankara, 1960.

Strayer J. et al. ed. *Dictionary of the Middle Ages.* 13 vols. New York: Scribner's, 1982–1989.

al-Tusi, Nasir al-Din. *Memoir on Astronomy.* 2 vols. Ed. and tr. F. Ragep. New York: Springer Verlag, 1993.

al-Uqlidisi, Abu al-Hasan. *The Arithmetic of al-Uqlidisi.* Tr. A.S. Saidan. Dordrecht and Boston: Reidel, 1978.

Ullmann, Manfred. *Islamic Medicine.* Edinburgh: Edinburgh University Press, 1978.

Walker, Paul E. *Early Philosophical Shiism.* Cambridge: Cambridge University Press, 1993.

Wolfson, Harry. *The Philosophy of the Kalam.* Cambridge: Harvard University Press, 1976.

Yarshater E. ed. *Encyclopedia Iranica.* 6 vols. London, Boston, and Henley: Routledge and Kegan Paul, 1982.

The Ethical Tradition in Islam

♦ Beginnings and Development: Foundational Values ♦ Theological and Traditionalist Approaches
♦ Philosophical Approaches ♦ Ethics in the Shia Tradition ♦ Sufi Perspectives
♦ Muslim Ethics in the Contemporary World

There are a number of concepts in the Quran that signify the ethical dimensions of human life. However, ethics in Islam cannot be treated apart from the larger moral universe portrayed in the Quran which crystallizes an interconnected world of ideals, standards and applications to daily life. In the contemporary world, Islam has become a worldwide phenomenon and Muslims are found in virtually every region of the globe. It is therefore important to develop historical insight into how the whole spectrum of Islamic values and their underlying moral and ethical assumptions have been shaped during the course of Muslim history, in order to appreciate the diversity of Islam's heritage of ethical thought and life.

♦ BEGINNINGS AND DEVELOPMENT: FOUNDATIONAL VALUES

The norms and assumptions that have characterized belief and action in Islam have their initial inspiration in two foundational sources. One is scriptural, embodying the message revealed by God to the Prophet Muhammad and recorded in the Quran. The second is the exemplification of that message in the perceived model pattern of the Prophet's actions, sayings and norms, collectively called the *sunna*. Muslims regard the Quran as the ultimate closure in a series of revelations to humankind from God, and the *sunna* as the historical projection of a divinely inspired and guided human life in the person of the Prophet Muhammad, who is also believed to be the last in a series of messengers from God.

The late Fazlur Rahman, noted University of Chicago scholar of Islamic thought and modernist Muslim thinker, argued that in its initial phase Islam was moved by a deep rational and moral concern for reforming society and that this moral intentionality was conceived in ways that encouraged a deep commitment to reasoning and rational discourse. Like other religious traditions, and particularly Christianity and Judaism, Islam, in answering the question, "What ought or ought not to be done?", had a clearly defined sense of the sources of moral authority. The *Quran* revealed God's will for humankind, who in turn could respond to that revelation through the exercise of reason to elaborate forms of ethical behavior. The emphasis on reflection and the necessity of cultivating a moral life based on revelation as well as the search for a rational understanding of human conduct is therefore critical for the development of a philosophically oriented system of Muslim ethics. The relationship between the Quran and the life of the Prophet, as a model of behavior, was also elaborated, to create a legal framework within which values and obligations could be determined. The process of determination and elaboration, however, involved a more limited and focussed application of human reasoning and it is this continuing interaction between reason and revelation and the potential and limits of the former in relation to the latter, provide the basis for formalized expressions of ethical thought in Islam.

In one of the chapters of the *Quran*, entitled the Criterion (*al-Furqan*, sura 25), revelation to all of humanity becomes the point of reference for distinguishing right from wrong. The same chapter goes on to cite examples of past Biblical prophets and their role as mediators of God's word to their respective societies. Like Judaism and Christianity, Islam's beginnings are thus rooted in the idea of the divine command as a basis for establishing moral order through human endeavor. Elsewhere in the Quran, a revealed morality presents humanity with a clear distinction between right and wrong, which is not subject to human whim. By grounding a moral code in divine will, an opportunity is afforded to human beings to respond by creating a rational awareness that sustains the validity of revelation. Thus a wider basis for human action is possible if rationality comes to be applied to revelation to elaborate criteria for encompassing the totality of human actions and decisions. These themes are played out in the Quranic telling of the story of Adam's creation and regress.

Adam, the first human, is distinguished from existing angels, who are asked to bow down to him, by virtue of his divinely endowed capacity to "name things," that is, to conceive of knowledge as capable of being described linguistically and thereby be codified, a capacity not accessible to angels, who are seen as one-dimensional beings. This creative capacity carries with it, however, an obligation not to exceed set limits. Satan in the Quran exemplifies excess since he disobeys God's command to honor and bow before Adam, thus denying his own innate nature and limits. In time, Adam too fails to live within the limits set by God, loses his honorable status, which he must attempt to recover subsequently by struggling with and overcoming his propensities on earth, the arena that allows for choice and action. Islam views Adam as recovering his former status by attesting to the capacity to return to the right course of action through rational understanding of his failure and by transcending the urge to set aside that rationality and test the limits of knowledge unmediated by God. Adam's story therefore reflects all of the potential for good and evil that is built into the human condition and is symbolic of the human response to a divine revelation within history. Adam's story exemplifies the ongoing struggle within humanity to discover the way that allows for balanced action and submission to the divine criterion. In this sense the word *Islam* stands for the original revelation, requiring submission to achieve equilibrium, and a *Muslim*, is one who seeks through action to attain that equilibrium in personal life as well as in society.

The human quality that encompasses the concept of the ideal ethical value in the Quran is summed up in the term *taqwa* which, in its various forms, occurs over two hundred times in the text. It represents, on the one hand, the moral grounding that underlies human action, while on the other, it signifies the ethical conscience which makes human beings aware of their responsibilities to God and society. Applied to the wider social context *taqwa* becomes the universal, ethical mark of a truly moral community:

O humankind! We have created you out of male and female and constituted you into different groups and societies, so that you may come to know each other—the noblest of you, in the sight

of God, are the ones possessing *taqwa* (Quran 49:11-13).

More specifically, when addressing the first Muslims, the Quran refers to them as "a community of the middle way, witnesses to humankind, just as the Messenger [Muhammad] is a witness for you" (Quran 2:143).

The Muslim *Umma* or community is thus seen as the instrument through which Quranic ideals and commands are translated at the social level. Individuals become trustees through whom a moral and spiritual vision is fulfilled in personal life. They are accountable to God and the community, since the community is the custodian through whom the covenantal relationship with God is sustained. The Quran affirms the dual dimension of human and social life, material and spiritual, but these aspects are not seen in conflicting terms, nor is it assumed that spiritual goals should predominate in a way that devalues the material aspects of life. The Quran asserts that human conduct and aspirations have relevance as acts of faith, within the wider human, social, and cultural contexts. In this sense the idea that Islam embodies a total way of life can best be understood.

An illustration of one aspect of such a vision is the Quran's emphasis on the ethics of redressing injustice in economic and social life. For instance, individuals are urged to spend their wealth and substance on: family and relatives, orphans, the poor, the traveling homeless, the needy, and freeing of the enslaved. Such acts define a Muslim's responsibility to develop a social conscience and to share individual and communal resources with the less privileged. These commands are institutionalized in the Quran through the duty of *zakat*, a term suggesting giving, virtue, increase, and purification. In time, *zakat* became an obligatory act assimilated into the framework of ritual pillars including prayer, fasting and pilgrimage. The Quran also sought to abolish practices of usury in the mercantile community of Mecca and Medina, stigmatizing such practices as reflecting the lack of a work ethic and an exploitation of those in need.

At the social level, the Quran's emphasis on the family includes a concern for ameliorating the status of women through the abolition of pre-Islamic practices such as female infanticide and by affording women new rights. Among these were the rights of property ownership, inheritance, the right to contract marriage and to initiate divorce if necessary, and to maintain one's own dowry. Polygyny, the plurality of wives, was regulated and restricted, so that a man was permitted to have up to four wives, only if he could treat them with equity. Muslims have traditionally understood this practice in its seventh century context, as affording the necessary flexibility to address the social and cultural diversity that arose with the expansion of Islam. However, some modern Muslims maintain that the thrust of the Quranic reform was in the direction of monogamy and an enhanced public role for women. Such modernists also hold that the development and occurrence of customs and practices of seclusion and veiling of women were a result of local tradition and customs and are antithetical to the spirit of emancipation they claim to envisage in the Quran.

Since Muslims are privileged in the Quran and cited as the "best of communities" whose function it was to command the right and prevent wrong, the Prophet Muhammad's mission, like that of past prophets, involved the creation of a just, divinely-ordained polity. The struggle towards this goal involved Muslims in warfare and the term in the Quran that encompasses this effort as a whole is *jihad*. Often simply and erroneously translated as "holy war," *jihad* carries a far wider connotation that includes striving by peaceful means, such as service and education. This striving can also take place in a more personal and internalized sense, as in the struggle to purify oneself. Where it refers to armed defense of a justly executed war, the Quran specifies the conditions for war and peace, the treatment of captives and the resolution of conflict, emphasizing that the ultimate purpose of God's word was to invite and guide people to the "ways of peace."

As the Muslim polity took shape it also became necessary for it to address the question of its relationship and attitude towards non-Muslims with similar scriptural traditions, particularly Jews and Christians. In the Quran they are referred to as the "People of the Book." Where they lived among Muslims, as subjects, they were to be granted "protected" status through a mutual agreement. They were to be subject to a poll tax and their private and religious property, law, and religious practices were to be protected. They could not, however, proselytize among Muslims. Although Muslims were encouraged to convert Christians and Jews. The Quran recognizes the particularity of all religious communities favoring common moral goals over mutually divisive and antagonistic attitudes when possible:

> For each community, we have granted a Law and a Code of Conduct. If God wished, He could have made you One community, but he wishes rather to test you through that which has been given to you. So vie with each other to excel in goodness and moral virtue. (Quran 5:48)

The need for congruence between the divine moral imperative and human life is also reflected in the preserved Prophetic tradition which is perceived as explaining and confirming Quranic values and commands. The recording of episodes of the Prophet's life, his words, actions, and habits, came in time to represent for Muslims a timeless model pattern for daily life. It also assumed an authoritative role in explaining and complementing the *Quran*. His personal character, struggle, piety, and eventual success, enhance for Muslims Muhammad's role as the paradigm and seal of prophecy. A rich tradition of poetry in praise of the Prophet exists in virtually all the languages spoken by Muslims, inspiring both the commitment to emulate his behavior and a sense of personal affinity and love for his person and family. For Muslims, the message of the Quran and the example of the Prophet's life thus remain inseparably related through all of history as paradigms for moral and ethical behavior. They formed the basis for Muslim thinkers to develop legal tools for embodying moral imperatives. The elaboration of the legal sciences would lead to a codification of norms and statutes that gave form to the concept of law in Islam, generally referred to as the *sharia*. Among the forms that developed to encompass the moral imperative, are the various schools of law in Islam, each of whom, through the legal discipline of *fiqh* (jurisprudence), elaborated legal codes to embody their specific interpretation of how Muslims should respond to God's commands in conducting their daily lives.

Parallel to the developing legal expressions, there also emerged a set of moral assumptions that articulated ethical values, rooted in a more speculative and philosophical conception of human conduct as a response to the Quran and the Prophet's life. Groups in Islam, as well as schools of law, were not as clearly circumscribed in the first three centuries of Muslim history as is generally thought. Most sects were still in formation, and their subsequent boundaries and positions were yet to be fully defined and elaborated. Public, legal, and educational institutions in the Muslim world of the time had not achieved the classical forms or purposes that came to be associated with them. A key to this process of definition and distinction is the nature of public discourse that characterized the growing Muslim society in its first three centuries. Muslim conquest and expansion resulted in contact with cultures whose intellectual heritages were selectively appropriated by Muslims then refined and further developed. The integration of the intellectual and philosophical legacies of Greece, India, and Iran, among others, created conditions and a tradition of intellectual activity that would lead to the cosmopolitan heritage of an emerging Islamic civilization. Christian and Jewish scholars, who had already encountered the above legacies in varying degrees, played a crucial mediating role as "translators," since they were also aware that the moral disposition of Muslims, like theirs, was shaped by common monotheistic conceptions based on divine command and revelation. The term *adab* has come to be used to define the wide connotation of meanings implied by the moral, ethical, intellectual and literary discourse that emerged. It was also during this period, from the eighth to the tenth centuries that we see the emergence of what later came to be clearly identifiable theological and intellectual traditions, within the Muslim community that are identified with groups such as the Sunni, Shia, Mutazila, and the Muslim philosophers.

The main features of the moral environment and perspective based on the Quranic message define the general ethical stances that came to be regarded as normative through their expression in legal language and terms. In the early period of Muslim intellectual history, these values also provided a frame of reference for the selective appropriation and development of philosophical, moral, and ethical assumptions from other traditions, for example, the Hellenistic. These incorporations served as a basis for widening the scope and application of an Islamic frame of reference to articulate ethical and moral values outside of merely juristically defined values. Since clear cut distinctions in Islam between religion, society, and culture are hard to sustain, it seems appropriate, in discussing Muslim ethics, to let the whole spectrum of tendencies, legal, theological, philosophical, and mystical, act as resources for disclosing moral assumptions and commitments in order to appreciate both development and continuity across the whole spectrum of Muslim thought and civilization.

♦ THEOLOGICAL AND TRADITIONALIST APPROACHES

The emergence of an intellectual tradition of inquiry based on the application of rational tools as a way of understanding Quranic injunctions led to the use among Muslims of a formal discipline devoted to the study of *kalam* (literally meaning speech, i.e., the word of Allah). The goals of this discipline were theological, in the sense that the application of reason was to make comprehensible and justify the word of God. The discussions involved Muslims in the elaboration and definition of certain ethical concerns, namely: the meaning of Quranic ethical attributes such as just, obligatory, good, evil, etc.; the question of the relationship between human free will and divine will; and the capacity of human beings to derive, through reason, the knowledge of objective ethical norms and truths.

Without doing too much injustice to the process of debate and discussion among various Muslim groups, it can be maintained that, in general, two clear positions emerged: one associated with the Mutazila and the other a traditionalist approach (generally associated with the Sunni tradition in Islam).

First, the Mutazila argued that since God is just, rewarding and punishing within this context, human beings must possess free choice in order that they might be held fully accountable. They denied that acts could therefore be predestined. Second, they maintained that since ethical notions had objective meaning, human beings possess the intellectual capacity to grasp these meanings. Reason therefore was a key attribute and capacity and, independent of revelation, the human being was capable of making empirical and rational observations and drawing ethical conclusions. Natural reason, however, must be supplemented and confirmed by divine revelation. Related to this was another Mutazili conviction, that God's just nature precluded any belief that He might deliberately lead believers to sinful acts.

Historically, the Mutazila school of thought died out and its views were not deemed acceptable to the majority of the traditionalists. The latter's refutation of the main points suggest a differing orientation towards the sources from which ethical values are derived, and the context of faith in which they have meaning. The traditionalist position, as embodied, for example, in the classic work of one founder of a Muslim juridical school, al-Shafii, was that the foundations of faith were a matter of practice, not speculation. Over against the Mutazila belief that natural reason enabled good and evil to be determined, al-Shafii emphasized revelation as the ultimate source of definition. Since the principle of human accountability was also the cornerstone of juridical thought, obligations implying the human capacity to undertake them, good and evil were to be determined on the basis of textual proof in the Quran and by what was contained in the Prophetic tradition. Acts and obligations were good and evil ultimately because divine commands defined them as such.

On the question of human freedom for action, the Mutazili portion was combated, in one respect, through a notion of acquisition. It was argued that the human power to perform acts was not one's own but came from God. Human beings "acquire" responsibility for their actions, thus making them accountable. It must be emphasized that traditionalist thinkers were not opposed to the use of reason. They parted company with rationalists only over the value placed on reason. They regarded reason as an aid and tool for affirming issues of faith, but purely secondary in its relation to the definition of ethical obligation.

The traditionalist position argued that the final basis for moral obligation was the data of Islam's foundational texts, the Quran and the *sunna* elaborated and applied as God's commands and prohibitions, conceived as the *sharia* and, formulated through the respective Muslim juridical schools. Such formulations of commands and prohibitions in Muslim books of law are expressed in ethical terms. Five categories are employed for evaluating all acts: (1) obligatory acts, such as the duty to perform ritual prayer, paying of *zakat* and the practice of fasting; (2) recommended acts, which are not considered obligatory, such acts of charity, kindness, prayer, etc.; (3) permitted actions, regarding which the law adopts a neutral stance (there are no expectations of reward or punishment for such acts; (4) acts that are discouraged and regarded as reprehensible, but not strictly forbidden; (Muslim jurists differ about what actions to include under this category; (5) actions that are categorically forbidden, such as murder, adultery, blasphemy, theft, intoxication, etc.

These categories were further set by jurists within a dual framework of obligations: towards God and towards society. In each instance transgression was perceived in both legal and theological terms, as constituting a crime as well as a sin. Such acts were punishable under the law and the jurists attempted to specify and elaborate the conditions under which this could occur. For example, one of the punishments for theft or highway robbery was the cutting off of a hand and, in minor instances, flogging. Traditionally, jurists attempted to take into account active repentance to mitigate such punishment, following a tradition of the Prophet, to restrict the applicability of such punishments to extreme cases.

Some of these categories have received attention in several Muslim countries in recent times where traditional juristic procedures have been re-instated, but there is a great deal of divergence in the Muslim world about the necessity and applicability of some of these procedures. Where applied, such punishment is meted out through *sharia* courts and rendered by appointed Muslim judges. Jurists or legal experts also function as interpreters of the *sharia* and are free to render informed legal opinions. Such opinions may be solicited by individuals who wish to be certain about the moral intentionality of certain acts, but, among most Muslim schools of law, such opinions need not be binding. The four major Sunni schools of law consider each other to reflect normative stances on matters of legal and ethical interpretation. For Muslim jurists, both law and ethics are ultimately concerned with moral obligations which they believed are the central focus of the Islamic message.

◆ PHILOSOPHICAL APPROACHES

The integration of the philosophical legacy of antiquity in the Islamic world was a major enabling factor in the use of philosophical tradition among Muslim intellectuals. It gave rise to figures such as al-Farabi, Ibn Sina (Avicenna), Ibn Rushd (Averroes), and others, who became well-known to medieval Europe as philosophers, commentators and exponents of the clas-

sical tradition going back to Plato and Aristotle. The public discourse of *adab* grounded in philosophical and moral language and concerns, represents a significant part of the cosmopolitan heritage of ethics in Islam and reflects efforts to reconcile religiously and scripturally derived values with an intellectually and morally based ethical foundation. The Muslim philosophical tradition of ethics is therefore doubly significant: for its value in continuing and enhancing classical Greek philosophy and for its commitment to synthesizing Islam and philosophical thought.

Al-Farabi (died 950) argued for harmony between the ideals of virtuous religion and the goals of a true polity. Through philosophy, one is able to arrive at an understanding of how human happiness is to be achieved, but the actual recourse to moral virtues and acts involve the instrumentality of religion. He compares the founding of religion to the founding of a city. Citizens ought to acquire the traits which enable them to function as residents of a virtuous polis. Similarly the founder of a religion establishes norms that must be upheld through action if a proper religious community is to be established. The thrust of Farabi's argument, particularly as it is articulated in his classic work *The Virtuous City* suggests a communal framework for attaining ultimate happiness, and defines therefore, significant social and political roles for religion as well as an engagement in similar concerns for politicians. In this respect, the emphasis on virtue and its ethical connotations suggests a common focus for both Greek and Muslim philosophies, namely the application of such standards and norms to political societies. The greater the wisdom and virtue of the rulers and the citizens, the greater the possibility of attaining the true goal of philosophy and religion, 'happiness'.

Ibn Sina (died 1037) develops the argument that the Prophet embodies the totality of virtuous action and thought, reflected in the attainment of moral virtue. The Prophet, he claimed acquired the moral characteristics needed for his own development which resulted in a perfect soul. This achievement not only imbued in him the capacity of a free intellect but also made him capable of laying down rules for other people through laws and the establishment of justice. This rationale implies that the Prophet goes beyond the philosopher and the virtuous ruler who possess the capacity for intellectual development and practical morality, respectively. The establishment of justice, in Ibn Sina's view, is the basis for all human good. The combination of philosophy and religion encompasses harmonious living in both this world and in the hereafter.

Ibn Rushd (died 1198) was faced with the daunting task for a Muslim philosopher of defending philosophy against attacks, the most well-known by the great Sunni Muslim theologian al-Ghazali (died 1111). The latter, through a work entitled *The Incoherence of the Philosophers*, had sought to represent philosophers as self-contradictory, anti-scriptural and, in some cases, as affirming heretical beliefs. Ibn Rushd's defense was based on his contention that the Quran enjoined the use of reflection and reason and that the study of philosophy complemented traditionalist approaches to Islam. He asserted that philosophy and Islam had common goals, but arrived at them differently. There is thus common interest between Muslims who adopt philosophical frames of inquiry and those who affirm juridical ones.

In summary, the various Muslim philosophers in their extension and occasional revision of earlier classical notions linked ethics to theoretical knowledge, which was to be acquired by rational means. Since human beings were rational, the virtues and qualities that they embraced and practiced were seen as furthering the ultimate goal of individuals and the community. This was the attainment of happiness.

♦ ETHICS IN THE SHIA TRADITION

The Shia differed from the Sunnis in attributing legitimate authority after the Prophet Muhammad's death to his cousin and son-in-law Ali and subsequently to his designated descendants known as Imams. They emphasized the Imam's role in contextualizing the faith but also in promoting the use of the intellect. Shiism, like the early theological and philosophical schools, affirmed the use of rational and intellectual discourse and was committed to a synthesis and further development of appropriate elements present in other religions and intellectual traditions outside Islam.

One well-known Shia writer is Nasir al-din Tusi (died 1275). Developing further the philosophical approaches already present among Muslims and linking them to Shia conceptions of guidance, Tusi draws attention to the need for ethical enactments to be based on superiority of knowledge and preponderance of discrimination, i.e., by a person "who is distinguished from others by divine support, so that he may be able to accomplish their perfection." Tusi blended into his ethical work elements of Neoplatonic as well as Shia Ismaili and Twelver Shia philosophical and moral perspectives.

The Twelver Shia are so-called, because of their belief that the twelfth in the line of Imams they recognized had withdrawn from the world and is to reappear physically at the end of time to restore true justice. In the meantime, during his absence, the community is to be guided by trained scholars called *mujtahids* who interpret for individual believers right and wrong in all matters of personal and religious life. In the Twelver Shia tradition, such individuals, called *mullahs* in pop-

ular parlance, play a significant role as moral models. In recent times in Iran and elsewhere *mullahs* have assumed a major role in the political life of the state, seeking to shape it in line with their view of a Muslim polity.

For Ismaili groups the Imam's presence is considered necessary to contextualize Islam in changing times and circumstances, and his teachings and interpretation continue to guide followers in their material as well as spiritual lives. An example is the role of the current Imam of the Nizari Ismailis, the Aga Khan, who leads a worldwide community. Among the Shia, continuity with Muslim tradition and values thus remains tied to the continuing spiritual authority vested in the *Imam* or his representatives.

♦ SUFI PERSPECTIVES

Sufism is the mystical and esoteric dimension of Islam, emphasizing the cultivation of an inner personal life in search of divine love and knowledge. Since a major part of Sufi teaching was to enable an individual Muslim to seek intimacy with God, it was felt that such seekers must embrace a commitment to an inner life of devotion and moral action that would lead to spiritual awakening. The observances of the *sharia* were to be complemented by adherence to a path of moral discipline, enabling the seeker to pass through several spiritual "stations," each representing inner, spiritual growth, until one had understood the essential relationship of love and union between seeker and Allah. Since the inner meaning of action was a significant aspect of Sufi understanding of ethical and moral behavior, Sufis emphasized the linkage between an inner, experiential awareness of morality and its outward expression so that a true moral action was one embracing and penetrating the whole of life.

In its institutional setting, organized Sufi groups taught conformity to traditional Muslim values but added the component of discipline and inner purification. Since the practices that instilled discipline and moral awareness varied across the range of cultures and traditions encountered by Islam, many local practices were appropriated. These included, for example, the acceptance of the moral customs and practices adhered to in local tradition, such as in Indonesia and other countries, where large-scale conversions had occurred. Sufi ethical practices thus provided a bridge for incorporating into Muslim moral behavior the ethical values and practices of local traditions illustrating the universality of Sufi Muslim perspectives on the oneness of the inner dimension of various faiths. Al-Ghazali, the Sunni jurist and theologian mentioned earlier, became a supporter of Sufi thought but sought to synthesize the moral perspectives of the *sharia* with the notion of inner piety developed by Sufis. He conceived of divinely ordained obligations as a starting point for cultivating a moral personality, provided that it led to an inwardly motivated sense of ethics in due course. He was, however, reluctant to accept the emphasis of some Sufis on a purely experiential and subjectively guided basis for moral action.

♦ MUSLIM ETHICS IN THE CONTEMPORARY WORLD

The practice and influence of the diverse ethical heritage in Islam has continued in varying degrees among Muslims in the contemporary world. Muslims, whether they constitute majorities in the large number of independent nation states that have arisen in this century, or whether they live in significant numbers and communities elsewhere, are going through an important transitional phase. There is growing self-consciousness about identification with past heritage and a recognition of the need to adapt that heritage to changing circumstances amidst a globalization of human society. Ethical questions faced by Muslims cannot be reflected in unified and monolithic responses. They must take into account the diversity and pluralism that has marked the Muslims of the past as well as the present.

Ethical criteria that can govern issues of economic and social justice and moral strategies for dealing with questions of poverty and imbalance have taken up the greater share of Muslim attention in ethical matters. Whether such responses are labelled "modernist" or "fundamentalist," they all reflect specific readings of past Muslim symbols and patterns and, in their rethinking and restating of norms and values, employ different strategies for inclusion, exclusion and encoding of specific representations of Islam. In terms of broad moral and ethical concerns, this ongoing discourse seeks to establish norms for both public and private life and is therefore simultaneously cultural, political, social and religious.

Since the modern conception of religion familiar to most people in the West assumes a theoretical separation between specifically religious and perceived secular activity, some aspects of contemporary Muslim discourse, which does not accept such a dichotomy, appear strange and often retrogressive. Where such discourse, expressed in what appears to be traditional religious language, has become linked to radical change or violence, it has unfortunately deepened stereotypical perceptions about Muslim fanaticism, violence and cultural and moral difference. As events and developments in the last quarter of the twentieth century indicate, no one among the many Muslim societies in the world can be regarded as normative for all Muslims.

In the pursuit of a vision that will guide Muslims in decisions and choices about present and future ethical matters, the most important challenge for Islam may not be simply be to formulate a continuity and dialogue with its own past ethical underpinning but, like the Muslims of the past, to remain open to the possibilities and challenges of new ethical and moral discoveries.

Azim Nanji

References

Arkoun, M. *Rethinking Islam: Common Questions, Uncommon Answers.* Boulder, Co.: Westview Press, 1994.

Fakhry, M. *Ethical Theories in Islam.* 2nd expanded ed. Leiden: E.J. Brill, 1994.

Hourani, G. *Reason and Tradition in Islamic Ethics.* Cambridge: Cambridge University Press, 1985.

Houvannisian. R., ed. *Ethics in Islam.* Ninth Levi: Della Vida Conference. Malibu, Calif.: Undena Publications, 1985.

Izutsu, T. *Ethico-Religious Concepts of the Quran.* Montreal: McGill University Press, 1966.

Khadduri, Majid. *The Islamic Conception of Justice.* Baltimore: John Hopkins University Press, 1984.

Metcalf, B. ed. *Moral Conduct and Authority.* Berkeley: University of California Press, 1984.

Mottahedeh, R. *The Mantle of the Prophet.* New York: Pantheon Books, 1985.

Nanji, Azim. "Islamic Ethics" in *A Companion to Ethics* ed by Peter Singer. Oxford: Blackwell, 1991.

Nasr, S. H. *Ideals and Realities of Islam.* Cambridge, Mass: Beacon Press, 1972.

Rahman, F. *Major Themes in the Quran.* Minneapolis, Bibliotheca Islamica, 1980.

Rispler-Chaim, Vardit. *Islamic Medical Ethics in the Twelfth Century.* Leiden: E.J. Brill, 1993.

———. *Health and Medicine in the Islamic Tradition.* New York: Crossroad, 1987.

Schimmel, A. *Mystical Dimensions of Islam.* Chapel Hill, University of North Carolina Press, 1976.

Walzer. R., trans. *Al-Farabi on the Perfect State.* Oxford, The Clarendon Press, 1985.

Part V:

The Spiritual and Devotional Tradition in Islam

17

Early Muslim Spirituality and Mysticism

♦ The Origins of Islamic Spirituality ♦ The Birth of Sufism
♦ The Development of a Synoptic Mystical Thought in Islam

Classical Islamic spirituality can be divided into four major periods of development: (1) the pre-Sufi phase, which would include the Quran, the central ritual elements of Islam, the legends of miraj, *the poetic traditions, and the thought of the Muslim-theologian and ascetic Hasan of Basra (died 728); (2) the period of the great early Sufi masters such as Rabia, Bistami, and Junayd (died 910) whose legacy has come down to us largely through collections of their sayings in the works of later writers; (3) the formative phase of Sufism as a self-conscious mode of spirituality embracing all aspects of life and society as exemplified in the monumental works of writers like Sulami, Sarraj, and Qushayri (died 1074); and (4) the full flowering of Islamic spirituality in the works of Ibn al-Farid, Ibn Arabi, Attar, and Rumi (died 1273). This chapter treats the first three stages.*

♦ THE ORIGINS OF ISLAMIC SPIRITUALITY

Nineteenth-century Western scholars as well as some Islamic modernists and reformers have imposed a dualistic opposition between Sufism and spirituality on the one hand and ritual Islam, which is embodied in the Islamic way of life (*sharia*) on the other. The premise of this chapter is that spirituality and embodiment are not in opposition in Islam, but, on the contrary, are mutually related and have been from the very beginning of Islam.

The word "spirit" (*ruh*) appears in the Quran only twenty-four times, yet it is one of the key terms in the Quranic lexicon. The spirit is associated with three primordial moments: creation (as exemplified in the "inspiriting" of Adam when the Creator breathed into him

the spirit of life and in the Quranic story of Jesus' conception through the Spirit); prophecy (exemplified through the spirit as the necessary accompaniment and aid to prophecy and in the famous Quranic passage, which describes the "night of destiny" in which the spirit of prophecy descends); and the moment of truth or day of judgment in which the spirits return to the celestial equivalent of the Kaba, the Muslim sacred house of God. At this final moment of truth, there is an ontological reversal: What seems secure (the mountains, the heavens, the earth, the instinctive nursing of a calf by its mother) is torn away, and what might seem ephemeral, "an atom's weight of generosity or an atom's weight of evil" (Quran: 99:8), becomes each person's absolute reality.

When the heavens are stripped away,
the stars are strewn,
the seas boil over,
the tombs burst open,
then shall each soul know
what it has given and what it has held back
(Quran 82:1–5).

At its most subtle semantic register, the Quranic language of spirit is the moment in which these three archetypal moments (creation, prophecy, moment of truth) are united, as well as the point at which the "signs" of reality—the polarities of day and night, male and female, odd and even—are brought together.

In the famous "light verse" (Quran 24:35), the Quran describes a cosmos of signs embedded within signs, meanings, within meanings and deeper realities within other realities:

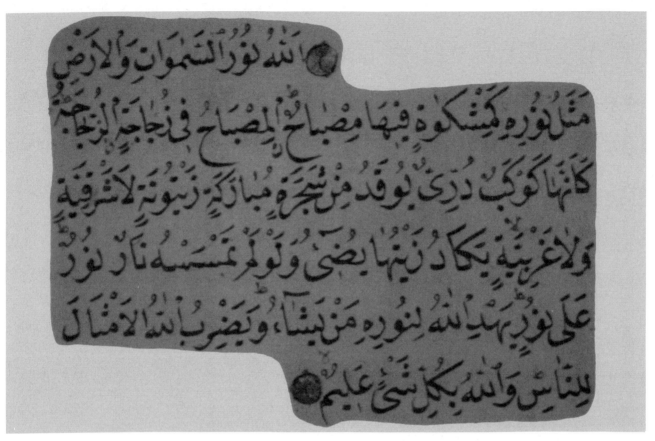

"Verse of Light" from the Quran (24:35).

Allah is the light of the heavens and earth
His light like the light of a lamp in a niche
The lamp enclosed in a glass
The glass like a pearl-white star
Kindled from an olive tree that is blessed
Neither from the East nor from the West
Its oil nearly glows forth without the touch of
fire
Light on light God guides to his light whomever
He wills
Allah strikes symbols for humankind
Allah in all things is most knowing.

A similar realm of embedded symbols of increased luminosity, transparency, blessing, and truth is presented in the account of Muhammad's prophetic vision (Quran 53:1–18; 97); the story of Joseph (Quran 12); the famous episodes in the *sura* titled "The Cave" (Al-Kahf) (Quran 18); Moses's prophetic encounters with the transcendent (Quran 7:142–43; 20:9–14); and the incomparably beautiful *Sura* of "The Compassionate" (Quran 55). The Quranic world is a world of signs (*ayas*) of the inherent existential generosity manifest in being, in the earth, in its fruits, in its life-forms, in consciousness. Each of these signs offer a clue to a deeper reality. The integrity and destiny of each individual is bound up with his/her interpretation (*tawil*) of these signs, an interpretation that is later made clearer by the prophetic revelations and culminating with the Quran.

The Quran—the divine revelation in Islamic belief—is preeminently an embodied text as it is performed within and throughout the life of the Islamic community. Quranic calligraphy and Quranic recitation permeate Islamic life. These Quranic arts entail a cultivation of nuance and a combination of awe and intimacy so distinctive of Quranic discourse. The epitome of the performed and embodied Quran is the call to prayer that resonates over Islamic communities five times a day, calling people away from their daily preoccupations and demanding a moment of reflection and self-composure before their God. The physical movements (*Raka*) of ritual prayer (*salat*) orient all Muslims toward the Kaba in Mecca and harmonize the body and spirit within that orientation.

The fasting (*sawm*) for the month of Ramadan more radically disrupts everyday senses of space and time, as daytime becomes a time of austerity and nighttime a time of communal celebration. The last days of Ramadan, after the intense psychophysical effects of a

The Tomb of Shah Rukn-I-Alam

month of fasting, culminate in the night of destiny (*lay-lat al-qadr*), a vigil reenacting the night of Muhammad's reception of the divine word and marking the moment of closest intimacy between the divine and the human. The ritually obligatory tithe (*zakat*), a word based on the concept of purification), institutionalizes the Quranic virtue of generosity and is a complex embodiment of the searing Quranic denunciations of acquisitiveness ("Do you think the wealth you have acquired will make you immortal") within a functioning social framework. Through constant generosity and sharing, and through avoidance of all predatory economic practices, wealth is purified.

All of these aspects of spiritual embodiment are embodied physically and are brought together in the pilgrimage to the Kaba. As the pilgrim moves through the stations of pilgrimage, founding events of Islamic life are reenacted. In the slaughtering of a sheep, for example, Abraham—whom Muslims believe built the Kaba—is remembered for his sacrifice of the sheep in place of his son. Simultaneously, around the Islamic world, an animal sacrifice is made, linking the pilgrims to those throughout the world celebrating the great *Id*, or holiday. On the plain of Arafat, there is a simultaneous reenactment of Muhammad's final sermon and

pre-enactment of the final day of judgment or moment of truth (*Yawm*) as the Islamic community stands on the plain of Arafat and chants "*labayka* " (Here I am, Lord). The circumambulation of the Kaba is a movement around that point where, for Muslims, the world and the transcendent meet. The Kaba itself represents the three archetypal moments in the Quran where the world of time and the world of eternity come together: the creation (the stone of the Kaba is viewed by tradition as a relic of the original creation), prophecy, and the day of judgment.

In Shia Islam, the reenactment of the martyrdom of Husayn, the grandson of the Prophet and the third Shia imam, becomes the occasion for a meditation on the tragic aspect of human existence and reaches a pitch of intensity when the audience in the play no longer perceives itself as watching a representation of an event that took place centuries ago, but rather as coparticipants in that event. While Sunni Muslims do not celebrate the *taziya* formally, they also venerate the figure of Husayn and remember the tragedy of his martyrdom.

In the story of the *Miraj*, Muhammad is taken up through the seven heavens to the divine throne. Based upon a brief mention in the Quran to a night journey (*isra*) (Quran 17:1), the Miraj account is elaborated upon in the *hadith* and *Sira* (The accounts of Muhammad), and collated with the key passages on Muhammad's reception of the divine word (Quran 53, 94, 99). Muhammad is taken on a night journey from the precinct of the *bayt al-haram* (the sacred house, i.e., the Kaba) to the *bayt al-muqaddas* (the house of sanctity). From there he is taken up through the seven heavens and is greeted by, and in effect validated by, the previous prophets who now occupy those heavens (Adam, Joseph, Aaron, Moses, Abraham, and Jesus). At the culmination he sees the lote tree of the furthest boundary, the divine throne (*arsh*), the "house of life" (*al-bayt al-mamur* —the celestial counterpart to the Kaba), and receives the divinely ordained prayers for his community.

The poetic heritage was another central mode of expression of early Islamic spirituality. The tradition of the pre-Islamic ode (*qasida*) was to supply key aspects of Sufi lexicon, sensibility, and emotive nuance, as well as key themes: the remembrance (*dhikr*) of the beloved, intoxication (*sukr*), love-madness, perpetual wandering, the secret (*sirr*) between lover and beloved, the stations (*maqamat*) of the beloved's journey away from the lover (these resonate strongly with the stations of the Arabian pilgrimages), the constantly changing states of the beloved (*ahwal*), and the meditation on the ruins of the abandoned campsite of the beloved, ruins that are signs both of her presence and her absence.

By the end of the first century of Islam, the beginnings of a new mode of spirituality were manifesting themselves around the figure of Hasan of Basra (died 728) who was a founder of both Islamic theology and Islamic ascetic piety. Hasan's probing of the key Quranic tensions between divine predestination and human responsibility, the all-one deity, and the plurality of its attributes led to a new movement of rational theological inquiry known as *ilm al-kalam* (scholastic theology; literally the science of discussion or debate). At the same time, Hasan's ascetic piety became a symbol of resistance to the new imperial culture. While grounding itself in the Quran and *sharia*, this ascetic piety began to develop a set of free devotions (not required by Quranic rule) forms of asceticism, fasting, meditations, and spiritual pedagogy.

◆ THE BIRTH OF SUFISM

Quranic spirituality, precisely because it is embodied in the performance of the Quran and in the signs and symbols of all aspects of the world, never stressed asceticism, and indeed, for some early thinkers, was not compatible with asceticism, particularly with the celibate model of asceticism that is important to some human interpretations of Christianity. While Hasan represented the movement toward integrating ascetic piety into Islamic spirituality, it was the next generation that succeeded in articulating the limits of ascetic piety, its relation to Quranic spirituality, and its relation to key theological issues of divine predetermination and affirmation of divine unity.

The tension between world-affirmation and world-transcendence is dramatized vividly in the life and sayings of Rabia al-Adawiyya (died 801), a freed slave from Basra. Rabia became the touchstone for a developing set of values that were to be the ethical ground of Sufism: *tawhid* (the affirmation of the divine unity, interpreted by her as a relational absolute in which only the divine beloved is a matter of concern or even consciousness); *tawakkul* (trust-in-God, interpreted as a refusal of all need for creature goods); and *rida* (acceptance; a relentlessly active acceptance of divine will to the point of refusing to ask the deity for anything other than for its will to be done). These virtues were consolidated in Rabia's radical affirmation of sincerity (*sidq*). In one story she is portrayed as running down the path with water in one hand, a lighted torch in the other. When asked why, she stated that she would be willing to douse the fires of hell and burn paradise, so that no one would ever love the beloved for any other reason than sincere love, without fear of punishment or desire for reward.

Rabia's focus on divine unity as something performed in one's life, not just verbally affirmed, clarified the limits of asceticism. When asked if she hated Satan

and loved Muhammad, Rabia said that she had room only for one concern, love of the divine beloved. Similarly, when an ascetic began showing his contempt for the world, Rabia answered dryly that anyone who spent so much time rejecting something must be very attached to it indeed; one whose only concern was love of the one beloved had no room for distractions such as rejecting the world.

Complementing Rabia's graphic affirmation of divine unity as a way of life was the rigorous and psy-

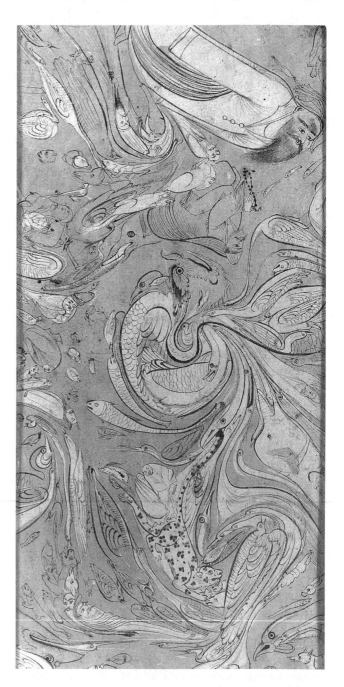

Mystical Journey, c. 1650. A Safavid painting depicting the spiritual quest.

Musicians performing at Salim Chishti's tomb.

chologically relentless critique of the human ego-self (*nafs*) offered by mystics such as Muhasibi (died 857). Muhasibi spent a lifetime examining the subtleties, seductions, and self-delusions of human pride. He divided pride into dozens of subcategories such as *riya* (the desire to make a show of oneself), and detailed the various manifestations of each category (*riya* in the world of affairs, religion, and Sufism) with an implacable moral critique.

To Jafar al-Sadiq (died 765), the sixth Shia imam is attributed an extraordinary set of writings, from philosophy to Shia jurisprudence to alchemy. The Quranic commentary attributed to Jafar is one of the earliest specifically mystical or Sufi commentaries. In it, the prophetic visions of Muhammad and Moses are viewed as archetypes for the Sufi mystical experience of *fana*, or the extinction of the ego-self in union with the divine. Within a hundred years of the death of Jafar as-Sadiq, the movement known as "Sufism" was in full blossom. Sahl al-Tustari (died 896) composed a Quranic commentary grounded in the Light Verse of the Quran, but more explicity based on the pre-eternal covenant verse in which Allah addresses the progeny of Adam prior to creation, and they affirm their allegiance. Tustari presents the essence of the Prophet

Muhammad as a column of light emanating from a pre-eternal "position of prayer." The notion of a pre-eternal position of prayer dramatizes the correlation of spirit and body. Even in the pre-created eternal realm, there are no disembodied spirits, but only a position of prayer, a human orientation and relationship in complete acceptance of and toward the source of being.

Out of the same circles came Junayd (died 810). Junayd's sayings and writings focus upon the trial or test (*bala*) that the Sufi must undergo to encounter reality, and the overpowering, even violent, nature of the manner in which such a person is seized, overwhelmed, and obliterated by the divine presence. Junayd's articulation of the concept of *fana* (extinction of the ego-self in union with the divine) became the centerpiece of Islamic mystical thought. Junayd and other early Sufis grounded this concept of mystical union in the famous divine saying (*hadith qudsi*): "When my servant draws near to me through obligatory and free devotions . . . I become the hearing with which he hears, the seeing with which he sees, the hands with which he touches, the feet with which he walks, and the tongue with which he speaks."

As is the case with many early Sufis, we only know the sayings of the most famous mystic from the

Khurasan region of Iran, Bayezid Bistami (died circa 875), through the oral traditions of his sayings. Bistami varies radically according to the collector of the sayings. In some accounts he is a radical ascetic and *sharia* absolutist who is unable to eat any food even touched by the possibility that it may not be ritually pure, both in being free of all Quranically condemned substances and purchased with money that was properly obtained. In other portraits, he is willing to publicly break the laws of ritual purity as a way of calling blame upon himself, in order to keep himself and his followers from falling into the trap of venerating his own person rather than the one deity. The two portraits are really complementary. In neither case does Bistami reject the Quranic polarity of sacred/prohibited (*haram*) and permitted (*halal*). Rather, he pushes it to its extreme, tapping into its energy as a channel for the sacred and grounding his famous mystical utterances (*shatahat*) within that channel.

Hallaj was another master of *shatahat*, including the famous *ana al-haqq* (I am the truth). This statement was interpreted by Hallaj's defenders in the same way that Bistami's famous saying, "Glory be to me" (*subhani*) was interpreted by his defenders as the divine voice speaking through the mystic whose ego-self had become annihilated in his love of the divine beloved. Hallaj pushed Sufi paradoxes to the extreme and, more dangerously, insisted upon confronting society with them in the most dramatic way possible. He was executed in Baghdad in 922. The real reasons for his execution are complex. Ironically, many of the Sufi paradoxes practiced and believed by Hallaj were repeated by other Sufis with scant political repercussions.

One of Hallaj's surviving works, the *Tawasin*, includes an unforgettable interpretation of Iblis, the closest spirit-being next to God who refused the divine command to prostrate himself before the newly created Adam (Quran 2:30–33; 38:71–75). He thus was expelled from heaven for disobedience and became the cursed Satan. In the *Tawasin*, Iblis defends himself by saying that he was an absolute monotheist and that he could never bow before any other being than the one deity, even at the divine command. Drawing upon the poetic tradition, he presents himself as the totally loyal beloved who will not abandon his loyalty (in his case, his monotheism) even at the cost of love-madness, deformation, torment, and, worst of all, eternal separation from the beloved. Drawing upon sophisticated theological disputes over human free will and divine predetermination, he states that God had eternally known that Iblis was an absolute monotheist and would never bow before an "other-than-God" and thus eternally prewilled Iblis's self-sacrificing disobedience to the command. Iblis also suggests a dynamic configuration of opposites in which farness and nearness from the beloved become the same to one totally consumed by love for the beloved.

◆ THE DEVELOPMENT OF A SYNOPTIC MYSTICAL THOUGHT IN ISLAM

Islamic spirituality entered a fundamental new phase with the emergence of the Sufi writer and thinker, Abu Nasr al-Sarraj (died 988), and his masterwork *Book of the Flashes*. By Sarraj's time, tensions were felt within Sufism (between various followers of Tustari and the followers of Bistami) and between the Sufis and other Muslim intellectuals. This was only natural given the explosive growth and power of the Sufi movement in the preceding two-hundred years. It was Sarraj who began the systematic explication of Sufism as a way of life, grounded in the Quran and in the *sharia*. He placed the paradoxes and ecstatic utterances of the Sufis into context, and harmonized the teachings of the Baghdad and Khurasan schools. Sarraj articulated the various virtues of earlier mystics like Rabia and Muhasibi (trust-in-God or *tawakkul*, active acceptance or *rida*, critical self-examination or *war*) into a rigorous and profound dialectical movement of "stages" (*maqamat*) along the Sufi path and ephemeral "states" (*ahwal*)—from bliss to awe to terror—that could come upon the Sufi without warning or will.

Abu Talib al-Makki (died 996) in his *Food for the Hearts* (*Qut al-Qulub*) combined the moral and psychological rigor of Muhasibi with the intellectual sweep of Sarraj to demonstrate the essential grounding and the mutual interrelation of Sufism and *sharia*. The more famous Abu Hamid al-Ghazali (died 1111) used Makki's *Food for the Hearts* as the basis of his own work, the *Revival of the Religious Sciences*. What original insights Ghazali may have added to Makki's work cannot be ascertained until the massive and much neglected work of Makki is given more thorough attention.

A third major Sufi writer, Sulami (died 1021), preserved the great early Sufi interpretations, including those of Tustari and Jafar mentioned above. His *Ranks of the Friends of God* portrays the early Sufi "friends of God" in a style that uses the *hadith isnad* (chain of authorities) for each saying, and which continually reinforces the grounding of Sufism in *sharia*. By using the *isnad* to support the sayings of the Sufis, and by beginning each chapter with a formal *hadith* of the Prophet, with full *isnad*, Sulami also aligns Sufism with the chain of authorities and the formal passing on of tradition whose spiritual aspect has often been neglected.

The culmination of early Sufism is found in the work of Qushayri (died 1074). In addition to a Quranic commentary, Qushayri composed a *risala* (treatise in letter form) that took the earlier writings of Sarraj, Makki, and Sulami to a new level of literary and philosophical intricacy. In the first section, Qushayri presents the lives of the "friends of God," and in the final section, he presents the principles of Sufism. In a short central section, Qushayri treats twenty-seven key Sufi concepts with a supple and brilliant analysis. Each concept is shown in its range of possible meanings and in both negative and positive lights. The section is perhaps the most lucid introduction to Sufi thought ever written, moving from vivid and sometimes comic anecdotes to sudden spiritual exortations. The section also brings to a new level the Sufi synthesis of the intricate poetic sensibility and symbolic cosmos (remembrance of the beloved, love-madness, perishing in love for the beloved, intoxication, effacement, lighting flashes of promise and absence) with the mystical experience of passing away. With Qushayri, Sufism achieved a fully self-conscious and integrated world of thought and discourse, and was ready to burst forth in the masterworks of the golden age of Sufi writings.

Michael A. Sells

References

Awn, Peter. *Satan's Tragedy and Redemption: Iblis in Sufi Psychology.* Leidenstate: Brill, 1983.

Ernst, Carl W. *Words of Ecstasy in Sufism.* Albany: State University of New York Press, 1985.

Qushayri. *Principles of Sufism.* Translated by Barbara von Schlegell. Berkeley, CA: Mizan Press, 1993.

Schimmel, Annemarie. *Mystical Dimensions of Islam.* Chapel Hill: University of North Carolina Press, 1975.

Sells, Michael. *Early Islamic Mysticism.* New York: Paulist Press, Classics of Western Spirituality, 1996.

Smith, Margaret. *Rabia the Mystic.* 1928, Reprint, Cambridge, England: Cambridge University Press, 1984.

Devotional Life and Practices

♦ Popular Islam ♦ Devotion to God ♦ The Quran in Popular Islam
♦ Devotion to the Prophet in Popular Islam ♦ Devotion to the *Auliya* in Popular Islam
♦ Devotional Life in Practice ♦ Muharram Celebrations in India: A Case Study

Throughout the world, Muslims engage in a myriad of devotional practices that go beyond those of the traditional "Five Pillars." Devotion to God, the Prophet Muhammad, and other holy persons is expressed through such diverse forms as sacred music, vernacular religious literature and poetry, local pilgrimages, and religious festivals. On any given day one can witness all manner of religious activities. In places as distant from each other as Egypt and Pakistan, one can hear highly trained singers expounding the mystical unity of God over the rhythmic percussion of drums, guiding their listeners into states of religious experience. In South Asia, Muslim women gather together to read aloud stories of the Prophet's daughter Fatima and seek her intercession. Somewhere in the Muslim world right now, a person is feeding the poor people of the neighborhood in order to fulfill a religious vow. Elsewhere a family has invited its neighbors into the courtyard to listen to the performance of a professional Quran reciter.

Every year millions of pilgrims visit the tombs of great Muslim saints (the *awliya-i Allah*) to offer prayers and fulfill vows. On the occasions of the birth and death anniversaries of these devotees, festivals are held that exhibit an extraordinary mixture of deep piety and light-hearted entertainment. These events allow participants to confront the sacred through the act of visiting the saint while simultaneously partaking in the delights of fairs and carnivals.

♦ POPULAR ISLAM

These sorts of activities and performances are part of a diverse tradition commonly referred to as popular Islam. For some people the notion of popular Islam implies beliefs or practices that are inherently inconsistent with "authentic" Islamic practices, such as those rooted in the *sharia*, or classical Islamic law. From this perspective, popular practices such as participating in ecstatic musical performances, going on pilgrimage to the tombs of saints, and making vows are questionable practices integrated with Islam from pre-Islamic cultures or, in the most extreme cases, blasphemous divergences from the true Islam intended by God and Muhammad. But for the Muslims who take part in them, these purely voluntary activities are as much an expression of devotion to God and to the Prophet as following the Islamic practices explicitly mentioned in the *sharia*.

For the purposes of this chapter, "popular Islam" refers to those expressions of Islamic piety that extend beyond the practices required and recommended in Islamic law. I specifically include those practices that express love and devotion toward the Prophet Muhammad and toward those persons understood as his legitimate successors. These activities include *ziyarat* (pilgrimage to the tombs of saints), *qawwali* and *inshad* (devotional music), and *urs* and *mawlid* (the commemoration of the death and birth anniversaries of Sufi saints).

Popular Islam is a diverse phenomenon. As Islam spread throughout the world, it did not erase all of the previous cultural practices it encountered. Even as Islam took root among the first generation of Muslims, it did not entirely eliminate the pre-Islamic culture of Arabia. Rather, as the Prophet struggled to Islamize the Arabs, some elements of pre-Arab culture were specifically condemned while other aspects of the culture were re-defined to bring them into accord with Islam. For example, the pilgrimage to Mecca, which was performed in pre-Islamic Arabia, continued under Islam, stripped of its polytheistic interpretation and transformed into an Islamic ritual. Similarly, in every region where Islam took root and flourished, elements of the

Salim Chishti's tomb in Fatehpur Siki.

local culture remained, were Islamized, and, were incorporated into the new Islamic worldview. Thus, every region of the Islamic world displays, on the one hand, certain cultural elements that are unique to it alone and, on the other, some which are to be found universally throughout the Muslim world. The "Five Pillars" of Islam and recommended practices, such as the prayers and fasts mentioned in the *sharia*, remain constant. But aside from these basic practices, devotional activities vary in their details from region to region.

The concept of popular Islam need not imply an inherent opposition to the classical textual tradition of Islam. Despite the diversity of most popular Islamic practices, a discernable and coherent worldview underlies and connects them. This popular Islamic worldview rests upon religious ideas that lie at the very core of the classical Islamic tradition: the necessity of devotion and allegiance to God and the Prophet Muhammad.

◆ DEVOTION TO GOD

Allah is the ultimate focus of all devotion in Islam. Belief in the unity of God (*tawhid*) is the core concept of Islam, and the necessity of obedience to God's will is the bedrock underlying all Islamic piety. The unimaginable majesty and sovereignty of Allah, his infiniteness, formlessness, and simultaneous transcendency and immanence is Islam's essential tenet. Thus, the central act of *salat*, the ritual prayer, prescribes complete prostration before God, symbolizing complete obedience to the Creator and ruler of the universe. The one unforgivable sin in Islam is *shirk*, the violation of divine unity by associating any partners with God. For many Muslims the majesty of God renders impossible any devotion short of absolute obedience.

But there also exists a long tradition of thought in Islam that has argued that mere obedience to God is insufficient. This tradition has stressed the necessity of the love of God. In particular, Islamic mysticism, or Sufism, has taught that if obedience to Allah is not rooted in love for God it is empty and hollow. Accordingly, the true Muslim should obey Allah, not out of a fear of hell or a desire for paradise, but out of a love for Allah. This longing for a greater intimacy with Allah has led to a myriad of popular devotional practices, which have as their focus the two concrete evidences of Allah in the world: the Quran, the word of God; and the Prophet Muhammad, God's messenger.

♦ THE QURAN IN POPULAR ISLAM

The Quran, in its original Arabic, is God's word made present in the world. To recite it or to hear it recited is to encounter the words of God as they first were revealed to Muhammad: One thus re-creates the cosmic event of the Quran's original revelation. As Allah's word it is a powerful and sacred presence for Muslims, and must be treated as such. Thus, a Muslim should never touch the Quran when in a state of ritual impurity. Muslims should never place another book on top of the Quran. The verses of the Quran, in their spoken and written forms, possess spiritual power for Muslims. The recitation of the Quran in Arabic provides an occasion for religious gatherings in private homes.

Muslims express their belief in the power and efficacy of the Quran in a myriad of less formal and more popular ways as well. Verses of the Quran written on posters are often hung on the walls of homes for protection. In particular, people believe that the Throne Verse (*Quran* 2:255) possesses powerful properties for protection from evil. Similarly, the opening line of the Quran, *bismillah al-rahman al-rahim* (In the Name of God the Merciful and the Compassionate), or its numerical equivalent, 786, is often found on the windshields of taxicabs and motorized rickshaws in the Muslim world. Students will often write 786 on the top of their exam papers. Talismans containing Quranic verses worn around Muslims' necks, particularly those acquired from Sufi saints, are another expression of belief in the power of the Quran. Such talismans are commonly thought to have the power to ward off sickness or protect one from the Evil Eye. Because of its sacred power, when a Quran is old and worn out it must be disposed of according to specific religious procedures. One prominent Sufi in Pakistan even maintains a "Quran Hospital" for the repair of used Qurans.

While not all of these practices are to be found in the *sharia*, they all rest on the assumption that the word of Allah is powerfully effective, not only because of its meaning and teachings, but also by its very presence. As such, these devotions ultimately rest on the core Islamic belief in the existence and the authority of Allah.

♦ DEVOTION TO THE PROPHET

Devotion to the Prophet Muhammad is a cornerstone of Muslim piety. Devotion to the Prophet is, ultimately, rooted in a love for God: All Muslims should love God, and what better way is there for humanity to show its love than to show love for those whom God loves best. As such, for the ordinary believer, what better expression of love for God can there be than to love Muhammad. There are many *hadiths* that report God's special love for Muhammad, who is traditionally known as the beloved of God (*habibullah*). Unlike God, who transcends time and space and whose attributes are largely abstract, the Prophet is a human being. Thus, the events of his life can be recounted and serve as paradigms for human action. Devotion to the Prophet, like that centered on the Quran, provides a concrete focus for a Muslim's religious fervor. Thus, a variety of expressions of devotion to the Prophet have emerged in the Muslim world. For example, in many parts of the world Muslims celebrate the birthday of the Prophet as a special holiday. In some places people organize huge processions to commemorate the birth of Muhammad.

Naat and Durud

Devotion to the Prophet permeates the religious lives of Muslims in other ways as well. For example, *naat* is the a cappella melodic recitation of devotional verse about the Prophet Muhammad in Arabic and vernacular languages. Recordings of *naat* are popular in many parts of the Muslim world, and renowned *naat* reciters are in great demand to perform at religious gatherings.

Another important form of devotion to the Prophet is the recitation of *darud*. Darud is a formulaic blessing of the Prophet recited in Arabic. Many forms of Sufi devotion consider *darud* to be a central act of piety. Often Muslims recite *darud* in conjunction with other religious activities such as pilgrimages to the tombs of Sufi saints. Specific *darud* are traditionally thought to yield different spiritual effects. For example, the recitation of certain *darud* can bring about spiritual results such as the appearance of the Prophet to the devotee in a dream. It is commonly believed that the Prophet actually hears the *darud* of his devotees at his tomb (*darbar*) in Medina. *Ziyarat* to the tomb of the Prophet in Medina for many Muslims means actually visiting the Prophet. Sufi hagiography contains numerous stories of *awliya* who are addressed by the audible voice of the Prophet while visiting his tomb.

The Continuing Spiritual Presence of the Prophet

Inherent in this notion that the Prophet hears the heartfelt *darud* of pilgrims to his tomb is the belief in the continuing spiritual link that Muslims maintain with the Prophet Muhammad. It is commonly held that although the Prophet died—as do all human beings no matter what their religious role—he is still available to his devotees as a spiritual presence. It is difficult to overemphasize the importance of this belief in popular Islam. It is perhaps safe to say that the majority of Muslims not only respect the Prophet as the founder of Islam, but they also venerate him as a continuing spiritual presence. They consider the Prophet to be present and available (*hazr-o nazr*) to members of his community. The belief in the Prophet's continuing presence is tied to the belief, based on classical sources of *hadith* or personal accounts of contacts with the prophet, that his very existence is a manifestation of a preexistent light—the prophetic *nur*. Thus, devotion to the Prophet is not merely an act of remembrance but also an act directed toward the Prophet himself as a spiritual entity.

Devotion to the Family of the Prophet (*ahl al- bayt*)

According to many Muslims, devotion to the Prophet should extend to his "legitimate successors." Just as Muhammad is the beloved of God and love for Muhammad is an expression of love for Allah, what better expression of love for Muhammad can there be than to love those whom Muhammad has loved best. In the Shia branch of Islam this devotion is directed toward the family of the Prophet (*ahl al-bayt*). Shia devotion has focused particular attention on the immediate family of the Prophet, the *Panjatan Pak* (Five Pure Ones), who are often represented iconographically by the five-fingered Fatimid hand. These include Muhammad, his daughter Fatima, his son-in-law Ali, and his two grandsons Hasan and Husayn. The Shia show special devotion toward Husayn whom they consider to be their third imam. The anniversary of Imam Husayn's martyrdom at the Battle of Karbala on the tenth of the lunar month of Muharram provides an occasion for public and private acts of devotional mourning, which are among the most intense and passionate of all Shia religious activities.

Reverence for the family of the Prophet is not limited to Shia Muslims. To varying degrees, they are venerated by Sunni and Shia alike. Ali has long been a focus of devotion among Sunni Muslims, and many Muslims, Sunni and Shia, believe that he, like Muhammad, maintains a continuing spiritual presence. The phrase "*Ya Ali Madad* " (Oh help me, Ali) is commonly invoked by Sunni and Shia alike in times of difficulty. In South Asia women often gather together in groups to read miracle stories about the family of the Prophet, especially about Fatima, in connection with spiritual vows called *mannats* in which they seek intercession of the family of the Prophet for spiritual and secular problems. Devotion to the *ahl al-bayt* is particularly strong in the Sufi tradition, where devotion to the Prophet Muhammad and Ali has long been a central theme.

◆ DEVOTION TO THE *AWLIYA* IN POPULAR ISLAM

Devotional practice is tied closely to the Sufi tradition. Sufism incorporates devotional allegiance to the Prophet and his family, and extends it to include the *awliya-i Allah*. Belief in the *awliya* exists in nearly every part of the Muslim world. It is commonly held that there are a series of hierarchical spiritual allegiances. The community of Muslims (*Umma*) forms a pyramid with ordinary believers at its base and the Prophet at its apex as the spiritual pole of this world. Within this system, the *awliya* inhabit the higher strata of the pyramid and function as agents of the Prophet's authority. They have spiritual dominion over the world and function as an invisible spiritual government. They have powers of intercession and the ability to affect life-transforming changes on those whom they encounter.

In the popular imagination, the court of the Prophet (*darbar-i Mustafa*) in Medina is the meeting place for the *awliya* and the center of their spiritual government. One popular booklet published in Pakistan explains it this way: "The *awliya*, who are called governors or officers, know the full (spiritual) condition of everyone who lives in the region (that they have been given dominion over) . . . (furthermore), *awliya* continually travel back and forth to the court of the Prophet" (Panipati 32).

This whole system hinges on devotion to the Prophet. Just as the *ahl al-bayt* are the familial descendants of the Prophet, the *awliya* are his spiritual descendants. All of the Sufi orders trace their lineage back to Muhammad, and most of them go back through Ali as well. Thus, the authority of the *awliya* is the direct result of their connection with the Prophet and his family. The power of the *awliya* is seen as proof (*hujjat*) of the Prophet's authority.

There is, of course, a voluminous and profound textual Sufi tradition. Some of the Sufis who have become known as great *awliya* were also great scholars of the Quran and *hadith*, having written great works on Islamic law. But the great mass of Muslims who are devoted to the *awliya* have likely never read these writings, nor would they necessarily know of their existence. Their understanding of the spiritual world comes from stories about the *awliya* they have read or more likely heard. Collections of stories about the *awliya* are readily available in vernacular languages throughout the Muslim World. Oral versions of these narratives are also to be found.

These stories relate the miraculous deeds and spiritual accomplishments of the *awliya*. They emphasize ethics and the necessity for allegiance and devotion. A good example of this type of tale is the story of the greedy sugar salesman who encountered the great medieval Indian saint, Baba Farid Shakr-Ganj. Baba Farid was famous for his sweet tooth. Upon seeing the approaching merchant carrying a large bag full of sugar, the saint asks him what he has in the bag. Not wishing to share his sugar as hospitality would dictate, the merchant replies that his bag contains not sugar but salt. Baba Farid replies, "Fine, it is salt then," and the merchant returns home to find that his sugar has indeed become salt! He is then forced to approach the saint for forgiveness. This story presents two types of messages. The first is ethical: Dishonesty, greed, and a lack of hospitality are wrong and can have dire consequences. The second is devotional: The *awliya* are powerful and must be respected. Furthermore, they can see beneath appearances to the reality of things. One cannot hide the truth from the *awliya-i Allah*.

Stories like this make people aware of the lives of the *awliya*. But while most people know the names and deeds of at least the most notable *awliya*, specific historical knowledge about individual *awliya* is relatively uncommon. What emerges through these narratives is, instead, a general belief in the existence of powerful individuals close to the Prophet who can be approached for intercession concerning spiritual or mundane difficulties.

Encounters with the Awliya

There are two main ways in which people encounter the *awliya*. One is an encounter with living *awliya*. Sufism is a living tradition in the Muslim world. Sufi masters, known as *shaykhs* or *pirs*, continue to attract disciples, called *murids*. While some people come to *pirs* in order to engage in the disciplined practices associated with Sufi mysticism, others come to visit them for more immediate concerns. People often seek out local *pirs*, not only for assistance in spiritual matters, but also for help with more worldly concerns—curing a sick child, help in passing one's exams, assistance in arranging a good marriage, or simply to obtain the *pirs* blessing. All of these actions rest on the belief that the *awliya* constitute the spiritual government of this world, and that their intercession is possible. Critics of this belief point out how easily belief in the intercession of *pirs* can degenerate into the worship of *pirs*, a form of *shirk*. They also point out the potential for abuse by charlatans who claim to be *awliya* or become *pirs* on a purely hereditary basis and make a living from the "voluntary" offerings of the poor and desperate people who come to them for help.

The practices of Sufism provide a basis for many devotional activities. A central Sufi practice is *dhikr* in which *murids* gather around their *pirs* and engage in the collective repetition of the name of Allah, Quranic verses, or prayers. *Dhikr* is intended to bring about heightened spiritual states called *hal* or *wajd*, and often *dhikr* sessions result in persons experiencing states of religious ecstasy. Sometimes *dhikr* sessions are held in public places such as the courtyard of Sufi tombs,

and ordinary people may attend simply to watch. A particularly well known form of *dhikr* is *sama* (to listen), which involves listening to special religious music. In Egypt this is known as *inshad* and the performers of this tradition display their art in traditional venues such as Sufi gatherings at tombs, and in more "secular" performance spaces such as recording studios and concert halls. The same is true for the South Asian music form called *qawwali*, which is perhaps most "authentic" when performed at the tombs of Sufi saints or in gatherings of *murids* sitting at the feet of their *pir*, but is also performed in concert halls. Recordings of great *qawwals* made by Nusrat Fateh Ali Khan and the Sabri Brothers have become hit records. The lyrical content of this music is devotional in nature and may speak of the unity of Allah, the excellences of the Prophet and his companions, or the wondrous lives of Sufi *awliya*, and is usually presented in the vernacular language.

Ziyarat

The other form this encounter can take is pilgrimage to the tombs of the great *awliya*. Pilgrimage (*ziyarat*) to the tombs of holy persons provides an opportunity for Muslims to physically affirm their allegiance to the Prophet and his legitimate successors.

It is significant that *ziyarat* involves visitation to tombs. According to Islamic tradition, graveyards are the site of "the punishment in the grave," which believers must undergo in preparation for the Day of Judgment. Whereas the fate of most of humanity in the grave is punishment, the *awliya*, who are beloved by Allah, are blessed in the grave. Unlike the graves of sinners, which contract to press in and punish them until the Day of Judgment, the graves of the *awliya* expand so as to give room and comfort to those who are beloved of Allah and his Prophet. They are transformed from mere tombs into places of intercession.

Ziyarat is performed throughout the Muslim world. In Turkey, the tomb of the great Persian poet and mystic Mawlani Jalal Al-din Rumi in Konya and the tomb of Hajji Bektash in central Anatolia are two major sites for *ziyarat*. Both of these tombs have been designated as museums by the Turkish government, and tourists and pilgrims alike must purchase tickets to enter them. They are still treated as a place of pilgrimage by believers. In modern Kazakhstan, the tomb of Ahmad Yasavi, who is commonly referred to as the Father of the Turks because he is credited with the conversion of the Turkic-speaking peoples to Islam, is also a place of pilgrimage for people throughout Central Asia. In south Asia, the tombs of Muinuddin Chisti and Baba Farid Shakr Ganj, among many others, are also places of frequent and enthusiastic visitation. In Egypt the tomb of Ahmad Badawi in Tanta is a site of a yearly major festival for the birthday, *mawlid*, of the saint.

Ziyarat Observed

People who visit the tombs of the *awliya* come for a variety of reasons, similar to those they might use to justify visiting a living saint. Some come simply to pay their respects to the saint. Sometimes pilgrims perform *ziyarat* in connection with a personal vow. Generally, this consists of a devotee making a request for intercession and offering to perform a pious action once that request is fulfilled. For example, a woman seeking the birth of a son may indicate that after she has given birth to a son she will make *ziyarat* to the shrine and recite certain Quranic verses or distribute food (*langar*) to the poor. At many tombs pilgrims initiate a vow by tying a thread or attaching a lock to the tomb grating. They then return for a second pilgrimage and remove it once the wish is fulfilled.

Sometimes a *ziyarat* is the result of a dream in which the saint has called the pilgrim into his presence. Some pilgrims come because they are *murids* of a living *shaykh* who has assigned them to perform *ziyarat* at a particular tomb as an act of spiritual devotion. Women are frequent pilgrims to certain shrines, usually coming in groups. Because they often lack access to other kinds of power, women often perceive the tomb

The Shrine-Complex of Mawlana Jalal al-din Rumi, Konya, Turkey.

of the saint as a court of last resort, a place of final refuge.

Despite some minor geographical variations there is a remarkable uniformity to the practice of *ziyarat* throughout the Muslim world. When a pilgrim performs *ziyarat*, he or she moves through a series of stages or doorways, from the world of ordinary reality to the "extraordinary" world of the tomb of the saint. Tombs of saints possess great *baraka* (blessing) and objects carried into the shrine become blessed through contact with it. Thus, the *baraka* of the shrine can be carried away by the pilgrim and either kept or transferred to others. At large urban shrines, the street leading to the outer gate is usually lined with shops selling religious artifacts. Flowers to be left at the tomb as a sign of respect are particularly popular. Both sweet and salty foods are carried into the shrine so that they can be blessed by the *baraka* of the tomb. Often these blessed foodstuffs are distributed to other pilgrims at the shrine. Sometimes they are carried back to the pilgrim's hometown to share with friends or neighbors. *Chadors* or "grave cloths" are available as well. These are placed over the grave by the pilgrims. Often these cloths are decorated with Quranic verses or other religious symbols. Souvenirs of the experience are also available, such as pamphlets about the life of the saint, religious pictures, or rosaries (*tasbih*). Sometimes toys are also sold near the shrine. These are especially popular with mothers who wish to keep their children occupied as they perform their *ziyarat*.

Normally the tomb is surrounded by a walled courtyard. The actual gateway to the courtyard is often crowded with beggars as pilgrims are often in a particularly generous mood. At the gateway there is usually a person who takes the pilgrims' shoes as well as individuals selling flowers, sweets, or other paraphernalia. Passing through this first gateway, one removes one's shoes and enters into the courtyard of the tomb. Before and after the actual *ziyarat*, people may linger here simply for conversation or a quiet place to relax.

There is a prescribed etiquette for behavior at shrines. When people enter the shrine, they enter on the right foot and may not actually touch the threshold with their foot since pilgrims often kiss the floor at that point. The pilgrims then circumambulate the tomb. They may stop at the "head" to touch the grave, or possibly sit at the "heart" side of the grave to read the Quran or other religious literature. Qurans are often kept in the shrine so they can be used by pilgrims during their *ziyarat*.

Pilgrims perform a variety of actions within the tomb. The basic *adab* (ritual propriety) of the shrine requires that the pilgrim greet the saint, recite some brief *suras* and *darud*, and then after first asking permission of the saint, depart, backing out to show re-

Rustem Pasa Caravanserai

spect. A great variety of activities also occur within the shrine proper. Some pilgrims may sit and read large portions of the Quran. Some simply sit in the presence of the saint. Some pilgrims may even enter into an ecstatic state. Sufi orders may come into the tomb to perform acts of devotion. At some tombs bridegrooms come to acquire blessings for their marriage on their wedding night. Pilgrims may present their sick children so that the saint might heal them.

Upon completing the *ziyarat*, pilgrims walk back through the same environment through which they crossed to enter the tomb. Along the way they may distribute alms. For many, the presence of the saint has reaffirmed devotional allegiance, both to the Prophet and the *auliya*, in a way that has reinvigorated their faith. They have also reaffirmed their belief in Allah, the ultimate source of the power of the saint.

Ordinary social and religious rules are subsumed under an overarching *adab* of personal allegiance to the saint who is seen as a proxy for the Prophet. Thus, a variety of activities that ordinarily might not be regarded as normative are sanctioned at the site of the shrine. This aspect of *ziyarat* can, at first glance, make these journeys seem deceptively nonreligious. There is an element of tourism in the act of *ziyarat*. The Pakistan Tourism and Development Corporation has even published a brochure, called *Journey into Light*, on arranging tours of spiritual places. In the city of Multan, soda stands, cafes, snake charmers, and a rather large amusement park surround the tombs of Bahauddin Zakariyya and Ruknuddin i-Alam. After performing *ziyarat* at the shrine, one can always go for a ride on the bumper cars or watch television on a huge outdoor screen.

But these visits do not simply constitute "spiritual tourism," even though elements of them may appear that way. Shrines remain places of deep religiosity. While certain aspects of *sharia* may be relaxed, for example, men and women may mix more freely than in ordinary circumstances; *adab* or ritual courtesy and propriety is taken very seriously. There are proper ways to enter a tomb and proper ways to behave when inside. The reason behind this concern for proper etiquette lies in the belief that the saint is actually present in the tomb. Like the corollary belief in the spiritual existence of the Prophet, the notion that the saint is present in the tomb is taken quite literally. *Ziyarat* is a visit to the court of a spiritual ruler, and like any visitation to a noble and powerful person, one must observe the rules of proper respect and conduct.

Urs and *Mawlid*

Among the most popular events that occur at Sufi shrines are *urs* and *mawlid*. *Mawlids* take place on the birthday of the saint. *Urs* is an old Arabic word meaning wedding, and the *urs* takes place on the anniversary of the saint's death in order to commemorate the marriage of the saint to his true beloved, God. All sorts of activities occur in the vicinity of the shrine during the period of time leading up to the actual anniversary. The number of pilgrims increases dramatically. Processions in honor of the saint are held. Religious music is performed, and people may enter into a "trance" and dance ecstatically. *Murids* come to offer special devotions. Wandering sufis, called *malangs* or *faqirs*, come dressed in colorful clothing, singing songs and playing percussion instruments. Merchants set up stalls to sell religious paraphernalia and other goods. In some parts of the world, circuses and fairs take place during the *urs*. In Pakistan and India, these fairs, called *melas*, are major attractions. Circuses travel from *mela* to *mela*, bringing with them such attractions as acrobats, midway rides, freak shows, transvestite performers, and motorcycle daredevils. In Egypt, the tomb of Sayyid Ahmad Badawi in Tanta is similarly the site of a major fair. During his *mawlid*, the various Sufi orders, who throughout the year hold regular *dhikr* in the tomb following Friday prayers, take part in processions that travel through the streets in the environs of the shrine.

The complex variety of activities that occur at Sufi tombs often make it difficult for the outside observer to make sense of these shrines as Islamic holy places. Indeed, some Muslims (and non-Muslim scholars of Islam) question to what extent these activities at Sufi tombs can be considered truly Islamic. Within these kinds of celebrations, scholars have identified the survival of pre-Islamic activities, particularly in South Asia where events at the meals often resemble certain pre-Islamic Hindu and Buddhist festivals. But the people who attend these celebrations are not thinking of the Buddha or Hindu gods when they celebrate the presence of the *auliya*. They have come to express their commitment to Allah and Muhammad. On one level, it really doesn't matter if some of the processions that take place at Sufi shrines in south Asia have their origins in centuries-old Buddhist processions. They are now Muslim processions where individuals may express their sense of devotion and commitment in a local setting and a vernacular language to express universal values and feelings.

♦ DEVOTIONAL LIFE IN PRACTICE

Questions about the legitimacy of *ziyarat* are part of a larger debate over the propriety of popular Islamic practices and beliefs. *Ziyarat* to Sufi shrines is only one manifestation of the tendency within Islam to emphasize devotional allegiance to the Prophet and his "legitimate successors." It is interesting to note that the strongest opposition to *ziyarat* and other popular Islamic practices comes from those same Muslim organizations who refute belief in the continuing presence of the Prophet.

Most Muslims participate to some degree or other in popular devotional activities in addition to the normal practices. They understand their actions to be firmly consistent with a larger tradition of Islamic piety going back to the Prophet and his Companions. Their position is often at odds with certain "rationalist" and "fundamentalist" tendencies within the Islamic world, which have attempted to characterize such acts of devotion as "un-Islamic." But educated defenders cite the Quran and *hadith* to support their position, and consider such practices as *ziyarat* to be a logical extension of devotion to God and the Prophet.

There are other Muslims less radical in their criticism of *ziyarat*. These Muslims accept the validity of some beliefs and practices but object to others, especially activities associated with shrine visitation: fairs, carnivals, music, and so on. They may accept the existence of the *awliya*, although often they tend to honor them primarily for their contribution in converting non-Muslims. They are likely to point out the dangerous possibility of *shirk*, associating others with God in saint veneration and objecting to the experience of trance and spiritual intoxication that takes place as a result of devotional acts at the shrines.

Indeed some people become spiritually intoxicated at the shrines. Spiritual intoxication has always been controversial in Islam. Those who argue for the permissibility of intoxication argue that, in the presence of one's beloved, one does not always behave according to ordinary rules. One follows the heart. They see this as the natural and acceptable result of devotion. Persian and Arabic sources give examples of people so consumed by their love of Allah or the Prophet that they behaved in unusual ways.

As for the more secular singing, dancing, and general celebration that occur at the shrines, these should again be seen as part of the piety of devotional allegiance. The question must be asked to what extent Muslims are expected to reflect gloomy dispositions in the practice of their faith. People at the shrines are often very happy. After all, many of them have come because a personal wish has just been fulfilled. Their sick children have become well. They have given birth to a son. They have done *ziyarat* to say thank you to the saint and to God. It is thus not surprising that they would be in a celebratory mood.

On a more metaphysical level there is a sense of great spiritual elevation in being in the presence of the *awliya*. The *awliya* are men (and occasionally women) who have achieved a proximity to Allah and his Prophet that most people can only dream of. Thus, the encounter with the saint that lies at the center of *ziyarat* is considered a blessing. It makes people feel fulfilled. In the saint's presence (and in his name) people distribute food to the poor, recite the Quran, recite *darud*, and so on. When asked whether or not gatherings by women to read miracle stories were an innovation, a Shia religious leader replied that it did not matter if they were or not. As he put it: women come together, they pray, they tell stories of the *ahl al-bayt*, and they distribute food in their name. Since all of these elements of these gatherings are recommended actions, how can one criticize them? This seems to represent the attitude of many Muslims toward such practices. It may not be rooted in the normative *sharia*, but it does resonate with the core values of Islam, and, as such, represents an important aspect of piety among Muslims that complements the observance of other established acts of devotion.

Vernon James Schubel

♦ MUHARRAM CELEBRATIONS IN INDIA: A CASE STUDY

The rituals and art associated with Muharram celebrations are linked to deeply held sentiments that have been decisively shaped by historical facts and the memories and expressions evoked by past events. The event that has given rise to its central passion is the martyrdom of Imam Husain, the grandson of the Prophet Mohammad. Muharram commemorates the cause and passion of Imam Husain at Karbala where he and members of his family were massacred in the year 680 by the army of Yazid, a despotic ruler in the year 680. The tragedy of Karbala has become one of the most powerful narratives in the history of Islam. It has captured the imagination of Muslims in many parts of the world and has been integrated into devotional practices, art, and architecture.

Every year during the month of Muharram Shia Muslims relive the tragedy and are joined by Sunni Muslims who also participate in this event as a symbol of the victory of Islam against evil and injustice. Alhough the Muharram celebration is generally regarded as a Shia observance, most Muslims and a large number of the Hindus in India commemorate the martyrdom of Imam Husain. Hundreds of *taziyas*, votive mausoleums for Imam Husain, are made and buried every year. The *ganga-jamuni* (gold and silver), stone, wooden trellises of Imam Husain's *zareehs* (symbolic sarcophagi) are covered with colored threads and locks of hair, in the hope that misfortunes will be erased and

aspirations fulfilled. Many folkloric practices from India and elsewhere have been integrated into the observance and express a variety of devotional sentiments. In the Shia tradition ritual art is placed near the shrines of the martyrs where they accumulate and decompose or are given back to the elements; Other objects are then made to take their place. It is the performance of this rite that is critical to Shia, not the objects.

Taziya is manifested in various forms across the Islamic world. It signifies an act of mourning for the death, but has come to be exclusively connected with the martyrdom of Imam Husain. In Iran the *tazia* is represented as a passion play where the tragedy of Karbala is acted out. In India it is manifested in architecture, generally in the form of votive artifacts symbolizing the tomb of Imam Husain. This tradition is particularly common in north India, and it is more popular among Sunnis. *Taziyas* are taken out in processions on the tenth day of Muharram, the day of the massacre, known also as *Ashura*, during which they are buried at the local *Karbalas*.

On the day of *Ashura*, *tabuts* (biers) of Husain are carried by the Shia to the local *Karbalas*. At intervals the processions halt and elegies are recited; some mourners flagellate themselves with knives and blades. The bloody deeds of Karbala are reenacted through mock burials and funeral themes.

The Muharram procession passes through streets and public squares with the participants weeping and beating their chests while reciting the saga of Karbala. This is a common form of expression during Muharram that reminds the devotees of the persecution endured by the Imam and his family.

A white, riderless horse representing the horse of Imam Husain, Duldul, is an important feature of the Muharram procession. It is a reminder of the experience of the women, who, while waiting in the camp during the original battle of Karbala, witnessed the riderless horse and were made aware of their loss.

The symbol of the hand represents the concept of Panj-tan-i-Pak, the five members of the household of the Prophet revered by the Shia, the "Pure Ones": Muhammad, Fatima, Ali, Hasan and Husayn. The swords and shields generally found on the *alam* emerge from the many stories glorifying the bravery of Ali, Hasan, and Husain.

Shiism came to India mainly through Iran, and over time the commemoration of Muharram developed its own indigenous framework. The *pahar* (literally a mountain) is an example of the influence of an Iranian model, an extension of Imam Husayn's *tabut*, (bier). The *pahar*, as the name suggests, is the mountainous weight of Imam Husayn's sacrifice which the believers carry on their shoulders. The immense weight of the *pahar* requires scores of people to carry it.

Family Imambara, Lucknow

Main Zareeh, Shahi Imambara, Calcutta

Ma'tam, the Bohra community of Pune

Effigies of Umar ibn Saad, the commander-in-chief of Yazid's army at Karbala, Lucknow

Punja, detail of Shia alam at Haji Karbalai Imambara, Calcutta

Sipar, Ashura procession, Shiekhpura, Bihar

Duldul, the horse of Imam Husain, Amroha

Offerings of clay horses to Imam chowks, Bengal

Asafiya Imambara, Lucknow

Husainabad Imambara Mosque, Lucknow

Tabut procession, Amroha in Uttar Pradesh

Pahar, Khambat, Gujerat

Bare Baba, the horse of Imam Husain, Indore

Imambara, Hooghli

Nade Ali, a detail from a Shia banner, Calcutta

Alam, representation of Imam Husain's standard, symbolizes the Shia faith

Tazia procession, Jaipur

Nade Ali, wood carving from Kashmir

Scene from Karbala, Bara-imambara, Meerut

The architecture of *imambara*, an addition to the religious architecture of Indian Islam, owes it beginning to the rituals associated with Muharram. *Imambara*, the house of the Imam, acquired complex dimensions and meanings during the rule of the Nawabs of Oudh in the eighteenth and nineteenth centuries. Besides symbolizing a shrine of Imam Husayn, with the *zareeh* (sarcophagus) of Imam Husayn as its central element, it was also built as the burial place of the Nawab.

In Lucknow, which is one of the centers of Shiism in India, there are hundreds of *imambaras*. Every family has its own *imambara*, normally just a part of a room or a model. Wealthier families have rooms set aside as *imambaras*, richly decorated with silver *zareehs* and *alams*. In addition, every neighborhood has its own *imambara*, and the Nawabs have their own. The Asafiya, built by Nawab Asafuddaulla (1775–98), and the Husainabad *imambara*, built by Nawab Mohammad Ali Shah (1837–42), are two nationally protected monuments of India.

The Shah Najaf *imambara*, build by Gihazi-uddin Haider (1814–27), is dedicated to the first imam, Ali who is buried at Najaf in Iraq. At the center of the building is the grave of Ghazi-uddin.

Imam Husain's horse, Duldul, is one of the many actors in Karbala celebrations that has developed its own iconography. Imageries of Karbala are vivified in various Muharram rituals and objects by the Shia the Sunni as well as participating Hindus. Each form and rite has its source in deeply rooted local myths and traditions. Votive horses are common features of Indian sacred folk art. Their presence provides the link between the perishable earth and heaven, and they are the symbols of protection in villages. Duldul, in the legends of Karbala, symbolizes courage and devotion. The brave horse stood undauntedly alongside its master, Imam Husayn, for the cause of Islam and justice. Such images are presented mainly by the Sunni community and the Hindus of Bengal.

This short, illustrated essay gives a glimpse of the complex symbolism and the intricate dimensions of Muharram in India. It provides an opportunity to look at the devotional aspects of Muslim life in India to illustrate the convergence of local tradition and vernacular art. The martyrdom of Imam Husian reflects its appropriation by different people for different reasons. In that way it provides alternative means of devotional expression outside the boundaries of traditional Muslim practice. It offers a dimension in Muslim practice where devotional expression links local tradition with the universal themes of Islam and of sacrifice, divine justice and compassion.

Shakeel Hossain

References

Currie, P.M. *The Shrine and Cult of Muin al-Din Chisti of Ajmer.* Delhi: Oxford University Press, 1989.

Hodgson, Marshall. *The Venture of Islam. Vol. 1, The Classical Age of Islam.* Chicago: University of Chicago Press, 1974.

Qureshi, Regula. *Sufi Music of India and Pakistan: Sound, Context and Meaning in Qawwali.* Cambridge and New York: Cambridge University Press, 1986.

Reeves, Edward B. *The Hidden Government: Ritual, Clientelism, and Legitimation in Northern Egypt.* Salt Lake City: University of Utah Press, 1990.

Schimmel, Annemarie. *Mystical Dimensions of Islam.* Chapel Hill: University of North Carolina Press, 1975.

———. *And Muhammad is His Messenger: The Veneration of the Prophet in Islamic Piety.* Chapel Hill: University of North Carolina Press, 1985.

Schubel, Vernon James. *Religious Performance in Contemporary Islam: Shii Devotional Rituals in South Asia.* Columbia, South Carolina: University of South Carolina Press, 1993.

Sharif, Jafar. *Islam in India, or the Qanun-i Islam. Translated by G.A. Herklots.* Oxford University Press, 1921; reprint ed., London: Curzon, 1975.

Subhan, John A. *Sufism: Its Saints and Shrines.* New York: Samuel Weiser, 1970.

Waugh, Earle H. *The Munshidin of Egypt: Their World and their Song.* Columbia, South Carolina: University of South Carolina Press, 1989.

⑲

Spiritual Life and Institutions in Muslim Society

♦ Early Sufi Leaders ♦ The Friends of God ♦ Sufi Orders ♦ The Modern Period

Muslim spiritual life takes its orientation from the Quran and the Prophet Muhammad. As an example, one may cite the famous Quranic passage on "the Night of Power," commonly regarded as the night on which the revelation of the Quran was delivered to the Prophet: "The Night of Power is greater than a thousand days. The angels and the spirit descended upon it, with the permission of their Lord, with every command" (Quran 97:3–4). The act of revelation as a descent of the spirit, and the corresponding movement of the ascension of the Prophet through the heavens to meet God, became the spiritual model for later generations of Muslims. The first examples of organized spiritual life in Muslim circles were formed around outstanding individuals such as Al-Hasan al-Basri (died 728) and Sufyan al-Thawri (died 778) who brought a pietistic intensity and an ascetic impulse to their meditation upon the meaning of the Quranic scripture. These early figures certainly had an impact on their contemporaries through public preaching and through their writings, and they drew attention to the need for psychological introspection and moral analysis as part of obedience to the commands of God. The first centuries of the Muslim era did not, however, produce formal social structures around these figures of notable piety. When modern scholars speak of a "School of Basra" or a "School of Baghdad" in early Muslim spirituality, it is more of a trend than an organized movement. These leaders formed relations with followers and associates that were informal and highly personal, a pattern that would endure until the formation of organized Sufi "orders" in the twelfth century. Perhaps the only exception to this observation was the retreat for devotees established by the Basran Abd al-Wahid ibn Zayd (died 794) at Abbadan in the Persian Gulf. While it is

possible that Christian or Manichaean monastic communities furnished models for this type of retreat, Muslim spiritual circles used a religious vocabulary based entirely on Arabic and Islamic sources. The figure of the Shia imam, Jafar al-Sadiq (died 765), also emerges in this early period as a model for future mystical teaching and leadership.

♦ EARLY SUFI LEADERS

The outstanding figures of the ninth and tenth centuries, such as Abu Yazid al-Bistami, Junayd al-Baghdadi (died 910) and others, later became known retrospectively as the central organizers of the Sufi movement. The term *Sufi* (from the Arabic word for wool) described their custom of wearing rough woolen cloaks in imitation of the prophets and holy ones of the past (and in deliberate contrast to the luxurious fabrics of court dress). The two regions of Baghdad (capital of the Abbasid caliphate) and northeastern Iran (or Khurasan) were the two most active centers of Sufism. Junayd's one-time disciple al-Hallaj (died 922) became the center of controversy because of his public proclamation of mystical attainments, and he was cruelly executed after a highly politicized trial. Awareness of tension between mystical experience and more conservative interpretations of Islam led to a series of writings that may be termed apologetic, defenses of the Islamic credentials of Sufism. By the beginning of the eleventh century, a number of Arabic texts had been written as guides to Sufism, summarizing the scriptural basis of Muslim spirituality and the psychological techniques of Sufi meditation. These texts also furnished a biographical and historical concept of Sufism in which early ascetics and pious leaders were viewed as a series of masters and disciples who safeguarded and

Al-Aqsa Mosque, Jerusalem, traditionally associated with the Prophet's ascent or miraj, alluded to in the Quran.

transmitted a mystical knowledge that had originated with the Prophet. Sufism was presented as parallel to the standard Islamic religious sciences to which it added the internal knowledge of divine realities.

Sufi leaders increasingly were associated with residential hospices (Arabic *ribat* or *zawiya;* Persian *khanqah*), an institution first developed in Iran by a puritanical religious movement known as the Karramiyya. Abu Said ibn Abu al-Khayr (died 1049) established such a center for Sufis in Iran with codes of conduct for the guidance of novices. Newly arrived Muslim rulers such as the Seljuk Turks found it attractive to sponsor the construction and upkeep of hospices along with academies (*madrasas*) for the teaching of the Islamic religious sciences. These hospices typically were places for prayer, the study of the Quran, meditation, and communal meals where travelers and the needy were welcome. Sufi masters would impart instruction and advice to their students and to visitors. Some hospices like the Said al-Suada in Cairo (founded by Saladin in 1173) depended entirely on royal patronage. Other hospices had a broad clientele among the artisan classes from which many of the Sufi masters came. The hospice of Ruzbihan Baqli (died 1209) was built in Shiraz in 1165 by stonemasons who were among his followers.

Yet the need of political leaders for religious legitimation put pressure on the new Sufi institutions to become part of the state patronage apparatus, typically through accepting endowment with land-tax income. Thus, by 1281 the Mongol rulers of Iran set up an endowment for the previously independent hospice established by Ruzbihan, in this way linking its fortunes with the state. In India the residences of Sufi masters of the Chishti order were typically one large room where everyone lived and pursued their discipline, unlike the multiple private cells of hospices in Syria and Iran. These "meeting houses" (*jamaat khanas*) tended to be supported, at least initially, by voluntary donations rather than fixed land income. In Turkey the hospices were known as *tekkes*. Because of hospitality regulations that required feeding and lodging guests for a limited time, the Sufi hospices became centers where members of different levels of society interacted with the Sufi master.

♦ THE FRIENDS OF GOD

The next noticeable institutional feature of Sufism was the tomb of the Sufi saint, which increasingly became a focus of local pilgrimage. The Sufi manuals had clarified the status of the "friend of Allah" or saint as one who is perfect in obedience to God and who is sustained by the love of God. The saints were seen as the invisible supports of the world, a hierarchy of holy men and women who were under God's protection, even after their death. In a hierarchical society where the average person had to approach authority through local notables, saints could be viewed as people with influence at the court of God. In this way saints became intercessors for those who approached them, both for everyday needs and at the Day of Judgment. This concept is based on the Quranic idea of *baraka*, meaning blessing, conferred by God on humankind. Particularly privileged individuals, such as the "friends of Allah," are believed to mediate this blessing for others.

The tombs of many Sufi saints were erected at or near their homes. Under Muslim law, the ownership and maintenance of these tombs fell to family members who may or may not have had any spiritual aspirations. The association of that space with the saint invested it with *baraka*. In subsequent generations, the devotion of many pilgrims created a class of hereditary custodians who were in charge of the finances and operations of the tomb-shrines. These operations often were combined with a functioning hospice where Sufi teaching took place or with other institutions such as mosques or *madrasas*. Increasingly, however, the Sufi tomb came to be an independent institution, in some cases functioning as the center of massive pilgrimage at the annual festival of the saint. These festivals were variously termed the saint's birthday (*mawlid*) in the Mediterranean region, or "wedding" (*urs*) in Iran and India. In the latter case the festival symbolically celebrated the death anniversary as the "wedding" of the saint's soul with God. The tombs of especially popular saints eventually were surrounded with royal burial grounds where kings and members of the nobility would erect their own tombs to acquire a borrowed holiness or to benefit in the afterlife from the pious exercises of pilgrims to the nearby saints. Examples of this kind of necropolis include the Sufi shrines of Khuldabad and Gulbarga in the Indian Deccan, Tatta in Pakistan, and the various graveyards of Cairo. At some Sufi shrines where the master's descendants did not possess the spiritual talent of their ancestor, dependence on royal support from land endowment made institutional Sufism into an arm of the government, what the Mughal emperor Jahangir called "the army of prayer." Numerous examples are known where the offspring of a Sufi master became government functionaries, as happened with the children and grandchildren of the leader of the Indian Shattariyya, Muhammad Ghawth. Institutionalized shrines added architectural features that incorporated the royal presence into the Sufi tomb itself. These features can be seen in royal

music galleries added to Chishti tombs in the Indian Deccan by eighteenth-century patrons. Secular court music would be played whenever the Nizam of Hyderabad chose to visit the shrines.

Sufi tombs and hospices also in many cases became cultural centers as well, where distinctive kinds of music and poetry were heard. The Arabic poetry of the noted Sufi poet Ibn al-Farid (died 1235) has been regularly recited at his tomb before mass audiences, particularly at his annual festival. Likewise, Indian Chishti shrines continue to be centers for recitation of poetry in musical sessions (*sama*, now known as *qawwali*). At major festivals, such as the *urs* of Baba Farid in Pakistan, one can hear dozens of singers compete for the honor of singing before the saint's tomb, mixing lyrics in Persian with verses in Hindi, Punjabi, Sindhi, and other Indian languages. Special local traditions of music developed in Turkish hospices and shrines with poetry of a style quite different from court poetry. Performance styles at musical sessions included the measured dance of the Mevlevi Sufis or "whirling dervishes." In North Africa, other distinctive musical styles developed in the Sufi shrines using Galenic humoral physiological theories to effect healing based on bodily sympathies of particular musical modes.

◆ SUFI ORDERS

The most decisive institutional formation of Sufism was the establishment and formalization of Sufi orders. A number of outstanding personalities of the twelfth and thirteenth centuries lent their names to associations that developed individual spiritual methods or "ways" (*tariqas*), including special formulations of the names of God for meditative repetition (*dhikr*). Each of these associations became known as a "way" or a "chain" (*silsila*), with masters and disciples constituting the links. Chains were plotted backward in time to end ultimately with the Prophet Muhammad as the final human figure. Some chains are duly depicted with the angel Gabriel and God as the ultimate sources. Nearly all of these chains reach Muhammad via his son-in-law and cousin Ali. Frequently, there are parallel chains consisting of the early Shia imams, who are commonly revered in Sufi circles, even though the majority of Sufi orders have a Sunni orientation. A notable exception is the Naqshbandi order, which reaches the Prophet via Abu Bakr, and thus preserves an anti-Shia tonality unusual in Sufism. While it is convenient to refer to these organizations as "orders" with an implicit analogy to the monastic orders of Roman Catholicism (Franciscans, Dominicans, etc.), the analogy is inexact. Sufi orders are not monastic and much less centrally organized than their Roman Catholic counterparts, and they have a more fluid hierarchical structure that is for-

Zawiya of Idris II in Fez, Morocco, a center for Sufi gatherings and devotion.

mulated in terms of different types of initiations. Complicating the situation is the phenomenon of multiple initiation, observable since the sixteenth century, through which individual Sufis could receive instruction in the methods of various orders while maintaining a primary allegiance to only one. The major impact of the Sufi orders in terms of religion was to popularize the spiritual practices of the Sufis on a mass scale. The interior orientation of the informal movement of early Sufism became available to a much wider public through participation in shrine rituals, the circulation of hagiographies, the dispensing of various degrees of instruction in *dhikr* recitation, and membership in the *tariqa*. Elaborate initiation rituals developed in which the master's presentation of articles such as a dervish cloak, hat, or staff would signify the disciple's entrance into the order. A frequent feature of initiation was the requirement that the disciple copy out by hand the genealogical "tree" of the order, which would link the disciple to the entire chain of masters going back to the Prophet.

Some of the Sufi orders, such as the Qadiriyya

(named after Abd al-Qadir Jilani, died 1166), are spread throughout Islamic lands from North Africa to Southeast Asia. Others are more regional in scope, like the Shadhiliyya in North Africa (named after Abu al-Hasan al-Shadhili, died 1258), or the Chishtiyya in India and Pakistan (named after Muin al-Din Chishti, died 1236). Particular orders are known for distinctive practices, such as the loud *dhikr* recitation of the Rifaiyya, in contrast to the silent *dhikr* favored by the Naqshbandiyya. Some orders, including the Chishtiyya and the Mevleviyya, have integrated music and even

dance into their practice, while other orders resolutely shun these activities as distractions to spiritual training. Sometimes Sufi leaders, such as the early Chishti masters, tried to keep political power at arm's length, and they advised their followers to refuse offers of land endowments. Some Sufi masters would demonstrate their disdain of the world by refusing to entertain rulers or visit them at court.

On the other hand, certain orders have a history of close association with political power. The Suhrawardiyya and the Naqshbandiyya in India and

Ali Qapu Mosque, Iran.

Iran felt it was important to influence rulers in the proper religious direction, and the Bektashiyya had strong links to the elite Ottoman troops known as the Janissaries. The Safawiyya, once a moderate Sunni order based at Ardebil, became widespread among Turkish tribes on the Persian-Ottoman frontier, and it emerged with a strongly Shia and messianic character to become the basis for the Safavid empire that ruled Iran from the sixteenth through the eighteenth century. During the period of nineteenth-century colonialism when much of the Islamic world fell under European domination, Sufi institutions played a variety of roles. Hereditary custodians of Sufi shrines in places like the Indian Punjab were treated as important local landlords by colonial officials, and they became further entrenched as political leaders due to British patronage. Ironically, the cooperation of these Sufi leaders became essential in later independence movements directed against British control. Similarly, the Senegalese order known as the Muridiyya became heavily involved in peanut farming as a result of being favored by French colonial authorities, and they have emerged in the postcolonial order as a prominent social institution. With the overthrow of traditional elites by European conquest, Sufi orders in some regions remained the only surviving Islamic social structures, and they furnished the principal leadership for anti-colonial struggles in places such as Algeria, Libya, the Caucasus, and China. French administrators in North Africa viewed Sufi orders with suspicion, and colonial scholars produced studies of the Sufi orders designed to predict their possible resistance to or cooperation with official policies.

♦ THE MODERN PERIOD

In the post-colonial period, Sufi orders and institutions have an ambiguous position. Governments in many Muslim countries have inherited the centralized bureaucratic organization of their colonial predecessors, and, in countries like Egypt and Pakistan, efforts are made to subject the orders and shrines to government control. Officials frequently appear at Sufi festivals and attempt to direct popular reverence for saints into legitimation of their regime. Nonetheless, many of the liveliest Sufi organizations flourish without official recognition. Some contemporary movements and leaders attack Sufism with a virulence only slightly less intense than that which is reserved for anti-Western diatribes. Pilgrimage to Sufi tombs is frequently denounced as an idolatry that treats humans on the level of Allah. Sufi orders have been illegal in Turkey since the 1920s when Kemal Ataturk secularized the Turkish state. The performance of the Sufi rituals, such as the "whirling dervish" dance of the Mevleviyya and the

dhikr of the Istanbul Qadiriyya, is tolerated as a cultural activity and is exported abroad through touring companies and sound recordings. The tomb of the great Sufi poet Jalal al-Din Rumi, which many visitors treat as a shrine, is officially regarded as a museum. Sufi activities are not publicly tolerated in countries such as Saudi Arabia since Sufi leaders and tomb cults would constitute an unacceptable alternative to existing authority. Still, it is remarkable that the founders of certain modern Muslim movements, such as the Muslim Brotherhood in Egypt and the Jamaat-i Islami in India, were exposed to Sufi orders in their youth, and they seem to have adapted certain organizational techniques and leadership styles from Sufism. The main difference between these and other Sufi orders is that these movements have substituted ideology for Sufi spirituality in order to become mass political parties in the modern arena.

In recent years, Sufi orders have extended their influence into Europe and the Americas, and today there are branches of orders from India, Iran, North Africa, and Turkey active in major urban centers in many Western countries. Some groups derived from Sufi orders have only tenuous associations with Islam, and they present Sufism as a mystical universal religion that may be pursued through dancing and chanting without requiring the practice of ritual prayer or other duties of Islamic law. Other groups have more explicit relations with Islamic tradition, including even insistence on the clothing and customs of the order's country of origin. While it is too soon to predict the future of Sufism in the West, it seems certain that it will take on some aspects of modern American and European culture such as joint participation of men and women in contexts where gender separation was the norm in many premodern Muslim societies. At the same time, Sufism in the West strives to preserve many of the distinctive rituals and institutions of traditional Sufism. One notes that the tomb of Bawa Muhaiyuddin in Philadelphia has already become a place of pilgrimage. In any case, Sufi orders are surviving despite the restrictions of modern governments and the opposition of fundamentalists, and they continue to act as channels that both preserve the influence of saints of the past and make possible a more direct personal access to Allah and the Prophet through spiritual discipline.

Carl W. Ernst

References

Bowering, Gerhard. *The Mystical Vision of Existence in Classical Islam: The Quranic Hermeneutics of the Sufi Sahl At-Tustari (died 283/896)*. New York: Walter De Gruyter, 1980.

Chittick, William C. *The Sufi Path of Love: The Spiritual Teachings of Rumi*. Albany, N.Y.: State University of New York Press, 1983.

Corbin, Henry. *The Man of Light in Iranian Sufism*. Boulder, Colo.: Shambhala, 1978.

Farid al-din Attar. *The Conference of the Birds*. Translated by Afkham Darbandi and Dick Davis. New York: S. Weiser, 1984.

Gilsenan, Michael. *Saint and Sufi in Modern Egypt*. Oxford: Clarendon Press, 1973.

Hoffman-Ladd, Valerie. *Sufism, Mystics, and Saints in Modern Egypt*. Charleston S.C.: University of South Carolina Press, 1995.

Murata, Sachiko *The Tao of Islam: A Sourcebook on Gender Relationships in Islamic Thought*. Albany, N.Y.: State University of New York Press, 1992.

Reeves, E. B. *The Hidden Government: Ritual, Clientelism, and Legitimation in Northern Egypt*. Salt Lake City: University of Utah Press, 1990.

Schimmel, Annemarie. *Mystical Dimensions of Islam*. Chapel Hill, N.C.: University of North Carolina, 1975.

Sells, Michael. *Foundations of Islamic Mysticism*. Mahwah, N.J. Paulist Press, 1996.

Trimingham, J. Spencer. *The Sufi Orders in Islam*. Oxford: Oxford University Press, 1971.

Part VI:

Law, Order, and Society in Islam

20

Law, Society, and Governance in Islam

♦ Theoretical Considerations ♦ Practical Implications
♦ Major Legal Schools ♦ Islam and Social Transformation
♦ Self-Sufficiency of the Islamic Revelation in Providing Fundamental Principles

♦ THEORETICAL CONSIDERATIONS

Islam is a religion based on a system of principles and rules designed to achieve the betterment of humankind. Its object, as proclaimed in the Quran, is to steer aright the human race along the long road of life, the end and the beginning of which are made known to humanity through the revealed path of religion. While the human intellect can perceive and discern this visible world, they cannot, according to the Quran, penetrate unaided through the screen that veils the great beyond. Through revealed religion human beings are enabled to catch a glimpse of the invisible world, which is inaccessible to the limited human faculties in the phenomenal world.

In Islam, life on this earth is believed to be transitory. It is a place of passage leading to everlasting bliss or everlasting damnation in the hereafter. Whether one goes to the one or the other is dependent upon the nature of one's conduct in life, whether it is in obedience or in defiance of the commands of God, the Muslim Creator. For the Creator of humanity, the Lord of the entire universe, knows best what is to human advantage and to his/her disadvantage. Hence, Muslims are urged to obey God and follow the course he has established for humanity in all things.

It is with the aim of directing humanity to realize its potential moral and spiritual worth that Islam undertakes to create a divinely sanctioned system known as the *sharia*. *Sharia* refers to God's divine law. In the *sharia*'s popular use it indicates the religion of Islam because it embodies the Islamic revelation in practical application. Muslim jurisprudence has attempted to understand and elaborate details of the law by explaining the specifics of the *sharia*, justifying them by copious references to the revelation, discussing and debating them and ultimately recording them in their juridical corpus for posterity. Accordingly, it represents the culmination of a long and comprehensive process of legal formulation. It deals not only with questions of faith, but it also regulates morals and human relationships. An underlying principle in this law is the well-being of the community through the pursuit of the good and the avoidance of evil.

Such a divinely ordained system is constructed upon five pillars: creed, worship, sacred law, moral principles, and religious-temporal authority.

Creed is designed to improve and enrich the intellect and to rid it of idolatry, superstitious beliefs, and illusions. Worship assists in the reform of the spiritual life as well as keeps watch over the soul, and serves as a constant reminder of the last reckoning, lest the soul be led astray by temptations, evil desires, and passions. Sacred law is based upon one of the most prominent principles that it does not impose undue burdens and intolerable restrictions upon those believing in its precepts and abiding by its rules. It regulates divine-human and human interpersonal relationships, making known duties and safeguarding rights with the aim of establishing justice. Moral principles direct the human being toward ethical knowledge and the best of human accomplishments. Religious-temporal authority invests with the power of governance to preserve and maintain the public order built on the four other pillars, and to protect these pillars from infringements and tampering from within or without the Muslim community. In pursuance of this goal the governing institution, or ruling authority, has discretion to determine, according to time and circumstances, how the purposes of God might best be effected for the Islamic community.

One can draw two conclusions from these theoretical considerations:

First, according to the Quran, the lawgiver is God who reveals the law through his prophets. Muhammad is the messenger through whom Allah transmitted the *sharia*, that is, the religious-moral norms necessary for the creation of the ideal Muslim society. These norms are communicated to the community through two channels:

First, the Quran is regarded by Muslims as the word of God, both in letter and spirit. The Quran is the source of law from which the fundamental principles employed in deducing particular legal decisions are derived.

Second, the *sunna* ("pattern of conduct" or "tradition") is transmitted through reports about the Prophet Muhammad's conduct with teachings and precepts, heard and/or witnessed by the companions who lived with him and related his teachings and precepts to succeeding generations through a chain of authenticated sources going back to the Prophet or the other members of the early Muslim community.

The *sunna* performs three crucial functions in the implementation of the *sharia*. First, it expounds the Quran by providing the intent of the divine synoptic account of revelation. Second, it elaborates the circumstantial and practical rulings not to be found in the Quran but already partially disclosed in the beliefs and practices of various religious groups. Third, the *sunna* supplies rights, duties, commands, and prohibitions derived in conjunction with the fundamental principles laid down in the Quran. The relation between the *sunna* and the Quran may be considered analogous to that of the current U.S. statute laws and the Constitution. The laws formulate in detail what the Constitution has laid down in general terms. The *sunna* thus supplies all that has been treated in most general terms in the Quran.

The second conclusion is that any power within the sovereignty of Islam is an executive and not a legislative power. When the Prophet is described as a lawgiver, he is regarded as the instrument that God used in transmitting his law to humanity. In this sense, the Prophet is essentially the authority that the prescriptive legislation will emanate from. Ultimately, the Quran being Islam's organic law in the large, its contents cannot be altered in any way.

◆ PRACTICAL IMPLICATIONS

The *sharia*, as the divinely ordained blueprint for human conduct, is a self-contained system, all-comprehensive and all-embracing. It encompasses all aspects of human life, on the individual as well as collective level in matters of faith, worship, human relations, and in personal and public rights. All avenues of life, whether political, economic, or any other, fall within its sphere of jurisdiction, for Islam ministers to the whole human and sees to material as well as to spiritual needs. Islam leads humans who are willing to be led. As the Quran says: "Let him then who will, believe; and let him who will, be an infidel" (Quran 18:29).

Islam, through its respect for the revelation given to the Prophet Muhammad and toward the wisdom granted to each generation of leadership, has made allowances for scholarly interpretation. It recognizes the fact that the road revelation has outlined for humanity is broad and multi-laned, and, as is, must be protected from deviation and violation. Hence, the application of Islamic legislation demands that revelation must be understood in letter as well as in spirit. This understanding requires *ijtihad* (independent judgment on a legal or theological question) by the *mujtahids* (those who reflect and exert these faculties). The exercise of one's individual judgment in the derivation of a judicial decision in the interpretation of Islamic principles and fundamentals, although defined by authoritative texts and governing rules, can produce agreement only insofar as general principles and broad outlines are concerned. There are numerous ways of understanding the texts, the intent of the legislator, of drawing analogies, and of applying the rules of discretion and preference regarding certain points where there is no fixed and clearly defined text.

◆ MAJOR LEGAL SCHOOLS

From the middle of the eighth century, a number of juristic scholars emerged whose independent interpretations of the words and actions of the Prophet Muhammad stimulated the development of separate legal schools in Islam. Islamic jurisprudence became a highly technical process, and disputes about method and judicial opinions crystallized into various legal schools designated by the names of prominent jurists.

The legal school that followed the Iraqi tradition was called "Hanafi," after Abu Hanifa (died 767). The Hanafi school is known for its endorsement of reason and logic as legitimate sources in the application of rules to the practical questions of life. Abu Hanifa's unusual ability to broaden the juristic practice with the use of analogy and "juristic preference" allowed Hanafi jurists to carry out meticulous investigation of legal sources to formulate their juridical decisions.

Those who adhered to the rulings of Malik ibn Anas (died 795) were known as "Malikis." In his legal formulations Malik depended upon the well-established practice of the early associates of the Prophet in Medina. Although in his legal doctrines he was bound by the *sunna* of Medina, he also utilized analogical deduction in cases not treated in the Quranic revelation to arrive at a rule. Maliki jurists regard "juristic preference" and "public interests" as valid sources of juridical decisions.

Muhammad ibn Idris al-Shafii (died 820) founded the "Shafii" legal school whose influence spread widely in the Muslim world. The Shafii school was the result of a synthesis conducted by a single scholar who was thoroughly familiar with the doctrines of the Maliki and Hanafi schools. Shafii adopted the essential thesis of the Malikis regarding the centrality of the Medina legal opinions as a juridical source. From the Hanafis he accepted the role of independent sound judgement and used it as a tool for analogical inference in his legal theory. Shafii's contribution lies in his magnificent synthesis of legal theory in Islamic jurisprudence.

Another school was associated with Ahmad ibn Hanbal (died 855) who compiled a work on the *sunna* that became the source for juridical decisions of the "Hanbalis." His juridical decisions are part of his monumental work on traditions that contains more than forty-thousand reports on various topics, not necessarily all legal. This compilation has become the source for juridical decisions undertaken by later Hanbali jurists.

Of other Muslim groups, the Twelver Shia, also known as the "Jafaris" after their leading authority Jafar al-Sadiq (died 748), were the only ones to generate a continuous and creative juristic tradition through a systematic reinterpretation and reevaluation based on the application of reason by the leadership in each generation. Besides the Quran and the *sunna* as sources for deriving religious practice, Shia legal theorists regarded human reason as an equally decisive basis in determining the scope of divine purposes for humanity. They believed that natural reason guides a person to ethical knowledge and can objectively determine good and evil as rational categories. However, for the Shia, reason needed to provide a more categorical verdict on religious injunctions. Such a verdict, in their minds, could only be derived from an absolute religious authority resembling that of the Prophet and his legitimate successors, the Shia imams or their representatives. Hence, in practice, the role of reason was confined to establishing the requirements of Quranic revelation in extracting the general principles from the Quran and the *sunna* and inferring rulings in particular cases through the use of reason. Besides the Quran and the *sunna*, the Shia saw reason as a valid source for judicial decisions that are deduced from Quranic revelation. In the Sunni jurisprudence, consensus of Muslim jurists does occupy a decisive status. The Shia jurists accepted consensus as evidence only if it included an infallible leader's opinion, sometimes transmitted by associates who had participated in reaching a consensus. Otherwise, consensus lacked authoritativeness for deducing law. The authority of the imam's utterances was so central to the decision-making process in jurisprudence that even when independent reasoning was admitted as a valid intellectual process in deducing judicial decisions, it was perceived as reasoning based on revelation, not simply on intellect and, as such, was regarded as valid.

Leading Sunni and Shia jurists remain committed to an interpretive task of developing and justifying the essentially religious sources based on Quranic revelation by demonstrating its continuity and its relevance to the concrete situations in the life of the community today.

The problem facing the contemporary Muslim community is to find ways of reconciling the basic concept of Islam to a modern world given that Islam, as creed and institution, is ideally to remain forever fixed and unaltered. Any authority professing Islam can be an executive authority only, not a legislative one. How can the community reconcile their belief in a doctrine that is perceived to be timeless and immutable with the needs of a human society that is developing. Life does not assume one fixed pattern for all times and places, without change or evolution. Will Islam adapt itself to the life of humankind in its development and change to keep pace with progress, or remain forever fixed?

♦ ISLAM AND SOCIAL TRANSFORMATION

Islam recognizes development in humanity through ideas, beliefs, values and attitudes, and morals and mores in material aspects and needs of life. Correspondingly it insists on the fixed nature of the revealed religions determined by fixed texts. Islam in itself is not subject to change since its original sources or texts are preserved and fixed, and any deviation therefrom or neglect or misapplication thereof in no way affects them. People's understanding of Islam may develop and change as a result of reassessment and new applications, necessitating a reconsideration of interpretations to be conducted in order to discover the design and purpose of God.

This need was recognized by the Prophet himself who termed this process a regeneration of the state of religion. He declared: "God sends to this community at the turn of each century someone who will regenerate its religion." The term "regeneration" is understood to mean purification of the Islamic faith from all the spurious innovations that have disfigured its original, pure features, and also the revival of binding duties and commendable actions that have been forgotten or forsaken.

To lead people to perform their individual as well as collective duties upon which the security and well-being of the Islamic community rests is a regeneration of

Islamic thought and practice. When Muslims are enmeshed in their own affairs and pleasures or are too distracted by internecine strife and passions to rush to the rescue of the community, the righteous authority must be the one to urge the people to fight a *jihad* (or holy war) against aggression to protect the country. As such, the authority is engaged in the "regeneration" of the faith, having similarly the right and power to meet new situations or developments in the society. Regeneration can also mean having the authority to wage *jihad* against superstition, prejudice, and stultification of human faculties.

Islam has provided humankind with guidelines that are basic and fixed. There are, however, certain exceptional or emergency situations where these may be discretionary. Sometimes the suppression of truth may be the only way to public welfare salvation or to the rescue of others from oppressive injustice, or the seizure of another's wealth may also prove the only way to save a person and society from starvation, or a severe penalty administered by the judiciary may be indispensable to the establishment of law and order. In all these exceptional and temporary situations, Islamic law has made allowances. On the basis of the texts, Islamic jurisprudence has pronounced that certain situations may legitimize certain prohibited actions to such an extent as to alleviate a given situation.

In the area of social legislation, Islamic law prohibits adultery because it undermines family life, corrupts it, and brings in its wake untold tragedies and evils as well as moral and physical harm. Any behavior or situation that might facilitate adultery is also prohibited. For instance, a man may not stay with a woman unrelated to him if alone, or a woman may not travel with a man unless she is in the company of her husband or any of her male relatives not legally a potential husband. Such a ruling is regarded as immutable because it is based on natural instincts that do not change. Similarly, a woman's modesty and decorum in her apparel and ornament has also been ordained. Women have been instructed to conceal their bodies from male eyes save those of their husbands or consanguine relatives. One of the basic principles indicated by the original texts of the law is the "blocking of expedients," that is, prevention of all that may lead to corruption and something virtually corrupt. That is why, also, the taking of small quantities of liquor, although not intoxicating, has been prohibited, for it may lead to more drinking, which is corruptive, not perhaps in the case of a certain person, but perhaps in the case of another.

In the legal as well as in the judicial system, Islamic law has dealt with two areas: the private law (civil and penal) and the public law consisting of its two divisions: the internal (constitutional, administrative, and financial) and external (international). The authoritative sources like the Quran and the *sunna*, provide the fundamental principles of the fixed kind that admits no change or transformation in human ideas or evaluations. The details and means of application are left to individual interpretation to fit developing temporal needs or interests, and the potential demands of time and place. The texts do not concern themselves with details or particulars or with matters of a secondary nature except when they prevent disagreement as in the rules dealing with inheritance, certain rules governing divorce, and the penalties for certain major crimes, which might have serious effects upon an Islamic society. These are known as *hudud* crimes (transgression of limits of the law for which sanctions are provided in the Quran). As for the punishments of other crimes, these have been left to the discretion of temporal authorities to be dealt with according to need and public interest. These are known as penalties of "chastisement" or "deterrence," since their purpose is to deter the offender himself or others from similar conduct. The guiding principle regarding this form of crime is that the punishment should fit the nature of the crime and the character of the offender. The broad purpose of *tazir* (deterrent) punishment is to prevent any conduct that would jeopardize the good order of the state. The state may intervene in cases of strictly civil nature.

The law has imposed impartiality in judgments strictly based on evidence, leaving the ways and means of achieving this end rather unspecified. It does not specify whether the judge should be one person or more, if there should be one or more levels of judicial administration, or whether different methods should be followed in different cases—one type for important cases, another for less important, a third for administrative justice, and a fourth still for civil or penal justice. There is one rule governing all the above, namely the "selection of the better course" or the "application of discretion" or "seeing fit" in legal decisions. The government invested with authority is to choose what fits the situation best, in accordance with time and place and that which is likely to achieve the desired end.

The same ruling applies to other aspects of life. For instance, in the area of constitutional affairs, Islam has laid down that the community should have a sovereign authority in charge of all its affairs, ruling in accordance with the revealed law. This is known as the legal doctrine of "governance in accordance with the *sharia.*" The sovereign in the management of all the affairs of state should always be prepared to consult the community and to listen to the representations of the community. Neither side is to act independently of the other or to impose its own point of view. This was the tradition of the early Muslim caliphs following the Prophet's death. However, the ways to assure such consultation and representation were not laid down in the texts for fear that if this had been done, they would have assumed a rigid form that might not have been flexible enough to adapt itself to varying future situations.

In public affairs the underlying rule was to work toward the achievement of the desired end. The Prophet cautioned against entrusting a public function to a certain person when there were others more qualified to discharge that specific function. This caution covers all functions connected with any type of public appointment or employment, even the elector's vote, which is given to a candidate whose success may not even depend upon that vote. What is important in this respect is not so much the methods used to achieve the end as the achievement of the end itself.

◆ SELF-SUFFICIENCY OF THE ISLAMIC REVELATION IN PROVIDING FUNDAMENTAL PRINCIPLES

Both the Quran and the *sunna,* are characterized by generalization and adaptability. They sketch the fundamental principles of the law as well as the ends it seeks to serve human interests in this world and the next without engaging in details and particulars. For instance, punishment by retaliation has been ordained to save lives. The pre-Islamic system of vengeance and blood-feud could potentially destroy the innocent as well as the guilty; retaliatory punishment inflicted on the murderer is, in consequence, more fair.

Muslims believe that the establishment of justice is to worship and fear God, for fear of God means the avoidance of anything that might incur God's wrath or displeasure, and this is perceived as injustice. The Prophet's saying "No harm and no harassment" illustrates the need for compensating every harm incurred.

These prescriptions have served as a basis for analogy in dealing with issues that are not covered in the Quran or *sunna.* Prohibition of the game of chance in the Quran is analogically extended to include all kinds of gambling, which have the same harmful consequences to society. Similarly, prohibition of cheating or fraudulence in contracts is stretched to include all kinds of deceit and fraud in human relationships.

Whether through personal interpretation or by the use of analogical deductions and inferences, Islamic law has the capacity to guide human activity. Finally, the role of custom and usage in the formulation of legal principles of every type is acknowledged by all Muslim jurists. Although their role is subordinate, serving only to explain contracts and other administrative measures, custom and usage define legal obligations and interpersonal commitments of every type. Custom assumes considerable importance in establishing the capability of the law to meet all legislative needs and to ensure necessary adaptability under changing and developing social mores. It is a basis in the enforcement of the law, without requiring a textual precedent to regulate each special case whether in matters pertaining to religion or to the everyday life of the community. When the Prophet was questioned about date-palm pollination, he responded, "You are more knowledgeable about your affairs of daily life." This response has served to encourage scientific and intellectual exploration in industry, agriculture, administration, and commerce under the guidance of the religious precepts of uprightness and integrity.

All human affairs for Muslims are thus circumscribed within a legal and juristic framework. There is no area in life that is not provided for by Islam. With each succeeding generation, jurists work out rules to meet any new situation. Over time, the corpus of Muslim jurisprudence has become an imposing structure capable of accommodating change, incorporating major theories and general principles by which particular cases can be determined and decided. With its flexible nature, resting as it does on malleable and not so rigid principles, Islamic law has provided for human activities and relations. This legal system is meant to be applicable at all times in appropriate contexts.

Muslim jurisprudence has been oriented toward serving the community with the aim of always giving the interest of the community precedence over that of individuals when the two come into conflict. The greater bulk of the judicial decisions have not been derived from definitive texts or formulated principles but rather have resulted from conclusions drawn by independent interpreters of the law. The basis for these conclusions is either legislative prototypes in the Quran or those set forth in the traditions of the Prophet, and appropriate historical precedence that can guide legal specialists in their exercise of discretionary judgment. But since these prototypes are limited, interpretations must be worked out to address cases as they arise.

An independent legal opinion formed by the discretionary method of *ijtihad* (independent judgment on legal or theological matters), not based on an authentic text but derived by logical inference, cannot be regarded as valid unless it has been logically deduced from premises supplied by Islamic law. The formulation of independent opinion should not be uniform, owing to the various guidelines that are followed for this purpose, and there is bound to be juristic differences as a consequence. These differences have served as a prolific resource for legislative enactments. They have also contributed to the progressive evolution of a vital Muslim jurisprudence.

In some cases, the jurists have even devised hypothetical cases for the purpose of finding legal solutions for them, considering that those cases might arise at a later date. As an illustration of how this might apply in a contemporary setting, consider the assumption of jurists that a woman may resort first to mechanical precautions against pregnancy or, secondly, may take a drug or a pill to postpone or delay it. By such methods, a married woman may protect herself against pregnancy. Translating the above instances into modern terms, judges have stated that the first mechanical method to prevent pregnancy, known as coitus interruptus (*azl* in Arabic), used traditionally to prevent pregnancy, corresponds to the modern devices such as IUDs used by women, or to devices used by men, such as condoms. The second resort mentioned in the legal decision is said to correspond to the contraceptive pill.

With the rise of Western hegemonic models of knowledge in the Islamic world and the emergence of secular educational systems that exclude traditional Islamic juristic structures and terminology in the nineteenth century, the indigenous intellectual activity in Islamic jurisprudence came to an abrupt halt. Shia centers of learning fared better than Sunni centers in pursuing new developments in legal theory, providing methods that were able to work through established political authority and effect changes that serve Muslim interests.

Muslim administrators and reformers alike were the catalysts that pushed Muslim jurists to rethink the sources of Islamic law so that independent legal decisions might respond to changing needs, particularly in cases concerned with human social relations and practices. The *sharia*, it was argued, ought to be practical, in the same way that Western codes of law are. The legal reform movement that began toward the end of the nineteenth century has advocated a new creative approach to independent reasoning as an important source of juridical decisions, a disregard of classical legal formulations, and an eclectic approach to tradition, as a whole. It is in the traditional practical areas of marriage, divorce, and inheritance that the influence of the *sharia* remains most pervasive. The magnitude of the achievement of modern Muslim states in creating and implementing their new legal structures is an achievement of immense importance and complexity. The history of Muslim jurisprudence has illuminated the way for the jurists and enabled them to exercise individual judgment guided by its sources. These judgments reflect a concern for the welfare of the Muslim communities. As new situations arise and societies and individuals encounter change, Muslim jurists are committed to base their decisions on Allah's law. Muslims all over the world ask how the heritage of the *sharia* can apply to their lives and seek answers on how their needs can be in accord with what they believe to be the appropriate response of their faith, Islam.

Abdulaziz Sachedina

References

Anderson, J. N. D. *Law Reform in the Muslim World.* London: Athlone Press, 1976.

Coulson, Noel J. *Conflicts and Tensions in Islamic Jurisprudence.* Chicago: University of Chicago Press, 1969.

Ghunaymi, Muhammad Talat al. *The Muslim Conception of International Law and the Western Approach.* The Hague: Mouton, 1969.

Kerr, Malcolm H. *Islamic Reform: The Political and Legal Theories of Muhammad Abduh and Rashid Rida.* Berkeley: University of California Press, 1966.

Little, D., John Kelsay, and Abdul-Aziz Sachedina. *Human Rights and the Conflict of Cultures.* Columbia, S.C.: University of South Carolina Press, 1988.

Mayer, Ann Elizabeth. "The Fundamentalist Impact on Law, Politics, and Constitutions in Iran, Pakistan, and the Sudan." In *Fundamentalisms and the State: Remaking Polities, Economies, and Militance.* Edited by Martin E. Marty and R. Scott Appleby, Chicago: University of Chicago Press, 1993.

Masud, Khalid. *Islamic Legal Philosophy: A Study of Abu Ishaq al Shatibi's Life and Thought.* Islamabad: Institute of Islamic Research, 1977.

Naim, Abd Allah Admad. *Towards an Islamic Reformation: Civil Liberties, Human Rights, and International Law.* Syracuse, N.Y.: Syracuse University Press, 1990.

Sachedina, A. A. *The Just Ruler (al-Sultan al-Adil) in Shiite Islam.* New York: Oxford University Press, 1988.

Ziadeh, Farhat. *Lawyers, The Rule of Law, and Liberalism in Modern Egypt.* Stanford, Calif.: Stanford University, 1968.

21

Islamic Law

♦ The Foundation of Islamic Law ♦ Development of Islamic Law ♦ Modern Developments

Muslim society has developed several approaches to define piety. Islamic law is one such approach; it stipulated that rules and regulations presumed to have been divinely revealed in the Quran are an ordained way of life for all Muslims. Mysticism, philosophy, theology, and esotericism also attempted to define Muslim life and these various approaches and have served to be mutually influential in religious spheres.

♦ THE FOUNDATION OF ISLAMIC LAW

Sharia, the Arabic term for Islamic law, literally means path or way to a water hole in the desert. Since many Arabs who lived during the time of the Prophet Muhammad were desert dwellers and/or were influenced by the ways of the desert, water and direction were essential to life. In the same vein, Muslim jurisprudence sees Islamic law as essential to Muslim life. The Quran explains that Allah has regulated the universe with certain laws (*sunna*). Laws that were revealed through his Prophets are referred to as the *sharia*. Like the *sunna*, the basic religious message (*din*) in these revelations is similar. Since the source of both *sunna* and *sharia* is the same, there is no perceived conflict between them for Muslims.

For Muslims obedience to Islamic law is voluntary. This approach to religion—obedience to revealed laws by choice and the surrender of individual will—is the essential meaning of Islam: submission.

Submission to Islamic law is accepted by Sufis, Muslim mystics, who stress complete surrender of individual will to the divine will of Allah. However, Sufis differ with the jurists (the most strict interpreters of the *sharia*) in their interpretation and understanding of *din* and *sharia*. Sufis insist that the legal approach focuses on external and formal meanings of religion, whereas the inner of spiritual meanings are quite different. Sufis acknowledge that, although *tariqa* (the

Sufi "way" or "path") represents a higher and ultimate approach, it cannot be completed without *sharia*.

The philosophical approach to religion in Islam focused on the inner meaning of revelation as understood by reason. A number of Islamic philosophers have borrowed extensively from Greek philosophy, trying to provide a rational framework for *sharia*. A group of them, known as *Ikhwan al-safa*, offered a complete system of philosophy of religion based on an understanding of inner meanings. The Ismailis, a branch of Shiism, who, according to some studies are identified with this group, also offer still an approach to *sharia*, that integrates the two aspects of faith.

The theological approach (*kalam*) focuses more on a strictly defined creed and belief and considers deeds as an outcome of that creed. Abu Hanifa's (died 767) treatise on creed was entitled *al-Fiqh al-Akbar* (*Greater Understanding*) and is an example of how Muslim theology and law is interconnected. During this period, law books also contained chapters on creeds, later, however, theological matters were separated from legal matters. The theological approach to religion rigorously prevailed among the Mutazila and Ithna Ashariyya (the Twelver Shia), who treat the question of *imam* (leader, religious authority) and related matters of creed as essential (*usul*, roots) and details about rituals and social life as secondary (*furu*, branches).

These approaches were not only in competition but were mutually influential. The literalist interpretation of Islamic law or *sharia* ultimately came to be accepted as the most fundamental expression of the Muslim faith. A more specific interpretation of Islamic law, though interpreted diversely in detail by various Muslim sects that recognize diverse methodologies, has been recognized as an essential component of the belief system.

The methodology of Islamic law has been opposed by the *hadith* scholars. The *hadith* (literally meaning "narration") comprises a record of the sayings or deeds of the Prophet Muhammad. Such scholars have insisted that only such narrations constituted exact law as it informed Muslims about the *sunna*, (the way) of the Prophet Muhammad, a model that every Muslim is obliged to follow. Other sources were to be regarded as mere conjecture or individual opinion. The legal approach insisted that law consisted in an understanding (*fiqh*). *Hadith* scholars saw the *fiqh* as being too conservative, literal and formalistic.

Islamic law has developed a system of classification of legal subject matters, categories and values of legal authority, and a methodology of legal reasoning. Those who adopted this approach were called *fuqaha* (jurist/scholars). They differed from *hadith* scholars who emphasized narrative precedents. The ensuing debate between them has given rise to the question of the definition and authenticity of sources. The jurists accept *hadith* as a source of law next to the Quran, but they differ with *hadith* scholars on the criterion of authenticity. The *fuqaha* insist on the application of analogical reasoning (*qiyas*) to rationalize Quran and *hadith* in order to extend their application to other cases. The *hadith* scholars disagree with rational analysis. The schools of law that emerged among the *hadith* scholars have denied the validity of this type of reasoning. The *hadith* approach was, however, influenced by the legal approach, as eventually all *hadith* literature came to be patterned on the model of *fiqh* books consisting of chapters on legal subject matters (i.e., Bukhari's (died 870) great work, *Al-Jami al-Sahih*).

Developed in this doctrinal context, Islamic law aims at total submission to God's will and consists of two parts, *sharia*, divinely revealed ordinances, and *fiqh*, interpretation of *sharia* by Muslim jurists. Islamic law expresses itself in three notable forums: courts, responsa, and texts and glosses.

◆ DEVELOPMENT OF ISLAMIC LAW

The history of Islamic law begins with the revelation of the Quran, which contains legal principles and injunctions dealing with such subjects as ritual, marriage, divorce, succession, commercial transactions, and penal laws. The Quran was revealed to the Prophet Muhammad gradually over a period of twenty-three years. An overview of the Quranic regulations reveals the following three principles of legislation: removal of hardship, limited obligations, and gradual introduction of laws. The Quran introduced two basic reforms in Arabian society. First, the pre-Islamic laws of inheritance, which were essentially patrilineal, were changed into fixed shares of inheritors, including female relatives. Second, the Quran altered the status of women, allowing women the right of property and transaction and enhanced their legal position within the family.

The Prophet Muhammad not only acted as the head of state in Medina, but also as arbiter and judge. After the Muslims conquered other territories, he appointed judges in these areas to enforce Muslim law. The Islamic system differed from the pre-Islamic tribal system, which rested on the agreement of the parties of dispute to accept a person as an arbiter. A Muslim judge derived authority by way of his appointment by the ruler. However, conflicts arose between some judges and caliphs. During the first two centuries of Islam, these conflicts resulted in the supremacy of *sharia* over the rulers. During subsequent periods, suggestions and attempts were made by rulers to permit them authority of interpretation and legislation, but jurists resisted such attempts. They even opposed the creations of uniform laws. Consequently, two parallel systems of law grew alongside each other: rules promulgated by the rulers, as well as the jurists' law.

Muslim jurists concentrated on practice of the faith and on personal law. When they speculated on other matters of law (e.g., laws relating to property, transactions, etc.), local customs in various parts of the Muslim world usually prevailed over their interpretations. When they wrote constitutional, administrative, and fiscal laws, these were not incorporated into regular legal manuals. In disputes concerning commercial and trade transactions, it was usually the local custom that prevailed. The jurists' law usually conformed with practice in these matters. On the other hand, matters relating to practices of the faith were excluded from court jurisdiction; cases relating to such matters as family disputes, and succession, were decided according to jurists' law.

Normally, the jurisdiction of a judge was defined in his letter of appointment. He abided by the school of law in which he had received his training, and the disputing parties would also be adherents of that same school of law. In these matters, judges followed the texts of the school. The judges were encouraged, and often required, to consult jurists on points of law. In practice, however, precedents based on court judgments developed separately from jurists' law. Since judges were not bound by preceding judgments, the judgments were not preserved as records of law. The biographies of judges preserves a record of a great number of such judgments.

In Spain and North Africa, the judicial aspect of Islamic law grew more distinctly from jurist law. In addition to literature on judicial documents, formularies, and procedural matters, local judicial practices emerged in the form of treatises. These treatises were local in nature defining judicial convention, developing on certain legal subjects as well as general judicial practices. Judges were required to follow these practices, even against the consensus of jurists, and were officially assisted by jurists known as *Mushawirs*.

In addition to regular courts, there were also three other significant institutions for the administration of Islamic law: *Hisba, Nazar fil Mazallim*, and *Ifta.*

Hisba *Hisba* (inspection) courts had summary jurisdiction. The holder of this post, the *muhtasib*, was an inspector of the market and a general guardian of morals. He was a controller of weights and measures, prices, and the quality of merchandise. He would also make sure that religious and moral laws of Islam were observed. Like the position of judge, this institution was established as early as the period of Umar (634–644), the second caliph. There is evidence that women were regarded as being equally qualified for this post and were appointed to such positions. Manuals for the function of a *muhtasib* were also written. This institution stills exists in Muslim societies in different forms. In Pakistan, for instance, the office of *muhtasib* has been established since 1980 to deal with public petitions against government offices and officers.

Nazar Fil Mazalim *Nazar fil Mazalim* courts were established by Abbasid caliphs separate from regular courts. Initially they were presided over by the caliphs; later judges were appointed to this position. These courts were not governed by *sharia* or *fiqh*, but by *Siyasa* (administrative laws). Procedural laws for these courts were given in books separate from *fiqh* texts, usually along with constitutional and administrative laws. Ibn Taymiyya appears to have been the first jurist to try to streamline this branch of law that was secular in nature with *sharia*, as recorded in his book *Al-Siyasat al-Shariyya.*

Ifta It was during the Mamluk period (1250–1382) in Egypt that jurists were attached to these courts as jurisconsults (*muftis*). A *Mufti* was a jurist who rendered opinions about Islamic law. The difference between a judgment rendered by a judge and an opinion by a *mufti* was that while the former is enforceable, the latter was not; both judge and *mufti* were considered equal as far as qualifications.

In the early days of Islam, no distinction appears to have been made between a teacher and a *mufti;* prominent scholars also functioned as *muftis.* Special training was, however, given to a person who wanted to be one. Usually such a person spent a certain number of years as apprentice with a qualified *mufti*, who on satisfaction, gave him his license (*ijaza*).

In the fourth century of Islam, manuals were written describing the qualifications of a *mufti*, along with the cautions, requirements, and etiquettes for writing a *fatwa.* Unlike judgments, the *fatawas* were systematically recorded and collected. This practice still continues, and such opinions and responses are published.

Two types of books appeared under the title of *fatawa.* The first consists of those that contained actual answers to questions. The second consists of those that were not answers but the accepted opinions of great jurists. Following the development of schools of law, the jurists classified this second type of literature as lower in grade of authority than the texts written by the founders of the schools.

The well-known *Fatawa Qadi Khan* (1196) and *Fatawa Alamgiryya* (1685–1707) are of the second type of collection in which the accepted and prevalent view of the Hanafi school is given (the Hanafi school being one of four schools of Muslim jurisprudence). The contents of the second type of collection are restricted to and classified by subjects. The previously mentioned collection has a wider scope, covering such subjects as philosophy, theology, political science, and economics, which are not the subjects of regular legal texts. Even the forms of communication of giving opinions have changed in modern times. A modern *fatwa* may be issued in a newspaper, on radio, by telephone, on a television program or on the Internet.

Schools of Law

Aside from the courts and official legal institutions, Islamic law also developed as local legal traditions that emerged later into systematized schools of law that produced a vast legal literature. These local traditions grew in various prominent cities during the early period of Islam. The companions and descendants of the Prophet were consulted by the community on religious matters and areas of proper Muslim behavior. During the Prophet Muhammad's life, about twenty-five companions distinguished themselves as interpreters of *sharia.* Toward the end of the first century some of them moved away from Medina and settled in Egypt and Yemen.

Two movements are notable in this period. One movement relied on *hadith* and its literal interpretation, despite the application of differing standards. For example, the Shia who followed Imam Ja far al-Sadiq (died 765) accepted narrations by persons of the house of Muhammad, whereas the Sunni accepted narrations from the Hanbali school of jurisprudence (established by Ahmad ibn Hanbal, d. 855). The second movement accepted *hadith* as a source of Islamic law but, like Abu Hanifa (died 767), preferred *hadith* that were narrated by persons of legal understanding or, like Malik (died 795), accepted those on which local consensus had emerged.

The Shafii school, attributed to Muhammad ibn Idris al-Shafii (died 820), grew out of a further refinement of these two movements. Shafii defined the sources of Islamic law to be the Quran, *hadith*, *ijma* (consensus of the companions of the Prophet), and *ijtihad* (legal reasoning). He wrote a treatise defining the principles of interpretation and assigned *hadith* the most vital position, as a source that explained Quranic verses, as he

ImamShaffii's Mausoleum, Cairo, Egypt.

felt that it was necessary to turn to *hadith* for explanation and understanding of these verses. He also adopted the methodology of the *hadith* school and further refined it for its use in legal reasoning. Shafii's emphasis on *hadith* and on the clear and expressed meanings of Quran and *hadith* gave rise to the school of Zahiris (literalists) attributed to Dawud ibn Khalaf (died 884).

The doctrine of *taqlid* (adherence to a particular jurist or school) solidified these schools. *Taqlid* was prompted by the policy of the Muslim rulers who usu-
ally appointed judges with official affiliation and adherence to a particular school. *Taqlid* gave rise to a conflict of laws that led jurists to develop *usul al-fiqh* (the principles of law) to justify the legal theories of the school. Early *fiqh* literature with the title of *usul* usually dealt with the basic principles of a particular school of law. These principles were either generalized to include all the doctrines of the school, or limited to a particular legal subject.

Later, when the question of authoritative sources for the interpretation of Islamic law became prominent, *usul* came to be referred to by its primary sources—Quran, *hadith*, *ijma* and *qiyas*. *Ijma* referred to the agreed opinion of scholars of a community. It gradually came to be defined as the consensus of jurists of the whole Muslim community. *Qiyas* referred to analogical reasoning by which a jurist deduces rules from a primary source.

The literature on the subject reflects continued intellectual activity by Muslim jurists about questions of legal theory. Philosophical, theological, and purely juridical interest in legal questions produced varying approaches. Abul Husayn Basri's (died 1085) *Al-Mutamad* is a theological approach and Ibn Rushd's (died 1198), *Fasl al-Maqal'* is philosophical.

The following are the major schools of law: Hanafi, Maliki, Shafii, Hanbali, Ibadi, Ismaili, Jafari, and Zaydi. At the present, the Hanafi school is followed in south Asia, Turkey, Eastern Europe, China, central and west Asia, and in some parts of the Middle East. Shafiis flourish on the coastal areas of South Asia, East Africa, East Asia, Egypt, and some parts of the Middle East. The Malik school is followed in North and West Africa and in some southern parts of the Middle East. Hanbalis are found mostly in Saudi Arabia. Among the Shia schools, Ithnaashari school are found in Iran, Iraq and south Asia, and the Zaydis in Yemen. Ismailis are found in many parts of the world. All of these schools have developed a large body of legal literature.

Legal Literature

The legal literature developed in all the schools along a similar pattern. The earliest texts consisted of the doctrines of the founder and his disciples. Later, abridgements, elaboration or compendia, glossaries, and commentaries were written on these texts. These books, although their orders varied, classified legal subject matters into the following categories:

Ibadat *Ibadat* includes rituals dealing with the practices of the faith and the pillars of Islam (i.e., prayer, almsgiving, fasting, and pilgrimage), and laws dealing with personal status (including marriage, divorce, custody of children, maintenance, testate and intestate succession, rights of divorce and inheritance. Also included in this group are transactions dealing with contracts and obligation, legal capacity of a person, and different kinds of transactions relating to property and services. Islamic laws dealing with transactions, though based on mutual consent and freedom, protect parties by assuming certain terms in the contract that provide options against defects, fraud, and one-party risk. Islamic transactions are also governed by the prohibition of *riba* (excess interest) in loans and exchange of certain valuable foods.

Jinayat *Jinayat*, or Islamic penal laws classify crimes and offenses according to penalties into three categories: (1) *Qisas* (retaliation) deals with offenses against the person, including homicide and assault. They are punishable exactly by the same treatment to the offender. (2) *Hudud* (fixed) laws deal with offenses against property and honor, including theft, robbery, false accusation, extramarital sex, and drinking. Severe punishments are fixed for these offenses, ranging in very severe cases, in some traditional interpretations, to amputation of hands for theft to severe punishment, stoning to death, for extramarital sex. (3) All other offenses are dealt with under laws in which punishment is left to the discretion of the judge.

Application of the Law

Local customs and social practices have contributed a great deal to the formation of most doctrines, since local linguistic usage and custom play an essential role in the understanding and interpretation of these laws. Several local practices have been incorporated into family law. Local customs play a more decisive role in punishments. *Fiqh* books therefore often contain chapters explaining these specific laws of judicial procedure. Laws about rituals, marriage, divorce, succession, and so on are largely derived from the Quran.

Islamic procedural laws attach burden of proof to the party who claims against the legal presumption. In principle, freedom is the basic assumption. Evidence is usually drawn on the basis of reliable witnesses or written documents; circumstantial evidence is acceptable only in the absence of an eyewitness. Even if a party fails to prove the case, the other party is asked to take an oath. The admittance of female witnesses in certain parts of the Muslim world is very limited.

◆ MODERN DEVELOPMENTS

It may be noted that *fiqh* was not the only law in force in Muslim societies. It was a source of law among others used by the courts, only in specific matters of family and personal status. State fiscal, administrative, and penal laws existed alongside each other. For commercial laws, *fiqh* often followed, rather than led the market. Consequently, reforms in Islamic law in the modern period pose very basic problems. European colonial rule treated Islamic law as a matter of religion and local custom, and limited its application to situations pertaining to personal status and ritual, preventing its growth as a modern legal system. However, when reforms were eventually undertaken in these areas, reformers often faced resistance. Two views developed on the question of reform. Reformers treated Islamic law like any other law that could be changed, amended, or repealed by state legislation. Many Muslims, conservative scholars, and orientalists regard Islamic law (*sharia/fiqh*) as religion and not law in the proper sense. Thus, reform in the strict sense of the word, according to them, cannot be undertaken as it would violate the sacred character of the faith.

Khalid Masud

References

Azami, Muhammad Mustafa. *On Schacht's Origins of Muhammadan Jurisprudence.* New York: Wiley, 1985.

Burton, John. *The Sources of Islamic Law: Islamic Theories of Abrogation.* Edinburgh: Edinburgh University Press, 1990.

Calder, Norman. *Studies in Early Muslim Jurisprudence.* Oxford: Clarendon Press, 1993.

Coulson, Noel J. *A History of Islamic Law.* Edinburgh: Edinburgh University Press, 1964.

Esposito, John L. *Women in Muslim Family Law.* Syracuse, N.Y.: Syracuse University Press, 1982.

Fyzee, Asaf A. A. *Outlines of Muhammadan Law.* Oxford: Oxford University Press, 1949.

————. *An Introduction to Islamic Law.* Oxford: Oxford University Press, 1964.

Hooker, M. B. *Islamic Law in Southeast Asia.* Singapore: Oxford University Press, 1984.

Khadduri, Majid, and Herbert J. Liebesny, eds. *Law in the Middle East,* 2 vols. Washington, D.C.: Middle East Institute, 1955.

Liebesny, Herbert J. *The Law of the Near and Middle East: Readings, Cases, and Materials.* Albany, N.Y.: State University of New York Press, 1975.

Masud, Khalid. *Islamic Legal Philosophy: A Study of Abu Ishaq al-Shaibi's Life.* Islamabad: Institute of Islamic Research, 1977.

Powers, David S. *Studies in Quran and Hadith: The Formation of the Islamic Law of Inheritance.* Berkeley: University of California Press, 1986.

Schacht, Joseph. *Origins of Muhammadan Jurisprudence.* Oxford: Clarenden, 1950.

Shafii, Muhammad ibn Idris al. *Islamic Jurisprudence: Al-Shafiis Risala.* Translated by Majid Khadduri. Baltimore: John Hopkins Press, 1961.

Tabatabai, Hossein Modarressi. *An Introduction to Shii Law: A Bibliographical Study.* London, 1984.

Weiss, Bernard G. *The Search for God's Law: Islamic Jurisprudence in the Writings of Sayf al-Din al-Amidi.* Salt Lake City: University of Utah Press, 1992.

Part VII:

Artistic and Architectural Expressions in Islam

The Arts of Islam

♦ Characteristic of Islamic Art ♦ Early Islam: the Formative Years (622 to 1050)
♦ Classical Period (1050 to 1250) ♦ Postclassical Period (1250 to 1500)
♦ Late Islam: the Age of Empires (1500 to 1800) ♦ The Modern Period (1800 to present)

Civilizations that profess the teaching of the Prophet Muhammad reveal a great diversity of ethnic, linguistic, and regional traditions as well as exposure to different political, social, and cultural changes throughout the centuries. The attempt to find common themes in the artistic traditions among Muslim societies that have spread to Asia, Africa, and Europe, and in recent years to parts of Australia and the Americas, as well as to define those that prevailed for over fourteen hundred years would be as challenging as applying the same criteria to all the Christian communities of the world. The artistic expressions of Muslims of Fatimid Egypt are as different from those of Mughal India as are the styles and themes of Medieval Italy from those of Baroque Germany. There is, nevertheless, something immediately recognizable as "Islamic" in the arts produced in areas as far removed in time and place as twelfth-century Egypt and seventeenth-century India.

♦ CHARACTERISTIC OF ISLAMIC ART

The first and foremost characteristic of Islamic art is the universal usage of the Arabic script. Arabic was the language of revelation of the Prophet Muhammad, and its script the means by which his message was transmitted and preserved in the Quran. The Arabic script was also adopted by non-Arab Muslims, including the Turks and Iranians, who used it for both religious and secular writing. While such nations as Turkey and Malaysia have changed their script to the Latin alphabet, which is better suited for their particular languages, Arabic remains the language of the Quran and the vehicle for religious education.

The art of transcribing the Quran in a beautiful and flawless hand was considered an act of devotion and piety, and its copyists, the calligraphers, have been highly esteemed. Renowned individuals excelled in different styles of writing and applied their talents to a variety of subjects, ranging from literary and historical texts to imperial edicts.

The significance of calligraphy in Islamic civilizations cannot be overstated. This form of art has retained the highest aesthetic and technical standards throughout the centuries (see fig. 33). In contrast to painters, potters, metalworkers, and other artists who, by and large, remain anonymous, the calligraphers frequently signed their works and many are thus known. Voluminous treatises were written about famous masters, discussing their stylistic innovations and recording their lives, works, and genealogies. Caliphs, sultans, and shahs collected the works of past and contemporary artists; several practiced the art of calligraphy themselves and were trained by celebrated masters. In addition, the rulers established large libraries attached to institutions of learning as well as extensive collections of all types of manuscripts for their personal use. They supported a large corps of copyists, painters, illuminators, and bookbinders who produced splendid books for their courts.

A second characteristic that seems to apply to all the Islamic arts, despite regional and stylistic variations, is the interest in surface embellishment that transforms a mundane object into a work of art, be it designated for a humble household or the treasury of a prince. While such objects are basically functional, they are decorated with designs that harmoniously balance a mixture of themes which enhance the shape. The decorative repertoire may include inscriptions, stylized scrolls, geometric motifs, and/or floral elements. Frequently the scrolls extend beyond the physical boundaries of frames and borders and are superimposed, or layered, creating depth or three-dimensionality on flat surfaces. This aesthetic approach can be found in manuscript illuminations, bookbindings, textiles, and rugs as well as in ceramics, tiles, metalwork, and other objects.

Surface designs on Islamic arts are further enriched by color through the application of polychrome pigments and glazes or contrasting materials. While there exist unadorned pieces whose bold yet elegant shapes are their only aesthetic appeal, the majority of objects are decorated with themes and motifs that symbolize the harmony of the universe, the beauty of creation, images of paradise, and the pleasures of earthly courts, in addition to phrases that bestow good wishes and prosperous lives to the owners.

Such designs are perhaps the greatest attraction of Islamic arts. The objects are devoid of any political or theological didactics. They were meant to be used and enjoyed, their messages universally understood and appreciated. Even the uninitiated can admire the elegance of shape, delicate flow of script, and intricacy of decoration.

The artistic productions of Islamic civilizations reveal a continual process of absorption, adoption, and synthesis of both internal and external influences. Each cultural entity had its own intrinsic traditions that became amalgamated with the faith and its vision of the world. With the arrival of newcomers to western Asia, the political and social scene changed. New ideas were introduced, and new patrons rose to power, both of which effected the arts.

In order to simplify the discussion of the artistic developments, a chronological progression will be followed, beginning with early Islam when the teachings of the Prophet spread from Arabia to inner Asia, North Africa, and Spain. The chapter will conclude with the modern age when new states were being founded.

During its formative years (622 to 1050), Islamic art selectively adopted certain themes and motifs from pre-existing traditions and created a unique artistic vocabulary. The following period, classical Islam (1050 to 1250), witnessed the rise and fall of numerous dynasties, each of which promoted a dynamic artistic production extending from Spain to India. In the postclassical period (1250 to 1500), the centers of power shifted, with the production in provincial courts rivaling that of the capitals. The arts became centralized in late Islam (1500 to 1800) with great and powerful rulers promoting imperial styles that came to identify their cultural traditions and glorify their regimes. Finally, the modern age (1800 to present) began with nationalistic styles that eventually gave way to international modes of expression. Needless to say, the arts are still in the process of evolving, and the final chapter has yet to be written.

♦ EARLY ISLAM: THE FORMATIVE YEARS (622 TO 1050)

During its formative years, Islam spread rapidly to dominate the vast region between the Indus River and the Atlantic Ocean, coming into contact with rich and

Fig. 1. Page from a Quran. Iraq (?), eighth-ninth century

varied cultural traditions. The first great empires were established by the caliphs, the successors of the Prophet: the Umayyads (661–750 in Damascus) and the Abbasids (750–1258 in Baghdad; 1261–1517 in Cairo). In time the authority of the Sunni, or orthodox Abbasid caliphs, was undermined by provincial governors who created independent states as well as by two rival caliphates. One was founded by the Sunni Umayyads in Spain (756–1031) and the other by the Shia Fatimids, who rose to power in North Africa and extended their control into Egypt and Syria (909–1171). The splendor of the courts of the Umayyads in Cordoba and the Fatimids in Cairo matched that of the Abbasids in Baghdad.

Although politically fragmented, the lands conquered by Muslims were united by the language of Islam and its unique script. This early period is best characterized by the development of the Arabic script and the evolution of calligraphy, the fine art of writing, which was first applied to the copying of the Quran and then spread to all the religious and secular arts.

The earliest Qurans were written in an angular script known as *kufic*, and embellished with illuminated frontispieces, chapter headings, and verse marks (Fig. 1). The manuscripts were horizontal in format; they were written on parchment in dark-brown, almost black ink while the illuminations made abundant use of gold, at times highlighted with touches of color.

The decoration of these volumes reveal the impact of two pre-Islamic traditions. Stylized floral motifs, such as symmetrical palmettes that extend into the margins, were adapted from the Sasanian art of Iraq and Iran. Geometric compartmentation used in the illuminations indicates influences from the Greco-Roman and Byzantine traditions of the Mediterranean.

Writing, or inscriptions, began to be employed in the other arts, including ceramics, metalwork, glass, and rock crystal, and were often combined with stylized floral motifs. A group of slip-painted ceramics pro-

Fig. 2. Slip-painted ceramic bowl. Iran (?), tenth century

duced in Iran and regions to the east contains proverbs, popular sayings, and aphorisms (Fig. 2).

Two great technical innovations in ceramics also date from this period: the use of blue derived from cobalt ore to paint designs on white surfaces; and the creation of luster, in which silver and copper oxides were employed to produce shimmering reflections. Some blue-painted white wares display floral motifs similar to those used in manuscript illuminations (Fig. 3), while others contain inscriptions, adding at times

other colors to enrich the composition. It was the innovative use of cobalt-derived blue that influenced the Chinese, who excelled in the production of blue-and-white porcelains after the thirteenth century. The Chinese called this pigment "Muhammedan" blue, honoring the artists who first employed it.

The commercial traffic of goods, particularly of ceramics, influenced the production of wares throughout Asia, parts of Europe and Africa. While the Chinese were enamored of blue painted ceramics from the

Fig. 3. Ceramic bowl painted in blue on white. Iraq, ninth century

Islamic world, their splash-glazed and incised pottery was copied by Muslims. The origin of some pieces painted with splashes of yellow and green (often with supplementary incised designs) is hard to determine, as the same type of ware was produced in eastern Asia as well as western Asia.

The greatest contribution of Muslim potters was the creation of luster-painted ceramics, the impact of which is still visible today. The most renowned and laborious as well as expensive type of luster was polychrome painted with ruby-red and golden-yellow

lusters, enhanced with several other tones. A less cumbersome type contained two tones of luster in which brownish-reds and greenish-yellows dominate. This was followed by the monochrome wares, which employed one or the other luster colors mentioned above. While polychrome and two-tone lusters generally depicted floral motifs, the monochromes tend to represent figural compositions, possibly due to the ease of production. On these pieces figures participate in banquets, hunts, and battles, recreating the activities associated with earthly courts. At times entertainers, such

Fig. 4. Luster-painted ceramic bowl. Iraq, tenth century

as musicians and dancers, become the main theme and depict the pleasant pastimes of sultans and caliphs (Fig 4).

While the art of the potter reached new heights in early Islam, producing wares for both domestic use and imperial households, metalwork remained more conservative, still tied to the materials and techniques of the past. In time the interest in coloristic effects also influenced the metalworkers, and items fashioned in brass or bronze began to be inlaid with copper and silver. Utilitarian pieces, including ewers, basins, buckets,

bowls, and cups, were generally cast or hammered, and embellished with chased, engraved, and inlaid motifs. While stylized florals and inscriptions were the most popular designs, animals began to be used as appendages for spouts, finials, or handles. Furthermore, a group of vessels were shaped as birds and other creatures; some used as drinking or pouring utensils were known as aquamaniles (Fig. 5), while others served as incense burners.

Items made of precious metals, namely gold and silver, have not survived in sufficient numbers to deter-

Fig. 5. Bird-shaped bronze vessel. Iran (?), late eighth century

mine the artistic vocabulary of these expensive pieces. Such metals were recycled throughout the centuries to make new pieces for personal adornment or melted down to be converted into currency. The few examples of gold jewelry that have remained indicate the continuation of the traditional techniques of granulation, twisted wire, and gem encrustation. It is difficult to differentiate Greco-Roman, Byzantine, and Sasanian ornaments from those made during the early Islamic period unless, of course, there are Arabic inscriptions on the pieces. Even figural designs are indistinguishable, with

the Islamic goldsmiths and silversmiths using similar real or fantastic creatures amidst stylized floral elements.

A type of floral motif, generally called a winged palmette (since the outer leaves of the symmetrical configuration extend and appear to flutter like wings), seems to have been unanimously accepted by artists and craftsmen. The winged palmette is found on a variety of early Islamic arts, ranging from manuscript illuminations to architectural decoration. On carved surfaces the design was cut at an angle, using a tech-

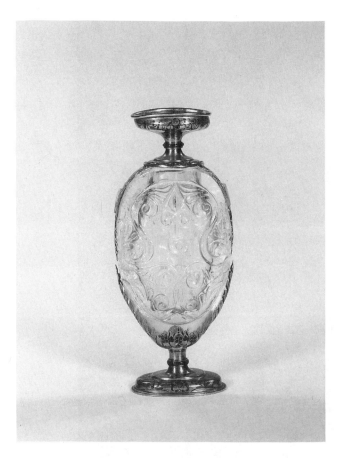

Fig. 6. Rock crystal flask with enameled gold mount. Egypt, ninth-tenth century (mount Austrian circa 1600)

nique known as beveling, which produced shadows of different intensities. Applied to stone and stucco as well as to glass and rock crystal (Fig. 6), this uniquely Islamic technique reveals the attempt to enhance surfaces, whether through the employment of color or the refraction of light.

Early glass wares were generally mold-blown and decorated with carved motifs, encrusted with pieces of contrasting glass (similar to the cameo technique in which pieces with contrasting colors are applied in relief to the flat backgrounds), or luster painted, the latter recalling the decoration of contemporary ceramics. The debate over which came first, luster-painted glass or ceramics, is still going on. Where this technique originated, whether in Egypt or Iraq, also remains contested.

If one work of art is to represent the stylistic and technical characteristics of this period, it is a lidded cylindrical ivory box, called a pyxis (Fig. 7). Decorated with carved floral scrolls, real and imaginary animals, figural compositions, and *kufic* inscriptions, the piece epitomizes the artistic production of the age. It indicates that by the tenth century the artists had synthesized the traditions of preexisting cultures and created a vocabulary that expressed their new world.

♦ CLASSICAL PERIOD (1050 TO 1250)

The beginning of the classical period of Islamic art coincides with the arrival of the Seljuq Turks from central Asia in the mid-eleventh century. They moved into Iran, Iraq, Syria, and Turkey and reinstalled the power of the Sunni caliphate in the central Islamic lands. By the mid-twelfth century the Seljuq sultanate disintegrated into a number of independent dynasties. Among these were the Ayyubids (1169–1260), who overthrew the Fatimids and claimed Egypt and Syria. Other autonomous states rose in central Asia, India, North Africa, and Spain, fighting for domination in these regions. In addition, the central Islamic lands were periodically invaded by waves of Crusaders from the West, who also established short-lived and rival states.

Despite the political turbulence and the rise and fall of new regimes, this period was one of great economic prosperity, during which the arts flourished. Competition for power was reflected in the arts, with each new ruler flaunting his real or assumed power by commissioning the most spectacular objects. Ambitious *wazirs, amirs,* princes, and commanders attempted to contest the authority and legitimacy of the reigning sultans not only by force but also through patronage of the arts. Competing with them were the affluent middle classes, merchants, and administrators. Cultural centers were spread all over the Islamic world, and the perpetual movement of peoples and armies, together with increased commercial activities, transmitted new ideas and artistic expressions from one region to another. While Cairo, Damascus, and Baghdad remained the major cultural centers, other cities, such as Isfahan and Kashan in Iran, Mosul and Raqqa in Iraq, and Konya and Diyarbakir in Turkey, became equally renowned for their artistic activities.

The artists produced an unprecedented quantity of all types of objects, experimenting with designs, techniques, styles, and shapes. Figural compositions depicting courtly scenes, daily activities, astrological themes, mystic and talismanic images, and literary and historic episodes dominate the secular arts and architecture. The high quality of execution and innovative surface decoration indicate the existence of a large scale and demanding patronage that compelled the artists to excel in their metier. Workshops were set up in all major cities, producing wares for both the average citizens and the wealthy courtiers.

Although Arabic was still the dominant language, Turkish and Persian began to be widely used in administrative and literary circles. The arts of the book reached new levels of excellence with an abundance of illustrated manuscripts requiring the talents of calligraphers, illuminators, painters, and bookbinders. The calligraphers devised different styles of angular and

Fig. 7. Carved ivory pyxis made for al-Mughira, son of Caliph Abd al-Rahman III. Spain, dated 968

cursive scripts, employing their best efforts in the production of Qurans, each folio splendidly designed, harmoniously combining text and decoration (Fig. 8). The format of book became vertical and paper replaced parchment, the latter continuing to be used in limited quantities in North Africa. Some Qurans were produced in thirty-volume sets, each volume containing the prayers of a Muslim month (the Islamic calendar is based on the lunar cycle in which each month has thirty days).

It is, however, in manuscripts devoted to medicine, engineering, astronomy, botany, zoology, literature, and poetry that the artists created new forms of expression. They not only illustrated the pertinent portions of the text but asserted their individuality by devising new themes and compositions, recreating contemporary figures and settings (Fig. 9).

Freedom of artistic expression is also found in ceramics and metalwork. A group of luster-painted wares made in Iran depicts princely hunters, polo players, warriors, and scenes of courtly entertainment as well as mystic and esoteric themes with remarkably sophisticated imagery (Fig. 10). Items made for religious establishments were limited to non-figural compositions with exquisitely rendered stylized florals combined with majestic inscriptions. Among the most renowned examples are large *mihrabs*, the prayer niches in the mosque, constructed of luster-painted tiles produced in Iran (Fig. 11). Other luster-painted wares made in Egypt are outstanding in their naturalistic portrayal of daily activities and figures.

While the luster wares of this period are monochromatic (using either brownish-red or greenish-yellow), a different but equally famous pottery known as *minai* (or enameled, as the pigments were applied both under and over the glaze) was polychrome painted with a wide range of pigments, rivaling the works of manuscript illustrators. Some of these wares depict scenes from ancient Persian sagas, such as the *Shahnam*, the epic history of Iran and Turan. Others represent courtly scenes and even contemporary events such as the conquest of a fortress by a group of Seljuq warriors (Fig. 13).

Other types of ceramics include wares painted in black under a transparent turquoise glaze. The majority have no specific stories to tell but display splendid brushwork with a perfect balance between the fulls and the voids in the composition. Luster-painted and *minai* wares were expensive to produce (requiring several firings, precious materials, and expert painters) and, hence, purchased by the wealthy classes. The other types were easier to make and targeted for popular consumption. They too had to conform to the tastes of an equally discerning clientele with an acute sense of aesthetics.

Metalwork of the period reflects the same criteria as the pottery. Both were made for the rulers and the ruled, who shared similar critical values. Items fashioned of precious materials were expensive and yet affordable by the affluent middle classes as well as the sultans and emirs. Many gold and silver pieces were cast, hammered, and molded; and embellished with coloristic effects, some with niello (a black alloy), others with enamels and gems. They were made into necklaces, bracelets, earrings, rings, pendants, and belt-hooks as well as bottles and bowls.

A more common technique of producing coloristic effects on the surfaces was to inlay the pieces (now predominantly made of brass) with silver, copper, and gold. Ranging from small utensils to large containers, these inlaid brasses display the same decorative themes as the other arts. Humans and real or fantastic animals are depicted alone, in pairs, or in groups. They are frequently set against varying types of floral scrolls and overall geometric patterns and combined with inscriptions. A type of inscription called 'animated' was unique to metalwork. In animated inscriptions either the terminals of the letters were transformed into human heads; or, in some cases, human and animal torsos, arms, and legs constituted parts of the letters. The concept of the living word was extended in the decoration of floral scrolls with humans and animals incorporated into the designs. Difficult to decipher but nevertheless readable, animated inscriptions generally bestow formulaic good wishes to the owner. There are also inscriptions using angular and cursive scripts that give pertinent information about the patron, artist, place of execution, and the date (Fig. 14).

A select group of inlaid brasses contain a different configuration of images that reflects the multifaceted cultural milieu of the age. A representative example is a large basin that depicts Christian themes (the exterior has scenes from the life of Jesus and the interior shows a row of saints standing under arches) combined with princely themes (polo games and musicians), animated scrolls, angular and cursive inscriptions, and real and imaginary creatures—all placed against a profusion of floral and geometric motifs (Fig. 15). A noteworthy aspect of the basin is the content of the inscriptions, which contain the name of an Ayyubid sultan who valiantly defended his lands and peoples against the Crusaders who invaded western Asia and devastated both local Muslim and Christian communities. This extraordinary piece exemplifies the cultural diversity and the rich artistic vocabulary of the classical age.

♦ POSTCLASSICAL PERIOD (1250 TO 1500)

This period is characterized by Turkish or Turkic domination of the Islamic lands, beginning with the rise

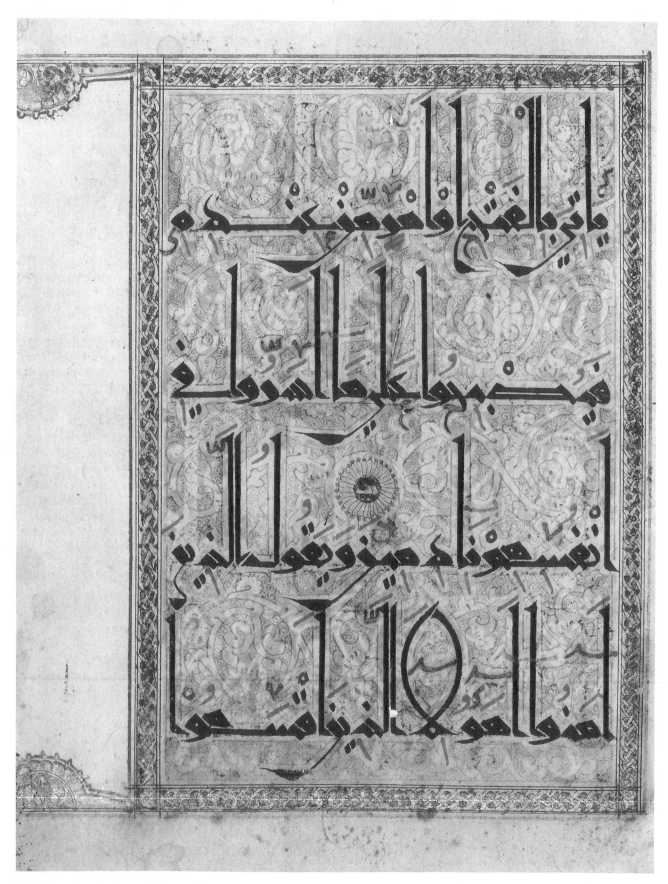

Fig. 8. Page from a Quran. Iran, twelfth century

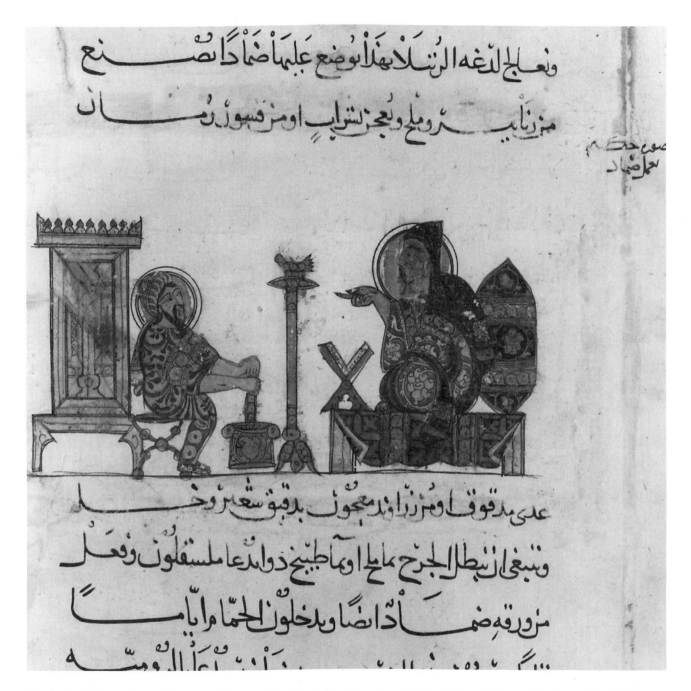

Fig. 9. Physician and attendant preparing medicine. Illustration from the *Materia Medica* of Dioscorides Iraq, dated 1224

of the Mamluks (1250–1517) in Syria and Egypt, and the Mongol invasion of the mid-thirteenth century. The Mamluks ousted the Crusaders from the central Islamic lands, and the Mongols were eventually conquered by the traditions of the regions they sought to rule, creating the Ilkhanid state (1256–1353) centered in Iran. The Ilkhanids in turn succumbed to other Turkish invasions from central Asia, namely the Turkmens under the Akkoyunlus (White Sheep; 1378–1508 in eastern Turkey and western Iran) and the Karakoyunlus (Black Sheep; 1380–1468 in western Iran and Iraq); followed by the

Timurids (1370–1506 in Iran and Afghanistan). While the Seljuq rule was undermined by various new Turkish emirates, Muslim Spain achieved a cultural renaissance under the Nasrids (1230–1492).

The calligraphers of the age formulated even more elaborate cursive scripts, employing them for both religious and secular manuscripts. The Qurans were profusely decorated with illuminated double frontispieces, opening pages, and finispieces in addition to large chapter headings and marginal ornaments rendered in polychrome pigments and several tones of gold. It be-

Fig. 10. Luster-painted ceramic plate made by Shams al-Din al-Hasani. Iran, dated 1210

came fashionable to produce sets of two or more over-size volumes, each with matching leather covers embellished with stamped, tooled, gold embossed, and filigree designs with the main motifs placed against contrasting grounds. The illuminations relied on geometric divisions with interlinked components, each unit filled with floral and/or geometric elements, frequently superimposing two or more designs to create the illusion of recessed and articulated surfaces (Fig. 16).

Illustrated manuscripts made during the Mamluk pe-riod were generally copies of earlier Arabic texts whose pictorial cycles had been established in the thirteenth century. While scientific books written in Arabic continued to be copied and illustrated, historical and literary texts composed in Persian became more and more popular. Persian had become the language of the courts, which sponsored illustrated manuscripts devoted to epic and mystic poetry. Among the first illustrated Persian epics was Firdausi's *Shahname*, which was produced in several Ilkhanid, Turkmen, and Timurid capitals in the fourteen and fifteenth centuries (Fig. 17).

Fig. 11. Mihrab with luster-painted tiles made by al-Hasan ibn Arabshah. Iran, dated 1226

Fig. 12. Overglaze-painted ceramic bowl. Iran, early thirteenth century

Other illustrated manuscripts were copies of the mystic poems of such celebrated Persian writers as Nizami, Sadi, and Hafiz, as well as Persian translations and adaptations of Arabic classics (Fig. 18). Royal courts, such as those in Granada, Cairo, Tabriz, Baghdad, Shiraz, and Herat, became centers of cultural activities, attracting renowned poets, historians, scholars, and a multitude of artists.

Although figural compositions continued to be employed on ceramics, metalwork, glass, and other works of art, inscriptions began to dominate the artistic vo-

cabulary. The exuberant production of luster-painted and *minai* wares observed in the classical period noticeably dwindled. The examples dating from this age show prosaic designs and techniques. One region, however, shows a revitalization of luster wares in the fourteenth century. Nasrid artists in Spain made a series of large bowls, plates, and exceptional vessels known as "Alhambra vases," as they were thought to have been commissioned for the Alhambra Palace in Granada (Fig. 19).

A more popular type of ware was underglaze painted,

Fig. 13. Ceramic bowl painted black under turquoise glaze. Syria, early thirteenth century

some reflecting designs inspired by the Chinese porcelains exported to the Islamic world. The interest in imitating Chinese blue-and-white porcelains, which began to be felt in this period, became far more pronounced in the following age, particularly in Turkey and Iran.

Metalworkers continued to employ silver, gold, and copper inlays on their brasses, and represented both figural and epigraphic compositions. A number of examples depict formulaic courtly activities, with riders and enthroned figures amid panels with large inscriptions that bestow good wishes or exaltations to anony-

mous rulers (Fig. 20). A peculiarity of the period is a large group of some one hundred candlesticks that have the same shape, size, and weight. They are assigned to northern Iraq, western Iran, Azerbaijan, or eastern Turkey and dated between the late thirteenth and early fourteenth century. Some follow the repertoire of courtly themes; others are covered with overall designs; and a number show personifications of the planets, signs of the zodiac, and the labors of the twelve months based on the solar calendar. Since the majority of the pieces were found in dervish convents

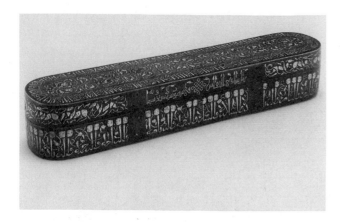

Fig. 14. Brass penbox inlaid with copper and silver made by Shazi for Majd al-Mulk al-Muzaffar (governor of Merv). Iran or Afghanistan, dated 1210/11

in Turkey, the candlesticks appear to have been produced for Sufi establishments, which combined mystic and religious practices.

The patronage of the Mamluks extended from illuminated and illustrated manuscripts and inlaid brasses to enameled and gilded glass. Glass items made for religious structures, predominantly hanging lamps, were

decorated with Quranic verses, while those for secular use depict figural scenes in addition to written messages. Mosque lamps, produced in large quantities, frequently contain the blazon (coat of arms) of the patrons. Some blazons are epigraphic with the titles of the patrons. Others show symbols of office or emblems that are thought to be the coat of arms of ruling families, including those of the neighboring states that ordered luxury items from the Mamluk artists.

The artistic traditions of the Mamluks had a long-lasting impact on the artists of the later periods as well as on contemporary Mediterranean cultures, more specifically on Italian metalworkers and glassmakers. It was, however, the Timurids with their impeccably refined designs who had a far greater impact on the arts of Islam. Extending from manuscript illumination to inlaid metalwork, Timurid artists set the standards for surface decoration while their painting styles provided models for sixteenth-century court studios in Turkish, Iranian, and Indian capitals.

◆ LATE ISLAM: THE AGE OF EMPIRES (1500 TO 1800)

In the sixteenth century three great dynasties rose to power in the world of Islam: the Ottomans (1281–1924)

Fig. 15. Brass basin inlaid with silver made for Sultan Najm al-Din Ayyub. Egypt or Syria, circa 1240

Fig. 16. Illuminated double page from a Quran made for Sultan Shaban II for his mother's theological school. Egypt, donated 1369

who controlled western Asia, northern Africa, and eastern Europe from their court in Istanbul, and who became the caliphs of orthodox Islam after the sixteenth century; the Safavids (1501–1732), who dominated Iran and Afghanistan, extending their rule into parts of the Caucasus and central Asia, and established courts in Tabriz, Kazwin, and Isfahan; and the Mughals (1526–1858), who expanded from northern India to govern the entire subcontinent, their courts spreading throughout the land to include Delhi, Agra, Fatehpur Sikri, and Lahore. Although Spain was lost to Christian control, Islamic dynasties controlled major portions of Asia and Africa.

Cultural activities were centered around the courts of great rulers, where artists of diverse traditions congregated and created indigenous styles and themes that reflected the magnificence of their patrons. Artistic traditions formulated in the courts radiated to all corner of the empires and influenced the arts of the neighboring states. Increased diplomatic and commercial missions between the Europeans and the Ottomans, Safavids, and Mughals resulted in a demand for Islamic goods, which were ardently sought after by European aristocratic and ecclesiastic circles. Items of greatest

demand were rugs and textiles, which transmitted Islamic designs to Europe; other popular wares included Ottoman ceramics, which were not only collected by the wealthy but imitated by French, Italian, and other European artists.

Ottoman, Safavid, and Mughal arts all thrived as a result of powerful and demanding imperial patronage that forced the artists to create innovative styles and themes, executing their objects with remarkable skill. All three empires had immense resources and spared no expense in the construction of monumental architecture and production of luxurious objects. Each created unique artistic expressions that combined several traditions. With the Ottomans it was the synthesis of western Islamic, native Turkish, and European cultures; the Safavids combined Turkmen, Timurid, and local traditions; and the art of the Mughals shows a configuration of Timurid, Safavid, and Indian elements, incorporated with certain European features.

Imperial patronage is best reflected in the arts of the book, with the court ateliers producing splendid manuscripts for the royal libraries. Calligraphy was the undisputed leader of the arts, with great masters establishing their individual schools of writing. • Their

Fig. 17. Alexander the Great at the talking tree. Illustration from the *Shahname* of Firdausi Iran, early fourteenth century

and sprays that covered the surfaces. There are, nevertheless, some examples of ceramics, metalwork, textiles, and rugs that contain figural compositions.

Ottoman ceramics and tiles became world renowned for their technical and aesthetic excellence, employing several brilliant colors under a crystal clear glaze. Among the earliest examples are blue or blue and turquoise painted wares that either copy Chinese designs or rely on indigenous compositions. A more common type represented fantastic or naturalistic flowers painted in vivid reds, greens, and several tones of blue (Fig. 26).

It is in this period that large quantities of blue-and-white Chinese porcelains were exported to the Islamic world and deposited into the royal kitchens of the Ottomans or the religious shrines of the Safavids. The designs of Chinese porcelains were first imitated by the Safavid potters who soon used the underglaze-painted blue pigment to create their own compositions (Fig. 27).

The opulence of the courts can be observed in the precious items made for ceremonial or daily use. Fashioned of gold, silver, and, for a brief period, of zinc, a variety of objects created for personal use were encrusted with gems and display infinitesimally detailed

Qurans, calligraphic exercises, and single-page compositions were avidly collected by the sultans and shahs (Fig. 22). Some rulers and members of the court also practiced the art of fine writing, several excelling in specific styles and calligraphic compositions.

The painters of the Ottoman court studios illustrated large quantities of secular manuscripts, the most outstanding artists working on contemporary histories of the sultans. These volumes were written by the official historians and illustrated by artists who personally witnessed the events, recreating historic personages and settings (Fig. 23). In contrast, the Safavids were more interested in copies of earlier Persian texts, such as the works of Firdausi, Nizami, Sadi, and Jami (Fig. 24). While the Ottoman artists were more concerned with the accurate depictions of historic events, their Safavid counterparts worked the scenes like jewelers, refining and embellishing the compositions. The Mughals also commissioned illustrated histories that commemorated the lives of the rulers, occasionally producing allegorical scenes that had political implications (Fig. 25).

The predominant decoration of the age, observed in Ottoman, Safavid, and Mughal arts alike, was floral with stylized and naturalistic blossoms used in scrolls

Fig. 18. Battle between the lion and the ox. Illustration from the *Kalila and Dimna* of Nasrullah. Afghanistan, dated 1429

Fig. 19. Luster-painted ceramic vase. Spain, early fourteenth century

Fig. 20. Brass bowl inlaid with gold and silver. Iran, early fourteenth century

surface decoration (Figs. 28 and 29). Other pieces made of equally rare materials such as ivory, jade, and rock crystal were similarly embellished, employing gold inlays and jewels. The court artists used several different techniques to create articulation and depth. They superimposed scrolls of diverse designs, carved and recessed the backgrounds, and added components with additional sunken or raised elements, producing both coloristic effects and surfaces that changed with the reflection of light. Ceremonial and functional arms and armor were lavishly decorated, frequently employing gems and gold inlays or overlays on steel items.

The artists employed every conceivable material and technique to embellish the pieces commissioned for royal libraries, dining rooms, and dressing chambers. Imperial suites were decorated with ceilings painted in gold. Walls were faced with tiles; wood doors, window shutters, and cupboards were inlaid with mother-of-pearl and tortoiseshell; divans and cushions were upholstered with brocaded silks and velvets; and woven or embroidered floor coverings were made of metallic threads, polychrome silks, and shimmering wools.

The textile industry reached unprecedented heights of technical excellence, manufacturing a variety of goods. The most expensive were brocaded silks and velvets made for ceremonial kaftans, followed by fabrics used as imperial furnishings. A number of kaftans were fashioned of unique textiles and were produced for a single garment, such as a brocaded floral silk woven for an Ottoman prince (Fig. 30). Cheaper textiles, that is, those with lesser amounts of metallic threads but with the same quality of execution, were designated for local and foreign markets.

A similar criteria was applied to rugs. Those woven with expensive materials were made for the courts; oth-

Fig. 21. Enameled and gilded glass bowl. Syria, mid-fourteenth century

Fig. 22. Page with calligraphic compositions made by Ahmed Karahisari. Turkey, circa 1540-50

Fig. 23. Sultan Suleyman being entertained in his palace. Illustration from the *Suleymanname* of Arifi Turkey, dated 1558

ers using cheaper materials were used for domestic consumption or exported. In the Ottoman world the centers for production varied, but the workshops of central Anatolia were the most prolific. Active since the fifteenth century, many are still manufacturing handwoven rugs today. Ottoman rugs were purchased in quantity by the wealthy classes in Europe. They were registered in royal and church inventories and often used as wall hangings, table covers, and altarpieces. After the eighteenth century Ottoman rugs were also exported to the Americas, becoming valued items in colonial manors.

Safavid and Mughal textiles and rugs enjoyed the same popularity. Some of the most beautiful examples were preserved in European treasuries and are now in public museums, attesting to their great appeal (Fig. 31). Still fashionable and expensive, they continue to be rare and precious collectibles.

◆ THE MODERN PERIOD (1800 TO PRESENT)

The nineteenth century was a period of great eclecticism. Islamic architectural styles and decorative mo-

tifs were copied in diverse European cities while European artistic traditions appeared in Islamic capitals. With the popularity of world fairs and exhibitions on Islamic arts organized in Paris, London, Vienna, and other European centers, artistic styles and forms identified with the Islamic world became easily accessible to the general public. Large European estates were embellished with "Oriental" pavilions and gazebos. Upper class homes had "Turkish" rooms furnished with items purchased in Istanbul, Cairo, and Damascus as well as with copies of Islamic decorative arts produced by local artists. Captivating the imagination of the intellectual elite, Islamic, or more specifically Turkish, themes became the rage in European music, opera, theater, literature, and the arts. A number of European artists visited the Islamic countries and recorded real or imaginary vistas and scenes, leading to a movement in painting known as Orientalism.

Archaeological expeditions together with extensive traffic of travelers involved with trade, tourism, or pilgrimage further increased European awareness of western Asian and North African traditions. There was a renewed fascination not only with the biblical sites of the Holy Land, but also with the ancient civilizations of these regions, including Pharaonic Egypt, Sumerian Iraq, and Hittite Turkey.

As Europe became more and more involved with the Islamic world, both politically and culturally, the Islamic world began to emulate the institutions and life-styles of Europe. By the turn of the 20th century the great empires of the past had disintegrated, giving birth to a number of new states. Each regime attempted to find its own national identity by both reverting to the past and experimenting with new modes of expression. For many the inspiration came from the vitality of European traditions, and soon a common artistic language developed.

European instructors were invited to teach in the newly-founded art schools, and artists from the Islamic world were sent abroad to be trained in European academies. The works of painters in Istanbul soon became indistinguishable from those of their colleagues in Paris (fig. 32). The arts entered the age of intercontinentalism with the same techniques, styles and themes practiced in all major centers in Europe, Asia, and Africa.

The final stage may be termed global, with artists no longer restricted by regional or cultural backgrounds, each expressing his or her individualistic view of the world, presenting personal reactions and perceptions in a manner that is universally understood. One can no longer identify a work of art as being a representative example of a particular nation, ethnic origin, or religious preference. Where an artist was born and trained, or where he or she works and exhibits, are irrelevant to judging the merits of a work of art. Some individuals

Fig. 24. Zulaykha arrives in Egypt. Illustration from the *Haft Avrang* of Jami

Fig. 25. Jahangir preferring a Sufi sheykh to kings made by Bichitr Illustration from an album India, ca 1615-18

Fig. 26. Underglaze-painted ceramic plate. Turkey, mid-sixteenth century

Fig. 27. Ceramic plate painted in blue on white. Iran, seventeenth century

Fig. 28. Jeweled gold canteen with jade plaques. Turkey, late sixteenth century

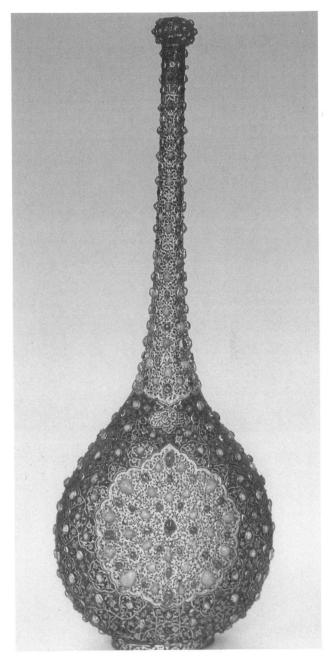

Fig. 29. Jeweled zinc bottle. Iran, early sixteenth century

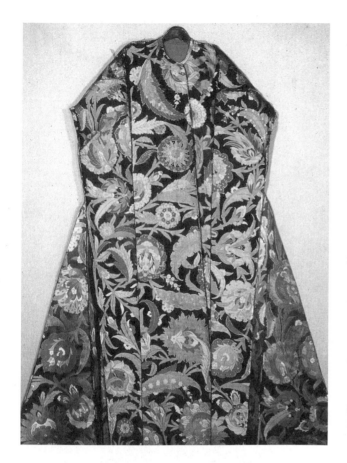

Fig. 30. Brocaded kaftan made for Prince Mehmed, son of Sultan Suleyman. Turkey, mid-sixteenth century

Fig. 31. Rug with floral pattern. Iran or Afghanistan, sixteenth century

Fig. 32. *Arms Merchant* signed by Osman Hamdi. Oil on canvas Turkey, dated 1908

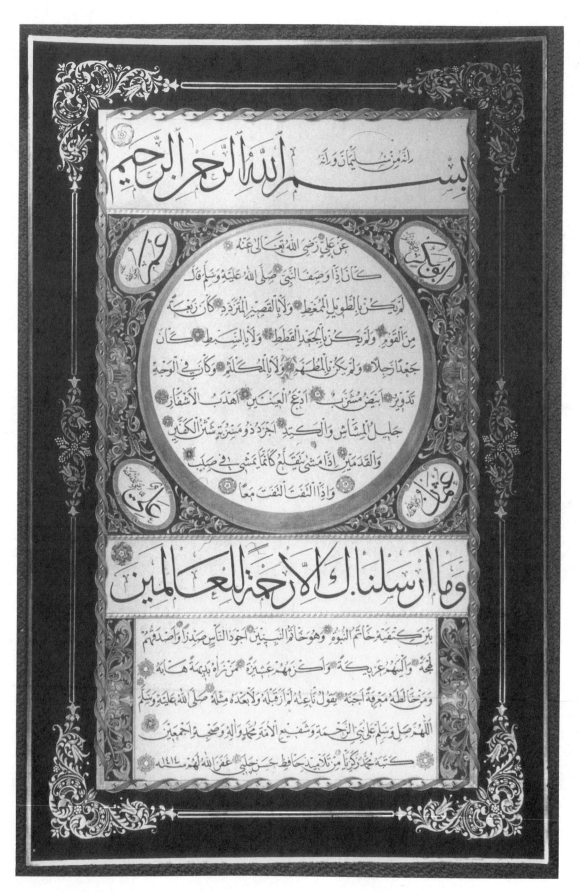

Fig. 33. *Hilye-i Saadet* signed by Mohamed Zakariya Color and gold on paper U.S.A., 1994

continue to practice and excel in the traditional arts. Others may be inspired by the past but use their own contemporary styles to represent their world.

Esin Atil

References

Atil, Esin. *The Age of Sultan Suleyman the Magnificent.* Washington, D.C. and New York: National Gallery of Art, 1987.

———. *Art of the Arab World.* Washington, D.C.: Smithsonian Institution Press, 1975.

—— —. *Ceramics from the World of Islam.* Washington, D.C.: Smithsonian Institution Press, 1973.

———. *Renaissance of Islam: Art of the Mamluks.* Washington, D.C.: Smithsonian Institution Press, 1981.

———, ed. *Islamic Art and Patronage: Treasures from Kuwait.* New York: Rizzoli, 1990.

———, ed. *Turkish Art.* Washington, D.C.: Smithsonian Institution Press, 1980.

Atil, Esin, W. T. Chase, and Paul Jett. *Islamic Metalwork in the Freer Gallery of Art.* Washington, D.C.: Smithsonian Institution Press, 1985.

Beach, Milo Cleveland. *The Imperial Image: Paintings for the Mughal Court.* Washington, D.C.: Freer Gallery of Art, Smithsonian Institution Press, 1981.

Blair, Sheila, and Jonathan Bloom. *The Art and Architecture of Islam, 1250-1800.* New Haven, Conn.: Yale University Press, 1994.

Brend, Barbara. *Islamic Art.* London: British Museum Press, 1991.

Dodds, Jerrilynn, ed. *Al-Andalus: The Art of Islamic Spain.* New York: Metropolitan Museum of Art: Distributed by H.N. Abrams, 1992.

Ettinghausen, Richard. *Arab Painting.* Geneva: Skina: Distributed by World Pub. Co., Cleveland, 1962.

Ettinghausen, Richard, and Oleg Grabar. *The Art and Architecture of Islam, 650–1250.* New Haven, Conn.: Yale University Press, 1994.

Lane, Arthur. *Early Islamic Pottery: Mesopotamia, Egypt and Persia.* London: Faber and Faber, Ltd., 1947.

———. *Later Islamic Pottery.* London: Faber & Faber, Ltd., 1971.

Lentz, Thomas W., and Glenn D. Lowry. *Timur and the Princely Vision: Persian Art and Culture in the Fifteenth Century.* Los Angeles: Los Angeles County Museum of Art, 1989.

Ward, Rachel. *Islamic Metalwork.* London: Published for the Trustees of the British Museum by the British Museum Press, 1993.

23

The Architectural Expressions in the Built-Environment of the Muslim World

♦ Building Types And Their Architectural Character ♦ Urban Character ♦ Conclusion

Muslim architecture has become incorporated as an indispensable legacy of the world's cultural achievements. Despite the unique architectural elegance of vernacular rural architecture, which is so well suited to its environment, inspiring in its mix of simplicity and sophistication, most of the architectural heritage in the societies of the Muslim world is concentrated in the urban areas. We will concentrate on that heritage and attempt to identify its common elements.

It is almost impossible to do justice to a topic as wide in scope and as varied as the Muslim world. After all, Muslim societies are found in dissimilar locales from Morocco to Indonesia, and from the coast of East Africa to the Himalayas. Terrains ranging in variety from the jungles of Java to the deserts of Arabia, from the fertile plains of the river societies of the Middle East and South Asia, to the Mountains of Anatolia, encapsulate climatic conditions so disparate that the architectural expression must be different to compensate for the difference.

The Concept of Overlay for Understanding Architecture

The concept of overlay is useful in understanding the manifestations of Islamic culture as reflected in the built environment of Muslim societies. Historically, Muslim experience was very distinct compared to that of Roman civilization, with its clearly defined architectural language resulting, for example, in identically designed forts being built in the deserts of Libya and the snows of northern Europe, irrespective of climate—a situation akin to the use of a giant rubber stamp in defining the boundaries of cultural identity of the em-

pire through the placement of icons. Muslim civilization, on the other hand, exported no uniquely defined architectural language from Arabia to the vast and varied regions it ultimately encompassed. Islam spread a more subtle, yet ultimately an increasingly more powerful presence through its method of defining itself and society by responding intellectually and culturally to the "codes of conduct" outlined in the Quran and the example based on Prophetic tradition. From Morocco in the west to Indonesia in the east, with the sole exception of the Iberian peninsula, these societies once established, have been able to retain their Muslim identity, even after prolonged periods of colonization.

Indeed, this process evolved mainly because Islam's contribution to a civilization functioned as an overlay which interacted with existing realities and cultural specificities, modifying them in subtle ways, thus creating a new synthesis by allowing it to evolve for an extended period and finding new expressions in response to interactions between different cultures. For example, the interplay between the Muslim empires of Central Asia and India led to a synthesis of form that belonged to both cultures. However, once established, almost any Muslim society is best understood as comprising several cultural systems as well as empires which function as states with all the power relationships and commercial transactions embodied in such an organization of human affairs. It is then that one finds architectural expression being affected by stylistic borrowings and transfers. These, however, are the manifestations of specific Muslim societies and their interactions, not the assertion of some universal Muslim identity that spread from one geographic center. For instance, although Timurid architecture was known in Egypt (indeed there are two well-preserved fifteenth-century Timurid domes in Cairo), Mamluk architecture which came later pursued its own stylistic development.

In architectural literature the value of "regionalism," like most other "isms," is a much-debated topic. Regionalism embraces the notion that any architectural work reflects the specificities of the region in which it is located. It accepts contexualism in the broader sense of including the physical aspects (site, climate, materials) and the socio-cultural context, stylistically and functionally. The Turkish architect, Suha Ozkan, has contributed a useful differentiation between what he terms "vernacularism" and "modern regionalism" in understanding contemporary architectural work which seeks to speak to a specific identity. To paraphrase: "vernacularism" refers to architecture which has evolved over time in any particular region and is therefore limited to existing building types and scales, whereas "modern regionalism" refers to a contemporary interpretation of local architectures and is not limited by scale, building types or technology. Ozkan stresses that regionalism does not exclude modernism; rather it presents another view of architecture that rejects the idea of internationalism, a tendency largely formented by the power of example and by wide media coverage and shifting fashions in a world growing ever smaller through technological advances in communications.

Regionalism is of considerable concern in different parts of the Muslim world today. Malaysian architect, Ken Yeang, a leading exponent of regionalism, has argued that the architectural significance of regionalism appears through relating its built configuration, aesthetics, organization and technical assembly and materials to a certain place and time. He has, in fact, produced cutting-edge contemporary work paying particular attention to climate.

More broadly, however, this view obviously defines regionalism as bridging both technology and culture and thus, the architectural debate on regionalism has a direct link to the recognition of societal particulars. Furthermore, the specificities of Muslim societies can be better appreciated by understanding the interaction which occurs between universalist Islamic principles and local realities as an enriching overlay which, although frequently subtle in its physical manifestation, was nonetheless pervasive and durable.

The cultural evolution of these societies particularly in its modern phase, however, has for the most part been subjected to historic rupture which permeates much of the present debate about cultural identity in Muslim societies. This has been the subject of recent critical writings, especially from Mohammed Arkoun.

The Menara Tower in Malaysia: architect Ken Yaeng's brilliant contemporary design for an office building in the hot tropical climate of Malaysia.

His scholarly enquiry traces, in large measure, the malaise which impels contemporary Muslim societies to a "rupture" in the evolution of the integrated and integrating framework within which individuals view self and society. An ossification of intellectual enquiry accompanied the imposition of central dogma by Muslim empires of the later Middle Ages. The European Renaissance and its subsequent intellectual ferment thus coincided with a time of intellectual stagnation in the Muslim world. This situation was exacerbated by the Industrial Revolution and the colonial experience. Attempts at modernizing Islamic thought, from Jamal al din Al-Afghani and Muhammad Abduh in the late nineteenth century to the philosopher Mohammad Iqbal and others in the twentieth century, sought to remedy this rupture in the evolution of Muslim intellectual development. Contemporary "fundamentalist" currents, with their emphasis on reviving the past, are also manifestations of this concept of arrested development. Each region of the Muslim world, however, retains its own distinct cultural, socio-political and architectural character. It is this last which is the focus of this essay.

The legacy of the Muslim architectural past, is still best studied in urban centers which continue to define both the legacy and the evolving modern conditions of the built environment of Muslims today. What, then, are the characteristics of that architectural and urban-situated legacy?

◆ BUILDING TYPES AND THEIR ARCHITECTURAL CHARACTER

Architectural character is, of course, held hostage to materials, technology, climate and the function of the building. In general, however, the architectural character of a place was defined by a number of important buildings: the Mosque, the *Qasr* (Citadel or Palace), Residences and Shrines. Cities in Muslim societies were also centers of commerce and learning, therefore, additional types of buildings were found in many areas: *Khanqa*, the place for spiritual contemplation and retreat; *Madrasa*, the place for education and learning; and *Sebil-Kuttab*, the place for teaching children and watering the wayfarer. Frequently, a number of these elements were joined together in a single complex structure.

It is difficult to explain the typology of these buildings in a stylistic sense, because, notwithstanding the common thread of overlays, there is much geographic and historic variation in architectural expression. Nevertheless, one can illustrate each type of building, using the medieval documentation available for Cairo and the Middle East as a primary source. The work of Laila Ali Ibrahim has been essential in elucidating many of the architectural terms of the medieval period, to which she devoted decades and produced a scholarly dictionary on the subject. It is based on her work that the following clarifications are made. For greater clarity we can group them into religious buildings, secular buildings, and buildings for investment.

Religious Buildings

Of all religious constructions the mosque is the most important and has the highest prestige. All mosques are *masjids*, a masjid where the Friday prayer takes place is called *masjid al-khutba, masjid al-Juma, al-masjid al-jami* and later simply *Jami*. From the Cairene documents, this development took place between the time of building of the Mosque of Ibn Tulun, 876–79, which is called by inscription *masjid* and the mosque at Esna built in 1077 by the Fatimid general, Badr al-Jamali, which is called *Jami*.

The *Jami* played a very important role in medieval Muslim society. It was a multi-purpose structure, used primarily for prayer, but also for teaching, debates and announcing decrees. This aspect of multi-use complex

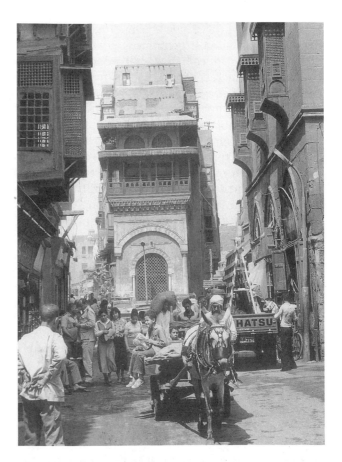

The Sebil-Kuttab of Abdel-Rahman Katkhuda in Cairo: An example from the Ottoman period of a combined structure with a Quranic school on the top floor and a public fountain on the ground floor.

characterizes many Mosque complexes to this day. A tribunal was sometimes located in the mosque and in early Islam it housed the treasury.

The design of the Mosque has changed considerably over the centuries even within the same general area of the Middle East. The simplest, oldest and original design, was the open courtyard and columned covered areas on four sides, called *Riwaqs*, with the one facing Mecca, known as the *Riwaq Al-Qibla* being larger than the other three. The center of the *Riwaq Al-* Qibla may be accentuated by a dome and the wall be marked by a niche called the *mihrab*. One or more minarets completed the composition. This is the style made famous by the great Ummayad Mosque in Damascus. Subsequently the four *riwaqs* were replaced by vaulted spaces opening onto the central courtyard called *Iwans*. The dome over the Qibla side became more accentuated, and the verticality of the composition enhanced, as was the case with the Mamluk mosques such as the Sultan Hassan Mosque in Cairo. The Ottoman mosques reached their apogee with the great architect Sinan in the 16th Century, and relied on a huge domed central space supported by four half domes. The enclosed structure was entered through an open forecourt with colonnades all around. In all cases one or more minarets served the dual function of landmark and call to prayer.

Mosques were utilized by a variety of different people: *ulama* (scholars), *fuqaha* (jurists), *mudarrisins* (teachers), *muhadithins* (hadith scholars), *sufi shaykhs*, Quran reciters, *muezzins* (those who call to the prayer) and others. The Muslim historian Maqrizi reported that there were seven hundred fifty people living in the Azhar mosque by the beginning of the 15th century, and that in 1416 the Emir Sudun had turned them out. While this action might seem appropriate by modern standards, in the 15th century it was not only deplored, but even harshly condemned. Emir Sudun was believed to have committed a major sin because a mosque has to be *mamur*, that is inhabited by pious people day and night.

Zawiyas, spaces for superogatory prayer outside mosques, were numerous, usually built by a ruler or a wealthy person for a certain *shaykh* who acted as the head of the center. The *shaykh* and his staff lived in the *zawiya* where he received his pupils. When the *shaykh* died he was usually buried in his *zawiya*, which accounts for the large number Shaykhs' tombs inside the city.

The *madrasa* (college) is listed second in prestige after the mosque. The term appears on a considerable number of Cairene monuments. There was, however, a considerable difference between teaching in mosques and teaching in a *madrasa*. Although, the scholar Maqrizi mentioned five earlier schools in Nishapur when speaking of the Nizamiyya Madrasa in Baghdad (1066–68), he regarded it as the most important *madrasa* because the teachers were granted a regular salary from the ruler, a practice that was begun in 989,

Courtyard of Al-Azhar Mosque-University: The great Mosque of Al-Azhar, founded by the Fatimids (10th century AD) and to which many later additions by Mamluks and others were made, is also one of the oldest universities in the world.

during the reign of the Fatimid Caliph al-Aziz bi-Allah at the Al-Azhar University-Mosque.

A *madrasa*, on the other hand, was a private institution in which teaching was confined to resident students. Friday public prayer, for example, did not take place in the *madrasas* until the fourteenth century. An example of this new development was found in the great complex of the Sultan Hasan, 1356–1362 in Cairo, which had both a *masjid Jami* and four *madrasas* (as stated in the endowment deed, (*waqf*) written at the time of its founding). It was the college mosque par excellence.

The terms used for sufi institutions, varied from one country to the other, hence the confusion sometimes caused from historical sources. Ibn Battuta, the famous traveller, who visited Egypt in 1326, said *zawiyas* in Egypt were called *khanqas*, the place wherein *sufis*, lived, and their gatherings held in a domed chamber. Other historians said that *ribats* and *khanqas* fulfilled the same purpose. *Sufi* institutions in Egypt are therefore known either as *khanqas* or *ribats*.

A major difference between *khanqas* and *madrasas*, according to medieval Muslim sources, was that while teachers could reside in and take allowances from any religious institution, a *sufi* could not stay in a *madrasa* and receive a pay from its endowment at the same time. He adds: a *faqih* is a *sufi*, but a *sufi* is not a *faqih*. Many *khanqas* also had *madrasas* which were attended by Sufis who stayed in them.

Secular Buildings

All buildings were called *dars*, in the early Islamic period, but by the Mamluk period (1250 AD) the term was usually applied to private houses. A princely residence was normally called a *qasr* or palace. Maqrizi, in his description of Cairo, mentions fifty-seven town houses, the majority of which he calls *dar*; while referring to four others as *qasr*. Early *dars* in Egypt were extremely large constructions comparable to the Roman *insulae*. Dar al-Tamr had twelve shops, five lounges, fifty-eight storerooms, fifteen huts, six halls, a yard, seventy-five residential units and five upper lounges. Another large house also had five *masjids*, two baths and several bakeries for its inhabitants who needed more than four hundred jars of water a day. Often, the term *makan* (place) which could be applied to any construction religious or secular, was adopted for princely residences.

Buildings For Investment

A *waqf*, (an endowment stipulated for a specific purpose), is the best source for different types of medieval investment constructions. For example, the *waqf* of al-Ashraf Barsbay, carved on the walls of his *madrasa*

The Azm palace in Syria: Is an example of a Qasr, fully restored to its erstwhile appearance with missing parts and the gardens fully reconstructed.

dated 1425, enumerates fifteen different types of constructions. We shall discuss only four terms which have generally been confused, *qaysariyya, khan, funduq* and *wakala.*

One important point which must be made is that the term used to designate the function of the building applies only to the ground floor. The upper stories are referred to separately. *Qaysariyyas* were not like *dars,* where craftsmen worked and sold their products. A *qaysariyya* was either rented as a whole by auction, or each unit separately in cash or on trade leases. There were *funduqs* in Fustat since the beginning of the Muslim conquest from 641, which had accommodation for foreign merchants. The governors of Misr for forty years, until the reign of Yazid ibn Muawiyya (680–83) stayed in Funduq Harmah in the *masjid* at its entrance. *Funduqs* were used for selling goods and products from the countryside or from other countries and were usually built at city gates, a strategic point where merchants had to unload and pay custom duties (*mukus*).

Khans were quite large, served as *funduqs* and had store rooms. It was only, however, in *khans* and *funduqs* that money was kept. *Khan* Masrur al-Kabir, also

called *funduq,* had ninety-nine *bayts* (living units) a *masjid Juma* and a safe where the money of orphans, and those out of town, was kept. Merchants kept their money in Funduq Bilal al-Mughisi; therefore *funduqs* and *khans* were well guarded places. The *wakala* was a bonded warehouse for trade, and it is probable that after the state tax was collected, the owner of the *wakala* got a share or perhaps a percentage on the value of the imports and the distribution in the city.

The buildings were often inviting, sometimes imposing. The remaining monuments were mostly public buildings, the bulk of old residences having succumbed to replacement and occasionally reuse. By and large, where there were noticeable deviations from the human scale, they tended to accentuate verticality. Most of all, buildings were primarily hostage to and a reflection of the townscape. Irregular shapes and their shadows created by the irregularly shaped lots of growing cities, the imaginative character of corners and details responding to the organic growth of the city as building reclamation and the linking of new to older buildings helped create the lively, vibrant character we still find so charming.

◆ URBAN CHARACTER

What then were the key elements of this urban character? They were: (i) The Friday Mosque; (ii) The Market; (iii) The Palace or citadel; and (iv) The residences, which included both individual homes and apartment complexes. A brief word about each is pertinent.

The Friday mosque: The central and most important building in the city, the Friday Mosque, like the cathedral in the Christian societies of the west, was both landmark and congregation point. It was frequently surrounded by the rest of the urban tissue, so that the approach through narrow streets led to a sense of discovery, very different from the broad approaches and public places found in western urbanism. Stylistically, the architectural expression varied by region and period, but key features such as the minaret and the gateway are common. The dome is found in Egypt, the Middle East and North Africa and arguably finds its greatest expression in the Ottoman architecture of Turkey.

The market, the center of economic activity, it was frequently found near the Friday Mosque and tended to be a series of streets with commercial stalls on both sides. Physical contiguity usually coincided with specialization in terms of the wares provided, thus creating sub-markets within the market area.

The palace or *citadel* tended to be the seat of temporal power, the expression of wealth of the ruler or the ruling elite and to affirm an elegance of construction, representing the best technology of the period. A detailed discussion of the citadel of Cairo and the Topkapi palace in Istanbul will be given later in this essay.

The residences, included apartment complexes known as Rab' (plural Riba') which consisted of several duplex units frequently but not always laid out around a courtyard. The individual homes of the elites were usually built around a courtyard, with a garden and water.

This brings us to the infrastructure that complements these elements. *The streets* were the essential element that defines the urban character and provides the contact for a sense of place. Characterized by broken alignments, variable land uses and a skillful combination of slight expansions that create the space for public interaction and tight spaces that highlight the human scale these tortuous streets were the organizing framework of the old city. Frequently the houses and activities were based on clan, ethnic or guild associations giving the space a strong social solidarity. *Neighborhoods* organized around cul-de-sac streets called Harat were the basic building blocks of the city.

Gardens were very important to provide privacy and enjoyment for the elites. The sanctity of the inner courtyards, frequently protected by a broken entrance, led to "oases in the city." *Water* was provided through public fountains in the streets and in the gardens.

Within the urban context, the characteristics mentioned above are valid for most of the cities of medieval Islam until the early nineteenth century, when technological change and the influence of models from the west created a profound transformation of the urban landscape of the cities of the Muslim world. In the twentieth century, and especially in the last forty years, dramatic population growth, modernization and increased urbanization have all contributed to the transformation of the cities into major metropolises not to say mega-cities, with all the problems and opportunities inherent to such a transformation.

Since it would be impossible to examine the transformation of all the different areas of the Muslim world here, we propose, to limit our discussion, to three cities and survey their urban development and evolving architectural character: Cairo, Istanbul, and Samarkand. Each of the three cities has a well documented history, and has exercised a profound influence on the region where they are located. They are sufficiently different to justify inclusion in a survey article such as this, yet sufficiently similar to exemplify the common thread believed to exist throughout the Muslim societies of the world.

Cairo: From Military Camp to City

Muslim general Amr Ibn al-Aas conquered the fort at Babylon in 636. To commemorate his victory, he first built a mosque near the site. Even in its much trans-

formed state, it reveals in its hypostyle formation, and open courtyards, the inspiration of the Arabian Hijaz. This area became known as *Al-Fustat,* or "the encampment," in which military tents slowly gave way to more substantial dwellings in mud brick. These were based on eastern models, more specifically on the open "T-shaped" *iwans* (vaulted spaces open on one side), some examples of which can be found in the Ukaider palace in Iraq, a nascent step toward the model internalized and refined in the tenth century in Cairo by the Fatimids. One example of that transition exists today in the Dardiri Qaa in Cairo which is now used as a space for light industry; the high square central tower with flanking covered iwans, an unmistakable descendent of the houses of *Al-Fustat.*

After the initial settlement of Amr ibn Al As at Fustat, expansion of the settlements proceeded between the river and the Mokattam mountain in a Northeasterly direction. The first expansion settlement was al-Askar, followed by Ibn Tulun's al-Qatai. All these settlements accompanied the strengthening of the role of the city as the center of administrative control, although Alexandria continued to be a very important city.

There is little left of these three early settlements, except for two major Mosques. The oldest, the Mosque of Amr, has been many times restored and there is no more than one or two bays of the original building still in place. The imposing structure that we see today is all built in subsequent periods and through subsequent additions and restorations. The Mosque of Ibn Tulun (ninth century AD) is a much more important building. It was the quasi-independent ruler of Egypt, Ahmad Ibn Tulun who had this imposing structure built. It is unique in having a minaret with an external staircase, apparently inspired by the Malwiya tower of Sammarra in Iraq. The square plan with the beautiful arcades on all four sides is elegant and unencumbered. The scale, although large, is not overwhelming. The Mosque was not used during the Fatimid period, and had fallen in disrepair., until a young Mamluk, Lasheen, hid from his enemies in the abandoned mosque and vowed to restore it if he escaped. He did and in the tumultuous politics of the period, became sultan and fulfilled his vow, returning the Mosque to its original grandeur. Because his restoration was faithful to the original, the building we now have is not very different from the Mosque that Ibn Tulun built in the ninth Century AD.

After the Tulunids, the return of Abbasid suzerainty was weak. Soon the country fell into the hands of the Ikhshid dynasty. The dissolute court and the weak administration of such a rich province, plus the general weakening of the Abbassid Caliphate in Baghdad, meant that Egypt was an easy and natural eastward expansion of the rising power of the Shia dynasty, the

Fatimids, who conquered Egypt from north Africa in 969 AD. The Fatimids established their capital city immediately to the northeast of the existing settlements and called it Al-Qahira, the victorious, today known as Cairo.

Today, we have little left of the older settlements other than the two big mosques. Because of their permeability, the mud brick residences there were always less secure than their masonry counterparts in the princely city of Al-Qahira. Al-Fustat and Bulaq served as the port and supply center for the new city with each representing a completely different character. Because the Fatimids at first excluded the general populace from the new city, Al-Qahira, they designed it to fit their vision. Its plan was inspired by the Roman cities they had seen in their trek across north Africa, it was orthogonal and axial, while the civil basis of Al-Fustat encouraged more organic development.

The plan of the Fatimid area, was a regular rectangle encircled by fortification walls and divided from north to south by a great thoroughfare. In the center, two palace complexes faced each other opening into a large square. Around this central complex of palaces, the city was divided into quarters that housed the different ethnic groups.

The Fatimid rule made Cairo the center of a vast and splendid empire. The walls of the city and its gates date from that period as do some of the mosques: Al-Hakim, and al-Saleh Tallai, named after a grand Vizier of the period, which shows that the mosque was on an upper floor with shops below it.

The most important builder for Cairo remains the famous ruler and warrior Saladin. This amazing individual started as the Vizier for the last Fatimid Caliph whom he deposed and established his own dynasty. He built the fortifications of Cairo and started the construction of the citadel that still dominates Cairo to this day. Saladin was not to reside in the citadel, but from 1206 AD, all rulers of Egypt resided there until the Khedive Ismail (builder of the Suez canal and much of modern Cairo) moved to the newly constructed Abdeen Palace in 1874.

The Citadel is a unique complex, a royal city that ruled over the rest of Cairo and Egypt for the next 800 years. It is one of the largest citadels in the world, and contains many buildings erected by successive rulers. A well for water, Bir Yusuf, runs 90 meters deep. An aqueduct, combining seven waterwheels links the citadel to the city. The citadel walls are vast and considered impregnable in its day. There are 36 towers, many of them larger than the towers at the Tower of London. Several mosques and palaces are built within its walls, and the stables were designed to accommodate up to 30,000 horses. So imposing is this complex that it is visible from almost any place in Cairo, and the

thin minarets of the Mohammed Ali Mosque, the last erected there in the 19th century, are the quintessential signature of the Cairo skyline.

The vast bulk of the monuments in medieval Cairo, however, date from the Mamluk period. After the end of the Ayyubid dynasty founded by Saladin, the slave warriors, the Mamluks, who had initially been imported into Egypt to protect the regime, became themselves the rulers. The transition occurred through the brief reign of a most remarkable woman, Shajarat Al-Durr ("tree of pearls"), who as wife and widow of the last Ayyubid sultan, ruled for a brief period initially in the name of her son then in her own name, including minting money with her name. She led the defense of Egypt against the IX crusade and imprisoned France's king (saint) Louis IX in Mansura (1249 AD). She married the most powerful of these warrior slaves, Aybak, and was subsequently murdered by his first wife. The succession started the first of two Mamluk dynasties the Bahri Mamluks, of whom the most illustrious was Al-Zahir Baybars, who stopped the westwards expansion of the Mongol warriors at Ain Galut (1260 AD) and completed the defeat of the crusaders in the Levant. He established the first of the great Mamluk monuments, the mosque that bears his name.

Under the Mamluks, Cairo became the center of a vast empire of great wealth and learning. The Mamluks, though themselves originally warrior slaves, had no loyalty other than to Egypt. They built for themselves and for posterity in Cairo and the rest of the country. It is their legacy, as well as the subsequent Ottoman heritage that most decisively defines the character of medieval Cairo.

The plethora of monuments that make up the unique richness of the Cairene urban environment date mostly from the Mamluk period. The great complexes of Qalawun and the Mosque and Madrasa of Sultan Hassan are exemplars of the architecture of the period that are widely studied. The urban character of the city, and imperial capital for about 400 years by that time, was developed into the characteristic guild quarters and system that one finds in all the other cities of that time. The emergence of the building types described at the outset of this essay are all well reflected in Mamluk architecture from the 12th to the 16th centuries.

The Mamluk state fell to the advancing Ottoman Turks in 1517. The Ottoman period saw a relative decline of Cairo, as many of the best artisans and architects moved, forcibly or voluntarily to Istanbul, the unquestioned center of the Muslim world after the 16th century. Ottoman rulers in Egypt were relatively less important persons, although the best traditional houses to be found date from the 16 and 17th centuries. Some splendid small structures were erected, including the *sabil-kuttab* of Abdel Rahman Katkhuda, one of the best examples of the charitable trust arrangements that was intended to educate youth in the upper floor while the ground floor provided water fountains for the travelers.

After the invasion of Egypt by Napoleon and his expedition, which provided an unparalleled description of the country, its flora and fauna, as well as its monuments and the socio-economic characteristics that prevailed at the end of the 18th century, the return of Ottoman rule in Egypt was accompanied by a major renewal and modernization program launched by the energetic and visionary Muhammad Ali Pasha. He modernized agriculture, built industries and educated youth. He also built one of the finest exemplars of Mosque architecture, sometimes known as the alabaster mosque, which dominates the Cairo skyline. The style of the Muhammad Ali Mosque is the quintessential Ottoman design perfected by Sinan, with Dome and squinches and pencil point minarets. The Dome is 52 meters high. The Minarets of the Mosque are among the most elegant in the world, reaching some 50 meters in height on a diameter of only 2.7 meters. So well built are these infinitely slender minarets, even though they are made of unreinforced stone and joined by mortarless masonry, that they did not break in any of the earthquakes that hit Cairo in the last 150 years.

Beyond the major monuments and urban character that we have been discussing, the houses and the texture of buildings that filled in the city deserve a few words. In 1171, following the Ayyubid takeover of Cairo from the Fatimids, the city was opened to general habitation and use, with a concurrent change in its linear street patterns. The pattern of growth and the concern for privacy eventually combined to convert the streets of medieval Cairo into a convoluted and seemingly chaotic, but essentially hierarchical system of major and minor streets, lanes, alley, and paths, incrementally interrupted by open spaces of various sizes. Additional studies, on the city have shown the extent to which the location of these spaces and the configuration of these circulation paths are far from random.

Green areas, now becoming increasingly rare in a city that is increasingly suffering from dust and pollution, acted as natural cooling and filtration devices for surrounding buildings. Also an analysis of the housing pattern and open squares reveals that a deliberate tactic of interlocking spaces was used. Typically, two courtyards were employed, with one being planted on the windward side and the other being paved. As the sunrise and the hot air generated by the paved area began to rise, the simple principle of convection pulled through the cooler air, trapped by the vegetation in the planted court from the previous evening, causing a cycle to begin. Since the planted courts in this symbiotic system were placed to intercept the desert breeze first,

Egyptian architect, Hassan Fathy.

the higher palm trees in them acted much like the cilia in the human lung, catching the air-born dust and sand, which was then filtered over the surface of the ground, not on every available horizontal building surface, as it is today. Larger open spaces in this system, such as the mosque courtyards, continued the process, turning the entire pattern of solids and voids in the medieval city into an effective air-conditioning system.

Even today, however, it is the density of outstanding monuments that is breathtaking in medieval cairo. The Shari Muizz li-din illah, the north-south artery of the Fatimid city, still retains its formal integrity, despite the severe pressures now placed upon it. Running from the Bab al Futuh (the northern gate) at the northern wall, to the Bab Zuwaila (the southern gate) in the south, it connects an unprecedented sequence of historically significant Islamic monuments, which still remain unknown to most of the world. Even a partial list will indicate their extent; the Mosque of Hakim, Bayt Kathuda and Souheimi, the extraordinary Qalaun complex, consisting of a *Mamluk maristan*, or hospital, *madrasa*, and mausoleum, to name just a few. Each of the four richest architectural periods in their turn, from Fatimid (969–1169) through Ayyubid, (1169–1260) Mamluk, (1254–1517) and Ottoman (1517–1924) are each well represented within the walls of the medieval city and, each, while readily recognized as different in detail, continues to speak the basic language spoken by its predecessor.

The more recent development of Cairo has seen the transformation of the city into a huge sprawling metropolis of over 12 million inhabitants. The medieval city with all its charm is but a tiny part at the center of the city, which is severely under stress from speculation, inappropriate land uses and rising damp. Efforts at conservation are still inadequate to the task, and more needs to be done if the unique treasure that Cairo represents is not to be lost to future generations.

The new city has not produced much new architecture and urbanism. The layout of Cairo, modeled after 19th century European models, did not cope well with the population explosion that followed the second world war. The architectural expression of new buildings tended to either reinterpret the past, as was artfully done by the great architect Hassan Fathy and his colleague Ramses Wisa Wassef, or to try to emulate the western modern style, with some competent but few notable buildings in that style.

The heart of Cairo was a three-dimensional textbook for Hassan Fathy, (1900–1991) who was undeniably the most important contemporary architect Egypt has produced. Through his influence and example, an entire generation of young architects are now exploring their heritage, which previously had been a source of embarrassment. This has occasionally led to unfortunate misreadings, particularly of the personalized vocabulary that Fathy had painstakingly established. The process of self-criticism has however proved to be a beneficial one. The new Cairo Opera House, By Suzaki Hiroyuki, indicates the extent to which this vocabulary has also penetrated the international consciousness, providing metaphors that would have been dismissed as retrogressive during the period immediately following World War II.

The powerful argument frequently used to curtail destruction of the rain forests, that there are untold species in them, still unknown, which may hold clues to the improvement of the human condition also holds true for medieval Cairo. The serious study of Cairene architecture started with the protean efforts of the British architectural historian, K.A.C. Creswell in categorizing this resource over half a century ago. Significant additional work was done by many scholars, including Laila Ibrahim, Doris Abu-Seif, Mona Zakaria, Nelly Hanna and Andre Raymond. Saleh Lamei Mostafa has been systematically recording and analyzing the monuments of Cairo and has recently co-authored a major reference work with Abdel-baki Ibrahim. Several scholars and specialists, including Ronald Lewcock, Saleh Lamei Mostafa, Oleg Grabar

and others have graphically traced the enormity of the forces now conspiring to eradicate this priceless heritage and steps are being taken to stop them, but these efforts are minuscule in comparison to the problems involved and time is running out. Rising ground water resulting from leaks in antiquated sanitary systems, excessive vibrations caused by heavy traffic along Shari al Muizz, which should be a pedestrian street, increasing air pollution primarily carried by stiff winds from the industries at Helwan in the south, are among the many issues urgently needing to be addressed. A clue to the singularity of this legacy may be found in the recognition that it has received as a part of the world heritage, not just of the Muslim peoples.

Samarkand

Samarkand, which is located on the ancient silk route through the Zerafshan Valley, in Uzbekistan, and one of the oldest cities in Transoxania, is no stranger to natural or man-made calamities. In the fourth century B.C. Alexander the Great and his army were one of the first to invade it. At that time the center was located to the north of Registan Square and the town was known as Maracanda or Afrasiyab. After Alexander the Great died, this city and other parts of central Asia made up a key part of the Selucid Kingdom.

Surprisingly, few sources on the spread of Islam into the area exist, but those that do, indicate that the Muslims first crossed the Oxus in 654 to begin a conquest made difficult by unfamiliar, rugged terrain, too extended supply lines, and fearsome opposition. They were assisted in their efforts, however, by a sharply divided aristocracy which was split among many autonomous rulers, and a landowning nobility which consisted of merchants who grew rich on trade with China. Both classes were called "dihqan." The city of Paykand, near Bukhara, was known as the "city of merchants," and recorded as having been equal to Samarkand in wealth and prestige. While the internal dissent which existed between the various classes of the aristocracy would initially seem to have paved the way for easy domination of the region, the invaders were opposed by brave warriors with a strict code of discipline. The Muslim historian, Al-Tabari relates how, each year at Samarkand, a table was set for the warrior considered to be the most courageous fighter in Soghd. Anyone wishing to challenge this claim sat down at the same table and there followed a series of individual combats that settled the matter decisively. Many stories exist of personal friendships encouraged by common respect, between members of the opposing armies, and some of these have now been elevated to the status of legend, because they had been passed down from generation to generation.

Samarkand was a particularly difficult part of that

struggle. A complex administrative organization was instituted. Despite precise record keeping, the name of the specific Turkish tribe that proved to be the undoing of the Samanid dynasty that ruled the area until about 1000, however, has not been recorded. However, Ibn-al-Athir, the historian, noted that in 960 that "200,000 tents" of various Turkish groups converted to Islam. The Seljuks, who were one of these, went on to free the Muslim population of Tand, before moving south. On October 23, 999 A.D., the entire Samanid treasury in Bukhara was captured and an important chapter in history was closed. Nearly thirty years later, dissension among the Karakhamids allowed Abul Qasim Mahmud, otherwise known as Mahmud of Ghazna, the son of a Turk named Sabuktagin, who had control of most of the province south of the Amu-Darya, to invade Transoxania on the pretext that his envoys did not have free access to eastern Turkestan. He crossed the river in 1025 on a bridge created by boats linked together, leading what finally amounted to an enormous army up to the walls of the citadel of Samarkand. The local ruler fled, but by negotiation was able eventually to regain control of the city. In his dealings with the Abbasid Caliph Qadir, Mahmud put himself forward as the inheritor of Samanid power. His death, in 1030, marks the end of an important period in the history of the region since. His reign was marked by the construction of many significant buildings, particularly a mosque and *madrasa* at Ghazna. Masud, the eldest son of Mahmud of Ghazna continued the policies of his father, renewing a treaty with the Caliph regarding relationships with the Karakanids and Ghaznavids.

The Saljuk sultans began raiding Transoxania at the beginning of the eleventh century. The Saljuk leader, Malik-Shah, captured Bukhara in 1089 and laid siege to Samarkand, ending a period of great prosperity for the city. After taking it, Malik Shah moved on to Uzgand, before returning to Khurasan, leaving a governor in Samarkand. The Mongol invasion followed in the early part of the thirteenth century.

Following the depredations caused by Genghis-Khan and his death in 1227, Transoxania, along with the lower half of Khwarazm and territories east of the Sir Darya river was given to his second eldest son, Chaghatay. In spite of the general devastation caused by the Mongol advance, Samarkand recovered rather easily after the death of Genghis-Khan, because of its position along a main commercial artery.

In 1336, Timur, known in history as Tamerlane, was born near Shahrisabz, son of a pious Muslim named Taraghay. He gained an early reputation as a mercenary, entering the army of Jalal-al-Din in Sistan in 1363. His skill soon began to worry his superior, who tried to kill him, but only succeeded in partially paralyzing his right arm and leg. This handicap was subsequently the reason for the addendum of "leng," or "lame" to his name, which was later corrupted to "Tamerlane." He built a force of archers based on the Mongol "Tuman." In 1370, he built a new citadel at Samarkand, used it as a training ground for his army and a base for his first major victory against Herat in 1381. He waged other campaigns against Zaranj in Sisten, Qandahar, Rayy on the Caspian Sea, Tabriz, and Shirvan, Tiflis, Mosul Edessa, Mardin, Kars, Sivas, Aleppo, Damascus, and Baghdad, always returning to Samarkand.

After these impressive victories, Timur made overtures to England and Spain, encouraging them to establish trade agreements with him and as a result, a Spanish ambassador named Ruy Gonzalez de Clavijo left for Samarkand in 1403, arriving one year later in a state of total exhaustion. In spite of his weariness, he wrote a glowing description of the city for the ruler of Spain, describing its architecture and urban features.

Ruy Gonzalez also referred to the Kok Sarai, Timur's famous "Blue Palace," which was visible from everywhere in the city. Today, however, little remains of the Citadel that Timur built. Many of his other projects have been rebuilt so that it is now possible to comprehend the enormity of Timur's architectural interests. The grand scale of his building projects changed the whole scope of the town with architectural complexes creating a strong and permanent effect on the form of Samarkand for centuries to come.

The grandest of these is the *Masjid-i-Jami*, or *"Bibi Khanum,"* Mosque which is one of the largest monuments ever built in the Islamic world. The axis linking the entrance to the courtyard was connected to the Registan by a covered bazaar. Timur also built the *Gur-i-Amir* mausoleum for his grandson, but he was buried in it too. Like the *"Bibi Khanum,"* the *Gur-i-Amir* was intended to be a complex with a *khanaqa* and a *madrasa*. This complex, completed around 1404 A.D., is generally regarded as one of the earliest examples of Timurid formal architecture, laid out with two public buildings enclosing an urban square. During this period a synthesis of the arts emerged in Samarkand, fusing local tradition with those of the arts "imported" from conquered lands which created an organic link between architecture and painting, wood and stone carving, ceramic and metal ware.

Although Timur was a great builder and has been credited with over thirty monuments (of which only eight survive), he preferred to spend his time in the suburban garden palace which he had built near the city. Here he constructed a number of pavilions and palaces decorated with paintings illustrating his campaigns, his family, courtiers and army. Its plan was based on the typical layout of Persian gardens and used the axial principle of many towns of the region. The scheme consisted of planted spaces intersected with paths and water channels. A palace or a pavilion was situated on the central axis. The pattern of these gardens, known as *Chahar Bagh* or "four gardens" is linked to cosmological symbolism. Many of these gardens had a raised central pavilion on a mound surrounded with water as part of this presentation. The largest garden was known as the Takht-i-Qaracheh, located on the main Samarkand-Shahrisabz road. Off the same road but closer to the capital was the Daulatabagh garden, which was surrounded by a 4-kilometer long wall and a wide canal which divided the garden in two parts. There was a large palace in the center overlooking the gardens.

After Timur's death in 1405, his son Shahrokh inherited his vast kingdom after a struggle. Unable to govern it alone, he divided the kingdom in two parts. He took Khwarazm, with its capital at Herat, and put Mavarannahr, with Samarkand as its capital, under the charge of his son, Ulugh Beg. Unlike his grandfather Timur, Ulugh Beg was not associated with expansionism, but with learning and science. He was an astronomer and mathematician, poet and scholar as well as a connoisseur of architecture. Construction continued under Ulugh Beg and additions were either made to the "*Bibi Khanum,*" *Gur-i-Amir* and *Shah-i-Zindeh* necropolis or they were completed. Ulugh Beg's eagerness to spread learning and scientific thought committed him to patronize the construction of *madrasas* in Bukhara, Merv and Samarkand. The *madrasa* in Samarkand, which forms part of the Registan square, was intended to include a *khanaqa*, a *caravanserai* and a mosque.

During the reign of Ulugh Beg, Samarkand developed into a great cultural center attracting the best scholars and craftsmen from all over Asia, including mathematicians and astronomers such as Qazizadeh Rumi, Mawlana Ghiyath-al-Din, Jamshid al-Kashi and others. Jamshid al-Kashi arrived in Samarkand when Ulugh Beg's greatest dream, the observatory, was nearing completion. This observatory was extraordinary. A gigantic cylindrical building, 48 meters in diameter and 40 meters in height, it was equipped with the most modern instruments of the time and its facade was covered in carved mosaics and decorative glazed tiles in the Moorish style of the fourteenth and fifteenth centuries.

The level of scholarship inspired by the patronage of Ulugh Beg was indeed unique. Ali Kashi for instance, known for his work on numerical analysis in *Miftah as Hisab* (The Key to Calculation), preceded similar breakthroughs in Europe by nearly two centuries. He dedicated this work to Ulugh Beg whose own monumental work on astronomy, *The Gurganor Tables* or The *Zij of Ulugh Beg* became a basic textbook for astronomers. Shahrokh's death in 1447 A.D., followed two years later by that of Ulugh Beg, brought this period of scholarship in Samarkand to an end, and Timurid power began to decline.

During this period Samarkand continued to be the center of the economic and political life of the region. (Construction of roads, bridges and irrigation canals continued.) Although it is recorded that two enormous *madrasas*, the size of the Egyptian pyramids, were built to the north of the Registan square, no trace of them remains. In fact, few monuments of this period have survived.

Education, however, continued to be important for the rulers of Samarkand. For example, the Uzbek Ashtarkhanide dynasty ruled Samarkand during the first half of the seventeenth century. Its chieftain, Yalangtash Bahadur, replaced Ulugh Beg's *caravanseri* at the Registan Square with the now famous *Tillya Kari Madrasa,* and the *khanaqa* on the same site was replaced by the Shir Dor and *Tillya Kari Madrasa* which surround the Registan Square.

These frequent dynastic changes do not seem to have diluted the richness of Samarkand's cultural heritage. The seventeenth century poet Malek Mohammed Bade-ibn-Mohammed Sharif Samarkandi mentions the names of 2300 poets who lived in Samarkand during this time. These poets held posts such as calligraphers, tentmakers, artisans, painters, bookbinders, and potters. The development of craft skills and handloom fabric-weaving in silk and cotton continued. Wine making and the paper making continued to thrive. By the beginning of the nineteenth century separate kingdoms emerged and the *khanates* of Bukhara, Ferghana and Khiva became separate entities. Samarkand was absorbed into the kingdom of Bukhara.

Towards the middle of the nineteenth century, Samarkand had become part of the Russian empire. The military siege of the town by the Czar's army resulted in damage and the destruction of a considerable number of the old monuments, including those on the Registan Square and the area near Timur's citadel. The redesign of Samarkand during this period follows the pattern of many other European colonial towns in the Muslim world. Samarkand was divided into two parts—the native or old town and the European town. European architecture was preferred to the indigenous Central Asian style and the administrative buildings and residential quarters took on radically new forms. In housing, the concept of the apartment block replaced the courtyard house.

Timur's citadel was also modified. By the latter half of the nineteenth century, the inner part of the citadel had been divided into two parts, one being used as the Khan's palace and for local administration and the other as a residence. After the citadel's capture by Russian troops, the palace was converted into a hospital. The *hammam* (public baths) adjoining it became

Registan Square in Samarkand: This complex of three great Madrassas covering some 200 years of history is the heart of Samarkand.

the mortuary. A Russian school and a church were constructed in the citadel's premises and also a square with a memorial to the fallen Russian soldiers. Some years after the October Revolution of 1917, the Uzbek Soviet Socialist Republic was formed with Samarkand as its capital from 1924 to 1930. Subsequently, the capital shifted to Tashkent and Samarkand became the second most important administrative center of Uzbekistan. Samarkand today is the second largest city in the newly independent Republic of Uzbekistan and remains an industrial and cultural center. It has a large university and important institutes specializing in teaching, architecture, medicine, agriculture, scientific research and sheep breeding. The town also has major theaters for opera, ballet and variety performances. There is an important museum of history, culture and the art of Central Asia located in the town. As in the past, Samarkand continues to export dried fruit, cotton, rice, and leather to other parts of the world.

Uzbekistan, situated in the heart of Central Asia, is located between the Amu Darya and Syr Darya Rivers, the Aral Sea, and the Tien Shan mountains. In its northwestern half, Uzbekistan is largely a desert, while its southern half includes the fertile valleys of the river

systems of Ferghana and Zerafshan that were the lifelines for the ancient cities of Bukhara, Ferghana, and Samarkand. The Uzbeks take their name from a fourteenth century ruler named Khan Uzbek, and have their origins in the Turko-Mongol tribes who were once nomadic pastoralists. Today, the city of Samarkand is multinational and its population of 390,000, as of 1989, comprises ninety nationalities. According to recent data, the region has a population of 20 million, which includes Uzbeks (68%), Russians (11%), Kazakhs, and Tajiks (each 4%), Kara-Kalpaks (2%), and Korlans (1%). In the last twenty years, the population of the city of Samarkand has increased by over 100,000. Samarkand, which now covers over 15,000 hectares, is also an important railway junction of the Krasnovodsk-Tashkent line and its airport is the second largest in Uzbekistan after Tashkent.

The pre-modern city of Samarkand has been the subject of a number of plans that have aimed at giving formal direction to its expansion and modernization. The basic approach taken by previous urban planners has been to consider the modern and the premodern settlements as one unit and to find ways of integrating them. The use of green avenues which pass through town has been one approach utilized to attempt this integration. Russian planners, in the last century, located their extension of the city along the curved avenues towards the west of the old town encircling the site of the citadel. At that time, clearing the remains of Timur's citadel and locating the military camp on the site had provided the only meeting point between the old pre-modern Timurid settlement and the new Russian colonial settlement. Subsequently, the political and administrative center built during the Soviet period was located on the site of the military camp.

This territory and the area between it and the Registan complex has remained the symbolic center of Samarkand. During the Timurid and post-Timurid period, the network of narrow streets and passages that linked the gates in the city walls all covered the area of what is known today as the Registan Square. Plans drawn up in the 1890s laid down a broad tree-lined avenue running northeast to southwest that connected the new settlement to the citadel. This avenue remains a focal spine for the master plan drawn up in 1981, which shows a major expansion of the town along this spine towards the southwest of the city. Today, Islam is once again practiced freely in the Ferghana Valley and the construction of mosques and madrasas has continued, making it possible for the architectural traditions of the past, which are so responsible for the individual character of Samarkand, to be re-established once again.

Istanbul

For many, the source of Islamic architecture in Turkey begins in Istanbul, just as that of Egypt does in Cairo. It is understandable that an event as cataclysmic as the Turkish conquest of the eastern capital of Christendom in 1453 would bring about other major adjustments in both the form and population of the city. Since Constantinople's population had gradually, but steadily, decreased prior to the conquest, Mehmet II found himself the sovereign of a virtually empty city. After tentative attempts at resettlement that were resisted because of the Sultan's initial refusal to grant ownership of real estate, a dual policy of land grants to prominent citizens and *waqfs* (religious endowments), as well as forced deportation and resettlement, totally reorganized the existing urban fabric, giving it a new social mix. New districts, bearing the names of origin of people resettled from Karaman, Trebizond, Belgrade, or elsewhere, began to spring up throughout Istanbul as people began to pour into the vacated city. Eventually, this chaotic and somewhat haphazard policy of repopulation became more systematic, once the various areas throughout the Ottoman empire also began to be relocated en masse specifically because they could be of some exact service to either the court or

the city. In addition to this influx of culturally diverse ethnic groups, Mehmet also drastically altered the Byzantine makeup of the city by introducing the Ottoman *kulliye* into common use. Basically a self-contained village unto itself, the *kulliye* is a complex providing social services symbiotically related to a mosque, providing housing facilities, kitchens, hospitals, schools, and libraries, which are meant solely for the welfare of the public. This new institutional type had within it the seeds of a totally distinct urban organization and it progressively transformed Istanbul into an Ottoman city. The imperial *kulliye* gradually occupied the key points of the urban fabric and the city's linear structure, which had been fixed virtually since the time of Theodosius, was progressively replaced by a discontinuous point-by-point configuration that has left an indelible mark upon it. This large scale system of monumental punctuation allows great readability of the urban area today.

Between the time of Sultan Sulayman (died 1566) and the end of the nineteenth century, Istanbul's population nearly doubled, growing from 500,000 to 900,000. In that time, the accumulation of *kulliye* and new settlements had completely altered the main axis of the Byzantine city, which had primarily paralleled to the Marmara coast, to one along the Golden Horn which linked the Bayezit, Sulayman and Fatih complexes together. With the opening of the first Ottoman customs office between the Sultan Ahmet and Bayezit Square near the Golden Horn, a new urban focus began to be established, but the old city walls on the west restricted further development. Because of this restriction, all new growth in the city extended along the Bosphorus, including Kadikoy and Uskudar, which at first were totally separate settlements of unique character divided by wide fields and gardens. Professor Dogan Kuban, the Turkish architect, has shown that fountains were central as the primary water source of the village, and a comfortable walking distance to each helped to determine boundaries. He has also estimated that prior to the sixteenth century, 62.4% of all Istanbul's mosques were located in the old city with the remainder scattered among the Bosphorus settlements. In the eighteenth century, this ratio dropped to 45% on the peninsula and 55% outside. All of the new settlements along the water's edge helped to establish the Bosphorus as a major water transport lane, gradually transforming the image of the entire region even further.

Along with the new axis of development along the Golden Horn, additional spines were established from Sircige to the west and from the Old City across the Golden Horn to Taksim and Harbeye, where a large influx of foreigners at the end of the seventeenth century established a vibrant colony which continued to grow for nearly two centuries. The growth of this second axis corresponded to a general move toward westernization in Istanbul at this time. Called the "Age of the Tulips" because of all the new gardens which seemed to spring up overnight, it was a period characterized by a general liberalization and social *joie de vivre*, as well as a growing governmental interest in cultural development. A series of military setbacks prompted several successive sultans, such as Abdulhamid I, Selim II, and Mahmud II, to make a determined effort to reorganize the Ottoman army between 1774 and 1839, despite stubborn resistance from both the elite army core of Janissaries and the *ulama*, the religious scholars. One important result of these reforms was the introduction of foreign military advisers and their dependents into the city and the creation of new military schools and barracks, built along Western lines, that became the focal point of expatriate compounds around them. These changes eventually led to a series of reforms, or *Tanzimat*, enacted in 1827, which inevitably altered the predominantly oriental customs and manners of Istanbul. The wearing of turbans, the headgear was officially banned in 1827, followed by the publication of the first newspaper in 1831, opening of a postal service in 1834, and the replacing the title of Grand Vizier by that of Prime Minister in 1836. Slavery was outlawed in 1846, followed by the opening of universities, as well as schools of medicine and art. Between 1846 and 1868, Ottoman embassies were established in many foreign countries, which also gave Turkish students the opportunity to study outside the country. As a final significant step, a Magna Carta was passed in 1856 that guaranteed the rights and equality of all of the people in the Empire regardless of religion or ethnic background.

As a result of the prevailing governmental attitude toward reform and with the advent of the industrial age at the turn of the century, the pace of westernization quickened. New railways were built that connected Istanbul to Europe as well as to other cities in Turkey, making it the hub of industry and trade and had a significant impact on its economic structure. New banks, attracted by this change, were established in the city to take advantage of its increased wealth. Steamship services started in 1850, with six ships, eventually led to the building of Hyderpasha port in the same year and Galata port in 1909, all of which were a great impetus to economic activity in Istanbul.

This new openness to western technology and culture also led to the first of what were to become an ongoing series of city plans which followed the lead of those then being implemented in the major cities of Europe. The first of these was prepared under the supervision of Marshal von Moltke who, in imitation of Baron Hausmann in Paris, proposed the opening of fourteen meter wide boulevards and avenues through the traditionally closed and dense urban fabric of the city. Aside from improving transportation links between different parts of the city, the most important rationale for this approach, apart from its being in vogue at the time, was the wish to create broad vistas to highlight large monuments more effectively by isolating them within wide open spaces. While the width of the avenues proposed by von Moltke was later reduced by half, the basic concept of the destruction of large sections of the traditional city fabric was firmly implanted and remained as a feature of all of the thirteen plans that were to follow.

These changes had a dramatic effect on traditional city plans in which over 30% of the buildings were devoted to religious use. The ideas instituted by von Moltke and refined later were finally crystallized in the famous Proust plan of 1937, which continued to be implemented through 1950. Focusing again on methods of transportation rather than the traditional values of the people, the Proust plan concentrated on establishing major highways on all three shores of the Istanbul peninsula, basically replacing the area previously taken up by the sea walls.

In addition, new cross axes were proposed at roughly the same places where the land walls of Septimus Severus, Constantine, and Theodosius had been built, linking the Marmara Sea and the Golden Horn with wide belts of asphalt that cut through the old city. This plan has been implemented incrementally and has completely disrupted the existing urban texture just as similar highways have destroyed the old city of Cairo, which previously was only capable of coping with pedestrian scale movement. Proust, in his "Archaeological Park" idea, has left buildings like the Hagia Sophia and the Yeni Cami stand alone in the midst of vast open spaces where in the past they had been an integral part of the urban context. Another far-reaching and often misunderstood impact of the Proust plan was a basic underestimation of Istanbul's potential for continued capital growth following the shift of the center of government to Ankara by the Turkish President, Ataturk in 1923. By proposing the location of what he felt would remain only light industry along the Golden Horn, Proust virtually assured the destruction of much of its natural beauty as that industry inevitably grew. All of the remaining urban plans commissioned since Proust, were ideologically based on the same philosophy of von Moltke and Proust, revolving around the creation of wider streets and a "social museum."

When Ataturk made the momentous decision to move the capital of Turkey from Istanbul to Ankara for security reasons in 1923, Istanbul lost political dominance within the country virtually overnight, but by 1950 had begun to find a new economic role for itself which became a turning point for the modern city. In

Hagia Sophia, Istanbul, Turkey.

the first part of what has been called the Republican Period (1923-50), Istanbul's loss of position as the political heart of Turkey brought about the loss of its social, economic, and cultural lifeblood as well. The aristocratic and bureaucratic associations of court life that the city had enjoyed for so long diminished as quickly as the empire it had once ruled. Prestigious residential areas, such as those around Bayezit and the Sultan Ahmet Square, which were just becoming fashionable among court officials at the time of the move, immediately lost value and were either demolished or suffered the slow destruction. The beginning of rural migration, which has so dramatically affected other countries such as Egypt in this century, also brought Anatolian farmers streaming into Istanbul at this time. This migration not only brought the city population above 1,000,000 for the first time in its history, but also started a critical shift in its social balance, from a traditionally polyglot ethnic mix of Turks, Armenians, Greeks, Levantines, Jews, and others, to a primarily rural Anatolian stock. Consequently, many minorities, who have historically formed the basis of a well-to-do bourgeoisie in Istanbul and who also gave the city a high degree of social texture, now found themselves being pushed out and started selling their property to

avoid being engulfed by the migrants moving in from the countryside. Many of these migrants did not find work easily. The peasant saying that the roads of Istanbul are paved with gold does not always prove to be the case and adjustment can be difficult. In 1979, for example, a survey of the Sulaymaniye area uncovered hundreds of itinerant workers living in one of the *kiosks* of the mosque complex, providing a specific example of the slow takeover of many parts of historical buildings, as well as a general profusion of squatter settlements, around Istanbul.

Following its loss of social and economic status in the Republican Period Istanbul entered a second phase of development after 1950. A switch to a multiparty system in the country at this time, and subsequently a more liberal attitude toward economic development meant that Istanbul has not only regained its old momentum, but today stands as one of the most cosmopolitan cities in the world. As a result of what might be characterized as mural, dendritic growth, the rings of Istanbul's walls, like the rings of a tree, have radiated out, one after another, from the first wall around the base of the old acropolis. This growth, when overlaid with the overlapping changes of axis in the Byzantine and Ottoman cities and the contemporary legacy of

Proust, have resulted in a city with totally separate, highly individual and identifiable zones. These zones, which give Istanbul a uniquely staccato character, are related in turn to the squares that have emerged from the archeological park idea, usually, but not always, centered around an Ottoman *kulliye* or mosque in their midst. A brief overview of several of them will help to clarify these ideas.

The Sultan Ahmet Square, which is the oldest of these, is completely dominated by the presence of the Hagia Sophia, which remains aloof as a perpetual symbol of the aspirations of two successive cultures. For nearly 800 years after it was first commissioned by the Emperor Justinian as a basilica, over a millennia ago, on the site of the original Constantinian church, it represented the largest covered space in the world, with a dome as high above the ground at its apex as the top of a modern fifteen story skyscraper. It was remodeled as a mosque and served as a formal progenitor for much of the religious architecture that followed Ottoman conquest.

The Sultan Ahmet, or "Blue Mosque," which lies southwest of the Hagia Sophia and gives this square its name, echoes this contention and received its name because of the beautiful tiles in its interior. Built under the patronage of the fourteenth sultan of the Ottoman empire, this mosque, was completed in seven years and opened to the public in 1616. Because of the difficulty in finding land of adequate size for the mosque, the units of its *kulliye* were scattered randomly all around the northern edge of the Byzantine Hippodrome, which is also located here.

The Sultan Ahmet Mosque, in its primary location at the tip of the Istanbul promontory, is the first in a series of mosques that seem to follow in line down the length of the peninsula. Covering a built area of 64 by 72 meters, excluding its courtyard, the building is modelled after the Sehzade Mosque, which was built by the great architect, Sinan, 68 years before. Following the pattern established by the Hagia Sophia, the main prayer space is covered by a dome that is 24 meters in diameter supported by four large round columns that stake out the corners of the square space below. This main dome is buttressed in turn by four semi-domes, which greatly expand that space.

Due to several hundred windows that penetrate both the domes and the walls, the mosque is generally better illuminated that the structure by Sinan after which it was patterned, allowing the tiles in its interior, the masterwork of a craftsman named Cinici Hasan Usta, to be seen to best advantage. An interesting aside in the design of the building is that a reduction in the anthropomorphic method of measurement which was used by the masons at this time from 24 to 60 fingers in width, has resulted in a marked difference in the proportions

of the mosque, making it quite unique among the others of the classical period.

Possibly, the most famous building on the Sultan Ahmet Square, however, is the Topkapi Palace, which stands at the highest point of the tip of the peninsula, exactly on the spot where the ancient acropolis has been. After Sultan Mehmet II conquered Constantinople in 1453, he first thought to build his palace in the Bayezit area because the *Saray-i Atik*, or Old Palace, as it was called was already there, having replaced Constantine's Great Palace as the residence of the Byzantine emperors after the eleventh century. Not totally satisfied with this choice, however, Mehmet decided to build at the Sarayburnu, perhaps because of its almost mythical connections with the city's imperial past. After the Byzantines abandoned it, a hospital and a home for the elderly had been built here in the twelfth century, as well as several monasteries, which stood on the Marmara side of the hill. Construction of a new palace, or Saray-i Cedid, began in 1467 A.D., on a slope overlooking the water, which ensured a constant breeze and sweeping views of Galata, Uskudar, Marmara, and the juncture of the Golden Horn and Bosphorus below. Continuously modified during the 400 years of its use, the palace constantly evolved into the eclectic complex seen today. In the course of that evolution, an extension of one of the pavilions built over the sea walls took the name *Topkapisi*, or Gungate Pavilion, because of the canons strung out along the shore below. This pavilion was removed, with the building of the railroad in this area in 1863, but the name remained and eventually replaced that of Saray-i Cedid for the whole complex. In 1478, Mehmet the Conqueror ordered the construction of the three meter thick Sur-i Sultan or Sultan's Wall around the palace, which joined with the old Byzantine walls to encircle the entire site.

Having reached its general form by 1465, the palace complex progressively decreased its size and degree of public access in successive courts, each surrounded by their own wall and each entered by a grand gate. The first of these is the *Bab-i Humayun*, or Imperial Gate, which leads to the *Alay Meydani*, or procession center, the scene of countless opulent audiences and reviews of elite Janissary corps in the past. The *Janissaries*, whose name is a corruption of the Turkish phrase Yeni-Ceri, or "new force," were an elite army recruited to serve the sultan. The *Alay Meydani* was relatively accessible to the public during ceremonies and was rimmed with utilitarian spaces such as bakeries, armories, servants' residences, and storage rooms.

The middle gate marks the transition from the first court to the second and only the sultan and his retinue, or invited guests, were allowed to pass through it. The *Babi-i Saadet*, or Gate of Felicity, is the entrance to the third court of the Topkapi complex. The entrance itself is domed and framed by extended arcades that give it a more delicate feeling than the *Ortakapi* that precedes it. The throne of the sultan was placed under the domed canopy of the gate on ceremonial occasions and it was here that he, as commander-in-chief of the army, would receive the holy banner of Islam before each military expedition. Also called the *Akagalar,* or the White Eunuchs' Gate after the troops that were used to guard it, it leads to the throne room of the Sultan, where foreign ambassadors and dignitaries were both presented to and took their leave of him. Moving in from the Gate of Felicity on the left hand side of the third court is the *Kutsal Emanetler,* or Treasury of the Sacred Relics, which is a square building divided into four sections, each covered with a dome. Known to those inside the palace as the *Hirkai Saadet,* or Pavilion of the Holy Mantle, this section not only housed the garment for which it was named, namely the mantle which the Prophet is said to have worn, but other sacred relics of Islam specifically brought here from Egypt by Sultan Yavuz Selim. Carefully guarded, these relics were ceremoniously visited only on certain special holy days, when the Sultan and his retinue would stay in the Presentation Room, and have the relics brought out to them. A number of the relics belonging to the Prophet Muhammad and the four Caliphs that succeeded him still survive here, so that many people from all over the Islamic world come to visit this section of the palace. In keeping with the religious nature of this section of the palace, the Agalar Mosque, as well as the Harem Mosque were also located here. The Agalar Mosque, which was intended for those in the *Enderun* (an important school for the higher education of the *Janissaries* who showed great promise), has since been turned into a library for rare manuscripts and houses many exceptional and priceless miniatures.

Vaulted passageways at the rear of the third court lead into the fourth and final compartment of the carefully differentiated succession of spaces that make the Topkapi Palace so unique. Where the second and third courts are enclosed, the fourth court is planned around the spectacular panoramic views of the Golden Horn far below. A series of kiosks are strategically placed on different levels across the narrow expanse of the terrace that both complement and contrast each other in form and personality, making this stepped garden a sculpture court of broad eaved pavilions. Perhaps the most famous of these is the Baghdad Kiosk, which was built in 1639 in honor of the Ottoman conquest of that city in the same year. Attributed to the architect Kasim Aga, this broad eaved kiosk rests on a high podium and is supported by many columns. It has four *iwans* that radiate out from a domed central space, all of which

are covered with the most beautiful tiles imaginable and lit with colored glass windows that create ever changing patterns on the walls and floor of the interior.

In contrast to other famous Islamic gardens, such as the Alhambra in Granada, or the Royal Maydan in Isfahan, Iran, the Topkapi Palace is unusual because of the progressive unity of its spaces. In the Alhambra, for example, such open space and the accompanying buildings that surround it are conceived as separate and distinct units, which are aesthetically self-contained, having little or no visual or physical connection with those adjoining them. In the Topkapi, however, the spaces, which are also interiorized and compartmentalized, are sequentially linked in scale, proportion, and overall character, based on the desired degree of public or private access to them. An oriental philosophy, similar to that found in the Forbidden City of Beijing, and which seems to indicate the common ethnic root of both designs, judges the royal procession from exterior to interior to be the unifying link in the spatial chain of spaces, rather than the highly individualized character to each.

The Sokullu Mehmet Mosque, which is a small treasure created by the architect Sinan in 1572, is located on the southern side of the peninsula at the far extreme of the Saraburnu, near the end of the hippodrome. Named after a famous Grand Vizier in the court of Sulayman the Magnificent, the complex was actually commissioned by the Vizier's wife, Esmehan, who also was the daughter of the Sultan Selim II. Originally consisting of *madrasas* (religious schools), baths, shops, and a *caravanserai,* which have not survived, the complex was skillfully organized on a sloping site, which the great architect Sinan turned from a liability into an asset at the main entrance.

The marble paved courtyard is surrounded by a portico of pointed arches, behind which are classrooms that were used for religious education. The interior of the building is dominated by a large dome, the drum of which is supported by arches resting on two buttresses that spring from the entrance, as well as from each of the sidewalls. The lateral areas are covered with small semi-domes which peak at the bottom level of the drum. A major feature of this mosque is its extremely fine, long, and narrow *mihrab* (niche), which is built of Mammara marble. The crown is gilded. The *minbar* (equivalent of a pulpit), which surrounds it, is widely recognized as one of the finest masterpieces of tile workmanship in Istanbul, incorporating calligraphy into the composition in a very integral way. Sinan, more than any other architect, has normally shown a preference for verticality in his medium-sized mosques, but here it is an essential compliment to the magnificent Iznik tiles which are used, so that space and ornamentation work together as one.

Sedad Eldem's Social Security Complex, a beautiful example of modern Turkish architecture and of fine contextualism.

Bayezit Square with its frenetic and closely packed mixture of commercial, educational, and religious institutions is far different in character from the stately and spacious vistas of Sultan Ahmet, where the full effects of Proust's idea of a "historic park" can be most readily visualized. Bayezit, in turn, is also more intimate in feeling and far more scaled down than Sulaymaniye, which is next in the sequence of major urban spaces in old Istanbul. As in the case with those that have preceded it, the focal point of this area is the religious complex of Suleyman the Magnificent, also known as Kanuni (the Lawgiver), the longest reigning sultan in Turkish history. Having extended the Ottoman empire to the apogee of its power between the years 1520 and 1566, he is also remembered for the racial and religious unanimity which characterized his reign. Sultan Suleyman, who made a habit of personally leading his army in battle, died in a military encampment in Hungary and was buried in a mausoleum in the courtyard of this mosque, which bears his name.

Sinan the Great, who was the architect of the complex, was almost fifty years old when he was given the title of Chief Imperial Architect in 1539, and lived to be nearly one hundred. In the course of that long career,

he also became an authority on public works, the professional guild system and organized architects, carpenters, and masons into cohesive groups. He was known to be a disciplined, never-ceasing worker. Born of Christian parents in Karamania in 1490, Sinan is known to have been trained in the elite Ottoman Janissary Corps and to have seen action in many military campaigns throughout Europe and Asia, where he learned mathematics, geometry, and acoustics in the design and construction of many military buildings. After leaving the military, he worked on nearly four hundred different projects, including many located throughout the empire. Many of the young people involved in this organization later went on to become famous architects in their own right.

The Sulaymaniye Mosque and the complex surrounding it, which is one of the most famous of Sinan's buildings, was built in 1557. In addition to the mosque, the *kulliye* consists of four *madrasas*, a Quran school, an elementary school, a medical school, a hospital, a public kitchen, a hospice, a post graduate school, a bath, and mausolea, with the various parts surrounding its vast inner courtyard, seeming to slowly build toward the hemispherical volume of the mosque's dome.

The harmony achieved in the massing of all of these different types of buildings is extraordinary, especially when seen over the tops of the low buildings in the streets nearby. Sinan's skills are evident in the way he opens up the mosque toward a vista of the Golden Horn and Bosphorus at its eastern end, it becomes obvious that Sinan deliberately built the *madrasas* to frame the view in that direction.

In the Sehzade Mosque, Sinan had previously created a wide central space, using four half domes to support a large dome in their midst. Yet, in the interior of the Sulaymaniye Mosque he rejects a similar approach, which would have yielded a larger volume in favor of two half domes, which reduce the prominence of the main dome and improve the overall incremental massing. In addition, the side aisles are covered with three successive domes with the one in the middle raised higher than the other two in order to link these aisles to the scale of the central space. The marble columns supporting the roofs of the side aisles follow this overall desire for volummetric unity by being so lean that they are hardly noticed and do not appear as dividing elements. Although the plan is not symmetrical, the interior space builds up uniformly, successfully, and sympathetically uniting a monumental building complex with the much smaller scale urban context that surrounds it.

Without getting involved in a discussion of Sinan's use of proportion and numerical harmony, it should be noted that he also indulged in some symbolism here as well, using four minarets to denote Suleyman's position as the fourth Sultan after the conquest of Constantinople and ten balconies on the minarets to signify his being the tenth Ottoman Sultan since Orhan Bey.

Along the European side of the Bosphorus at Besiktas, the area is dominated by the long, linear elevation of the Dolmabahce Palace, a Balyan creation that was built for Sultan Abdul Mecit. This, represents the first true defection from time honored royal residence at the Topkapi Palace, which had been the home of every Sultan since Faith the Conqueror until this time. Costing the present day equivalent of about eighty million dollars and taking twelve years to build (1844-56), the Dolmabahce Palace is an enduring symbol of both the strong desire for westernization and the level of extravagance which, as in Egypt, eventually led to bankruptcy and the virtual mortgaging of the state to foreign powers. The Dolmabahce continued to be used as a royal residence up to and through the reforms instituted by Ataturk in 1922. The only exception was Sultan Hamid II, who built his own palace at Yildiz in the park of the same name. This palace, which was designed by an Italian architect named Raimondo d'Aronco, broke the Balyan monopoly on royal com-

missions and introduced the art nouveau style into Istanbul. It was followed by many other works executed between 1883 and 1909. D'Aronco attempted to fuse the Viennese succession style with Ottoman forms with mixed success. Works such as his Hyder Pasa army medical school, Karakoy Mosque (now demolished), the Botter house at Istiklal, the Mamdoh Pasa library at Arnavutkoy, and Cemil-Beyhouse at Kirecburnu; however, pale in comparison to his Seyh Zafir tomb in Yildiz, built in 1883. This, as well as the summer house built for the Italian Ambassador at Tarabya in 1905 are almost surreal and show the full extent of Olbrich's influence upon this gifted architect.

The reforms of Ataturk ran deep. They brought about the secularization and the westernization of Turkey to a degree not seen in any other imperial Muslim country. The character of Turkey, however, remained profoundly Turkish. Its legacy and its genius unique. Contemporary architectural giants like Sedad Eldem have not only brought about the transformation of the architectural landscape with many modern buildings, but have created a new form of regionalism, built on a profound study of traditional Turkish architecture. Eldem's massive study of the Turkish house must count as one of his unique achievements. The style of his best work is truly contemporary and elegant and yet contextual in the best sense of the word, as can be seen in his social security complex in Istanbul.

♦ CONCLUSION

The evolving character of the built environment of Muslim societies is the product of the interaction between people and their rapidly changing conditions. It reflects the rich legacy of the past and the adaptive genius of a people in the process of profound transformation. The fruits of their current labors and imagination will create the rich legacy of the future.

There is today evidence of a new direction, a "new traditionalism," which amalgamates the best from modernism and those who would have us learn the lessons from the past. Not related to post-anything, this initiative is contemporary and seeks to express the basic principles of Islam, layered over regional considerations and takes into account the complex historical factors partially indicated here. This is a challenging time and a critical one for the architects searching for this synthesis.

Ismail Serageldin and James Steele

References

Abu-Lughod, Janet. Cairo: 1001 Years of the City Victorious. Princeton: Princeton University Press, 1971.

Asher, Catherine. B. *Architecture of Mughal India.* The New

Cambridge History of India, vol. 1, pt. 4. Cambridge: Cambridge University Press, 1992.

Bierman, Irene A., Rifaat A. Abou-El-Hah, and Donald Preziosi, eds. *The Ottoman city and Its Parts.* New York: A.D. Caratzas, 1991.

Blair, Sheila and Bloom, Jonathan. *The Art and Architecture of Islam 1250–1800.* New Haven and London: Yale University Press, 1994.

Cantacuzino, Sherban, ed. *Architecture in Continuity: Building in the Islamic World Today.* New York: Aperture, 1985.

Celik, Zeynap. *Displaying the Orient.* Berkeley: University of California Press, 1992.

Chadirji, Rifat. *Concepts and Influences: Towards a Regionalized International Architecture.* London: 1986.

Evin, Ahmet, and Renata Holod, eds. *Modern Turkish Architecture.* Philadelphia: 1984.

———. *Architecture Education in the Islamic World.* Singapore: Concept Media, 1986.

Golombek, Lisa and Donald Wilber. *The Timurid Architecture of Iran and Turan.* Princeton: Princeton University Press, 1988.

Goodwin, Godfrey. *A History of Ottoman Architecture.* London: 1971.

Grabar, Oleg. *The Formation of Islamic Art.* New Haven and London: Yale University Press, 1973.

Hillenbrand, Robert. *Islamic Architecture: Form, Function and Meaning*: New York: Columbia University Press, 1994.

Hoag, John. *Islamic Architecture.* New York: H.N. Abrams, 1975.

Michel, George, ed. *Architecture of the Islamic World.* New York: 1978.

Nanji, Azim, ed. *Building for Tomorrow.* London: Academy Editions, 1994.

Rastorfer, Darl, J. M. Richards, and Ismail Serageldin. *Hassan Fathy. A Mimar Book.* Singapore and London: Concept Media, 1985.

Sakr, Tarek Mohamed Rifat. *Early Twentieth-Century Islamic Architecture in Cairo.* Cairo: 1993.

Salam, Hayat. *Expressions of Islam in Buildings: Proceedings of an International Seminar Sponsored by the Aga Khan Award for Architecture and the Indonesian Institute of Architects held in Fakarta and Yogyakarta, Indonesia, 15-19 October 1992.* Geneva: Aga Khan Awards for Architecture, 1993.

Serageldin, Ismail, ed. *Space for Freedom: The Search for Architectural Excellence in Muslim Societies.* London and Geneva: Butterworth, 1989.

Steele, James, ed. *Architecture for a Changing World.* London and Geneva: Academy Editions, 1992.

———. *Architecture for Islamic Societies Today.* London and Geneva: Academy Editions, 1994.

Wright, Gwendolyn. *The Politics of Design in French Colonial Urbanism.* Chicago: University of Chicago Press, 1991.

Part VIII:

Literary Expressions in Islam

㉔

Muslim Literature in Arabic

♦ The Arabic Language ♦ The Quran ♦ Early Religious Literature in Arabic
♦ The Belles Lettres: Forms of Expression
♦ The Historical Development of Muslim Literature in Arabic ♦ Early Muslim Literature in Arabic
♦ Modern Muslim Literature in Arabic ♦ Modern Arabic Literature in the Vernacular
♦ Themes in Modern Muslim Literature in Arabic

Arabic has been the linguistic medium for vast numbers of peoples, Muslims and non-Muslims, Arabs and non-Arabs. The literature with which we are concerned has been created and developed by Arabs, Turks, Iranians, Kurds, Muslim Malays, Indonesians and Filipinos, as well as by non-Muslim, Arabic-speaking Christians, Jews, Berbers, and others. Arabic literature, therefore, is really the literature of Islamic civilization as a whole, and not merely the literature of a particular region or linguistic group within the Islamic world.

♦ THE ARABIC LANGUAGE

Arabic is a Semitic language, like Hebrew, Ethiopic, and Aramaic, and shares with these and other Semitic languages common features such as triconsonantal roots, case endings, and the capacity to provide a variety of meanings through a recognized system of prefixes, infixes and suffixes. For example the root (j m/), which has the general meaning of "to gather," can be made into several recognized verbal forms and other patterns, each of which has different semantic implications: (jama/a) means to gather, to collect; (jamma/a) to amass, to assemble parts of a machine; (jama/a) to have sexual intercourse; (ajma/a) to agree;, (ijtama/a) to come together; (jam/un) indicates the plural of a noun; (jami/un) means a mosque; and (jami/atun) means university, union, or league.

Arabic is the language of the Quran and the language of prayers for Muslims, as well as much of their formal and devotional literatures. For this reason, the majority of Muslims learn at least some rudiments of Arabic in order to perform their religious duties. It

should be noted that what is known as the Arabic language is in fact composed of several forms of Arabic: Classical Arabic, Modern Standard Arabic, and Colloquial Arabic. Classical Arabic is the language of the Quran and most of the formal literature, such as works of theology, law, philosophy, and medieval literature. Modern Standard Arabic has maintained the syntactical and the morphological patterns of Classical Arabic, and some of its stylistic features and vocabulary, but has, in some aspects, developed new features under Western-inspired modernistic movements that swept the Arabic-speaking lands in the second half of the last century. Colloquial Arabic is the form of Arabic spoken in each Arab country; for example, there are spoken idioms of Egypt that are different from those of Morocco, and Syrian Arabic that is similar to Lebanese but different from Algerian Arabic. These linguistic variations are artificial yet convenient ways in which to chart the linguistic map of Arabic-speaking communities. In no way should they be taken as pure types since a great deal of interpenetration of these divisions occurs, especially among the educated classes of Arabic speakers, whose conversation may range from the very formal standard Arabic to the informal and colloquial.

For the most part, formal elite literature is written in Modern Standard Arabic. But there is a form of popular literature that is couched in one or the other spoken varieties of Arabic. In modern times one finds a thriving literature in the vernacular languages of Egypt, Lebanon and Morocco, in poetry as well as prose. Any definition of Muslim literature in Arabic has to incorporate works composed in literary, as well as colloquial Arabic.

331

♦ THE QURAN

Muslims consider the Quran to be the word of God, which was revealed to the Prophet Muhammad from about 610 until his death in 632. It has long been regarded by Muslims as being exemplary of literary excellence, and writers over the centuries have endeavored to emulate its style and imagery. Scholars have sought to understand this sacred text through the science of the Quran (*Ulum al-Quran*). One of its main branches seeks to elucidate the literary excellence of the style and diction of the Quran. This is known as *ijaz al-Quran* (the incapacity of mortals to imitate the miraculous style and diction of the Quran). For this reason, many Muslims believe that the Quran cannot be truly appreciated in a non-Arabic version. Even when renderings in other languages are available to facilitate understanding of scripture, the Arabic text is the ultimate reference point.

♦ EARLY RELIGIOUS LITERATURE IN ARABIC

Tafsir

This branch of Muslim literature in Arabic seeks to interpret the Quran. Such works of commentary draw on a number of disciplines such as Arabic linguistics, grammar, and logic to provide an exegesis of the Quran.

Sira

There is a separate body of Muslim scholarship devoted to the biography of the Prophet; it is called *sira* (lifestory, literally path or way taken). Traditionally, it is a paradigmatic type of biography, full of praise for the person of Muhammad, extolling his achievements, character and spirituality. The sources for this literature go back to orally-transmitted stories about Muhammad's life that circulated during his lifetime and were committed to writing at a later date.

From the earliest period to modern times, Muslims have continued to compose biographies of Muhammad based on traditional sources. In the course of time, three types of literature, closely connected to Muhammad's biographies, emerged: *Dalail*, *Shamail*, and *Mawlid*. *Dalail* contains proofs of Muhammad's prophethood, citing evidentiary miracles to establish that he was indeed God's messenger, while *Shamail* addresses the personal attributes of the person of Muhammad, both physical and spiritual. *Mawlid* (plural *Mawalid*, birth) literature, in prose and verse, details in highly laudable terms the life and miracles of Muhammad, and is usually recited in gatherings during the celebration of the anniversary of Muhammad's birthday. In modern times numerous biographies have been published in which the figure of the Prophet has at times been interpreted in modern secular terms and often made to anachronistically represent ideas such as socialism or Arab nationalism. Some of these biographies are apologetic in character, seeking to refute the negative portrayal of Muhammad in some Western writings. One of the most well-known and, perhaps, most influential of these modern biographies is that of the Egyptian writer, Muhammad Husayn Haykal.

Hadith

Although Quranic teachings include directions regarding practices and institutions of the faith, they did not always provide detailed rules that would govern various aspects of daily life. That is why the sayings and the acts of the Prophet Muhammad become important as guidelines for issues that elaborate Quranic teaching and provide further interpretation. The words and actions of the Prophet Muhammad came to be known as *hadith* (reports, traditions), which were transmitted through a chain of narrators from generation to generation. This presentation of the Prophet's life as a model of behavior is know as the *sunna*.

In the beginning such reports were transmitted orally, as it was felt that writing them down might result in their being misconstrued as parts of the Quran. However, as early as the eighth and ninth centuries, once the Quran was firmly established and such fears became groundless, collections of traditions were produced. These traditions were named after those who collected them, for example, the collections known as Sahih al-Bukhari and Musnad ibn Hanbal were produced by the Muslim scholars al-Bukhari (died 870) and Ibn Hanbal (died 855), respectively. From the early days of the *hadith* collections, Muslim scholars have been concerned about the authenticity of these reports, a concern involving both the text and the chain of individuals who transmitted it. A science known as *ilm al-hadith* developed in order to establish the veracity of these reports and their attribution to the Prophet Muhammad. The personal integrity of the scholar became the focus of *hadith* scholars, and biographical dictionaries were produced in order to record the life and career of individual *hadith* scholars. *Hadith* collections that are regarded by Sunni Muslims as reliable date from the ninth and early tenth centuries. The Shia developed their own tradition of collecting *hadith*, which were authenticated on the basis of transmittal from their Imams.

♦ THE BELLES LETTRES: FORMS OF EXPRESSION

Qasida

The principle belles lettres genre is the monorhymed multi-thematic ode (*qasida*), normally composed of be-

Page from the Quran showing script used for early religious literature in Arabic.

tween thirty and fifty lines, but at times of one hundred. Each line is divided into two hemistichs, with a standard rhyme scheme that goes: aa, ba, ca, da, ea, and so forth. This genre of poetry was invented by the pre-Islamic poets. Its classical form consisted of fixed parts: the amatory prelude (*an-nasib*), the description of the poet's journey, and finally the eulogy of the poet's tribe or patron or hyperbolic self-praise or satire of foes. The *qasida* was also the form used to express praise of God and for panegyrics in honor of the Prophet Muhammad and his family (particularly al-

Husayn, his grandson, martyred in 680), or any of the Sufi saints.

Ghazal

The *ghazal* is a form of love-poem that developed out of the prelude of the pre-Islamic ode. It ranges from five to twelve full lines (ten to twenty-four hemistichs). It was used for both sacred and profane topics—the beloved was either a beautiful maiden or a youth and sometimes God.

Qita

As the name indicates, the *qita* reads like a "section" taken from a larger poem. Its main characteristic is that the two hemistichs do not rhyme, as is the case with the ode or the love-poem. It dealt with mundane topics, word-play, and light-hearted satire.

Rubai

The rubai is a quatrain in fixed meter with the rhyme scheme a a b a, originated in pre-Islamic Persia. It was mainly employed by Persian-born Muslim poets, such as Omar Khayyam, who composed the popular poetic collection the *Rubaiyat of Omar Khayyam*, translated freely by Edward Fitzgerald in 1859.

Muwashshah

Originated in Muslim Spain in the eleventh or the twelfth centuries, the *muwashshah* is a strophic poem, mainly about love, composed in short metres and arranged in four to six-line strophes (stanzas) differing rhyme each, but with internal rhymes at times and ending with a foreign word or phrase. Among its practitioners was the accomplished Ibn Zaydun (died 1071), who dedicated some of his *muwashshah's* to his beloved Wallada, an Umayyad princess.

Zajal

The *zajal* was another strophic form that originated in Muslim Spain, at around the same time as the *muwashshah*. It was sung—hence the name *zajal* (melody)—and composed in the vernacular of the day, with phrases in Romance languages. One of the best known *zajal* composers was Ibn Quzman of Cordoba (died 1160), whose corpus awaits a major study in English.

Zajal was also employed by mystically inclined poets such as Ibn Quzman's contemporary Abu l-Hasan ash-Shushtari (died 1136), who was perhaps the first to use the Arabic vernacular in religious verse.

Prose

Apart from some orally-transmitted tales of heroic deeds known as the "Days of the Arabs" (*Ayyam al-Arab*), samples of ancient rhymed prose and a few proverbs, no major works of prose of pre-Islamic Arabia are known to us.

Risala

Belles lettres are also referred to in Arabic as *adab*, a word that also denotes good etiquette and sophistication of manners. *Risala* was one of the major prose forms and ranged in length from one page to a small booklet. The topics of the *risala* are varied. What would start as an ordinary letter to a friend could end up as a formal treatise on a philosophical, mystical, political, or literary topic. The early master of that form was the Persian-born Ibn al-Muqaffa (died 757) who was a scribe in the Abbasid bureaucracy. He composed works of great polish such as *al-Adab al-Kabir*, and *al-Adab as-Saghir*, and translated from the Pahlavi the famous work *Kalila and Dimna*, which is a collection of animal stories with didactic purposes. The form was perfected, however, at the hands of the prolific Iraqi-born master al-Jahiz (died 869). His epistles range widely in subject and scope. He composed serious as well as humorous topics and works such as a compendium *Hayat al-Hayawan* on the life of animals, *al-Bayan wa t-Tabyin* on eloquence, and the satirical work, *al-Bukhala*, on the class of misers. His epistles dealt with subjects such as singing girls, blacks and whites, and men and women.

Maqama

As an anecdote about the adventures of a rogue, the *maqama* (assembly, session) was composed in embellished, if not pedantic, rhymed prose by masters such as Badi az-Zaman al-Hamadhani (died 1008) and al-Hariri (died 1122). The choicest words, and sometimes the most obscure, were employed, logographs and double-entendres abounded, and the meaning was at times obscured by rhetorical acrobatics. The stories betrayed the folk origin of the stock characters, and came very close to the Western pattern of the short story. This style of rhymed prose continued to enjoy a measure of popularity among writers of diverse interests and disciplines until around the middle of the nineteenth century, when, as a result of contact with the West, the need arose for a matter-of-fact, plain style of writing that made clear the intended meaning. This need gave rise to journalism and a class of professionals who sought a straightforward style of writing devoid of artificiality.

Adab ar-Rihla

Travel accounts (*adab ar-rihla*) constitute a large portion of Muslim literary output. The most famous of these were composed by Ibn Battuta (died 1377) and Ibn Jubayr (died 1217).

Al-Tarikh

Historical chronicles or al-tarikh also make up a large body of Muslim literature in Arabic. The most famous Muslim historian was the Tunisian-born Ibn Khaldun (died 1406), who wrote the multi-volume *al-Muqaddima* (*The Prelogomenon*, translated into English by Franz Rosenthal, 1958). Other major Muslim historians of the earlier period are al-Tabari (died 923), al-Masudi (died 956), Ibn al-Athir (died 1234), and Ibn Taghribardi (died 1470), to name but a few.

♦ THE HISTORICAL DEVELOPMENT OF MUSLIM LITERATURE IN ARABIC

The Early Period

Poets in the early years of Islamic period were regarded with some suspicion since certain kinds of poetry were condemned in the Quran as being composed by those who "err in every valley, and say what they do not do. Only the perverse follow them" (Quran 26:225). Poetry, in general, was regarded as being capable of being a subversive verbal art that idealized pre-Islamic ways, ways that were unacceptable to the spirit of the new Islamic faith.

Yet, pre-Islamic poetry was preserved in the eighth century and generally upheld as exemplary of poetic excellence and as a guide to the obscure meaning of some of the Quranic phrases. Some modern critics, such as the Egyptian Taha Husayn (died 1973) and the English orientalist Margoliouth, have raised serious doubts about attribution of this poetry to the pre-Islamic period, contending that most, if not all, of it was forged by medieval compilers. Whatever the truth about the exact date of this pre-Islamic poetry, many of its features survived into the early period of the Islamic era, such as the amatory prelude in the ode expressing nostalgia for the lost beloved; extolling manly virtues of endurance, bravery, and skill in hunting and war; revelling in drinking and feasting; and eulogizing oneself, tribe or patron. What can be fairly described as a new phenomenon was the kind of ascetic poetry composed by the mystically-bent poetess Rabia al-Adawiyya; a sample of her poems is offered below.

Poetry in praise of the Prophet Muhammad was composed during his lifetime by Kab ibn Zuhayr and the Prophet's own poet, Hasan ibn Thabit. This panegyric poetry (*madih*) borrowed much of its diction and imagery from the pre-Islamic model and is, on the whole, mannered and artificial.

Umayyad Period (661–750)

Both Jarir and al-Farazdaq (both died circa 728) continued to produce poetry in the pre-Islamic style, as can be seen in their polemical poetry (*naqaid*) in which each extolled the virtues of his tribesmen and satirized his opponent's. Love poetry was also composed during; this period; some in the pure and "virginal" type (*udhri;* it may also be attributed to a tribe called Udhra) composed by Jamil (died 701), and other in the erotic and ironic mode produced by Umar ibn Abi Rabia. Jamil

was in love with a woman called Buthayna, about whom he says in one of his poems:

> Shall I ever meet Buthayna alone again
> Each of us full of love as a cloud of rain?
> Fast in her net was I when a lad, and till
> This day my love is growing and waxing still.
>
> I have spent my lifetime, waiting for her to speak,
> And the bloom of youth is faded from off my cheek
> But I will not suffer that she my suit deny,
> My love remains undying, though all things die!

> (R.A. Nicholson,
> *A Literary History of the Arabs*)

Compare Umar's erotic love poem for the coquettish Hind:

> Tender is she, cool in the season of heat when thevehemence of the summer has burst into flames,
> Warm in wintertime, a coverlet for a lad under the night when the bitter cold wraps him around
> . . . .
> When I said, "When shall be our tryst?" Hind would
> laugh and say, "After tomorrow!"

> (A. J. Arberry, *Aspects of Islamic Civilization as Depicted in the Original Texts*)

A different kind of love poetry was composed by the mystic Rabia al-Adawiyya, in which she expressed her love for God:

> Two ways I love Thee: selfishly,
> And next, as worthy is of Thee.
> Tis selfish love that I do naught
> Save think on Thee with every thought;
> Tis purest love when Thou dost raise
> The veil to my adoring gaze.

> (R.A. Nicholson,
> *A Literary History of the Arabs*)

The Early Abbasid Age (749–1055)

With the demise of the Umayyad dynasty at the hands of the Abbasids, the seat of power shifted from Damascus to Baghdad. Such shift also signalled the introduction of non-Arab converts into the new empire, which had a vast cultural impact on the fields of literature, philosophy, science and art.

The new caliphs patronized men of letters, intellectuals and artists. One of them, al-Mamun, set up an academy called *Bayt al-Hikma* (House of Wisdom) in the early years of the ninth century whose members translated a good number of works from Greek and Syriac. These translations contributed to the advance of Arabic literature and sciences.

The Development of Poetry

In the early Abbasid age, Arabic poetry developed both in content and diction. New topics ranged from ascetic poetry to what was popularly termed wine-poetry. New styles were elaborately discussed in the works of medieval writers who detailed the rules of composition in diverse forms. The immoderate use of style sometimes provoked a backlash of literary criticism.

Known as the father of the ascetic poetry, Abu al-Atahiya expressed the transience of this life and the hope to gain the lifeafter:

What ails me, World, that every place perforce
I lodge thee in, it galleth me to stay?
And, O Time, how do I behold thee run
To spoil me? Thine own gift thou takest away!
O Time! inconstant, mutable art thou,
And o'er the realm of ruin is thy sway.

(R. A. Nicholson,
A Literary History of the Arabs)

Then there is the carefree Abu Nuwas, devoted to a life of the carnal pleasures of wine and love:

Ho! a cup, and fill it up, and tell me it is wine,
For I will never drink in shade if I can drink in shine
Curst and poor is every hour that sober I must go,
But rich am I whene'er well drunk I stagger to and fro
Speak, for shame, the loved one's name, let vain disguise
alone:
No good there is in pleasures o'er which a veil is thrown.

(R. A. Nicholson,
A Literary History of the Arabs)

By far the most famous poet of this time was al-Mutanabbi, (died 965), whose patron was the Aleppo prince Sayf ad-Dawla al-Hamadani. In the following example, al-Mutanabbi rebukes his patron for being less generous to him and unappreciative of his talents:

O justest of the just save in thy deeds to me!
Thou art accused and thou, O sire, must judge the plea.
Look, I implore thee, well! Let not thine eye cajoled
See fat in empty froth, in all that glistens gold!
What use and profit reaps a mortal of his sight,
If darkness unto him be indistinct from light!
My deep poetic art the blind have eyes to see,
My verses ring in ears as deaf as deaf can be.
The desert knows me well, the night, the mounted men,
The battle and the sword, the paper and the pen!

(R. A. Nicholson,
A Literary History of the Arabs)

If Abu al-Atahiya lamented the vanity of this ephemeral world and hoped to gain God's favors in the hereafter, Abu al-Ala al-Maarri (died 1057), a blind Syrian poet, expressed a rather pessimistic view of this life and a skeptical attitude toward the religious assurances of the rewards for the pious in the hereafter. He outraged the pious by his open skepticism and irreverence; some accused him of parodying the Quran in his book *al-Fusul wa l-Ghayat* (*Paragraphs and Periods*), in which he provided a series of precepts in rhymed prose. He also composed the epistle *Risalat al-Ghufran* (*The Epistle of Forgiveness*), in which he described a journey to the hereafter with sardonic comments on Arabic belles lettres. These lines show his pessimism and skepticism:

Falsehood hath so corrupted all the world
That wrangling sects each other's gospel chide;
But were not hate Man's natural element,
Churches and mosques had risen side by side.

Elsewhere, Abu al-Ala says:

How have I provoked your enemity?
Christ or Muhammad, tis one to me,
No rays of dawn our path illume,
We are sunk together in ceaseless gloom.
. . . .
Take Reason for thy guide and do what she
Approved, the best counsellors in sooth.
Accept no law the Pentateuch lays down:
Not there is what thou seekest—the plain truth.

(R. A. Nicholson,
A Literary History of the Arabs)

It has been suggested that Abu al-Ala's book about a journey to the hereafter may have influenced Dante's *Divine Comedy*.

The Development of Prose

Unlike Umayyad prose, as can be seen in the epistles of Abd al-Hamid al-Katib (died 750), Abbasid prose developed great precision and articulation. The best example of this new prose is found in the works of Persian-born scribe Ibn al-Muaqaffa (died 756), who initiated what has been termed "secretarial literature"—compositions on a variety of subjects produced by secretaries in the official chancelleries. He translated into Arabic examples of Persian court literature such as *Khawatay-namak* (*The Book of Kings*). Al-Muqaffa and others helped create "Mirror for Princes" literature in Arabic, which provided guidelines for rulers on how they should behave in matters of politics and governance of society. He also adapted and translated into Arabic the Indian fables of Bidapai, known in Arabic as *Kalila wa Dimna*. His writings contributed to the development of the rules of proper conduct (*adab*). As mentioned, the term has been used by Arabs to refer to literature in general.

With the expansion of the Islamic empire into different lands with different cultural traditions, there was a noticeable change in literary concerns and tastes. The writings of the erudite al-Jahiz (died 869) reflected some of these changes; the wide range of subject-matter, the vast amount of anecdotal information, and the lucid and entertaining prose style point to the new urban society. Al-Jahiz wrote about theological issues (he was a Mutazili), misers, singing girls, thieves, and even zoology. His writings are full of information about Arab life in the first part of the ninth century, and are a gold mine for Arab traditions, proverbs and theological debates, which afford a glimpse into the underworld of the social derelicts and outcasts, prostitutes and thieves. His style is eloquent without being pedantic, precise without being curt, stylized without being flowery. However, his writings are disorganized and lack discipline; more often than not they sound more like a learned man's table talk.

An indication that *adab* moved beyond the limited meaning of "rules for proper conduct" can be seen in the way it began to be applied to works of any literary claim. Persian-born Ibn Qutayba (died 899) wrote a ten-volume book entitled *Uyun al-Akhbar* (*The Fountains of Stories*). Each volume addressed a different topic and was replete with anecdotal information and, at times, sharp critiques of long-accepted views, as when he challenged the prevailing belief in the superiority of pre-Islamic poetry in *ash-Shir wa sh-Shuara* (*On Poetry and Poets*). Ibn an-Nadim (died 988) wrote a bibliographical work entitled *al-Fihrist* (*The Index*), in which he compiled a list of all the works of the tenth century that dealt with diverse branches of knowledge. Works on Arabic linguistics and philology were also produced; al-Khalil ibn Ahmad wrote a lexicon of Arabic, and Persian-born Sibawayhi wrote a comprehensive reference on Arabic grammar (a remarkable feat for a non-native Arab!).

A grand master of these multifaceted *adab* works, without a doubt, is polymath Abu Hayyan al-Tawhidi (died 1023), a tragic genius who was torn between the desire to attain worldly success and the desire to pursue knowledge, which could only be afforded through the patronage of sharp-tongued, pretentious regional rulers he strongly, and at times openly, despised. It was after his bitter experiences with two of these rulers, Ibn al-Amid and Ibn Abbad, that he wrote his mordant lampoon *Mathalib al-Wazirayn* (*The Vices of the Two Viziers*). The venom of his satire was so potent and his bitterness so profound that the book was believed to bring misfortune on those who possessed a copy of it. Al-Tawhidi's style is characterized by vigor, witticisms, and sardonic tone. Other topics he treated include friendship, treatises on theological and philosophical concerns, and correspondence with the Muslim ethicist Ibn Miskawayh (died 1030).

The mannerism (*badi*) that became the mark of some Abbasid poetry and was extolled in manuals of literary composition (*insha*) was also applied to prose. The writer showed off his linguistic skills by filling his composition with *saj* (rhymed prose), unusual metaphors, puns and verbal acrobatics. An example of this highly mannered writing is found in the *maqama* (assembly, session), first composed by Badi az-Zaman al-Hamadhani (died 1008) and elaborated by al-Hariri (died 1122), whose *maqamas* narrated the adventures of the rogue-hero Abu Zayd as-Saruji. It could be said that the *maqama* foreshadowed the emergence of the modern Arabic short story. The highly literate style of the *maqama* and its narrative about humble and low-born characters appear to be in conflict, for example in abrupt shifts from the serious to the humorous; at times, the *maqama* reads as a mock-heroic piece of writing. It is a striking example of the blend of high and folk literature and the confluence of the preoccupations of the literati with those of the humble. Such a blend, as we will observe time and again, appears to be a characteristic of Islamic literature in Arabic.

Developments in the Maghrib (North Africa) and Muslim Spain

Literary developments in the Maghrib and Muslim Spain matched those of other regions in the Muslim world. New genres in poetry originated in Muslim Spain: the strophic lyrical poems the *muwashshah* (in classical Arabic) and the *zajal* (completely in colloquial Arabic). Ibn Zaydun is a good example of the poets who employed the *muwashshah*, whereas Ibn Quzman (died 1160) was the uncontested master of *zajal*, Ibn Quaman's oeuvre betrays a curious affinity to the vernacular troubadour poetry of Spain and France, and still awaits more studies in English (he was studied by the Spanish orientalist Garcia Gomez).

Both genres became popular in the east, particularly in Egypt and Iraq. Their melodic quality, multiple rhymes and accessible diction made them a good vehicle for love as well as mystical verse. Ibn Zaydun of Cordoba and Ibn Sana al-Mulk of Egypt employed the *muwashshah* in their love pieces, whereas Ibn Arabi and Abu l-Hasan ash-Shushtari employed it and *zajal* in their mystical verse, and in so doing provided an example of the seemingly "Islamic" blend between the highly sophisticated mystical content and the pedestrian idiom of everyday life of the common folk.

Prose works of considerable merit were produced by Muslims of the Maghrib and Spain. Ibn Abd Rabbihi (died 940) wrote the *adab* work *al-Iqd al-Farid* (*The Matchless Necklace*); Ibn ar-Rashiq (died 1064) and Hazim al-Qartajanni (died 1285) wrote works of literary criticism. The Zahirite theologian Ibn Hazm (died 1064) wrote a book on the "science of love" entitled *Tawq al-Hamama* (*The Dove's Neckring*), which purported to be an investigation into the stages and kinds of love. It provides fascinating and moving stories of lovers.

Philosophical writings were produced by Ibn Rushd

Scribe writing, seventeenth century.

(Averroes). He wrote a commentary on Aristotle, treatises on the harmony between reason and revelation, and a famous rebuttal of al-Ghazali's refutation of the philosophers; al-Ghazali's work is entitled *Tahafut al-Falasifa* (*The Incoherence of the Philosophers*), Ibn Rushd's is entitled *Tahafut at-Tahafut* (*The Incoherence of the Incoherence*).

A noted Maghribi philosopher, Ibn al-Tufayl (died 1185), composed the allegorical work *Hayy ibn Yaqzan* (*Alive Son of Awake*), translated into Latin in 1671 under the title *Philosophus Autodidactus*). It is the story of a child, abandoned on a deserted island and reared by a gazelle, who grows up and manages by the use of reason to attain the full range of truths taught by both prophets and philosophers.

Travel literature was enriched by the accounts of the Sicilian traveller ash-Sharif al-Idrisi, who wrote *Nuzhat al-Mushtaq fi Ikhtiraq al-Afaq* (*The Joy of Him Who Desires to Trot the Globe*) and attached to it a map of the world; Ibn Jubayr (died 1217), who described his journey to Mecca; and Ibn Battuta, one of the most widely travelled Muslim writers of the period (died circa 1377), who wrote extensively about his travels to China, India, and parts of Africa.

Mention must be made of the great Tunisian-born historian Ibn Khaldun (died 1406), who wrote the important *al-Muqaddima* as an introduction to his planned universal history, *Kitab al-Ibar* (*The Book of Lessons*). His was the first attempt to construct a general philosophy of history. Previous historians had for the most part written chronicles and accounts of ruling dynasties without attempts at organizing or analyzing the material within a philosophy of history.

◆ MUSLIM LITERATURE IN ARABIC (1258–1800)

The year 1258 witnessed the destruction of the Abbasid caliphate at the hands of the invading Mongols and the rise of the Mamluk dynasty (Turkish and Circassian military caste of slave origin) in both Egypt and Syria. The Mamluks ruled independently until 1517, when the armies of the Ottoman sultan invaded Egypt and Syria and both fell under Ottoman control until the French invasion in 1798.

Arab literary historians usually refer to the Mamluk and Ottoman period as the "Age of Decadence" because of the general decline in creativity and the spread of mannered compositions that were replete with hackneyed and outworn cliches. There was also a deterioration of the Arabic language, as can be evinced in the history chronicle *Badai al-Zuhur* by the Egyptian Ibn Iyas (died 1521?). The great Muslim traveller Ibn Battuta was dismayed to hear some of the learned men of Basra, an old center of Arabic grammarians, make deplorable grammatical mistakes in their sermons. But there were some major developments in popular literature during this age. The first of these was the popular prose epic (*as-siyar ash-shabiyya*) of tribal heroes and heroines in their struggle against Muslim and non-Muslim rulers (Crusaders in some cases), which were couched in semi-classical Arabic diction and interspersed with rhymed prose and verses borrowed from the literature of the elite. Some examples of these popular epics are *Sirat Antar*, about the heroics of a pre-Islamic warrior and poet; *Sirat Baybars*, about the Mamluk ruler Baybars (died 1277), who had defeated the Mongols. *Sirat Bani Hilal* recounts the migration of the Banu Hilal tribesmen from Egypt to Tunisia, and extolls the heroic deeds of Abu Zayd. The second development was exemplified in the book *Alf Layla wa Layla* (*The One Thousand and One Nights*, known in the West as *The Arabian Nights*). Much of its content originated in pre-Islamic Persian tradition, but appears to have been crystallized in its present form during this period of Mamluk rule in Egypt. These works of popular literature show the skillful use of the colloquial idiom and the imaginative and captivating stories of kings and paupers and their struggles against fate.

There is also an inexhaustible fount of humorous literature surrounding the character of a semilegendary humble theologian, known to the Arabs as Juha, to the Turks as Nasreddin Hoca, and to the Iranians as Mulla Nasiruddin. Anecdotes about this comic figure abound in Arabic, and other Muslim literatures, and they range from the extremely witty to the extremely absurd, betraying at times an astonishing degree of satiric irreverence. The figure of Juha awaits a major study in English. The period from 1500 to 1800 reflects a certain stagnation in literary creativity. Some works on theology, Arabic grammar, biography, and mysticism were produced by writers such as as-Suyuti (died 1505); ash-Sharani (died 1565); an-Nabulsi (died 1731); and Turkish Muslims such as Tashkopruzade (died 1560), who compiled a biographical dictionary, and Hajji Khalifa (died 1656), the well-known Ottoman bibliographer. In India a number of theological, philosophical and biographical works in Arabic were produced. Poetry in the conventional monorhyme ode continued to be composed in the sixteenth and the seventeenth centuries. Azad Bilgrami (died 1786) became known as the Hassan of Hind (after the name of the Prophet's poet, Hassan ibn Thabit) for having composed, in Arabic, panegyrics in honor of the Prophet Muhammad. The lexicographer as-Sayyid Murtada az-Zabidi (died 1791), famous for his *Taj al-Arus* (*The Bride's Crown*), was of Indian origin.

♦ MODERN MUSLIM LITERATURE IN ARABIC

The history of modern Muslim literature in Arabic, or other Muslim languages for that matter, is essentially the story of Muslim encounter with the modern culture of the West in the nineteenth and the twentieth centuries. The demonstrated superiority of Western armies and their speedy conquest of Muslim lands, particularly the French occupation of Egypt (1798–1801), raised the desire to know the "secret" of Western superiority. This eventually helped create a more direct, informative kind of literature, which was a departure from the then-prevailing literary modes characterized by verbal embellishment and worn-out motifs.

In the early nineteenth century, many Western works were translated into Arabic by figures such as Egyptian Rifa Rafi at-Tahtawi and Lebanese Ahmad Faris ash-Shidyaq. These works introduced the public to aspects of Western society hitherto unknown. Al-Tahtawi wrote about Parisian society in his famous work, *Takhlis al-Ibriz ila Talkhis Bariz*, whereas al-Shidyaq talked humorously about English life in his autobiographical work *as-Saq ala s-Saq fima huwa l-Fariyaq*. Both books have rhymed titles that betray an attachment to the literary convention of rhymed prose, but their contents introduced a new genre to the public.

As the nineteenth century continued, Syro-Lebanese Christian writers revived a sense of pride in classical Arabic and the need increased for more direct prose that conveyed information clearly and succinctly. Such revival of the classical Arabic received a boost in the establishment of the press in 1860 and some nationalist stirrings. Literature became more concerned with the national causes of each country and less with the universal spirit of the Muslim legacy.

Development of Modern Poetry

Poetry was less subject to change than prose. The classical ode with its motifs and diction were still held in esteem by neo-classical poets, although they started to express new concerns. Egyptian poets Mahmud Sami al-Barudi (died 1904), Ahmad Shawqi (died 1932), Hafiz Ibrahim (died 1932), and the Iraqi Maruf ar-Rusafi (died 1945) revived the classical *qasida* and expressed their concerns about the political and social issues of their day. On the whole, however, their poetry were embellishments on the classical models. Lebanese-born Khalil Mutran (died 1949) introduced some measure of organic unity and subjective lyricism to the classical ode, which earned him credit for being among the first to compose "Romantic" poetry as well as the narrative poem. Such romantic tendency received some encouragement from literary men such as Ibrahim Abd al-Qadir al-Mazini (died 1949) and Abbas Mahmud al-Aqqad (died 1964) as well as the Apollo group of romantic poets headed by Ahmad Zaki Abu Shadi.

It is important to mention that such a romantic trend in Arabic poetry must have had its first inspiration in the works of a group of Syro-Lebanese emigres to the

Americas known as the Mahjar school. Among their number was the well-known Gibran Kahlil Gibran (died 1931). In their works they tried to free themselves of the monorhymed ode by using free verse, unconventional symbols and diction, and a more self-indulgent style.

But it was in the late 1940s that one witnessed important formal changes in Arabic poetry, changes that brought about what is known as *ash-Shir al-Hurr* (free verse). The pioneers of these changes were the Iraqi poets Nazik al-Malaika (1923–) and Badr Shakir as-Sayyab (died 1964), and, to some extent, the Egyptian Liwis Awad (died 1991). Now Arab poets could divest themselves of the conventions of monorhymed ode and express their inner thoughts in multi-rhymed lines of unequal lengths. The subject matter, tone, imagery, and diction changed to keep in step with events of immediate relevance. Now there was concern expressed for the individual, rebellion against tradition, and an examination of social and political issues that impinged on the individual and society. This concern can be found in the poetry of the Egyptian Salah Abd as-Sabur (died 1982), the Iraqi Abd al-Wahhab al-Bayyati (1926–), and the Palestinian "poets of resistance" such as Mahmud Darwish (1941–).

In recent years, Arabic poetry has developed many innovations in form and diction. It has even shown a tendency towards the excessive use of obscure, mystical and surrealistic images, to the extent of being unintelligible at times, as in the poetical works of the Iraqi poet al-Bayyati as well as the Syro-Lebanese poet Adonis (Ali Ahmad Said) (1931–). Here is an example from Adonis's poem "The Tree of Fire":

A Family of leaves
Sitting beside a water spring
Wound this earth of tears
Reading aloud to the water from the book of fire
My family did not wait for my coming
They went and now there is
Neither trace nor fire.

(M. M. Badawi,
A Short History of Modern Arabic Literature)

Poetic Forms The more commonly known poetic forms in modern times are the: *mawwal, dubayt, bullayq, kan-wa-kan, quma,* and *waw*. Each of these non-classical metrical forms is used for a particular topic; for example, the *bullayq* is employed for satirical purposes, whereas the *kan-wa-kan* for long narratives.

Mention should be made of humorous or nonsensical verse comprising contrived arguments between entities such as a cat and a dog or two kinds of fruit. Usually the poem alternates between stanzas of "rational" content and "irrational" or nonsensical content

(*dawr aqil/dawr majnun*). The following is from a collection of the nineteenth-century Egyptian vernacular poet Hasan al-Alati:

[Rational Stanza:]
If my Lord, the Preserver, wishes you well
He would make you a preacher
Many are the times you heard the Quran and sermons
But you go on in your waywardness

[Irrational Stanza:]
I saw a louse with shoes on
And a flea with a pick-axe destroying things
And a baby mosquito that has such strength
It carried Paris and moved it to Egypt's countryside

In the twentieth-century, particularly in Egypt, poetry couched in the colloquial has arisen, in part to assert political and nationalistic causes. This can be seen in the colloquial compositions of Egypt's Abdallah an-Nadim (died 1896), Yaqub Sannu (died 1912), Bayram at-Tunisi (died 1961), Badi Khayri, and Muhammad Shafiq al-Misri; in Lebanon's Umar az-Ziinni (died 1961); and in Iraq's Abbud al-Karkhi. In the 1920s, there was also a spate of prose compositions in the colloquial, such as the "memoirs" of several working-class or underworld types: (*Mushakkirat Arbagi (Memoirs of Carriage Driver), Mudhakkirat Fitiwwa (Memoirs of a Strong Man),* and *Mudhakkirat Nashshal (Memoirs of a Pick-Pocket)*.

In recent years, vernacular compositions, particularly in verse, have been used to express opposition to local regimes or to support political causes. This is evident in the vernacular poetry of the Egyptians Fuad Haddad, Salah Jahin, Ahmad Fuad Nigm, Abd ar-Rahman al-Abnudi, and Samir Abd al-Baqi, the Iraqi Muzaffar an-Nawwab, and the Palestinian Rajih as-Salfiti, among many others.

Developments in Prose

By the end of 1980s, almost all Western literary genres—the novel, the short story, drama, and non-fiction—had been attempted in Arabic. Existentialism, socialist realism, romanticism and even surrealism had been adopted.

The new generation of writers did not wish to reject their heritage. They maintained that they were engaged in renewing not discarding it. These modernists were to some degree the disciples of Shaykh Muhammad Abduh (died 1905), the Egyptian religious scholar based in Cairo who led a reform movement. Taha Husayn (died 1973) and Mustafa al-Aqqad can be said to have contributed significantly to modern Egyptian culture. Taha Husayn, educated in Egypt and France, wrote many books on literary criticism, and history, as well as novels, including his prominent three-volume autobiography, al-Ayyam (*The Days*, 1926, 1939, 1972). Al-Aqqad, influenced by nineteenth-century English thought and literary criticism, formed with other modernists the Diwan school, which called for new modes of expression in poetry and was critical of the neoclassical poets such as Ahmad Shawqi and Hafiz Ibrahim.

The Novel and the Short Story

At the turn of the century, writers, such as Egyptian al-Muwaylihi, employed the medieval genre *maqama* (assembly, composed in rhymed prose) as a way in which to address modern concerns. The attempts at writing this genre and the increasing amount of Western fiction published in Arabic translation must have whetted the readers' desire to read fiction with indigenous characters and settings. The novel *Zaynab* (published in 1913) by Egyptian writer-statesman Muhammad Husayn Haykal (died 1956) is generally regarded as the first Arabic novel.

The development of the novel moved from simply imitating western models to the episodic until it reached a high degree of cohesiveness and skill in the hands of the Egyptian Najib Mahfuz (commonly spelled Naguib Mafhouz) (1911–). At the beginning of his career, Mahfuz wrote a series of historical novels. Then, in the mid-1950s, he produced his well-known trilogy, which narrates the story of an Egyptian family caught between holding on to the traditional ways of the past and the pressing need to accommodate to the changing conditions of modern life. His work incorporates religious, philosophical and spiritual concerns, particularly the allegorical *Awlad Haritna (The Children of Our Qurter*, tr. into English as *The Children of Gebelawi*), and *al-Liss wa l-Kilab (The Thief and the Dogs)* In recent years Mahfuz has been turning to the narrative modes of the folktale and away from the Western model that he spent the better part of his career trying to master. Other noteworthy novelists from across the Arab world are Hanna Mina, Suhayl Idris, Ghada as-Samman, Hanan ash-Shaykh, Abd ar-Rahman Munif, Emile Habibi, Ghassan Kanafani, Ahmad al-Faqih, Muhammad Barrada, Abdallah al-Arwi (Laroui), Mahmud al-Masadi, al-Bashir Khurayyif, Abd al-Hamid ibn Hadduqa, and at-Tahir Wattar.

The single most important Muslim short story writer in the twentieth century was the Egyptian Mahmud Taymur (died 1973), whose corpus contains about thirty collections of short stories that deal with a variety of social topics, including the coming of age, loss of innocence, and the good will of the common and poor people. The short story became better crafted, with characters skillfully portrayed and new themes and techniques undertaken, in the hands of Yahya Haqqi (1905–) and Yusuf Idris (died 1991), Other important short story writers are the Syrian Zakariyya Tamir (1931–) and the Iraqi Fu'ad al-Takarli (1927–).

Drama

Arabic literature contained some forms of dramatic art as early as the fourteenth century, as can be seen in the shadow-plays of the Egyptian Shams ad-Din Muhammad ibn Danyal (died 1311). But drama as a Western form was imported by the Arabs in the middle of the nineteenth century, first in Syria by Marun an-Naqqash (died 1855), who wrote and produced the first Arabic play, entitled *The Miser*, loosely based on Moliere's *L'Avare*. In Egypt, it was Yaqub Sannu (died 1912) who wrote a number of plays in the colloquial Egyptian in which he satirized the social and even the religious customs of his fellow Egyptians. Between 1870 and 1872 he wrote and acted in over ten plays, one of which, entitled *id-Durriten (The Co-Wives)*, was a daring attack on Islamic-sanctioned polygamy.

A thorny problem facing early dramatists was the chasm between literary Arabic and the dialect of everyday life. While it was difficult to abandon literary Arabic for the pedestrian language of the marketplace, it was unnatural to make peasant and intellectual alike speak classical Arabic. Compromise, not totally satisfying, was reached wherein dialogue would be in the colloquial and instructions in literary Arabic.

Among the well-known playwrights in Egypt were Shawqi, known for his historical dramas in verse, Muhammad Taymur (died 1921) and Tawfiq al-Hakim (died 1987). Al-Hakim, the most accomplished of all, adapted the Western dramatic form, which he studied in France, to explore a variety of philosophical and social issues. More recently Yusuf Idris, Numan Ashur, Alfred Faraj, and Najib Surur in Egypt along with the Syrian Sad Allah Wannus (1941–) have attempted to reproduce the life-story of folk heroes and prominent figures in Arab history in order to present a new vision of national heritage. Among the active playwrights in the Arab world are the Syrians Mamduh Udwan (1941–) and Ali Uqla Arsan (1940–); the Iraqi Walid Ikhlasi (1935–); the Lebanese Isam Mahfuz (1939–); the Tunisian Izz ad-Din Madani (1938–); and the Moroccan at-Tayyib as-Siddiqi (1938–), among others.

◆ MODERN ARABIC LITERATURE IN THE VERNACULAR

Alongside the established literature, has been a body of writings couched in colloquial Arabic, representing a more popular expression of the literary imagination.

Literature in the vernacular is not one homogeneous body; its innocuous, unpretentious form can be regarded as "folk" literature (*al-adab ash-shabi*), encompassing folk songs, proverbs, riddles, jokes, and so forth. But there exists in modern times a body of literature, known as *al-adab al-ammi* (vernacular literature), that takes its inspiration from the language and lore of the common folk, as well as the vernacular poetry of Muslim Spain (*zajal*), but infuses modern ideas (nationalism or socialism, for instance). Poetry in the vernacular is known in the Arab world as *ash-shir al-ammi* or *shir al-ammiyya* (Egypt) and *ash-shir al-malhun* (North African Arab states), which derives from *lahn*, that is, the ungrammatical use of classical Arabic. This label, which may have been given to it by its opponents, denotes both its ungrammaticality in the eyes of the elite as well as its musicality, for the word *lahn* means also melody. In Saudi Arabia it is called *ash-shir an-nabati* (Nabatean poetry).

◆ THEMES IN MODERN MUSLIM LITERATURE IN ARABIC

Tradition/Modernity; East/West Encounters

A look at modern Muslim literature in Arabic reveals both a sense of continuity as well as a break with the past. Some literary genres have disappeared, and others have been borrowed from the West. Rhymed prose (*saj*), the *maqama*, and the *risala* (epistle) have been discontinued as serious forms—only satirical imitations in the vernacular are at times attempted (for example, the parodies of Bayram at-Tunisi (died 1961) in Egyptian Arabic). Meanwhile, the short story, the novel, drama, free verse, and children's literature have become common.

A number of ideologies and literary movements originating in the West have had an impact on modern Muslim literature in Arabic. One encounters examples or echoes of Romanticism, Existentialism, Social Realism, Surrealism, *literature engage*, the theatre of the absurd, and even postmodernist trends. There are also clear indications of the influence of particular English literary figures: Shelley, Keats and Wordsworth in the poetry of the Romanticists Ahmad Zaki Abu Shadi (died 1955), Ibrahim Naji, and others; Franz Kafka in the plays of Mikhail Ruman (died 1973) and the novels of Sunallah Ibrahim (1937–); T.S. Eliot in the poetry of Salah Abd as-Sabur (died 1981); Paul Eluard and Pablo Neruda in the "committed" poetry of Abd al-Wahhab al-Bayyati (1926–); and Galsworthy and Dickens in the fiction of Najib Mahfuz (1911–), to cite but a few examples.

These influences can also be seen in the literature produced by Christian and Muslim Arab emigres to the Americas, which is known as the Mahjar literature. In prose as well as poetry by Mahjar figures such as Gibran Kahlil Gibran, Mikhail Nuayma, Amin ar-Rihani, and Ilyas Abu Shabaka, one senses the influence of American writers such as Edgar Alan Poe and Walt Whitman.

The adoption of ideas about literature is but one aspect of Muslim encounter with the West in modern times. A recurring theme in the Muslim literature in Arabic is the encounter between a native (usually a young man in pursuit of higher education in a European capital) and a Western woman. More often than not the encounter fails to produce a healthy or lasting relationship, and ends in separation or even in violence. This East/West encounter can be seen in novels such as *Usfur min ash-Sharq*, and *Adib* by the Egyptians Tawfiq al-Hakim and Taha Husayn, respectively, *al-Hayy al-Latini* by the Lebanese Suhayl Idris, and *Season of Migration to the North* by Sudanese at-Tayyib Salih. This theme has also been broached by vernacular poets and writers such as the Egyptian Bayram at-Tunisi, who composed many poems in the Egyptian colloquial about his encounters with French women and is at the heart of his two-volume, *is-Sayyid wi-Mratu fi Bariz* (*Sayyid and His Wife in Paris*) and *is-Sayyid wi-Mratu fi Masr* (*Sayyid and His Wife in Cairo*) on exploring the encounter between a lower-class Egyptian couple and Parisian society.

The Use of the Colloquial in Elite Literature

Arabic has undergone changes in modern times; the literary language is freer from the rhetorical embellishments of the classical compositions and the prose style is, by and large, more direct and purposeful. Standard Arabic has come closer to the colloquial, due in part to the development of Arabic drama (using the colloquial) and colloquial dialogues in works of fiction, not to ignore the important role mass media have played in bridging the gap between the two linguistic poles of Arabic. There is now an entire corpus of literary compositions written completely in the colloquial, particularly the poetical works produced by Egyptian, Lebanese, Saudi Arabian and Moroccan vernacular poets.

The Use of Folklore in Elite Literature

Literature of the elite sometimes makes use of themes derived from Arab or Muslim folklore but, of course, tends to infuse the folk material with all kinds of modernistic ideas. Some elite writers made use of tales from the *Arabian Nights* (e.g., Shawqi Abd al-Hakim's *King Maruf* and Alfred Faraj's *The Barber of Baghdad*) or modern Egyptian narrative ballads (e.g., "Hasan and Naima," "Shafiqa and Mitwalli," and "Yasin and Bahiyya"), as in the case with the dramatists Shawqi Abd al-Hakim and Najib Surur, or the folk theatre of as-

Samir, which involves audience participation and free-flowing comments, the puppet-show Aragoz, or the Sufi dervish dances utilized by Yusuf Idris of Egypt.

The Emergence of Women Writers and Feminist Literature

Modern literature has forged a new path by producing a body of literary works by women and feminists, notably in Egypt, Lebanon, and Morocco, which include the works of the Egyptian Nawal as-Sadawi, the Moroccan Fatma Mernissi, the Lebanese Ghada as-Samman, and the Palestinian Hanan ash-Shaykh.

Themes Relating to the Arab-Israeli Conflict

A whole body of works is devoted to the Arab-Israeli conflict. Vast amounts of prose and poetry have been produced to express the anguish of the dispossessed Palestinians and the bitter feelings of Arabs over their repeated defeats at the hands of the Israelis. Political poetry, the so-called "poetry of resistance" (*shir al-muqawama*), has been written by Palestinian poets such as Fadwa Tuqan, Mahmud Darwish, Samih al-Qasim, and Tawfiq Zayyad, among others.

As the Nobel Prize Award to the Egyptian writer Najib Mahfuz in 1988 indicates, Arabic literature has once again claimed international recognition. New patterns are emerging that include a return to aspects of the classical heritage to new and contemporary ways of literary expression. It is clear that a complex literary discourse is emerging as a major element in the cultural life of the Arabic speaking Muslim world, as vital and diverse as that of the past, but more inclusive of minority trends, and individual voices.

Kamal Abdul Malek

References

Abdel-Malek, Kamal. *A Study of the Vernacular Poetry of Ahmad Fuad Nigm*. Leiden: E.J. Brill, 1990.
————. *Muhammad in the Modern Egyptian Ballad*. Leiden: E. J. Brill, 1995.
Allen, Roger. *Modern Arabic Literature*. New York: Unger Publishing Co., 1987.
————. *The Arabic Novel: An Historical and Critical Introduction*. Syracuse, N.Y., 1982.
Arberry, A.J. *Aspects of Islamic Civilization as Depicted in the Original Texts*. Westport, Connecticut: Greenwood Press, 1977.
Badawi, M.M. *A Short History of Modern Arabic Literature*. Oxford: Oxford University Press, 1993.
Beard M. and Haydar, A. eds. *Naguib Mahfouz: From Regional Fame to Global Recognition*. Syracuse: Syracuse University Press, 1993.
Bakalla, M.H. *Arabic Culture Through Its Language and Literature*. London and Boston: Kegan Paul International, 1984.
Boullata, I. *Critical Perspectives on Modern Arabic Literature*. Washington, D.C.: Three Continents Press, 1980.
Brugman, J. *An Introduction to the History of Modern Arabic Literature in Egypt*. Leiden: E.J. Brill, 1984.
Cachia, P. *An Overview of Modern Arabic Literature*. Edinburgh: Edinburgh University Press, 1990.
The Cambridge History of Arabic Literature: Arabic Literature to the End of the Umayyad Period. Cambridge: Cambridge University Press, 1983.
The Cambridge History of Arabic Literature: Abbasid Belles Lettres. Cambridge: Cambridge University Press, 1990.
The Cambridge History of Arabic Literature: Modern Arabic Literature. Cambridge: Cambridge University Press, 1993.
Gibb, H.A.R. *Arabic Literature*, 2nd revised edn. London: Oxford University Press, 1963.
Hamori, A. *On the Art of Medieval Arabic Literature*. Princeton: Princeton University Press, 1974.
Haywood, John A. *Modern Arabic Literature: 1800-1970*. New York: St. Martin's Press, 1971.
Kritzeck, J. comp. *Anthology of Islamic Literature: From the Rise of Islam to Modern Times*. New York: Holt, Rinehart, and Winston, 1964.
————. *Modern Islamic Literature: From 1800 to the Present*. New York: New American Library, 1970.
Malti-Douglas, Fedwa. *Structures of Avarice, The Bukhala in Medieval Arabic Literature*. Leiden: E.J. Brill, 1985.
————. *Woman's Body, Woman's Word: Gender and Discourse in Arabo-Islamic Writing*. Princeton: Princeton University Press, 1991.
Nicholson, R. A., *A Literary History of the Arabs*. 1907. Reprint. Cambridge, Mass.: Cambridge University Press, 1969.
Stretkevych, J. *The Zephyrs of Najd: The Poetics of Nostalgia in the Classical Arabic Nasib*. Chicago: University of Chicago Press, 1993.

Muslim Literature in Persian and Turkish

♦ THE PERSIAN LANGUAGE

Persian is an Indo-European language, belonging to the Iranian language group, that includes Kurdish and Pashto. Linguistically, it is not related to the other major languages spoken by Muslims, such as Arabic, Turkish, Urdu, Hansa, or Malay. At the time of the Arab Muslim conquest of Iran during the mid-seventh century, Persian had a millennium-old lettered tradition and had already undergone a significant linguistic evolution. Not much is known about the history of the language during the period from 650 to 900, when Persian was displaced by Arabic as the language of high culture. Persian retained its liturgical and scholarly status, however, among the Zoroastrians, and never ceased to be spoken. At the end of this long period of cultural abeyance, a linguistic renaissance set in during the tenth century, and Persian reemerged, written in the Arabic script. Its grammar simplified, and a large portion of its vocabulary Arabized, this new Persian became the major language of art, administration, literature, and scholarship in Iran and beyond, and has remained the main linguistic medium of high culture in Iran to date.

♦ GENERAL CHARACTERISTICS OF THE PERSIAN LITERARY TRADITION

The most noticeable trait of Persian literature is the preponderance of poetry. A remarkably sophisticated and unified poetic tradition has occupied the center of this literature ever since its emergence over a millennium ago. In spite of continuous and vigorous experimentation throughout this period, the formal, thematic, and lexical core of the poetic tradition has remained distinct and vibrant into the modern era. As a result, anyone proficient in modern Persian can find easy access to an incredibly rich and inexhaustible poetic storehouse dating as far back as the tenth century.

Another prominent feature of Persian literature, especially lyric poetry, is its infusion with Sufism, the tradition of Muslim spirituality and mysticism. This development dates back to the very beginnings of New Persian literature, and became pervasive during the mid-twelfth century, when both panegyric and lyric poetry assumed mystical dimensions. There took place an almost complete merger between profane and sacred agendas, particularly in lyric poetry, which Persian poets exploited to its full potential with utmost skill and verve. The resultant corpus constitutes, without doubt, a zenith in lyric/mystical poetry worldwide.

Persian literary traditions are notable for the enormous influence they have exercised in the cultural life of Islamic societies in West, Central, and South Asia since about the eleventh century. Not only was Persian literature enthusiastically cultivated outside the boundaries of the Iranian plateau, especially in Anatolia and India, by both Iranians and non-Iranians well into the modern period, but its literary achievements remained the chief models in the formation of other literary traditions in the eastern part of the Islamic world (Azeri, Chaghatay and Ottoman Turkish, Bengali, Punjabi, Pashto, Sindhi, and Urdu).

Throughout the premodern period, Persian literary life depended heavily on the patronage of monarchs as well as urban notables. The significance of the courtly setting in particular for the cultivation of literary taste was most obvious in the formative period when Persian evolved as a new literary idiom under the patronage of Iranian rulers, most notably the Samanids based in Bukhara. Although protection and sponsorship by the wealthy and powerful remained the norm after this initial phase, the ascendancy of religious, especially mystical, themes in both verse and prose meant that literary production did not always have to be harnessed to the agendas of powerful patrons. Social function, however, does not directly inform artistic perfection, and it should not be assumed that such patronage detracts from the value of Persian literature.

Forms and Themes

In its formal aspects, Persian poetry has its roots in the Arabic poetic tradition, though ancient Iranian literature probably also played a role in its development. The influence of Arabic is most clearly visible in the adoption of quantitative meters (*artuz*) and the *qasida*, the basic form of Arabic poetry. However, Iranian poets forged distinctively Persian patterns in both prosody and form so that the usual meters and forms of Arabic and Persian poetry do not normally correspond.

Persian poetry can be divided into two forms, the lyrical and the epic. The major lyrical forms are the *qasida*, the *ghazal*, and the *rubai*, while the basic form of all epic poetry is the *masnavi*. The *qasida*, a long monorhyme (aa, ba, ca), was normally used for panegyric, though it was also adapted to the cause of secular and religious moralism. It traditionally consists of three parts, a prologue, the actual panegyric, and a final appeal to the patron. The *ghazal*, prosodically the same as the *qasida* though shorter in length, was distinguished from the latter by its concentration on profane and/or mystical love and the practice of including the poet's penname in the last distich. The *rubai*, the Persian quatrain, is not only defined by the number of lines but also further delimited in rhyme (aa ba) and meter. There were also several strophic forms and fragmentary pieces in lyric poetry.

All epic poetry is composed in the form of a *masnavi*, where each distich has a separate internal rhyme (aa, bb, cc). Ideally suited for lengthy compositions, the *masnavi* was used extensively in a wide range of poetic works. These can be divided into three broad, though not mutually exclusive, groups: the heroic, the romantic, and the didactic. The heroic epic, normally based on material from ancient Iranian mythology, related the lives and exploits of Iranian kings and warrior heroes. The romantic epic, which narrated quintessential love stories, drew on a wider range of sources, incorporating material of Iranian, Hellenic, Arabic, and

Quranic background. The didactic epic, the most diffuse in subject matter, usually aimed to transmit religious, especially mystical, views.

Prose played a more modest role in literary production. Prominent literary types in prose included didactic/moralistic treatises, the popular heroic romance that was religious or amorous in emphasis, popular fables, and collections of anecdotes or short stories. Mention should also be made of mystical and philosophical treatises as well as historical chronicles, since some of the finest examples of Persian prose were produced in these fields. Among the conspicuous traits of this prose literature are the interspersion of prose with poetic fragments and the increased prominence of rhymed prose, which led to highly embellished compositions in the later stages of Persian literary history in particular.

The most commonly accepted periodization of premodern Persian literary history, both in and outside Iran, is a fourfold division according to stylistic criteria: (1) the style of Khorasan, (2) the style of Iraq, (3) the Indian style, and (4) the neo-classical style. The style of Khorasan is so defined after the relatively pure and simple yet vigorous and harmonious poetry produced in Northeastern Iran during the eleventh and the twelfth century. The style of Iraq, which emerged from a shift in the center of literary activity towards western Iran, reflected growing rhetorical and intertextual sophistication along with a heavier presence of Arabic vocabulary. This style, also marked by the predominance of the *ghazal* form, represented the mainstream until the formation of the Safavid Empire at the beginning of the sixteenth century. The Indian style, so called after another shift in the geographical core of literary production towards Mughal India, was characterized by an expanded stock of poetic images and metaphors, a predilection for abstract, philosophical ideas, and a tendency to allegorize. This style eroded during the second half of the eighteenth century and was replaced by a neo-classical movement, advocating a return to the classical models. Unchallenged during the nineteenth century, neo-classicism has remained popular until the present.

This periodization needs to be completed by the addition of a modern period, encompassing the late nineteenth and the twentieth century. It is impossible to characterize the modern period on the basis of any particular literary style. The most conspicuous traits of this latest phase of Persian literature are the emergence and increasing popularity of fiction (the novel, the novelette, and the short story) and the development of an extremely vibrant free verse movement in poetry. Drama, while perhaps less commonly cultivated than fiction, has also been fully adapted to Persian.

◆ HISTORICAL SURVEY OF PERSIAN LITERATURE

Tenth to Thirteenth Centuries

During the tenth to the thirteenth centuries, poetry was mostly produced in courtly settings under the patronage of rulers based in eastern Iran. The predominant form was the *qasida*, though the *ghazal* steadily grew more popular. The famous lyric poets included Rudaki (died circa 940) the preeminent figure of Samanid literature; Farrukhi (died circa 1037), Unsuri (died circa 1039), and Manuchihri (died circa 1040), three poets of the Ghaznavid school; Sanai (died circa 1150); Anvari (died circa 1187); and Khaqani (died circa 1198). The undisputed master of the *rubai*, Umar Khayyam (died 1131), lived in this period:

Neither you nor I know the mysteries of eternity,
Neither you nor I read this enigma;
You and I only talk this side of the veil;
When the veil falls, neither you nor I will be here.

(P. Avery and J. Heath-Stubbs, trans.,
The Rubaiyat of Omar Khayyam)

This period also witnessed the production of classics in all branches of poetry. Sanai's acclaimed *masnavi Hadiqat al-haqiqa* (*The Garden of Truth*) laid the foundation for all future didactic epics. Nizami (died 1209), the unrivalled master of the romantic epic, left behind a series of five romances known as the *Khamsa* (*The Quintuplet*), which became the classical models of romance in all later Islamic literatures. Firdawsi (died circa 1025) composed the *Shahnama* (*The Book of Kings*), the celebrated Iranian national epic. Here is an excerpt from the prologue to the tragedy of Suhrab and Rustam, in which the national warrior hero Rustam inadvertently kills his young son Suhrab in battle:

A vagrant wind springs up quite suddenly,
And casts a green unripened fruit to earth.
Shall we call this a tyrant's act, or just?
Shall we consider it as right, or wrong?
If death is just, how can this not be so?
Why then lament and wail at what is just?
Your soul knows nothing of this mystery;
You cannot see what lies behind this veil.

In prose, many prominent examples of the "mirror for princes" genre date back to this period: *Kabusnama* (*The Book of Kabus*) by Kay Kaus (died circa 1098), the *Chahar maqala* (*The Four Discourses*) of Nizami Aruzi (died 1164?), the *Siyasatnama* (*The Book of Government*) by Nizam al-Mulk (died 1092), and the *Nasihat al-muluk* (*Advice for Kings*) by al-

Page from a *Shah Nama*.

Ghazali (died 1111). Also circulating at this time were many Persian renderings of Indian fables and stories such as the *Kalila va Dimna* (*Kalila and Dimna*) and *Sindbadnama* (*The Book of Sindbad*), as well as popular romances mostly based on ancient Iranian lore such as the *Darabnama* (*The Book of Alexander the Great*). On another front, Iranian gnostics and mystics produced masterpieces of Persian prose. In this connection, mention could be made of the works of Ahmad al-Ghazali (died 1126), Ayn al-Quzat al-Hamadani (died 1132), and Shihab al-Din Yahya Suhrawardi (died 1191).

Thirteenth to Sixteenth Centuries

The lyric poetry of the thirteenth to sixteenth century period is marked by the prominence of the *ghazal*. Only a few out of the long list of the famous *ghazal*-composers can be mentioned here: Rumi (died 1273), Iraqi (died 1289), Sadi (died 1292), Amir Khusraw (died 1325), Ahadi (died 1338), Maghribi (died circa 1406), Svaju of Kirman (died circa 1351), Salman Savaji (died 1376), Hafiz (died circa 1389), Kamal Khujandi (died 1400). Among these Hafiz, Rumi, and Sadi stand out by consensus as the undisputable masters. The following *ghazal* is engraved on the tomb of Hafiz in Shiraz:

Where are the tidings of union? that I may arise—
Forth from the dust I will rise up to welcome thee!
My soul, like a homing bird, yearning for Paradise,
Shall arise and soar, from the snares of the world set free.
When the voice of thy love shall call me to be thy slave,
I shall rise to a greater far than the mastery
Of life and the living, time and the mortal span:
Pour down, oh Lord! from the clouds of thy guiding grace
The rain of a mercy that quickeneth on my grave,
Before, like dust that the wind bears from place to place,
I arise and flee beyond the knowledge of man.
When to my grave thou turnest thy blessed feet,
Wine and lute thy shall bring in thine hand to me,
Thy voice shall ring through the folds of my winding-sheet,
And I will be arise and dance to thy minstrelsy.
Though I be old, clasp me one night to thy breast,
And I, when the dawn shall come to awaken me,
Rise up, let mine eyes delight in thy stately grace,
Thou art the goal to which all men's endeavor has pressed,
And thou the idol of Hafiz' worship shall bid him come forth and arise!

(A. J. Arberry, ed., *Fifty Poems of Hafiz*)

The mystical didactic epic its culmination during the thirteenth century in the works of Attar (died after 1221) and Rummi. Rumi's long composition, known simply as the *Masnavi*, is by common consent the

Manuscript of the Guy u Chawgan.

greatest mystical work in verse and a true masterpiece of Persian literature. Moralistic literature also attained its zenith during the same century in two works of Sadi, the Bustan (*The Garden*), in verse, and the *Gulistan* (*The Rose Garden*), in prose interspersed with verse. These became two of the most influential works in Persian as models of elegance, felicity of expression, wit, and robust moralism. The romantic epic continued to enjoy popularity, especially in the works of Amir Khusraw and Abd al-Rahman Jami (died 1492); the latter is commonly acknowledged to be the greatest poet of the fifteenth century.

Sixteenth to Mid-Eighteenth Centuries

Lyric poetry, in particular the *ghazal* in the Indian style, dominated the literary scene from the sixteenth to the mid-eighteenth centuries. The major poets were Baba Fighani (died 1519), Ahli of Shiraz (died 1535), Muhtasham of Kashan (died 1587-88), Vahshi of Bafq (died circa 1583), Urfi of Shiraz (died 1590), Fayzi (died 1595), Zuhuri (died 1616), Naziri (died 1612), Saib of Tabriz (died 1675), Kalim of Hamadan (died 1650), Talib of Amul (died 1626), and Bidil (died 1721). Of these, Saib is commonly acknowledged as one of the best Persian poets ever. Some of his lines have become proverbial:

When a man grows old, his greed grows young.
Slumber becomes heavy at the time of dawn.
All this talk of faith and unbelief leads to one end.
The dream is the same, only interpretations differ.
Only light-headed people grow excited by every empty word.
A slight breeze makes a bamboo grove reverberate.
From the insignificance of dust on top of the wall I concluded That a nobody does not become a somebody by sitting on high places.

(Esan Yarshater, ed., *Persian Literature*)

Prose works of the period, particularly strong in religious and historical subjects, have received little scholarly attention.

Mid-Eighteenth Century to the Present

In poetry, the neo-classical poets of the eighteenth and the nineteenth century shunned the Indian style, attempted to return to earlier styles, and rehabilitated the *qasida*. Saba (died 1822) and Qaani (died 1854) were among the most successful. The leading representatives of neoclassicism in the first half of this century were Muhammad Taqi Bahar (died 1951) and the female poet Parvin Itisami (died 1941). The period after World War II, up through today, is dominated by the free-verse movement initiated by Nima Yushij (died 1960), and championed, among many others, by Furugh Farrukhzad (died 1967), Akhavan Salis (died 1989), Ahmad Shamlu (died 1925), and Suhrab Sipihri (died 1989). The following is a short poem of the poetess Farrukhzad called "Gift":

I speak out of the deep of night
out of the deep of darkness
and out of the deep of night I speak.

If you come to my house, friend
bring me a lamp and a window that I can look through
at the crowd in the happy alley.

(A. Karimi-Hakkak, ed.,
An Anthology of Modern Persian Poetry)

In the modern period, the long monorhyme disappears, displaced by the popularity of prose genres developed under the influence of European literatures—the novel, the novelette, and the short story. Some of the significant figures for prose were Muhammad Ali Jamalzadah (died 1892), Muhammad Hijazi (died 1977), Sadiq Hidayat (died 1951), Sadiq Chubak (died 1916), Buzurg Alavi (died 1904), Ali Dashti (died 1982), Jalal Ali-i Ahmad (died 1969), and Simin Danishvar (died 1921). The most notable feature of Persian fiction after the 1960s is the predominance of female writers such as Shahnush Parsipur (died 1946) and Muniru Ravanipur (died 1954), a trait that became particularly visible after the Iranian revolution of 1979.

◆ THE TURKISH LANGUAGE

Turkish is the generic name of a variety of closely related languages that belong (along with Mongolian) to the Altaic language group. The language is not related to either Arabic or Persian. The entry of the Turkish speakers into the Islamic cultural sphere from the tenth century onwards played a decisive role in the development of Turkish languages, most visibly in the formation of a literate tradition written in the Arabic script and the adoption of loan-words from Persian and Arabic. Nowadays, Turkish is spoken in a vast area stretching from Eastern Europe to Siberia (Azeri, Kazak, Kirghiz, Turkish of Turkey, Turkmen, Uzbek).

◆ GENERAL CHARACTERISTICS OF THE TURKISH LITERARY TRADITION

Turkish Muslim literature can be divided into three broad categories based on on stylistic and sociological criteria: court literature, mystical-religious literature, and folk literature. Court literature, which required the patronage of the political and cultural elite, developed and remained under the influence of Persian literature. The Turkish cultural elite, mostly proficient in Persian, produced sophisticated poetic and prose traditions that paralleled and, in the opinion of many Turks, rivalled their Persian counterparts. By adapting Persian models to Turkish, Muslim Turks participated enthusiastically in the literary adventures initiated by Muslim Persians which they carried to new heights in a different linguistic medium. This elite tradition existed side by side with a vibrant and extensive folk literature, mostly oral in form. Here the influence of non-Turkish literary traditions was largely absent, and forms and themes were predominantly Turkish in origin. In between court and folk literature, and with roots in both, there developed a vast intermediate literary domain of mystical and popular religious discourse. This literature, cultivated chiefly by Sufis, had a broad appeal across all social strata.

In addition to the horizontal tripartite division based on social and literary criteria, Turkish literature is also divided vertically into two groups based on linguistic and geographical grounds: Eastern Turkish and Western Turkish. The former, also known as Chaghatay in the premodern period, is used to refer to the shared written literary tradition of Turks living to the east and northeast of Iran in an area that primarily corresponds to the Central Asian Republics. The latter, consisting of the Ottoman and Azeri areas, denotes the literary tradition for the Turks of Western Asia.

Forms and Themes

In their court literature, Turks adopted Persian literary models. In poetry, the quantitative *aruz* meter was used, and the *ghazal*, the *qasida*, the *masnavi*, and the *rubai* were the principal forms (discussed in the section on Persian literature above). The themes of court poetry also largely reproduced those of the Persian poetic tradition: divine/human love and eulogy. In prose, mostly given to historical and legendary subjects, the tendency to intersperse the prose narrative with poetic fragments and the predilection to use rhymed prose, both characteristic of Persian, were also predominant in Turkish.

The major poetic forms in mystical poetry, normally composed in syllabic meter, were the *ilahi* and the *nefes*, as well as the *mesnevi* for long compositions. Apart from its standard Sufi repertoire, some of this poetry also preserves a strong Shia influence. The most popular prose genre in this literature was the *menakib*, the sacred biography, devoted to the exposition of the lives of famous saintly figures.

Folk poetry, mostly produced in syllabic meter, had its own store of forms, the *mani* (quatrain), the *turku*, *kosma*, *destan*, *semai*, and *varsagi* (all strophic forms roughly comparable to the ballad). Folk poetry was devoted to the standard rural themes of human love, yearning, sorrow, and the beauty of nature. The folk tradition also included a remarkably broad range of oral epics, certainly one of the richest epic treasures in the world. A significant portion of these epic cycles have been recorded in writing at different stages of

their development. The heroic, romantic, and didactic (mostly religious) subjects are equally well represented. In addition, Turkish folklore has preserved an unusually large number of popular tales and fables.

Periodization

The formation of Muslim literature in Turkish started during the eleventh century. The timeframe for Eastern and Western Turkish traditions, however, was different. The formation of a central lettered tradition in the East occurred during the eleventh and the twelfth centuries, largely under the patronage of the Karakhanid dynasty; a comparable development in Western Asia, primarily in Asia Minor, emerged during the late thirteenth century and was not complete until the mid-fifteenth century. In both cases, the matrices established for literary activity remained in effect well into the nineteenth century, when the influence of European literatures began to displace them.

◆ HISTORICAL SURVEY OF EASTERN TURKISH LITERATURE

Eleventh to Twelfth Centuries

A new Muslim literary tradition in Turkish emerged in Transoxania under Karakhanid patronage. This Turko-Islamic literary culture utilized the Uighur script and was a result of a synthesis of Inner Asian traditions and Islamic religious values. The first and best known work of this new literary idiom was the *Kutadgu Bilig* (*The Wisdom of Royal Glory*), a long *mesnevi* in the "mirror for princes" genre composed in 1069 or 1070 by Yusuf Khass Hajib. The author introduces the main characters of his narrative at the end of his prologue:

First I speak of the king, Rising Sun—I shall explain this name, gentle reader! Then I speak of Full Moon—the sun of blessed Fortune receives its light from him! Rising Sun stands for Justice and "Full Moon" for Fortune. Then I speak of Highly Praised—he is the personification of Intellect, which raises a man's estate. Finally I speak of Wide Awake—he represents the Last End. Upon these four things have I based my discourse. It will become clear as you read it, so keep your eyes sharp.

(R. Dankoff, trans.,
*Wisdom of the Royal Glory (Kutadic Biliqk):
A Turko-Islamic Mirror for Princes*)

The other well-known work of this period is the *Diwan lughat al-turk* (*Compendium of the Turkic*

Dialects), a remarkable piece of linguistic scholarship rich in literary lore compiled by Mahmud al-Kashgari in 1077.

Thirteenth to Fifteenth Centuries

The Karakhanid tradition was continued in the areas of Khwarazm and Southern Russia, especially under the Golden Horde. Apart from a lively religious literature, well represented by the *Kisasul-enbiya* (1310) of Rabguzi, an elite literary culture began to emerge under the Persian influence. Qutb's *Husru u Shirin* (1341), modeled after Nizami's Persian romance, and Khwariami's *Mahabbetname* of 1353, based on Gurgani's *Vis u Ramin*, are prominent examples of the ascendancy of Persian literary patterns. It is likely that the popular mystical literature, especially of the Yesevi mold, also crystallized during this period, as suggested by the presence of several hagiographies that date back to the fifteenth century.

Fifteenth to Ninteenth Centuries

The fifteenth to nineteenth century span is known as the Chaghatay period, which developed under Timurid patronage. During the fifteenth century, poets such as Gadai (flourished mid-century), Sakkari of Samarkand (second half of the century) and Lufti of Herat (died circa 1460) completed the adaptation of Persian poetic models to Eastern Turkish literature. The unrivalled literary master of the Chaghatay tradition was Ali Sir Nevai (died 1501), a poet, scholar and statesman who was a close friend of the Timurid ruler Husayn Baykara (reigned 1469–1506), himself a poet. His literary output in both verse and prose, spanning the gamut of classical Turkish court literature, exercised a major influence on all later literary figures of this tradition and earned Nevai his reputation as one of the greatest Turkish poets of all time. Mention should also be made of Muhammed Babur (died 1530), the founder of the Mughal empire, whose fame largely rests on his unusually frank and perceptive autobiography in prose, the *Baburname*. His collection of poems clearly places him as a major poet also.

The history of Eastern Turkish literature during the seventeenth, eighteenth, and nineteenth centuries is still in need of much scholarly attention. Some major figures of this long period were Abul-Gazi Bahadur Han, the ruler of Khiva (reigned 1644–1663) and the author of two celebrated prose histories; the mystic poets Baba Mesreb (died 1711) and Sufi Allah Yar (died 1723); and the popular Turkmen poet Mahdum Kuli (died 1782). The folk literature of Eastern Turkish is exceptionally rich, though we do not have written records of it prior to this period. Most significant in this connection are oral epics known as *dastan*, well-represented

Illustration of Timur holding a feast to celebrate victory in battle.

by the Manas epic of the Kirghiz and the popular romance.

Twentieth Century

The unified literary tradition of Eastern Turkish gradually gave way to new national literatures in Kazah, Kirghiz, Uzbek, Tatar, and Turkmen, especially during the Soviet era. This period of Turkish literary history has not yet been studied adequately.

◆ HISTORICAL SURVEY OF WESTERN TURKISH LITERATURE

Thirteenth to Mid-Fifteenth Centuries

The thirteenth to the mid-fifteenth centuries were the formative age of Western Turkish literature in its three branches under the patronage of the Turkish rulers of Asia Minor and Azarbaijan. Court poetry modelled after Persian models was developed by the poet Kadi Burhaneddin (died 1398) and attained maturity at the end of this period in the work of Ahmedi (died 1412) and Seyhi (died 1431). Mystical poetry was fully developed by the towering figure of Yunus Emre (died circa 1320), by consensus one of the greatest poets of all Turkish literature. His stature was such that no later poet of the mystico-religious tradition could emerge from under of his shadow. The following is a selection from his poem:

Now hear this, lovers, my friends:
Love is a precious thing;
It doesn't grace everyone,
Love is a decorous thing.

Like the winds, it shakes the hills,
Into hearts it blazes trails,
Turns sultans into vassals—
Love is a courageous thing.

The man struck by love's arrow
First feels no pain nor sorrow
But then weeps and screams with woe:
Love is a torturous thing.

It makes the seas rage and boil,
Throws huge waves into turmoil,
And moves the rocks off the soil:
Love is a vigorous thing.

Mystic Yunus is helpless;
On one feels for his distress.
His feast is the Friend's caress:
Love is a delicious thing.

(Talat Halman, trans.,
Yunus Emoc and His Mystical Poetry)

Other mystic-religious poets of this period included Kaygusuz Abdal (died after 1424), the Hurufi Nesimi (died early fifteenth century), and Suleyman Celebi (died 1422), whose *Mevlid* (*The Birth*), a monorhyme composition on the life of the Prophet Muhammad, became one of the most widely read and recited works in Turkish. Esrefoglu Rumi (died 1469) and the Yazicioglu brothers Ahmed Bican (died 1465?) and Mehmed (died 1451) contributed significantly to the formation of mystical poetry and prose. In folk literature, *The Book of Dede Korbut*, the celebrated heroic epic of the western Turks, probably took its final shape in the early fifteenth century, though it was recorded somewhat later.

Mid-Fifteenth to Mid-Ninteenth Centuries

Court poetry was at its height during the mid-fifteenth to the mid-nineteenth centuries. Major figures included Necati (died 1509), Zati (died 1546), Hayali (died 1557), Tashcali Yahya (died 1582), Nevi (died

1599), Ruhi (died 1605), Nefi (died 1635), Naili (died 1666), and Nabi (died 1712). The greatest names, however, were Fuzuli (died 1556), Baki (died 1600), Nedim (died 1730), and Seyh Galib (died 1799). Literature in prose also flourished, most notably in the genre of historical chronicles, though there are some significant exceptions such as the religious and ethical works of Sinan Pasa (died 1486) and the voluminous travelog of Evliya Celebi (died 1684?).

Mystical literature attained new heights in both quantity and quality, especially in prose. Its most notable feature is the preponderance of the genre of sacred biography, *menakib* or *vilayetname*. The voice of Shia poetry was felt very strongly in the poems of Shah Ismail (also known as Hatai) (died 1524) and *Pir* Sultan Abdal (mid-sixteenth century).

The historical record for folk literature is much richer for this period than it is for earlier ones. In poetry, Koroglu (sixteenth century), Kayikci Kul Mustafa (seventeenth century), Dadaloglu (nineteenth century), but above all Karacaoglan (sixteenth century), were the major voices. Heroic, religious, and amorous romances enjoyed unprecedented popularity throughout this era. Stories of religious heroes such as the *Battalname*, the *Ebu Muslimname*, the *Saltukname*, and *Koroglu Destani*, as well as love stories such as *Kerem ile Asli* and *Tahir ile Zuhre* circulated among the western Turks and some even spread to the Eastern Turkish world.

Mid-Ninteenth Century to the Present

The modern period witnessed the displacement of court literature by free verse and prose genres of Western origin such as the short story, novel, and drama. Simultaneously, there occurred a certain revalorization of folk and, to lesser extent, mystical literary traditions. The initial critical reaction to court literature was led by such figures as Ibrahim Sinasi (died 1871), Fath Ali Ahundzade (died 1878), Namik Kemal (died 1888), and Tevfik Fikret (died 1915). After World War I, Western prose genres were fully naturalized at the hands of short story writers such as Omer Seyfettin (died 1920), Refik Halit Karay (died 1965), Sait Faik Abasiyamk (died 1954), novelists Halit Ziya Usakhgil (died 1945), Yakub Kadri Karaosmanoglu (died 1974), Ahmet Hamdi Tanpinar (died 1962), Kemal Tahir (died 1973), Yasar Kemal (1922–); and humorist Aziz Nesin (died 1915). The free verse movement, initially overshadowed by brilliant neoclassicists like Yahya Kemal Beyath (died 1958) and Ahmet Hasim (died 1933), gained the upper hand during the 1940's and produced such poets as Nazim Hikmet Ran (died 1963), Fazil Husnu Daglarca (1914–), Atilla Ilhan (1925–), and Turgut Uyar (died 1985). Throughout this period, the appeal of the quantitative *aruz* meter steadily diminished, while the Turkish syllabic meters enjoyed renewed popularity best demonstrated by the poems of Sehriyar (died 1991). The most notable feature of most recent Turkish prose is the prominence of female writers such as Adalet Agaoglu (1929–), Nazh Eray (1945–), and Latife Tekin (1957–). One of the leading younger writers is Ismet Ozel (1944–).

Ahmet T. Karamustafa

References: Persian Literature

Arberry, Arthur J. *Classical Persian Literature.* London: Allen & Unwin, 1958.

Browne, Edward G. *A Literary History of Persia,* 4 vols. Cambridge University Press, 1902–24. Reprinted 1964.

DeBruijn, J.T.P. "Iran Literature." In *The Encyclopedia of Islam.* Leiden: D.J. Brill, 1960–.

Farrukhzad. "Gift." In *Ahmad Karimi-Hakkak, An Anthology of Modern Persian Poetry.* Boulder: Westview Press, 1978.

Firdawsi. "Shahnama." In *The Tragedy of Sohrab and Rostam.* Translated by Jerome W. Clinton. Seattle: University of Washington Press, 1987.

Hafiz. "Ode of *Hafiz.*" Translated by Gertrude Bell and reproduced in Arthur J. Arberry, *Fifty Poems of Hafiz.* Richmond: Curzon Press, 1993.

Khayyam, Omar. *The Rubaiyat of Omar Khayyam.* Translated by Peter Avery and John Heath-Stubbs. New York: Penquin, 1981.

Morrison, George, ed. *History of Persian Literature from the Beginning of the Islamic Period to the Present Day.* Leiden: E.J. Brill, 1981.

Rypka, Jan. *History of Iranian Literature.* Dordrecht: D. Reidel Publishing Company, 1968.

Saib frag. Translated by Ehsan Yarshater in "The Indian Style: Progress or Decline?" in *Persian Literature.* N.p.: Bibliotheca Persica, 1988.

Yarshater, Ehsan, ed. *Persian Literature.* Albany, N.Y.: Bibliotheca Persica, 1988.

References: Turkish Literature

Barthold, W. "Turks, Caghatai Literature." In *The Encyclopaedia of Islam,* 8 vols. Leiden: E.J. Brill, 1913–38.

Birnbaum, Eleazar. "Turkish Literature through the Ages." In *Introduction to Islamic Civilization,* edited by R.M. Savory. Cambridge University Press, 1976.

Deny, Jean, et al., *Philologiae Turcicae Fundamental,* 2 vols. Wiesbaden: Franz Steiner, 1959–64.

Emre, Yunus frag. Reproduced in *Yunus Emre and His Mystical Poetry,* 3rd ed., edited by Talat Halman. Bloomington: Indiana University Turkish Studies, 1991.

Hajib, Yusuf Khass. "Kutadgu Bilik." In *Wisdom of Royal Glory (Kutadgu Bilik): A Turko-Islamic Mirror for Princes,* translated by by Robert Dankoff. Chicago: The University of Chicago Press, 1983.

Gibb, E.J.W. *A History of Ottoman Poetry,* 6 vols. London: Luzac and Company, 1900–09.

Iz, Fahir. "Turkish Literature," In *The Cambridge History of Islam,* vol. 2, *The Further Islamic Lands, Islamic Society and Civilization,* edited by P.M. Holt, Ann K.S. Lambton, and Bernard Lewis. Cambridge: Cambridge University Press, 1970.

Koprulu, M.F. "Turks, Ottoman Turkish Literature." In *The Encyclopaedia of Islam,* 8 vols. Leiden: E.J. Brill, 1913–38.

Menemencioglu, Nermin, ed., *The Penguin Book of Turkish Verse.* New York: Penguin, 1978.

Muslim Literature in South Asia

♦ Literatures of the Turko-Persian Culture
♦ Literature of Islamic Reform in the Contemporary Period

The largest concentration of Muslims in the world today reside in the South Asian nations of India, Pakistan, and Bangladesh. For over twelve centuries the region has been home to a magnificent Islamic civilization that has profoundly affected all aspects of South Asian culture and life. The achievements of this civilization are legendary. The Taj Mahal, the monumental mosques, palaces, forts, and pleasure gardens that dot the Subcontinent's landscape, as well as exquisite miniature paintings and intricate marble lattice-work, are just a few of its more notable products. The civilization has also nurtured several of the world's greatest rulers, artists, mystics and poets, many of whose writings have endured as literary masterpieces still recited today.

♦ LITERATURES OF THE TURKO-PERSIAN CULTURE

Turko-Persian culture was associated with various ruling dynasties and the *ashraf*, the aristocracy of foreign origin. Its sphere of influence extended also to the intelligentsia and the literati, some of them Hindu, who were directly or indirectly patronized by the courts and the nobility. Physically, this culture was largely confined to the major cities and towns, the centers of political, economic, and religious dominion. At the same time, because the Persian language was primarily used, it was an international culture that influenced, at least until the eighteenth century, Central Asia, Afghanistan, Iran and even Turkey. Its cosmopolitan character meant that the literati in Indian cities such as Delhi, Lahore, Bijapur and Dacca spoke the same language, read the same books, enjoyed the same poems as those in Herat (Afghanistan), Bukhara (Central Asia), Isfahan (Iran) and Istanbul (Turkey). It also meant that poets, artists, and scholars were free to move between courts within this great cultural nexus in search of new or better patronage.

Persian was not only the language of intellectual and artistic life in Islamic South Asia but was also the official language of government and administration. The significance of Persian extended far beyond its use as a medium of communication among the elite, however. Persian became such a prominent cultural component in medieval India that Persian vocabulary features prominently in all of the major North Indian languages. Furthermore, it so strongly influenced the literary forms, idioms, and scripts of several Indic languages such as Urdu, Sindhi, Pushtu, and Balochi, that a knowledge of Persian becomes critical to an appreciation of their literatures. This is particularly true of Urdu, whose poetry cannot be truly understood in all its nuances without a thorough knowledge of the Persian poetic tradition.

Over the course of several centuries, the total quantity of Persian literature produced in South Asia greatly exceeded that in Iran proper. The corpus is so vast that we can here only provide a summary of its contents. Every major and minor genre of Persian literature flourished here: from mystical poetry and biographies of saints to treatises on medicine, music, war and works of belles lettres. Of special significance are the many historical works in Persian chronicling the reigns of almost every dynasty and ruler. These records have become important sources for reconstructing the history of Muslim India. Several important works of Indian literature in Sanskrit such as the *Mahabharata* and the *Atharvaveda* were also translated into Persian, often under royal patronage. The Emperor Akbar (died 1605), for example, ordered the learned scholar Abdulqadir Badauni (died circa 1615) to translate the Hindu epic *Ramayana*, an assignment which this ultra-conservative Muslim viewed as a curse and a form of spiritual punishment. Akbar's great-grandson, the Prince Dara Shikoh (died 1659), was himself responsible for translating the *Upanishads* into Persian under

Prince Dara Shikoh meeting with Muslim and Hindu scholars and mystics.

the title *Sirr-i Akbar* (*The Greatest Secret*). It is through a Latin translation of this work that nineteenth century European circles first became aware of the Hindu philosophical texts.

Poetry was by far the pre-dominant and most popular form of literary composition in Persian. Poets in medieval India utilized all the major Persian forms, including the *qasida*, a panegyric extolling the virtues of a ruler or patron, the *ghazal*, a mystically-tinged love lyric, and the *masnawi*, a "double-rhymed" epic form used particularly for romances. In the religious sphere, the *madh* and *nat* were employed in praise of Allah and the Prophet Muhammad, while the *marsiya* or elegies mourned the martyrs of Shia Islam, particularly the tragic massacre of Imam Husayn and his family at Karbala in 680. In addition to these verse forms, poets adhered strictly to poetic conventions regarding symbols and imagery as developed in Iranian and Central Asian traditions. The vast majority of them delighted in composing *naziras*, poems imitating the classical models of renowned Persian authors, as well as those of their peers, as a way of demonstrating their literary prowess. Not surprisingly, as they hardly ever drew

themes and subjects from the Indic literary traditions, the vast corpus of Persian poetry composed in the subcontinent consequently has very little that is distinctively Indian in character.

The rare exception, in this regard, was Amir Khusrau (died 1325), the so-called "Parrot of India," the greatest Persian poet medieval Muslim India produced. Unlike his fellow-poets, he ventured into the territory of the local milieu, forbidden by convention, to search for new ideas. He was the first and only of the Persian poets who alluded to Indian customs in his lyrics, incorporating a number of Indian stories into his Persian epic romances and attempting to compose verse in a local language, Hindawi. Interestingly, he introduces his Persian *diwan* or collection of poems with a typically Indian idea inspired by indigenous poetry: associating the rainy season with separated lovers:

> The cloud weeps, and I am separated from my friend—
> How can I separate my heart from my heart's friend on such a day?
> The cloud weeps, and I and my friend standing, bidding farewell—
> I weeping separately, the cloud separately, the friend separately. . . .

(Annemarie Schimmel,
Islamic Literature in India)

Though Persian was the primary language of Turko-Persian culture, literatures in Arabic and Turkish were also cultivated. Despite the long-standing connections between Arabia and South Asia, Arabic language literature did not develop to the same extent as did Persian. Arabic was employed in a limited capacity, primarily for writing works on religious subjects and matters of Islamic jurisprudence. A significant portion of this religious literature consisted of collections and commentaries on the *hadith*, the corpus of accounts that recorded the sayings and actions of the Prophet Muhammad. The study of *hadith* was so highly developed that medieval India could boast of several renowned and acclaimed scholars of this important religious genre, many of whom had travelled extensively in the Arab world. Many commentaries and supercommentaries on the Quran were also written. The Muslim rulers of kingdoms of the Deccan as well as Gujarat, perhaps to counter the Persian cultural ethos so dominant in the north, also patronized Arabic literature of a more secular type by attracting to their courts prominent Arabic scholars and poets from Hadramawt and Yemen. Finally we must note that the Arabic language was also employed (as it still is today) as the medium of instruction among the elite who wished to preserve

Mirza Ghalib

their cultural identity in an environment in which they were a minority. In the late seventeenth and eighteenth centuries, with the collapse of the last major Mughal dynasty, the "literary tyranny of Arabic and Persian" as Richard Eaton states, was overthrown.

The Turko-Persian ethos, however, continued to remain strong and exert an influence on the vernacular literatures in a variety of ways. When, for example, the literati in the eighteenth century began to express themselves in an indigenous language, they called it by a Turkish name, Urdu, meaning "military camp," presumably because the language originated as a means of communication between Turkish soldiers and the local population. They heavily persianized its vocabulary, incorporating literary forms from classical Persian. The symbols they employed in Urdu poetry were intimately connected with those from the Persian tradition. The most renowned writer of Urdu prose and poetry, Mirza Ghalib (died 1869), considered his Urdu poetry, persianized as it was, to be inferior to his Persian works.

Pioneering the use of Indian languages for Islamic literatures were various Sufis or mystics. By virtue of their esoteric interpretation of Islam and their focus on a personal relationship between the human and the di-

vine, they were suited in temperament to assimilating Islamic concepts and ideas to the Indian environment. While it may be too simplistic to conceive of them as missionaries who converted substantial populations to Islam, the overwhelming evidence suggests that the Sufis, and not the tradition-bound theologians and religious-lawyers, were initially responsible for popularizing Islamic ideas among the masses. Literature composed by Sufis in local languages played an instrumental role in this process of the Indian acculturation to Islam.

The most significant characteristic of this literature was that it was folk in character, intended for the illiterate classes of society who lived mostly in the rural areas. This audience understood neither Arabic nor Persian, the languages of religion, theology, and secular learning in literate circles. Consequently, in order to overcome the language barrier, some Sufis began composing religious poems in Indian vernaculars. These poems they then incorporated in popular Sufi rituals such as the *sama* (listening and dancing to mystical music). Of course, by choosing to write in the vernaculars, the Sufis encountered the deep-seated prejudice among the Muslim elite towards the use of local Indian languages. As a consequence, they would sometimes have to preface their compositions with an apology or pleas to readers to look beyond the medium to the meaning. In this regard, many Sufis would agree with the sixteenth century religious leader, Pir-i Raushan, who declared:

> God speaks in every language, be it Arabic, Persian, Hindi or Afghani. He speaks in the language which the human heart can understand.

By the late seventeenth century, when Islamic literatures in vernacular languages from Punjab to Bengal attained maturity, an overwhelming number of poets and writers were Sufi or affiliated with Sufi orders. Annemarie Schimmel suggests that the pioneering role of the Sufis in the development of Indic languages is analogous to that played by the mystics, monks and nuns of medieval Europe in the growth of modern European languages.

Much more was involved in the use of Indic languages for Islamic literatures than simply a new medium of communication. Islamic religious concepts needed to be expressed in terms that would be familiar and sensible to South Asian audiences from a variety of backgrounds. Sometimes this meant explaining an Islamic idea within a religious framework indigenous to the South Asian context, resulting in the blurring of religious boundaries that religious conservatives found objectionable. For example, in the folkloric *punthi* literature in the Bengali language, the Islamic concept of *nabi/rasul,* a prophet/messenger sent by God to guide humanity, is identified with the Indian idea of *avatara,* a divine descent into the world to vanquish evil and maintain the good. Consequently, many works from this genre portrayed Muhammad, the prophet of Islam, as the last and most powerful of a long series of prophet-*avataras* that included Hindu deities such as Rama and Krishna. Other works, motivated by the desire to elevate Islam over local religious traditions, depicted the triumph of the Prophet Muhammad and other legendary Islamic heroes over the gods and demons of the Hindu pantheon, creating, in effect, an alternative Islamic mythology for South Asian converts to Islam. There was also a similar juxtaposing of concepts from the yogic and tantric traditions with Islamic mystical ones in many Sufi poems in Indic languages.

Muslim poets and writers of the vernacular tradition also freely adopted the literary structures and forms prevalent in the indigenous folk-poetic tradition, a tradition that was predominantly oral in character, meant to be sung or recited often with musical accompaniment. This tradition was maintained and preserved by women, who were the most important custodians of folksongs, proverbs and folk customs. Thus, in addition to employing various indigenous verse forms, Sufi poetry adopted extensively the forms and symbols of songs sung by women as they performed their daily household chores. Within these songs they incorporated basic teachings about Islam. As an example, we cite the *chakki-nama,* a song recited by women in certain regions of Southern India while grinding grain at the *chakki,* the grindstone. Drawing parallels between various parts of the grindstone, the poet explains in a simple way the fundamental precepts of Islam:

> The *chakki's* handle resembles [the letter] *alif,*
> which means *Allah* . . . the axle is Muhammad. . . .
> In this way the truth-seeker sees the relationship:
> *Ya bism Allah.*

(R. Eaton, *Sufis of Bijapur*)

In trying to explain the link between God, the prophet Muhammad and the reciter, these songs make reference to *dhikr* (remembrance), a Sufi mediational practice involving the rhythmical repetition of one or more religious phrases invoking the ninety-nine names of God. In those regions of South Asia, such as Punjab, Sind and the Deccan, where the cultivation and processing of cotton was a major source of livelihood, poetry is replete with references to *dhikr,* for the spinning of cotton could be easily compared to the humming sound produced by constant *dhikr.* Shah Abdul Latif (died 1752), the great poet of Sind, stretches even further the parallel between the woman at the spinning

wheel and the soul occupied in recollection of God. In a series of spinning poems intended to be sung in traditional folk tunes, he extends the Quranic image of God as the purchaser of the soul (Quran 9:111)—just as finely spun thread fetches a good price from a buyer, so also the human heart has to be refined and prepared with utmost care before the merchant-God can purchase it.

> Wondrous devotion spinners have,
> who tremble, spin and spin;
> For earning good, in the spinning-yard
> at sun-rise they begin—
> Such soul beauty the connoisseurs [God]
> even for themselves would win.
> Yarn spun by spinners so genuine,
> without weighing they buy.

(E. Kazi, *The Risalo of Shah Abdul Latif*)

Perhaps the most interesting Indian literary convention that the Sufis incorporated into their poetry is representing the soul as the *virahini,* a woman, usually a bride or bride-to-be, who longingly awaits her groom, symbolically representing God. Though the woman-soul symbolism is quite rare in Arabic and Persian poetic traditions, it is quite common in Indian literature. Its most renowned use is in Hindu devotional poetry addressed to the Hindu deity Krishna. The *gopis* (milk-maids), in particular Radha, express their longing for union with their elusive beloved. Muslim poets adapted this symbol to an Islamic framework, varying the identity of the Muslim *virahini's* beloved according to the context.

In many *qawwalis,* the popular songs typically sung at the shrines of many Sufi saints in South Asia, the bride-soul expresses her longing to offer herself up in utter devotion to her groom, who is either Allah or the Sufi master. We are reminded here of the popular *qawwali* attributed to Amir Khusrau the "Parrot of India," one of the earliest Muslim poets to whom poetry in Hindi is attributed. This song, expressing Amir Khusrau's yearnings for his spiritual master, is still recited today in Deli at the shrine of Nizam al-Din Awliya. Sometimes, devotion to the Prophet Muhammad is also expressed using the symbol of the *virahini.* Characteristically, in *mauluds,* or poems in praise of the Prophet from the region of Sind, the yearning soul or bride-to-be longs for marriage with Muhammad, the bridegroom of Medina. Abd ur-Rauf Bhatti (died 1752), one of the earliest Sindhi poets to write such poems, sings:

> Welcome to that bridegroom Muhammad, from
> the Hashimite clan

He comes; the master for whom the fragrant bed
has been spread.
He comes attended by ten million angels!
The prince's attendants have seated their hero in
their midst.
The beloved came and strolled around Abd ur-
Rauf's court-yard!

In some cases, as in the *ginans*, the devotional
hymns of the Subcontinent's Shia Muslim Ismaili community, the *virahini's* beloved can even be in the Shia
Imam, who is venerated on account of his spiritual and
physical lineage from the Prophet and his role as spiritual guide to this particular sect.

Muslim writers in the vernacular tradition could express their ideas through a wide variety of other Indic
literary forms and devices. In areas of northern India
where various dialects of Hindi, such as Awadh, Braj,
and Bhojpuri were spoken, they used the romantic epic
as a vehicle, probably inspired by the well-established
tradition in classical Persian literature of retelling romances such as Layla-Majnun or Farhad-Shirin within a
mystical framework. The use of popular Indian romances can be dated to 1379 when the Hindi poet
Maulana Daud, disciple of a Chishti Sufi master, illustrated in the Awadhi Hindi epic *Chandayan* the use of
the Indian romance between Lurak and Chanda as a
mystical allegory. This epic was so famous that
Badauni, the celebrated chronicler, records in the
Muntakhab at-tawarikh (composed after 1596); a
Muslim preacher used excerpts from this epic during
his sermons because of its ability to capture the hearts
of his audience when sung by the sweet singers of
Hindustan. Maulana Daud's work initiated a brilliant
tradition of Islamic mystical epics in Hindi that was to
continue well into the late nineteenth century, and included masterpieces such as Kutuban's *Mrigavati*
(composed 1503), Malik Muhammad Jaisi's *Padmavat*
(composed 1540), and Manjhan's *Madhulmalati* (composed 1545). This epic tradition was an important factor in the development of Hindi prose literature in the
nineteenth and early twentieth centuries.

The use of popular romances for conveying Islamic
mystical instruction was not confined to Hindi speaking areas. By the late fourteenth-century, Shah
Muhammad Sagir, a pioneer Muslim poet of the Bengali
language, had composed in his mother tongue the epic
of Yusuf and Zulaykha, the first of many such works in
Bengali. Similarly, Muslim poets in the Punjab were responsible for an impressive series of romantic epics in
Punjabi. Yet, it is in the region of Sind where poets developed interesting and innovative ways of utilizing the
region's romances as a tool for mystical education. By
1600, some of the region's poets were using traditional
Sindhi tales as themes for their Persian epics. Later

writing in their native language Sindhi, they used the
heroine of the romance—and in keeping with the *virahini* convention it is always the heroine and never
the hero—as the symbol for the soul longing for union
with God through suffering and death. The heroine in
these poems always searches for her lost beloved until
she either finds him, or dies of thirst and heat in the
mountains, or drowns in the river Indus. She becomes
the parable of the seeking soul on the mystical path
who, separated from the Divine Beloved, must undergo
great tribulation and a painful purification process in
her quest:

My body burns. With roasting fire
I am consumed but make my quest.
Parched am I with the Beloved's thirst
Yet drinking, find in drink no rest
Nay! did I drain the ocean wide,
'Twould grant in not one sip a zest.

(H. T. Sorley, *Abdul Latif of Bhit:
His Poetry, Life, and Times*)

In the skillful hands of these folk-poets, the traditional heroines are ingeniously endowed with interpretations that recall Quranic verses such as "Verily from
God we are and to Him we return" (Quran 2:151) or
Quranic concepts such as the primordial covenant between each soul and God (Quran 7:171). The heroine
becomes so sublime that her physical and external
quest for her Beloved is transformed into a spiritual
and internal one. Thus, Shah Abdul Latif's heroine
Sassui, who out of negligence lost her beloved Punhun,
sings:

As I turned inwards and conversed with my soul,
There was no mountain to surpass and no
Punhun to care for;
I myself became Punhun . . .
Only while Sassui did I experience grief.

(M. Jotwani,
Shah Abdul Latif: His Life and Work)

In addition to the romantic epic and its heroine,
Muslim poets had at their disposal the whole repertoire
of inherited images derived from the range of activities
common in rural life such as ploughing, sowing, hunting, and milking. In coastal regions, the worlds of fishing and seafaring were a particularly favorite source of
inspiration. Lalan, the famous Baul poet of Bengal, explains the role of the Prophet by comparing him to a pi-
lot steering the boat of the faithful to salvation:

You are a companion of God's,
Helmsman to the far shore of truth.

Without you, the world on the shore
We shall not see again.
And who but for you could govern
In this way, Oh instrument of faith.
Lalan says, no other such lamp will ever burn so.

(Q. A. Mannan and C. Selly, *Lyric Poetry*)

Many poets also turned to the world of nature and the countryside that surrounded them for symbols: from the swan that has a keen discriminating taste for pure pearls to the lotus flower that symbolizes the preservation of purity in the midst of an uncongenial, sullied world. The possibilities were endless as long as the poet was able to effectively blend his religious message into the image, retain its simplicity, and not weigh it down with burdensome theoretical speculations.

Indeed, vernacular literature frequently condemns barren intellectualism and bookish learning as a means of approaching Allah. As in the case with Sufi poetry in Persian and Turkish, the main targets of criticism were the *ulama*, the learned theologians and religious jurists who claimed exclusive authority over the interpretation of the Quran on account of their training and education. According to most vernacular poets, all the knowledge and scholarship in the world was useless in comparison to the experience of a person who has seen the Beloved. The rustic peasant-farmer felt reassured that he, too, his illiteracy notwithstanding, could enjoy a loving relationship with his God when he listened to poets declare that in the path of divine love, it was not necessary to read or write more than the first letter of the Arabic alphabet, the *alif*, with which begins the name Allah:

Those who have found the Lord *alif*, they
do not read again the Quran; O He.
They respire the breath of love and
their veils have been lifted; O He.
Hell and heaven become their slaves
their faults they have forsaken; O He.

(Rama, Krishna, Lajwajti,
Panjabi Sufi Poets A.D. 1460–1900)

Far more significant than formal education in nurturing a person's spiritual development was the instruction and guidance of the appropriate mystic guide, the *pir*. Poetry in every vernacular language of South Asia extols the importance and the necessity of having a *pir*. He has a special relationship to God, that of *wali*, (friend) and, as perceived representative of the Prophet, could help the individual soul through all kinds of perplexities, material or spiritual. Poets employed a variety of images, usually drawn from the activities of daily life, to explain the *pir's* role. For example, he was compared to a *dhobi*, a washerman who beats his laundry with a stick to thrash out dirt, or to a dyer who cleans off the spots of impurity from the soul by dipping it in a vat that contains, to use an expression from the Quran (2:132), the *sibghat Allah*, "the coloring of Allah" (Schimmel, *Pain and Grace*, 180). Although the *pir* may seem to be harsh and cruel in his method of education, he may see this as the best means of furthering the disciple's spiritual development. Not to have a *pir* was the greatest disaster, for, as a Bengali poet puts it:

When one who did not accept a spiritual teacher dies,
Azrail [the angel of death] will take him
And will force him to drink cups of urine;
A filthy cap will be placed on his head,
The angels will beat him with iron clubs,
And drive him to hell.

(Q. A. Mannan,
*Heritage of Bangladesh: Sufi Movement and
Sufi Literature in the Medieval Period*)

Naturally, the importance that most folk poetry accorded to the *pir* and his authority was objectionable on theological grounds to many *ulama* (religious scholars) and the religious establishment. According to them, no human could be elevated to such a lofty status. From their point of view, the most disturbing aspect of the vernacular tradition was that it was often permeated with heretical ideas emanating from the *wahdat al-wujud* (unity of existence) theory popularly associated with the Arabo-Hispanic mystic Ibn Arabi (died 1240). This system of mystical speculation, whose fundamentals are summed up in the formula, "Everything is He," greatly influenced the expression of much mystical literature in the Islamic world after the fourteenth century. Thus, while the conservatives were alarmed by the theory since it seemed to blur the distinction between creation and the Creator, poets influenced by it wrote pantheistic-sounding verses claiming the fundamental unity of all outward forms of creation. The Sindhi poet Sachal Sarmast (died 1826) describes the immanence of God thus:

Sometimes He is Rama or Sita;
Sometimes He appears as Laksmana.
Sometimes He is Nimrud or Abraham;
Several are the guises He adopts.

Not surprising, this philosophy, which is strongly reminiscent of the advaita, a non-dualistic philosophical system in Hinduism, has led several scholars to detect a preponderance of "Vedantic Hindu" influences in much poetry written by Muslims in Indian languages.

While the extent of Hindu influence is debatable, what remains beyond question is the central role that the vernacular literary tradition accords Muhammad, the Prophet of Islam. Devotion to him is the hallmark of Islamic identity. The Punjabi poet Sultan Bahu, who has been considered by some as the prime example of a Muslim poet influenced by Hindu *vedanta*, says in this regard:

This heart is burning with separation;
it neither dies nor lives.
O He, the true path is the path of Muhammad,
along which God is found, O He.

(Rama Krishna)

Love for the Prophet, as Constance Padwick has emphasized, is the strongest binding force in the Islamic tradition, for it is an emotion in which all levels of society, from the peasantry to the intelligentsia, can share (Muslim Devotions, 145). The Prophet is the loyal friend, the most trustworthy companion, the intercessor on the Day of Judgement. Just as the poets of the classical languages Arabic and Persian composed erudite eulogies for the Prophet, the vernacular poets wrote moving verses to spark Prophetic love in the hearts of their audience, whether they spoke Sindhi, Punjabi, Hinsi, Gujerati, Bengali, Malayalam or Tamil. Lalan, the Baul poet of Bengal, pleads to the Prophet:

I shall not find again a compassionate friend like
you,
You showed yourself, now do not leave, oh
Prophet of faith.
We all were inhabitants of Madina,
But were as though in forest exile,
Then from you we gained wisdom,
We gained solace.

(Mannan and Seely)

A variety of images, metaphors and verse-forms, many of them derived from the Indian literary milieu, were employed to express themes ranging from the love the Prophet's followers felt for him to the protection and kindness that Muhammad extended to his community. A Sindhi poet could adopt in his *maulud* the persona of the *virahini*, the young woman yearning for the bridegroom Prophet; a Tamil poet could choose to compose a traditional *pillaittamil*, or a "baby-poem," to describe the Prophet's birth and his charming play as a baby, his radiance as a child, and the loving way in which his nurse rocked him in a cradle, which reflected his greatness:

Your cradle
is like the sky chariot
that the lord of the star-filled sky
joyously rides

Its frame is inlaid
with gems so full of color
that they radiate sunlight
as if lightning stolen from the sky

(Paula Richman, *"Veneration of the Prophet
Muhammad in an Islamic Pillaittamil"*)

Perhaps the most beautiful image frequently associated with the Prophet is the cloud of mercy which brings the rain of mercy to a parched and thirsty earth—a clever reference to the Quranic epithet for the Prophet, "a mercy for the worlds" (Quran 21:107).

◆ LITERATURE OF ISLAMIC REFORM IN THE CONTEMPORARY PERIOD

Since the eighteenth century, Muslims in South Asia have experienced drastic changes in the manner in which they articulate their identity and the contexts in which they practice their faith. On the one hand, they have had to respond first to the loss of Muslim political power in the subcontinent and, later, to the creation of an Islamic state, Pakistan. On the other hand, they have had to address a deeply felt need to find a cure for a widespread spiritual and religious malaise. To convey their ideas on these and other issues to the wider Muslim community, reformers and activists, liberal and conservative alike, turned to various literary genres, especially poetry. Notwithstanding the rich diversity of languages spoken by Muslims in South Asia, the Urdu language, due to a complex set of factors, became the symbol of Islamic culture in South Asia and hence the most important literary medium for advocates of reform and change.

The pioneer of religious reformers in South Asia was Shah Wali Allah (died 1762), the great theologian of Delhi. Although the most important work in which he expressed his thought was in Arabic, the *Hujjat Allah al-Baligha*, Shah Wali Allah's ideas had a deep impact on later reformist writers in Urdu and other languages. Shah Wali Allah felt strongly that the Muslims of South Asia would be better able to live in accordance with the precepts of their faith and begin resolving their socio-religious problems if they could understand the Quran for themselves without relying on the secondary interpretations offered in commentaries. Hence he translated the Holy Book into Persian, paving the way for his two sons Rafi ud-Din (died 1818) and Abd al-Qadir (died 1813) to translate it into Urdu; the latter appropriately called his Urdu translation *Mudih al-quran,* (*Explainer of the Quran*). In the subsequent decades, translations of the Quran began to appear in several other Indian languages as well.

Shah Wali Allah and many of his disciples were affiliated with a branch of the activist Naqshvbandi Sufi order known as the Tariqa Muhammadiyya (The Muhammadan Path). As its name suggests, this movement placed strong emphasis on the figure of the Prophet Muhammad as a true and stable paradigm and guide for the Muslim community in a period of political and social flux. The ideology of the Muhammadan path influenced the writings of many prominent Urdu poets, including the so-called "pillars of Urdu," the stern Mazhar Janjanan (died 1781) and the mystic poet Mir Dard (died 1785). It also inspired numerous biographies of the Prophet and studies of *hadith* not only in Urdu, but also Sindhi and other languages.

From a literary point of view, the most prominent group of writer-activists in the nineteenth century were associated with Sir Sayyid Ahmad Khan (died 1898). As a young man, Sir Sayyid was well-trained in theology in the tradition of Shah Wali Allah, as well as Mutazila rationalism. He was also affiliated with the Tariqa Muhammadiyya. After the traumatic 1857 rebellion against the British, he was convinced that the best path for the Muslim community to follow was that of absolute and unwavering loyalty to British rule. Furthermore, he felt that Muslims should fully participate in the Western-style educational system being established by the British in India so that they would not become a social and economic underclass. He did not hold Western thought, in particular Western science, to be in fundamental conflict with Islam. To promote his ideas and provide young Muslims with Western-style higher education, he founded at Aligarh the Anglo-Muhammadan College, which later became Aligarh Muslim University.

Sayyid Ahmad Khan was a fairly prolific writer in Urdu and hoped to influence Muslims through his books as well as his journals. The most significant of these was the monthly Urdu periodical, *Tahzib al-Akhlaq* (*The Cultivation of Morals,* also known as the *Mohamedan Social Reformer*), which revolutionized Urdu journalism. Its pages, written in simple and clear prose, contained articles reflecting Sir Sayyid's views on a wide range of issues from public hygiene to rational speculation on religious dogma.

Sayyid Ahmad Khan's approach enjoyed the support of several important personalities in Indo-Muslim society and formed the basis for the so-called Aligarh movement. Among the members of the movement were several important literati who wrote both Urdu poetry and prose to disseminate its ideas. Most prominent among these was Altaf Husain Hali (died 1914), the founder of Urdu literary criticism. He published in 1879 his *Madd o gari-i Islam* (*The Ebb and Flow of Islam*), an epic poem considered to be the Aligarh movement's most enduring literary monument. Popularly known as the "*Musaddas*," after its six line stanzas, it contrasts the past glories and achievements of Islamic civilization with the poor and miserable status of the Muslims of Hali's time. The poem, which was recited aloud at conferences and boldly calligraphed on journals and newspapers, sharply attacked the evils prevalent in all segments of the Indian Muslim community.

Some of Hali's poems, such as "Ek biwi ki munajat" ("A Woman's Petition"), focus on the plight of women in Muslim society. This theme was taken up by several reformist writers, including Nazir Ahmad (died 1912), one of the pioneers in the development of the Urdu novel. By profession a teacher, he was a firm believer in the importance of educating young people, in particular young women. Most of his novels, therefore, illustrated social or moral themes, showing the need for reform and change. His most famous book, *Mirat al-arus* (*The Bride's Mirror*), emphasized the need for female education by highlighting the miseries of an uneducated Muslim bride. In other works he addresses the evils of polygamy and attacks the taboo in Indian society against the remarriage of widows, which he felt was contrary to the spirit of Islam. Notwithstanding their didactic and moralistic tone, his works were tremendously popular for their realistic descriptions of middle-class Muslim life. They also inspired similar works in other languages such as Sindhi. Other members of Sir Sayyid's circle were equally concerned about improving the status of women, particularly Mumtaz Ali. He devoted most of his energies to this important issue and even published a special journal, *Tahzib al-niswan,* containing articles on women's issues. In his major work, *Huquq al-niswan* (*The Rights of Women*), he advocates complete equality between men and women.

In the twentieth century, the personality whose literary works have had the most profound influence on the Muslim community is Sir Muhammad Iqbal (died 1938). The reformist poetry of this poet-philosopher had such a powerful impact that he is counted among the most significant thinkers of modern Islam. He is also widely considered to be the spiritual father of Pakistan, as he was the first to advocate the idea of a separate Muslim homeland.

Iqbal received his early education in Lahore, influenced in his thought by, among others, the modernist Sir Sayyid Ahmad, the historian Shibli, and Sir Thomas Arnold, an Orientalist who attempted to revive a less polemical and more sympathetic understanding of Islam in western scholarship. In many ways Iqbal was also the inheritor of the ideas of Shah Waliullah and

Hali whose poetic style he followed. At the turn of the century he had become well-known for his Urdu poems expressing nationalist ideas, Hindu-Muslim solidarity and freedom for India. One of his poems from this period, "Tarana-yi Hind," praised the glories of Hindustan and is still popular in India today.

In 1905 Iqbal went to Cambridge where he studied Hegelian philosophy, proceeding in 1907 to Munich where he received his doctorate for a thesis entitled *The Development of Metaphysics in Persia.* Iqbal's stay in Europe was instrumental in the further evolution of his reformist ideas and allowed him to become familiar with the philosophy of Nietzsche and Bergson. On his return to India, though he was offered a position at Aligarh, Iqbal preferred to practice law. At heart, however, he was primarily a poet and used his poetry to articulate his thought in a manner that is unprecedented in modern Islamic history. His verse, with its direct style devoid of the traditional flowery language and literary acrobatics, had a tremendous appeal for the Indian Muslims who were searching for leaders with an intellectual and political vision.

In his first major reformist Urdu poem—"*Shikwa*" ("The Complaint"), written in 1911— he complains to Allah for being fickle and having abandoned the faithful Muslims in favor of the infidels. A year later he composed a reply in the form of "*Jawab-i Shikwa*" ("The Answer to the Complaint"), in which Allah points out the defects in the way Muslims practice and understand their faith. Both poems were clearly inspired by Hali's "*Musaddas.*" During the war, Iqbal composed two major works, "Asrar-i Khudi" ("Secrets of the Self") and "Rumuj Bekhudi" ("Mysteries of Selflessness"). These, like all his major philosophical poems, he chose to write in Persian, for he intended his ideas to reach an audience beyond the Subcontinent. It is here that he reinterpreted the Persian mystical concept of *khudi* (ego) in a positive sense, articulating the dynamic role of the individual in society. His stress, here and in his other Urdu and Persian poems, was on activity and dynamism at both the individual and communal level. He believed that each human, as the vicegerent of God on earth, had a duty to actively develop himself or herself to the highest potential. In 1924 Iqbal published a major collection of Urdu poems under the title, *Bang-i dara* (*The Call of Caravan Bell*). The title is significant for it reflects Iqbal's perception of his role and his message: he is the bell at the head of the caravan arousing the sleeping and erring Muslims of India into activity, leading them to the center of Islam, the Kaba in Mecca. By this time his poetry was considered so important and had garnered so much attention, he was knighted in 1922 by the British monarch.

For the next ten years, Iqbal published most of his significant writing in either English, as with *Reconstruction of Religious Thought in Islam*, or Persian, as with *Zabur-i ajam* (*The Stroke of Moses*). The former contains some of the finest of Iqbal's Urdu poems (including a renowned piece on the Mosque of Cordoba that recalls the past glory of Muslims). The poems of the latter are mainly critiques of the existing political and social order, critical of the British and of Muslims who ape Western ways blindly.

Iqbal is the most famous of several authors whose writings have had a deep impact on the Muslim community in recent times. Like other Muslim writers in the contemporary period, he draws extensively on the Turko-Persian and the Indic heritage of Indo-Muslim literature, yet incorporates also the legacy of Western thought. Iqbal's fame lies in the unique way he interprets and expresses Islamic concepts and ideas through a skillful combination of Western and Eastern intellectual and literary tools. That he and other poets such as Faliz Ahmad Faiz (died 1984) could effectively use poetry as a medium to spread their ideas far and wide attests to the fact that literature, oral and written, continues to be a vibrant force in South Asian Muslim culture today as it has been in centuries past.

Ali Asani

References

Ahmad, Aziz. *Studies in Islamic Culture in the Indian Environment.* London: Oxford University Press, 1964.

Ahmad, Zubaid. *Contribution of Indo-Pakistan to Arabic Literature from Ancient Times to 1857.* Lahore: Shaikh Muhammad Ashraf, 1946.

Asani, Ali. "Sufi Poetry in the Folk Tradition of Indo-Pakistan." *Religion and Literature* 20:I (1988): 81–94.

Bausani, Alessandro. *Storia della litterature del Pakistan.* Milan: Nuova Accademis Editrice, 1958.

Eaton, Richard. *Sufis of Bijapur 1300–1700.* Princeton: Princeton University Press, 1978.

Haq, Muhammad Enamul. *Muslim Bengali Literature.* Karachi: Pakistan Publications, 1957.

Jotwani, Motilal. *Shah Abdul Latif: His Life and Work.* Delhi: University of Delhi, 1975.

Kazi, Elsa, *The Risalo of Shah Abdul Latif.* Selections. Hyderabad: Sindhi Adabi Board, 1965.

Mannan, Qazi Abdul. *Heritage of Bangladesh: Sufi Movement and Sufi Literature in the Medieval Period.* Monograph. New York: Learning Resources in International Studies, 1974.

Mannan, Qazi Abdul and Selly, Clinton. *Lyric Poetry.* Monograph. New York: Learning Resources in International Studies, 1974.

Padwick, Constance. *Muslim Devotions.* London: S. P. C. K., 1961.

Rama, Krishna, Lajwanti. *Panjabi Sufi Poets A.D. 1460–1900.* 1938. Karachi: Indus Publications, 1977.

Richman, Paula. "Veneration of the Prophet Muhammad in an

Islamic Pillaittamil." *Journal of the American Oriental Society* 113:1 (1993): 57–74.

Robinson, Francis. Perso-Islamic Culture in India from the Seventeenth to the Early Twentieth Century," in *Turko-Persia in Historical Perspective*. ed. Robert Canfield. Cambridge: Cambridge University Press, 1991, pp. 104–131.

Roy, Asim. *The Islamic Syncretistic Tradition in Bengal*. Princeton: Princeton University Press, 1983.

Rypka, Jan. *History of Iranian Literatures*. Dordrecht: D. Reidel. 1968.

Schimmel, Annemarie. *As Through a Veil: Mystical Poetry in Islam*. New York: Columbia University Press, 1982.

———. "Reflections on Popular Muslim Poetry." *Contributions to Asian Studies* XVII (1982): 17–26.

———. *Islam in the Indian Subcontinent (Handbuch der Orientalistik*, 4:3). Leiden: E.J. Brill, 1980.

———. *Pain and Grace: A Study of Two Mystical Writers of Eighteenth Century Muslim India*. Leiden: E.J. Brill, 1976.

———. *Mystical Dimensions of Islam*. Chapel Hill: University of North Carolina Press, 1975.

———. *Classical Urdu Literature from the Beginning to Iqbal*. Wiesbaden: Otto Harrassowtiz, 1975.

———. *Islamic Literatures of India*. Wiesbaden: Otto Harrassowitz, 1973.

———. *Gabriel's Wing: A Study into the Religious Ideas of Sir Muhammad Iqbal*. Leiden: E.J. Brill, 1963.

Sorley, H. T. *Shah Abdul Latif of Bhit: His Poetry, Life and Times*. Lahore, Karachi and Dacca: Oxford University Press, 1966.

Storey, H. T. *Persian Literature. A Bio-Bibliographical Survey 1927–1953*. London: Luzac, 1970–72.

Muslim Literature in Sub-Saharan Africa

♦ Common Features in Sub-Saharan Literature ♦ Fulani Literature ♦ Hausa Literature
♦ Wolof literature ♦ Somali Literature ♦ Swahili Literature

Muslim literature in sub-Saharan Africa may be divided into two categories. The first category is a product of Islamic learning and scholarship; it includes books, pamphlets, and various other media that expound on Islamic law, jurisprudence, obligatory and voluntary rituals, codes of conduct, and other aspects of Muslim thought. The second category consists of works of creative writing, particularly in modern times, in which Muslim beliefs, identity, and education find expression and creative interaction within the context of modern inquiry and challenge. The latter forms the focus of this survey, which, to remain meaningful within the limited scope of this chapter, discusses the literatures of five peoples that, between them reflect the salient features of Muslim literature in Africa: the Fulani, the Hausa and the Wolof in West Africa; and the Somali and the Swahili in Eastern Africa.

♦ COMMON FEATURES IN SUB-SAHARAN LITERATURE

Although the five literatures span wide geographical areas, the initial phases of their history are remarkably similar. The first phase was influenced by the introduction of Islam and, with it, the Arabic language and script. Both were utilized as tools for producing theological works, as well as historical documents and chronicles of the various rulers and wars. But out of this phase also developed early poetry on religious and theological themes, written at first in Arabic and later in the respective vernacular languages employing the Arabic script. Certain themes were common: praise of the Prophet Muhammad, the transitoriness of this world and the permanency of the hereafter, the rewards of heaven, the punishments of hell, the practice

of faith, and personal conduct. Where Sufi brotherhoods exercised a strong influence, especially the Qadiriyya and the Tijaniyya *tariqas*, poems were composed in praise of their founders or of the local leaders and model figures who had introduced and developed Islam in these regions.

The next phase involved the change of orthography from Arabic to a standardized Latin script. Standardization was brought about or initiated by the colonial administrators primarily in the 1930s, although the Fulani did not use a Latin script until 1966 and the Somalis until 1972. Standardization helped to widen readership, especially after the introduction of the printing press. The schools established by the colonial regimes helped to introduce new genres: the novel, drama, and free verse. These genres were employed by Muslim writers from the 1950s on to project views that, sometimes were not favorable to orthodox clerics. The schools also gave wider exposure to the didactic poems of Muslim scholars by incorporating them in the curriculum; translations of the Arabian tales, *The One Thousand and One Nights* is an example.

The significant and influential role of oral literature should be noted as common to all five literatures. With the spread of Islam, Muslim motifs came to be reflected in some of its genres, especially in songs and stories advocating a morality underpinned by Muslim ethics.

♦ FULANI LITERATURE

The historical beginnings of Fulani literature have a common link with Hausa literature in the person and family of Shehu (Sheikh) Usman dan Fodio (1754–1817), a Fulani leader who waged a series of religious wars (*jihad*) against the Hausa kings of northern Nigeria, and successfully overthrew their dynasties by 1812. Poems and writings attributed to Shehu Usman, written in Hausa and Fulfulde, appeared at this time and educated the people about *jihad*, in order to retain their support. The poems also discussed the tenets of Islam and the obligations of Muslims. Some poems were attributed to his brother Abdullahi (circa 1763–1829), his son Muhammad Bello (died 1827), and daughter Nana Asmau. A contemporary, who may even have preceded Shehu Usman with his compositions, was Muhammadu Samba of Guinea (circa 1765–1852).

The poems were based on Arabic originals and written in *ajami*, a modified Arabic script. The themes (from which were derived the names of some of the genres unique to Fulani literature) were: the oneness of God, praise of the Prophet, astrology, Muslim law, admonition, and the lives of paradigmatic individuals. The poems were copied in manuscripts and disseminated by students and followers over large areas under Fulani hegemony. Today's poems still reflect such themes, but poems with secular topics are also composed, for instance in praise of modernity. Such secular viewpoints, of course, are condemned in the stricter religious poems. Poems composed by professional singers combine features of oral literature and traditional "formal" poetry. As the singers derive their livelihood from the public, they choose topics that readily hold people's interest.

Mention must be made of Amadou Hampate Ba (1901–), a poet and scholar who has done an indepth analysis of Fulani and Bambara oral literature and religious traditions, as well as treating those of the Dogon and Malinke peoples. In his view, the relationship between Islam and traditional religions is one of fusion, particularly as "strong capabilities may be shown to exist between Islam (particularly the Tijaniyya and Hamaliyya Sufi confraternities) and the tenets of African traditional religions, whose cosmogony lies at the heart of traditional oral literatures in West Africa." Ba considers traditional religions to have provided the foundation for the growth of Islam in sub-Saharan Africa. He demonstrates this compatibility in his poetic works on Fulani initiation, which reflects the esoteric dimensions of Islam.

♦ HAUSA LITERATURE

Parallel streams of oral literature exist among the Hausa, as they do in the other literatures surveyed here. One carries notions that were present in the pre-Islamic period—mythical tales and stories associated with the spirit cults, for example. The other reflects moral and ethical norms introduced during and after the consolidation of Islam, such as tales about the ethical dimensions of one's relationship with God. Other tales include animal fables, tales about human charac-

ter, didactic tales, tales that comment on historical events, and tales praising rulers and conquerors. Oral traditions have also retained "sermon-songs" which were preached by peripatetic Muslim scholars, and court poetry, which, according to the Kano Chronicle, existed as far back as the fourteenth century.

Examples of written traditions date at least from the years of the *jihad*, and the writings of Usman dan Fodio and his family (as described above), although the existence of written traditions among the Hausa well before this date is possible. Hausaland had contacts with the Arabs (and hence with Islam and the Arabic script) from at least the sixteenth century. A renowned Muslim Sufi scholar, Muhammad Abd al-Karim al-Maghili (died 1504), taught at Kano and primarily at Katsina, as did Ibn al-Sabbagh, known among the Hausa as Dan Marina (died 1655). But it was during the process and aftermath of the *jihad* that written Hausa literature came to be consolidated.

Some of the classic forms of Islamic poetry—*waazi* (admonitory verse), *madahu* (panegyric verse), *tawhidi* (theological verse), *sira* (biographic verse), and mystical Sufi verses and variations of these categories—bear close resemblance to those of Fulani literature. After the Second World War, poets gave increasing attention in their poetry to secular matters. The profile of the poets also changed in that they came from different walks of life; the genre was not dominated as it had been previously by Muslim scholars. Radio, television, and newspapers aided in this process by providing wider public audiences. Radio Kaduna and the weekly newspaper, *Gaskiya Ta Fi Kwabo*, which was incorporated by the Northern Nigerian Literature Bureau in 1943, were particularly responsible for stimulating the creative interests of poets and of Hausa writers in general.

Since most Nigerian literature had been based on religious themes, in 1932, a Translation Bureau, the predecessor of the Literature Bureau, was set up in 1932 to lay the foundations of a vernacular literature. A competition was held toward this purpose the following year, in which five novels won prizes. Among them was *Shaihu Umar* (*Sheikh Umar*) by a former Nigerian political leader, Abubakar Tafawa Balewa (died 1966).

Shaihu Umar is the story of a Muslim scholar, who narrates his biography to his students. His life reflects the realities of nineteenth century Nigeria, including war, slave-raiding, and the unlimited power of the ruler over his subjects. According to Pilaszewicz, Balewa refrains from making an overt moral assessment of his characters, but does focus on their virtues of "piety, honesty, erudition, diligence, and complete submission to God's decrees." The main character, Shehu Umar, "is almost too good to be true. He is almost too good a Muslim: never shows passion of any sort, never despairs, never does anything contrary to what his religion lays down."

Drama is not alien to African audiences, as the traditional craft of story-telling incorporates ingredients of theater. As an imported genre, however, it has been incorporated successfully into Hausa literature. The themes have tended to be current, including aspects of family life (particularly the question of polygamy), the status of women, politics, and dependence on Muslim scholars. Schools have encouraged creativity in this genre as well by teaching and staging locally-written plays.

◆ WOLOF LITERATURE

Wolof literature from Senegal exhibits two distinct features related to its development. Its oral genres, mainly the stories and tales, were the earliest of sub-Saharan literatures to be published in the West. Consequently, these stories received early attention from French and Senegalese intellectuals—the latter, writing in French, being prominent in literary circles by the 1930s. These two aspects influenced the production of literature and artistic works, including film which express the Wolof artists' view of their Muslim heritage. An analysis of Wolof literature identifies five groups within a spectrum whose extremes are represented by those who embrace Islam with zeal and those who consider it an impediment to progress and fulfillment.

The first group comprises the traditional promoters of Islam, who are well versed in Arabic and whose works are in Arabic and "Wolofal" (Wolof using the Arabic script, *ajami*). Among the foremost contributors in this group are Amadou Bamba, the founder of the Muridiyya brotherhood, and his disciple, the poet Moussa Ka, who translated Bamba's poems into Wolof. Their works form part of the poetic repertoire of the Muridiyya brotherhood. One of Wolof's poetic masterpieces is Ka's "Ma dyema burati" ("I'll try to uplift myself again . . . "), an ode to humility, piety and devotion that retells the history of the prominent figures of Islam within the Quran and addressing the nature and mortality of human existence.

The second group follows in the footsteps of the first, but its members are less didactic. Cheikh Hamidou Kane and Aminata Sow-Fall, the main representatives of this group, are themselves products of African, Arab-Islamic, and Euro-Christian education. They write in French, and their chosen literary medium is the novel. Kane's *L'aventure ambigue* (*The Ambiguous Adventure*), published in 1962, draws a contrast between Islamic mysticism and Western materialistic individualism. The main character of the novel, Samba Diallo, becomes the focus of a conflict between the two. The climax is ambiguous in that, although Diallo dies, his death can be understood as the transcendence of the eternal over the transitory material world. Sow-Fall's novel is on *zakat* (the giving of alms from one's income, one of the principles of Islam), the purification it brings to an individual, and the social and ethical value of sharing. The late Mariama Ba's first novel, translated into English as *So Long A Letter* (1981), explores the plight of educated Muslim women who have to negotiate between tradition and modernity.

The third group, "the irreverents," use popular oral literature as their medium. Stories and satirical narratives are employed to poke fun at religious figures and their own lack of the virtues they preach. They are satirized and castigated for their greed, hypocrisy, and for yielding to temptation without much effort, and are characterized as charlatans who use Islam to further their own interests by exploiting the faithful. Examples are given in the tales translated into French by Birago Diop.

The iconoclasts, the fourth group, are rather similar to "the irreverents" except that the media they employ are films in African languages and fiction in French. An example is Mahama Traore's film, *Njangaan*, which portrays what he sees as the exploitation of children in the *dara*, the Quran school, with its outdated and misapplied methods of education. In the film, a six-year-old child is sent away from his village to be educated in the same *dara* that had educated his father. As part of their training, in order to teach them humility, children are sent out to beg in the streets. But here, begging becomes an overt money making scheme to benefit the teacher. The child not only has to go begging, but has also to bring back money to fulfil a given quota. The criticism is directed towards the teachers and other intermediaries of the faith. Islam itself is not under indictment; those who practice it for self-gain are.

The well-known Sengalese director Ousmane Sembene may be regarded as the complete iconoclast, or the fifth group. His films not only depict individuals who misbehave, but portray religion and tradition as obstacles to the true integration of individual and society in Senegal. Islam is seen as another intrusion into African society, an intrusion that is used as a mask for exploitation. More recent filmmakers in Senegal have developed a more balanced perspective on the Wolof heritage, accepting the contributions of both Islam and local traditional cultures.

◆ SOMALI LITERATURE

Most of the religious literature of the Somali is in Arabic. This is because Arabic is considered a more appropriate medium for religious communication, and because an official orthography for Somali was only established in 1972. Prior to that, individuals formulated their own orthographies, most based on a modification of the Arabic script.

Another cause for religious literature to be written in Arabic involves local culture. Traditional patterns of thought in Somali divide men into *wadaad* (religious scholar) and *waranle*, (spear-bearer or layman). The scholars exercise spiritual power; their main language of liturgy, learning, and literature is Arabic. The laymen were employed in secular matters, the domain of their control. Since Arabic was assimilated into Somali, it has been accepted, not as a colonial language, but as a language of religion that has been adopted and integrated into national life and culture. However, two poems written in Somali, using the Arabic script, are well known: one is by the Sufi theologian, Shaykh Uways Muhammad of Brava (died 1909), and the other by Shaykh Ismail Farah (died 1910), a poem in praise of the Prophet Muhammad.

A majority of Somali religious literature is oral poetry attributed to *shaykhs* and *walis* (saints), mostly of the Qadiriyya brotherhood. Among those well known are Sheikh Abdulrahman Seylici (died 1882), Shaykh Abdulrahman Abdalla, also known as Shaykh Sufi (died 1905), and Shaykh Uways, mentioned previously. Their tombs are places of annual pilgrimage; their poems are sung by the pilgrims. Some of their compositions are regarded efficacious as prayers in situations of need and danger. The following extract is from a poem composed by one of the followers of Shaykh Uways, Shaykh Abdulrahman Shaykh Umar (1896–1982) in praise of his leader.

> O God, we turn to you through the intercession
>   of our shaykh
> Our Uweys, beloved of the Qadiriya disciples.
> In his name I invoke help in every calamity.
> Through his worthiness bring us relief in our
>   concerns,
> Through his mysteries grant me success in my
>   pursuits
> In this world and the world to come, and cure
>   the disease of our hearts.

> (B.W. Andrzejewski,
> *Literature of Somalia*)

Such poems echo the oral narratives about the miracles performed by the *sheikhs* for the benefit of their followers. These oral poems were related by religious teachers and preachers who roamed from place to place in the countryside.

Poems with a religious theme, or with an intrinsic religious slant, have also been used by leaders of the Sufi movement to mobilize support of the people to fight against the British. A well-known leader of the movement in Somalia was Sayyid Muhammad Abdallah Hasan (1856–1921). In many of his poems, he preached against the occupation of Somalia by foreigners and called for a struggle against them. His poetry also provides a profile of an ideal Muslim, who is described as having the determination not to be subservient and oppressed by others.

It may be noted, finally, that some modern novels, short stories and plays also discuss aspects of contemporary social life affected by religion. In parallel with literatures elsewhere, the media (newspapers, radio, periodicals) has been particularly instrumental in developing these genres. One of the plays, *Shabeelnaagood*, first performed at the National Theater in Mogadishu in 1974, reflects a reformist argument against the disintegration of traditional family life in urban areas. Another play, published in 1975, depicts the events of the Dervish war, the principal character being Sayyid Muhammed Abdallah Hasan, some of whose poetry is incorporated.

◆ SWAHILI LITERATURE

An understanding of the Muslim dimension in Swahili literature requires an appreciation of the historical process through which the cultures of the East African coast came to be influenced by Muslim thought and values. Four ingredients were salient to the process: the gradual introduction from the ninth century onward of Islam to the East African coast; settlement since the sixteenth century by Arab Muslims and their general integration into Swahili society through intermarriage (though there were always ethnic groups that attempted to retain a distinct identity); the growth of Arab and, later, Swahili and mainland African cadres of influential and renowned Muslim scholars; and, finally, the adoption of the Swahili-Arabic script, alongside Arabic, as an orthography of literary expression.

The earliest phase of Swahili written literature from the seventeenth to the nineteenth centuries is dominated by poetry with religious themes. The life of the Prophet Muhammad provided inspiration for the earliest extant, work the *Hamziyah*, composed in 1652 by Idarus Othman, who based it on an Arabic poem of the same name by the eminent poet Abdallah Muhammad al-Busiri (died 1296). Several events in the Prophet's life inspired early Swahili poets: his ascent to heaven (*miiraj*), his character, virtues, struggles and wars, and his intercessionary powers on behalf of Muslims.

A common topic in Muslim literatures derived from the Quran is the ephemeral nature of life on earth and the necessity of proper conduct. A classic poem on this topic in Swahili is *al-Inkishafi* by Sayyid Abdallah Nasir (died 1820). The poet uses the city of Pate as his focus, a city that had once been splendid and powerful but which had fallen into decline by 1810, with its imperial palaces in ruins. By early nineteenth century, Swahili poets were no longer seeking inspiration solely from the Middle East for their topics, but were integrating the local realities of East African life into their works as an alternative means of advocating the precepts of Islam.

One such historical reality was the spread and adoption of Swahili itself as the lingua franca for the coastal region, and then, after independence, as a national and official language in Tanzania and Kenya respectively. Swahili literature was developed and enriched by contributions from both Muslims and non-Muslims alike who faced common concerns during the colonial and post-colonial periods. The poems of Muyaka Mwinyi Haji (1776–1840) contain socio-political themes. Similar themes are reflected in the poems of the more renowned modern poets such as Shaaban Robert (died 1962) of Tanzania and Ahmad Bhalo (b. 1937) of Kenya. But references to matters of faith are not altogether absent from the repertoire of modern writers. Ebrahim Hussein wonders in his poem *"Ngoma na Vailini"* ("The Drum and the Violin) whether God would listen to a person of divided faith. One of the leading poets of today, Abdilatif Abdalla, who is widely known for his 1973 work *Sauti ya dhiki* ("The Voice of Agony"), written while he was a political prisoner in Kenya from 1969–1972, has also written a long poem on Adam and Eve. However, the major emphasis of the modern writers, and this includes novelists and dramatists, is on social and political matters that affect them primarily as Kenyans or Tanzanians.

Newspapers in East Africa carry a weekly page of poems on a variety of subjects submitted by poets from different parts of the respective countries. Here, one finds comments and sometimes debate on religious or, more often, on socio-religious matters such as the rights of women in Islam, the status of husbands, and the payment of *mahr* (dowry). Incidentally, as Swahili poems are meant to be recited, such debates are also "sung" on the radio on weekly poetry programs.

Farouk Topan

References

Abdulaziz, M.H. *Muyaka: 19th Century Swahili Popular Poetry*. Nairobi: Kenya Literature Bureau, 1979.

Ahmed, Ali Jimale. "Of Poets and Sheikhs: Somali Literature". edited by K. Harrow. Nairobi: Kenya Literature Bureau, 1991.

Andrzejewski, B.W. *Islamic Literature of Somalia*. Hans Wolff Memorial Lecture. Bloomington: Indiana University, 1983.

Andrzejewski, B.W., S. Pilaszewicz and W. Tyloch, eds. *Literatures in African Languages: Theoretical issues and sample surveys*. Warszawa: Wiedza Powszechna & Cambridge: Cambridge University Press, 1985.

Ba, Amadou Hampate. *Kaidara: A Fulani Cosmological Epic from Mali*. Translated by Daniel Whitman. Washington, D.C.: Three Continents Press, 1988.

Boyd, Jean and Graham Furniss. "Mobilise the People: The Qasida in Fulfulde and Hausa as Purposive Literature." In *Qasida: The Literary Heritage of an Arabic Poetic Form in Islamic Africa and Asia*. Edited by S. Sperl and C. Shackle. 1993.

Harrow, Kenneth W. *Faces of Islam in African Literature*. Portsmouth, NH: Heinemann Educational Books, Inc., 1991.

Hiskett, Mervyn. *A History of Hausa Islamic Verse*. London: School of Oriental & African Studies, 1975.

Kane, C.H. *L'aventure ambigue*. Paris: Julliard. Translated into English by Katharine Woods. *The Ambiguous Adventure*. London: Hehnemann Educational Books, 1962.

Knappert, Jan. *Swahili Islamic Poetry*. Leiden: E.J. Brill, 1971.

———. *Four Centuries of Swahili Verse*. Nairobi: Heinemann Educational Books, 1979.

Nasir, Abd Allah A. *A Soul's Awakening*. Translated by W. Hichens. London: Sheldon Press, 1972 Reprint, Nairobi: Oxford University Press, 1972.

Pouwels, Randall L. *Horn and Crescent: Cultural Change and Traditional Islam on the East African Coast, 800–1900*. Cambridge: Cambridge University Press, 1987.

Robinson, Charles H. *Specimens of Hausa Literature*. Cambridge: Cambridge University Press, 1986.

Topan, Farouk M. "Modern Swahili Poetry," *Bulletin of the School of African & Oriental Studies* 37, no. 1 (1974): 175–87.

Muslim Folklore and Folklife

♦ The Concept of Folklore and Folklife ♦ Muslim Identity

The richness of Muslim folklore and folklife lies in the range of expressive cultural forms represented from across the Muslim world including: folk arts and crafts, local musical traditions, cuisine, customary activities such as local rituals and festivals, standards and styles of social behavior, games, theater, folk poetry (whether lyric or narrative, chanted or sung), oral history and other forms of prose narrative, proverbs, riddles, verbal dueling, and other kinds of folk speech and folk play. These diverse cultural forms seem to be a common denominator capable of drawing the local and world community of Muslims together.

Every Muslim nation-state or subnational community has had to respond to local historical circumstances in its construction and maintenance of a Muslim community. Both at the folk level and in reflections of scholars of religion and history, varied experiences from Southeast Asia to certain West African states and on to the New World, before and during colonialism and beyond, provide keys to understand both the largest-scale and the most detailed ramifications of Muslim culture and its complex relations with other world cultures, from the local to the transnational level.

♦ THE CONCEPT OF FOLKLORE AND FOLKLIFE

The term "folklore" was coined by the British folklorist William Thoms in the mid-nineteenth century, replacing the term "popular antiquities," and designating the study of rural peasant culture, which was perceived to be eroding under the influence of European industrialization. Folklore is cultural property that has been handed down from person to person as an inheritance. It is a connection to a past that is recognized by individuals to be unalterably theirs. This shared past is a major aspect of communal and personal identity and is a resource for meaningful expression in new and dif-

ferent situations—thus tradition itself is eventually changed, improvised, and reinvented, thereby affecting subsequent traditions. Both the analytic definition of "tradition" as a type of socially meaningful invention and the experiential definition of "tradition" as cultural property received from the past are "valid" and necessary to adequately define either local culture or folk religion; both definitions are key to refining the idea of Muslim folklore and folklife. Folklife is a term that was introduced into the English language in the mid-twentieth century. It encompasses not only verbal lore, but the nonverbal forms, customs, rituals, festivals, technologies, and the relations among these bodies of worldview, knowledge, and practice.

The German Romantic nationalist Johann Gottfried von Herder conducted work in the study of folklore. Von Herder defined "Volk" as people, as a group with a shared territory and identity based especially on shared language and the cultural understandings conveyed by and in a "mother tongue." The notions of racially or biologically shared knowledge conveyed by a mother tongue are important to von Herder's concept of nationhood. His basic argument served to help formulate the late eighteenth and early nineteenth century concept of German nationalism and addressed the strong need felt by German intellectuals to find an emotional and ideological center for nationhood as a response, in part, to French imperialism. Concepts of "folk" and "folklore" have been and remain historically entangled in political issues, technological change, and population displacement.

The ethnic and local implications of the nineteenth-century European terms folklore and Volk seem antithetical to Islam, as Islam implies a commitment of will or (submission) to a faith that cuts across linguistic and ethnic communities and creates a higher-level community, the *umma*. Note that the term, *umma* like mother tongue or von Herder's "Vaterland," evokes concepts of kinship, similarity of background, and understanding among community members. In Islam there is the recognition that human kinship need not be limited by ethnic or linguistic difference, as one does in Romantic nationalist thought. Muslims see all humans as *bani Adam*, "sons of Adam." Converted populations and Muslim communities in diaspora, living among non-Muslims, are often highly self-conscious about maintaining their faith within a culture; the central precepts of Islam are often most debated among these groups. Muslim communities nearer the perceived Arabic-speaking religious centers also maintain elaborate cultural traditions unique unto themselves.

The cultural history of Islam may not be best viewed in terms of the history of European ideas (e.g., folklore). However, European concepts may be useful in understanding the tension between the Islamic concept of community and Western European loyalties to national language and/or regional, local, or kinship identities. These differences require exploration in order to adequately evaluate the concept of Muslim folklore and folklife.

The notion of "folk groups" in more recent European and American thought has evolved beyond von Herder's concept of ethnic or linguistic cultural groups and Thoms's focus on preindustrial peasant communities which include all sorts of other groupings: local, professional, kin-based, groups based on shared age, gender, work, social status, or shared bodies of knowledge or belief. Folklorist Alan Dundes took the position in the mid-1960s that a "folk" could be any group of two or more people who share any feature (cultural or physical) and have some shared attitudes about it. Others in the field, such as Richard Bauman, tried to mitigate the problems of this radical definition by showing how, over time, the sharing of a cultural feature or property may lead to group membership. Whatever its difficulties, Dundes's definition served to shift the academic definition of "folk" away from using identities such as race or mother tongue, and, in the process, rejected the aspects of Herderian Romanticism that formed the basis for Nazi thought.

The fact that "folk groups" may come in all shapes and sizes and may be based upon varied degrees of historical longevity (and self-consciousness) and the widest range of cultural features means that any one person is simultaneously a member of an indeterminate number of folk groups. Multiple membership may or may not be a harmonious experience; for example, debates arise over the Javanese Muslims' sense of responsibility toward dead ancestors and the validity of Muslim feast practices known as *slametan*. One may find contradictions in the core meanings and goals of various groups to which one belongs. Choosing which group membership to make primary is often a point of contestation in human social life and is not necessarily conscious or calculating. The concept of Muslim folklore and folklife might imply that "Muslim" be taken as the dominant group identifier in a particular setting. However, it would be rash to say that what counts most at all times in the performance or communication of Muslim folklore is being Muslim. Non-Muslims and Muslims as well sometimes have tended to reduce recognition of local cultural forms to a kind of sectarian consciousness: "They do that because they're Muslims." Generalizing in such a way denies the wide range of human experience mediated by folklore, that is, the local, vernacular expressive forms that can become the recognized cultural properties of social subgroups, both in Muslim and non-Muslim societies. This chapter emphasizes local culture, which more explicitly evokes awareness of Muslim identity, but folk culture in the Islamic world by no means defines the sense of "being Muslim."

The concept of "folk society" developed by Robert Redfield in the mid-twentieth century maintains "folk culture" as an ideal that might not exist in pure form anywhere (i.e., within an isolated, culturally and economically self-sufficient, and homogeneous group, as in a tribe or peasant village). The terms "isolated," "self-sufficient," and "homogeneous" all break down under direct scrutiny in almost any ethnographic study. Fredrik Barth and others have argued since the 1960s that the sense of group solidarity is derived more from not being isolated, than from being near people who are perceived as different. This is in contrast to the belief that the so-called homogeneity of a group can be perceived by its contrast with outsiders. Even in situations where the sense of group boundaries and differences is acute, there may be a considerable exchange of personnel between these boundaries. Individuals learn different styles and approaches to social situations as they move between diverse groups. Barth's studies specifically focused on Muslim Pashtuns and Baloch in Afghanistan and Pakistan. As a result of this study, Barth identified "folk groups" as groups among groups or groups of different sizes organized on similar or different lines. Individuals may feel themselves to be members of several different groups (whether nested within each other or overlapping), such that their sense of cultural homogeneity is multilayered and must be explored, not assumed. This complex and dynamic concept of folk groups, makes it more possible to work with the concept of "Muslim folklore and folklife."

◆ MUSLIM IDENTITY

The ideal of Muslim identity transcends ethnic or cultural distinctions, which are secondary to the Muslim's experience of relationship to the community of believers. Muslims share a relationship to God, and from this derive their ideas about human beings' relationships and responsibilities to one another. This ideal would seem to imply a high degree of cultural and social homogeneity, but as Clifford Geertz remarks in *Islam Observed*, "Religious faith, even when it is fed from a common source, is as much a particularizing force as a generalizing one."

Henry Glassie, an American folklorist active in Turkish and Bengali cultural studies, remarked in a letter on his experience in Bangladesh, "The deep force of order in traditional communities is religion" (Khan, p. 197). In as much as "tradition" or "traditional" is a complicated concept, the term "community," like "folk group," must be evaluated if it is to be useful. Looking at Geertz's and Glassie's statements with reference to Islam in south Asia and other regions, we find, among both Muslim writers and outside observers, serious debates over the nature of Muslim tradition; it is considered either as a given practice or viewpoint properly canonical (based on the *hadith* or *sunna*) or something else based on the knowledge of local custom (sometimes called *mirasi*, "legacy" or "inherited"). In North India and Bengal, to which Glassie refers to in his observation, there is a coexistence of two or more well-established religions, Islam and Hinduism. The reconciliation or perhaps lack of polarization between the two has been accomplished and sustained among the different social groups. "Folk" ways can often be seen to parallel those of "high" culture in important ways. For instance, the highly philosophical, abstract arguments for *tawhid* (the unity of all creation in God) among Muslim Sufis exist side by side with universalist tendencies or Vaishnavism in Hindu theology. Muslims and Hindus also share shrines, saints, ritual practices, healing systems, and certain, but not all, food preferences, and so on. However, indigenous and foreign observers in northern India and Bengal have argued that British colonialist and postcolonilist documentation and implementation of local customary law at the district level ("divide and rule" in the view of some), and the reactions of different parts of the population to these policies, resulted in forms of spiritual reform in both the Muslim and Hindu experience. These reforms tended to create or highlight distinctions between the two sets of believers, and these distinctions were used to draw more stringent communal boundaries. "Religion" is certainly a "deep force for order," but the kinds of order it enforces change with time and political circumstances. Local beliefs and practices can be eclectic; communal boundaries can be porous or become culturally exclusive with a rigid effect both on political borders and on expressive culture. In South Asia in particular, "traditional" has come to mean something not static and authoritarian, but rather eclectic and flexible.

Language

Islam provides a vantage point from which to examine von Herder's notion of shared language as a key to membership in a "Volk." Many Muslims do, indeed, share a common language, the Arabic of the Quran, which is regarded by them as a most perfectly expressive language and a key to their group membership. The Arabic of the Quran is perceived as sacred by Muslims because it is the language through which God revealed the Quran, and it is the language of formal address to God in daily prayer. The canonical tradition in Islam (the *hadith* and *sunna*) is transmitted through the Arabic language. But the language of the Quran is not one that most Arab Muslims use to express everyday thoughts and feelings. Their mother tongues are a variety of colloquial languages based on what is termed a modern standard Arabic that is quite different from the Arabic of the Quran.

Oral Tradition

Another aspect of Islamic social institutions that challenges or defies the applicability of European notions of folk culture is orality or oral tradition. Oral communication or transmission is one of the qualities often taken as basic to local folk culture or folklore. The Quran is by definition a recitation, and its most powerful and proper means of transmission is through highly trained, specialized techniques of oral recitation. Islamic religious teaching is also, in many explicit ways, highly committed to oral transmission; the Prophet Muhammad himself was said to be unlettered. Sufi missionary teachers emphasize oral teaching and interpretation in local languages rather than unguided solitary study of the canonical written documents. Thus, the Arabic of canonical Islam is constantly being interpreted in vernacular oral teachings and interpretations. Some modern-day examples of this is the circulation of sermons on cassette tapes which now extends the listening audience for individual preachers and for philosophical tales, or anecdotes of the lives of prominent religious teachers (*malfuzat*) similar to the reports given in the *hadith* and *sunna*, (the officially sanctioned reports of reliable witnesses attesting to the deeds and words of the Prophet). The fact that the Arabic of the Quran is not a spoken vernacular has in no way compromised the existent vernacular languages in the Muslim world or diminished the requirement that the language of the Quran be learned and articulated for religious purposes. There is, however, visible anxiety among teachers who face the challenge of imparting sacred knowledge in the vernacular because the mediated meanings can be falsified or obscured.

The place of orality in Muslim pedagogy is not the

same as the European concept of folklore orality. Conventional European and American thinking sees the oral tradition as of lesser importance than the literary or written culture; oral variability is used by some scholars as evidence of the weakness of memory in comparison to the strength of written script. The complete training of a *Qari* (Quran reciter) challenges this Western European belief, as *Qari* training necessitates mastery of all seven major strands of traditional enunciation as well as a critical understanding of their implications for interpretation. Oral tradition and the uses of memory have had quite a different effect on Muslim history and modern Muslim scholarship than they have had in European history and scholarship. Stress placed on oral, rather than literary culture, affects the kinds of authority granted to oral communication processes in all dimensions of culture.

The preference for oral religious instruction attempts to bring each individual to a state of common, canonical understanding. The proper degree of accommodation to local, idiosyncratic conditions of knowledge and beliefs (such as practices of divination or appeals for the intervention of saints or other venerated dead) thus becomes an intense field for debate among Muslims in locales from east Asia to west Africa where local belief systems are only somewhat acknowledged within the Muslim canonical view.

Literary Tradition

What might be called "folk books" mediate between the highly literary world of Muslim theology and the life and work of ordinary Muslims. The twenty-four page Pashto-language *Potters' Book* details special prayers for four crucial phases of the potter's work: leaving home to dig clay, digging the clay, firing the kiln, and opening the kiln and removing the pottery. The book includes appropriate quotations from the Quran in Arabic and apparently was translated from Persian and sold by itinerant booksellers to village craftsmen. Similar books were produced for carpenters, blacksmiths, washermen, barbers, and others. These crafts are considered low status positions in South Asia and are identified as such in the ancient Hindu grammarian Panini's discussion of craft castes. The *Potters' Book* served to help members of low-caste groups assure the orthodoxy of their Islamic practice and to experience religious consciousness and legitimacy in their daily activities.

Traditional crafts, their techniques, themes, and styles are visibly connected in Islam, between elite to folk. Prayers and invocations from the Quran that have been written in calligraphy are common components of decorative and protective folk paintings (works that serve to protect the individual from evil) on everyday surfaces from house walls to lorries and taxis.

Local Beliefs

The mediation of Islamic ideas, from Arabic into the colloquial languages and then passed on to non-Arabic speakers and non-literates, has entailed complex procedures that ensure the equivalency of terms and ideas between Arabic and the target languages. Concepts of supernatural beings (*jinn*) and the devil (*shaytan*) are a case in point. These concepts of *jinn* are mentioned along with angels and humans as beings capable of thought and faith (or lack of faith) in the Quran and have been confused with non-Arabic terms and concepts deriving from other local culture histories. In Iran and Afghanistan, *jinn* are to some extent aligned with *div*, the latter term being from pre-Islamic Zoroastrian cosmology denoting a class of malevolent supernaturals. *Pari* is another term that has survived from the pre-Islamic past and is a cognate to the English word *fairy*. The *paris* are regarded as benign supernaturals in Iran and Afghanistan and commonly appear as characters in fictional magic tales (*afsaneh*). They are sometimes perceived as the recipients of votive meals (*sofreh*) offered to solicit their protection and aid. Other beings, also called *pari*, are widely known in the mountains of the Hindu Kush and Northern Pakistan, where they are somewhat less benign but quite powerful and present, causing psychic abductions, possession states, and sometimes debilitating illnesses and even death.

Healing for these conditions is specifically religious and may involve the breathing of prayers onto the sufferer, the ingestion or inhalation of religious formulae written in ink then dissolved in water, or the fumigation of bits of paper burnt to free the patient from the evil spirit. The healers may be male or female. The healer's view of the process may differ from the sufferer's. As the Pir of Chatorkhand (a local hereditary spiritual leader in northern Pakistan) told this author in 1989, his prayerful blessing of small packets of sugar brought to him by women, on behalf of suffering members of their families, has some curative results because: "It is faith, pure faith." The believer's faith, not the particular practice, is what he saw as effective. Folk healing through religious faith is a large and diverse topic in Islam. But within Islam's broad reach, some ailments may be seen as "culture-bound syndromes." Both the agents and the particular array of symptoms of illness are defined and dealt with in local terms.

Similar arrays of symptoms may not even be seen elsewhere. In South Asia, *jinn* are sometimes equated with *preta*, a local class of evil spirits regarded as malevolent ghosts of the dead in Hindu and Buddhist thought. There are two basic concepts supported by the Quran that allow for such local interpretation:

The first principle is that God sent a prophet

(*payghambar*) to every group of people, up to 124,000 of them, only some of which are named in the Quran. Thus, many beings locally deemed gods by non-Muslims may be viewed by Muslims as earlier prophets whose mission was misunderstood. This leads to a remarkable range of tolerance. In Sri Lanka one can visit the great shrine complex of the God Skanda at Kataragama, venerated by both Tamil Hindus and Singhala Buddhists. There is a mosque within the shrine precincts that stages a *milad* (birth celebration) for Skanda with special devotional activities in connection with Skanda's great annual pilgrimage and festival, attended by hundreds of thousands of Hindus and Buddhists as well as Sri Lankan Muslims. The imam of the mosque explains to visitors that Skanda, deemed a deity by Hindus and Buddhists, was actually a prophet. He added in conversation with this author (July 1993): "They say he died, but we say he is alive." That the name Skanda is said to derive from Iskandar (Alexander), who, in turn, is identified by Muslims with Dhul Qarnayn (Alexander the Great), mentioned in the Quran and linked in legend both to the Old Testament Prophet Elias (Ilyas) and to Khidr, the eternal, undying, and ever-wandering friend of God, reveals further possible dimensions of the imam's brief explanation.

The second inclusive principle derived from the Quran permitting local interpretations is that God created other intelligent beings in addition to humans and angels who reside in the air and earthly regions and may interact with humans. Thus, as illustrated above, local demonologies can be subsumed under the category *al-shaytan* (the devil), and local spirits under the category of *jinn*, righteous or unrighteous. Some Muslims claim that the Prophet Solomon converted some populations of *jinn* to Islam. Demons are to be warded off, and spirits may be treated with respect (perhaps placated when they are inadvertently wronged), avoided, or warded off if they are of the unrighteous sort. Ill-intentioned and unrighteous humans may be accused of approaching such spirits for unholy purposes, often with the technologies of other religions. Whether such malign magic is deemed actively evil and dangerous, or just ignorant and foolish, depends on the observers' interpretive position in this flexible cosmology and their understanding of the powers ancillary to those of God.

A humility about the limits of human understanding concerning the whole range of God's creation allows for local ideas about the supernatural to be accommodated in various ways and degrees. Observers, both Muslim and non-Muslim, have viewed in different ways Muslim participation in non-Muslim devotional activities such as Hindu *pujas* (worship ceremonies for deities) or solicitations of help through votive rituals, or divinatory or incantatory activities dedicated to be-

ings other than God. Reformers may view such activities extremely negatively, as *shirk* (putting other beings in partnership with God), and as claiming powers and purposes rightfully reserved for God. A Muslim, however, may see his or her participation in such rites as a way to maintain positive relations and communication with other powers which are a part of God's creation or as a sign of respect and fellowship toward a fellow human. As one Bangladeshi scholar explained to the author: "He comes to my *Idd* (Muslim festival) so I go to his *puja* (worship ceremony)." Leaving aside the question of differences of belief and instead focusing on the theme of shared humanity and reciprocity, especially the sharing of offered food, is a powerful social value diffused throughout Muslim thought in many explicit and implicit ways.

The reconciling of different beliefs is not merely a "cover all the bets" folk religious sensibility. Islamic scholars have attempted to take on the task of interpreting local beliefs and practices to show to what extent they are deviations from orthodox cosmological thought. At the folk level, Bengali Muslim farmers explained to John P. Thorp that the *jati* castes is the result of the conflict between Eve's children, Muslims having descended from Habel (Abel), Hindus from Kabel (Cain). These Daripalla residents see themselves as converts to Islam, though, in fact, the conversion was some generations back. They claim that their ancestors were faithful and proper followers of previous prophets (from among the 124,000), and thus they were able to accept Islam when it arrived. Their readiness to convert was, for them, what proves their descent from the righteous Habel.

Local Practices

Across the Muslim world, the abundant local pilgrimages to the graves of saints or sites connected with miraculous events, often condemned by reformers as superstitious and wasteful of resources, can be viewed as substitutes for the *Hajj*, the great pilgrimage to Mecca, for those unable to undertake it. The concept of *niya* or intention, which is the ultimate determiner of the righteousness or unrighteousness of an action, is invoked by Sufis and others to ensure that worship is acceptable in its intention, even if its form is unorthodox.

It has been argued by some outsiders that the core of spiritual identity for many Muslims is not in textual experience but in ritual experience. Hence, the traditional value of a shared ritual meal may be felt without the participant recalling which *hadith* or *sunna* established the sharing of a particular food. The choice of foods for such events (the sort of thing folklorists like to explore) might be supported by scripture and/or by various interpretive elements at a local level. For example, on the Iranian plateau and in Turkey, wheat bread (and by extension, some other wheat-based foods) is featured in certain rituals and customary practices, including various *sofreh* or *nazr* (charitable food distributions where special bread is ritually prepared and sanctified through prayer). After sanctification, this bread is offered to the solicited saint or *pari* or distributed to the poor or to neighbors. This ritual use of wheat products reflects indirectly to the Muslim belief that the food that tempted Eve to disobey was a grain of wheat. As a result, wheat, the staple food for the region, is fixed at the very center of symbolic thinking about food. In Malaysia and Thailand the food that provides the essential blessing in Muslim votive rites and memorial meals is likely to be rice (or a rice preparation). In either case, the local staple grain on which human life depends quite logically epitomizes God's blessing. These regional preferences in ritual foods may predate the advent of Islam and cut across local Muslim and non-Muslim communities. Such examples provide a basis for understanding diverse Muslim practices at the local level and demonstrate coherency, rather than fragmentation or conflict, in vernacular religion. At the same time, it must be acknowledged that the "particularizing" tendency in Islam to adapt to local cultures, as noted by Geertz, may be seen by Muslims or outsiders as a threat to religious coherency. Geertz's own interpretation of Javanese Islam tends to downplay its "Islamicness," despite the Javanese intention to be and act as Muslims.

The Role of Women in Local Customs

Some Islamic reformists have also viewed local practices as threatening the unity or coherency of both the faith and the community of believers. Maulana Ashraf Ali Thanawi's *Bihishti Zewar* (*The Ornaments of Heaven*) is an interesting example of such contested beliefs. This late nineteenth century Urdu book of instruction in proper Islamic behavior was aimed at women, particularly because women were regarded by the Deobandi Muslim reformer-educators in India as the predominant bearers of local customary culture which contradicted "pure" Islam. The perception of women as bearers of potentially heretical vernacular religious practices and beliefs has been linked to women's exclusion from central communal liturgical practices and from formal education. Thanawi and others have advocated religious and general education for women as an effort to replace their involvement with local vernacular knowledge systems, thus directing their devotional energies to the "five pillars" in a more restricted sense. Entire sections of *Bihishti Zewar*, and of a similar but shorter document, Khwaja Altaf Hussein Hali's *Majalis un-Nissa* (*The Assemblies of Women*), lists specific vernacular ritual practices of

question, including the ceremonial use of henna, or ongoing gift exchanges within women's networks on occasions of Muslim life-cycle celebrations such as weddings and circumcisions. Such practices are presented in these texts, as not merely irrelevant or innocuous to religion but, as actually sinful or leading to sin by implication. Thanawi's criticisms tend to suggest the elimination of such customary practice. However, Thanawi's vivid and alarmist portrayals of women's participation in local customary activities clearly illustrates how female culture can be taken as essentially local, as well as irrational, emotional, and socially disorderly. The control of women for Thanawi and others became an important part of a call for Muslim men to assert spiritual renewal, moral and political self-control, and self-determination in colonized India, where there was then, an atmosphere of loss of power, spiritual direction, and cultural marginalization. Women were consequently made to feel that their religious contributions were of lesser importance. One fictional female speaker in *Majalis un-Nissa* expresses acute embarrassment and shame that a British man had published a book describing local customs in India, with the result that the ignorance of the community, especially that of its women, would become notorious.

Under conditions of wartime displacement, as seen in both the Afghan and Palestinian struggles, women have found the bonds of *purdah* customs (domestic seclusion rules) tightened upon them. While women often are the designated bearers of local vernacular culture, they also are held as icons to be controlled and defended. Although, under conditions of threat, individual women may elect more constrained styles of dress and interaction in solidarity with their community's resistance to non-Muslim encroachment or aggression, the tendency for Muslim (and other) women to wear local traditional costume for longer periods of time than men in circumstances of rapid urbanization and expanding Western influence, is an example of the mutual conceptualization of women's bodies as a site of vernacular territorial maintenance. Such phenomena are by no means unique to Muslim societies, but can help us understand the range of meanings implied by the use of cultural markers labeled "Muslim," including the many and highly varied local forms of modest dress or veiling (*hijab*).

♦ CONCLUSION

On a historical note, the Shia practice of *taqiya* (concealment of religious affiliation under circumstances of sectarian hostility) could, under social pressure, explicitly allow for social conformity to local priorities without giving up one's inner commitment to Muslim beliefs and practices. So participation in ritual events or customs across apparent communal boundary lines can be tolerated or not tolerated, done or not done, and quite variously interpreted in a complex mix of outward behavior and inward beliefs and sentiments. As Kirin Narayan has advocated in a recent paper on post-colonialism and folklore, one can only understand other people's actions if one understands the interpretations of these actions and the wider experience upon which these actions are based. A good deal of their subjective views we will probably never understand, but we will do well to attend to as much of people's own interpretations of their cultural activities, as they are willing to share. Only then will we be able to understand some dimensions of the complex relations between belief, spiritual experience and cultural expressions, and the debates in progress within communities, variously influenced from without, about the contents and significance of local culture.

This chapter has attempted to illustrate issues and examples encompassed by the concept of "Muslim folklore and folklife," abundantly revealed in the very large literature on localism in Islam. The subject has been of major interest for Western observers beginning with early travel writers and ethnologists of the colonial era, and it has been a topic of great interest and concern to Muslim scholars. The dynamic relationship between religious faith and vernacular culture defies summarization, but the glimpses obtained of it through lenses that juxtapose local practice and interpretive argument continue to intrigue us and to teach us things about cultural process and cultural authority among Muslims all over the world.

Margaret A. Mills

References

Barth, Fredrik, ed. *Ethnic Groups and Boundaries.* Boston: Little, Brown, 1969.

Bauman, Richard, ed. *Folklore, Cultural Performances, and Popular Entertainments.* Oxford: Oxford University Press, 1992.

Boddy, Janice. *Wombs and Alien Spirits: Women, Men and the Zar Cult in Northern Sudan.* Madison: University of Wisconsin Press, 1989.

Caton, Steven C. *"Peaks of Yemen I Summon:" Poetry as Cultural Practice in a North Yemeni Tribe.* Berkeley: University of California Press, 1990.

Geertz, Clifford. *Islam Observed.* New Haven, Conn.: Yale University Press, 1968.

Glassie, Henry. *Turkish Traditional Art Today.* Bloomington: Indiana University Press, 1993.

Grima, Benedicte. *The Performance of Emotion among Paxtun Women.* Austin: University of Texas Press, 1992.

Handler, Richard, and Jocelyn Linnekin. "Tradition, Genuine or Spurious." *Journal of American Folklore* 97, 1984.

Jamzadeh, Laal, and Margaret Mills. "Iranian Sofreh: From Collective to Female Ritual." In C. W. Bynum, S. Harrell, and P. Richman, eds., *Gender and Religion: On the Complexity of Symbols.* Boston: Beacon Press, 1986.

Kanafani, Aida S. *Aesthetics and Ritual in the United Arab Emirates: The Anthropology of Food and Personal Adornment among Arabian Women.* Beirut: American University, 1983.

Metcalf, Barbara. *Perfecting Women: Maulana Ashraf 'Ali Thanawi's Bihishti Zewar, A Partial Translation and Commentary.* Berkeley: University of California Press, 1990.

Khan, Shamsuzzaman. *Folklore of Bangladesh.* Vol. 1. Dhaka, Bangladesh: Bangla Academy, 1989.

Mills, Margaret A. "Folk Tradition in Jalal ud-Din Rumi's *Mathnavi* and the *Mathnavi* in Folk Tradition," In *Poetry and Mysticism in Islam: The Heritage of Rumi.* Edited by Georges Sabagh and Amin Banani. New York: Cambridge University Press, 1994.

———. *Rhetorics and Politics in Afghan Traditional Storytelling.* Philadelphia: University of Pennsylvania Press, 1991.

———. "Sex Role Reversals, Sex Changes and Transvestite Disguise in the Oral Tradition of a Conservative Muslim Community in Afghanistan." In *Women's Folklore, Women's Culture.* Edited by R. Jordan and S. Kalcik. Philadelphia: University of Pennsylvania Press, 1991.

———. "A Cinderella Variant in the Context of a Muslim Women's Ritual." In *A Cinderella Casebook.* Edited by Alan Dundes. New York: Garland Publishers, 1982.

Minault, Gail. *Voices of Silence: English Translations of Khwaja Altaf Hussain Hali's Majalis un-Nissa and Chup ki Dad.* Delhi: Chanakya Publications, 1986.

Narayan, Kirin. "Banana Republics and V.I. Degrees: Rethinking Indian Folklore in a Postcolonial World," *Asian Folklore Studies* 52, 1993.

Pugh, Judy. "Divination and Ideology in the Banaras Muslim Community." In *Shariat and Ambiguity in South Asian Islam.* Edited by K. Ewing. Berkeley: University of California Press, 1986.

Roy, Asim. *The Islamic Syncretistic Tradition in Bengal.* Dhaka, Bangladesh: Academic Publishers, 1983.

Ryan, Patrick J., and S. J. Imale. *Yoruba Participation in the Muslim Tradition.* Missoula, Mont. Scholars Press, 1979.

Rye, Owen S., and Clifford Evans. *Traditional Pottery Techniques of Pakistan.* Washington, DC: Smithsonian/Islamabad: Lok Virsa, 1974.

Sanneh, Lamin O. *The Jakhanke: The History of an Islamic Clerical People of the Senegambia.* London: International African Institute, 1979.

Sowayan, Saad A. *Nabati Poetry: The Oral Poetry of Arabia.* Berkeley: University of California Press, 1985.

Thorp, John P. "The Muslim Farmers of Bangladesh and Allah's Creation of the World," *Asian Folklore Studies* 11:2, 1982.

von Oppen, Renata. *Art on Wheels.* Karachi, Pakistan: Ferozsons (Pvt.), 1992.

Weir, Shelagh. *Palestinian Costume.* Austin, Tex.: University of Texas Press and the British Museum, 1989.

Woodward, Mark R. "The *Slametan:* Textual Knowledge and Ritual Performance in Central Javanese Islam," *History of Religions*, 28:1, 1988.

Part IX:

Women and Their Contributions to Islam

Women, Men, and Gender in Islam

♦ Quranic and Other Normative Teachings regarding Women ♦ The Family and Gender Roles
♦ Development of Public and Private Roles of Men and Women in Muslim Societies
♦ Diversity in Status and Role across the Muslim World ♦ Contributions of Women
♦ Contemporary Developments and Issues

The Islamic religion embraces not only ethical injunctions and spiritual teachings, but also prescribes specific and practical behavior that has an impact on all aspects of everyday life. As a consequence, the implications of its teachings in fashioning and sustaining gender roles and relationships have permeated the widely diverse societies to which Islam has spread.

♦ QURANIC AND OTHER NORMATIVE TEACHINGS REGARDING WOMEN

The Quran repeatedly addresses both "the believing men" and "the believing women" and, according to Islamic teachings, every human being is accountable for his or her own actions. Specific Quranic pronouncements that affect women are ones that involve inheritance, marriage and divorce, testimony in disputes, and modesty.

Inheritance

The Quran brought about a significant improvement in the status of women from that of pre-Islamic times, in that it allocated regular inheritance shares for women (Quran 4:11). A widow receives one-eighth of the estate if there are descendants and one-quarter if there are not. In the case of a man and woman with equal degrees of relationship to the deceased, such as a brother and sister, the inheritance share of the woman is set at one-half that of the man. This law acknowledges the fact that land was owned by families; the daughters of these families married into other families holding separate lands or resources. As a result, women received a dowry at the time of marriage while men did not.

Marriage and Divorce

The Quran often speaks of the relationship between the spouses as one of love and mutuality (Quran 30:21). Several Quranic verses do, however, suggest an asymmetry of roles. Examples are: "Women have rights similar to those [of men] in kindness, and men are a degree above them" (Quran 2:228) and "men are in charge of women because God has made one of them to excel the other, and because they spend their property [to support women]" (Quran 4:34).

Muslim modernists and feminists, uncomfortable with the implication of inherent male superiority, link the meaning of such verses to the sense that the higher-level economic responsibility of men in traditional contexts entailed a veto right in family decision making.

Some Muslims feel that polygamy was only allowed as a sociohistoric necessity and that the Quranic injunction "Marry of the women who seem good to you, two, three, or four, but if you fear that you can not be just (to so many) then marry only one" (Quran 4:3) is tantamount to a discouragement of multiple marriages. In practice, the command for equal treatment of wives has been left up to the man's conscience. Polygamy always has been relatively rare (less than 5 percent). Some Muslim countries such as Tunisia and Turkey have banned it outright in recent decades, while others have legally restricted it.

Testimony in Disputes

An asymmetric tendency is also noted in the Quranic prescription that the testimony of two female witnesses should be considered equivalent to that of a single man (Quran 2:282). This unfortunately has been interpreted by some commentators to imply that women are intellectually inferior to men, unreliable in

A women's credit group in Bangladesh.

their judgment, or easily swayed by emotions. Modernist commentators contend that this stipulation had applied only in limited cases and that this injunction does not apply today due to women's higher level of education and greater experience in worldly affairs and commercial transactions.

Men and women criminals are subject to the same punishments according to the *hudud* laws stipulated in the Quran regarding theft, drinking alcohol, committing adultery, and bearing false witness.

Modesty

Modesty on the part of both sexes is exhorted in the Quran (Quran 24:30 ff), which states that women should not reveal their charms to male who are beyond a certain degree of kinship, such as their fathers, brothers, sons, and husbands. Such close male relations are known as *mahram*, and Islamic law forbade women to travel alone unless accompanied by a *mahram*.

In addition to the Quran, the *hadith*, or reports of the Prophet Muhammad's sayings and actions, are considered authoritative textual sources in Islam. Some contemporary Muslim scholars have claimed that the *hadith* contains negative material concerning the status of women and have suggested that this is the result

of the Arabian background of its time. Many of the Quran's ethical pronouncements that raised women's status seem to have been diluted in the ensuing centuries, during which the formal contours of the Islamic law (*sharia*) took shape. This was due to the fact that under *sharia* the cultural status quo was upheld, as long as it was not in conflict with the Quran.

Legal pronouncements, including those which impact gender relations, have been interpreted somewhat differently among the Sunni and the Shia schools of law. For example, the Hanafi school of law and Shia law permits mature women to contract their own marriages, while the other schools require a male guardian's (*wali*'s) consent. Islamic law guaranteed property rights and personal status to free women who were entitled to stipulate monogamy at the time of writing the marriage contract.

In mosques and during ritual prayer, men and women are separated, with the women generally praying behind the men—often on an upper balcony, in a separate room, or behind a partition. This is generally explained as allowing both sexes to avoid the distraction of potential attraction to one another during times of worship. However, during the annual pilgrimage to Mecca, men and women may pray beside each other

Men and women in prayer in a mosque.

due to the crowded conditions. While women have equal spiritual status according to Islam, they are to refrain from ritual prayer and fasting during their menstrual periods.

◆ THE FAMILY AND GENDER ROLES

While there is some evidence of matrilineal forms of social organization in pre-Islamic Arabia, the society was primarily patriarchal when Islam emerged—providing a pattern that is patrilineal and emphasizes recognition of paternity. One example of this is the legal stipulation that a divorced or widowed woman must observe a waiting period of approximately three months, known as the *idda*, in order to conclusively prove that she is not pregnant before she may remarry (since it might confuse paternity).

Children

During early childhood a ritual known as the *aqiqa* is performed on both girls and boys in which the child's first growth of hair is shaved. A *hadith* report suggests that two sheep should be sacrificed to celebrate a boy's birth and one sheep for a girl's, but many parents no longer perform this aspect of the ritual.

Circumcision is required of male Muslims. While it is a medical procedure performed during infancy in many societies, in others such as Morocco and Turkey it has come to symbolically represent a rite of passage to manhood and is performed with some ceremony on older boys. Although female circumcision is not a religious requirement, it is practiced in some Muslim cultures, especially in certain regions of Africa and Southeast Asia.

Marriage

Muslim societies maintain a strong emphasis on family ties and solidarity. In the Arab world and South Asia, cross-cousin marriage remains a common practice among more traditional, rural populations. Marriages usually are arranged by the families, although some urban young couples may have a chance to meet independently of their families and then subsequently ask their parents' permission to marry. Most Muslim societies stipulate minimum ages for marriage, usually mid or late teens—women generally marry by their early twenties and are somewhat younger than their husbands.

Traditional views regarding female chastity are emphasized in Muslim society; dating is therefore not com-

For some Muslim women, traditional forms of dress express a commitment to cultural identity, modesty, and privacy.

mon. In some cultures, for example, South Asia, the couple may only have exchanged photographs at the time of the actual wedding ceremony.

Today, dowry (*mahr*) practices seem to be largely based on cultural rather than religious precedents. When the Prophet Muhammad gave his daughter Fatima in marriage, the *mahr* she received from her husband, Ali, was very modest. This moderation has not been maintained by Muslims. In South Asia the bride's family is usually responsible for the major contribution, including the furnishings of the new household. In the Arab world and in Persian and Afghan culture, the husband must often pay a large sum as *mahr* and be able to afford housing for the new couple. This *mahr* is generally kept as a kind of insurance to be paid to the bride if the marriage ends in divorce, although in principle the wife can request payment at any time during the marriage. The husband is also responsible for limited spousal and extended child support in the case of divorce.

Marriage is formally established by contract, and marriage parties include large public displays where guests may be feted over several days and hundreds may attend. It may be months or even years before the spouses actually live together and consummate their union.

Traditional interpretations of Islamic law stipulate that the man support his family and that women not have to work outside the home. If a woman holds her own property or has her own source of income, she is free to retain control of them and to spend them as she wishes.

Divorce

According to Islamic law, divorced or widowed women retain custody of children for a limited time. For example, in Hanafi law husbands are legally entitled to custody of male children over seven years of age and female children over nine. Many men, however, waive this right. It should be noted that, even if the mother has physical custody, guardianship in terms of certain matters is still the legal prerogative of the husband or his nearest male kin. Today, many Muslim societies allow the courts to rule in the best interests of the child in custody cases.

Divorce is relatively rare in traditional Muslim societies but is on the rise among the "modern" elite. In some regions it is highly stigmatized, while in others it has become relatively common. Statistics indicate that divorced and widowed men remarry more frequently than women.

According to Islamic law, men are allowed to initiate divorce in a number of ways, generally by pronouncing their intent to divorce. A three-month waiting period is recommended, during which attempts are made to reconcile the couple. An immediate repudiation of the wife known as the "triple divorce" is legal but is not condoned. Women are less able to request a divorce, although certain grounds such as the husband's insanity, dangerous illness, impotence, desertion, cruelty, or failure to maintain his wife legally constitute grounds for her to initiate a divorce.

While some level of personal chastisement of wives appears to be recognized by the Quran (Quran 4:34), contemporary societies such as Egypt have defined unacceptable treatment in terms of cultural and class expectations. Modifications in divorce procedure, as in other aspects of Islamic law, have been written into many of the legal codes currently applied in Muslim societies.

Family

Persons rarely live on their own in Muslim societies. Single women stay with their families until marriage; bachelors generally live at home unless they have to migrate for education or work. In fact, many couples reside with the husband's parents after marriage, if the residence is large enough to accommodate an extended family. Older people are cared for by their children or other family members.

In Muslim societies the social interaction between unrelated men and women is restricted. Traditional house design often allowed the women the inner part of house, which would be off-limits to outsiders. This is the concept of a *harim*, which literally means a sacred or restricted space. In earlier times windows were screened with grilles or elaborately carved wooden shutters, which allowed light and air to enter while concealing the interior from outside scrutiny. The veil was used, and is still seen by some, to permit women more independent movement outside of their dwelling quarters. Until the twentieth century total seclusion might mean that women who had to leave their home would be transported in enclosed palanquins. Today, a much higher degree of independent movement by women in public spaces is the norm, and the concept of modesty is internalized in these contexts by avoiding inappropriate glances or conversations. Public facilities such as transport or restaurants may offer separate rooms for women passengers or "family" parties.

In terms of actual practice, Muslim societies permit a range of gender roles but normatively, women generally are seen as the primary homemakers and caretakers of the children. Religious norms are often cited that discourage women working publicly, unless in case of dire economic need—this need has become a reality in many developing societies. Since the rationale for modest dress is to avoid the temptation of sexual indiscretion, postmenopausal women do not have to observe the same degree of segregation and veiling.

◆ DEVELOPMENT OF PUBLIC AND PRIVATE ROLES OF MEN AND WOMEN IN MUSLIM SOCIETIES

Contemporary discussions of the Islamic position on women have attempted to separate religious norms from cultural traditions. Men in pre-Islamic Arab society often held a disparaging view of women. At times of famine the practice of female infanticide was sanctioned, a custom strongly forbidden by Quranic teaching. Some women in pre-Islamic times did acquire their own wealth and were recognized as poetesses and warriors. A variety of marriage practices giving women the direct freedom over marriage alliances seem to have existed at that time. However, these were ultimately

Here a group of men socialize together.

limited by Islamic norms reinforcing paternity and punishing adulterous liaisons.

The first person to follow the Prophet Muhammad was a woman, his wife Khadija. In the early period of Islamic history large numbers of women accepted Islam and took allegiance to the Prophet. During the time of the Prophet and the early caliphs, Muslim women attended the mosques, transmitted legal decisions, and even fought alongside men.

Muslim historians of the early Umayyad period (661–750) have recorded the activities of independent women such as Sukayna bint al-Hussain (died 735), a dynamic and cultured woman who was married at least four times. Scholars conclude that women's social roles were freer and more prominent during this period than during the later Abbasid period (750–1258), when the interpenetration of Persian cultural practices and the ready availability of slave women tended to encourage concubinage and make women commodities. While full veiling restrictions on women and their seclusion seems to date from this period, it should be kept in mind that the loss of female labor that this seclusion traslated into could only have been afforded by wealthy urban classes. In rural and nomadic populations, veiling practices and segregation have always

been less prevalent. As Islam spread to South and Southeast Asia, these veiling and seclusion practices also were adapted to local norms.

In mystical circles women seem to have been accorded more independence and sometimes even lived unmarried communally in institutions known as *ribats*. Popular mysticism also gave more scope to female leadership roles and independent activities such as traveling to participate in religious sessions or charismatic healing ceremonies like the trance-inducing *zar* dances that take place in North Africa.

In the pre-modern period women's education was limited to those with learned or privileged male relatives who encouraged their talents. The historical sources list occasional women experts in Quranic, legal, and mystical studies, who taught both men and women students and traveled, under the supervision of their male relatives, in order to further their knowledge.

The tradition socializing patterns of men and women is primarily either family or gendercentric. Middle Eastern men traditionally gather in "male" spaces, such as coffeehouses, while women visit the homes of their close female friends and relatives during leisure hours. Mosques have traditionally been "male" spaces, while

A family at study.

the shrines of Sufi saints would be frequented more often by women supplicants, who used the opportunity to relax and socialize with friends. This pattern is currently under modification, with increased woman education and the contemporary woman's desire to participate in the intellectual and political spheres.

◆ DIVERSITY IN STATUS AND ROLE ACROSS THE MUSLIM WORLD

Today, women have risen to the position of head of state in such Muslim societies as Turkey, Pakistan, and Bangladesh. The traditional family structures, where parents often reside with or near their children, allow many Muslim women to excel in such demanding careers as medicine and law since child care is handled by the extended family; upper-class families in many developing Muslim countries may employ servants to allow career women to work outside the home.

In certain Muslim societies, the government restricts the movements of women in ways that might limit their choice of career. For example, in Saudi Arabia, women are forbidden to drive. At the same time, Saudi Arabia and other oil-rich nations have attempted to provide separate educational opportunities for women. Women graduates, including many in technical and scientific fields, currently outnumber men. However, in less wealthy or rural regions women's literacy rates still lag far behind those of the male population.

With material development in these regions, there is an increase in literacy and a decrease in fertility as resources increase to allow women further education. The number of live births per woman varies from a high of 7.6 in Yemen and Gaza to 3.0 in Indonesia. It should be noted that geographical region is a more significant variable in predicting fertility and other material indexes of female status than religious affiliation.

Religious law can be interpreted to place certain limits on female leadership roles. For example, a woman cannot lead men in prayer. Conservatives consider that even hearing the female voice is sexually provocative, therefore severely limiting a woman's public role. More recently greater scope for women's activities in religion have been advocated by Islamic modernists. For example, women have been invited to give Friday speeches following the regular sermon in the mosques in Iran, South Africa, and elsewhere.

Women's political participation has constituted an important, if not controversial, dimension of the anticolonialist movement in the Iranian revolution. Revolutionary and Islamist rhetoric seeks to define a role for Muslim women that sanctions the traditional norms of modesty, while encouraging political mobilization, religious consciousness, and modern education. This, in turn, contrasts with the often negative stereotype of the westernized woman as a sex object or "painted doll."

Dress

Dress in Muslim countries varies across ethnic, class, and ideological lines. The Quran stipulates basic norms of modesty in dress and deportment for both men and women. Many Muslim women cover their hair either with a separate scarf or with a longer garment, which also envelops the rest of the body but leaves the face exposed. Arms and legs are to be covered up to the hands and feet, and clothing should not be tight fitting or revealing in other ways. While this extent of female covering is considered religiously obligatory, some women also choose to wear a *niqaba* or face veil in emulation of some of the Prophet's wives who received visitors only from behind a curtain at the request of the Prophet. Male norms of modesty include covering the body from the navel to the knees. The Persian term for curtain, *purdah*, has come to refer to the system of gender segregation in Muslim south Asia. In South Asian regions baggy pants and a long tunic is the standard regional attire for both men and women, whereas traditional Arab dress is a loose one-piece robe reaching to the ankles. Weddings and festive occasions are usually marked by the exchange of textiles and the wearing of expensive and intricately embroidered clothes.

Women in many Muslim societies have preserved traditional ways of dressing more tenaciously than men who generally adopt Western suits and ties in professional situations. However, the latest Paris fashions may be favored by westernized elites as a status symbol in the Middle East. In Indonesia, women have largely adopted European dress, while in Malaysia, Malay identity has come to be symbolized by a form of Islamic dress, the *baju kurung*, a brightly colored ankle-length straight skirt with a long tunic. At present, most but not all Malay women cover their hair with scarves. Stricter norms for female "Islamic" dress are publicly enforced by the state in Saudi Arabia and Iran. In other regions and situations, family or social pressure may be put on women to dress either more modestly or less modestly than they would personally choose.

◆ CONTRIBUTIONS OF WOMEN

Religious role models for women in the Quran include Mary (or Miriam), the mother of Jesus, after whom an entire chapter is named. Asiya, the wife of Pharaoh, is portrayed as a heroine, since she saved Moses and stood up to her tyrannical husband. Hagar, the slave wife of Abraham, figures prominently in the symbolism of the *Hajj* pilgrimage; the ritual of *say*, or running between two hillocks near the Kaaba, mirrors her action when she desperately sought water to sustain herself and her infant son, Ismail, in the desert.

Among the most prominent women associated with the Prophet Muhammad is his wife, Khadija, the prototype of the ideal helpmate and the wise, older woman. Aisha, whom he married after Khadija's death, was both a respected legal consultant and a political activist. Fatima, his daughter, is depicted as pious, ascetic, and, in Shia spirituality, as a benevolent and compassionate intercessor imbued with spirituality. Umm Umara is another of the heroic female associates of the Prophet. She was wounded in combat thirteen times and defended Muhammad in battle, perhaps saving his life by her timely action. Sayyida Zaynab and Nafisa are saintly female descendants of Muhammad whose tombs are places of refuge and supplication for the urban poor of Cairo.

Female rulership is sometimes seen as being sanctioned by citing the sovereignty of the Queen of Sheba who appears in the Quranic narrative about Solomon. A few pre-modern Muslim women came to rule in their own right such as Sayyida Arwa (died 1138) in Yemen, Shajarat al-Durr (1257) in Mamluk Egypt, and Raziyya Sultana (1240) in India, while many more were the powers behind the throne as queen mothers and royal spouses.

Islamic biographical compendia, which memorialized the achievements of the preceding generations of Muslims, began to be compiled during the third Islamic century. Many included separate chapters or entire volumes devoted exclusively to women's lives. Statistical analysis has shown that the relative percentage of women cited in such collections decreased over time, reflecting a corresponding decline in their public participation. Among the roles cited for women in these collections is that of legal expert, which included in the first generations Aisha, Amra d. Abd al-Rahman, and Hafsa d. Sirin. Later, in Baghdad, Umm Isa d. Ibrahim (died 939) and Amat al-Wahid (died 987) issued legal decisions. Several hundred learned women are mentioned in al-Sakhawi's fifteenth-century biographical dictionary.

Women in religious roles are especially prominent in the field of Islamic mysticism, which seems to have allowed more leeway in exercising traditional gender roles. Rabia al-Adawiyya of Basra (ca. 801) was a famous saint who abjured marriage and was acknowledged to surpass the male saints of her age in spiritual accomplishments. Ibn al-Jawzi (died 1200), a man compiler, mentions 240 women Sufis in his biographical work on mystics.

The public contributions of wealthy patronesses who endowed mosques, schools, and public works such as hospitals, cisterns, and water fountains are also abundantly recorded. Many of the trusts and buildings

Women are often the major contributors to the cultural achievements of Muslim societies.

endowed by women still survive. Occasionally, these women also administered these charitable foundations.

Women's accomplishments in the traditional folk arts such as embroidery, carpet weaving, food preparation, or music are more difficult to trace due to the lack of individual recognition for such skills. These areas, in which women were often the major contributors, represent a significant component within the cultural achievements of Muslim societies.

Even in pre-Islamic times the roles of poetess and soothsayer were open to Arab women. Al-Khansa was a poetess who accepted Islam and eulogized her brother and sons, who died fighting for the faith. Other notable Muslim poetesses have included Rabia Balkhi, (circa 1100), an Afghan princess who was murdered by her brother, and Wallada al-Mustakfi (1001–1080) an Andalusian noblewoman.

Today, Muslim women are active in all fields of artistic and intellectual activity. While roles in the popular artistic or entertainment world such as actress, dancer, or popular musician are still considered somewhat risqué, such women have certainly attained wealth and adulation, the most striking example being the Egyptian star Umm Kulthum (1910–1975). Muslim women poets and novelists in recent years have written more openly about previously taboo topics such as love and have assorted their own cultural and social critique, generating both controversy and admiration. Examples are the Persian poetess, Furugh Farrukhzad (1935–1967), the Lebanese writer Layla Balabakki (1936–), and the Algerian Fadela Mrabet (1935–). Currently, cultural feminists from Muslim societies attract international attention as part of the global women's movement. Nawal el-Saadawi, an Egyptian doctor and activist, is well known for her novels and other writings criticizing the position of women in Arab society. She headed the Arab Women's Solidarity

Association (AWSA), a feminist organization founded in the early 1980s. Fatima Mernissi is a Moroccan intellectual who, early in her career, criticized contemporary gender relations in Muslim societies. More recently, she has assumed the role of cultural feminist in attempting to recover the roles of active and creative women in early Islam. In post revolutionary Iran, a flourishing cinema includes a number of women directors such as Rakhshan Bani-Etemad.

♦ CONTEMPORARY DEVELOPMENTS AND ISSUES

The feminist movement in Muslim societies began by addressing such goals as education for women and the right to vote. Only in the nineteenth-century had education for women become available in public institutions. Early advocates of improved status for women included the Egyptian lawyer, Qasim Amin, who wrote *Freedom of the Woman* in 1899. The famous Egyptian activist, Huda Sharawi (1882–1947), came from an elite background, and after participating in the Egyptian nationalist movement, dramatically removed her veil in 1923; she rallied other Egyptian and Arab women to the cause of women's rights. In general, the early rhetoric of Arab feminism called for educating women to be better citizens, wives, and mothers, rather than for their own personal enrichment.

Notable woman participants in nationalist struggles include the Turkish writer Halide Edib Adivar (1883–1963) and Fatima Jinha of Pakistan. In the Algerian and Iranian revolutions and in the Palestinian struggle, women fought alongside men and sacrificed their lives for the national cause.

Islamist movements are also not without their share of female activists. For example, the Egyptian, Zaynab al-Ghazzali, founded the Association of Muslim Women in 1937; her association with the Muslim Brotherhood led to her imprisonment. Aisha Abd al-Rahman, also known by her pen name of Bint al-Shati, is a noted Quranic scholar and university professor in Egypt; she has authored studies of prominent Muslim women of the past and articulates a role for Muslim women today that combines traditional Islamic norms of modesty with education and integration into public life.

Contemporary developments in Muslim societies include raising the status of women and ensuring their rights. While previous legal reforms had often been modeled on European codes, many Muslim societies are trying to maintain the essence of the Islamic norms, particularly in the area of family law, while adjusting to contemporary situations. Among controversial issues are laws governing birth control; polygamy, divorce, and the weight of a woman's testimony in courts of law. On the basis on Quranic and *hadith* pronouncements, family planning is generally considered acceptable,

while abortion is not, unless the mother's life is endangered.

The issue of dress is imbedded in a web of cultural mores, including a quest for authenticity and a rejection of colonial and neocolonial incursions. Since female veiling practices among the urban middle classes and elite are perceived as signs of opposition to the government in some situations, women covering the hair or face have on occasion been banned from attending universities in such countries as Turkey and Egypt. On the other hand, women from rural backgrounds and the urban nonelites often practice veiling as part of traditional behavior without this constituting a political statement.

The participation of women in all aspects of life, including religious roles, is undoubtedly increasing. The Islamist movements prominent in many societies are also focusing on the interests of women participants who are putting on new forms of Islamic or shari dress in rising numbers. Many younger and educated women are active participants in Sufi-influenced movements such as the Said Nursi movement in Turkey or Al-Arqam of Malaysia. The rhetoric of even the most conservative movements is shifting away from limiting women to domestic roles. One of their appeals to activist young women is the call for them to be educated and work for the improvement of their societies.

At the same time, a new generation of feminists who have been trained in the Islamic sciences is beginning to reinterpret the scripture and laws from a woman's perspective and is thereby challenging some of the previous readings.

Other women's movements across the Muslim world are organizing to protest social and economic inequalities. Some, such as Women Living under Muslim Laws founded by Marie-Aimee Helie-Lucas, an Algerian living in Paris, monitor laws affecting the status of women and publicize gender-related acts of violence or oppression. Others, such as the Malaysia-based Sisters in Islam, are trying to work within the Islamic tradition by encouraging women to study and interpret the Quran and to recover Muslim women's history.

Marcia K. Hermansen

References

Ahmed, Leila. *Women and Gender in Islam.* New Haven, Conn: Yale University Press, 1992.

Badran, Margot, and Miriam Cooke. *Opening the Gates: A Century of Arab Feminist Writing.* Bloomington: Indiana University Press, 1990.

Bodman, Herbert. *Women in the Muslim World: A Bibliography.* Providence, R.I.: Association for Middle East Women's Studies, 1991.

Fernea, Elizabeth Warnock. *Women and the Family in the Middle East.* Austin: University of Texas, 1985.

————, and Basima Qattan Bezirgan. *Middle Eastern Muslim Women Speak*. Austin: University of Texas, 1977.

Kimball, Michelle. *Resources for the Study of Women in the Muslim World: A Bibliography with Select Annotation*. Santa Barbara: University of California, 1994.

————. *Women and Islam: A Historical and Theological Enquiry*. Oxford: Basil Blackwell, 1991.

Mernissi, Fatima. *Beyond the Veil: Male-Female Dynamics in Modern Muslim Society*. Rev. ed. Bloomington: Indiana University Press, 1987.

Moghadam, Valentine. *Modernizing Women: Gender and Social Change in the Middle East*. Boulder, Colo: Lynne Rienner, 1993.

Mumtaz, Khawar, and Farida Shaheed. *Women of Pakistan: Two Steps Forward. One Step Back?* London: Zed Books, 1987.

Qasim Amin. *The Liberation of Women: A Document in the History of Egyptian Feminism*. Translated by Samiha Sidhom Peterson. Cairo: American University in Cairo Press, 1992.

Roded, Ruth. *Women in Islamic Biographical Collections: From Ibn Sad to Who's Who*. Boulder, Colo.: Lynne Rienner, 1994.

Smith, Margaret. *Rabia the Mystic and her Fellow Saints in Islam*. Cambridge, Mass.: Cambridge University Press, 1928.

Stowasser, Barbara. *Women in the Quran, Traditions, and Interpretation*. New York: Oxford University Press, 1994.

Wadud-Muhsin, Amina. *Quran and Woman*. Kuala Lumpur, Malaysia: Fajar Bakti, 1992.

Wiebke, Walther. *Woman in Islam*. Translated by C. S. V. Salt. London: George Prior, 1981.

Women and Revolution in Iran. Edited by Guity Nashat. Boulder, Colo: Westview Press, 1983.

Women in the Muslim World. Edited by Louis Beck and Nikkie Keddie. Cambridge: Harvard University Press, 1978.

Zuhur, Sharifa. *Revealing Reveiling: Islamist Gender Ideology in Contemporary Egypt*. Albany: State University of New York, 1992.

30

Muslim Women Writers

♦ Muslim Women Writers in Arabic ♦ Muslim Women Writers in Turkish
♦ Muslim Women Writers in Malay ♦ Muslim Women Writers in South Asia

♦ MUSLIM WOMEN WRITERS IN ARABIC

The early history of Islam includes a number of prominent women who, though unpublished, are credited with playing an influential role in the life of the Prophet, as well as the Muslim community; two such women were Muhammad's first wife, Khadija, and Aisha, who has been regarded, after Khadija, as his favorite wife. In later times, women such as these acted as a vitalizing force in battle, and became theologians and interpreters of the *sunna*; others, like Shajarat ad-Durr, who became Sultana during the Ayyubid dynasty (1250), ascended to power. Other women ruled from behind the scenes either as wives of caliphs or mothers of young Caliphs before their ascension to the throne. The most important of this group is Khayzuran, wife of the Abbasid Caliph al-Mahdi (775–785) and mother of the most famous Abbasid Caliph, Harun al-Rashid.

Early Women Writing in Arabic

In ancient times, the voice of the poetess al-Khansa (580–640) immortalized her brothers, Sakhr and Muawiya. Although fulfilling a duty incumbent upon women in the Jahiliyya (pre-Islamic period) to mourn their blood relatives, al-Khansa was driven by more than the call of duty to write her elegies. Sakhr, in particular, was his sister's lifeline, providing her with many of life's necessities when her husband failed to support his family. Al-Khansa's opportunities to express her independent nature and individuality were due in part to the support of the male members of her family. The mystic Rabia al-Adawiyya (717–752) contributed to the body of spiritual writings of the eighth century by dwelling on the concept of divine love. Born in Basra, Iraq to a very poor family, Rabia chose a life of asceticism and sang of her love of God in beautiful poems. Her words, like her actions, express her deep faith in and love for God:

O God, if I worship Thee for fear of Hell, burn me in Hell, and if I worship Thee in hope of Paradise, exclude me from Paradise; but if I worship Thee for Thy own sake, grudge me not Thy everlasting beauty.

Even cursory examination of the lives and works of Muslim women writers discloses that most of them worked for the improvement of social conditions. The titles of many of the modern novels carry a defiant tone, for example, *Ana Ahya* (*I Live*) by the Lebanese writer Layla Balabakki (1936–) and *Lam Naud Jawari Lakum* (*We Are Not Your Slaves Anymore*) written by the Palestinian writer Sahar Khalifa (1941–). The texts themselves are quite challenging, revealing inquisitive minds and an unwillingness to accept established norms. Most heroines demonstrate their defiance by refusing conventional marriages and choosing education instead, against parental opposition.

Subjects which have been taboo were openly debated and analyzed by women. Love, for example, is an important theme in the literature of the women writers, even in the more conservative societies of the Arabian Peninsula. Dhabya Khamees, a native of the United Arab Emirates, writes in one of her poems, "Love Poems in Time of War":

When the summer came, you had hidden in it
two wings for love.
The summer is long and encompassing.
The summer lured me, pulling my feet to the
foam of the sea.
It used to be the arms of a lover and now it has
become
A winter in the heart of warm months.

Between 1088 and 1091, another Muslim woman poet, Wallada bint al-Mistakfi contributed to the cultural life in Cordoba and challenged the political scene of the time. The image that Wallada reflected was in total contradiction to that of a traditional Muslim woman, who was expected to be modest and withdrawn. The Andalusian poet worked with two personas: one which praised her own poetic achievements unabashedly, and one describing the men who loved her and sang of her charms, both physical and mental. The two most famous of these men were Ibn Zaydun and Abu Amir bin Abdus. Wallada describing her own physical appeal and superior intellect writes, "Worthy am I, of the highest and/Proudly I walk, with head aloft." These verses bordered the right side of her robe, while the left side carried the following inscription: "My cheek I give to my lover and to those who wish them, I yield my kisses." Wallada's case is an especially interesting one as she was the daughter of al-Mustakfi, Caliph of Cordoba, who reigned briefly in 1025. This connection increased her sense of pride without suppressing her playfulness.

Muslim Spain had a second famous poetess, Hafsa bint al-Hajjaj (1136–1190). She was famous for the love poems she exchanged with the poet Abu Jafar ibn Said, whom she loved deeply. Both Hafsa and Wallada were recognized for their strong attachment to the classical poetic tradition and expressed their emotions in a natural manner.

Modern Women Writing in Arabic

The liberation of the Arab woman in modern times coincided with the Arab renaissance, or the "Awakening," as it is called. Men had become conscious of the need for and importance of women in building a modern society and made public appeals calling on women to free themselves from the yoke of debilitating traditions. The most prominent of these men were the Tunisian al-Taher al-Haddad (1899–1935) and the Egyptian Qasem Amin (1863–1908). This attitude greatly helped women find the daring and courage to fulfill their dreams. For some women, this support took the form of husbands cooperating and encouraging their wives, fathers educating their daughters, and brothers providing intellectual guidance. The Iraqi poet Jamil Sidqi al-Zahawi wrote enthusiastic verses supporting the emancipation of women:

Tear your veil, Iraqi woman
Uncover yourself, life needs change.
Tear it, burn it, don't hesitate
It was no more for you than a false curtain.

The road to women's emancipation was education. Education enabled women to voice their concerns directly through written texts (prose or verse) and facilitated their access to positions that served as platforms for their message. It must be noted that upper class and

Christian families were more inclined to educate their daughters and less apprehensive about the consequences. As a result, the emancipation movement was led by the elite and Christian Arab women, who served as role models for the middle and lower classes and facilitated the journey for them.

The demonstration led by women against the exile of Egyptian nationalist leader, Saad Zaghoul was organized by Hoda Sharawi, daughter of Muhammad Sultan Pasha, president of the first chamber in Egypt. The activities of Hoda Sharawi, an Egyptian philanthropist and member of Muslim royalty, are an example of the role played by the royal family in promoting charitable organizations that provided both medical and educational facilities for the less fortunate. When she decided to establish an intellectual association for Egyptian women, Sharawi looked to the royal family for support, as she explains in her *Memoirs:*

I mentioned the idea to some of the princesses and asked for support, which they willingly agreed to give. We met in my house to conclude plans. Princess Amina Halim presided over the gathering of princesses, Egyptians and foreign women. Thus in 1914 the Intellectual Association of Egyptian women was born.

Members of the association also included the well-known writers such as Mayy Ziyadeh and Labiba Hashim, editors of the magazine *Fatat al-Sharq (The East).*

Most women writers from all social classes rebelled in one way or another against the colonial power in their respective countries. The nobility of the goal overruled male objection to their public involvement and it gave these women a great deal of respectability. But the concerns of the writers, whether poets, novelists or journalists, encompassed a wide range of topics, including women's rights in society and within the family and literary research. These concerns are best illustrated by the writings of Iraqi poet Nazik al-Malaika (1923–1993). She is well known for her contribution to the liberation of the Arabic poem from the rigors of classical form to the ease of free verse. It is with this new form that she expresses her personal sentiments, both joyful and sad, as well as more general philosophical concerns about life and humanity.

The struggle of Arab women in modern times is also illustrated by Aisha Taymour (1840–1902), who wrote and published from her home. Her task was facilitated by an understanding father who provided her with private tutors for her education, much to the dissatisfaction of her mother. Aisha Taymour was multi-lingual and published two collections of poetry, one in Arabic, *Hilyat At-Tiraz (The Garment Ornament)* and one in

Turkish, *Shakufah*. Her poetry centers on metaphysical subjects and includes a significant number of elegies stirred by the premature death of her eldest daughter Tawhidah. While some of her poems deal with the subject of love, an even larger number deal with the *khedives* in Egypt. Taymour was a conservative in many respects. She supported the wearing of the veil and remarked disapprovingly on the growing independence of women due to what she perceived to be men's failure to protect them. Taymour also published a nonfiction work entitled *Nataif al-Ahwal fil-Aqwal wa al-Afal* (*Consequences of Conditions Regarding Matters of Speech and Actions*).

The first glimpses of feminist outlook came from a contemporary of Taymour's, Bahithat al-Badiya, pseudonym of Malak Hifni Nasef (1886–1918). She attended school, encouraged by her learned father, and taught until her marriage in 1907. Her articles were collected and published under the title *Al-Nisaiyyat* (*Women's Issues*). In her writings, Bahithat al-Badiya called for the education of women, the removal of the veil and the transformation of society, such that it would accept these changes.

Another example of a politically-minded woman writer is the Palestinian poet Fadwa Touqan (1917–) who, unlike Taymour and al-Badiya, was educated in Europe. She never married, and after the deaths of her father and brother she became active on behalf of the Palestinian issue. Touqan's brother Ibrahim played a major role in her life, particularly in the formative years of her poetic career. She acknowledged his contribution in these words: "Ibrahim looked at me in silence. Then all of sudden he said:

"I'll teach you to write poetry. Come with me." It is significant that the first poem Ibrahim used to teach his sister was an elegy by al-Khansa. Poetry for Touqan was a gate to freedom, as it allowed her to explore the spheres of the mind and the heart without encountering the obstacles posed by tradition.

A distinctive and controversial woman writer was Qout al-Qulub al-Dimirdash (1899–1968), who continued the tradition of the Demerdashiyyah Sufis. She demonstrated great respect for education and learning and hired renowned French professors to complete her education. She successfully managed her large estates and complex finances. Qout al-Qulub wrote three short stories and six novels in French, portraying Egyptian life and denouncing debilitating traditions in *Zanouba*. In another novel, *Harem*, she describes Egyptian religious and national celebrations.

Journals founded by women for women appeared as early as 1892 with Hind Nawfal's *Al-Fatah* (*The Girl*). Others followed, many of which were established by Christian Arab women. Yet, this literature did not fully achieve its mission of promoting the emancipation of Arab women, due to the high illiteracy rate among them. It was not until the middle of the twentieth century, with the spread of education, that women's journals reached their full bloom and became an important medium for women to air their problems and concerns, publish their creative works and reach a large audience.

As the majority of the first modern generation of Arab women to receive an education were Christians, names of Muslim women writers did not begin to dominate the literary scene until after the first World War. A change in the social structure of the Arab countries and a greater openness to Western culture gradually altered people's attitudes towards women's education.

The second quarter of the twentieth century is dominated by names of Muslim women who contributed to the field of creative writing and achieved high levels of education. The most outstanding names are those of Egyptian Suhair al-Qalamawi (1911–), the first Muslim woman to receive a doctorate in Humanities, and her compatriot Bint al-Shati, who received a doctorate in Arab Literature in 1950. Other Muslim women made their impact in the realm of journalism as editors of women's journals, such as Amina al-Said (1914–), who edited *Al-Misriyyah* (*The Egyptian Woman*) and *Hawwa* (*Eve*). Although very prominent in the Arab world, these three women are less known for their creative writings than for their scholarly research.

Al-Qalamawi's fiction includes a novel, *Ahadith Jaddati* (*My Grandmother's Tales*), and a collection of short stories entitled *Al-Shayatin Talhu* (*The Devils Fritter Away*), which serve to illustrate life in Egypt before 1882. Ali-Said's first novel, *Al-Jamiha*, revolves around the inner problems of a woman and her efforts to define her identity. The book marks a movement away from biographical works. Some writers have criticized conservative Islamic doctrine, while others have attempted to reexamine it as it pertains to women. Bint al-Shati (pseudonym for Aisha Abd al-Rahman), takes a modernist view of Islam's position on women's rights. She explains that the principle of women's equality with men is an Islamic concept and not one imported from the West.

Bint al-Shati voices her concern and criticism of society in her two fictional works, a collection of short stories entitled *Sirr al-Shati* (*The Secret of the Beach*) and a short novel, *Sayyid al-Izba: Qissat Imraa Khatia* (*Master of the Estate: The Story of a Sinful Woman*). The book deals with society's hostile attitude toward female children and with the sexual exploitation of women. Bint al-Shati also wrote a number of biographies of famous Muslim women, often approaching her topics from a religious perspective. She, along with Zainab al-Ghazali, is one of the few writers dealing with religious themes. The latter's approach is, however, more militant. She did not write fiction but published a biography, *Ayyam Min Hayati* (*Days of My Life*), which describes Zaynab al Ghazali's imprisonment and torture for political and religious protest.

Arab Muslim women writers have participated in all literary genres, but have made no significant contribution to the theater. Although their early concerns were the social problems that assailed their countries, they remained close to the national and political struggle of the people during the colonial rule. A few wrote in the language in which they were most proficient, which, for historical and cultural reasons, was not always Arabic. The two foreign languages most commonly by Muslim women writers are French and English. The Maghrib (northwest African) countries and Lebanon count the largest number of writers using French. The use of English by Muslim women as a medium for creative writing is a more recent phenomenon.

Most of the literature of the second half of the twentieth century follow the general trend of other world literatures. It seemed inappropriate for many writers to tackle personal themes while their countries were crushed under the yoke of colonialism. The Algerian writer Assia Djebar (1936–), who chose not to write about the personal in her first novel *La Soif*, later apologized due to political pressure. Her later novels, particularly *Les Enfants du Nouveau Monde* (*Children of the New World*) and *Les Alouetts Naives* (*Naive Larks*), were deeply anchored in the struggle for national liberation. Most writers, whether poets or novelists, succeeded in incorporating personal issues within the framework of the larger nationalistic setting. Women writers often traveled parallel paths, the sociopolitical and the personal, by which they tried to assert themselves and their rights as women.

The major socio-political issue that has polarized women writers of various nationalities is the Palestinian issue. This conflict gave birth to a huge emigration movement, spread to other geographical locations, and created major psychological repercussions that did not leave women indifferent. Some, like Sahar Khalifa, contributed to the national struggle, particularly in the *Intifadah* (uprising), and reflected her rights as a woman. Feeling betrayed by what had happened in Algeria, where women lost much of the short-lived freedom during the liberation war, the Palestinian women remained on the defensive. Khalifa portrays this difficult resistance in her novels. While the heroines are primarily preoccupied with mere survival to assure the livelihood of the family in the absence of men in *As-Sabbar* (*The Cactus*), they gradually become involved in political life in *Abbad ash-Shams* (*Sun-Flower*), and reach total participation within society in the *Intifadah* in *Bab as-Saha* (*The Gate*). Another of her novels, *Muthakkarat Imraa Ghayr Waqiiyya* (*The*

Memoirs of an Unrealistic Woman), demonstrates the close link between the feminist struggle and the national one: a woman who remains in an unhappy marriage for fear of taking responsibility for her own life is equally incapable of fighting for her own country.

The civil war in Lebanon was reflected dramatically in the fiction writings of Syrian-born Ghada al-Samman (1942–), particularly in her novels *Kawabis Beirut* (*The Nightmares of Beirut*) and *Hekayet Zahra* (*The Story of Zahra*). Al-Samman portrays the sense of imprisonment of the individual resulting from conditions in Lebanon. Corruption and hypocrisy are the dominant themes in most of Ghada as-Samman's novels. She denounces the exploitation and abuses of the poor and defenseless by the rich and mighty. In *Beirut 75*, her compassion extends to all exploited members of society, whether women in love or men struggling to survive. Another Lebanese writer, Ethel Adnan (1925–), expresses in her novel *Sitt Marie Rose* (*Miss Marie Rose*) both the unlimited forces of evil and the limitless possibilities of good.

A feminist whose militant spirit overshadows the art of fiction in her writings is Egyptian Nawal as-Sadawi. A Psychiatrist turned novelist, Sadawi uses the medium of writing to condemn a society that exploits women and muzzles their freedom, especially when women voice their rights as human beings. Sadawi has been the most vocal Arab woman activist in the last quarter of the twentieth century. Her publications are too numerous to list here, but it is informative to read her semiautobiographical novel *Muthakkarat Tabiba* (*Memoirs of a Woman Doctor*) to gain an understanding of her position. The heroine of the novel ponders society's attitude toward men and women when she asks:

"Why had society always tried to convince me that manhood was a distinction and an honour, and womanhood a weakness and a disgrace? Who was society anyway? Wasn't it men like my brother brought up from childhood to think of themselves as gods, and weak, ineffectual women like my mother?"

A close examination of Sadawi's writings reveal, in addition to the feminist streak, a deep dissatisfaction and even disgust with human vices such as exploitation of others, hypocrisy, greed, injustice, corruption, and all kinds of fraudulent behavior. She denounces society in Searching through the character Saati, who cheated his way in academia by exploiting young, aspiring researchers, and who rose in politics through flattery.

Writing by women has gradually achieved a greater maturity, which is reflected in a better understanding of the self. The Arab Muslim woman is still, however, living her revolution. She is in the experimental stage, engaged in a search for new depths through a variety of processes. For some the search will lead back to traditional Islam; for others it might lead to secular feminism.

Aida Bamia

♦ MUSLIM WOMEN WRITERS IN TURKISH

In the Turkish context modern refers to the period that begins with the foundation of the Turkish Republic under the leadership of Mustafa Kemal Ataturk in 1923. Ataturk was the commander-in-chief of the Turkish army that fought and won the Independence War (1919–1923) after the Ottoman government lost the First World War (1918), and Ottoman lands were divided between Britain, France, Italy, and Greece. Elected as the first president of the republic, Ataturk undertook a series of reforms in order to create a westernized Turkey. In 1924, the institution of the caliphate was abolished and secularism was embraced as the basic principle of the republic. The Equal Education Law of the same year brought about a number of changes. The unveiling of women was encouraged, but fell short of rendering veiling illegal, however, Ataturk continued to stress the necessity of unveiling Turkish women in his speeches. The Civil Law of 1926 ended polygamy and gave the right of divorce and child-custody to women. In 1928, with the Alphabet Law, Arabic script was replaced with Latin script. Women received the vote in local elections in 1930 and in national elections in 1934. Eighteen women deputies were elected to the National Assembly in 1934.

Ataturk emphasized cultivation and utilization women's potential because they constituted half of the population, and, therefore, half of the work force. Through the concept of civic duty that applied to women, as well as to men, a place was made for women outside the home. However, the central role of women was still the care of the family, since it was believed that the education of future generations depended on the mother. Ataturk claimed that in order to fulfill the duty of shaping the minds of children, women had to be even more educated than men. As Deniz Kandiyoti argues, the image of the new, enfranchised, unveiled woman, working side by side with men became a powerful symbolic marker of the break with the Ottoman past.

Modern Women Writers in Turkish

Halide Edip Adivar (1918–1964) started her writing career in the controversial journal *Train*, following the Young Turk revolution of 1907. She wrote primarily about educational issues, especially women's education. Her first novel, *Raikin Annesi* (*Raik's Mother*),

was published in 1909 and was followed by *Seviyye Talip* in 1910, and *Handan* in 1912. She explored the psychology of women and dilemmas of love in the figures of heroines, who saw themselves equal to men. *Yeni Turan* (*The New Turan*), published in of 1912, shows the influence of her friend the great writer, Ziya Gokalp, whose ideas on the celebration of Turkishness were just becoming popular, spurred on by the model of nationalism of other ethnic groups in the Ottoman Empire. Patriotic themes were later developed in the figures of her self-sacrificing heroines in *Atesten Gomlek* (*The Shirt of Flame*), published in 1922 (an English translation was published in 1924) and *Vurun Kahpeye* (*Strike the Harlot*) in 1926. This last work is also a strong critique of the misuse of religion by corrupt individuals for their own ends.

Halide Edip's most renowned novel is *Sinekli Bakkal* (1936); The novel, originally written in English, appeared under the title *The Clown and His Daughter* in 1935. It is centered around a grocery store in a poor neighborhood during the reign of Abdulhamid II (1876–1909). The protagonist is Rabia, a *hafiz* (one who has learned to memorize and recite the Quran) and the daughter of a grocer. She connects the neighborhood to palace circles, specifically to the mansion of a minister through her musical activities. The negotiation of different classes and their ideologies, dramatized in the juxtaposition of these social circles, is made more complex by Rabia's love affair with Peregrini, an Italian music teacher at the minister's mansion. Peregrini is also a former priest. The couple's ensuing marriage and Peregrini's conversion to Islam function as the means of synthesizing Eastern and Western values in their contribution to new Turkish identity.

Halide Edip has written twenty novels, including *Kalp Agrisi* (*Heartache*, 1924), *Zeynonum Ogul* (*Zayno's Son*, 1928), *Yopalas Cinayeti* (*The Murder of Yopalas*, 1938), *Doner Ayna* (*The Revolving Mirror*, 1954), *Akile Hanim Sokagi* (*Akile Hamin Street*, 1958), and *Hayat Parcalari* (*Bits of Life*, 1963), among others. Her stories are collected in three books; her play *Maske ve Ruh* (1945) was translated into English as *Masks or Souls?* (1953). The memoirs *Memoirs of Halide Edip* (1926) and *The Turkish Ordeal* (1928) recount her years of teaching in Istanbul, her participation in the Independence War at the rank of sergeant major, and her ensuing conflict with Ataturk, which forced her to live abroad from 1926 to 1939. Returning to Turkey following Ataturk's death, she served as deputy at the National Assembly (1950–1954) and as a professor of English literature at Istanbul University from 1940 to 1950, and again after 1954. Her historical writings include: *Turkey Faces West* (1930), *The Conflict of East and West in Turkey* (1930), and *Inside India* (1937).

Halide Edip dominated the literary scene as the only canonical female writer until the 1960s, although Suat Dervis (1905–1972), prolific author of fifteen socialist realist works such as *Kara Kitap* (*Black Book*, 1920), *Emine* (1931), *Fosforlu Cevriye* (*Flashy Cevriye*, 1968), and *Ankara Mahpusu* (*The Prisoner of Ankara*, 1968), is currently being rediscovered.

The recent history of Turkey has been marked by three military coups which have shaped literary tastes and practices. The first took place in 1960, leading to greater social liberties and rights with the constitutional changes it brought. It is in this climate that women authors turned to the treatment of gender-related issues, since most women authors tended to share the ideals of leftist politics. The second coup of 1971 was geared toward suppressing anarchic Marxist activity. This coup brought into literature the type of revolutionary who fights against the wrongs of the social order only to be punished for his or her misunderstood and unappreciated self-sacrifice. The third coup of 1980, which temporarily outlawed all political parties, depoliticized life and literature, and ushered in the age of individualism. As argued by sociologist Sirin Tekeli, this depoliticization engendered an indigenous feminist movement. Women activists who had directed their energies to the class struggles of the Marxist cliques that promised them liberation were freed from the male-dominated, hierarchical structures of these groups when they were banned. In the absence of these groups, in which men claimed to speak also for women, women acquired their own voice. Currently diverse feminist groups continue to challenge the boundaries of female liberties defined by the state feminism put in place by Kemalist reforms.

During the 1960s and 1970s the number of women writers increased; currently women writers outnumber male writers. Women writers brought not only new themes, but also new styles of writing into Turkish literature. Experiments with multiple narrations that contrast the differing points of view of the characters is common. Contemporary women authors have played with linear sequences of time, altering the order of the past, present and future through memories, dreams, and flashbacks.

Leyla Erbil (1931–) is the author of *Hallac* (*The Wood-Carver*, 1961), *Gecede* (*In the Night*, 1969), *Tuhaf Bir Kadin* (*A Strange Woman*, 1971), and *Karanligin Gunu* (*The Day of Darkness*, 1985), among others. In her most widely discussed work, *Tuhaf Bir Kadin* (*A Strange Woman*), she follows the life of a university student/poet who is initiated into political activity by her first lover and who devotes her life to raising the consciousness of working classes, only to be rejected by them at the end. The novel intertwines the perspectives of three protagonists, culminating in a dream sequence which questions whether any of the events in the novel happened after all.

Adalet Agaoglu (1929–), a playwright, essayist, and author, is most famous for her trilogy *Olmeye Yatmak* (*Lying Down to Die*, 1973), *Bir Dugun Gecesi* (*A Wedding Night*, 1979), and *Hayir* (*No*, 1987) which portray the life of Aysel, a sociology professor in Ankara. The novels present a wide social panorama of Turkish society from 1930 to 1980. Inner monologues of the characters, who come from all classes, are broken up and complemented with a collage of newspaper articles, official government reports, diaries, and letters. The first novel depicts Aysel's suicide attempt caused by her unhappy realization that her professional accomplishments do not save her from the fate of being a woman and a second-class citizen. In the last novel of the trilogy, Aysel decides to reject a prize that honors her academic work and to attempt suicide for a final time.

Furuzan (1935–) revitalized the writing of the short story with such books as *Parasiz Yatili* (*Room and Board Free*, 1971), *Kusatma* (*Conquest*, 1972), *Benim Sinemalarim* (*My Cinemas*, 1973), *Gecenin Oteki Yuzu* (*The Other Side of Night*, 1982), among others. She depicts single women who are able to survive on their own. In her writing she champions the ethnic Turkish refugees who came to Turkey from the Balkans in the twenties and thirties by celebrating their dignity, honesty, and work ethic. Inner voices of several characters coexist in the web of her richly complex narratives, which move forward with inner epiphanies rather than external events.

Nezihe Merc (1925–), Sevim Burak (1931–1983), Sevgi Soysal (1936–1976), Tomris Uyar (1941–), Aysel Ozakin (1942–), Pinar Kur (1943–) and Inci Aral (1944–) are a few of the many prolific women writers who have challenged the traditional themes and/or structural notions of plot, time, and character in realist fiction. They have critiqued the institutions of marriage and family and have analyzed the concepts of love, motherhood, and sexuality through the lens of female identity. Sexuality emerges in their writing as the discourse of suppressed female identity, which can be reclaimed in the name of an autonomous and freed self. Their writing is socially contextualized, with women and the lower classes becoming interchangeable metonymies for the powerless under patriarchy. Their overall voice is individualistic, rebellious, and in opposition to the traditional definitions of both society and literature.

One of the most innovative authors is Nzali Eray (1945–). Since her writing debut in 1976, Nzali Eray has exploded the unity of time, place, and identity in her fantastic, surrealist stories that liberate the individual through imaginative openings of definitions. Through a joyful deconstruction, she creates a new world in which boundaries of established categories are transcended. For example, in these new worlds, the dead can come back to visit their relatives for a daily outing, man can become pregnant, characters can fly over the world on a magic carpet, and past and present selves of the same person can call each other on the phone. Her books include *Hazir Dunya* (*Ready World*, 1983), *Deniz Kenarinda Pazartesi* (*Monday by the Sea*, 1984), *Yoldan Gecen Oykuler* (*Stories that Pass by the Road*, 1987), and *Arzu Sapaginda Inecek Var* (*Somebody Wants to Get Off at the Sidestreet Called Desire*, 1989).

Latife Tekin (1957–) has interjected into Turkish fiction a new description of the squatter settlement, derived from her own experience of growing up in a squatter area outside Istanbul. Although she depicts the poverty and harshness of the lives of the people there, she celebrates their ability to survive through gentle humor, sharp irony, and a striking sense of magical realism. Each of her four novels is a different experiment with postmodernism: *Sevgili Arsiz Olum* (*Dear Cheeky Death*, 1983), *Berci Kristin Cop Masallari* (An English translation, *Berci Kristin: Tales from the Garbage Hills*, appeared in 1993), *Gece Dersleri* (*Night Lessons*, 1986), and *Buzdan Kulichar* (*Swords of Ice*, 1989).

This is only a general survey; there are many other Turkish women authors. Furthermore, their number is growing every day, which indicates that women writers will continue to be a dominate presence in Turkish literature.

Sibel Erol

♦ MUSLIM WOMEN WRITERS IN MALAY

Women have played an important part in shaping the history of Malaysia. They worked alongside men to gain independence from British colonial rule in 1957 and have made their mark in politics, education, academia, literature and the media. A survey of women writers in modern Malay literature, however, reveals that women's literary contributions remain in the minority compared to those of men. This status and the cultural conditions behind it are slowly being reformed.

Early Women Writers in Malay

One of the pioneers and champions for the education of girls was Zainon Sulaiman, who was fondly known as Ibn Zain. She was a teacher as well as political activist. Through her initiative and foresight, she founded the Persatuan Guru-Guru Perempuan Melayu Johore (The Jahore Malay Women Teachers Association) in 1929.

In her paper on "Women Fiction Writers and Images of Women in Modern Malay Literature," Ungku Maimunah M. Tahir said that *Bulan Melayu* (*Malay Monthly*), the Association's official mouthpiece, was considered the first women's magazine published in Malaysia. It also was the first and only magazine to be run and managed by women. Founded in 1930, the *Malay Monthly* recognized the need for a women's forum through which they could voice their opinion on issues affecting them and create space for an exchange of ideas. Special columns such as "*Cerita*" ("Stories") gave the opportunity for women to submit their stories, usually centered around the theme of marriage and family.

Malay Monthly paved the way for the publication of other women's magazines, for example, *Kemajuan Perempuan* (*Women's Progress*), *Dewan Perempuan* (*Women's Council*), *Lidah Ibu* (*Mother's Tongue*) and *Dunia Perempuan* (*Women's World*). The titles themselves spoke of the ambition of these women.

Although opportunities were there, literary works by women were not particularly encouraged from the 1930s through the 1950s. This reflected a general bias against women's involvement in public life at the time of British rule. During the twenties and up to World War II, Malay parents did not give great emphasis to the education of their daughters. They were reluctant to send their daughters to schools, especially to English schools, as they felt that it was more appropriate to provide a traditional upbringing that would be necessary for marriage and raising a family. English schools run by Christian missionaries were also seen as a threat. Parents felt that, if their daughters went to these schools, they would be converted to Christianity. The few Malay families, who sent their daughters to English schools, tended to be ostracized by society and were objects of gossip. Daughters generally received basic education in Malay schools until attaining puberty. Parents would then arrange for them to be married. Early writings by women writers are thus in the Malay language, a medium used by the majority of Malay women writers until today.

As far back as the year 1900, the weaknesses of and problems faced by Malays were highlighted in the newspaper *Al-Imam*, run by a group of young Malay men. One such writer was Syed Sheikh al-Hadi, whose ideas were considered advanced for the time. As editor of *Al-Imam*, he focused on important social issues of the Malays, who were perceived by the British as backward and lacking in initiative. The editorial provided a platform for him to champion the importance of education, and to encourage the Malays to better themselves through education while at the same time upholding the values and spirit of Islam.

In his novel, *Faridah Hanum*, written in 1925, al-Hadi became the first Malay male Muslim writer to address the social status of women. According to the thesis by Rosnah Binti Baharudin on the "Role and Status of Women in Malaysia Between 1957–1975 based on Novels by Women Novelists," *Faridah Hanum* marks the emergence of a form of literature new in Malay. This novel is about the love story of Faridah Hanum and Shafik Affendi. In the story Faridah Hanum is forced by her father to marry her cousin, although she initially refuses his proposal. As a result, the marriage fails. Finally, after overcoming several obstacles, she is reunited with Affendi.

In another novel, *Iakah Salmah* by Ahmad Rashid Talu, the main character, Salmah, fights for her rights. Between the 1930s and 1950s there was already a movement by Malay youths to raise the question of education for women, frowned upon by Malay society in general. These young male writers were fighting for women's rights as early as the 1920s, before women themselves became vocal enough to fight for their own rights. It was at this time that the Sultan Idris Training College was established. Most of these young men were the products of this College which, over the years, was to produce literary and nationalist figures.

With the development of modern education in Malaysia for women, Muslim women writers, following the new literary trend, began to write short stories, novels and poetry. The majority of these pioneer writers were either teachers or journalists.

The first short story by a woman writer to appear on the Malay literary scene was "Kesedihan Perkhawinan Paksa" ("Grief of a Forced Marriage") by Hasnah. Published in 1934, it was followed by another short story "Waktu Ishak Menangkap Pencuri" (At Night to Catch a Thief") by Siti Nurmah.

In 1941, Rafiah Yusuf became the first Malay woman to write a novel, which was entitled *Cinta Budiman* (*Wise Love*). Kamariah Saadon followed suit with the novel *Dua Pengembara* (*Two Adventurers*). Soon the various women's magazines were flooded with literary works by women. The themes centered around family and home issues, as these publications were an extension of their lives. Compared to the writings by North American women at the same time, whose works were about oppression and gender bias, the writings by Malay women appear domestic and perhaps somewhat "unliberated."

Most of these writings during the period up to the fifties were believed to be lacking in literary quality. Some of these women stopped writing after the completion of a few novels. It should be noted that the majority of them were from urban centers, especially from Johor (in the southern part of Peninsular Malaysia, and considered at that time to be progressive and modern), and the island city of Singapore. The liberal attitude of parents in these big cities toward education for girls

and the exposure to modernization were among several factors that contributed to the emergence of women writers.

In spite of this, the participation by women on the literary scene was minimal. Various programs were created to encourage more women to write. One of them was a writing competition. For instance, the magazine *Ibu* (*Mother*) had a short story competition for its first issue in October 1952. Again the theme was centered around women and the family.

Critic and journalist, Rayuan Sukma has said that this state of affairs was related to parental attitudes, which circumscribed their daughters' education pursuits. Even when the girls were given an education, they were made to leave school half-way through to set up a home. It was, thus, unlikely that women's names would crop up in the literary scene.

Modern Women Writing in Malay

It was during the 1960s that literary production by women in Malay began to make its mark. Several notable women novelists who had some formal training in the art of writing appeared on the scene. The most prolific among them was Saleha Abdul Rashid, who is better known by her pseudonym, Salmi Manja. Salmi received her education in an Arab school as well an English school in Singapore. She was fortunate to take courses in creative writing and literature from a well-known editor, Harun Aminurrashid. Because of her desire to learn and to improve her skills in creative writing, she corresponded with well-known male writers like the poet laureates Usman Awang and A. Samad Said. She later married A. Samad Said.

Salmi's writing career began when she was a journalist at a Malay language newspaper. She wrote poetry and short stories that appeared in several Malay language newspapers and magazines. Her first novel, *Hari Mana Bulan Mana* (*What Day, What Month*) was published in 1960. In 1968, she published three novels, *Sayang Ustazah Sayang* (*A Pity, Ustazah, A Pity*), *Rindu Hilang Di Tapak Tangan* (*Longing Vanishes in the Palm of the Hand*) and *Entah Mengapa Hatiku Duka* (*Why Does My Heart Grieve*).

Yahaya Ismail, the writer and critic, has referred to most of Salmi's fiction as "love stories and women's chatter." Such criticism seems typical of male literary critics in Malaysia. One of the reasons why Salmi and other women writers of her time portrayed women as main characters in their writings was because novels written by men depicted women in secondary and degrading roles, and avoided the domestic issues and problems faced by women. These women writers wanted to provide a balance to the thematic stereotyping of women.

It was during this period that a teenager by the name

of Khalidah Adibah Amin appeared on the literary scene with her novels focusing on the lives of young women. Her first novel, *Puteri Asli,* was published in 1949. This was followed by two more novels, *Gadis Sipu* and *Bangsawan Tulen.* Her novels addressed the concerns of younger women and acted as a moral guide. Her *Bangsawan Tulen* addressed social issues, especially criticizing the Malay royalty for their ostentation and pride. She also contributed short stories to the magazine, *Ibu,* with the encouragement and support of her mother, Ibu Zain. Eighteen years later, in 1968, she came out with another novel, *Seroja Masih de Kolam* (*The Lily is Still in the Pond*), a story about a young girl who is engaged to a man she does not love. In 1983, she published another novel, *Tempat Jatuh Lagi Dikenang,* considered to be an autobiography of her childhood days.

Adibah Amin is a prolific writer, very conversant in both Malay and English, a rare combination since the majority of writers are skilled in only one language. She was educated in Malay, English and Arabic. She started her career as a teacher, later becoming a columnist under the pseudonym Seri Delima in the column "As I Was Passing" for *The New Straits Times,* one of Malaysia's leading English language dailies. She shows great insight into the lives and customs of the different ethnic groups in Malaysia, and has a flair for painting a delightful picture of common everyday things that she sees and hears as she passes on her way through life. Her column "To Know Bahasa Malaysia" expresses the cultural diversity of different groups and the linguistic and literary variety of the uses of Malay.

Besides being a columnist, she was appointed Special Advisor to the Group Editor, a post never before held by a woman. She has won several awards for her writing, including the Asian Journalist of the Year Award by the Press Foundation of Asia-Matsui in 1979 and the South-East Writer Award in 1983. She was also conferred an honorary degree for literary works from English to Malay by the National University.

Among other writers concerned with the position of women, especially Malay women, is Anis Sabirin. As a daughter of a Malay book publisher, she was fortunate to be exposed to literary works published in Malaysia and Indonesia. She began writing short stories when she was at the university. Her works revealed the conflicts and tensions that she experienced as she observed the discrimination faced by women, especially among the educated who are intelligent and ambitious, but are not given the same recognition as their male counterparts. Thus her feelings and views about herself and other women not only become the main theme of her poems and short stories, such as *Dari Bayang ke Bayang,* but also the main issue discussed in her collected essays entitled *Peranan Wanita Baru* (*The Role*

of the New Woman). She believes very strongly that women have an important role to play and can contribute a great deal to society.

At a forum on "Women and Sex in Malay Novels" organized by the National Writers Organization in 1963, Anis Sabrin was the only woman to debate the topic. She boldly opposed the views of other well-known presentors, and was very critical about the negative image of women being portrayed in novels written by men. She has a Ph.D. in economics from the Claremont Graduate School in California and worked at the Malaysian Commercial Section in Los Angles for many years. She is currently a guest writer at the Language and Literary Agency in Kuala Lumpur.

Another writer and well-known artist, Siti Zainon Ismail, who wrote her dissertation on the concept of Malay traditional costumes, has won several awards for her literary contributions, including Malaysia's Literary Award and the South-East Asian Writers' Award. Her poems and short stories deal with her personal experiences and use symbolism to express her feelings about life. Some of her major publications include *Tekstil Tenunan Melayu* (*Malay Woven Textile,* 1986), *Rekabentuk Kraftangan Melayu Tradisi* (*Design of Malay Traditional Handicrafts,* 1986), and *Alam Puisi* (*The World of Poetry,* 1994).

The late poet Zaihasra concentrated on religious themes in her poems during the last five years of her life. Another prolific poet and winner of several literary awards is Zurinah Hassan. The main themes of her poems are women's experiences and issues of patriotism.

The resurgence of Islamic fundamentalism in the late seventies brought about different perceptions of what Islam really means within the Muslim community in Malaysia. It was during this time that a young journalist, Zainah Anwar, decided to do her Masters thesis on the religious fervor affecting students who were just coming back from their studies abroad. The result of her research was published in a book titled *Islamic Resurgence in Malaysia.*

About the same time, another young journalist, Rose Ismail, also became concerned about the impact of fundamentalist ideas on women. She felt that the Islam she knew and grew up with was being questioned. Rose Ismail is the feature editor of one of Malaysia's English dailies, *The New Straits Times.* Her articles focused on the discrimination of women in the name of Islam. She believes that it is not Islam that looks down on women, but rather some religious leaders who have interpreted it in a way that presents men as superior to women. The spirit of Islam—love, mercy and respect of one human being for another as enshrined in the Quran—has not been addressed by those who take a narrow and literalist view of Muslim teaching.

Both Zainah Anwar and Rose Ismail are members of

a newly formed group of eight women who call themselves "Sisters in Islam." In 1987, they started as a support group for women and women's organizations interested in women and Islam. In the course of sharing their experiences, they evolved into a study group looking at issues of gender and women's rights in the context of Islam. In 1991 the group published two booklets, *Are Women and Men Equal Before Allah?* and *Are Muslim Men Allowed to Beat Their Wives?* in English and Malay.

A Women Writers Seminar in March 1969 brought together women writers throughout Malaysia. It was the first time that such a gathering of literary women took place. At this seminar a resolution was passed urging publishing houses to have more publications on women for women. A few months later, one of Malaysia's leading language dailies, Utusan Melayu Group, came out with a monthly magazine called *Wanita* (*Woman*), which touches on topics ranging from fashion and cooking to health and women in politics. Following the success of this magazine, other women's magazines written in Malay and English began to flood the market such as *Jelita* (*Beautiful*), *Keluarga* (*Family*), *Her World*, *Female*, *Nona* (*Woman*), and *Women At Work*. There is a fiction feature in most of these publications.

There was a shift in the portrayal of women in novels published from the seventies onwards. Writers like Khadijah Hashim and Zaharah Nawawi present their women characters in a more positive light. Khadijah's novels *Badai Semalam* (1968), *Pelangi Pagi* (1971), *Dekat Disayang Jauh Dikenang* (1985), and *Laila Azwa Gadisku* (1986) emphasized the importance of education for girls, who were then free to choose their careers. Zaharah Nawawi's *Sebelum Berhujungnya Musim Bunga* (1972) and *Jalur Sinar di Celah Daun* (1981) also portray her women characters as strong and decisive. Zaharah has been described as a feminist writer because of her characterization of women. In most of her writings, she addresses issues of education for women and women's right to make decisions for themselves so that they become a model for the younger generation. She also writes children's stories. She was a journalist and is currently the editor of the magazine *Timang*, a publication of the National Population and Family Development Board.

Like Zaharah, Kahdijah was also a journalist. Prior to working for the Malay language daily, *Berita Harian*, she was also a religious teacher. She left *Berita Harian* to form her own publishing house. A very successful publisher, her novels are very popular among the young. One of her books, *Badai Semalam*, is used as a text book in schools, and her novel *Merpati Putih Terbang Lagi* (*The White Dove Flies Again*) has been translated into English. This latter novel won a

consolation prize in a novel competition organized by the Language and Literary Agency, making her the first woman novelist to win such a prize.

An exhibition on "Women and Creativity" in 1990 brought together women artists and writers for the first time. The writings by women included not only literary works, but also academic writings. Recently, the Language and Literary Agency launched a publication entitled *Mustika Diri: Bunga Rampai Karya Wanita 1930–1990*. At a panel discussion in November 1994, the participants discussed how writings by women can address broader issues of gender, the public's perceptions of women and their changing roles, and critical social issues such as domestic violence and discrimination based on gender. The broader participation of Muslim women in all aspects of national life is bound to translate into a continuing growth in literary and artistic activities.

Shariafah Zuriah Aljeffri

◆ MUSLIM WOMEN WRITERS IN SOUTH ASIA

As yet, no major scholarly exploration of the contribution made by Muslim women to the rich and linguistically varied literary traditions of South Asia has been undertaken. That task is likely to gain impetus as scholars in the field of South Asian studies continue to recover what could be called the "silent voices" of the many literate and erudite women who have contributed to the oral tradition and written Muslim literatures of South Asia. That task will entail a systematic examination of a vast corpus of oral and textual materials. This chapter represents only a preliminary exposition of some of the figures and themes.

Early Women Writers in South Asia

One major resource for the contribution of women writing from the tenth to sixteenth centuries, is the collection of South Asian biographical dictionaries that might yield information concerning the existence of the activities and writings of women of note. Rabia al-Quzdariya, from Quzdar, was one of the earliest women poets to write in Persian during the tenth century. However, neither Abul-Fazl nor Badayuni, the two well-known compilers of biographies from medieval Muslim India, name any women poets or writers. Gulbadan (born circa 1523), the daughter of the first Mughal emperor, wrote an account of all she had heard and remembered of the reigns of her father, Babur (1483–1530), and brother, Humayun (1508–1556), at the behest of her famous nephew, the Emperor Akbar. This work, entitled the *Humayun-nama* (*The History of Humayun*), probably served as a source for Abul-Fazl, Akbar's court historian. The *Humayuni-nama* is a concise and sensitive portrait of the major events occurring during the reigns of these emperors and provides much information about the *harim*, or women's quarters, with respect to both to the engagement of Mughal royal women with affairs of court and state and to the minute details pertaining to *harim* life and customs. From Gulbadan's account, it is clear that a tradition of schooling in the religious sciences and literary erudition was accessible to royal women, especially during the reign of Akbar, who took a great deal of interest in the education of the princesses and established a school for girls at Fathepur Sikri. Several women connected with the court were appointed as tutors for the young princesses, including Sati un-Nisa and Hafiza Maryam. Gulbadan also makes frequent mention of the storyteller and singer Sarv Qad.

Akbar's son, Jahangir, and his queen, Nur Jahan, herself a poet who wrote under the *takhallus* (nom-de-plume) Makhfi (the Hidden One), were patrons of poets. Their granddaughter, Jahanara (1614–1689), the daughter of Shah Jahan, authored several works in Persian. Jahanara wrote a biography of the Sufi saint Khwaja Muin al-Din Chishti titled *Munis ul-Arwah*, as well as a mystical treatise titled *Khazain ul-Asfiya*. One of her short works is dedicated to Mulla Shah Badakhshi (died 1661), who served as spiritual director for Jahanara and her ill-fated brother, Dara Shikoh, a writer of mystical treatises. Just as the most powerful Mughal queen, Nur Jahan, authored an epitaph expressing humility ("Let there be neither a light nor a flower/ On the grave of this humble person/ Nor the wings of the moth burn [in the flame of love]/ Nor the *bulbul* send out her wailing cry"), Jahanara's self-written epitaph bears testimony to her mystical outlook on poverty in the face of divine wealth ("Let nothing cover my grave except the green grass/ For the green turf is covering enough for the poor").

Jahanara's niece, Zaib un-Nisa (Zebunnisa) (1638–1689?), the daughter of Emperor Aurangzeb, was tutored by Hafiza Maryam and by Mulla Said Ashraf Mazandarani, a poet. A proficient mathematician, Zaib un-Nisa also developed poetic skills in the company of other poets and was known as a patron of the arts, endowing and sponsoring artists with her wealth until her imprisonment by Aurangzeb in 1681. She initially wrote in Arabic, but composed her better-known *Divan-i Makhfi* in Persian. The following example reveals the mystical tenor of her *ghazals*, or love poetry:

I have no peace, the quarry I, a Hunter chases
me,
It is Thy memory;
I turn to flee, but fall; for over me he casts his
snare,
Thy perfumed hair.

Who can escape Thy prison? no mortal heart is
free
From dreams of Thee.

Her *ghazals* reveal a masterly hand and are filled at once with sorrow, despair, mystic love, and a refusal to bow to the tragic circumstances that surrounded her life. Zaib un-Nisa's letters also have been collected and translated, and bear testimony to her literary contributions in prose.

Very little information can be uncovered about women writers from the decline of the Mughals to the advent of British political control of the Indian subcontinent. Annemarie Schimmel, in her *Classical Urdu Literature from the Beginning to Iqbal*, mentions Ganna Begum (circa late 18th century), as a noted Urdu poet, but does not give any additional information except that she was the wife of Imadulmulk (died 1800) and wrote under the pen-name Nizam. Nor does Schimmel mention any women writers in her purview of Sindhi Literature; apart from the aforementioned Jahanara and Zaib un-Nisa, women writers are not mentioned in *Islamic Literatures of India*. This is not to say that women did not compose poetic or literary works, only that such works were not included in the literary canons of the day and, hence, may be lost to posterity or require deeper investigation to be reclaimed. T. Grahame Bailey's landmark study, *A History of Urdu Literature*, similarly omits mention of any women writers, underscoring the point that women writers were consistently marginalized.

It is possible that the sphere of women's contributions to literature, whether preserved or not, may lie within the realm of the Sufi world. Jahanara entered one of the major Sufi orders in Muslim India, the Qadiriyya, and earned the esteem of her master, Mulla Shah, while Bibi Jamal Khatun (died 1639), the sister of Jahanara's first preceptor, Mian Mir, was considered to be one of the foremost saints of the Qadiriyya order. In addition, there are many shrines to women saints throughout the Indian subcontinent, including the province of Sind, suggesting that there were oral accounts associated with these saints that may or may not have been preserved for later generations. In this context, the oral compositions of Sayyida Imam Begum (circa mid-nineteenth century) may be mentioned. Although she may have composed many works, only a handful of her devotional songs or *ginans* dealing with mystical themes are preserved in Ismaili Khoja literature. Women's oral compositions may have also originated among the artistic castes, that is, women who were renowned for their education, high culture, mastery over the musical and performing arts, and who were often also high-class courtesans. The *ghazals* of one such accomplished singer and poet, Mahlaqa Bai

Chanda (1767–1824), were posthumously compiled in a work titled *Gulzar-i Mahlaqa* (*Mahlaqa's Garden of Flowers*) in which the use of Sufi tropes suggests poetry embodying the vicissitudes of both physical and spiritual love.

Modern Women Writers in South Asia

Nineteenth- and twentieth-century literary writings by women span the period in Indian history that saw the birth of the Reform and Nationalist movements, the agitation for Independence, and the post-Independence era. Susie Tharu and K. Lalita, in their pathbreaking anthology *Women Writing in India: 600 B.C. to the Present*, have treated "women's texts as engaged in negotiation, debate, and protest, invariably in areas that directly concern, or are closely related to, what it means to be a woman. [They] are therefore documents of historical struggles over the making of citizen-selves and nation-worlds." That is, women's writings are not unconnected to the larger discourses of defining freedom and equality under colonial rule, reconfiguring Indianness in the movement toward nationhood, and the "internal restructuring" of the nation after Independence within the policies defined by government leaders. At the same time, writings by women raise, examine, renegotiate, and protest issues that are connected intimately to their concerns with the politics of gender, class, tradition, and access to political institutions.

These issues are explored in far greater depth and detail than it is possible to recount here; suffice to note that, although the writings of Muslim women address issues that are their "real tasks in a real world," these writings must be understood within the larger frameworks of both the social re-imagining that was, and is, taking place within the Indian subcontinent as well as the reconfiguration of gender politics. Further, it should be mentioned that in recent decades Muslim women sociologists, anthropologists, and historians, among other Muslim women intellectuals, have created a wealth of literature that has addressed the legal, social, and educational aspects of Muslim women's lives.

In a short story titled "Sultana's Dream," Rokeya Sakhawat Hossain (1880–1932) constructs a utopian fantasy in which men are relegated to a *murdana* (comparable to the *zenana* or women's quarters) and women are in charge of the public sphere. An untiring activist against what she termed "the *purdah* (veil) of ignorance," she set up a school for girls and was involved in the Anjuman-e Khawatin-e Islam (the Association for Muslim Women). Her many essays and writings include the two-volume *Motichur* (*Pearl Dust*), published in 1905; *Pipasa* (*Thirst*), written in Urdu and published in 1922; and the novel *Padmaraga* (*Ruby*), written in Bengali. In her essays she tackles

with wit and humor the often ridiculous predicaments of women restricted by *purdah*, a stance that met with censure in orthodox religious circles.

While Rokeya Sakhawat Hossain wrote in Calcutta and was educated at home, Nazar Sajjad Hyder (1894–1967) was born in the North-West Frontier Province into a literary family. Her paternal aunt Akbari Begum gained popularity as the author of *Goodar-ka-Lal* (*A Gem in Rags*), published in 1908. Nazar Sajjah Hyder (also known by her maiden name Bint-e-Nazrul Baqar) began publishing articles and stories at an early age in prestigious journals such as *Makhzan*, *Khatoon*, *Ismat*, and *Tehzib Niswan*. She gave up wearing the veil in 1923, and her writings evince a keen engagement with social issues such as bigamy, forced marriages, the constraints of *purdah*, and the impact of Westernization. Among her writings are the well-known *Akhtarunnissa Begum*, published in 1910; *Ahi-Mazlooman* (*The Sigh of the Oppressed*), published in 1913; *Jan Baaz* (*The Valiant*), published in 1930; *Suraiya*, published in 1933; and *Najma*, published in 1939. In addition to writing, she was also involved in setting up girls' schools, including the Muslim Girls' College at Aligarh, and is credited with the decision many leading North Indian Muslim families made to send their daughters to college and to discard *purdah*. Her literary legacy is continued by her daughter, the famous writer Qurratulain Hyder.

The social issues addressed by Nazar Sajjad Hyder were fervently taken up by Rasheed Jahan (1905–1952), a passionate and eloquent campaigner for changes in women's conditions. She graduated from medical school in 1931, the same year in which an anthology titled *Angare*, containing two of her works, was published. One of these, a play entitled *Parde ke Piche* (*Behind the Veil*), discussed the plight of women rejected by their husbands for trivial reasons and addressed issues pertaining to abortion. Such subjects earned her, as well as her near contemporary Rokeya Sakhawat Hossain, the spirited wrath of religious leaders. She was warned that she would be kidnapped if she did not desist from writing about such issues. Very much a part of the Progressive Writers' Association, Rasheed Jahan was a strong Marxist and directed some of her energies toward the Communist cause. In addition to editing a political journal called *Chingari* (*Sparks*), Rasheed Jahan was committed to combatting poverty and illness, and addressed issues of social injustice in her writings. Her short stories and plays were collected posthumously under the title *Woh aur Dusre Afsane wa Drame* (*That One and Other Short Stories and Plays*), which was published in 1977, a quarter century after her premature death at the age of forty-seven. The impact of both her charismatic personality and writings has been acknowledged by such writers as

Faiz Ahmad Faiz, Ismat Chugtai, and Siddqa Begum Sevharvi, among others.

Ismat Chugtai (1915–1992) trained as a teacher at Aligarh Muslim University, despite family resistance, and turned to full-time writing after a short stint at teaching in 1943. Like many of the writers belonging to the Progressive Writers' Association, Ismat Chugtai wrote about the oppressed with a distinct subtlety and brilliance. Her masterly critique of middle-class family life comes through in her stories written in Urdu and compiled in such works as *Choten* (*Wounds*), published in 1943; *Kaliyan* (*Buds*), published in 1945; and *Chui Mui* (*Touch-Me-Not*), published in 1952. In a story written in 1941 titled *Lihaf* (*The Quilt*), Ismat Chugtai cleverly—and courageously—explores alternative forms of sexuality through the eyes of a child witnessing a lesbian relationship, leading to charges of obscenity that she successfully withstood. The novels *Ziddi* (*The Stubborn One*), published in 1941, and *Terhi Lakir* (*Crooked Line*), published in 1943, are explicitly feminist works.

Another subtle challenge to middle class mores comes from the writer Razia Sajjad Zaheer (1917–1979), who married the socialist thinker and political revolutionary Sajjad Zaheer, who compiled and co-authored the collection *Angare* that rocketed Rasheed Jahan to fame. In her story "Neech" ("Lowborn"), published in 1984 in a collection of her short stories entitled *Allah De Banda Le* (*God Gives and the Devotee Takes*), Razia Sajjad Zaheer explores how a working class woman questions her mistress' morality, middle-class complacency, and inner strength. Her publications include a short novel, *Sar-e-Sham* (*At Dusk*), published in 1953; *Kante* (*Thorns*), published in 1954; *Suman*, published in 1963; as well as the collection of short stories *Zard Gulab* (*The Yellow Rose*), published in 1981. Known also as a translator, Razia Sajjad Zaheer received public acclaim with the prestigious Nehru Award in 1966 and the Uttar Pradesh State Sahitya Academy Award in 1972.

Siddiqa Begum Sevharvi (1925–) was introduced to European thought and the Progressive Writers' Association by Rasheed Jahan, who thus inspired her to begin a literary career. Devoted to causes pertaining to social injustice, Siddiqa Begum Sevharvi published an anthology of her short stories entitled *Hichkiyan* (*Hiccups*) in 1944, and went on to edit and publish the magazine *Nauras* (*The Mellowing*). More anthologies of her short stories followed with *Palkon Mein Ansu* (*Tears in Eyelashes*) in 1947, *Raqs-e-Bismil* (*Dance of the Wounded*), *Dudh Aur Khun* (*Milk and Blood*) in 1952, and *Thikre Ki Marg* (*Engagement at Birth*) in 1957. In a short story titled "Tare Laraz Rahe Hai" ("The Stars are Trembling"), she addresses the issue of access to education, which is denied to a young bride while her husband supports his younger sister's college education. It poignantly explores the shutting of life's windows once marriage takes place, as expressed in the mother-in-law's words: "The moment a girl is married—she may be only twelve—she is no longer young. These glowing cheeks last only a few days. Then, when something stirs in the belly, it's all up."

Siddiqa Begum Sevharvi's contemporary, Sajida Zaidi (1926–), was educated at Aligarh University and the University of London, and taught education at Aligarh from 1955 until her retirement. She began writing poetry in Urdu in 1958, having been introduced to the verses of Ghalib, Iqbal and Hafiz by her father. Her works evince her exploration of the religious frame of mind, of socialism as an ideology, of humanism, and, in her current stage, of existentialism. Her first anthology of poetry, *Ju-e-Naghma* (*Stream of Melody*), appeared in 1962; this work was followed by *Aatish-e-Sayyal* (*Liquid Fire*) in 1972 and *Sel-e-Wujud* (*Flow of Existence*) in 1986. Sajida Zaidi has named Nietzche, Jung, Sartre and Kafka among those who have influenced her work, which bear traces of existentialist themes. "Existentialism is, in the West," she says, "the inevitable result of people's alienation in a machine-ridden society, and in the East, a result of religious and political tyranny and the breakdown of human values and relationships."

Another eminent Muslim woman poet is Zahida Zaidi (1930–), who was educated at Cambridge and taught English at the University of Delhi and at Aligarh University. Her first collection of poems, *Zahr-e-Hyat* (*Life's Poison*), appeared in 1970 and won the Urdu Academy Award in 1971. *Dharti ka Lams* (*Touch of Earth*) was published in 1975, and two collections of poetry written in English, *Beyond Words* and *Broken Pieces*, were published in 1979. In addition to being a poet and scholar, Zahida Zaidi is renowned as a translator of the plays of Anton Chekhov, Luigi Pirandello, Jean-Paul Sartre, and Samuel Beckett as well as the poetry of Pablo Neruda, among others, into Urdu. She has also staged several plays.

The poetry written by the renowned tragic–actress and singer, Meena Kumari, was posthumously compiled in *Tanha Chand* (*The Solitary Moon*). Born in 1932 to Iqbal Begum, an actress, and Ali Bux, a music director, Meena Kumari, began acting at age four to help support the family upon her father's illness, and in time gained both fame and wealth. She wrote under the pen-name Naz, and although not formally educated, was well-read. Her writings and lyrical compositions display a keen sensitivity to the existential predicament.

Perhaps the most prolific author of the twentieth century is Wajeda Tabassum (1935–), who was orphaned at age two along with her seven siblings. Raised by her grandmother in a religious household, Wajeda Tabassum was educated at Osmania University, married in 1960, and has five children. Her writing explore issues of social injustice and middle-class hypocrisy, and her *magnum opus* entitled *Zar, Zan, Zamin* (*Money, Woman, and Land*) was published in 1989. This work, which spans over 1600 pages, addresses the victimization of two women, one Muslim and one Hindu. Her other works include *Teh Khana* (*The Cellar/The Room Underground*), published in 1968; *Kaise Samjhaoon* (*How Can I Make You Understand ?*), published in 1977; *Phul Khilne Do* (*Let the Buds Bloom*) and *Utran* (*Castoffs*), both published in 1977); and *Zakm-e-Dil Aur Mahak Aur Mahak* (*Let the Fragrance of My Wounds Envelope You More and More*) and *Shehar-e-Mamun* (*The City of Peace*), both published in 1978. Although she has been criticized for creating characters who hold attitudes inappropriate for a Muslim woman, as in her short story "Utran" ("Castoffs"), her work has received much acclaim. That particular story has been translated into eight languages and filmed for television.

Jeelani Bano (1936–) is another writer whose work has been translated into several Indian languages as well as English, and who has won several awards. She is the daughter of the well-known scholar and poet Hyrat Badayuni. Jeelani Bano was raised in Hyderabad in an environment filled with artists and intellectuals committed to social causes and active in the Progressive Writers' Association in Hyderabad. She counts Niyaz Hyder, Maqdoom, Ismat Chugtai and Rasheed Jahan among those who have influenced her literary development. Her writings include *Roshni Ke Minar* (*Towers of Light*) published in 1958; *Nirwan* (*Deliverance*), published in 1965; and *Paraya Ghar* (*House, But Not One's Own*), published in 1979—all collections of short stories. Two novels— *Aiwan-e-Ghazal* (*Palace of Song*), published in 1967, and *Barish-e-Sang* (*Shower of Stones*), published in 1984— were followed by another collection of short stories, *Roz Ka Qissa* (*Everyday Questions/Stories*) in 1987.

Meherunnisa Parvez (1944–) takes up themes more directly related to the difficult existence of women due to social and religious mores, and has earned much criticism as a result. She has worked with and written about the tribal peoples in Madhya Pradesh in addition to her literary writings, which are largely devoted to the injustices and suffering faced by women. Her works include the short stories "Gardish" ("Travails") and "Talaq" ("Divorce") for which she was heavily criticized; the novels *Ankhon ki Dahliz* (*The Threshold of Eyes*), published in 1969; *Korja* published in 1977, which has won several awards; *Uska Ghar* (*His Home*), published in 1972, which explores longterm unmarried relationships; *Akash Neel* (*The Blue of the Sky*), published in 1978; and *Akela Palash* (*The Lonely Palash Tree*), published in 1982. Collections of her short stories are *Adam aur Avva* (*Adam and Eve*), published in 1972; *Galat Purush* (*The Tainted Man*), published in 1978; *Antim Chadhai* (*The Last Ascent*), published in 1982; and *Ayodhya Se Wapasi* (*Returning from Ayodha*), published in 1991.

Hajira Shakoor (1950–) is a lecturer in sociology at Jamia Milia University in Delhi. Discussing the themes in her writings, she says, "Since I am interested in social work, my stories reflect the problems faced by women. They ask questions about tolerance, equality, and human rights." Her work has been published in Indian and Pakistani journals, and the collections of her short stories that have appeared to date are *Gardishen* (*Vicissitudes*), published in 1970; *Band Kamron Ki Khuli Khidkiyan* (*Open Windows in Closed Rooms*), published in 1987; and *Barzach* (*Purgatory*), published in 1991.

There are many other writers of note whose writings are just beginning to be available. One of them is the writer Taslima Nasreen (1962–), a medical doctor by profession who has written many works in Bengali, one of which, *Lajja* (*Shame*) published in 1993, has been translated into English. Others include Janaki Bai (1889–?), whose writings are preserved in *Diwan-e-Janaki*, published in 1931; Sughra Humayun Mirza (1884–1954), one of the early women activists in Hyderabad, who was also a prolific writer and editor as well as a poet who wrote under the pen name Haya; Rukhsana Ahmad, who is a playwright and short story writer currently living in the United Kingdom; and Attiya Hosain, who writes about pre-Independence India. Other emerging writers who deserve mention are Banu Quddisa, Jameela Hashemi, Qurratulain Hyder, Muhammadi Begum, Anees Jung, and Khalida Husain, the last of whom has been studied in a dissertation by Ghazala Anwar completed at Temple University in 1993. This survey is by no means exhaustive. There are many other voices that have not been included and remain to be studied—those who continue to preserve oral tradition or compose material for performance, the many traditional teachers and compilers, who act as educators and exponents of Muslim tradition and practice, and those of the distant past, whose legacy has not been recorded and may be lost to us.

Zayn Kassam-Hahn

References: Muslim Women Writers in Arabic

Adan, Etel. *Sitt Marie Rose*. Paris: Des Femmes, 1978. Translated by Georgina Kleege under the title *Miss Marie Rose* (California: Post-Apollo Press, 1982).

A.J. Arberry, trans. *Muslim Saints and Mystics*. The University of Chicago Press, 1966.

Khamees, Dhabya. "Love Poems in Time of War," in *The Literature of Modern Arabia*. Salma K. Jayyusi, ed., Austin: University of Texas Press, 1989.

Mernissi, Fatima. *Beyond the Veil*. London; Al-Saqi, 1985.

———. *Le Harem Politique*. Paris: Albin Michel, 1987.

———. *Sultanes Oubliées, femmes chefs d'état en Islam*. Paris: Albin Michel, 1990.

Al-Sa'dawi, Nawal. *Muthakkarat Tabiba*. London: al-Saqui Books, 1988. Translated by Catherine Cobham under the title *Memoirs of a Woman Doctor*.

Shaarawi, Huda. *Harem Years: The Memoirs of an Egyptian Feminist*. Badran, Margot, trans. New York: The Feminist Press, 1986.

Touqan, Fawada. *A Mountainous Journey, An Autobiography*. London: The Women's Press, 1990.

———. *Alone With The Days*, 1955; *I Found It*, 1957 and *Give Us Love*, 1960.

References: Muslim Women Writers in Turkish

Erol, Sibel. "Discourses on the Intellectual: The Universal, the Particular and Their Mediation in the Works of Nazli Eray," *New Perspectives on Turkey* 11 (Fall, 1994):1–17.

Gun, Guneli. "The Woman in the Darkroom: Contemporary Women Writers in Turkey." *World Literature Today* 60:1–2 (1986):275–9.

Kandiyoti, Deniz. "Slave Girls, Temptresses, and Comrades: Images of Women in the Turkish Novel." *Feminist Issues* 8:1 (Spring):35–51.

Mitler, Louis. *Contemporary Turkish Writers: A Critical Bio-Bibliography of Leading Writer in the Turkish Republican Period Up to 1980*. Bloomington: Indiana University, 1988.

Paker, Saliha. "Unmuffled Voices in the Shade and Beyond: Women's Writings in Turkish." *Textual Liberation: European Feminist Writing in the Twentieth Century*. Helena Forsas-Scott, ed. London: and New York: Routledge, 1991. 270–300.

Reddy, Nilufer Mizanoglu. *Twenty Stories by Turkish Women Writers*. Bloomington: Indiana University Turkish Studies, 1988. (Pages viii–xii present a useful introduction.)

Sirman, Nukhet. "Feminism in Turkey: A Short History." *New Perspectives on Turkey* 3:1 (Fall 1989):1–35.

Tekeli, Sirin. *Kadin Bakis Acisindan 1980'ler Turkiyesinde Kadinlar*. Istanbul: Iletism, 1990. (An English translation entitled *Women in Turkey* is scheduled to appear from Zed Books.)

References: Muslim Women Writers in Malay

Adam, Askiah. "Muslim Personal Law: Some Reflections on Rights Mobilization in Malaysia." Paper presented at a regional meeting of the Asia Pacific Forum on Women, Law and Development: Women, Religion and Family Law, October 1992.

Anwar, Zainah. *Islamic Resurgence in Malaysia*. Kuala Lumpur: Pelanduk Publications, 1987.

Hashim, Khadijah. *De Ruang Mu Aku Di Sini*. (Translated into English under the title *Exile* by Adibah Amin. Kuala Lumpur: K Publishing, 1992.

———. *The White Dove Flies Again*. Translated by Harry Aveling. Kuala Lumpur: Dewan Bahasa danPustaka, 1987.

Hassan, Zurinah. *Kuala Lumpur & Other Places*. Kuala Lumpur: Penerbitan al-Huda, 1986.

Ismail, Siti Zainon. *The Moon is a Candle*. Translated by Harry Aveling. Kuala Lumpur: Dwan Bahasa dan Pustaka, 1992.

Kassiim, Azizah. "A Matrilineal Society in the Context of Development: The Adat Perpateh Case." *Federation Museums' Journal*, n.s. 21 (1976): 41–52.

Othman, Norani, ed. *Sharia Law and the Modern Nation State: A Malaysian Symposium*. Kuala Lumpur: Sis Forum (Malaysia) Berhad, 1994.

Samah, Asiah Abu. *Emancipation of Malay Women (1945–1957)*. Singapore: 1960.

Shaikah, Zakaria. *Muslim Women and the Law of Islam in West Malaysia*, Master's Thesis, University of Kent at Canterbury, 1973.

Sisters in Islam. *Are Women and Men Equal Before Allah?* Kuala Lumpur: Sisters in Islam, 1991.

———. *Are Men Allowed to Beat Their Wives?* Kuala Lumpur: Sisters in Islam, 1991.

Sweeney, Amin. *A Full Hearing: Orality and Literacy in the Malay World*. Berkeley: University of California Press, 1987.

Winstedt, Richard. *A History of Classical Malay Literature*. Kuala Lumpur and Oxford: Oxford University Press, 1969.

Yun, Hing Ai, Nik Safiah Karim, and Rokiah Talib. *Women in Malaysia*. Kuala Lumpur: Pelanduk Publications, 1984.

References: Muslim Women Writers in South Asia

Beveridge, Annette S., trans. with introduction. *The History of Humayun (Humayun-nama)*, by *Gulbadan Begum (Princess Rose-Body)*. 1901. Reprint. Delhi: Idarah-i Adabiyat-i Delli, 1972.

Findly, Ellison Banks. *Nur Jahan: Empress of Mughal India*. New York: Oxford University Press, 1993.

Ishaque, M. *Four Eminent Poetesses of Iran*. Calcutta, 1950.

Lal, K.S. *The Mughal Harem*. New Delhi: Aditya Prakashan, 1988.

Masse, H. "The Poetess Rabia Gozdari" in *Yadnama-yi Jan Rypka*. Prague, 1967.

Schimmel, Annemarie. *Islamic Literatures of India*. Wiesbaden: Otto Harrassowitz, 1973.

Tharu, Susie and K. Lalita, eds. *Women Writing in India*. *Volume I: 600 B.C. to the Early 20th Century. Volume II: The 20th Century*. New York: The Feminist Press at The City University of New York, 1991–93.

Zebunisa. *The Diwan of Zaib-un-nisa*. Translated from the Persian by Magan Lal and Jessie Duncan Westbrook. Wisdom of the East Series. London: John Murray, 1913.

Part X:

Muslim Education

31

Learning and Education

◆ Education in the Early Period ◆ The Impact of Developments in Education on the Muslim World
◆ Education in the Contemporary Muslim World

The earliest revelation to the Prophet Muhammad evokes powerful symbols of learning and knowledge: "Read! Your Lord is full of generosity, instructing by the Pen, educating humanity about that which they do not know" (Quran 96:3–5). In addition, the Quran distinguishes Adam from other created beings by virtue of the capacity gifted to him to "name everything" (2:31). The value placed on knowledge in the Quran became the foundation for the development of education in all its different expressions among Muslims. This spirit was further reinforced by the need to remember and preserve the traditions of the Prophet. Among the sayings of the Prophet were statements encouraging education. The acquisition of knowledge thus came to be perceived as part of one's daily life and as a way of enhancing knowledge of the faith and its practices; faith and learning were seen to be interactive and not isolated from each other.

◆ EDUCATION IN THE EARLY PERIOD

The incentive to read and learn the Quran provided the early Muslim community with its initial educational settings, in which instruction of the Quran, the life of the Prophet and knowledge of the Arabic language, its grammar, structures and forms took place. The mosque and the early Quran schools were the first examples of Muslim educational institutions. In addition, those who assumed responsibility for establishing such institutions and implementing regulations promulgated in the Quran and by the Prophet, felt the need to create meeting places where such matters could be discussed. Informal schools of learning on legal and theological questions came to be developed in mosques and other public places, as well as in private homes. Moreover, during this period Muslims were coming into increased contact with peoples in the areas to which Islam was

spreading. Such encounters with other cultures and their more developed traditions of learning served as an added incentive for Muslims to establish a system of learning to fit their needs and to enhance their understanding of their faith and its practice.

A variety of institutional settings developed during the early period of Muslim history, comprising a great deal of diversity in subject matter and function. The most important of these institutions were the *maktab* or *kuttab*, the *masjid* and *majlis*, *jami*, and libraries.

Maktab or *kuttab* were places where children received instruction in the Quran and in Islamic subjects, whereas *masjid* and *majlis* were meeting places associated with mosques where adults organized themselves into study groups. The groups varied in the subjects discussed which ranged from the study of the Prophet's life and sayings, issues pertaining to legal matters, devotional practice and poetry.

Many *jami*, or the Friday mosque, eventually became a seat of higher learning as exemplified in the rise of major mosque/centers such as the Kairouan in Morocco. A more comprehensive model developed later, as exemplified by the al-Azhar mosque in Cairo.

As Muslims engaged in learning and writing, a number of libraries began to develop, often attached to the court, where collections of books were organized. These largely informal institutions also housed books from other cultural traditions. The most important of these institutions was the *Bayt al Hikma* (House of Wisdom) in Baghdad established by the Abbasid caliph, al-Mamun (reigned 813–833). The *Bayt al Hikma* became an institution where the philosophical and scientific works of the Greeks were translated into Arabic. An observatory for the study of astronomy was also developed. The center's work and influence represents one of the most remarkable educational efforts to assimilate new learning into Arabic during the medieval period.

Maktab or *kuttab* were places where children received instruction in the Quran.

Emerging Models of Learning

While there were Muslims during the early period who felt that it was necessary to focus primarily on Quranic and related subjects, many others were influenced to integrate such learning within a broader context. An example of how learning was conceived as a way to increase one's knowledge and to serve as model for the pursuit of an ideal education can be seen in a parable preserved in a series of well-known and influential writings, known as the *Rasail Ikhwan al Safa* (*The Writings of the Pure Ones*), whose collective authors were a group of Muslim intellectuals living during the tenth century. The parable may be rendered as follows:

It has been related that there was a wise and noble king with children who were very dear to him and whom he venerated greatly. He wished to educate, refine, and train them, in order that they might become competent before reaching his Court; because none, except for those refined by good breeding, trained in the sciences, molded by good morals, and free from imperfections, is suited for the Court of kings.

He deemed it wise that he should erect for them a palace—among the most solid that had ever been built. Then he assigned to each a *majlis* and wrote on its walls every science that he wished to teach them. He portrayed in the *majlis* everything in which he wished them to be instructed. Then he settled them in the palace, seating each one according to the share allotted to him, and entrusted them with servants and slaves of both sexes. He then said to these children: "Observe what I have portrayed before you, read what I have written there for your sake, ponder upon what I have expounded for you, and reflect upon

it, so that you may perceive its significance and become outstanding and righteous men of learning. Then, I shall conduct you to my Court, and you will belong among my happy and honored intimates, forever blessed, as long as I remain and as long as you remain with me."

Among the sciences that he wrote for them in that *majlis*, he represented the form of the celestial spheres on the ceiling explaining how they revolved, the signs of the zodiac in their ascendancy, and likewise that stars and their movements, making clear their signs and rules.

He illustrated on the courtyard of the *majlis* the configuration of the earth, the division of the regions and a map of the mountains, oceans, deserts, and rivers. He explained the boundaries of the countries, cities, trade routes, and the kingdom.

In the foremost part of the *majlis*, he wrote the sciences of medicine and the natural sciences, il-

Masjid and *majlis* were meeting places associated with mosques where adults organized themselves into study groups.

lustrating the plants, animals, and minerals in their species, genus, and particulars, and explained their characteristics, uses, and dangers.

On another side he wrote the science of crafts and vocations and explained the mode of ploughing and production. He then portrayed the cities and market-places, explaining the regulations governing buying and selling, profit making, and trading.

On another side he inscribed the science of religion and creeds, the laws and the traditions, elucidating the lawful and the unlawful, the penalties and the legal judgments.

Then on yet another side, he wrote concerning political administration and the organization of the states, explaining the mode of levying taxes, and also with regard to the secretaries and the administrators of the *Diwan*, explaining the payments to be made to the soldiers and the protecting of the borders by the army and the auxiliaries.

These are six kinds of sciences by which the children of kings are edified. This is a parable struck by wise men; that is to say, the wise king is God, the Most High, and the young children are humanity. The erected castle is the firmament and the perfectly constructed *majlis* is the human form. The illustrated rules of conduct are the wonderful composition of his body, and the inscribed sciences in it are faculties of the soul and its knowledge.

Analysis of the Model

The above story summarizes the type of learning available at the time. It serves as a metaphor on the whole meaning and purpose of life and is illustrative of a very comprehensive approach to education. In fact, the section itself is part of a chapter which treats human beings as a microcosm. It is clearly stated that since life is short, and the scope of knowledge of the world too large, individuals must learn to attain a realization of the whole creation by studying themselves, since persons epitomize the universe. Thus, by relating the microcosm to the macrocosm through rational means, one can proceed from understanding the smaller model to understanding the larger one.

A place of learning is a preparatory ground to enable one to acquire the tools necessary to face life. Likewise, the body is seen as a preparatory place for the soul, in which to acquire all that the soul needs to perfect itself. In the story, the school symbolizes the body, and the

various subjects relate to the knowledge the soul has to acquire before it can reach the "Court of the King."

While educational philosophy is based on acquiring self-knowledge, as shown in this model, it is balanced with the recognition that one needs to acquire skills to live in the world. Besides this comprehensiveness, another practical and important aspect of this model is its concept of a suitable environment in which to acquire learning. The provision for a well-built structure and all the amenities of good living seems to emphasize the need for an enabling environment for learning.

Knowledge is divided into various fields: the first concerns knowledge of the celestial spheres and heavenly bodies; the second is that of the earth and its geographical makeup; and the final comprises all that pertains to the physical, cultural, and religious aspects of human life. Education also pertains to this life and its needs. This practical and pragmatic aspect of the Muslim theory of learning is illustrated by including within the sciences those pertaining to agriculture, and economic and political organization. Thus skills and the sciences have an immediate practical goal of coordinating the everyday life and needs of an individual and an ultimate goal where he learns to acquire self-knowledge and perfection for the time when he must leave this world.

Another theme that is included in the story is the role of religion in their educational system. In the story, the study of religions, law, and traditions is included in the curriculum. These, however, represent organized religion which in the Ikhwan's framework is swallowed up in a wider concept of learning that is termed *hikma* (i.e, wisdom).

The model of learning reflected in the story was characteristic of intellectuals who constituted informal discussion circles, rather than in full-fledged educational institutions. In time, particularly from the tenth century onwards a more organized institutional development, supported by the state took place in the Muslim world.

Al-Azhar

Conceived and founded initially as the main mosque of a new capital city, Cairo, in 970, al-Azhar became a fully integrated mosque-university during the early period of Shia Fatimid Ismaili rule. Its role was enhanced by the various Fatimid caliphs who through a series of gifts and endowments developed it into a major center of learning. At its height, the curriculum taught at al-Azhar and related institutions in Cairo included the study and interpretation of the Quran, law, metaphysics, philosophy, the natural sciences, and poetry and literature. Many teachers and scientists lived at al-Azhar, including the great physicist, Ibn al Haytham. The endowments supported students as well as professors.

The well-known poet, philosopher and traveller Nasir-i-Khusraw (died 1088) was very familiar with al-Azhar and the programs of education developed under the Fatimids in Egypt and other parts of their territory. Reflecting on his own education, he provides a list of the many disciplines in which he was trained and educated: language and linguistics; poetry and literature, astronomy, astrology and the mathematical sciences; politics and commerce; philosophy and metaphysics; and the traditional sciences of the Quran, law and Prophetic tradition. Since he acted as a representative and teacher of the Shia Ismaili movement, his own training was probably more intensive and comprehensive, but the range of subjects indicates the disciplines that were available in Cairo at the time.

In succeeding centuries, when Fatimid rule was replaced by various other dynasties which were Sunni in orientation, the function of al-Azhar changed and it became a prestigious center for the study of religious sciences and law. Such an institution came to be known as a *madrasa*.

The Madrasa

With the systematization of Muslim schools of law, the focus of legal scholarship and transmission shifted to another institution which evolved in an organized form by the eleventh century called the *madrasa*. Devoted primarily to the study of law, but including other subjects integral to the development of religious sciences, the *madrasa* incorporated the instructional role of early informal education such as in the mosque and study circles, becoming a major institution of learning in Sunni Islam. It received state support, had endowed professorships and residential facilities for teachers and students.

An early example of such an institution was the Nizamiyya *madrasa* established by the powerful *vizier*, (chief minister) of the Saljuq rulers, Nizam al Mulk (died 1092), in Baghdad in 1067. He founded it to create a strong Sunni institution to balance the influence of al-Azhar in Cairo. Like al-Azhar in Cairo, it too was established through an endowment. Such endowments, known in Islam as *waqf*, represented the philanthropic spirit in the Islamic tradition expressed through institutional means which provided the impetus for encouraging and developing education by the state as well as by individuals and families. Nizam al-Mulk went on to establish similar institutions in other parts of the Muslim world that were under Saljuq rule at the time, creating a network of centers of learning patronized by the rulers and guaranteeing the financial means and support for scholars to pursue their legal and theological studies. In all of the major cities of the Muslim world in the medieval period, the *madrasa* became the primary center for religious and legal education.

The scholarship generated in the *madrasa* had great significance for the development of thought among Sunni Muslims. One of the towering intellectual figures associated with the Nizamiyya *madrasa* was Abu Hamid al-Ghazali (1058–1111). He became a professor of law noted both for his scholarship and teaching. For a time, he took an extended leave, pursuing other interests, primarily the private pursuit of a mystical and spiritual life. On his return, his role became even more significant as he integrated the results of his personal quest to broaden perspectives among Muslims about the role of reason and spirituality in the practice and understanding of their faith.

Women's Education

The Prophet Muhammad's first wife, Khadija was a well-established business woman. His subsequent wife, Aisha became well known for her role as a transmitter of tradition. His daughter, Fatima, and several other women associated with his household were acknowledged for their love of learning. In the foundational period therefore there existed several reference points to encourage the participation and pursuit of women in learning.

In general women's education throughout medieval Muslim history was conditioned by local cultural factors, which put limits and set boundaries on their training and role in society. Prior to attaining the age of marriage, women remained with the immediate or extended family and received their knowledge of the Quran and Islamic practice at home or at an informal Quran school, where they were taught mostly by elderly women. After marriage, it was rare for most women to pursue formal education, since their role as wives and mothers and their custody of the household restricted their movements and activities outside the home. However, their influence on their children's education, particularly their daughters, was strong. Women also developed skills such as midwifing, embroidery, weaving, carpet-making, calligraphy and design. Others were recognized for there skills as poets and story-tellers and acted as transmitters of oral tradition and folklore.

Some women belonged to Sufi groups and participated in devotional and social networks that varied in their organization and educational activities, from urban to rural areas. There were women in the court or those brought up in families with a long tradition of learning who were more privileged and received formal education and excelled in several areas such as the collection and teaching of prophetic tradition and law, poetry and literature.

In historical terms, as with other major civilizations and religions in China, India, and Europe that flourished at the same time, the public role of women in education and learning in the medieval Muslim world was marginal. There are, nonetheless, outstanding examples of women who gained fame for their learning, their poetry and their patronage of knowledge.

Scientific Learning and Knowledge

The translation efforts of such centers as the *Bayt al-Hikma* in Baghdad and the presence of major classical academies and centers of learning in places like Alexandria and Jundishapur, provided Muslims with direct access to the sciences and learning of Greece and the Near East. In addition to centers for the study of specifically theological and legal subjects, many Muslim intellectuals were attracted to scientific inquiry and the techniques of investigative research and discussion. An example of such a group is the Ikhwan al Safa cited earlier and Muslim philosophers and scientists. The eleventh century scholar, philosopher and physician, Ibn Sina (Avicenna), provides an excellent model of how such learning was appropriated, further developed and then refined and reformulated in the context of Muslim thought.

Ibn Sina was instructed in the religious sciences at an early age and took up the study of philosophy and logic in his teens; eventually mastering Aristotle, Euclid, Ptolemy and other ancient Greek scholars, to gain as comprehensive a philosophical and scientific education as he could. In his autobiography, he describes his passionate devotion to philosophical study and his obsession with learning every subject available to him in the field. He also developed the skills of a physician and because of his reputation for healing and curing physical as well as psychological ailments found himself invited to various courts to be physician to the king. He managed to evade the pitfalls of being at various courts during a time of conflict between various rulers, seeking opportunity whenever it presented itself, to write and systematize his work. His most important works in philosophy, medicine and metaphysics reflect the breadth of his knowledge and the spirit of rational inquiry present in Muslim education at the time.

Twelver Shia Centers of Learning

The role of promoting education and learning under the patronage of Shia rulers was affected by the downfall of the Shia Fatimid dynasty in 1171. The next three centuries marked the steady growth and consolidation of Sunni *madrasa* education in the major centers of medieval Muslim society. Ironically, al-Azhar, founded originally by the Fatimid Shia Ismaili dynasty, became under Sunni patronage a prestigious seat of learning and training of Sunni scholars. Shia learning and perspectives, though less influential, were preserved and developed in several different places: in Yemen, where

Mustali Ismaili centers survived and Zaydi Shia law and sciences were also taught; in parts of Iran and Syria, where the Nizari Ismailis followed the Fatimid tradition; and among Twelver Imami centers in the cities of Najaf and Karbala in Iraq.

At the beginning of the sixteenth century a new dynasty took power in Iran. The Safavids, as they were called, imposed Twelver Shiism as the religion of the territories that they ruled and supported the establishment of *madrasas*. This royal patronage attracted Shia scholars to Iran from many parts of the Muslim world and led to the emergence of a revitalized tradition of learning and scholarship of Twelver Shiism in Iran.

In addition to the study of traditional religious sciences, students learned grammar, rhetoric and logic, philosophical theory, and advanced jurisprudence. The curriculum was fairly uniform in all of the *madrasas* and the advanced students and teachers became part of a flourishing and influential system of learning, representing an institutionalized guild of scholars and religious teachers, referred to as *mullas* or *mujtahids*.

Sufi Centers of Learning

The tradition of Muslim mysticism and spirituality affected all Muslim groups and institutions in varying degrees. It is not therefore entirely accurate to represent education and learning in their Sufi contexts as something entirely apart from other forms of educational activity in the Muslim world.

Congregational spaces where Sufis gathered to practice acts of devotion, piety, and meditation were also centers of training and learning. They are variously known as *ribat*, *khanqa*, *zawiya*, or *jamaat-khana*. Their evolution represents an aspect of the institutionalization of Sufi *tariqas*, the umbrella organization which defined one's sense of affiliation and identification with a particular group of Sufis. In these various centers, through a hierarchy of teachers and disciples, individuals were educated to learn the Quran and its spiritual meaning, to develop an understanding of the Prophet's role as a reference point for cultivating an inner life, and to read the writings of many great poets and writers in the Sufi tradition. Such environments were important centers of educational activity, which combined devotional practice and learning. They were also the most important vehicles for the transmission of Islam through oral learning and education and balanced the emphasis on classical learning based on Arabic or Persian texts with an encouragement to use vernacular models.

Pesantren Education in Indonesia

One example of a local indigenous Muslim educational institution is the *pesantren*, a boarding school developed in Southeast Asia as a place of learning. Based in rural areas, and supported by parents and members of the local community, such schools depended on commitment and prestige of local teachers who were willing to establish schools for pupils in the area. The subjects taught in the *pesantren*, included Quranic studies, law, ethics, logic, history and Sufism. Students who felt that they had developed sufficient learning would return to contribute to their own communities. As contacts between Southeast Asia and other major centers of Muslim learning increased, many students went overseas for further training and specialization. Often such schools also provided practical training in farming, crafts and trade.

Oral Tradition and Learning

Oral methods of transmission and learning co-existed with the use of the written word, from the beginnings of Islam. The Quran was taught and transmitted orally, the traditions and sayings of the Prophet were passed on through oral transmission and oral communication remained one of the most effective methods of passing on the history and memory of individuals, families, and dynasties.

In many Muslim cultures oral tradition continues to play an important role in the preservation and acquisition of knowledge. An illustration of how this process was institutionalized, can be found in West Africa. Among Muslim populations there, the responsibility for communication of history and religious tradition, often lay with individuals called *griots*. They preserved local history, genealogies, and the social history of their groups and rulers. Such individuals were also accomplished musicians and singers, and the use of music and poetry served as an important vehicle for passing knowledge from generation to generation. Similar oral forms of communication are found all over the Muslim world.

The Spread of Muslim Educational Institutions

The plurality of educational institutions in the medieval and pre-modern Muslim world represented a vast network. From Bukhara to Timbuktu, well-endowed institutions, learned scholars and thousands of students made Muslim societies among the most literate of the time and greatly facilitated communication and transmission across geographical boundaries and cultural differences. A broad spectrum of populations in the various urban centers benefitted from these networks, including in a limited way, women and children.

In many Muslim cultures oral tradition continues to play an important role in the preservation and acquisition of knowledge.

While colonial governments set up their own school systems to train people, many Muslims responded by returning or further developing traditional institutions with community support.

They reached their greater number during the period of the Ottoman, Mughal, and Safavid empires in the Middle East and under the rule of many other dynasties in Africa and Southeast Asia in the seventeenth and eighteenth centuries.

Muslim educational institutions profoundly affected the development of learning and education in all the areas to which Islam spread. Moreover, Muslim scholarship and institutional development also influenced in different ways, the development of education in Europe through the transmission of philosophy and the various sciences. The cultural and economic exchange between Europe and the Muslim world also facilitated parallel developments of institutions and practices in the field of education.

One illustration of the scope of learning in medieval times, is reflected in the work of Ibn Khaldun (died 1406), probably one of the most important figures in Muslim intellectual life in the fourteenth century. He lived, studied and taught in the Maghreb, in Spain and in Cairo and had a truly cosmopolitan background and outlook. He wrote an encyclopedic work of history which was prefaced by a *Muqaddima*, a meditative prologue on the significance and nature of history. In this preface he undertook a survey of all fields of learning. In addition, he attempted a comprehensive analysis of the significance and inter-relationship of the various disciplines. But much more so, he critically analyzed historical events and developments to establish the underlying causes and effects of social change. Ibn Khaldun's encyclopedic grasp of knowledge enabled him to develop for his own time, an assessment of the value of learning and its application to the problems affecting his own society, a model that may have great relevance for Muslims today.

◆ THE IMPACT OF DEVELOPMENTS IN EDUCATION ON THE MUSLIM WORLD

Probably the most important change affecting Muslim education in the nineteenth and twentieth centuries resulted from the contact, conflict, and interaction with external influences, primarily Europe. The period of internal self-sustained development over centuries was interrupted by European expansion, economic dominance, and military superiority. The colonization of major regions of the Muslim world in Asia and Africa, altered dramatically the structure of

In the past twenty-five years, a number of developing countries enriched by oil or mineral wealth economies have built schools and universities.

educational institutions in these areas and brought them into contact with the dual systems of European education, secular and church-related. The encounter generated ambiguity as well as opportunity. The new horizons of learning often presented themselves in alienating forms, through missionaries intent on conversion of peoples to Christianity or through official government policies by colonial powers that often took a patronizing attitude to local institutions and forms of education.

This sense of ambiguity and alienation is perhaps best captured in a fictional representation of the situation, in a novel by the highly regarded West African Muslim intellectual Hamidou Kane (died 1962). The novel, written in French, is called *L'Aventure Ambigue* (*Ambiguous Adventure*). At its center, is Samba Diallobe, future leader of his people who grows to adulthood in a traditional African Muslim world, increasingly altered by the influence of the French colonial presence. He is pulled in two directions, towards France to acquire education to best assure the future of his people or to stay home and strive to preserve a tradition that his people feel is under increasing threat and erosion. Samba's Quran teacher and mentor, fears

the consequences of Western education. He perceives it as lacking in spiritual and moral value and senses that its primary ethos is technological and secular. In his view traditional Muslim education encompassed the whole of the person, enabling all aspects of one's development to be nurtured. He fears that Western education is linear, adding together knowledge in fragmenting fashion, but not relating persons, the cosmos and God to each other. However, there are others who challenge this view and argue that the emphasis on rationality in the new approach to education would not only enable people to recognize their present condition but to transcend it and free themselves from colonial rule. This somewhat simplified dichotomy summarizes the broad set of responses that arose among Muslims, faced with the impact of new educational institutions and conceptions of knowledge.

Where choices were made to adopt or adapt Western forms of education, the existing systems were dichotomized and institutions whose primary function had been to transmit religious knowledge and learning became isolated from newly created institutions, adopting a primary custodial role as preservers of traditional learning and religious identity.

In the novel, *Ambiguous Adventure*, the hero chooses to go to France, is drawn into the world of new learning and thought, but is eventually alienated by it and returns to his spiritual and traditional roots, perhaps in the hope that some reconciliation can be negotiated between differing systems. What is recognized in the novel is that the traditional world cannot exist as a self-enclosed entity any more. Even in its most idealized representation, education in the Muslim world was always diverse and pluralistic. It would henceforth continue to be so, though the lines of demarcation and the goals of various institutions would not be as integrated as they once might have been. Thus in the contemporary Muslim world one finds a spectrum of institutions and modes of learning serving many different constituencies.

Education in the Nineteenth Century

One model of response to colonial rule and European influence was the establishment of primary and secondary schools and colleges and universities based on Western models. While the colonial governments set up their own school systems to train people, many Muslims responded by returning or further developing traditional institutions with community support. In countries such as Turkey, the rulers created academies for the military and the court administration to provide training similar to those of European nations. Some established institutions like al-Azhar in Cairo, the Qarawiyin in Morocco, the Mustansiriya in Baghdad, the Sulaymaniya in Istanbul, and the Fayziyeh in Iran, reinforced their traditional curriculum. New centers such as Deoband in India were created to consolidate religious education. One negative consequence of this development was the evolution of a dual system, whereby the secularized, Western models became isolated from developments at other institutions. The governments and rulers who sponsored such institutions simply bypassed the traditional institutions and their teachers, diminishing their role and impact in society. Where modern institutions of higher learning were created, such as Aligarh in India, they became influential but not universal. Attempts were made by enlightened scholars such as Shaykh Mahmud Shaltut (died 1963), rector of al-Azhar, to bring about reforms based on the earlier efforts of Muhammad Abduh. However, the changing pattern of state control over such centers of learning made it increasingly difficult for them to play a role in combatting the disjunction resulting from the dual systems that were already in place in many Muslim countries.

The University of Kerman, Kerman, Iran

◆ EDUCATION IN THE CONTEMPORARY MUSLIM WORLD

Two sets of statistical data are relevant to an understanding of the state of education in the Muslim world today. The first is demographic, and the second institutional. The fastest growing segment of the Muslim population in the world today is of school-going age. In order to accommodate this growth, the number of institutions for elementary and secondary education has grown rapidly. From Uzbekistan in Central Asia to Bangladesh thousands of schools have been built by the respective states in the last twenty five years to accommodate this growth. The same is true for university education. The number of state and private universities range from seventy in Indonesia to over thirty in Iran. Every country with a major Muslim population has at least one university. The tremendous growth in population was paralleled by an increase in centralized control over schooling at all levels.

In the past twenty-five years, a number of developing countries enriched by oil or mineral wealth economies have built schools and universities. Countries like Saudi Arabia, Oman, and Brunei boast several universities endowed with all the advantages of information technology and the latest advances in equipment. On the other hand poorer countries have had to struggle to sustain the institutions already in existence and foundering from shortage of resources and increased demand.

Some new academic institutions have been created which have self-consciously adopted the rubric "Islamic." Their purpose is to create institutions that will reflect an intellectual profile that emphasizes the centrality of Muslim subject-matter. Some of these institutions have been formed as a result of efforts by the Organization of the Islamic Conference (OIC) established in 1973 through the combined resources of Muslim nations. Whether this pattern will further segregate educational modes and institutions remains to be seen.

More recently, a number of private initiatives have also led to the establishment of private schools, universities, and academies. Some of these are highly specialized, seeking to create institutions that will serve the need of the greatest number through professional training suited to the needs of developing countries. An example is the creation in Pakistan of the Aga Khan University whose first initiative was a medical and nursing school of an international caliber to train physicians, nurses and health-care professionals to meet the medical needs of urban and rural areas through an innovative program of training and a primary health-care system. Similar institutions are being created through other private initiatives to meet local needs by networking with international agencies but retaining local control and autonomy. The Grameen Bank initiative in Bangladesh, though aimed at improving housing conditions and women's employment has developed support institutions such as schools to enable development in rural communities. Similar programs can be found in many Muslim countries of Africa and Asia, and increasingly in Europe and North America.

Major problems remain, particularly in the realm of education for women and young children, who are often deprived of their basic educational needs. While such difficulties are part of the historical legacy of centuries old traditional systems and of the heritage of some colonial practices, there is a major transformation evident across that Muslim world. Communication across communities, cultures and peoples, increasing access to the global media and the recognition that education is indeed the key to improving the quality of life of society and of future generations, has fostered a commitment to life-long learning and an acceptance that learning has to do with understanding more than what is known in one's own tradition and history. Perhaps like the ninth century Muslim philosopher, al-Kindi, this quest for the future will be influenced by his enlightened approach:

We should not be ashamed to acknowledge truth and to assimilate it from whatever source it comes to us, even if it be brought to us by former generations and foreign peoples. For those who seek the truth, there is nothing of higher value than truth itself; it does not diminish nor leave those who reach for it, but honors and ennobles them. [cited by S.H. Nasr, _Three Muslim Sages_, p. 11]

Azim A. Nanji

References

Ahmad Anis. _Muslim Women and Higher Education: A Case for Separate Institutions for Women._ Kuwait: I.F.S.O, 1984.

Ahmed, Akbar S. _Toward Islamic Anthropology: Definition, Dogma and Directions._ Ann Arbor, New Era Publications, 1986.

Ahmat S. and Siddique, S. eds. _Muslim Society: Higher Education and Development in Southeast Asia._ Singapore: Institute of Southeast Asian Studies, 1987.

Antoun, R. _Muslim Preacher in the Modern World._ Princeton: Princeton University Press, 1989.

Ashraf S.A. _New Horizons in Muslim Education._ Cambridge and London, 1985.

Barazangi, N.H. "Education: Religious Education" in _The Oxford Encyclopedia of the Modern Muslim World_, Vol. 1.

Berkey, J. _The Transmission of Knowledge in Medieval Cairo._ Princeton: Princeton University Press, 1992.

Callaway, B. _Education and the Emancipation of Hausa_

Muslim Women in Nigeria. East Lansing: Michigan State University, 1982.

Dodge, B. Al Azhar: *A Millennium of Learning*. Washington, D.C.: The Middle East Institute, 1961.

Eickelman, D. F. *Knowledge and Power in Morocco: The Education of a Twentieth-Century Notable*. Princeton: Princeton University Press, 1985.

Faruqi, J. R. *Islamization of Knowledge: General Principles and Work-plan*. 2d revised and expanded edition. Herndon, Va.: International Institute of Islamic Thought, 1989.

Geertz, C. *The Religion of Java*. Chicago: Chicago University Press, 1960.

Iqbal, M. *The Reconstruction of Religious Thought in Islam*. Lahore: M. Ashraf, 1934.

Kane, H. *L'Aventure Ambigue*. trans. by K. Woods, as *Ambiguous Adventure*. Portsmouth, N.H.: Heinemann, 1972.

Lacoste, Yves. *Ibn Khaldun: The Birth of History and the Past of the Third World*. London: Verso Traditions, 1984.

Lelyveld, D. *Aligarh's First Generation: Muslim Solidarity in British India*. Princeton: Princeton University Press, 1978.

Makdisi, G. *The Rise of Colleges: Institutions of Learning in Islam and the West*. Edinburgh: Edinburgh University Press, 1981.

Menashri, D. *Education and the Making of Modern Iran*. Ithaca, N.Y.: Cornell University Press, 1992.

Metcalf, B. *Islamic Revival in British India: Deoband, 1860–1900*. Princeton: Princeton University Press, 1982.

Mottahedeh, R. *The Mantle of the Prophet: Religion and Politics in Iran*. New York: Simon and Schuster, 1985.

Nanji, Azim. "On the Acquisition of Knowledge: A Theory of Learning in the *Rasail Ikhwan al Safa*." *The Muslim World*, Vol. LXVI (4) 1976, 263–271.

Nasr, S.H. *Traditional Islam in the Modern World*. London and New York: Kegan Paul International, 1987.

———. *Three Muslim Sages*. Cambridge: Harvard University Press, 1964.

Rahman, F. *Islam and Modernity: Transformation of an Intellectual Tradition*. Chicago and London: Chicago University Press, 1982.

Reid, D.M. *Cairo University and the Making of Modern Egypt*. Cambridge: Cambridge University Press, 1990.

Rosenthal F. *Knowledge Triumphant*. Leiden: E. J. Brill, 1970.

Shalaby, A. *History of Muslim Education*. Karachi: The University Press, 1979.

Stanton, C.M. *Higher Learning in Islam: The Classical Period*. Savage, Maryland: Rowman and Littlefield, 1990.

Szyliowicz, J.S. *Education and Modernization in the Middle East*. Ithaca: Cornell University Press, 1973.

Thomas, R.M. ed. *Schooling in the Asean Region: Primary and Secondary Education in Indonesia, Malaysia, and the Philippines, Singapore and Thailand*. New York: Pergamon Press, 1980.

Tibawi, A.L. *Islamic Education: Its Tradition and Modernization into the Arab National Systems*. London: Luzac and Co., 1972.

Totah, K.A. *The Contribution of the Arabs to Education*. New York: Teacher's College, Columbia University, 1926.

Unesco. *Learning Strategies for Past-Literacy and Continuing Education in Mali, Niger, Senegal and Upper Volta*. Hamburg: Unesco Institute of Education, 1984.

Zebiri, K. *Mahmud Shaltut and Islamic Modernism*. Oxford: Clarendon Press, 1993.

Part XI:

Islam and Other Faith Communities

Muslims, Jews, and Christians: Relations and Interactions

♦ The Foundational Period ♦ The Early Centuries of Muslim History ♦ The Medieval Period ♦
♦ The Modern Period ♦ The Future

Seen from the vantage of the late twentieth century, relations between Muslims, Jews, and Christians look both better and worse than at any time in the past. In many parts of the world, Muslims are engaged in dialogue with Jews and Christians. Islam has become the fastest growing religion in the multiconfessional mix of (New World) religions, and Muslim leaders are now found alongside rabbis, priests, and ministers in many civic and religious organizations. Beyond this dialogue, Islam is becoming indigenized in many areas once almost exclusively Christian. Yet, at the same time, members of all three religions find themselves fighting one another in territorial and nationalistic wars that have taken on sectarian and religious overtones. In sorting out this mixed state of Muslim, Jewish, and Christian relations, it is important to keep in mind that all three religious groups point to the historical past to justify how they relate to the other groups. Interpretations of history, as well as sacred text and traditional doctrines, thus far have become the determining factors for how well or badly Muslims, Jews, and Christians interrelate. Understanding history and the ways history has been interpreted becomes, then, central in understanding the various claims made by the members of each religion.

Relations among Muslims, Jews, and Christians have been shaped not only by the theologies and beliefs of the three religions, but also, and often more strongly, by the historical circumstances in which they are found. As a result, history has become a foundation for religious understanding. In each historical phase, the definition of who was regarded as Muslim, Jewish, or Christian shifted, sometimes indicating only a religious identification, but more often indicating a particular social, economic, or political group.

While the tendency to place linguistic behavior, religious identity, and cultural heritage under one, pure definition has existed for a very long time, our modern age with its ideology of nationalism is particularly prone to such a conflation. Ethnic identities have sometimes been conflated with religious identities by both outsiders and insiders, complicating the task of analyzing intergroup and intercommunal relations. For example, Muslims have often been equated with Arabs, effacing the existence of Christian and Jewish Arabs (i.e., members of those religions whose language is Arabic and who participate primarily in Arab culture), ignoring non-Arab Muslims who constitute the majority of Muslims in the world. In some instances, relations between Arabs and Israelis have been understood as Muslim-Jewish relations, ascribing aspects of Arab culture to the religion of Islam and Israeli culture to Judaism. This is similar to what happened during the Crusades, during which Christian Arabs were often charged with being identical to Muslims by the invading Europeans. While the cultures in which Islam predominates do not necessarily make sharp distinctions between the religious and secular aspects of the culture, such distinctions make the task of understanding the nature of relations among Muslims, Jews, and Christians easier, and therefore will be used as an analytic tool in this chapter.

Another important tool for analyzing Muslim-Jewish-Christian relations is the placement of ideas and behaviors in specific temporal and geographic contexts. Visions of the past have had a strong influence on each of the religions, and none more strongly than Islam. Many Muslims have as keen an awareness of the events around the time of the Prophet as they do their own time. It is important for a practicing Muslim to know what the Prophet did in his relations with Jews and Christians as a means of shaping their own behavior toward them. The Quran and the *sunna* of the Prophet are key guides for a Muslim in dealing with Jews and Christians, as they are in all areas of conduct. This same historical consciousness is also present among Jews and Christians, as each group makes claims for positions and status in Islamic societies. What is important to remember is that the historical interactions of Muslims, Jews, and Christians have resulted in each constituency being shaped, affected, and transformed by the others, such that it is difficult to imagine how each religion would be as it is without the presence and influence of the others.

♦ THE FOUNDATIONAL PERIOD

When Prophet Muhammad was born in 570, Arabia was deeply involved in the political, religious, and economic rivalries between the Byzantine and Sassanian Persian empires. Arabia was an important trade route for goods coming from the Far East and Africa and was strategically important for each empire's defense. Arabs were recruited into the armies of both sides, providing horse and camel cavalries, and each empire had maintained Arab client states as buffers and bases of operation. Around fifty years earlier, the last Jewish kingdom in southern Arabia allied with the Persians and was defeated and replaced by a Christian Monophysite army from Abyssinia allied with Byzantium. According to early Muslim historians, this army, led by a general named Abraha, tried to invade Mecca in the year of Muhammad's birth because the pagan Arabs had defiled one of the Christian churches in southern Arabia. Abraha and his forces were, however, defeated. Because the Abyssinians used war elephants for their attempted invasion, many think that this is the elephant referred to in the *sura* titled *al-Fil* in the Quran: 105.

There were numerous Christian settlements throughout the southern and eastern parts of Arabia, but few in the Hijaz, the area of Muhammad's birth. The Hijaz had numerous Jewish settlements, most of long standing, dating to at least the time of the destruction of the Second Temple in 70. According to some scholars, the earliest Jewish presence in the Hijaz was at the time of Nabonidus, about 550. The Jews in these settlements were merchants, farmers, vintners, smiths, and, in the desert, members of Bedouin tribes. The most important Jewish-dominated city was Yathrib, known later as Medina, which featured prominently in Muhammad's career. The Jews of the Hijaz seem to have been mostly independent, but we find evidence of their being allied with both Byzantium and the Persians. Some made the claim to be "kings" of the

Hijaz, most probably meaning tax collectors for the Persians, and, for a variety of reasons, more Jews were loyal to Persian interests against those of the Byzantine empire. Jews, as well as Christians, seem to have been engaged in attempting to convert the Arabian population to their religious and political views, often with some success. The loyalties of the Jews and Christians to one or the other of the two empires meant that choosing either Judaism or Christianity meant also choosing to ally with a superpower interested in dominating Arabia.

Arab sources report that, at the time of Muhammad's birth, some Meccans had abandoned Arabian polytheism and had chosen monotheism. In Arabic these individuals were referred to as *hanif* in a Jewish, Christian, or nonsectarian form. From Quranic and other evidence, it is clear that Meccans were conversant with the general principles of Judaism and Christianity and knew many details of worship, practice, and belief. During Muhammad's formative and early adult years, the character of his birth city, Mecca, was very cosmopolitan.

When Muhammad had his first revelation in 610, his wife Khadija sought the advice of her cousin, Waraqa ibn Nawfal, a *hanif* learned in Jewish and Christian scriptures. Muhammed eventually declared that he was a continuation of the prophetic traditions of Judaism and Christianity, claiming that he had been foretold in Jewish and Christian scripture. A central doctrine of Islam places Muhammad at the end of a chain of prophets from God, starting with Adam and embracing the major prophetic figures of Judaism and Christianity, including Abraham, Moses, and Jesus. Denial of this central idea by Jews and Christians is said to be a result of the corruption of the sacred texts, either inadvertently or on purpose. This disparity of perspective underlies much of what Muslims believe about their Jewish and Christian forebears, and conditions Islamic triumphalist views about the validity of Islam against the partial falsity of the other two traditions.

The Quran and the *Sira* (the traditional biography of Prophet Muhammad) present ambivalent attitudes toward Jews and Christians, reflecting the varied experience of Muhammad and the early Muslim community with Jews and Christians in Arabia. Christians are said to be nearest to Muslims in "love" (Quran 5:82), and yet Muslims are not to take Jews or Christians as "close allies or leaders" (Quran 5:51). The Quran often makes a distinction between the "Children of Israel" (i.e., Jews mentioned in the Bible) and members of the Jewish tribes in Arabia during Muhammad's time. This distinction is also present in the *Sira* and other histories. Some Jews are represented as hostile to Muhammad and his mission, while others become allies with him. The Quranic revelations that Muhammad received in regard to Christians and Jews seemed to correspond to the degree of acceptance that he was awarded by these two communities. Initially, Muhammed sought their acceptance, but when the leaders of the Christian and Jewish communities rejected him as a false prophet, he received revelations that commanded him to distance himself from them. In the "Constitution of Medina," which Muhammad negotiated with the Ansar, the Muhajjirun, and the Jews of Medina, Jews were included in the *Umma*, the community, and were allowed freedom of association and religion in return for the payment of an annual tax. This agreement and the subsequent treaties negotiated by Muhammad with the Jews of Tayma, and other cities in the Hijaz, establish the precedent of symbolically including "People of Scripture" (*Ahl al-Kitab*) in the *Umma*. As the armies of conquest encountered communities of Jews, Christians, and Zoroastrians, the model of Muhammad's accommodating behavior extended the original notion to incorporate all these recipients of God's revelation as *Ahl al-Dhimma*, or *Dhimmi*, protected peoples. There were fewer Christians in the Hijaz than Jews, so Christians are featured less prominently in the political history of the establishment of the Muslim community. Nevertheless, Muhammad had frequent contact with Christians from the southern areas of Najran and Ethiopia, disputing with them as he had with the Jews over matters of religious belief and practice. The traditions surrounding the sending of the Muslims to Ethiopia represent the ruler as seeing little difference between Islam and Christianity. The Quranic presentation of the life of Jesus and Christian belief shows that Muhammad and the early Muslims understood eastern Mediterranean Christian belief and practice, particularly if one acknowledges the importance of the "infancy" Gospels in Christian thought at the time. The Quran, however, denies the deity of Christ.

The death of Muhammad and the subsequent expansion of Islam out of Arabia brought about a definitive break with the Jewish and Christian Arab communities, so that subsequent relations were built on Jewish and Christian interactions with Muslims who knew the Prophet's actions only as idealized history. During the first Islamic century, the period of the most rapid expansion of Islam, social and religious structures were so fluid that it is hard to make generalizations. Jews and Christians were theoretically expelled from Arabia, or, at least, the Hijaz, but later evidence shows that Jews and Christians remained for centuries afterward. As late as the eighteenth century, for example, Jewish Bedouin roamed northwestern Arabia, and Christian Arabs were found in numerous settlements throughout Arabia.

◆ THE EARLY CENTURIES OF MUSLIM HISTORY

The period of the first caliphs and the subsequent era of the Umayyads was a time in which Muslims, Jews, and Christians negotiated the new power arrangements. The parameters of *Dhimmi* status were developed, and both head and land taxes were paid to the Muslim rulers. Jews and Christians related to the Muslim caliphs through representatives and not individually. For the Jews, the Resh Geluta or Exilarch was designated as a "prince" in the Muslim court, representing all the Muslims. Because the Exilarch was from the Rabbinic branch of Judaism, it became the dominant form, generally displacing other groups. Also, because Muslims expanded to include most of the world's Jews in their polity, Rabbinic Judaism was able to develop its institutions within the context of the Islamic *Umma*. For the newly forming Islamic state, the loyalty of the Exilarch, and, by extension, the Jews, added legitimacy to Muslim claims to legitimate rule over its various non-Muslim populations. The interaction between Jews and Muslims thus produced profound effects on both Judaism and Islam.

Christians acted as physicians, architects, clerks,

Fragment of a Syriac book on canon law dealing with the status of Christians in Muslim Society.

and advisors in the courts of the early caliphs. Greek and Coptic were the administrative languages for several centuries before Arabic became established enough to be the general medium of public discourse. Even the occasional uprisings against Muslim rule, as the Coptic uprisings of the early ninth century and the Jewish revolts against the Umayyads a century earlier, were local, over specific grievances, and not anti-Islamic as such. In fact, the Jewish revolt against the Umayyads, driven, it seems, by messianic visions, was sympathetic to early Shia views and attempts to overthrow the last Umayyad caliph.

The first two Islamic centuries was a time of translating Christian and Jewish scripture into Arabic, along with a vast body of commentary, particularly on biblical figures. Quranic *tafsir* (commentaries) became the repository of much Jewish and Christian tradition concerning such figures as Abraham, Moses, Solomon, Jesus, and others. The beginnings of Islamic theological speculation were stimulated by translations of Hellenistic thought from Aramaic, Coptic, Greek, and Syriac. One of the effects of this trend was to produce tension between those inclined toward greater cosmopolitanism of the intellectual and cultural heritage of Hellenism and those who felt that Islamic society should be centered only on the Quran and traditions from Muhammad, presaging the debates about the inclusion or exclusion of outside ideas. The resulting balance between religious and scientific learning became such a part of Islamic societies that even in periods of political fragmentation, Jews and Christians contributed along with Muslims to the intellectual and cultural life of the Islamic communities.

♦ THE MEDIEVAL PERIOD

In the western Islamic lands of the Iberian peninsula and North Africa, Jews, Christians, and Muslims combined in a society that is often described by later historians with the adjective "golden." The areas of poetry, music, art, architecture, theology, exegesis, law, philosophy, medicine, pharmacology, and mysticism were shared among all the inhabitants of the Islamic courts and city-states at the same time that Muslim armies were locked in a losing struggle with the Christian armies of the Reconquista. In the eastern Mediterranean, similar symbiotic societies could be found. The universities of al-Azhar in Cairo and Cordoba in Spain, both founded in the tenth century, followed the older model of the Bayt al-Hikma in Baghdad as places of shared learning among scholars from the three traditions. Both the concept of these types of institutions of learning, as well as the learning itself they produced, had profound influence on European institutions of higher education and European scientific advance-

ment. Within the intellectual circles of the Islamic world, Jews contributed and participated in this civilization through contact with Muslim philosophers and theologians, just as Muslims had from contact with Christians earlier. In the areas of commerce, world trade was dominated by trading associations made up of Muslims, Jews, and Christians from Islamic lands.

The twin attacks on the Islamic world in the Middle Ages by the Crusaders from the West and the Mongols from the East transformed Muslim attitudes toward the *Dhimmi*, and also the attitudes of the Jews and Christians in Islamic lands toward their relations with Muslim polity. Many Islamic areas develop in accordance with an already existing tendency to organize society along military lines. This becomes particularly true in areas where Turkic peoples take over the leading governmental and military roles. Converted by Sunni merchants and organized as military brotherhoods imbued with the spirit of military *jihad*, the Turks became the defenders of the Islamic lands. In their vision of society, the influence of Christians, Jews, and non-Sunni Muslim groups was circumscribed and made more rigid, but it was not eliminated. Muslim religious scholars used depictions of Jews and Christians found in the foundation texts as cautionary models for Muslims, but actual communities of Jews and Christians were treated with strict adherence to legal precedent. The *Dhimmi* had to wear distinctive clothing and badges to indicate their position in society, as did Muslims, as part of a general "uniform" indicating rank and status. Certain occupations became common for Jews and Christians, such as tanning, which was regarded as imparting ritual impurity to Muslims, and it became less common in this period to find Jews and Christians in the highest ranks of advisors to the rulers. Jews and Christians usually lived in separate quarters of cities, and, while they were inferior to Muslims in public and barred from riding horses or blocking the public way with religious processions, they lived autonomously with respect to their communal affairs. This autonomy, while somewhat protective of individuals, was to prove to have long-term consequences. Some Christian communities, caught in the middle of the conflict during the Crusades, actively expressed their loyalty to Rome and Constantinople and looked to the Crusaders as protectors of their interests. This association began a process of separation of some of these communities from the matrix of Muslim polity, and they became viewed as foreign by Muslims and themselves.

When Jews and Muslims were expelled from Spain in 1492, the majority of Jews chose to move to Islamic lands, the area of the Ottoman Empire in particular. The Iberian Jews were so numerous, well educated, and prosperous, that Iberian Jewish culture often supplanted that of the older Jewish communities, so that Sephardic became the general term for Jews living in Islamic lands. The trading and manufacturing skills and the capital of these immigrants to the Ottoman empire provided much of the wealth for Ottoman expansion. Under the Ottomans, Jewish and Christian communities achieved the greatest degree of autonomy. Through the *millet* system, each community was distinct and responsible directly to the Sultan. The most famous intrusions into communal life occurred with the Ottoman institution of the Jannisary corps. Young Christian males were conscripted by the Ottoman military, trained as soldiers, converted to Islam, and placed in high positions in Ottoman administration. The process sometimes produced resentment among Christians, but some families actively sought to have a member chosen because of the possibilities of favors and preferential treatment later when the candidate assumed official duties.

◆ THE MODERN PERIOD

Napoleon's invasion of Egypt in 1798 is generally regarded as the beginning of the modern period of the history of the Islamic Middle East and the beginnings of Western colonialism that was to encompass most of the Islamic lands in Asia and Africa. In reality, it signified the decline of Muslim polities against the economic and technological rise of Western Europe. By the eighteenth century, most Muslims found themselves living in or dependent on one of the three great Muslim empires: the Ottoman, the Mughal, or the Safavid empire. All three empires were agrarian and relied on peasant labor for wealth, military strength, and products for worldwide trade. As Western Europe underwent the technological transformation usually termed the Industrial Revolution, with the concomitant rise of capitalism, it also underwent a social and religious revolution that placed great value on the individual and stressed individual effort and initiative. This reorganization produced societies generally freed from family and clan constraints on labor allocation, rewards, and relations with governing powers such that the societies became more efficient in manufacturing and trading goods on the world market. In the worldwide competition, major areas of the Islamic world became providers of raw or only partially manufactured goods for the industrialized West. When the West sold back the manufactured goods, which often drove superior local goods from the market, it also exposed the Muslim customers to the ideals of the reorganized, industrialized society: individualized human rights, democracy, secularism and secular law, universal education, science, nationalism, and the subordination of religion to the greater ideology of the nation-state.

Western military and economic success proved attractive to many members of the Islamic states who sought to adopt Western ways as a means of securing part of this success.

In the Ottoman Empire, the British and French found Jews and Christians to be willing agents for their commercial activities, and the Ottomans, in turn, were pleased to employ the *Dhimmi* for these purposes as well. Many Jews and Christians sought to secure the benefits of Western societies for themselves and their offspring by asking for and getting Western protection, passports, and, in some instances, citizenship. The *Dhimmi* often fell under the protection of the foreign powers. The increasing identification of Jews and Christians with non-Muslim powers served only to isolate these non-Muslims from the rest of Islamic society. Even in places where there was not an indigenous Jewish or Christian population to be exploited for economic gain, Western European powers arrived as colonialists with professedly Christian institutions, expectations, and ideologies. The British were able to separate Egypt from the Ottoman empire and establish a protectorate in 1882, as they were able to put India under direct British rule in 1857. The French colonized Algeria in 1830 and Tunisia in 1881. The Dutch competed with the British for Southeast Asia, so that by the end of the nineteenth century, most Muslims were under Western political and legal influence. The secular legal systems devised in the West supplanted both Christian and Muslim customary and religious law, seriously challenging or eliminating the category of *Dhimmi* in those countries. The result was often a complete separation of Jews and Christians as groups from a relationship in law with Muslims.

The dissolution of the Ottoman Empire at the end of World War I, resulting in the creation of a number of small nation-states, resulted in a further separation of non-Muslims from Muslims. The ideology of nationalism reduced religion to the status as one of the components of a nation-state ideology. Education became Western, technological, and secular, further reducing religion to peripheral status. By the eve of World War II, most Islamic countries were prepared to overthrow colonialism and establish nation-states. When this happened after World War II, constitutions were modeled after such countries as Switzerland, the United States, and France, usually guaranteeing freedom of religion but providing no particular safeguards for religious expression. Other religious and ethnic groups also desired nation-states. Nominal Christian states were formed in the Balkans, and the state of Israel was formed in the formerly British mandate territory of Palestine. The creation of the state of Israel in 1948 became a central focal point for Muslim-Jewish relations, which had steadily deteriorated since the end of World

War I. The worsening conflicts in Palestine increased Jewish-Muslim conflict in the Arab states, where Jews were seen as both foreign and instruments of Western colonial designs. Within twenty years after the formation of the state of Israel, the majority of Jews living in Arab lands migrated to Israel, thus crystallizing the conflict in Palestine into a Jewish-Muslim conflict. Rulers in predominantly Muslim countries no longer had a constituent Jewish population. Jews were an abstract and hostile other, and Judaism, now increasingly identified with Zionism by Jews and non-Jews alike, was revalorized as the ever-present opposition to Muslims in Islamic history. This last notion, while having its roots in the foundation texts of Islam, was now abstracted in a way unlike any time in the past, and Jewish-Muslim relations took a new direction.

A common thread among many Islamic intellectuals concerned with the role and direction of Muslims in the postcolonial world is the role of the Jews in Islamic history. As mentioned above, the historical circumstances of a strong Jewish presence in the Hijaz during Muhammad's time and the opposition of most of the Jewish tribes to Muhammad's mission embedded numerous seemingly anti-Jewish statements into the early literature. For a few, in a quest to use the Islamic historical past to explain the present, the negative accounts of Judaism and Christianity became abstracted so as to conflate the past with the present Arab-Israeli and East-West conflicts; for example, biblical descriptions of Jews rebelling against God's commands. Medinan Jewish opposition to the forming Muslim state and Israeli actions against Palestinians were read together as an eternal Jewish character, a view sometimes informed by Western anti-Semitic literature. The Egyptian intellectual, Sayyid Qutb's article "Our Struggle with the Jews," is one example as are the views expressed by leaders of the American Nation of Islam.

Other Muslim intellectuals read the same foundation texts with an emphasis on the special relationship between God and People of the Book. While deploring the problems in Palestine, they separate the Arab-Israeli conflict from discussions about Jews and Christians. Some at al-Azhar in Egypt cite the Quran and *sunna* to support peace accords between Israel and the Palestinians, and Warith D. Muhammad, the son of Elijah Muhammad, in the United States has countered the anti-Jewish essentialist reading of the past with a Quranic-based message of mutual cooperation among Muslims, Jews, and Christians.

♦ THE FUTURE

As Islam spreads to new places in the world, more and more Muslims are living as minorities in non-Muslim lands. This, too, has proved to be an intellectual challenge. Some Muslim states and organizations have tried to revive a notion of *Dhimmi* in reverse, seeking to be the protectors of the rights of Muslims in non-Muslim countries, as, for example, the Muslim World League and the Islamic Call Society. Linked to these ideas is the notion of the *dawa*, or attempt to convert non-Muslims to Islam. The situation of minority Muslim communities in Africa, North America, and Asia, many of whom express Islam in ways different from those in Islamic countries where Islam and indigenous cultures are intermixed, is prompting a form of inter-Muslim ecumenism parallel to the willingness of Muslims to participate in the essentially ecumenical dialogues with Jews and Christians, the aims of which are understanding without attempts at conversion.

Discourse about Muslim-Jewish and Christian relations has been dominated in the first half-century by the problems of forming new group identities after the dissolution of colonialism. Muslim, Jewish, and Christian communities have all suffered from conflicts pitting one group against another. As with any conflict, this period has produced considerable polemic. It has also produced positive calls for mutual respect and cooperation. The World Council of Churches has called for positive dialogue with Islam as part of its movement to reach out to people of all religions, and at the Vatican II Council, the Roman Catholic Church called on its members to esteem Muslims. Among synagogues in America, groups are expanding to promote Jewish-Muslim dialogue. As peace treaties are negotiated and conflicts are reduced to nonbelligerency, members of all three religions find themselves in a position to build on the traditions of common heritage and common experience.

Gordon Newby

References

Armstrong, K. *A History of God: the 4000 Year Quest of Judaism, Christianity and Islam.* New York: A.A. Knopf, 1993.

Brinner W.M. and Stephen D. Ricks ed. *Studies in Islamic and Judaic Traditions.* Atlanta: Scholars Press, 1986. Brown Judaic Studies, no. 110.

Burrell, D. and B. McGinn ed. *Creation in Judaism, Christianity and Islam.* Notre Dame: University of Notre Dame Press, 1989.

Cohen, M.R. *Under Crescent and Cross: the Jews in the Middle Ages.* Princeton: Princeton University Press, 1994.

Cragg, Kenneth. *The Call of the Minaret.* New York: Oxford University Press, 1956.

———. *Sandals at the Mosque.* New York: Oxford University Press, 1959.

Cutler A. H. and H. E. Cutler. *The Jew as Ally of the Muslim: Medieval Roots of Anti-Semitism.* Notre Dame: University of Notre Dame Press, 1986.

Ellis, Kail C. *The Vatican, Islam, and the Middle East.* Syracuse: Syracuse University Press, 1987.

Firestone, R. *Journeys in Holy Lands: the Evolution of the Abraham-Ishmael Legends in Islamic Exegesis.* Albany: State University of New York Press, 1990.

Goitein, S.D. *Jews and Arabs: Their Contacts Through the Ages.* New York: Schoken Books, 1955.

Hourani, A.H. *Europe and the Middle East.* Berkeley: University of California Press, 1980.

King, N.Q. *Christian and Muslim in Africa.* New York: Harper and Row, 1971.

Lewis, Bernard. *The Jews of Islam.* Princeton: Princeton University Press, 1984.

McAulliffe, Jane. *The Quranic Christians: An Analysis of Classical and Modern Exegesis.* New York: Cambridge University Press, 1991.

Newby, G. *History of the Jews of Arabia From Ancient Times.* Columbia, S.C.: University of South Carolina Press, 1988.

————. *The Making of the Last Prophet.* Columbia, S.C.: University of South Carolina Press, 1989.

Parrinder G. *Jesus in the Quran.* New York: Oxford University Press, 1977.

Peters F.E. *Judaism, Christianity and Islam: the Classical Texts and Their Interpretation.* Princeton: Princeton University Press, 1990.

Stillman, N.A. *The Jews of Arab Lands: A History and Source Book.* Philadelphia: Jewish Publication Society of North America, 1979.

————. *Studies in Judaism and Islam.* Jerusalem: Magnes Press, 1981.

Wassenstrom, S. ed. *Islam and Judaism: Fourteen Hundred Years of Shared Values.* Portland, Or.: The Institute for Judaic Studies in the Pacific Northwest, n.d.

Watt, Montgomery W. Muslim-Christian Encounters: Perceptions and Misperceptions. *London and New York: Routledge, 1991.*

Part XII:

Contemporary Developments in Islam

33

Islam in the Modern World

♦ Early Reform Movements ♦ Modern Islamist Movements ♦ Popularity of Islamist Movements

The expansion of European power during the eighteenth and nineteenth centuries brought most of the Islamic world under European control. Although Muslim institutions and economic development were seriously disrupted, the impact of the West was far from being wholly negative. Scientific and technological advances and the dissemination of new kinds of knowledge and secular ideas through the medium of print (and later, by audio and visual means) undermined the role of the ulama *(Muslim scholars and jurists) as guardians of traditional values. The transformation of small-scale economies, the opening up of trade, and the introduction of new modes of transport generated educated Muslims able to respond to the challenge of reformulating the message of Islam. In West Africa colonial rule facilitated the spread of Islam. In Southeast Asia the arrival of steamship navigation under colonial auspices placed the* Hajj, *or annual pilgrimage to Mecca, within reach of increasing numbers of peasants and townsfolk who could never have hoped to fulfill the religious duty of the pilgrimage in preindustrial times.* Hajj *savings clubs stimulated local investment. Access to reformist currents spreading from Egypt and India encouraged a more universalist outlook, strengthening mainstream Sunni orthopraxy against local syncretic tendencies, while stiffening anticolonialist activity. In the core areas of Muslim high culture, however, the triumph of Western imperialism and loss of Muslim power generated a series of social, intellectual, and religious crises whose consequences have yet to be resolved.*

♦ EARLY REFORM MOVEMENTS

From the eighteenth century Islamic reformers had prepared the intellectual ground for a modernist movement by seeking to purge Islamic belief and ritual from the accretions and innovations acquired over the centuries, particularly the cults surrounding the Sufi *walis*

(saints), living and dead. It should be noted that these reform movements were not purely antimystical. In India the movement's two leading reformers or "renewers" of Islam were Shaykh Ahmed Sirhindi (1564–1624) and his most famous follower Shah Waliullah (1702–1763). They espoused the moderate Sufism of the Naqshabandi order, while insisting on strict observance of the *sharia* and the purging of Hindu influences. In North Africa the reformist Sanusiya used a typically Sufi network of *zawiyas* (congregational centers) to sustain a movement of renewal that advocated a return to basic principles of the Quran and *hadith* while developing agriculture and trade. Only in Nejd, in the Arabian uplands, did an antimystical renewal take place with the teachings of the Hanbalite scholar Muhammad ibn Abdul Wahhab (1703–1787).

An Islam pruned of its medieval accretions was better able to confront the challenge of foreign power than a local cult bound by the intercessionary power of a particular saint or family of saints. The movements of resistance to European rule during the nineteenth century and early twentieth century were led or inspired by renovators (*mujaddids*), most of them members of Sufi orders who sought to emulate the Prophet Muhammad's example by purifying the religion of their day and waging war on corruption and infidelity. Such movements included the rebellion led by Prince Dipanegara in Java (1825–1830), the *jihad* (holy war) preached among the Yusufzai Pathans on India's northwestern frontier by Sayyid Ahmad Barelwi in 1831, the Naqshabandi Chechen leader Shamil's campaign against the Russians in the Caucasus (1834–1859), and Abdul Qadir's *jihad* against the French in Algeria (1839–1847). However, all such movements were confined to resisting Europeans. The Mahdi Muhammad ibn Abdullah in the Sudan originally campaigned against the imperial ambitions of the Egyptians or "Turks" whom he believed had abandoned Islam to foreigners. The "New Sect" in China, led by another

Naqshshbandi shaykh, Ma Ming Hsin, was behind a series of major revolts against the sinicizing policies of the Manchu emperors during the nineteenth century.

Once it became clear, however, that Muslim arms were no match for the overwhelming technical and military strength of the Europeans, the movement for renewal inevitably took a more intellectually radical turn. Among the elite that had been exposed most directly to the European presence, Muslim failure was seen to lie in the lack of education, economic and cultural attainment, as well as being a result of military defeat. A return to the pristine forms of Islam would not be enough to guarantee the survival of Islam as a civilization and way of life. The more sophisticated nineteenth-century renovators may be divided very broadly into modernists and reformists. Generally speaking, modernism was the doctrine of the political elite and intelligentsia, which had the most exposure to European culture. They recognized that, in order to regain political power, Muslims would have to adopt European military techniques, modernize their economies and administrations, and introduce modern forms of education. On the religious front a new hermeneutic or reinterpretation of the faith in light of modern conditions was required. The modernists' fascination with Europe and all its works often led them to adopt Western clothes and Western lifestyles, which in due course separated them from the more traditionally minded classes. Reformists generally came from the ranks of the *ulama* and were more concerned with religious renewal from within the tradition. However, they absorbed varying amounts of modernist thinking into their reinterpretations of the faith. There are no clear lines dividing the two tendencies, which sometimes merged with each other according to circumstance.

The best-known reformist institution in India, the college of Deoband founded in 1867, not only attacked the cult of saints but adopted a modernist stance in emphasizing personal responsibility in observance of the *sharia*. The Deobandis made full use of modern techniques of communications, including the printing press, the postal service, and the expanding railway network. Deoband contributed significantly to the emergence of India's Muslims as a self-conscious denomination. Unlike the modernists, however, the Deobandis tried to have as little as possible to do with the British or their government. "To like and appreciate the customs of the infidels," wrote a leading Deobandi, Maulana Asraf Ali Thanawi, "is a grave sin." The Tablighi Jamaat, founded by a Deobandi alumnus, Maulana Muhammad Ilyas (1885–1944) in the 1920s and 1930s, reached the population, of the rural areas, which made it harder for the Deobandis to reach their reformist work.

In contrast to the reformist *ulama*, the modernists engaged directly with colonial powers. The most influential modernist thinker to appear in nineteenth-century India was Sir Sayyid Ahmed Khan (1817–1898), founder of the Muhammadan Anglo-Oriental College at Aligarh where, in contrast to Deoband, modern arts and sciences were taught in English alongside traditional Islamic studies. An employee of the East India Company, Khan's aim was to produce an elite of educated Muslims able to compete with Hindus for jobs in the Indian administration. As an aristocrat with family connections with the old Mughal court, the experience of the 1857 "mutiny" or rebellion convinced him of the impossibility of resisting British power. Survival lay in modernizing Islamic thought and institutions. Exercising personal *ijtihad* (or judgment) based on a study of the Quran's Arabic idioms, Sayyid Ahmad Khan made a fundamental distinction between the details of revelation (*furu*) which, he argued, referred to specific historical circumstances, and the general principles (*usul*) underlying them. In principle he believed that the laws of God as revealed through the *sharia* were identical with the laws of nature since, as the Final Cause or Creator, God ultimately determined the causal relationships governing all material and nonmaterial things. Thus, all human ethics derived from these laws. In practice, however, he accepted that the *sharia*, as currently constituted, reflected the ideas and attitudes of the first generations of Muslims. Questioning the *sunna* as an infallible source of law, Ahmad Khan developed a critical methodology of the *hadith* that addressed the content (*matn*) as well as the provenance (*isnad*) in terms very similar to those later employed by such Western scholars as Ignaz Goldziher and Joseph Schacht. All laws, Ahmad Khan declared, were subject to change according to circumstances, excepting the *ibadat* (religious duties). Ahmad Khan's modernist positions would be adopted by subsequent reformers, especially his radical questioning of some *hadith* and his ultimate identification of the *sharia* with the laws of nature. They were fiercely attacked by the Indian *ulama* whom he placated by placing in charge of Islamic studies at Aligarh, thus opening up a cultural division between modern and religious studies that conflicted with his original intentions. The most outspoken attack on Khan, however, came from Jamal al-Din al-Afghani, the pan-Islamic activist who spent much of his life trying to persuade the Muslim world's remaining independent rulers, the shah of Persia and the Ottoman sultan, to stiffen their resistance to European power. Although he shared Ahmad Khan's liberal theological outlook, Afghani regarded Ahmad Khan as a collaborator with the British, and polemically misrepresented his views as amounting to naturalism or materialism. In his view, any weakening of the faith could only undermine the resolve of Muslims to resist European power and cultural encroachments.

In his critique of Sayyid Ahmad Khan, Afghani exposed a dilemma that would continue to haunt Islamic modernists, especially in Sunni countries, up to the present. To harmonize Islamic thinking with the discoveries of modern science, the modernists would have to bypass the traditional *ulama*, and this meant collaboration with those foreign forces that were the agents of modernity. Those same foreign forces were experienced by most Muslim peoples as exploiters and agents of oppression. The desire for modernization clashed with the need to protect the community from foreign domination.

The problem was illustrated in the career of Afghani's famous disciple, Muhammad Abduh (1849–1905). After a period of exile in Paris when he assisted Afghani with the reformist magazine *Al-Urwa al-wuthqa* (*The Indissoluble Link*), Abduh came to the conclusion that he could only achieve his reforms by collaboration with the British-dominated government in Egypt, a decision that set him against both his former master and the *ulama*. Like Ahmad Khan and Afghani, he believed that the truths of science and those of revelation, if understood properly, were in harmony. The purpose of revelation was to help human reason determine what was true and false from a rational utilitarian perspective, not, as the traditionalist *ulama* were inclined, to arbitrarily endow certain acts with the character of good or bad. In some of his legal rulings, Abduh adapted the principle of *maslaha* (public interest) as a means of adjusting the *sharia* to modern requirements: "If a ruling has become the cause of harm which it did not cause before, then we must change it according to the prevailing conditions." He also introduced the principle of *talfiq* (piecing together) previously employed by Shah Waliullah in India, whereby rulings could be arrived at by systematically comparing the views of the four *madhhabs*, the schools of Sunni law, the Quran, the *hadith*, and the practice of the *salaf al salih* (pious ancestors). For this he is regarded as the founder of the *Salafiya* movement, a term sometimes misleadingly translated as "fundamentalism."

Despite his collaboration with the British, Abduh's influence spread westward from Egypt to the Maghreb (North Africa) and eastward as far as Indonesia. Yet in both these regions as well as in the Muslim heartlands, it helped inspire not just religious renewal but anti-colonial resistance by offering understandings of Islam as capable of challenging the traditional, mystical, or quietist persusions within the faith and generating educated Muslims to be independent of the colonial regimes. In French-occupied Algeria, for example, the schools founded by the principal exponent of the reformist (*islah*) movement, Abd al-Hamid bin Badis, became the eventual source of educated opposition to French rule. The same pattern of modernist collabora-

tion leading to resistance occurred in India where the alumni of Aligarh became leaders of Muslim resistance to British rule and, later, supporters of the Pakistan movement. The Europeans recognized the dangers reformist Islam posed to their imperial ambitions and generally came to support more traditionalist and mystical traditions or tendencies, such as those represented by Muridiyya in Senegal founded by Ahmadu Bamba (1850–1927), the Barelwi movement in India founded by Ahmad Riza Khan Barelwi (1856–1929), or the Shia Ismailis under their imams, the Aga Khans.

However, while they contributed to the stiffening of resistance against colonialism, the Salafi movement and its offshoots generally failed in their original objective of reforming the *ulama*. The lack of a centralized religious institution in Sunni Islam militated against comprehensive reform. Instead, the reformist movements tended to develop their own structures parallel to the traditionalist institutions. In due course these became divided into mutually hostile camps: the out-and-out secularists who applied reformist ideas to largely nationalist aims, effectively reducing Islam to the sphere of personal belief; and the fundamentalists or neotraditionalists who sought to reintegrate society into an Islamic framework from beyond the margins of the state.

◆ MODERN ISLAMIST MOVEMENTS

The principal intellectual forbears of the modern Islamic or "Islamist" political movements, which would challenge governments from the Maghreb to Malaysia during the latter decades of the twentieth-century were to be found in Egypt and south Asia, with increasing cross-fertilization between the two regions. In the West Abduh's more conservative disciple, the Syrian Rashid Rida, became the first important advocate of a modernized Islamic state. Rida formulated his views during the crisis surrounding the abolition of the Ottoman caliphate by Kemal Attaturk and the Turkish National Assembly in 1924, a move that was blamed on the colonial victors over the Ottoman empire during the 1914–1918 war and led to a mass agitation among Muslims in India. Although originally a supporter of the caliphate, Rida came to accept its demise as a symptom of Muslim decadence. While being no advocate of secularism, he saw the assembly's decision as a genuine expression of the Islamic principle of consultation (*shura*). The ideal caliph, according to Rida, was an independent interpreter of the law (*mujtahid*) who would work in concert with the *ulama*. In the absence of a suitable candidate and of *ulama* versed in the modern sciences, the best governmental alternative was for an Islamic state ruled by an enlightened elite in consultation with the people, able to interpret the *sharia* and legislate when necessary.

Many of Rida's ideas were taken up by the most influential Sunni reform movement, the Muslim Brotherhood, founded in 1928 by Hasan al Banna, an Egyptian schoolteacher. The Brotherhood's original aims were moral as much as political. It sought to reform society by encouraging Islamic observance and opposing Western cultural influences rather than by attempting to capture the state by direct political action. However, during the mounting crisis over Palestine during and after World War II, the Brotherhood became increasingly radicalized. In 1948 Egyptian Prime Minister Nuqrashi Pasha was assassinated by a Brotherhood member, and Hasan al Banna paid with his life in a retaliatory killing by the security services the following year. The Brotherhood played a leading part in the disturbances that led to the overthrow of the monarchy in 1952, but after the revolution it came into increasing conflict with the nationalist government of Gamal Abdul Nasser. In 1954, after an attempt on Nasser's life, alleged to have been carried out by the Brotherhood, the movement was again suppressed, its members imprisoned, exiled, or driven underground. It was during this period that the Brotherhood became internationalized with affiliated movements springing up in Jordan, Syria, Sudan, Pakistan, Indonesia, and Malaysia. In Saudi Arabia, under the newly established, vigorous leadership of Amir (later King) Faisal ibn Abdul Aziz (reigned 1964–75), the Brotherhood found refuge as well as political and financial support that included funding for the Egyptian underground and salaried posts for exiled intellectuals.

The Islamist or "fundamentalist" movement, which has come to dominate the political agenda of the Muslim heartland during the latter decades of the twentieth-century, owed much to the new synergy between India and Egypt as the works of its leading Muslim thinkers in both countries became available in translation. The seminal thinker of Indian Islam in the first half of the twentieth century was Muhammad Iqbal (died 1938), a poet, mystic, philosopher, and a moving spirit behind the Pakistan movement. Unfortunately, he did not live to see the establishment of this Muslim state. Drawing on a broad range of Islamic and Western thinkers, he developed a modernist theology free from historicism. The Islamic state, he argued, should not be confused with the model of the caliphate established after the death of the Prophet Muhammad, despite the fact that it was an ideal still dormant in the consciences of men and women. Political activity must be directed not at the restoration of an idealized past, but toward a future in which the caliphate, or vicegerency under God, would be equated with service to humankind. Although Iqbal was liberal in his outlook, his ideas had a major impact on the ultraconservative thinker, Abul Ala Mawdudi (1903–1979), who became a powerful influence among Sunni radicals. Unlike Abduh and other liberal reformers, Mawdudi included much of the traditional body of *fiqh* (jurisprudence) in his definition of what constitutes the *sharia* law. For example, he advocated strict *purdah* (seclusion) for women. But he shared Iqbal's vision of the *sharia* as a dynamic system of law that could be continually added to by the exercise of *ijtihad*. In effect, he wanted to extend the intricate and detailed structure of *fiqh*, traditionally restricted to matters of personal status, to include every aspect of modern life. One of Mawdudi's doctrines, in particular, was to have a major impact on Islamic political movement. It was the idea, adapted from Iqbal, that the struggle for Islam was not for the restoration of an ideal past, but for a principle vital to the here and now: the vicegerency of human society under God's sovereignty. The *jihad* was, therefore, not just a defensive war for the protection of the Islamic territory or Dar ul Islam. It might be waged against governments that prevent the preaching of true Islam, for the condition of *jahiliyya* (the state of ignorance before the coming of Islam) was to be found everywhere.

Such ideas were adopted and developed in the Arab world by Sayyid Qutb, the Muslim Brotherhood's most influential theorist, executed in 1966 for an alleged plot to overthrow the Egyptian government. During his years in prison, Qutb, who had spent some time in the United States as a member of an Egyptian educational delegation, wrote a comprehensive account of the modern *jahiliyya* in his book *Maalim fi-tariq* (*Signposts along the Way*).

> Today we are in the midst of a *jahiliyya* similar to or even worse than the *jahiliyya* that was "squeezed out" by Islam. Everything about us is *jahiliyya:* the ideas of mankind and their beliefs, their customs and traditions, the sources of their culture, their arts and literature, and their laws and regulations. [This is true] to such an extent that much of what we consider to be Islamic culture and Islamic sources, and Islamic philosophy and Islamic thought> . . . is nevertheless the product of that *jahiliyya.*

Qutb advocated the creation of a new elite among Muslim youth that would fight the new *jahiliyya* as the Prophet had fought the old one. Like the Prophet and his Companions, this elite must choose when to withdraw from the *jahiliyya* and when to seek contact with it. His ideas set the agenda for radicals, not just in Egypt but throughout the Sunni Muslim world. Groups influenced by them included Shukri Mustafa, a former Muslim Brotherhood activist and leader of a group known as *Takfir wa Hijra* (excommunication and emigration) who followed the early Kharijites in designating their enemies (in this case the government) as *kafirs* (infidels); Khalid Istambuli and Abdul Salaam Farraj, executed for the murder of President Anwar Sadat in October 1981; and the *Hizb al-Tahrir* (Islamic Liberation Party) founded in 1952 by Shaykh Taqi al-Din al- Nabahani (1910–1977), a graduate of al-Azhar whose writings lay down detailed prescriptions for a restored caliphate.

While Qutb's writings remained an important influence on "Islamists" from Algeria to Pakistan, the major thrust to the movement came from Iran where the Ayatollah Khomeini came to power after the collapse of the Pahlavi regime in February 1979. During the final two decades of the twentieth-century, the Iranian revolution has remained the inspiration for Muslim radicals or "Islamists" from Morocco to Indonesia. Despite this, the revolution never succeeded in spreading beyond the confines of Shia communities and, even among them, its appeal remained limited. During the eight-year war that followed Iraq's invasion of Iran in 1980, the Iraqi Shia who form about 50 percent of the population conspicuously failed to support their coreligionists in Iran. The revolution did spread to Shia communities in Lebanon and Afghanistan but generally proved unable to cross the sectarian divide. The new Shia activism it generated in these countries and in Pakistan tended to stir up sectarian conflicts.

Within Iran the success of the revolution had rested on three factors usually absent from the Sunni world: the mixing of Shia and Marxist ideas among the radicalized urban youth during the 1970s; the autonomy of the Shia religious establishment, which, unlike the Sunni *ulama*, disposed of a considerable amount of social power as a body or "estate"; and the eschatological expectations of popular Shiism surrounding the return of the Twelfth Imam.

The leading exponent of Islam as a revolutionary ideology in Iran was Ali Shariati (died 1977), a historian and sociologist who had been partly educated in Paris. Though without formal religious training, Shariati reached large numbers of youth from the traditional classes through his popular lectures at the Husayniyeh Irshad (Husayn Guidance Center), an informal academy he established in Tehran. Shariati's teachings contain a rich mix of ideas in which theosophical speculations of mystics like Ibn al-Arabi and Mulla Sadra were blended with the insights of Marx, Jean-Paul Sartre, Albert Camus, and Franz Fanon (whose friend he was and whose books he translated into Farsi). The result was an eclectic synthesis of Islamic and leftist ideas. God was virtually identified with the "people," justifying revolutionary action in the name of Islam. An outspoken critic of those members of religious leaders who acquiesced in the Shah's tyranny, Shariati drew a distinction between the official Shiism

of the Safavid dynasty (1501–1722), which made Shism the state religion in Iran, and the "revolutionary" commitment of such archetypical Shia figures as the Imams Ali and Husayn and Abu Dharr al Ghifari (a Companion of the Prophet often credited by some modern Muslims with having socialist principles). Shariati's ideas, disseminated through photocopies and audiotapes, provided a vital link between the student vanguard and the more conservative forces that brought down the Shah's regime. The latter were mobilized by Sayyid Ruhallah Khomeini, an ayatollah or senior jurist and scholar from Qom, who had come to prominence as the leading critic of Shah Muhammad Reza Pahlavi's "White Revolution" during the early 1960s. This was a series of agricultural and social reforms that threatened the interest of the religious establishment, not least because the estates from which many of the *ulama* drew their incomes were expropriated or divided up. Exiled to Najaf in Iraq, Khomeini developed his theory of government, the *Wilayet-i-faqih* (jurisconsult's trusteeship), which radically broke with tradition by insisting that government be entrusted directly to the religious establishment:

> The slogan of the separation of religion and politics and the demand that Islamic scholars should not intervene in social or political affairs have been formulated and propagated by the imperialists; it is only the irreligious who repeat them. Were religion and politics separate at the time of the Prophet?

Popular Shiism focuses on the martyred figures of Ali and Husayn and the expected return of the Twelfth Imam to restore justice and peace in the world. These motifs were skillfully deployed in the mass demonstrations preceding the fall of the Shah of Iran in 1978–1997. Though Khomeini never claimed to be the Hidden Imam, there can be no doubt that, by allowing his followers to address him as "imam," a title normally reserved by Shias for the imams of the Prophet's house (*ahl al bait*), Khomeini allowed popular eschatological expectations to work on his behalf.

Contrary to the view widely held in the West, however, Khomeini did not impose a fully "Islamic" system of government. The 1979 constitution is really a hybrid of Islamic and Western liberal concepts. As Sami Zubaida points out, there is a "contradictory duality of sovereignties." Article 6 of the constitution refers to the "sovereignty of the popular will" in line with democratic national states, but the principle of *Wilayet i faqih* gave sweeping powers to Khomeini as "chief jurisconsult" or trustee. The constitution is the keystone of a range of institutions, including the *majlis i shura* (consultative assembly) composed of elected members under the supervision of a Council of Guardians. Though the *sharia* is supposed to be the basis for all law and legislation, many of the civil codes from the previous regime were retained. There were three court systems: the *madani* (civil) courts, the *sharia* courts, and the "revolutionary courts," which handed out often arbitrary punishments by the *komitehs* or revolutionary guards.

♦ POPULARITY OF ISLAMIST MOVEMENTS

Several factors accounted for the increasing popularity of the Islamist movements and ideologies as the twentieth-century draws to its close. The collapse of communism and the failure of Marxism to overcome the stigma of "aetheism" made Islam seem an attractive ideological weapon against regimes grown increasingly corrupt, authoritarian, and sometimes tyrannical. As a center of opposition, the mosque enjoyed privileged status. If governments dared to close down "rebel" mosques, they merely confirmed the charges of disbelief leveled against them by their opponents. The explosion of information technology and particularly the revolution in audiovisual communication undercut the authority of the literate elite, while exposing ever-growing numbers of people to the transgressive and often lustful images created by the Western entertainment and advertising industries. An exponential leap in the rate of urbanization decisively altered the cultural and demographic balance between urban and rural populations, creating a vast new proletariat of recently urbanized migrants susceptible to the messages of populist preachers and demagogues. In some cases, the Islamist movements, through their welfare organizations, were able to fill the gaps caused by government failure to deal with housing shortages and other social problems created by overrapid urbanization.

The responses of governments to the challenge of political Islam ranged from outright repression to co-optation and accommodation. In the Syrian city of Hama a rebellion by the Muslim Brotherhood in 1982 was suppressed by the government of President Hafez al-Asad at a human cost estimated at between five-thousand and twenty-thousand lives. In Algeria the army's cancellation of the second round of the national elections after the Islamic Salvation Front won the first round in December 1991 led to an increasingly bloody civil war that came to resemble, in its barbarity and carelessness for the lives of noncombatants, the campaign fought by the French against Algerian nationalists nearly two generations earlier. In Jordan, however, King Hussein has proved relatively successful in containing militancy within the parliamentary system. In Egypt the government adopted a broadly similar strategy, co-opting the moderates by allowing the Muslim Brotherhood to be represented through other parties in

the National Assembly. Brotherhood members also found outlets in the Islamic banking sector, financed from the Gulf and Saudi Arabia, which developed into new sources of power and patronage. The more militant Islamist elements led by the *al-Jihad* group and *al-Jamaat al-Islamiya* (the Islamic Associations), active on university campuses since the 1970s, continued to wage a sporadic war of attrition against the regime, attacking Christians, government officials, "secular" intellectuals, and foreign tourists.

In Sudan co-option by the military went further than anywhere else (except Pakistan during the administration of the late President Zia al-Haqq), with the veteran Muslim Brotherhood politician Hasan al-Turabi actually holding power under the military government of General Omar al-Bashir. In Malaysia where the dominant Muslim Malays form only just over half the population, the ruling coalition made gestures toward "Islamic correctness" in response to the demands of the pan-Islamic "Dakwa" movement while trying to avoid putting off foreign investors or stirring sectarian tensions. In Indonesia, the world's most populous Muslim state, President Suharto has made similar symbolic gestures in response to the influence of the Nahdatul Ulama, an Islamic education and welfare organization that claims twenty-million followers. However, *Pancasila*, a syncretic concept drawing on the country's Islamic, Hindu, Buddhist, and Christian traditions, remains the official ideology of the state.

Elsewhere, "Islamization" policies, whether imposed "from above" by governments or applied locally "from below," have led to restrictions of the rights of women and religious minorities as modernist interpretations of Islamic precepts have given ground to more traditionalist attitudes. The increasing tendency to articulate political aims in religiously perceived terms has found constituencies in newly urbanized migrants whose understandings were typically formed in rural village milieus by *mullas* or *ulama* with minimal access to modernist influences. Consequently, the modernist tendency, which formed an important strand in the discourse of Abduh, Qutb, Banna, and even (to a lesser extent) Mawdudi, has been swamped by the traditionalism of the recently mobilized masses. This has by no means happened everywhere, however. In Central Asia the people rejected the "Islamist" alternative after the collapse of the former Soviet Union, despite a resurgence of activity among the young and a revival of Islamic education in schools and colleges. While Russian manipulation partly accounted for the return of the old communist *nomenklaturas* under new nationalist labels, it has become clear that in societies where literacy was universal, a consensus in favor of religiously conceived forms of government is conspicuously absent.

In the Muslim heartlands, as Olivier Roy points out, modernization has already occurred, but it has not been absorbed within a commonly recognized and accepted conceptual framework. Modernization has happened "through rural exodus, emigration, consumption, the change in family behavior (a lower birthrate) but also through the cinema, music, clothing, satellite antennas, that is, through the globalization of popular culture." The resulting confusion has particularly affected the position of women, formerly the protected and symbolically "invisible" half of traditional Muslim societies. As in most other parts of the world, the global economy is breaking down old extended family structures, leading to a growing necessity for women to earn cash incomes or to increase their earnings and be recognized for their efforts. Some patriarchal laws enshrined in the Muslim jurisprudential works of the past are being applied in response to populist demands that doubtless reflect anxieties about the loss of male status. The removal of traditional restrictions on female mobility is not only leaving women less protected, leading to increasing attacks by men, it is also being accompanied by demands for the application of Quranic penalties for sexual misbehavior under court proceedings where women are at a legal disadvantage. However, women's voices and organizations, both in their traditional and modern frameworks, are increasingly being heard and becoming visible.

Similar considerations apply to sectarian issues. Under modern conditions, sectarian or ethnic rivalries that coexisted in a rough or ritualized manner in premodern times acquire a violent dimension. In contrast to their predecessors, modern Muslim governments have tried to enforce religious and ideological uniformity on all their citizens, regardless of religious background. The result has been a significant increase in sectarian conflicts in countries with different Muslim traditions, including Turkey and Pakistan.

The legitimacy of the territorial governments established after decolonization was always open to challenge on Islamic grounds. The new national states were, in most cases, being imposed on societies where culture of public institutions was weak and where ties of kinship prevailed over allegiances to corporate bodies. In most Middle Eastern countries and many others beyond the Muslim heartlands, the ruling institutions fell victim to manipulation by factions based on kinship, regional, or sectarian loyalties. Even when the army took power, as the only corporate group possessing internal cohesion, the elite corps who buttressed the leadership were often drawn from a particular family, sect, or tribe. In the period following decolonization, the new elites legitimized themselves by appealing to nationalist goals. Their failure to "deliver the goods," either economically or militarily (especially in the case

of the states confronting Israel and in Pakistan, which has proved unable to recover the disputed part of Kashmir from India), led to an erosion of their popular bases and the rise of movements pledged to "restore" Islamic forms of government after years of *jahiliyya* rule.

Following the collapse of communism, "Islamism" is likely to dominate the political discourse in Muslim lands for the foreseeable future. For all the anxieties expressed in the West about a future "clash of civilizations," it seems unlikely to effect significant external political change. Existing Muslim states are locked into the international system. Despite the turbulence in Algeria and episodes of violence in Egypt, there have been fewer violent changes of government in the Middle East since 1970 than in the preceding two decades when different versions of nationalism competed for power. At the same time, the political instability in Pakistan and the continuing civil war in Afghanistan demonstrate that, in its current political or ideological forms, such "Muslim" models of governance are unable to transcend ethnic and sectarian divisions. The territorial state, though never formally sanctified by Muslim legal precedent or tradition, is proving highly resilient, not least because of the support it receives militarily and economically through the international system. For all the protests by Islamist movements that Saddam Hussein's invasion of Kuwait in August 1990 was a "Muslim affair," the result of Operation Desert Storm (in which the Muslim armies of Egypt, Pakistan, Syria, and Saudi Arabia took part) demonstrated conclusively that where major economic and political interests are at stake, the status quo wins.

In the long term, the globalization of culture through the revolution in communications technology must lead to a form of secularization in Muslim societies, not least because of the increasing availability of religious and cultural choice. A significant factor will be the presence of a large and growing Muslim diaspora (educated in the West) able to rediscover in Islam a voluntary faith freed from the imperatives of national enforcement while finding an expression for Muslim values through voluntary activity. The record of African American Muslim communities in combating economic and social problems, particularly drug dependency in the inner cities in the United States, is well documented. A very different example of voluntary activity inspired by Islamic values is provided by the Ismaili community who, through their philanthropic and development activities, regularly raise funds for the Aga Khan Foundation and other development agencies on a nonsectarian basis. British Muslim organizations have been active in raising funds for the relief of Muslims in Bosnia. The Grameen Bank concept by Muhammad Yunus, which enables poor, rural populations, particularly women, to be financially self-reliant, is being replicated in many parts of the world.

Although the political dimensions of Muslim activity appear to be in the ascendant, it is the community development and the devotional and spiritual traditions that promise to open up significant possibilities in the future. Both Mawdudi and al-Banna built faith and piety into their systems, believing that society must be transformed before the state could be conquered. Though the militants and activists who followed them, obsessed with corruption of governments and embittered by the appalling treatment many of them received at the hands of the state, have tended to focus on political action, not least because killings and bombings are bound to attract attention in an international culture dominated by television, there is evidence that quietist, moderate versions of Islam are rapidly gaining ground. The Tablighi Jamaat, originally founded in India, has spread to more than ninety countries from Malaysia to Canada and is now becoming thoroughly internationalized. Though active in promoting the faith, it is explicitly nonpolitical. Even within Muslim countries "it does not concern itself with the argument that Islam should provide the framework of political life." In the diaspora there is clear evidence that another major evangelical (*dawa*) organization, the Jamaat al-Islami founded by Mawdudi, is moving away from the hard political line it sustained in the past in order to attract Western converts. With globalization eroding the classic distinction between the traditional world of Islam and the outside world, it seems likely that the coming decades will see a retreat from direct political action and a renewed emphasis on the personal, private, community, and development aspects of faith.

For all the efforts to conquer the state on the basis of new collectivist ideologies constructed on the ruins of Marxism and with the use of some of its materials, the processes of historical and technological change point remorselessly toward increasing individualism and personal choice, primary agents of secularity. While regional conflicts such as Palestine or Kashmir or a political struggle for power as in Algeria may continue to be articulated in Islamic terms, the long-term prospects for Islam point to inevitable modernization. In an era when individuals are ever less bound by ties of kinship and increasingly exposed to urban alienation, Muslim souls are likely to find the path of inner exploration and community development more rewarding than revolutionary politics.

Malise Ruthven

References

Ahmad, Aziz. *Islamic Modernism in India and Pakistan.* Oxford: Oxford University Press, 1967.

Ahmed, Akbar S. *Discovering Islam: Making Sense of Muslim History and Society.* London: Kegan Paul, 1988.

Akhtar, Shabbir. *A Faith for All Seasons: Islam and Western Modernity.* London: Bellew, 1990.

Ali, Shariati. *On Sociology of Islam.* Translated by Hamid Algar. Berkeley: Mizan Press, 1979.

Arjomand, Said A. *The Turban for the Crown: The Islamic Revolution in Iran.* New York: Oxford University Press, 1988.

Arkoun, Mohammed. *Rethinking Islam.* Boulder, CO.: Westview Press, 1994.

Binder, Leonard. *Islamic Liberalism: A Critique of Development Ideologies.* Chicago: University of Chicago Press, 1988.

Burgat, F., and W. Dowell. *The Islamic Movement in North Africa.* Austin: University of Texas Press, 1993.

Denny, Frederick Mathewson. *An Introduction to Islam.* 2d ed. New York: Macmillan, 1994.

Evans-Pritchard, E. *The Sanusi of Cyrenaica.* Oxford: Clarendon Press, 1949.

Fundamentalism, the Family and Global Conflict. Edited by Martin E. Marty and R. Scott Appleby. New York: Foreign Policy Association, 1994.

Gammer, Gammer. *Muslim Resistance to the Tsar—Shamil and the Conquest of Chechnia and Daghestan.* London: F. Cass, 1994.

Gladney, Dru C. *Muslim Chinese: Ethnic Nationalism in the People's Republic.* Cambridge: Council on East Asian Studies, Harvard University, 1991.

Holt, P. M. *The Mahdist State in the Sudan.* Oxford: Clarendon Press, 1958.

———. *A History of the Arab Peoples.* Cambridge: Harvard University Press, 1991.

Hourani, Albert. *Arabic Thought in the Liberal Age.* Oxford: Oxford University Press, 1962.

Hussin, Mutalib. *Islam and Ethnicity in Malay Politics.* Singapore: Oxford University Press, 1968.

Islam and Development—Religion and Sociopolitical Change. Edited by John L. Esposito. Syracuse: Syracuse University Press, 1980.

Keddie, N. *An Islamic Response to Imperialism.* Berkeley: University of California Press, 1968.

Kepel, Giles. *The Prophet and Pharaoh: Muslim Extremism in Egypt.* London: University of California Press, 1985.

Khumayni, Ayatullah Ruh Allah. *Islam and Revolution: Selection of Speeches and Writings.* Translated and edited by H. Algar. Berkeley: Mizan Press, 1981.

Lapidus, Ira. *A History of Islamic Societies.* Cambridge: Cambridge University Press, 1988.

Lewis, Philip. *Islamic Britain: Religion and Politics and Identity among British Muslims.* London: I. B. Taurus, 1994.

Mayer, Ann. *Islam and Human Rights.* Boulder, Colo.: Westview Press, 1991.

Mitchell, Richard. *The Society of the Muslim Brothers.* New York: Oxford University Press, 1993.

Muslim Identity and Social Change in Sub-Saharan Africa. Edited by L. Brenner. Bloomington: University of Indiana Press, 1993.

Muslim Travellers Pilgrimage, Migration and the Religious Imagination. Edited by Dale E. Eickelman and James Piscatori. Berkeley: University of California Press, 1990.

Naumkin, Vitaly. *Central Asia and Transcaucasia: Ethnicity and Conflict.* Westport, Conn.: Greenwood Press, 1994.

O'Brien, Donald Cruise. *The Mourides of Senegal: The Political and Economic Organization of an Islamic Brotherhood.* Oxford: Clarendon Press, 1971.

Peters, F. *Islam and Colonialism: The Doctrine of Jihad in Modern History.* The Hague, Netherlands: Mouton, 1979.

Poston, L. *Islamic Dawah in the West: Muslim Missionary Activity and the Dynamics of Conversion to Islam.* New York: Oxford University Press, 1992.

Roy, Oliver. *The Failure of Political Islam.* Cambridge: Harvard University Press, 1994.

Ruthven, Malise. *Islam in the World.* London: Oxford University Press, 1984.

Troll, C. W. *Sayyid Ahmad Khan—A Reinterpretation of Muslim Theology.* Dehli: Vikas Publications, 1979.

Zubaida, Sami. *Islam: The People and the State.* London: Routledge, 1993.

34

Displaced Muslim Populations

♦ Defining Displacement
♦ Involuntary Displacement: Refugees, the Internally Displaced, and Oustees
♦ Voluntary Displacement: Migrants and Immigrants ♦ Magnitude of Muslim Displacement
♦ Voluntary Displacement of Muslims: Migration ♦ Afghan Refugees in Pakistan
♦ Characteristics of Afghan Refugees

A pattern of migration, coupled with disruptions caused by economic, social, and political factors, has resulted in the displacement of Muslims around the world in the twentieth century. In the recent past, the treatment of displaced Muslims has caused grave concern, particularly the plight of such displaced groups as Bosnians, Kurds, Palestinians, Tajiks, and North Africans, to mention some contemporary examples. The whole question of the voluntary or involuntary movement of Muslims around the world has yet to be studied in any detail. There are as yet no reliable estimates of displaced Muslims around the world. This chapter provides an overview of the displacement of Muslims in broad terms and uses the case study of Afghanistan to illustrate the problem. The example is used to highlight characteristics and reasons for displacement, the impact of displacement within a population that shares or has a different set of religious and cultural values, the international and national response to displacement including the effects of displacement on the host society, and patterns of settlement and integration. The study is intended to encourage discussion to improve people's understanding of the situation of displaced Muslim individuals, families, and communities, and to identify strategies which respond genuinely to their needs. A special attempt is made to provide an understanding of the impact of displacement from the perspective of the affected Muslim group and to identify the role religion and culture play in providing support or in creating conflicts between the newcomers and the host society.

♦ DEFINING DISPLACEMENT

Displaced populations share a major common characteristic: uprootedness from an established location or lifestyle. There are two major categories of displaced populations: involuntary migrants who are forced to move due to war, political strife, natural disasters or as a result of development projects; and voluntary migrants, legal or undocumented.

Involuntary migrants (whether they are victims of disasters, wars, political strife, or ethnic conflicts) who cross national boundaries become refugees, while those who are forced to disperse within their own countries become internally displaced. Despite commonalities among the two groups, one can divide each of these displaced groups into: refugees who cross borders; internally displaced who are within the borders of their own countries both due to civil wars and persecution; and oustees who are uprooted by development projects. These are discussed separately in literature as three distinct groups. Nevertheless, all displaced groups share many common characteristics; whether they migrate voluntarily or are forced to relocate, all of them suffer social, psychological, and economic losses.

♦ INVOLUNTARY DISPLACEMENT: REFUGEES, THE INTERNALLY DISPLACED, AND OUSTEES

Refugees

The term *refugee* is defined by the United Nations Convention Relating to the Status of Refugees as a person who:

"Owing to well-founded fear of being persecuted for reasons of race, religion, nationality, membership of a particular social group or political opinion is outside the country of his nationality and is unable, or owing to fear, is unwilling to avail himself of the protection of that country; or who, not having a nationality and being outside the country of his former habitual residence as a result of such events, is unable or, owing to such fear, is unwilling to return to it." The Organization of African Unity extended this definition to cover any person who "owing to external aggression, occupation, foreign domination or events seriously disturbing public order in either part of or whole country, is compelled to seek refuge outside his country of origin" (Organization of African Unity, 1989).

The concept and definition of refugees are derived largely from two periods in history. The first period followed the dissolution of colonial rule, during which the inhabitants of past colonies fled terror and oppression related either to their association with colonial powers or conflicts left in the wake of colonial rule. Britain, for instance, accepted many refugees from the Indian subcontinent and from former African colonies; many never returned to their homes. The second period followed World War II and the decades during which much of Eastern Europe fell under communist rule and millions of Europeans were displaced.

The Internally Displaced

While there is no internationally agreed upon definition, one suggested in a United Nations report but not adopted, defines *internally displaced* as: "persons who have been forced to flee their home unexpectedly in large numbers, as a result of armed conflict, internal strife, and systematic violation of human rights or natural or man-made disasters; and who are within the territory of their own country" (Analytic Report of the Secretary General, February 1992). The factors that trigger displacement for refugees and internally displaced are often identical and result in similar consequences.

Oustees

Another major group of internally displaced persons are the *oustees*. The term *oustees* is used to refer to people who are forcibly displaced from their "habitat through government intervention" for development projects. Economic, social, and psychological losses and trauma experienced by oustees from forced resettlement within their country is comparable in scope to the trauma and loss of those internally or internationally displaced due to natural or man-made disasters such as famines, civil wars, ethnic strifes, or political persecution.

◆ VOLUNTARY DISPLACEMENT: MIGRANTS AND IMMIGRANTS

Immigrants are persons who voluntarily cross national boundaries to take up permanent residence in other countries. Many move from their place of origin in search of improved economic opportunities and/or education. The move may be temporary or permanent. Those who move temporarily are referred to as migrants, while those who established legal permanent residency are referred to as immigrants. Temporary migrants are admitted for limited periods and are provided with work permits. Many temporarily displaced individuals and families, though they have strong emotional ties to their families and communities in their home countries, do not return home; they live under the "myth of return" and become permanent migrants.

◆ MAGNITUDE OF MUSLIM DISPLACEMENT

Major international crises as in Afghanistan, the Middle East, Chechnia, Iraq, and Somalia have forced Muslim individuals, families, communities, and nations to come to terms with the evils of displacement. In the case of Bosnia, ghosts of ethnic cleansing and genocide have reappeared. Such crises have confronted the international community to develop mechanisms for refugee protection and to establish temporary safe havens. Similarly, global economic integration, communication, and transportation networks have created large flows of voluntary international migrants, legal and illegal. In recent times an estimated twenty-three million refugees have been uprooted worldwide against their will, displaced from their homes and forced to seek asylum in other countries. An equal number are displaced within their own countries for reasons similar to those that precipitated international displacement. They suffer severe hardships and, in turn, adversely effect hundreds of million of people among whom they seek haven and succor; mass displacement has become a truly global phenomena in which Muslims have been both victims and perpetrators.

Most of the estimated forty million refugees are found in the developing countries whose economic, environmental, and political resources have, as a result, been stretched to breaking point. Statistical data on numbers of refugees are not reported by religious affiliation, but by country of origin and country of asylum or resettlement. In this survey the displacement of Muslims as refugees, and the impact of displacement on Muslim countries for provision of asylum and haven, have been identified by locating countries with a Muslim population of over 90 percent.

Afghanistan

It is estimated that five million Afghan Muslims fled to Pakistan and Iran during the then Soviet occupation of Afghanistan, creating the single largest refugee population in the world. Despite the withdrawal of the former Soviet Union from Afghanistan and efforts on the part of the United Nations High Commission for Refugees (UNHCR), the United States, and Pakistan, two million refugees still reside in Pakistan. In addition, there has been a recent reverse flow after the repatriation efforts because of internal conflicts in Afghanistan.

Burma

In Myanmar (formerly known as Burma) tens of thousands of Muslims poured into southeastern Bangladesh. Since Burmese independence from Britain in 1948, the government has carried out terror campaigns with the aim of evicting the Arakanese Muslim population. Over 250,000 Rohingya Muslims fled to Bangladesh between December 1991 and April 1992, accusing junta soldiers of torture, rape, and murder.

Refugees and Asylum Seekers in Need of Protection from, or Who Receive Assistance in Countries of the World with Muslim Populations of 90 percent

MIDDLE EAST
· Afghanistan
· Iran
· Iraq
· Arab Republic of Yemen
NORTH AFRICA
· Algeria
· Egypt
NORTHEAST AFRICA
· Somalia
WEST AFRICA
· Guinea
· Mauritania
ASIA
· Bangladesh
· Pakistan
EUROPE
· Bosnia

Reports indicate that large numbers of Muslims have been victims of persecution and displaced voluntarily in Africa and Asia, two continents with the largest number of refugees in the world.

Iraq

During and after the Persian Gulf War in 1991, approximately two million Kurds were forced to flee their homes in Iraq to various destinations such as Iran and Turkey. Over the last sixteen years, it has been estimated that the Iraqi army has destroyed four-thousand Kurdish villages and towns and deported their inhabitants. The Kurds are one of the world's largest ethnic groups without a homeland.

Bosnia

According to statistics from the UNHCR, there were 1.2 million displaced people inside the former Yugoslavia as of 1991 (*The Economist*, 23 May 1992). This includes Serbs, Croats, and Muslims. More than 2 million Bosnians are refugees, and out of these, 1.2 million are internally displaced. Out of 24 million people from the six republics that formed Yugoslavia, 3.5 million are refugees (internally and externally displaced); many have lost their homes and families and have been without adequate food and medical care. The emergency in the former Yugoslavia has been described as one of the largest in the history of UNHCR. In the last three years the situation has become increasingly worse.

Palestinians

An ongoing controversy has been the uprooting of Palestinians in the occupied territories. A large percentage of the Palestinians are Muslims who have received safe haven in neighboring Muslim countries. This struggle over land in that region of the world has an ancient history. It is estimated that there are roughly 2 million Palestinians in the occupied territories, with 1.2 million in the West Bank and 800,000 in the Gaza. There are 6 million Palestinians worldwide (*National Geographic*, June 1992) most of whom are registered as refugees. Current peace efforts raise hope for these displaced Palestinians and for tranquility among various groups in the region.

Somalia

More than one million people have left Somalia to escape war and famine. In January 1991 alone, the collapse of the military regime forced two-hundred-thousand new Somali refugees into Ethiopia. Yemen, one of the world's poorest countries, was housing fifty-thousand Somalis as of early 1993. Another one million residents of Yemen are estimated to be from Saudi Arabia and other countries in the Gulf as a result of the Gulf War.

The Former Soviet Union

The breakup of the Soviet Union has led to ethnic tensions and military conflict in Central Asia, affecting many thousands, if not millions, of Muslims. It is possible that the worlds' refugee population could be doubled due to strife in Azerbaijan, Uzbekistan, and Tajikistan

.Another factor which may cause involuntary displacement is natural disasters. The cyclone in Bangladesh and the earthquake in Iran in 1990 left approximately 500,000 people homeless. Such disasters usually lead to internal displacement, and have taken a great toll on Muslim lives. With proper prevention, the effects of earthquakes do not have to be as devastating as they often are. Unfortunately, many poor countries are unable to take the necessary precautions. Many structures in San Francisco, for example, are made of steel and wood with a timber frame. While not totally earthquake-resistant, they are certainly more resistant than the mud-baked or concrete houses in hillside villages in Iran.

Most of the over forty million refugees (twenty million internationally and twenty million internally displaced persons) are found in developing countries whose economic, environmental, and political resources are stretched to the breaking point. Statistical data on the numbers of refugees are not reported by religious affiliation. Rather, refugee data are reported by country of origin and country of asylum or resettle-

ment. To estimate the impact of displacement on Muslim countries that provide asylum and haven, we first identified countries with a Muslim population of over 85 percent, using data form the World Almanac (1995). We then listed the number of refugees in those countries as reported in the World Refugee Report (1994). Our analysis is presented below.

The 20 countries listed above, each with a predominantly Muslim population, hosted 8,142,100 refugees, which constitutes 50 percent of a grand total of 16,255,000 refugees listed in the World Refugee Report as of December 1993. The discrepancy between the total number of 16 million listed here and over 20 million listed by other sources can be partially accounted for by the fact that the numbers listed in the World Refugee report do not include refugees who are permanently resettled in other countries.

♦ VOLUNTARY DISPLACEMENT OF MUSLIMS: MIGRATION

Muslims who choose to migrate voluntarily live in many different countries on many different continents. Among the voluntarily displaced are the growing num-

East Wahdat Project in Jordan for Palestinian Refugees.

Facilities for Afghan refugees.

INVOLUNTARY MUSLIM DISPLACEMENT; REFUGEES

THE TOP TWENTY REFUGEE HOSTING MUSLIM COUNTRIES COUNTRY	POPULATION	MUSLIMS POP.	REFUGEES
IRAN	65,612,000	62,331,000	1,995,000
PAKISTAN	84,501,000	81,966,000	1,482,300
GAZA STRIP & WEST BANK	1,082,000		
JORDAN	3,961,000	3,644,000	1,073,600
SUDAN	633,000		
GUINEA	5,571,000	4,457,000	570,000
SYRIA	14,887,000	13,398,300	319,200
AZERBAIJAN	7,684,000	6,500,000	251,000
BANGLADESH	125,149,000	103,873,670	199,000
ALGERIA	27,895,000	27,000,000	121,000
BOSNIA	70,000		
SENEGAL	8,731,000	8,032,520	66,000
YEMEN	11,105,000	11,000,000	60,500
DJIBOUTI	413,000	388,000	60,000
MAURITANIA	2,193,000	2,193,000	46,000
IRAQ	19,541,000	18,954,000	39,500
AFGHANISTAN	16,903,000	16,733,970	35,000
SAUDI ARABIA	18,197,000	18,197,000	25,000
EGYPT	59,325,000	55,765,500	11,000
NIGER	8,635,000	6,908,000	3,000
TOTALS	480,303,000.00	441,341,960.00	8,142,100.00

Source: *U.S. Committee for Refugees. (1994).* 1994 World Refugee Survey. *Washington, DC: Author.*

ber of Muslims in Europe, the United States, Canada, and Australia. There are an estimated ten to twelve million Muslim immigrants living in Western Europe, in Belgium, Britain, France, Germany, and Holland, among others.

In the United States, for example, there are an estimated three to five million Muslims as a result of migration. After 1965 many immigration restrictions were lifted in the United States, and Muslim immigrants arrived in large numbers, the majority of whom were people from Africa and Asia.

These groups of displaced Muslims and their families throughout the world have migrated voluntarily from one part to the other for economic or educational opportunities; for many an initial temporary move has become permanent. Some have integrated successfully in host societies, while others have experienced serious difficulties arising from differences between their cultural and religious beliefs and those of the host societies, and from misperceptions of Islam because of global problems. Millions of Muslim refugees who have crossed national boundaries are surviving and adapting to life in countries of first asylum with a hope of repatriation or resettlement.

◆ AFGHAN REFUGEES IN PAKISTAN

During the 1980s—a third of the Afghan population—over six million people— became refugees. Over three million each reached Iran and Pakistan. In addition to the over three million registered refugees in camps administered by the government of Pakistan and the UN-HCR, Pakistan has been a host to an additional four-hundred to five-hundred-thousand unregistered refugees through-out the country. Humanitarian aid was offered generously and continues to have a profound impact on the refugees and the host country, which itself is poor and overpopulated. Recent research and writing have provided information and analysis on the condition of self-settled Afghan refugees and those in camps, and of vulnerable groups among Afghan refugees (i.e., women and children). However, there is little information on the impact of refugees and refugee programs on the different groups of Muslim hosts in Pakistan, least of all those who are poor, vulnerable, and less able to articulate their problems.

In the Pakistani context the status of Afghan refugees as Muslims has been a very important factor for both the Afghan refugees and the Pakistani hosts. This status has defined and guided the decisions of the Pakistan government and people. Seeking refuge from religious persecution, as well as providing refuge historically, have an important reference point in Muslim history. During the time of the Prophet Muhammad, those who fled to avoid persecution and death were called *muhajirin* (mi-

grants) and those who hosted and helped them *ansar* (helpers). As a result, Pakistanis regard the offer of sanctuary and support to their Muslim brothers and sisters as a religious duty. This religious context is embedded within the cultural context of customs that value autonomy, honor, and self-determination.

◆ CHARACTERISTICS OF AFGHAN REFUGEES

Afghan refugees first fled to Pakistan in 1973 with the overthrow of King Zahir Shah. The 1978 coup that established the Marxist government of Nur Muhammed Taraki dramatically increased the flow of refugees. The largest group of families reflecting the agrarian nature of Afghan society—farmers, merchants, craftsman, settled herdsmen, and nomads—came after the Soviet invasion between 1980 and 1982. The refugees continued to arrive at a lesser pace throughout the 1980s, except for increases in flows during the times of heavy fighting, which reflected the intensity of civil conflict in Afghanistan. In 1990, after the Soviet withdrawal, repatriation was encouraged and began but did not occur in large numbers until the fall of the regime at the time. In 1992, 1.2 million Afghan refugees in Pakistan turned in their ration cards prior to returning home. However, fighting in the capital city of Kabul between contending groups has caused a new exodus and reversed the flow of tens of thousands of refugees back to Pakistan.

Afghan refugees, like other refugees throughout the world, have relocated in neighboring provinces in Pakistan in areas that are closest to their homes. They share with their hosts language, culture and religious practices. Two thirds are located in the North West Frontier Province (NWFP). The second largest group is in the Baluchistan, another province that shares its borders with Afghanistan.

Seventy-five percent of the registered refugees in Pakistan were women and children. Of these, two-thirds were children, resulting in an estimate of over half the refugee population being under fifteen years of age. The age distributions according to the government of Pakistan are 48 percent children under the age fifteen, 28 percent adult females, and 25 percent adult males.

The occupational structure of the refugees has changed considerably in Pakistan. Unlike the involvement in the agricultural sector in Afghanistan, two-thirds of the men, ages eighteen to forty-nine, have found gainful employment as casual wage laborers in construction and unskilled work. One in ten were employed as chauffeurs or truck drivers or in sales and service jobs. A substantial number are semiskilled or in small businesses. For example, one in six were self-employed as shopkeepers, long-distance traders, mechanics, carpenters, or tailors. Over 10 percent of the women are also gainfully self-employed in their homes in tailoring, sewing, or embroidery.

Each displaced Muslim carries with him/her a different history. Yet, among displaced Muslims, there are many commonalities. Many share the same values such as group loyalty, family affiliation, strong kinship relations, and interdependence. Muslim families and family structures have changed due to both modernization and displacement. While some say that kinship networks have been weakened, many disagree. Strong evidence exists that shows kin relationships are still strong. Families keep in touch across borders, seeking ties as well as information about the home country.

Impact of Afghan Refugees

The presence of a large number of refugees has had dramatic impact in the provinces and centers where the refugee population is concentrated. International humanitarian aid benefits not only the refugees but also the economy of the provinces. The economy of the Northwest province boomed with the resources, skills and equipment that were brought in to support the refugees during a decade. Several segments of the society benefitted from the presence of the refugees. However, the presence of over three-and-a-half million refugees created tremendous problems, including crowding in municipal facilities, increased tensions among ethnic groups, damage to a fragile ecosystem by depletion of the forest for fuel and by overgrazing, penetration of Afghans in local and national economies, and overall competition of scarce resources, specifically for those who were poor or marginal before the refugees flow in the 1980's.

Overall, the problems of the presence of Afghans have been handled well both by the government and people of Pakistan, primarily as the result of common ethnic and religious bonds between the refugees and their hosts. However, there have been several instances of turmoil and civil strife over the presence of Afghans in Pakistan, specifically in large centers such as Peshawar, Islamabad and Karachi. Refugee Afghan youth have been scapegoated for problems that are not their creation, and political parties have used religious sentiments and exploited refugees to further their causes in the names of Islam.

Most of the refuges in Pakistan, as in other parts of the world, are in camps supervised by the United Nations High Commission on Refugees. In the camps, a number of nongovernmental agencies assist in the resettlement of individuals and families. Since the end of the war and the signing of the peace accord, as of the summer of 1992 the efforts for repatriation have been intensified. Hundreds of thousands have returned home to Afghanistan, and face hurdles such as deadly land mines and destroyed infrastructures. Office for the Coordination of United Nations Humanitarian and Economic Assistance Programs Relating to Afghanistan has concentrated its efforts on clearing mines, existing inhabited villages and important access roads and general security. However, mutually destructive fighting between the various political factions in the capital city of Kabul has caused a reverse flow of refugees.

Women and children who constitute over 75 percent of the refugees have been innocent victims of this brutal war will require substantial support. The trauma of having been uprooted, deprived of normal family support, the abrupt changes in their roles and status, in addition to the absence of male heads of households have left these Muslim women more vulnerable than any other group of refugees. Many have suffered from a wide range of problems including sexual harassment, violence, abuse, torture and other forms of exploitations. In the refugee camps, health centers have played a major role in allaying their fears and providing not only physical health services but also social and mental health support for many Afghan women. International Non-Governmental Organizations (NGOs) have trained Afghan nationals and served Afghan refugees during the war to provide resources and expertise for local NGOs and for work in diverse sectors including irrigation, agriculture, health, education, road repair and clearance of land mines. If and when civil war subsides, the transition is not expected to be easy. It will take years to create stability and will require substantial development aid. While Muslim professionals have been a significant part of these NGOs, who served both during the war and are involved in the rebuilding of the country, their contribution has been within the international, European and American context. Their distinct role as Muslims has not been discussed in the Western press or in current American literature.

Muslims in France: Voluntary Immigrants

Muslims in France represent a category of displaced, voluntary immigrants moving from Muslim countries to the predominantly Christian, industrialized countries of the West. This displaced group represents a mass migration of Muslim people who are seeking or have sought a new life in European countries where Muslims have confronted new problems.

The immigrant Muslim population in France is estimated to be about three million. They are a diverse group which varies on the basis of many characteristics, including country of origin (e.g. Algeria, Iraq, Pakistan, Turkey, and sub-Saharan African countries), ethnicity and language (e.g. Arab, Turk, Wolof, etc.), current citizenship, (e.g. French, Algerian, Iranian Senegalese, Malian, etc.), period of residency (between a decade and a century), and social and economic status. A majority of the elite, who hold French citizenship either through naturalization, reinstatement or by virtue of dual *jus sali* as a result of being born in French Territories, are highly educated, upwardly mobile, successful, and are represented among the intellectual, economic and political segments of the society. Among them are five hundred councilors of Maghrebi origin who in the recent past have entered the political arena. At the other extreme are working class, disenfranchised immigrant families, with children in special schools and unemployed immigrant Muslim youth who are linked with petty crime and the social ills typical of depersonalized urban environments. Thirty percent of the Muslims in France are French-born children and grandchildren of Algerians who were loyal to France.

As is the case in many other parts of Europe, the voluntary displacement of Muslims to France represents a legacy of colonialism. However, unlike the Belgians, British, Dutch and Germans, the French implemented a policy of assimilation, spreading their culture and civilization through the colonies. This policy of assimilation, referred to by France as integration, is implemented with respect to immigrants and their children. It is implemented at an individual level and remains an intrinsic part of the ethos of French society.

French citizenship is a cementing force for displaced voluntary migrants and their progeny. Children of immigrants in France demonstrate attitudes and levels of school performance that are similar to those of long-term residents with comparable backgrounds. A substantial proportion, specifically those from the higher socioeconomic group, view themselves as citizens in the full sense and do not get drawn into controversies associated with their home countries such as during the Rushdie affair or the Gulf War. However, they have felt pressured to take sides and put to the test despite their allegiance to France, their country of adoption.

As the European countries experience economic recession, resentment towards the immigrants, especially Muslims has risen. Recent ethnic tensions, xenophobia, and economic constraints in times of increased levels of unemployment and polarization of social groups is creating political upheavals and social stress. France, which has welcomed immigrants for two centuries, is closing its doors and placing the blame for social and economic problems on immigrants, specifically Muslims.

Muslim immigrants of Maghrebi origin (from North Africa) are being blamed for the country's high birth rates and deterioration of neighborhoods. They are described as having low educational motivation and living off the French welfare system. They face hostilities in the form of displays of social violence and right wing extremism, and are blamed for the ills of society.

Resettlement and Adaptation

Each displaced Muslim carries with him/her a different history. Yet, among displaced Muslims, there are many commonalties. Many share values such as group loyalty, family affiliation, strong kinship relations, and interdependence. One study found that language choice greatly influenced values. The study examined Muslims that were displaced in Britain in terms of whether they chose to use their native language or English. For Muslims who spoke their own language, the values of self-control, cleanliness, and responsibility were given the highest ratings, while English-speaking Muslims chose social justice, self-respect, and freedom.

Muslim families and family structure have changed due to both modernization and displacement. While some say that kinship networks have been weakened, many disagree. Strong evidence exists that shows kin relationships are still strong. Families keep in touch, even long-distance when possible, by letter or telephone. Families who are displaced and live in the United States, for example, help their kin back home financially. For Iranian families, old kinship networks may have weakened, but they have been replaced with new kinship networks. Another change cited within families is intermarriage. For example, because of displacement, marriages of Kuwaitis to non-Kuwaitis has increased.

Assimilation to a new culture can be measured in numerous ways—cultural (food, dress, language), structural (work, education), and identificational (future plans, importance of ethnic customs). Assimilation is best thought of as a complex process with varying rates of adaptation. Studies have found that assimilation varies with ethnic group, sex, and age of the individual. One study examined food habits of Muslims in U.S. society in terms of assimilation and integration. The study found that more males than females and more younger than older people were more acculturated to U.S. food habits and possibly more acculturated in general. Another study found that Muslims were less adapted to British society than were Hindu and Sikh immigrants. Among Muslim immigrants, men and younger people adapted faster than women and older people.

Regarding employment, ethnic and kin ties influence migration and work opportunities for displaced persons. "Chain migration" is a term that describes a form of migration in which immigrants follow others from their country or city or origin to a new location. The new arrival is then helped by other immigrants in getting a job, a place to live, etc. Immigrants take care of one another in an environment that is sometimes hostile. Similarly, refugees settle for long periods of time or permanently and achieve self sufficiency among those who live across their borders. Many Muslims, who have resided for long periods ranging from a few years to over a decade that they are better off in their adopted home land where they see their children come home safely from school and think of the mined fields back home.

Whether as involuntarily displaced refugees or as immigrants who have elected to migrate, most displaced persons are resilient, have strength to endure hardships and eventually settle well in their new homeland. How they resettle and adopt depends to a large extent on their experiences. The displacement experiences are generally viewed in three phases: preuprooting, transition, and resettlement. The preuprooting phase, the period before leaving home, may involve a number of traumatic events including natural or manmade disasters, persecution, violence of unspeakable atrocities or just preparation to leave home for a new life for a voluntary migrant. The transition phase is fraught with danger for refugees who may be subjected to violence and even death. Even for voluntarily displaced persons who migrate for better opportunities, the transition period results in social and psychological turmoil because they have left their homes, relatives, friends, and familiar surroundings. This phase lasts from a few days for voluntary migrants to years for refugees who may be restricted in camps, prisons, or detention centers, who after flight and asylum may seek settlement in a third country or return home. Service providers must take into consideration levels of stress, trauma, loss and bereavement experiences of displaced persons. Cultural, religious and social supports can play a significant role in alleviating stress and psychosocial consequences of displacement.

Summary & Conclusions

This article represents an attempt to sharpen the focus on the experiences of Muslims with displacement, both as displaced people and as members of host societies. It seems clear that the need for attention to these experiences is great, since they are indeed vast and multifaceted, and have received little examination up to this point. Millions of Muslims are uprooted each year, whether voluntarily or in an effort to flee sociopolitical crises or natural and man-made disasters. Furthermore, millions more Muslims are faced with the stresses and opportunities of welcoming displaced persons, whether they are immigrants, migrants or refugees from other countries or internally displaced people from another part of their own land. It must also be noted that some predominantly Muslim countries also generate large numbers of internally or internationally displaced people due to conditions of sever political strife.

The widespread phenomenon of the displacement of Muslims raises a number of challenges for Muslims and non-Muslims alike. Muslims who are displaced must cope with the many stresses of being uprooted. These include confronting the loss of social support networks and familiar physical and cultural surroundings, and in some cases the death of loved ones and the destruction of material possessions. The experience of displacement also involves the many stresses of movement to another location, sometimes under dangerous conditions, and the challenges of building a new life in an unfamiliar and possibly hostile environment.

Displaced Muslims who have settled in Muslim countries, such as Afghan refugees living in Pakistan, are faced with a unique set of challenges and opportunities. Because these newcomers often share common ethnic or religious bonds, both among themselves and with members of their host countries, they are more likely to find support for the establishment of a lifestyle founded upon familiar values and beliefs. However, they may also be faced with conditions of overcrowding and poverty as well as implication in the political and economic tensions of their host society.

Muslims who have relocated into non-Muslim societies, such as those who have emigrated to France, must cope with their displacement under somewhat different circumstances. As voluntary migrants, they tend to have more economic resources than those who have been forcibly displaced. However, because they come from a wide variety of social and cultural backgrounds, these immigrants do not form a cohesive group and must adapt to life in a society in which there is little support for or understanding of their values and practices. Like many newcomers in any society, Muslims in non-Muslim countries also must run the risk of being targeted as problems in a competition for scarce resources. However, this situation is especially volatile in European countries, where many Europeans are quick to brand Muslims as "the other" and to use them as scapegoats for the fear and frustration they feel in an exploitative and rapidly changing global economy.

As some of the world's most frequent hosts to refugees, predominantly Muslim societies also face a number of challenges and opportunities. In Pakistan and elsewhere, many Muslims welcome the opportunity to be of service and assistance to their fellow Muslims. Host societies can also reap economic advantages from the skills, resources and humanitarian aid that newcomers can bring. However, they often must also cope with an increased demand on already overtaxed infrastructures and natural resources. Furthermore, like their European counterparts, predominantly Muslim host countries may also face the tendency to use newcomers as pawns and scapegoats in times of political tension and confusion.

Thus, the many ways in which Muslims are involved in the phenomenon of displacement carry a number of implications for future action and research. First, all members of the world community, Muslim and non-Muslim alike, must strive to achieve a greater understanding of the causes and consequences of displacement in an effort to prevent and alleviate the problems associated with involuntary movements and to cope with the challenges of voluntary population shifts. It is particularly important that societies strive to develop an appreciation for the many contributions that newcomers can make to their host societies and an effort to avoid placing the blame for economic and political insecurity on these newcomers.

In the context of non-Muslim societies, this understanding must include a willingness to accept responsibility for the devastating effects of colonialism, which continue to be deeply felt in the developing world, and a commitment to achieving an appreciation for the richness, diversity and inherent worth of all cultures.

In the context of predominantly Muslim countries, it must be recognized that, although the impact of European colonialism is great, these societies are sometimes also responsible for helping to create the conditions which lead to the displacement of many of their members. As host societies, these countries need to deepen their understanding of the difficulties faced by uprooted people, to strengthen their efforts to welcome and support their fellow Muslims who are newcomers, and to avoid any tendency to use these newcomers as pawns in political and economic struggles.

Muslim families, communities and organizations have supported displaced persons and groups through providing asylum and support. However, there is a critical need for all Muslim communities and organizations to unite and work proactively to influence in their own governments as well as internationally to prevent displacement. Additionally, they should advocate humane laws and assistance that affect those who are displaced voluntarily or by force. Lastly, Muslim organizations must work towards educating people from all groups, Muslims as well as non-Muslims to clarify misperceptions and myths about Islam that result in unfounded prejudices against Muslims, especially in the western world.

Fariyal Ross-Sheriff

35

The State, the Individual, and Human Rights: A Contemporary View of Muslims in a Global Context

♦ The Emergence of the Modern Nation-State ♦ The Contemporary Global Context

The state, the individual, and human rights are three major concepts that have been the subject of constant debate, discussion, and conflict since the seventeenth century. Major institutional changes occurred in France and the United States following their respective revolutions in the eighteenth century, and that pattern of transformation in the realm of constitutional and legal change has since affected virtually every part of the world. The concept of the individual-citizen emerged in Europe after a long historical process that involved economic, social, intellectual, scientific, cultural, and technological forces. Religious institutions, particularly the Catholic Church, resisted these changes in certain parts of the world, arguing for the recognition of a theology of the person as a creature of God, called to a spiritual vocation, namely the full respect of the rights of God, without which they perceived human rights to be empty, mere legal, values. This debate is not over. Secularism with its juridical, philosophical underpinning continues to prevail in most Western societies, but many churches, religious institutions, and civil organizations are making claims for articulating an encompassing theological-philosophical vision integrating the three concepts, person-individual-citizen, which they regard as inseparable.

♦ THE EMERGENCE OF THE MODERN NATION-STATE

The emergence of the modern nation-state after World War II has resulted in continuing confusion and crises in the developing world, including Muslim countries, as they have struggled to improvise new constitutions, institutions of governance, legal codes, and administrative mechanisms without necessarily basing them on any indigenous, established tradition of governance from which they could draw principles or legitimizing values. Unlike the history of the modern West, these Muslim nation-states, emerging after decades of colonial rule, found themselves facing immediate and overwhelming problems of organization and development. In the pursuit of civil order and national identity, they borrowed fragments of modern political philosophy, adopted elements of various European legal codes, and imposed military rule, often invoking models that had no grounding in traditional frames of reference.

Among some of these newly emerging societies identifying themselves as belonging to the Islamic tradition, there has developed an ideological attitude that seeks to identify their own personality against what has been perceived as the "cultural-intellectual aggression" of the West or a desire to resist "westoxication," a form of obsession with the West that was believed to have poisoned their society. An ideological *bricolage* that has been able to mobilize considerable support in a younger, alienated generation has impacted all Muslim societies.

One of the main features of this development has been to project from the time of the Prophet to today, the notions, concepts, institutions, and ideas that relate to human rights, democracy, the concept of the individual, civil society, citizenship, the emancipation of women, and so on. All these values are presented as being already present in the Quran and in the society founded by the Prophet Muhammad in Medina and Mecca. According to this view, the West negated this historical authenticity and has gone astray through secularization. The task of every Muslim, therefore, is to struggle to reactivate and revive the authentic legacy of Islam and to eradicate all influences to the contrary from Muslim societies. While this discourse by no means represents the views of all Muslims, its visibility and articulation in our times has been sufficiently prominent that it has marginalized other voices. It has also been a factor that has affected the policies of many Muslim and non-Muslim countries.

In understanding this process, it is misleading to concentrate attention on Islam, as most observers have done, by simply focusing on "Islamists" who represent a radical integration of religion and politics or on "fundamentalism." Rather than representing a static view of a normative Islam, it is necessary to elaborate a global context for this complex phenomenon that has manifested itself among diverse societies—from Indonesia to Morocco and from Central Asia to Africa south of the Sahara. It is also important to focus attention on many thinkers who may not necessarily be part of established theological centers of learning, but who represent important new constituencies concerned with reconciling values across cultures and not necessarily assuming a divide between traditional values and intellectual modernity.

A reexamination and reworking of the concept of truth-right (*al-haqq*) and of its foundations in Islam are both possible and necessary. The Quranic term *al-haqq* applies to God himself as well as to absolute, transcendent truth. By respecting these truths one puts oneself in the right, recognizing God as true reality, and benefits from the rights that follow from it. In the Arabic language, the movement from the singular *haqq* to the plural *huquq* translates as a desacralization of right extracted from the religious force of *al-haqq* and disperses it in the realm and organization of contingent, profane, individual rights. Given this background, any anlaysis must proceed in two directions.

First, to understand the apologetic tendency to show that Islam as a religion is open to the proclamation and defense of human rights, but also that the Quran, the word of God, articulated a concept of such rights. One finds the need to define rights in such a way among contemporary Jewish and Christian apologists also. Although this tendency appears unhistorical, one must not lose sight of the current value of seeking a basis for resistance within religious tradition to oppose and defend oppressive political environments. Latin America affords a good example of such a tendency in the Christian context.

Second, the critical and historical reexamination of the actual contents of the Holy Scriptures, on the one hand, and of the modern culture of human rights, on the other, must become an urgent and indispensable intellectual task. It offers an excellent opportunity to shore up religious thought in general by forcing it to recognize that the highest religious teachings and revelation itself in the three monotheistic religions are subject to historicity and review.

The ideological conditions and the cultural limits that distinguished the birth and development of human rights in the West must be the object of the same sort of critical reexamination to illuminate the weaknesses not only in the traditional religious image but in the image of civil religion as a product of the secular revolutions in the West. There is a need to open a new field of inquiry that goes beyond the archaic differentiation between traditional religions and civil religion.

Islamic thought has always included a discourse on the rights of God and the rights of the person (*huquq Allah/huquq adam*), with the former having primacy and priority over the latter. That is why traditional thought obliges each believer to practice the traditional pillars of Muslim faith. It is through obedience that the faithful internalize the notion of the rights of God. Summoned to obey in this way, all creatures find themselves constrained to respect the social and political conditions for fulfilling this relationship between divine right and personal rights. In other words, the respect for human rights is an aspect of and a basic condition for respecting the rights of God.

However, while the rights thus defined within the fundamental covenant between creature and Creator affect the Muslim *Umma*, or community, first, they are, however, potentially applicable to all human beings and are universal insofar as all human beings are called upon to be part of the relationship between Allah and humankind.

◆ THE CONTEMPORARY GLOBAL CONTEXT

The scope, content, and rules that govern the global context of knowledge today cannot be seen in terms of separate, independent traditions. The global geopolitical context comprises several societies that are interconnected.

In analyzing the global context there needs to be a reappraisal of important cultural, intellectual, and spiritual zones of the past, particularly where Muslim societies, such as in the Mediterranean, were part of civilizational clusters open to each other and reflecting greater permeability in their cross-cultural relations.

What we call "modernity" made a brutal eruption into the "living space of Islam" with the intrusion of colonialism as a historical fact. Seen strictly in terms of the development and diffusion of human rights in the framework of intellectual modernity, the colonial fact poses problems for both the West and Muslim countries. Colonial endeavors of nineteenth-century Europe sought justification in what was called a civilizing mission. It was a matter of raising "backward" peoples to the level of a "universal" culture and civilization. According to this perspective, for colonizing countries such as France, human rights appeared to be exported along with modern culture and civilization. The Catholic and Protestant churches participated in this movement to some extent by establishing missionary outposts in Muslim lands. It is difficult to speak to a Muslim audience today about the Western origin of human rights without provoking indignation about the colonial period. The memory of wars of independence and liberation against Western "imperialism" still constitutes the psychological and ideological climate within which discourse on human rights has developed in recent years.

In the nineteenth century, Muslim countries encountered only fragments of the philosophical values of the Enlightenment. A very small number of intellectuals, scholars, journalists, politicians, and travelers had access to the schools, universities, and literatures of the West. During this era, often referred to as the liberal epoch, Arab, Indian, Indonesian, Turkish, and Iranian thinkers believed that the light cast by science and the political revolutions of Europe would benefit their societies. The reformist movements initiated by Jamal al-Din al-Afghani and then continued by Muhammad Abduh showed themselves hospitable to the philosophy of human freedom that inspired the discourse on human rights. Subsequently, nationalist leaders and movements in many parts of the Muslim world made reference to the great principles of 1776 and 1789.

However, the intellectual and political elites of the Muslim world, unlike those in France and England, were unable to assist in the development of institutions and of a sustainable state apparatus corresponding to these new ideas. In the new nation-states that emerged in the Muslim world, human rights/concerns remained a set of ideals and demands as a basis for the anticolonial struggle, but lacked cultural and social roots.

The present situation of Muslim societies is further complicated by two events following the collapse of the communist ideology in the former Soviet Union. As this disintegration had led to stress in Western contexts, it has created an even more intense conviction among certain Muslim groups that their vision of the world demands a dogmatic and violent rejection of intellectual modernity. Modernity remains, for these reasons, the unthought and, for large sections of these societies, the unthinkable. They perceive the contestation of what appears to be issues of "civil religion" in the West as evidence that the basic assumptions that have guided modern, Western society are morally bankrupt.

The text of al-Ghazali (died 1111) quoted as an epigraph at the beginning of this chapter describes with striking precision the discontinuity of the imamate, that is, the concept of medieval Muslim order that governed the state even though the conditions to uphold it no longer existed. Such a theory of the ideal state inspired by religious values continued to be expressed until the time of Ibn Khaldun (died 1406). There does not appear to be any universal, indigenously grounded theology or philosophy that has emerged to provide a reconsideration of the issues of state, civil society, individual, and human rights by Muslim intellectuals that would have general acceptance. It appears that al-Ghazali's rather resigned and pragmatic statement, "The lesser evil is relatively speaking the better, and the reasonable person must choose the latter possibility," still holds for many Muslims.

Many Muslims today feel the same sense of resignation in the face of various alternatives where states seem to be lacking legitimacy, both from the point of view of an idealized Muslim theory of state or from that based on political values of democracy. Many studies on political and social thought in Islam seem to focus on theoretical aspects rather than on concrete historical development in the different phases of Muslim political order in past history and in modern times. The history of the Ottoman state, for example, is crucial in evaluating the interaction between political power and religious authority at the time the modern state and secularized order were emerging in Europe. The commonly repeated theory that Islam confuses religion and politics is not well founded since, as in Ottoman times, there was always a close working relationship between the state and Muslim scholars and jurists. This relationship disappeared in its institutional form as most Muslim societies attained liberation from colonial domination. From 1945 to 1970, religion was controlled by the state, which favored a secularist trend. During the 1970s, Islamist attitudes became more prevalent in direct reaction to state policies, attempting to devise an overall language and program of political control of religion, as well as all aspects of social, economic, and cultural life.

In this context, what can one expect with regard to the future of the state, the individual, and human rights? Can we interpret fundamentalist movements as conjunctural and as local responses to the pressure of military or one-party states supported by Western geopolitical concerns? Or should this phenomenon be considered an expression of a demographic shift in which a massive young population, excluded from democratic participation, is expressing a voice for a new balance? If the second explanation is closer to reality, then there will be the need for a series of policy commitments and steps and use of resources that can enlarge the possibility for a new and peaceful contract between state and religion in Muslim contexts.

The possibility of realizing material and intellectual modernity requires a broader social basis, particularly because traditionalizing forces have already gained massive sociological support and appear to be resisting intellectual modernity. Until the collapse of the former Soviet Union, intellectual and political elites in most developing countries propagated a socialist state-driven model of development. After 1989 some observers in America prefer to speak of "the end of history," or to point out how the dramatic failures in the societies of the Third World were prefigured. This has obstructed constructive ways of creating solidarity within the changing world order.

It is very likely that this situation will still prevail for some years to come. There are no effective leaders or movements in place or on the horizon that inspire confidence in their ability to deliver a strong message mobilizing a commitment to build bridges between rich and poor societies. Leading academic voices, particularly in America, have tended to develop theories of future international political scenarios that involve the "the clash of civilizations." These theories are based on a fragmentary and distorted grasp of Muslim and non-Western cultures.

Waiting in the Future for the Past to Come is the evocative title of a significant novel published two years ago by a young Tunisian artist, Sabiha Khemir. Millions of Muslims wait for an imagined future in which a mythologized past is invoked as authentic, unchangeable, and with divine norms and values. The use of the most radical and concrete political struggle to achieve this goal is unexpectedly combined with imaginary collective constructs. This is not an unprecedented historical manifestation. However, social sciences have been unable so far to provide a relevant analysis and interpretation of all its dimensions. This is why we cannot predict in which direction the quest for the rule of law, the definition of the individual-citizen-person, and human rights will lead in the next few years. It is clear that if any development is to take place, the mentality generated by the Cold War and the assumption of opposing civilizations must be transcended. The evolution of an effective process necessitates the elaboration of common international values to combat the rise of national and ethnically driven conflicts that might destroy and delay the opportunities to enhance the required culture of human rights.

The Muslim intellectual must today fight on two fronts: one against a disengaged social science merely concerned with narrative and descriptive style; the other against the offensive/defensive apologia of Muslims who compensate for repeated attacks on the authenticity and the identity of the Islamic personality with dogmatic affirmations and self-confirming discourse. Beyond these two obstacles, always present but at least identifiable, the Muslim intellectual must contribute through the Islamic example to an even more fundamental diagnosis, especially regarding questions of ethics and politics. What are the blind spots, the failings, the non sequiturs, the alienating constraints, and the recurrent weaknesses of modernity? From Hegel to Nietzsche, Enlightenment thought was invoked as the opposite of myth in an effort to escape the clutches of religious dogma. At the same time that reason performed this liberating critique, it also fell back into a nostalgic celebration of the origins of civilization, especially the Greek polis and the first Christian communities that parallel the concept of the "Pious Elders" among Muslims.

Scholars moved beyond Enlightenment thought by integrating myth. Hence, the accumulated symbolic capital, was carried and maintained by religion into the cognitive activity of reason. The comparative history of religion, conducted within this perspective, furnishes a particularly fertile ground for the elaboration of new kinds of rationality. It goes without saying that forms of religious expression cannot be detached from symbolic and artistic creativity. It is not a matter of extending indefinitely the horizons of meaning open to the scrutiny of reason. Instead of exchausting ourselves in an effort to reclaim contingent values tied to abandoned forms of culture and bygone systems of civilization, Muslim scholars and others today must propose new opportunities for the emancipation, exaltation, and enhancement of human existence and for the thought and action of men and women.

Mohammed Arkoun

References

Arkoun, M. *Rethinking Islam: Common Questions, Uncommon Answers.* Translated and edited by Robert D. Lee. Boulder, Colo.: Westview Press, 1994.

Concept of Islamic State. London: Islamic Council of Europe, 1979.

Esposito, John. *The Islamic Threat: Myth or Reality.* New York: Oxford University Press, 1992.

The Ethics of World Religions and Human Rights. Edited by Hans Kung and Jurgen Moltmann. London: SCM Press, 1990.

Islam, Muslims and the Modern State. Edited by H. Mutalib. New York: St. Martin's Press, 1994.

Lewis, Bernard. *The Political Language of Islam.* Chicago: University Chicago Press, 1988.

Little, David, John Kelsay, and A. A. Sachedina. *Human Rights and the Conflict of Cultures: Western and Islamic*

Perspectives on Religious Liberty. Columbia, S.C.: University of South Carolina Press, 1988.

Maudoodi, Syed A. *Human Rights in Islam.* 2d ed. Leicester, England: Islamic Foundation, 1983.

Mayer, Ann Elizabeth. *Islam and Human Rights: Tradition and Politics.* Boulder, Colo: Westview Press; London: Printer Publishers, 1991.

Mottahedeh, Roy. *The Mantle of the Prophet.* New York: Simon & Schuster, 1985.

Naim, Abd Allah Ahmed. *Toward an Islamic Reformation: Civil Liberties, Human Rights and International Law.* Syracuse: Syracuse University Press, 1990.

Tibi, Bassam. *Islam and the Cultural Accommodation of Social Change.* Boulder, Colo.: Westview Press, 1990.

36

Fundamentalism and the Future in the Islamic World

♦ Fundamentalism Defined ♦ The Heart of Muslim Law
♦ Causes for Differences Among Muslim Nations ♦ Fundamentalism in the Media
♦ Muslim Identity

Islamic fundamentalism is a contemporary slogan popularized by journalistic despair in the aftermath of the 1979 Iranian revolution. No one was ready for the reentry of religion into global politics in the 1980s. The imam came unannounced and largely unexpected. Islamic fundamentalism was discovered to explain the sudden success of the Ayatollah Khomeini. Without the furor and the fear unleashed by the ascent to power of a medieval cleric in a seemingly prosperous and secular nation-state, there would be no Islamic fundamentalism. There might be fuming and fussing about airport terrorists or hijack specialists claiming Islamic inspiration for their crimes, but there would be no Islamic fundamentalism.

♦ FUNDAMENTALISM DEFINED

Yet, some people have questioned the very use of the term fundamentalism to describe either Khomeini or the Islamic Republic of Iran. They deny that the category fundamentalism can be applied to any Muslim, whether he or she is motivated by political interests or not. Equally they protest its applicability to all other religious activists, Jewish or Catholic, Sikh, Hindu, or Buddhist. Since fundamentalism began its semantic career in defense of Protestant scripturalism at the turn of the century, it technically should only be applied to Protestants. Reviewing all these arguments in a recent, elegant article, the Syrian philosopher Sadik al-Azm wonders aloud "if the beautiful souls making such recommendations ever give any thought to the political and epistemological implications of the kind of advice they are dispensing to themselves and to others." He

answers his own rhetorical question by "arguing broadly for the epistemological legitimacy, scientific integrity and critical applicability of such supposedly modern Western and Christian-derived concepts as fundamentalism and revivalism in the study of the contemporary Islamist phenomenon."

Sadik al-Azm supports the use of Islamic fundamentalism as much more than a journalistic caption or a mere ideology of convenience. He believes, as do I, that fundamentalism is shaped, above all, by its interaction with modernity and modernism. It is an interaction that has taken place, and continues to take place, on a global scale, affecting all religious traditions, including Islam. Moreover, Muslim fundamentalists would not be newsworthy had they not also absorbed some aspects of modernity even while counterposing to modernism their own traditional value system.

Beginning with the Ayatollah Khomeini, Muslim fundamentalists have enjoyed a measure of success precisely because they have come to terms with the modern world that they oppose. Islamic fundamentalists, like other fundamentalists, are antimodernist moderns. They are moderns because they accept the instrumental benefits of modernity. They talk by telephone, drive cars, and fly in airplanes. They also use hospitals, attend universities, and extol scientific advances. But at the same time, they oppose the ideological norms of the high tech era. Against laissez-faire secularism, they assert a chaste communitarianism with scriptural and historical antecedents. They embrace radical patriarchy as the ideal social system. And they dally with nationalism because it is such an entrenched system historically. Nationalism poses a peculiar problem for all fundamentalists: It is inherently against their beliefs, since all movements of national liberation or those advocating recovery of territory culturally or historically related to a nation but now subject to a foreign government have been secular. Yet they can only succeed by coopting the nation-state. In some cases, such as Jordan and Algeria, fundamentalists may seek to gain political power as antinationalists, while in other cases, such as Iran and more recently Sudan, they seek to redefine the nation-state as itself the divine instrument promoting both purity and patriarchy. Ambivalence about nationalism does not change the nature of Islamic fundamentalism, it only confirms its flexibility. In all cases, Islamic fundamentalists remain avowedly modern yet adamantly anti-modernist.

◆ THE HEART OF MUSLIM LAW

Two Jordanian spokesman reflect the anti-nationalist mood of Sunni Arab Islamism, not only as it is experienced in Jordan but also as it exists in many countries where the citizens are caught between the ascendant West and their own memory of a glorious Muslim past. A leading jurist who has authored over forty books, Abd al-Aziz Khayyat, once summed up the five divinely mandated preservations that were at the heart of Muslim holy law (*sharia*). They are: (1) self-preservation, enjoining what is proper to eat and drink while prohibiting indulgence in prolonged fasting; (2) preservation of the mind, or mental health, encouraging literacy and education while prohibiting alcohol, hashish, or drugs; (3) preservation of the species, requiring marriage while also limiting the number of wives to four, and making even that option remote by mandating conjugal parity; (4) preservation of wealth and property, by honoring labor and investment of money while also prohibiting unfair interest or usury or excessive accumulation of wealth; and (5) preservation of belief in God as One, in Muhammad as his final Prophet, and the Quran as his perfect revelation are enjoined on Muslims while superstition and idolatry in all forms, including the elevation of country above God and nationalism, are prohibited.

The basic creed of Islam comes only as the fifth preservation. While it may seem to deserve a higher priority, the effect of its final positioning is to add weight to the list as a whole. Not only does the fifth preservation reinforce monotheism, it also suggests that true compliance with Oneness supersedes loyalty to one's country. Many Jordanians, especially those of Palestinian origin, would read this as a rationale for demurral from honoring the monarchy too highly. At the same time, it could be seen as a not so veiled message to the Palestinians that they should honor their own commitment to a Palestinian homeland less intently than their devotion to God.

The very fact that the document could allow for alternate readings illustrates its appropriateness as a list of fundamentals. They are all terms that most observant Muslims would deem important, but at the same time, they are terms that Muslims would not apply uniformly to the day-to-day issues of their own lives.

Equally adept at stressing general assertions and avoiding specific contexts is Dr. Mohammed Sakr, an economics professor at the University of Amman and a member of the Jordanian branch of the Muslim Brotherhood. In an interview given to *World Link* magazine in the spring of 1991, Dr. Sakr, who earned a Ph.D. in Economics from Harvard, blasts the West. Without once naming a particular Western country as the culprit or villain, he is adamant that "the West is against us." Having lived in the United States, he claims to know it as "a civilization stricken by forces from within." The alternative to the West, he suggests, is a united Muslim world, one that would allow countries to share their resources in a complementary fashion. "Some countries like Saudi Arabia and Qatar have money, and others like Jordan and Egypt have the labor force. Unity would bring greater benefits for all." Unity would allow benefits of oil extraction to be shared because "today the wealth of the region is in the hands of a few shaykhs, and the majority of the people are poor." In the end, the masses will take decisions into their own hands, he warns. What then should the West do? Two things. First, it should take note that "we [Arabs] have millions of people who have U.S. educations and who are not slaves of the West" and second, Euro-American firms should stop squeezing profits out of the region Middle East, instead allowing its citizens to govern themselves "without dictation from Washington, Paris, or Bonn."

Though admittedly fragmentary because it was merely an interview, the above captures the tone of the discourse common to Islamic fundamentalists. The finger of accusation points with equal pique to enemies at home and abroad. Those who are the real Muslim culprits are "the few shaykhs" who take money from the West for oil. Yet, in the same breath, these *shaykhs* are asked to join an Islamic unity movement that would provide their countries labor from Jordan and Egypt in return for "fair" wages. It is a plea likely to fall on deaf ears in Riyadh and Kuwait City.

Nor will its parallel plea evoke assent in the United States. We are not told how this patchwork Islamic giant will govern itself, only that we are not to interfere with its interests. We are to be wary of them because they know us; they were, after all, educated in the West, not just a few hundred or a few thousand of them, but millions of Arabs have U.S. educations and, yet, are not slaves of the West.

The incoherence of this argument would seem self-defeating except that it exactly mirrors the dilemma of

Islamic fundamentalists in the 1990s: to have the best of the West, its education, its technology, and also its dollars, and yet to evolve into a separate, Islamically renewed, world order.

◆ CAUSES FOR DIFFERENCES AMONG MUSLIM NATIONS

To understand Islamic fundamentalism one must go beyond the pronouncements of self-styled Islamists or Islamic fundamentalists. One must begin by looking at structural causes for the rift between Muslim countries and the advanced industrial democracies. It was the sudden dramatic increase of oil revenues in the 1970s that produced the phenomenon known as Islamic radicalism or fundamentalism. Oil was not the necessary, but rather the sufficient cause of the latest wave of Islamic fervor. The necessary cause was the structural realignment of global power—economic and social as well as political and military—that preceded the rise of OPEC. The precursor to Islamic fundamentalism was Islamic revivalism. Just as Islamic revivalism cannot be separated from the introduction of European commerce at a certain moment in time, so Islamic fundamentalism cannot be divorced from the unleashing of petromania at a later moment in time. Petromania is linked to the 1970s and to the ascendancy of OPEC. But "the tyranny of oil," in George Corm's apt phrase, had begun well before the 1970s. It culminated then, due to the coincidence of political frustration after the latest of successive Arab-Israeli wars (the October war of 1973) with the overdue readjustment of oil prices leveraged through the newly founded union of oil-producing states named OPEC. OPEC was a union rather than a cartel, as is often supposed. By any standard of proportionality, its members were more than justified in seeking a fairer share of profits for their extraction of a nonrenewable resource.

However, the high profits gained by OPEC members did not pave the way to higher status in the international community, nor did it ensure independence from the skills and ambitions of others. The new wealth was monetary. It had to be invested or distributed in a way that would allow these preindustrial societies to enter the post industrial or high tech era. The way was never found. The wand of prestige never appeared. Instead, there was a frenzy of both consumption and expenditure that redounded, and continues to redound, against even the principal members of OPEC. Drawn into an economic order where OPEC members remain marginal, they can only function with the assistance of other more advanced and more powerful countries. They require foreign assistance in everything from agricultural goods to military weapons, from construction projects to transport vehicles. They house an enormous number of expatriate workers to implement development plans that project them belatedly into the modern world. Some do recognize the irony of sudden riches. As a Saudi official once lamented, "We Saudis are rich while you Americans are wealthy. I'd rather be wealthy." By this he meant that the true criterion of national prosperity is not import-export surpluses or per capita income but rather the potential to construct and maintain an economic infrastructure that is globally competitive without foreign assistance. By that criterion, Saudi Arabia, like every OPEC country including Iran, remains underdeveloped and, therefore, dependent on others for what it needs to exist and to compete as a modern nation.

As long as the greatest field of play in the high tech era remains science, technological adaptation, and commercial development, Muslim countries will remain at a disadvantage; Islamic fundamentalism will function as a spoiler. Its ideological appeal is strengthened by the failure—the inevitable failure—of other ideologies, namely nationalism, capitalism, and socialism. Yet the state against which the fundamentalists rail is a durative institution. Not only have governments proven their ability to survive insurgency, with the solitary exception of Iran, but the state, in the words of a seasoned Egyptian observer, "has become the strongest dominant shadow over the lives of the individual and society." From control of the army and secret police, and from ownership of major industries to recruitment in administrative bureaucracies, the new postcolonial state exercises centripetal pressures unimaginable in the pre-World War II era. Fundamentalists can challenge the state. They can even, as happened in Egypt in 1981, kill the "pharaoh," i.e., the head of state, but there will be other "pharaohs" and other centrist deployments of power.

◆ FUNDAMENTALISM IN THE MEDIA

Despite the very real threat that fundamentalists do pose in some parts of the Muslim world, it is an unwarranted exaggeration to suggest either that they represent all Muslims or that they constitute the vanguard of a tidal wave of aliens whose civilization clashes with the West and whose ultimate aims are to destroy the West.

In *The End of History and the Last Man* (1992), Frances Fukuyama of the Rand Corporation argued that post-1989, the whole world has been redivided between haves and have-nots, with the result that Japan, the United States, and Europe, despite some differences, find themselves on one side, arrayed over and against disadvantaged others, that is, certain Third World countries. Theirs is not merely a competition between rival ideologies but between different cultures. Above all, he conjectures, it will be "empires of resentment" (Iran) and "empires of deference" (People's Republic of China) who will forge alliances to attack the West in addition to Japan.

Hardly had the furor over Fukuyama's thesis subsided when it was revived by a still more dire prognosis, this time from Samuel Huntington of Harvard University. In *Foreign Affairs*, Professor Huntington traced "a clash of civilizations" that would supplant, and possibly surpass, the Cold War rivalry between the United States and the former Soviet Union. People would come to define themselves much more acutely by common history, language, culture, tradition, and also religion, with the result that "differences and animosities stretching or thought to stretch back deep into history would be invigorated."

As if to distance himself from Fukuyama, Huntington, again in *Foreign Affairs*, answered his numerous critics by suggesting that the end of history and the universal victory of liberal democracy, which Fukuyama had predicted, "suffers from the Single Alternative Fallacy." In other words, the defeat of one ideology does not lay the ground for the victory of its opposite. Instead, argues Huntington, there are many contenders for cultural dominance, especially "the religious alternatives that lie outside the world that is perceived in terms of secular ideologies. In the modern world," he asserts (without a shred of evidence), "religion is a central, perhaps the central, force that motivates and mobilizes people."

The initial difficulty with Huntington's approach is that it does exactly what Islamic fundamentalism does. It assumes that religion is a single, self-evident category, and that the major problem of the modern world has been the neglect of religion by zealous secularists. The "secular" person, we are told, remains fearful of religion, seeing religion as a fire too dangerous to play with. When experts like Professor Huntington try to redress the balance, they stoke the smoldering embers of secular resentment against religion, and their own writings are attacked.

The deeper problem with this solipsistic argument is its blatant neglect of what it claims to redress: religion. What I have argued repeatedly, both in *Defenders of God: The Fundamentalist Revolt against the Modern Age* (1989) and elsewhere, is that religion cannot be overloaded either as an explanation for all the ills of the modern world or their panacea. It is impossible to disentangle religion from ideology, economics, society, or politics. What Fukuyama did as an initial disservice and Huntington as a large-scale deception is to assume that generalization requires abstraction. Huntington gives away the rampant illogic of his own approach at the outset of his rejoinder to critics: "When people think seriously," he declares, "they think abstractly; they conjure up simplified pictures of reality called

concepts, theories, models, and paradigms." "Bah, humbug!" in the words of a famous popular philosopher.

The definitive riposte to Huntington's scaffolding of abstraction over the raw experience of human history comes from no less a figure than George F. Kennan. Kennan, more than any other American statesman, saw the myopia of this country's demonization of the former Soviet Union. Ironically, it was in *Foreign Affairs* that Kennan first published his warning—in the late 1940s! Earlier this year, when asked on the occasion of his ninetieth birthday to offer a few sage words for future generations of America abroad watchers, he declared: "Do not look for a single grand design—no vast common denominator—that will tell you how each troublesome situation should be approached. Above all, discard this traditional American fondness for trying to solve problems by putting them into broad categories. What you need are not policies—much less a single policy. What you need are sound principles . . . . "

What are sound principles? A minimal listing would include principles of free expression, human dignity, and social justice. These principles are as American as apple pie, the Stars and Stripes, and Mother's Day. Yet they become lost in a lockstep, binary worldview of us versus them. Models of abstract reality, whether teleological, such as Fukuyama, or apocalyptic, such as Huntington, do not accord with the reality of a Muslim world where at least some current spokesmen share the ideals of American foreign policy.

Consider, for example, the leader of the Islamic movement in Tunisia. Often cited as a quietly charismatic revolutionary, Rashid Ghannouchi has had to seek refuge in Great Britain because of the unpopularity of his views with authorities in Tunis. Unlike the leaders of the Islamic movement in neighboring Algeria, he does not stress Islam over all other world systems; rather he enunciates the principle that is at the heart of Islam and stresses loyalty to that principle. What is that principle? Freedom. "I believe," he said in an interview with a reporter who sought him out in London, "I believe that societies where freedom enjoys more life are closer to Islam than those that declare themselves Muslim." In other words, he defines Islam as freedom not the reverse, and as if to leave no doubt as to how he feels that principle would apply, he adds, "I believe that the [ideal] Islamic state is much closer to Western democracy than the states that exist now in the Arab world."

◆ MUSLIM IDENTITY

This is not to say that Rashid Ghannouchi is more representative of all Islamic movements than was Ayatollah Khomeini in the 1980s; there exist Muslim leaders, who in the name of God, confirm the Huntington hypothesis. One such would be Hassan al-Turabi, the French-educated spokesman for the National Islamic Front in contemporary Sudan. Yet for Al-Turabi, as for other Islamic fundamentalists of the 1990s, it is the absence of viable alternatives within their own societies, not the strength of their opposition to the West, that allows them access to power and continued ascent over others. The real problem is not Islam nor Islamic civilization but statism, the manipulation of Islam as a religious ideology to enforce loyalty to the center, its institutions, and its custodials. Like Christians and Jews, like Hindus and Buddhists, like humanists and even atheists, there are both good and bad Muslims. The bellwether of hope for future debates about Islam and Western interests remains George Kennan, not his younger and less subtle look-alikes.

The issue is more clearly understood if one does not focus exclusively on Islamic fundamentalism but rather on Islamic identity as the key concept. Islamic identity can be defined either from the bottom up or from the top down. From the bottom up, it is at once transnational, its rhetoric appealing to the entire *Umma*, or community, and also subnational because it is antielitist, often being invoked by marginal urban groups opposed to authoritarian ruling elites. At the same time, Islamic identity can be invoked from the top down. Dominant elites can claim it as their property and support nationalism. This is the case with the Islamic *dawa* (or call) that comes not only from Al-Turabi in the Sudan but also from the Muslim World League supported by some Saudis, the prophetic system (*nizam-i-mustafa*) propounded by some Pakistanis, and the national Islam limited to Malays, while excluding Chinese and Indians, in Malaysia.

In the 1990s, national structures and ethnic loyalties continue to prevail throughout the Muslim world. Ideologies, whether Islamist or liberal, exist as a corrective to, not a substitute for, nation-state ideologies; oppositional Islamists and liberals alike frame their protest in the context of the nation-state. Even though nationalism has failed to deliver on early promises, and even though its agencies elicit frustration, anger, and calls for change, nonetheless, at the very moment that opposition crystallizes and oppositional forces succeed, they are forced to work within the nation-state rubric. They adapt it to their needs at the same time that they accommodate their ideals to its realities.

As long as nation-states persist, what most deserves our attention when we consider the prospects for vital expressions of Muslim loyalty during the decades ahead is nationalism. In the near future there remain but three forms of nationalism in the Arab/Muslim world: status quo, Islamic protest, and liberal/progres-

sive. To the extent that one must use summary labels to distinguish between them, the first is nation-statism, the successor to nationalism stripped of its utopian hope but still having its centrist administrative apparatus, conferring both power and privilege. Its representatives, alas, are legion. The second is Islamic formalism, demanding that all symbols and resources be adopted to explicitly Islamic systems of law, commerce, and gender representation. Whether labeled fundamentalism, revivalism, or Islamism, it also has many advocates. The third alternative, which proposes a kind of Islamic democracy, represents a minority group critical of both nation-statism and Islamic formalism. Its members have become acquainted, often firsthand, with Euro-American norms and values but, like Sadik al-Azm and Rashid Ghannouchi, they see the universal applicability of these norms and values rather than their local origin. Though few in number, the impact of Muslim democrats persists, if only because they alone assure some possibility of the long-range integration of Muslim nation-states into a global system marked by tolerant cosmopolitanism rather than strident nationalism. Such power-sharing Muslims are at work in Jordan, Kuwait, Indonesia, and Malaysia as well as Algeria, Tunisia, and Egypt and elsewhere in the Muslim world, working at the national or non-governmental level, through foundations and other networks. They remain voices from the margins, yet their clarion cry echoes that of the greatest American Islamist of his generation, Marshall Hodgson, who urged that Muslims anticipate and prepare for a future marked, above all, by "creative vision."

Bruce B. Lawrence

References

Abu Amr, Ziyad. *Islamic Fundamentalism in the West Bank and Gaza: Muslim Brotherhood and Islamic Jihad.* Bloomington: Indian University Press, 1994.

Choueiri, Youssef M. *Islamic Fundamentalism.* London: Pinter, 1990.

Dekmejian, R. Hrair. *Islam in Revolution: Fundamentalism in the Arab World*, 2nd ed. Syracuse, NY: Syracuse University Press, 1985.

Esposito, John L. *The Islamic Threat: Myth or Reality?* New York: Oxford University Press, 1992.

Lawrence, Bruce B. *Defenders of God: The Fundamentalist Revolt Against the Modern Age.* New York: Harper and Row, 1989.

Marty, Martin E., and R. Scott Appleby, eds. *Fundamenatalisms Observed.* Chicago: University of Chicago Press, 1991.

Mohaddessin, Mohammed. *Islamic Fundamentalism: The New Global Threat.* Washington, DC: Seven Locks Press, 1993.

㊲

Faith, Development and the Built Environment of Muslims

♦ Faith and Development ♦ General Principles ♦ The Built Environment

As the Muslim world shakes and stirs in a fitful search to reaffirm its independent identity, it confronts the cultural as well as the political realities of a world dominated by others. This has led many in the Muslim world to define their identities by emphasizing their own "otherness" from the hegemonic world context. Such emphasis leads to a rejectionist approach that can be narrow and constrictive and does not do justice to the richness and variety of Muslim culture past and present. This diversity in culture could be valorized again through the process of adaptive assimilation that characterized the Muslim encounters with Hellenistic and Mediterranean cultures at the time of the early Muslim conquests of the seventh and eighth centuries.

♦ FAITH AND DEVELOPMENT

The built environment as it relates to Muslim societies and to the natural world has been subjected to a search for authenticity, widely interpreted as Islamization. Strident cries have arisen to reject foreign imported models of architecture and development, and to return to Muslim sources. Unfortunately, this move has taken place within the same narrow general conceptual framework that has guided many other aspects of the contemporary Islamic revival.

An alternative to this rejectionist mode of thinking is grounded in the original sources of Islamic doctrine: The Quran and the *sunna* of the Prophet Muhammad as they are related to the historical context of past experience and present realities. Such an alternative seeks to derive an appropriate approach to dealing with the built environment of Muslim societies at the beginning of the fifteenth century and the end of the twentieth century regardless of how this derived approach is similar to, or different from, Western experiences. There is, however, a subtle danger in initiating the search for a Muslim identity (in any specific domain of cultural expression) solely in terms of Muslim sources. It may lead to a bending of source texts, ignoring the context, to provide literal guidelines for contemporary action that fit a particular viewpoint.

A reading of the Quran or a study of the *sunna* will not provide instructions on how to design a house in Morocco or Indonesia, or how to design the thoroughfares of Cairo or Istanbul. Those who have tried to derive specific examples from these sources are doing both themselves and the sources a disservice. By ignoring the wider context in which we live, and that must provide the major "givens" of the problems to be addressed, one can reduce and demean the sources to the level of a handbook or textbook. If God had desired to give people specific instructions on how to build structures in the twentieth century, He could certainly have done so explicitly. What then is the return to the sources likely to produce? Surely no instructions have been given as to the size of rooms or height of doors. Rather, this systematic review of the sources should produce a general set of principles that should help guide the searcher towards what is an appropriate response to the problems confronting Muslim societies today and tomorrow.

In developing this appropriate response to contemporary problems, the past experience of Muslim societies must be taken into account. Not only is such experience the basic determinant of the heritage that provides Muslims with examples of the achievement of past generations, but it also serves as the basis for defining the elements of a cultural continuity that are essential in any search for authenticity and assertion of self-identity. Nevertheless, one must be wary of accept-

The built environment as it relates to Muslim societies has been subjected to a search for authenticity; cries have arisen to reject foreign imported models of architecture and development, and to return to Muslim sources.

ing the actions of past generations too readily. The history of the Muslim peoples (like that of all other peoples) is replete with failed attempts to live up to the ethical and behavioral norms of their credos. Sifting the wheat from the chaff is the task of the historian, the philosopher, the jurist, and the theologian. At this point it may simply suffice to state this concern and proceed with a search for general principles and an attempt to spell out their application to the problems confronting contemporary Muslim societies.

♦ GENERAL PRINCIPLES

Stewardship of the Earth

The starting point must be a search for a definition of the Muslim approach to the environment based upon God's intended role for men and women in this world as "stewards of the earth." References to stewardship are plentiful in the Quran. It is apparent that this special assignment was central to the very role of humans in the cosmos: It was God's design that a vicegerent be placed on earth, as evidenced by this passage from the story of Adam:

Behold, thy Lord said to the angels: 'I will create a vicegerent on earth.' They said: 'Wilt Thou place therein one who will make mischief therein and shed blood? Whilst we do celebrate Thy praises And Glorify Thy holy name?' He said: 'I know what ye know not' (Quran 2:30).

The intent that this injunction be universal comes through more clearly in the Arabic, where the word *Khalifa*, which here appears as vicegerent, is the same as that used for inheritors or successors in other passages addressed to all believers, such as the following: "He it is that has made You inheritors in the earth: If, then, any do reject [God], their rejection [works] against themselves" (Quran 35:39).

The privilege attached to this assignment is subject to the execution of special responsibilities, hence the concept of stewardship: "Then We made you heirs in the land after them, to see how ye would behave" (Quran 10:14).

The exercise of stewardship involves two premises. First, the natural resources of this world must be developed so that society may benefit from the rewards of this development. A minimalist, anti-developmental approach cannot be maintained in the face of injunctions to the contrary. However, this pursuit is that of a steward, not a rapacious exploiter. Such development is balanced with limits imposed on greed and personal ambition. Second, a society capable of working this earth and enjoying its fruits and bounty must be organized in a just, mutually supportive, and balanced manner. In the remainder of this chapter, these two themes are analyzed by looking at various principles in which the expected behavior of the "stewards of the earth" is spelled out to provide guidance for the appropriate development of the natural as well as the built environment.

These principles are grouped in a descending hierarchy based on scale: (1) Relationship with Nature: relevant to rural settlement, ecological considerations in urban settlements, and conservation issues; (2) Interpersonal Relationships: relevant to the congested, intricate patterns of settlement associated with urbanization, where the organization of space is closely tied to economic, financial and social issues; and (3) Individual behavior: relevant to the design of individual dwellings, the choice of decorative expression, etc. The boundaries between these levels are permeable. Indeed, almost any issue is best studied by reference to more than one of these levels.

Relationship with Nature

There is an order in the cosmos and in this world that must be respected. This leads to the need for environmental protection, including respect for living creatures of all types. The need to respect the intrinsic balance in the natural order is referred to throughout the Quran, where mention is made of God's meticulous order in all things, starting from the scale of the cosmos, of the sun and the moon:

And the Sun runs his course for a period determined for him: that is the decree of the Exalted in Might, the All-Knowing. And the Moon. . . . We have measured for her Mansions [to traverse]. . . . (Quran 36:38–39)

This meticulous order runs through all things: "Verily all things have We created in proportion and measure" (Quran 54:49). Clearly, therefore, the implicit proportion all things must be respected by those to whom God has granted stewardship of the earth. In today's jargon one would say that we are enjoined to respect the ecological balance and to promote development that is sustainable.

Furthermore, we are reminded that our co-inhabitants on this planet are to be treated as communities like ourselves. The systematic destruction of species would be indefensible in this scheme of things: "There

is not an animal [that lives] on the earth nor a being that flies on its wings, but [forms part of] communities like you" (Quran 6:38). Thus, conservation of wildlife is part of our human responsibility on this earth. Elsewhere (Quran 6:59) we are told that all things dry and green are of His domain, and not a leaf falls but by His will. Thus the protection of wildlife, vividly referred to as "communities like you," is expanded to all the natural environment.

Yet these injunctions should not act as a barrier against the use of the world's resources for the benefit of humanity: "Say: Who hath forbidden the beautiful [gifts] of God, which He has produced for His servants, and the things, clean and pure [which He has provided] for sustenance?" (Quran 7:32). Humanity is enjoined to develop these wonderful endowments and enjoy the fruits of these labors, but humans are enjoined to do so with respect for the environment and to partake of all things in moderation, and under no circumstances to be wasteful. These are prescriptions that any rational human being should welcome, especially in the light of the environmental degradation that unchecked greed and thoughtless exploitation of resources have brought about.

Interpersonal Relations

The domain of *muamalat* (transactions) that covers the relationship between humans in the context of societal organization has been well addressed in the scriptures and the *sunna* and has developed over centuries by the corpus of Islamic law (*sharia*) and *fatwa* rulings. It is not necessary here to elaborately retrace these developments, but rather to sum up some of the more relevant highlights. All Islamic jurisprudence is based on the concept of the welfare of the community and the interest of the majority tempered by the protection of the rights of the minority. In accordance with the principles of Islam, the organization of society would have the following broad features: freedom; the search for knowledge and truth; action and effort; justice; the public interest; and concern for the poor and the weak.

It sets the believer free from all the fears and constraints that might hinder development and growth. This freedom however, is not a license to rampage on the earth, the strong destroying the weak. It is a freedom that is circumscribed by the bounds of law:

O ye who believe! The law of equality is prescribed to you. . . . In the Law of Equality there is [saving of] life, to you O people of understanding; that ye may restrain yourselves. (Quran, 2:178–179)

It is imperative therefore that any society that tries to live within Islamic principles be one where freedom and the dignity of all its members are carefully protected by a legal framework that does not allow the humiliation of any minority or individual, male or female. This freedom should be reflected in familial as well as societal contexts, and interpreted in its broadest sense.

The pursuit of knowledge is the single most striking feature in a system of great revelation such as Islam. Knowledge, or *ilm* in Arabic, and its derivatives occurs 880 times in the Quran. However, knowledge is not perceived as neutral. It is the basis for better appreciating truth (*haq*), which can be seen by the knowledgeable in the world around them. Indeed, believers are enjoined to observe and to learn the truth. The Prophet exhorted his followers to seek knowledge as far as China, which was then considered to be the end of the earth. Scientists and scholars are to be held in high esteem. The Prophet said that the ink of scholars is equal to the blood of martyrs. The very first word of the Quranic revelation is an order to read and then to learn and seek knowledge.

Action and effort are the way of salvation. The faithful are enjoined to act: " . . . do good deeds, and your actions will be seen by God, His prophet and the believers" (Quran 9:105). Such actions should be for the common good, but even when the religious instructions are oriented towards an individual's task, humans are exhorted to undertake such a specific task with discipline and precision and to produce quality work.

The Muslim faithful are told that they are responsible for their fellow men and women, and they are asked to take an active role in redressing inequity where they see it to the full extent of their abilities:

> If one of you sees something that is wrong, then let him set it right; first with his hand, and if he cannot then with his tongue, and if he cannot then with his heart, and that is the weakest of all possible forms of faith. (A *hadith* or saying of the Prophet Muhammad.)

These exhortations clearly place a heavy emphasis on being in this world and acting well at all levels. Contemplative meditation is looked upon as a means of self renewal in order to undertake better tasks in the future, not as an end to itself.

The concept of justice is absolute in Islam. Muslims perceive all their actions defined within a context of accountability. They should succeed by acting in a just manner. The idea of justice is translated through interpretation into legislation which seeks to set the limits for what is permissible among human beings. It defines the foundations of a theory of rehabilitation and punishment and the manner in which punishment should be meted out. Muslim jurists are expected to update and enforce the law in the pursuit of a form of justice

that should be as absolute as it can be on earth. Scholars still recognize that some things are beyond the means of the Muslim community and are in the hands of the Creator [in the hereafter]. However, an essential feature of Muslim society is that it should seek to establish justice here on Earth and not simply await "the kingdom of heaven."

The concept of the public interest governs legislative innovation and is perceived as a justification for changing past forms and adjusting to an ever-changing present and future. The systematic means of introducing legislative innovation is both checked and spurred by the demands of public interest. It is aided by a framework for interpretation that states that "all that is not expressly forbidden is allowed." Mechanisms and processes of introducing these innovations have been worked out in great detail in order to ensure that they are still consonant with the ethical principles of the Quran and that evolution does not, over time, lead to the abandonment of the basic ethical principles set out in the founding Muslim community of the seventh century.

Justice must be tempered by mercy, and compassion must be a prevalent feature in the Muslim community. The faithful are enjoined time and again to show mercy towards those who are less fortunate, to show compassion to the needy, and to be magnanimous in victory and forgiving when in power. It is relevant that the early Muslim society introduced a form of social security and welfare assistance whereby the poor and the weak had a right to part of the public treasury and did not have to rely simply on charity from those who were more fortunate.

In order to promote a development pattern consonant with the above, an entirely new approach is required. Without falling prey to the excessive emphasis on "otherness" decried earlier, it is still possible to mention the conceptual difference that this approach implies vis-à-vis some Western neo-classical economic approaches: it requires a holistic view of development, cultural, physical, economic, social, and political factors; it is primarily focused on human beings, not on economic considerations.

Individual Behavior

Much of the behavior demanded of Muslims is implicit in the preceding discussions in terms of relations with nature and relations with members of the community. Other aspects (such as piety and charity) are implied and do not need further elaboration. One additional aspect, however, is of particular relevance to this discussion. This is a call for humility in individual behavior, a quality referred to in many passages in the Quran, for example: "And swell not thy cheek [for pride], nor walk in insolence through the earth; for God loves not any arrogant boaster" (Quran 31:18).

These and many other passages, when combined with other injunctions, lead to a composite picture of the appropriate behavior of the individual Muslim as one based on moderation and humility. These attributes seem to be in sharp contrast to much of the ostentatious consumption and self-glorification that are reflected in some of the buildings constructed by those who have exulted in newfound wealth. The Quran admonishes: "Exult not, for God loveth not those who exult [in riches]. But seek, with the [wealth] which God has bestowed on thee, the Home of the Hereafter . . . " (Quran 28:76–77).

♦ THE BUILT ENVIRONMENT

Rural Settlements

The majority of Muslims today are rural dwellers. The mass of silently suffering, impoverished peasants who constitute the bulk of Muslim society today must be the starting point of our discussion, even if the urban scene is where the most exciting, innovating and challenging confrontations between Islamic values and Westernization seem to be taking place.

In the rural world the relationship with nature is essential. Carefully and joyfully tilling the soil to produce its bounty while being charitable towards others and husbanding these precious resources is vividly depicted in this Quranic passage:

It is He who produces gardens, with trellises and without, and dates, and cultivated land with produce of all kinds, and olives and pomegranates, similar [in kind] and different [in variety]: Eat of their fruit in their season, but render the dues that are proper on the day that the harvest is gathered. But waste not by excess: for God loves not the wasteful. (Quran 6:141)

The Quran additionally advocates the appropriate use of animals: "And cattle He has created for you: from them ye derive warmth, and numerous benefits, and of their [meat] ye eat" (Quran 16:5); "And you have a sense of pride and beauty in them" (Quran 16:5); "And [He has created] horses, mules, and donkeys, for you to ride and use for show; and He has created

The majority of Muslims today are rural dwellers.

[other] things of which ye have no knowledge" (Quran 16:5,6,8,). It is interesting to note in this passage that animals are referred to as more than beasts of burden. Indeed, they may be pedigreed animals bred for beauty and show, for grace, elegance and refined enjoyment. Nonetheless, passage is in no way contrary to the large-scale mechanization of agriculture or the modernization of agricultural production, with its consonant changes in the pattern of life in the rural built environment.

The heart of the issue of rural development, however, is the possession of land and the problem of land tenure. Here, Muslim historical experience reflects a clear-cut preference for encouraging the development of unused land, what we would call today land reclamation projects, and giving ownership to those who develop it: "He who brings life to a dead piece of land owns it" (Hadith). The accumulation of vast land holdings is discouraged by the mechanism of the inheritance code. More generally, the type of exploitation of peasants and share-croppers by absentee landlords that is so prevalent in much of the developing Muslim countries has been thoroughly condemned. Property ownership is recognized as a social function and not an absolute right or privilege: " . . . And send out of the substance whereof He has made you heirs [stewards] . . . " (Quran 57:7).

These principles indicate a more equitable treatment of the rural (vis-à-vis the urban) world, and a more enabling environment for those who till the soil. Though their voices are seldom heard in the political arenas of today, they deserve our attention and respect. They should not be disenfranchised, as is often the case. Rather, they should be empowered to build the dignified productive environment to which they are entitled and to live in symbiotic harmony with the natural environment characteristic of well-balanced rural societies. To respond to the pressures of population growth on fragile ecosystems will require research and the modernization of agriculture. Thus, a new pattern of harmony will be required if the rural societies of the future are to remain well-balanced. The key will be to maintain and reinforce an enabling environment. This enabling environment, however, will mean that rural dwellers will respond to their changing socio-economic surroundings in a manner that is compatible with their own self-image, which may differ markedly from the romantic images of bucolic rurality that many contemporary architects hold.

In terms of construction and building techniques, it is clear that the injunctions against waste and for a just balance argue in favor of what is today called the appropriate technologies approach. This is not only the result of Quranic injunction but also the course of practical wisdom. That such an approach can yield structures and compositions of outstanding beauty and evocative power has been definitively demonstrated by the work of the late Egyptian architect Hassan Fathy, who stands as an exemplar for all designers who would tackle the problems of building in the rural Muslim world.

The Quranic injunction waste argue in favor of what is today called the appropriate technologies approach in construction and building techniques.

Urban Settlement

The principles governing human relations clearly come into play in the congested and contested articulation of urban spaces. Property rights, while fully recognized and protected, are not absolute. For example, access to water cannot be denied. Also the right of the neighbor to purchase or reject purchase of adjacent property is a fundamental organizing principle. Investment is encouraged, and those who hoard gold and silver are warned of dire punishment.

Within this broad framework, flexibility is the hallmark in guiding relations. Again, all that is not expressly forbidden is allowed. Neighbors are encouraged to reach agreement by mutual consent rather than by arbitration. This approach has led to a variety of subtle and charming air-rights developments in old cities. It has also allowed organic linkages between different structures that abut to help accommodate expanding families and changing needs. Communication and cooperation between neighbors therefore helped to create a living and changing environment that we have come to appreciate in the unique character of the old *Medinas*, the core of traditional Muslim towns and cities. Indeed, this emphasis on the relations between neighbors is exceptionally strong in Islam. Its comprehensive character emphasizes practical service above and beyond mere sentiment.

While no specific model for the form of cities or even urban dwellings is prescribed, Islam's urban ethos does encourage designers to create public spaces that

While no model for the form of cities or urban dwellings is prescribed, Islam's urban ethos does encourage designers to create public spaces that promote social interaction between individuals.

enable social interaction between neighbors and wayfarers and immediately brings to mind images of a living and thriving dense townscape. The key element in articulating this townscape becomes the street, its alignment, its scale, and its availability for pedestrian as opposed to motorized use. Broken alignments built on the human scale, with possible overhangs, air-right developments and adequately-spaced enlarged areas for social interaction are characteristics to be encouraged. Activities allowed in the street are key determinants of the area's character: commercial, residential, mixed, etc. The mixed use pattern is again implied in the heavy emphasis on social interaction. It is interesting to note in this context that Western town planning has now come full circle after experimenting for a century with exclusionary single use land zoning. It is now promoting mixed-use developments that today carry a substantial economic premium for the developers. Some of these developments appear to be no more than artificially recreated modern versions of the old bazaars, the *suq* (market place) so characteristic of any traditional Muslim city.

For a variety of other reasons, not the least of which is respect for privacy, this townscape should also en-

able a transition from the public domain to the private sphere without damaging either. When coupled with the general prohibition against ostentation and self-aggrandizement, I believe we are led to favor a high-density low-rise residential environment which can also be quite economic in aggregate terms, i.e., in the interest of the community as a whole. It would also avoid much of the collapse of social structures and ensuing alienation that has accompanied large scale high-rise residential complexes.

The pattern of urban settlement is largely determined by a wide spectrum of technological and geographic considerations that may have nothing to do with Islam. However, within the broad skeleton so determined, the flesh that is so definitive in determining character and defining the experiential aspects of architecture and urbanism remains in the domain of the designer.

One is still confronted by the problem of the scale of the modern metropolis and the tall building so characteristic of this century's technology and economics. With regards to the former one must recognize the need to strike a balance between the imperative of rapid modernisation and growth, on the one hand, and the need to preserve historic districts, on the other. This can surely be done without losing sight of the character of new developments, avoiding what Charles Correa has rightly called the bureaucratic solutions of cloning structures.

Individual Structures

When addressing individual structures we should first distinguish between individual dwellings and other types of structures. For dwellings it would be beneficial to recall the Muslim injunctions on humility and the respect for privacy as well as the sanctity of the home as the refuge of rest and peace and joy.

The physical layout of the house should provide for adequate articulation of public and private spaces and an appropriate transition to the public domain beyond, i.e., the street. The building should not conspicuously project an image of wealth to generate the envy of neighbors and passers-by, but, at the same time, it should not be an ascetic structure devoid of decoration. On this latter point it is appropriate to note the position of the distinguished Muslim scholar Muhammad Abduh, who gave a ruling as Mufti of Egypt in the last century

that paintings and sculptures were acceptable in Muslim societies since the prohibitions against them derive primarily from the fear of idolatry. Since today this fear is irrelevant in the direct sense of idolatry, the prohibition is also irrelevant. Decoration and the use of paintings and sculptures are all elements to be used by Muslims in making their homes a place to delight in, along with the more traditional uses of plants and water. In shaping the interior of the home to make it a place of restfulness, joy and beauty, Muslims are at liberty to do as they please, provided they observe the general dictum of chastity: "To every religion there is a character and the character of Islam is chastity" (Hadith).

Beside dwellings, no discussion of individual structures in Muslim societies can ignore the role of the mosque. It is central in the design of any Muslim agglomeration. It is not only the place of worship, but also the key to community activities. Granted that the complexity of modern life has forced many communal public activities into specialized structures, the tendency towards limiting the mosque to its liturgical function, a "churchification of the mosque," is to be deplored. This is all the more true since, in Western Christian cultures, there is at present an active move-

The interior of a Muslim home.

ment to open up churches as foci of community activity to improve the communications between the church and the community and to better utilize the building at times when there are no religious services.

The architecture of the mosque is a complex subject that has received some critical attention, but certainly not enough. Some of the recent writing opens up avenues for speculation and reflection, but considerably more needs to be done if we are to appropriately re-integrate the mosque building as an organizing element in the increasingly complex patterns of contemporary settlements.

Tall buildings remain an important if puzzling question. Clearly, there is nothing in Muslim teaching that prevents men and women from reaching for the stars and building ever higher structures if these are justified design solutions to particular problems, i.e., if the purpose of building such a tall structure is not mere self aggrandizement but to provide an effective response to a set of economic, functional and technical criteria. Indeed, old Muslim towns like Shibam and Sanaa in Yemen are comprised of skyscrapers. One can easily visualize new problems arising in geographically constrained commercial downtown spaces under the pressure of an ever increasing urban population. Although skyscrapers are indeed synonymous with the *zeitgeist* of this century and have been the focus of much attention, relatively little critical concern has been given them. The cultural dimensions of the tall building as an evocation of art, an element of societal cultural expression rather than just as a symbol of commercial success and a projection of an "image of progress" remain ambiguous. Skyscrapers have been insufficiently studied in the West and totally unstudied as they relate to the value structure and self-image of contemporary Muslim societies.

Muslim societies are as entitled as any other to have their sensibilities engaged by imaginative, beautiful landmark buildings provided they do not pander to mere vanity, but respond appropriately at the level of function. The Muslim saying "God is beautiful and loves beauty" certainly inspires the appreciation of beauty as one of the qualities that makes the human habitat distinctive and pleasing.

♦ CONCLUSION

The guidelines for dealing with the environment, both natural and built, that have been suggested here based on Muslim sources are broad and all-encompassing. Some would argue that these guidelines are universal and basically what rational minds would propose for sound design principles and, therefore, are not specifically Islamic. This, of course, may be true, but this in no way diminishes the validity of the rea-

soning or the arguments. With the exception of some particularly value-specific injunctions such as chastity, humility and neighborliness, most of the principles are those that rational humans would propose by themselves in order to maintain the natural habitat and develop pleasing living surroundings.

The fact that specific physical attributes of architecture are absent in a discussion of these principles may be viewed as a shortcoming by those seeking recipes and simple answers. But, in reality, this constitutes a very real strength because this is precisely what allows Islamic culture to be adapted to the cold climates of the Himalayas and the hot tropical forests of Indonesia as well as the deserts of Arabia. It is this subtle overlay of Islamic principles over regional particularism, the former fully recognizing and working with the latter to help improve the inhabitants' response to it, that has enabled Islam to have its true universal impact, creating the "diversity within a unity" that the flowering of Muslim culture has demonstrated through the ages.

The Muslim essence of any building or set of buildings is much more subtle than can be captured exclusively by attending to the physical attributes of these buildings. To seek to define any architecture as Islamic exclusively through the detailed analysis of the architectonic features of the building would be like trying to measure the temperature or the humidity of a room with a yardstick. The yardstick is a useful tool to capture one aspect of the reality of that room, but temperature and humidity are equally valid aspects of that same reality even if they totally escape the yardstick's ability to interpret them.

This analogy is indeed suitable for our subject. To the extent that (some aspects of) the suitability of the structure's design can be measured by the comfort of temperature and humidity, the specific materials, layout, and dimensions of the physical structure must also be well adapted to geographic localism to achieve these goals. So it is with a truly successful Muslim architecture: its physical attributes will be primarily determined by the specificities of geographic localism, but the end product will produce a certain spiritual harmony and facilitate a pattern of social interaction that are truly in conformity with an Islamic world-view.

Clearly, however, the application of these principles will be far from homogeneous throughout the Muslim communities of the world, and the quality of the results within each community will themselves show a very large degree of variability ranging from the absurd to the sublime. These results are reflective of the concerns of different groups: the architecture of the elite, that of the commercially dominant classes, and the anonymous vernacular architecture of the poor. But the quality of the product in each cell, or its Islamicity, is still an elusive property to assess. Here, there are no simple answers. There can only be an ongoing patient exploration of the essential nature of beauty that a work of art achieves through momentary fusion between artist and task, what Sir Kenneth Clark called "moments of vision" and what is now being elucidated by an increasing number of Muslim scholars in the context of the Muslim world. This self-knowledge, developed through painstaking analysis of past achievements and present realities, ought to enrich the collective intellectual resources of architects practicing in the Muslim world. The views, images and stimuli that they can bring to bear on any design problem must be enriched with the type of concepts that transcend the simplistic physical reading of a monumental heritage and promote a deeper understanding of self and society within the context of an Islamic world view.

Only thus can we hope to promote a greater harmony between the built environments of Muslims and the eternal message of Islam.

Ismail Serageldin

References

Ardalan, N. and L. Bakhtiar. *The Sense of Unity: The Sufi Tradition in Persian Architecture.* Chicago: University of Chicago Press, 1973.

Burckhardt, T. *Art of Islam: Language and Meaning.* London: World of Islam Festival, 1976.

Cantacuzino, S., ed. *Architecture in Continuity: Building in the Islamic World Today.* New York: Aperture, 1985.

Correa, Charles. *The New Landscape.* Bombay: The Book Society of India, 1985.

Dessouki, Ali, ed. *Islamic Resurgence in the Arab World.* New York: Praeger, 1982.

The Expanding Metropolis: Coping with the Urban Growth of Cairo, Seminar Nine in the series Architectural Transformations in the Islamic World, Cairo, Egypt, Nov 11–15, 1984. Singapore: Concept Media for the Aga Khan Award for Architecture, Singapore, 1985, pp. 3–15.

Huxtable, Ada Louise. *The Tall Building Artistically Reconsidered: The Search for a Skyscraper Style.* New York: Pantheon Books, 1984.

Mikellides, Bryon, ed. *Architecture for People.* New York: Holt, Reinhart and Winston, 1980.

Mumtaz, Kamil Khan. *Architecture in Pakistan.* Singapore: Concept Media, 1985.

Richards, J.M. Ismail Serageldin and Darl Rastorfer. *Hassan Fathy (A Mimar Book).* Singapore: Concept Media, 1985.

Serageldin, I. *Space for Freedom: The Search for Architectural Excellence in Muslim Societies.* London: Butterworth Architecture and The Aga Khan Award for Architecture, 1989.

———. "The Aga Khan Award for Architecture: The Anatomy of an Approach to Promoting Architectural Excellence" in *Building for Tomorrow*, ed. Azim Nanji. London: Academy Edition, 1994.

Expressing an Islamic Identity in the West

♦ The Expression of Identity ♦ Early Buildings ♦ The Islamic Center in Washington, D.C.
♦ The London Central Mosque ♦ The Mosque of Rome and the New York Center Mosque

A new phase in cultural exchange and encounter be-
tween Muslims and the West in the twentieth century
(internationalism) took place in the 1970s as ideas of
progress, development, and economic and cultural in-
dependence took new forms. This followed an earlier
phase (nationalism), in which many countries with
majority Muslim populations achieved independence
during the 1940s and 1950s. A more recent shift, "re-
Islamization," can be discerned beginning in the
1980s and continuing through the 1990s from the
Middle East to North and West Africa, the Central
Asian republics of the former Soviet Union, India to
western China, and in Southeast Asia. This shift is
different from the Islamic experience of the 1970s and
early 1980s (Iran in 1979, Lebanon after 1982, or
Egypt in the late 1970s, etc.) in that, in general, the
stimulus for change has come from internal factors
and forces, including the shift in demography in pre-
dominantly Sunni regions. This assertion of identity
within what has been called an "Islamist" tradition,
tests not only the expressions of Islamic nation-states
but also that of individual and collective aspirations.

♦ THE EXPRESSION OF IDENTITY

The expression of identity can be perceived in many
ways. Perhaps one that is clearest and most apparent is
its manifestation in architecture. Identity is tested
when contexts and boundaries of definition change; for
instance, when one migrates or is displaced and becomes a "foreigner." The notion of building boundaries
as a means of self-definition is common in anthropology and sociology and in terms of identifying oneself in
relationship to "the other." What a foreigner builds in
his or her adopted land is an externalizing of identity.

This shall be explored here in looking at the public aspect of the religious and social life of Muslims in non-
Muslim societies via the mosque.

Architecture is interpretation and mediates realities.
Buildings by their very state of being communicate directly to people. Creating an environment that "feels
right" raises the issue of simulation. The questions by
which we judge achieved simulation are these: How do
we judge a satisfying simulation? How do we, in an increasingly global culture where regions are not easily
definable, project the authenticity of locality? What relationship does the architectural expression in a new
situation have with the object "back home" born within
a definable architectural tradition? To speak of inherit-
ing and extending a tradition, sometimes into different
realms, does not mean copying what has gone before
but rather absorbing the principles behind earlier solutions and transforming them into new vocabularies
suitable to changed attitudes. It gives rise to ideas of
transfer and transformation that begin to address issues of understanding and operation in cultures other
than our own. For regional architecture, or indeed new
architecture, to express cultural roots, what may be
called the "deep structures" have not only to be transferred but also to be transformed if they are to take
root in new situations.

Manifestations of a self-conscious identity and the
role as self-conscious guardians of Islam relate individual experience to community. Muslims entering a community in the West express their collective identity
most clearly through the mosques that they commission. In general, these "symbolic" mosques are found in
cities and are built by Muslims of different origins and
backgrounds, and they serve as indicators of how a particular religious group sees itself within a new or dif-

The expression of identity can be most apparent in its manifestation in architecture. Pictured, the interior of Sherefudin's Mosque, Sarajevo, Bosnia.

ferent cultural setting. These may be distinguished from mosques built by communities for their own everyday use such as the African American storefront mosques in Philadelphia or New York, or local buildings such as the Islamic Center in Plainfield, Indiana, or Sherefudin's White Mosque in Visoko, Bosnia-Herzegovina. It can be argued that the older immigrant populations, such as those in the United Kingdom and African American Muslims of the United States, are now an integral part of their countries' settlements and that their expressions of identity cannot be seen as expressions of "the other" within their adopted homeland. However, I believe that the process of assimilation is nowhere near completed and that the different Muslim populations, such as the Pakistanis living in England, still, by and large, view themselves as apart and distinct from "the British." Hence, the characterization of the expression of "difference" and a separate reality still holds even in such situations.

♦ EARLY BUILDINGS

Projects for mosques expressing Muslim presence in non-Islamic countries started to take shape in the 1950s, although there are earlier examples. The colonial connections between countries like Britain and India, France and Algeria, or Italy and Libya remained. Early mosques, like England's first purpose-built mosque in Woking, Surrey, founded in 1889 by Shah Jehan Begum, the wife of the then Nawab of Bhopal, was a version of the Indian Mughal mosques of Lahore and Delhi. Similarly, the Paris Mosque built in the late 1920s was modeled on North African architecture. By the 1960s the burgeoning immigrant Muslim communities in Europe and North America began to express their identity and existence through the building of new mosques. Projects that had been initiated in the 1950s, like the Islamic Center in Hamburg built between 1960 and 1973 and funded jointly by the Iranian community in Germany and religious institutions in Iran, were finally seeing completion.

Like their counterparts in Islamic countries—the state and local authority-sponsored mosques—mosques built in foreign cultural settings are characterized by four tendencies: First, they accommodate multiple social and cultural activities such as classes and lectures, wedding ceremonies, and house facilities such as libraries and nurseries. Second, their design is tempered by the local context, modified by local laws and regulations, and sometimes by local community pressures. Third, the design refers back to historical or regional Islamic traditions, and the physical form is usually influenced by one dominant style from a country or region depending on who is financing, designing, or leading the project. Lastly, the interiors of the prayer halls tend to be exuberant and often eclectic collections of styles and ornamentation that proclaim the space as being particularly Islamic. The following examples are presented as outline case studies, emblematic of the periods and images that Muslims seem to wish to project to the society at large.

◆ THE ISLAMIC CENTER IN WASHINGTON, D.C.

In the United States, the 1957 Islamic Center in Washington, D.C., was established by a group of Muslim ambassadors stationed in the capital. The project is particularly remarkable for the perseverance of the initiators and for its breadth of vision. In addition to religious and prayer-related facilities, the scope of the initial project included a wide range of services such as a museum to exhibit artwork from different Islamic countries; an institute of higher learning for history, art,

law, and Arabic and religious studies for children; an academic magazine and various publications dealing with Muslim issues; a lecture series; and library facilities. Many of the clients' objectives were never fulfilled due to lack of funds, personnel, space, and differences of opinion within the Muslim community itself. It is probably the first such center in the United States, although the first mosque designed as such in North America is in Ontario, Canada, built at the turn of the century. It is interesting to note that the inception of the idea for the D.C. mosque was contemporaneous with that of the London Central Mosque. The two undertakings influenced each other in regard to community action though not in design.

The site of the D.C. mosque is in the prominent heart of the embassy quarter on Massachusetts Avenue. During the long years it took to realize the building, many Muslim countries, persuaded by their diplomats, substantially funded the work, which was also supported by donations by individuals and communities both in North America and abroad. The Egyptian ambassador persuaded the Egyptian Ministry of Waqf to design the center. In Cairo, the Ministry assigned an Italian architect, Mario Rossi, employed by the Ministry of Works, to design the center. Rossi was an influential

Paris Mosque

architect in Egypt at that time and designed several mosques in the country. His design shows an adherence to tradition using the Ottoman centralized dome type, stylistically reflecting Cairene models.

Fronting onto the avenue, the mosque is accessed by a flight of steps that lead to a main colonnaded portico entrance decorated with a tall band of calligraphy. The building is two stories high with pointed arched windows on the second floor, covered by a sloping green tiled roof reminiscent of Andalusian architecture. The whole structure is crowned by crenallations and by a 50-meter-high (160-foot) Mamluk-inspired minaret. As a result of the zoning requirements in Washington, the building had to be modified, especially in its alignment with the street, causing the entrance facade and the prayer hall's Mecca orientation to create an angled, courtyard-transitioned space. The actual prayer hall for eight hundred worshippers is almost square in plan and covered by a dome. The lower part of the external walls are ornately decorated with a band of Turkish tiles based on Iznik designs (donated by the Turkish government), as is the *mihrab* (donated by the Egyptian government), which consists of thousands of pieces of hand-carved wood inlaid with bone and ivory. The 18-meter high (60-foot) dome is supported on an octagonal drum with arched windows thats upon a square base, which, in turn, is on stone columns. Egyptian craftsmen executed the plaster work and the calligraphy that features Quranic verses and the names of Allah, the Prophet, and the four caliphs in *Kufic* script. At the time of the center's construction, the question of whether to admit women to prayer remained unresolved, but today a small curtained space is provided for female worshippers in the southeastern corner of the prayer hall.

♦ THE LONDON CENTRAL MOSQUE

Another mosque that also bases itself on traditional historical models is the 1977 London Central Mosque, perhaps better known as the Regents Park Mosque. This structure was built to provide a focus and inspiration to the over half million Muslims in the United Kingdom, which already has over five hundred mosques.

In 1940 the Egyptian Ambassador to the Court of St. James approached the then prime minister, Neville Chamberlain, to purchase a site for a mosque as a reciprocal gesture to the Egyptian government, which had donated land in Cairo for the building of an Anglican cathedral some years earlier. The site at Hanover Gate in the park was formally obtained in 1944 by the Mosque Committee, at that time made up of twelve ambassadors from Muslim countries. The project was designed by an Egyptian architect, Ramzy Omar, but

abandoned because of objections from the London County Council and the Fine Arts Commission. Finally, through an international design competition, a design by the British architect Sir Frederick Gibberd was selected. After modifications to the design, construction began in early 1974 at an estimated cost of $4.5 million donated by the Mosque Trust (*waqf*) made up of a number of Muslim governments.

The triangular site in Regents Park is almost entirely taken up by the mosque and Cultural Center. The *qibla* wall, the most important element of the mosque as it determines the direction of worship for believers, is pushed up to the edge of the site facing Mecca so that all other functions occur behind it. With the exception of the dome, which rises to a height of 25 meters (80 feet), and the minaret, 43 meters (140 feet) high, both of which function as important signs of the mosque's presence, the structure is built relatively low, 9.5 meters (30 feet), so as not to dominate the surrounding park land and Nash's terrace just across the road. The layout of the facilities is linear in terms of the transition of spaces, from the courtyard to the entrance hall and from these to the prayer hall. The prayer hall for about one thousand people is rectangular with the women's gallery, which represents about 20 percent of the hall's floor area, recessed into the west hall. The hall is covered with a steel-framed dome based on the form of the Iranian four-centered arch, which is a repeated formal element in the building.

The London Central Mosque was designed to be an expression of an Islam that uses modern technologies and pan-Islamic design elements that are considered to be recognizably Islamic to all Muslims, and not limited to any one culture. The treatment of the arches, for instance, was a reinterpretation within modern technological language concerned with the formal expression of contemporary building materials as developed by the architects Rifat Chadirji and Mohamed Makiya in the early 1960s. However, the new technology, as expressed by the arches and modern materials, is somewhat inconsistent with the traditional forms of the minaret and the dome.

♦ THE MOSQUE OF ROME AND THE NEW YORK CENTER MOSQUE

In contrast to the preceding examples, the Mosque of Rome and the New York Islamic Cultural Center Mosque propose an architectural expression in a contemporary vein and, although they refer back to historical models, they both reinterpret traditional styles and principles in a modern idiom. The Mosque of Rome, which was substantially completed in 1992, had its official inauguration in 1994. It offers a contrastive solution to the problem of establishing a link with the past

The Mosque of Rome had its official inauguration in 1994.

by evoking the historical model of the Great Mosque of Cordoba in terms of horizontality and the organic image of a forest of columns that the architects felt captured the atmosphere of spirituality in older mosques. In addition to the Moorish influence, Turkish and Persian styles are combined with Italian and specifically Roman imagery to reflect both the eclectic client and the *genus loci* of Rome.

Before the construction of the mosque, the international Muslim community had used rented premises for religious and cultural gatherings. In 1963 the Vatican Council agreed that it would allow the building of a mosque in Rome on condition that it not be in sight of St. Peter's Basilica and that its minaret be no taller than St. Peter's dome. This cleared the way for formation of the center in 1966. However, it was a visit to Italy in the early 1970s by the late King Faisal of Saudi Arabia that seems to have triggered the building of the mosque. The design is the outcome of a 1975 competition where two projects, one by the Iraqi architect Sami Moussawi and the other by the Italian team of Paolo Portoghesi and Vittorio Gigliotti, were ultimately selected by a jury composed of professors from Islamic universities, Italian historians, and a number of ambassadors to Italy from Muslim countries. The architects were asked

to collaborate in a joint effort to produce a final design. A committee of thirteen ambassadors sponsored the project, twenty-four Muslim countries financed it, and the 2.5-hectare (6-acre) site was donated in 1974 by the Rome city council. The design was approved in 1979 and work began but was soon interrupted because of insufficient funding. Building resumed in 1984 with an infusion of funds from Saudi Arabia.

The complex is divided into two distinct parts: the prayer area and the library and cultural center; the two are separated by a colonnaded court. On the sloping site, the prayer hall is set against the mass of the Monte Antenne, while the rest of the construction is kept lower in order to maintain a harmonious relationship between the architecture and the natural environment. The landscape brings to mind Persian gardens, and the strong geometric layout—its horizontality of colonnades with their dynamic curves—relates well to the site. The H-shaped complex creates continuously moving perspectives reminiscent of Michelangelo's Campidoglio in Rome and the inflected surfaces of Borrominis's architecture.

The most successful element of the complex is the large prayer hall itself that accommodates over two thousand people and combines the modular and circular systems of the classical Arab hypostyle hall and the central domed Ottoman model with its palm treelike structure inspired by the mosque of Cordoba. The central dome and sixteen minor domes are supported by an intricate system of interwoven arches and columns reminiscent of the elegant mosque of Tlemcen. The seven-stepped central dome, which measures almost 24 meters (78 feet) in diameter supported on eight columns, has mixed historical references in the cosmological image symbolizing the seven heavens according to the tradition of Prophet Muhammad's *Miraj*, or ascent to heaven, in his lifetime. The hall is lit naturally by glazed apertures in the domes, an effect that is replicated by artificial lighting. The circular geometry of this project is a recurring theme in Portoghesi and Gigliotti's work, observable in their projects for Amman and Khartoum, amongst others.

A women's section, raised as a gallery covering some 10 percent of the prayer area, runs along the sides of the prayer hall, screened by carved latticework. The interior is decorated richly in *zellige*, mosaic work from Morocco. The tiles and the screens are executed with great delicacy, and their rich traditional patterning and colors contrast strikingly with the monochrome interior and structure as do the carpets. Using modern technology and materials, the architects' aim was to create an atmosphere of sacredness and solemnity, using, according to Portoghesi, "the effects of lightness, dematerialization and static paradox found in classical Islamic architecture" that would evoke the atmosphere of ancient mosques. In this the architects have been successful in the prayer hall. Rather than make overt references to precise regional traditions or styles, the Mosque of Rome is a neutral expression of pan-Islamism in the sense that it attempts an architectural expression for all Muslims, regardless of their origins.

Similarly, the Islamic Cultural Center of New York uses easily recognizable elements associated with mosques to produce a modern building. The center, sponsored by the Islamic nations of the United Nations (U.N.), is located at 96th Street on New York's Upper East Side. Greater New York, which in the 1970s had no more than a dozen mosques, now has some 250 mosques and centers. Currently, there are over 800 mosques and Islamic centers operating in the United States serving some three to five million Muslims. The Muslims of New York form a wide ethnic and cultural mix: African Americans, Lebanese, Iranian, Pakistani, Yemeni, and Turkish being predominant, but virtually every other region of the Muslim world is represented. This population represents the most highly educated of the Muslim *Umma*, or community, in the world. It appears that an "American Islam" may be emerging in the United States. A general wish by Muslims living in the United States is to be seen as part of the modern American religious and cultural landscape. This also holds true for the Muslim states represented at the U.N. It is, therefore, not surprising that the New York mosque, seen as a pan-Islamic symbol, is conceived both as a place of prayer and social exchange—a model that reflects diversity. The problem faced by the mosque committee of U.N. ambassadors was the same as the one in London, Washington, D.C., and in Rome: Namely, what should the building look like?

Like earlier mosques, the source of funding and decision making was diverse, even though the Kuwaiti ambassador was the prime mover of the project. The wish to be seen as being "progressive" vis-à-vis the city and its non-Muslim inhabitants was an imperative in the mind of the building's sponsors. The building was first designed as a "skyscraper mosque" in the 1970s. This proved to be too ambitious, and the whole project was scaled down and put on hold. The project was relaunched in the 1980s and was given to the New York office of the firm Skidmore, Owings, and Merrill (SOM) under the leadership of the project architect Michael McCarthy who was known for his work in Kuwait. The architects were advised by two special committees of experts selected to assist project definition. Unfortunately, the two committees had conflicting viewpoints: One urged the architect to follow literal historic motifs and the other encouraged total freedom of expression with a respect for Muslim beliefs and architectural tradition. The architects chose to follow the latter and the project was adapted to include a dome and a minaret.

The building, angled to the street grid because of orientation requirements, is based on a square grid and is itself essentially a vertically extended cube covered by a central dome. The design was modeled on the single-domed Ottoman mosque, proposed by the project architects, which included the Turkish architect, Mustafa Abadan. The original idea remained, but it was revised and substantially reworked over time. The central space, which can house some one thousand worshippers, has a 27-meter (90-foot) clear span made up of four trusses supporting the steel and copper-clad concrete dome above and suspending the women's mezzanine below. The mezzanine to the rear of the prayer hall covers an area about 20 percent of that given to men. The whole space is carefully articulated and designed. The simplicity of monochromatic materials contrasts with panels of blue tiles and greenish opaque glass in the upper areas of the hall and with the striking blue *muqarnas mihrab*, which is bordered by a frieze consisting of Quranic verses in *Kufic* script. The main entrance portal also uses the same device of the glass *muqarnas*. Artificial lighting is provided by a circle of steel wire—supported lamps, similar to the suspended circles of oil lamps found at the Ibn Tulun mosque in

Cairo and elsewhere in Turkey. The corners and the top of the main structure are grooved to emphasize the dome with its gilded crescent finial or ornament on the outside. The minaret, some 40 meters (130 feet) tall, placed as a free-standing element, is a square shaft with an internal staircase with a balcony for the *muezzin's* call to prayer. However, as with most new mosques, the call to prayer is a recording transmitted through loudspeakers. Also included within the structure is a conference hall and ablutions facilities. The first stage of the center was completed and opened in 1991 and, although a second stage that includes a library, classrooms, offices, and other facilities was envisaged, no further work has yet been executed.

The illustrations are emblematic of trends in how Muslims present themselves to the outside world. As mentioned earlier, these expressions reflect a multicultural, multiethnic viewpoint conceived through official state representation as symbols of Islam in non-Muslim societies. These structures differ both in scale and program from those mosques/centers built by local communities for their own use. Image, in the case of these representative mosques, is a primary concern, and the presence of an international Muslim community is stressed. It is also generally apparent that, in spite of the break with their home societies, the ambivalent attitude by Muslims in general toward women in the mosque remains in their continued separation from men in the place of prayer. Only some 20 percent of the space is given over to women even though they make up a much larger percentage of the population.

Mosque design in the West seems to have changed over the years. The earlier twentieth-century buildings were, in the main, more literal in their historicist expressions, while the later buildings from the 1980s onward reveal a concern for projecting the "modern Muslim." However, tradition and modernity are seen as two sides of the same coin, and the buildings reflect experiments in expressing the identity of populations acquiring new roots in the West. Interestingly, and by contrast, buildings commissioned by national governments (such as state mosques) and local authorities in Islamic countries appear to be architecturally more conservative and tradition-bound, referring to past models that are seen as manifestations of political and religious authority and legitimacy.

There is a clear need to be able to deal simultaneously with an overlay of aspirations and material conditions. The simultaneous reality of global and local cultures is upon us. It is with reference to these that the multiplicities of actualities are now merely parts of the same web in which we all find ourselves, and with which we must deal. Twentieth-century realities of pan-national multiculturalism and multinational economic forces with global communications are also bringing with them the expression of a lowest common denominator, understood by individuals and the nation-states.

These building expressions of Muslim communities in transition raise wider issues about cultural assimilation. The architecture of the mosques provides one set of clues to understanding the needs of recent Muslim immigrants foreigners in a foreign land in societies of cultural diversity and ever-increasing immigration. If public buildings and spaces are to reflect the multicultural and intercultural realities of today's societies, the many fragmented boundaries that are created by a diversity of populations need to find a voice and a place. The "other" needs not only to be recognized as such but considered as an important participant in the formation of a "new world order" and new societies. How Muslims view themselves and express themselves within such contexts becomes important for cross-cultural understanding and development. The current message that seems to be transmitted by the mosque in the West is: We have our own identity and yet we wish to be part of the society into which we have entered, but we are not yet part of this world we inhabit because we are still unsure of ourselves and of our place within it.

Hasan-Uddin Khan

References

Abdul-Rauf, M. *History of the Islamic Center*. Washington, D.C.: The Islamic Center, 1978.

Ahmed, Akbar. *Living Islam: From Samarkand to Stornoway*. New York: Facts on File, 1994.

Bateson, Gregory. *A Sacred Unity: Further Steps to an Ecology of Mind*. New York: Cornelia and Michael Blassie Brook, 1991.

Haddad, Y. *Islamic Values in the United States*. New York: Oxford University Press, 1987.

The Mosque. Edited by H. Khan and M. Frishman. London: Thames and Hudson, 1994.

39

Islam and Modernity: Intellectual Horizons

It is now more than sixty years since Sir Hamilton Gibb, one of the father figures of Islamic studies in the West, reflected on the prospects of the Muslims world by raising the question, "Whither Islam?" Since then the world has undergone profound changes. But at the close of the century, the question itself remains as meaningful as it was in his day. But if the world has changed, so, indeed, has the context of the question. This transformation is best highlighted if we reflect for a moment on the following fact. Today we can hardly consider the question of the destiny of Islam without also asking in the same breath: "Whither the West?" For, despite the fact that this latter question would have been only too pertinent in 1932, a year before the election of Hitler to the chancellorship of Germany, nothing less than superhuman clairvoyance could have discerned, in the storm-clouds then gathering on the horizon, the shape of things to come: the dissolution of Muslim European empires and the corresponding loss of supremacy in the world; the rise of America to the position of a superpower; the Cold War and its impact on the entire political, economic and cultural map of the world; the end, decades later, of communism and the abrupt termination—practically overnight—of the Cold War; and the rise, in the meantime, of Islamic revivalist ideologies in sections of Muslim societies throughout the world. Neither in the 1930's nor in the ensuing decades—not until close to our own time—did the idea of the West transform itself from an assumption into a question or a problem. Nor do the questions, "Whither Islam?" and "Whither the West?" stand by themselves. They arise side by side with several fundamental perplexities of our time. Thus we may ask: "Whither the state?" or: "Whither society?" Or again: "Whither science and technology?" Or indeed: "Whither the world of human meanings and values?" Like the chords of a piano, each of these questions invites or solicits, by the logic of resonance, the others.

It is commonplace nowadays that in contemporary times the nations and peoples of the world are largely interdependent. Several key features of modern life have contributed to this fact: the revolution in modern communications brought about by the electronic media; the increasing susceptibility of national economies to currencies and trade cycles abroad; and the steady eclipse of the nation-state, owing partly to the foregoing features, partly to the movements of populations, and partly too to the role of the international media in the molding of political opinion and sentiments. Thus the state is increasingly dwarfed by both supra-territorial entities (such as the European Common Market, the North American Free Trade Association etc.), by a political culture led by the media, and by an international language and ethos of management.

If we were to confine ourselves, for a moment, to the subject of Islam, one can safely make the following assertion at the outset. There is no proper way to understand the position of Islam today unless we grasp, first of all, that it is complicated by positions adapted, in contemporary Muslim societies, *about* Islam. One might put it in this way: the question of Islam is, at bottom, a question of "Islam." What this means is that in the first instance we must learn to put aside the habit, common to religious realists or essentialists, of treating "Islam" (or "Christianity," or "Judaism," or whatever) as an entity independent of the mental constructs of the society in which the term is invoked. The *fact* of Islam is constituted, in large part, by the *idea* of Islam. It is best approached, therefore, as a phenomenon (or better still, phenomena—for there is today, just as there has always been, a plurality rather than a singularity of expressions which go by this name).

The first few centuries of Islamic history demonstrate a certain plasticity of religious identity. They exhibit a series of cultural endeavors, of debates and confrontations, which may be compared to chemical reactions, as opposed to the precipitate left once the reactions have followed their course. In other words, the period represents not the crystalline deposit, but the process, under way, of crystallization. And it is as erroneous to treat the precipitate as an original essence, rather than the contingent product of a reaction of specific elements, specific combinations, as it is to treat a world view, a system of doctrines, evaluations, and practices, as anything but an outcome of specific historical forces.

Furthermore, one of the most striking characteristics of this period is the immense variety of forms of thought and expression, of style as well as substance. They represent not just different interpretations of Islam, but rather different interpretations of life, of which Islam was the horizon.

Islam is part of the interpretation of Muslim societies of who they are. It is part of their way of being, which includes the totality of their institutions, practices, and above all, the self-image and world-image embedded in their way of life. The interpretation of life that Islam represents is, moreover, a changing, evolving, developing phenomenon. This is vividly borne out by the first four centuries of Islamic history. What is noteworthy about this period is the scarcity, in Muslim literature of the time, of definitions, reminders of, and references or appeals to "Islam." Why should this be so? The reason is obvious if one were to set aside the assumption of Islam as an *entire system* handed down, from its inception, from one generation to another; and to substitute, instead, a historically formed outlook. Many a historical account, however competent in detail, however, original in dating, placing, and discovering new or disputed materials, is rendered lame by failing to question and analyze the unit of its study. Thus there are histories of Islam which take the term "Islam" simply for granted; and are thus oblivious, for instance, of shifts in the *use* of the term over time and space. It is only fair to add that this problem is endemic to historical study, and by no means confined to scholarship on Islam.

In scholarly terms, we think of Islam as an entity, a system, sub-divided historically into a number of branches—"Sunnism," "Shiism," "Sufism," "law," "philosophy" and "theology", these being so many different "interpretations" (in the static, self-contained sense) of the Quran and Hadith. In a word, we *objectify* it. The defectiveness of this objectifying outlook becomes apparent if we reflect on the fact that in actual history, none of these "sects" or "interpretations" sprang into existence as a complete, codified organism. They evolved, but to note this is hardly enough. For it was not only their ideas, their inner content, that underwent a process of development; it was also their sense of boundaries—their self-image as a people within the Muslim *Umma*, and a people within the world. This is not to say, for example, that there there are no distinctively

Shia beliefs or traditions. It is only to say that these traditions are neither static nor self-contained. The ethos which forms their background is one of continual and shifting overlap with a vast variety of ideas and sensibilities, reflecting the variety of languages, cultures, and social classes which was a feature of the lands of classical Islam. For this reason, "Shiism" or "Sufism" are, in the last analysis, unsuitable as topics or units of study, though, obviously, the history of Safavid Iran cannot be written without an analysis of the state's appropriation of Shia ideas or loyalties; just as the sociology of Islam in West Africa cannot be written without the important role of the brotherhoods or *tariqas*. But in this latter case the units of study are other than "Shiism" or "Sufism" as holistic, homogeneous entities. There is, of course, an over-arching, unifying ideal. And this ideal is the Islamic faith. But Islam in this sense is the horizon, the framework within which the thoughts, the habits of feeling and conduct—the self-interpretation (again at the deepest, pre-reflective level)—of the particular society in question, are shaped and organized.

But if this is true of classical Islam, there is every reason to expect that it would be true of contemporary Islam. The term contemporary Islam is only a vague unsatisfactory shorthand for a set of highly complex realities.

The challenge facing Muslim societies overlaps largely with the challenge facing the world as a whole, and that a response defined in terms supposedly peculiar or idiosyncratic to Islamic culture at this juncture in our history is bound to be off the mark. It may be said that the problem of contemporary secular modernity is a western problem, and that Muslim societies need not be bothered by it. But this would be sheer make-believe. In actual fact, the best of Muslim thought for many years has grappled credibly with this very problem. Modernity is now a global phenomenon. It used to be thought, as late as half a century ago, and even later, that all that the new nations of Asia and Africa needed to do for their development was to take the best that the West had to offer—its technological know-how for instance—and for the rest, simply maintain their own traditions. But this is possible only up to a point. Reality defies such neat expectations. There is no "know-how" which does not embody, in itself, a particular interpretation of the world. The material as well as cultural constituents of modernity are now omnipresent on the globe. And they pose both common opportunities and common predicaments before the citizens of the world at large.

Commonality of problems implies commonality of response. In turn, this implies commonality of historical memory and foundations. For some time now, there has been a conceptualization of Islam in the West which casts it in terms not only of dissimilarity but of antithesis to itself. This conclusion is sustainable only through several intellectual maneuvers. One of these is to ignore subtle, or even substantial variations between different expressions, in different parts of the Muslim world, and to sum them up under the heading of the "protest of Islam against the West." Another tactic is to ignore all those expressions and viewpoints by intellectuals or others in Muslim societies that do not conform to the established stereotype, and to brand them as somehow idiosyncratic, minority, or "secular" in character, thereby excluding them from what is defined as "Islamic." It is as though to extend the same hearing to these other views would be to complicate things. It would mean being obliged to confront the complexity and untidiness of the real world as opposed to the neatness of fiction; to discriminate and differentiate where otherwise one may well get away from clinging to handy generalizations. It is only at the price of this oversimplification that the image of a revival of Islam as a diametric opposite to literally every ideal associated with the European Enlightenment, can be credibly sustained.

There is an important reason for refusing to identify the ideology of Islamic revival with the revival of Islam. And this, in a nutshell, is the fact that "revival" is a misnomer. Fundamentalism claims to be returning to fundamentals. In fact, what it proposes is something new. The language of fundamentalism is nothing if not polemical; polemics implies a rival against whom to react; and reaction to a new rival has new characteristics, not to be found in what went on before the new rival came onto the scene. The new phenomena with which modern Muslim societies have to reckon are first, the nation-state; second, the culture of modernity—the joint product of modern economic practice, urbanization, demographic mobility, and global communication; third, the predominance of western power and influence in this new culture. Each of these novelties is of immense and far-reaching magnitude. An Islamic response to them cannot, of necessity, correspond to the Islamic response to an earlier, substantially different world. An invocation of the past is not necessarily a restoration of the past. Whether the new phenomenon is an adequate response to the new challenge is a separate question. What is important to note first, is the novelty beneath its affect to antiquity. It will be seen that is this respect, fundamentalism joins with traditionalism, and is open, therefore, to the same criticism.

The vagaries of modern communications are such that fundamentalism, receiving a regular press, has crowded out all subtler expressions of Islamic piety. Among those which have been thus overshadowed, is the endeavor of re-interpretation. The modern tradition of re-interpretation owes itself to the work of figures of the later nineteenth and the first half of the present century. Impressed by modernity in the form incarnate in western civilization, then at the peak of its imperial triumph these individuals—men like Sir Syed Ahmad Khan, al-Afghani, Mohamed Abduh, and Sir Mohamed Iqbal (See Ch. 33)—sought, on behalf of their societies, to avail of the fruits of modernity while fortifying their own traditions, so as to ensure their independence from the West. To do this meant, on one hand, to be selective about the modern world, as as to be masters of their fate; and on the other hand, to revivify loyalty to their past. This in turn meant linking modernity to tradition. The task of which they conceived was not simply to bridge the two experiences, but rather, more substantially, to make the first flow from the second. This meant interpreting classical Islamic history in such a way as to show that the fruits of modernity were already contained in it—that they had indeed once flowered impressively, to be nearly blighted, since, by a frost for which post-classical Muslim societies were themselves to be blamed. But slumbering under centuries of neglect were the seeds of the old blossoms, dormant but not dead. Would Muslim societies rise to the occasion, and turn cultivators of their land, transforming the battle-field that the West had made of it, into an orchard ripe with the fruits that had once brought so much joy and vigor? This was the challenge that they saw before them.

The appropriate starting-point for Islamic thought today is the need of the hour. At the same time, by definition, Islamic thought must be rooted in its past. It must grow organically out of it. Each of the systems of thought falling under the broad categories of traditionalism, modernism, and fundamentalism in the Muslim world today, are fuelled by the needs of the moment; and, in the process of answering to them, operate with different images of the past. But in each case there is a summons to *return*: to return to tradition; to a bygone but recoverable dynamism; or to an erstwhile military and political glory. Is there a way forward, which is not a simple return? A way with a built-in dialectic between past, present, and future?

A coherent theology is intellectually of the utmost importance. Such a theology would entail a systematic elaboration, on the basis of tradition as well as reason, of pivotal concepts like the word of God, interpretation, etc. Being guided by tradition, a theology of this kind will not be the prisoner of modernity. Being guided by reason, it will be relevant to the issues of modernity. "Relevant" here means informed, but not dictated. For, a criticism of the times—that is to say, a reasoned argument against, rather than a rhetorical denunciation of them—is as relevant to the times as an enthusiasm for them.

A crucial question, then, which a modern theology

has to take up is how to realize what, following Charles Taylor, an important contemporary philosopher of religion, one can refer to as the question of meaning in the Judaeo-Christian-Islamic tradition— the central promise of divine affirmation of the human, more total than humans can ever attain unaided while guarding against the suppression, in the name of the divine, of the affirmation of the human spirit, intellect, and imagination.

If historical and religious consciousness are to come together rather than go their separate ways, it is essential to recognize the historical dimension *within* religion, and, conversely, the religious imagination *within* history. Religious life is the vehicle through which the ideal makes its appearance in human affairs. By definition, the ideal surpasses what exists. It is what immediacy is not. It holds a rebuking mirror to the way things are. In the mirror of the ideal, the real is humbled. What the ideal releases in human culture is the power of aspiration: a vision of what might be, what could be, in place of what happens to be. It is, in a word, counterfactual. A moment's thought will suffice to show how close we are, in these reflections, to the pulse of religious experience. Consider the Book of Isaiah, or the Gospels, or the Quran. What is at the center of these texts, if not the juxtaposition of warnings with glad tidings, of a critique of what is, with a promise of what shall come to be?

The doctrines of monotheistic faiths are specific propositions. But the impulse to transcendence to which they attest is far more general. It seems to be inherent in the human condition that its drive for meaning must travel the path of a vision of radical otherness. This "otherness" answers to unrealized possibilities and unresolved contradictions in the here and now: the frailties, wounds, and iniquities which are part and parcel of the human estate on earth. This is vividly symbolized in the notion of the hereafter. So important was this notion in the evolution of society that it has persisted, as though in an unconscious mimicry, and in an altered form, in secular culture. The materialist philosophies of the nineteenth century European sociologists Auguste Comte (died 1857) or Karl Marx (died 1883), contesting preceding theologies, succeeded only, in part, by dressing old figures in new clothes. Comte's dream of the eventual victory of reason over magic, theology, and metaphysics, is a religious hope, not a scientific prediction. Clearly audible, in the ideas of Marx are nearly exact echoes of the tenets of monotheistic faith. Thus, the story of the rise of alienation through the division of labor repeats, at an abstract remove, the scriptural narrative of Adam's error and descent from Eden. Again, the dream of a distant time when the state shall wither, and the war of man against man give way to universal harmony, recalls the

kingdom to come. No philosophy, whether religious or secular, has ever succeeded in yielding effective meaning without envisaging a beyond, first revealed in symbols of faith. Total immanence, it would seem, is the arch enemy of meaning.

An Islamic thought or theology equipped to master the challenges of contemporaneity would thus need to discover its past anew, not as a legacy, not as a deposit, not even as a body of tenets and principles, but as a vision of which the principles were, in their time and place, an expression. Undoubtedly, the vision does not exist anywhere else but in the density of a culture—indefinite ideas, institutions, practices, in legal, social, and artistic traditions. The sacred is always *mediated*. The mediations are symbolic, which means that the sacred remains inexhaustible, and never finally and concretely formulated or epitomized.

The way beyond these entrenched habits of cultural imagination is not a way for one group or community alone. It cannot but be a common project, embracing in particular the "Abrahamic faiths," the three monotheistic traditions which draw their inspiration, directly or indirectly, from the Abrahamic paradigm. Of Islamic thought, this principle requires a renewed appreciation of its universalist potential. This, in its turn, would mean a critical revision of all those assumptions which identify the pursuit of ethnic or cultural identities—whether Arabian, Turkish, or Indo-Pakistani—with an Islamic cause. In this politics of identity, Islam and ethnicity become fatally intertwined. And, in effect, Islam comes to be an "Eastern" religion, separate from, even antithetical to the "West." But why could future Muslim generations in the West not remain true to their spiritual vocation while achieving a harmony with their cultural surroundings, with the languages and the scientific and humanistic knowledge of modern times at their disposal—and indeed, placing these resources in the service of the spiritual and ethical vision of their faith?

Sir Hamilton Gibb, whom I quoted at the outset, had this corrective word to say to his Western audience: "We are so accustomed to think of Islam as an oriental religion and of its culture as an oriental culture that we are apt to overlook the real character of Moslem civilization and to miss its true place and significance in the history of human society. From the very first it belonged, in consequence, to what we may call—in contradistinction to the Indian and Chinese religious groups—the western group . . . To call it "oriental" is a misnomer; it is oriental not in the absolute sense, but only in its local extension—and it has at all times been shared by Jews and eastern Christians as well as Moslems."

The salutary lesson in this remains as pertinent today as it was for Gibb's contemporaries. By the same token, it is of relevance to Muslim societies lest, by too absolute an identification of the faith with ethnic and regional mores, its universal potentialities become occluded. And lest that surplus of possibilities which we identified above with the very nature of faith become truncated by the victory of determinate forms over the primordial vision.

It may be objected that universalism, while inspiring as a sentiment, is in practice an impoverishment rather than an enrichment. Is it not conclusive, ultimately, to a levelling of sorts, hereby all identities are lost in a *melange* of cultural superficialities?

But universalism, in the perspective argued for in this essay, need not imply erosion of particular identities. A pluralistic, universalist point of view, which the conditions of the modern world seem to call for, does not necessitate the abdication of particular viewpoints and commitments. Breadth is not incompatible with depth. For, the community of man flourishes nowhere but in and through communities of particular men and women. It is true that when locked in its own specificity, a culture is liable to retreat into isolation. But escape from introversion lies not in the obliteration of specific memory, but in an enlargement of its intellectual horizons. Universal awareness is a movement from the inside to the outside. It is not a cancellation of inwardness. It calls for an opening of windows, not the demolition of homes.

Aziz Esmail

References

Gibb, Sir Hamilton. *Whither Islam? A Survey of Modern Movements in the Moslem World* New York: AMS Press, 1973.

Raison, Timothy ed. *The Founding Fathers of Social Science.* Baltimore: Penguin Books, 1969.

Taylor, Charles. *Philosophy in An Age of Pluralism: The Philosophy of Charles Taylor in Question.* Edited by James Tully. New York: Cambridge University, 1994.

Appendices

♦ Islamic Calendar ♦ Bosina Herzegovina ♦ The Muslim Life-Cycle

♦ ISLAMIC CALENDAR

The migration of the Prophet Muhammad from Mecca to Medina, known as the Hijra, marks the beginning of the Muslim calendar. The twelve-month year is based on lunar pattern and consists of 354 days. The twelve months are:

1. Muharram, the tenth day of the which has become associated with the mourning of the martyrdom of the Prophet's grandson, Husayn.

2. Safar.

3. Rabi al Awwal, the month in which Muslims celebrate the birthday of the Prophet and commemorate his death.

4. Rabi al Thani.

5. Jumada al-Ula.

6. Jumada al-Akhira.

7. Rajab, the month during which the Prophet experienced the Miraj or journey to heaven.

8. Shaban.

9. Ramadan, the month of fasting which also contains the Laylat al-Qadr, the night of power, when the Quran was first revealed.

10. Shawwal, the first day marks the Idd, festival commemorating the end of the period of fasting.

11. Dhu al-Qada.

12. Dhu al Hijjah, the month of pilgrimage when Muslims undertake the Hajj. On the tenth day of the month, Muslims celebrate the festival, Idd al Adha, with acts of sacrifice and sharing. The lunar calendar generally falls short of the solar calendar by about 11 days. Thus, 33 lunar years corresponds to about 32 years of the solar calendar.

While most Muslim countries now use the Common Era, the Hijra calendar is continued alongside.

♦ BOSNIA HERZEGOVINA

This region was formerly part of Yugoslavia. Its Muslim population has always co-existed with Orthodox and Roman Catholic Christians in the region. Most of the population shares a common Serbo-Croatian ethnic and linguistic heritage. Islam spread to the region and was adopted during the 15th to the 19th centuries. The number of Muslims in the region is about 3 million and Islamic influence is reflected in the arts, culture and architecture of the area. In 1992, Bosnia declared independence from Yugoslavia with the expectation that any resident, Muslim, Serb or Croat who deserved to live in a multicultural nation, could do so in a democratic and secular state. However, the various groups in the region have since been engulfed in a brutal civil war across mainly sectarian lines. Bosnian Serbs aided by fellow Serbs from Yugoslavia have embarked on a brutal policy of ethnic cleansing and seizure of Muslim towns. The persecution and suffering of Muslims has aroused international indignation and reprisals, but the internal strife has continued inspite of efforts to resolve the question of national boundaries.

In spite of close ethnic and language ties, the population has always been influenced by historical and religious differences and past conflict, most of them a product of the region's turbulent history. The period of Islamization took place largely under Ottoman rule from 1463- 1878. Many people in the Balkans became Muslim and Islamic cultural and religious institutions became well-established in the region. Following European conquest of Ottoman territory, in 1878, by the terms of the Congress of Berlin, Bosnia and Herzegovina were mandated to Austria- Hungary and remained part of the Austro-Hungarian Empire until 1918. A Kingdom of Yugoslavia, including Bosnia, then came into existence lasting until World War II, after which there followed a period of Communist rule and dictatorship until 1989.

The Balkan region of which Bosnia-Herzogovina is a part, also contains other Muslim populations. They are found in Albania and Bulgaria.

Since 1992, the Serb army has also systematically targeted and destroyed many important Muslim buildings, including mosques, libraries and restored centers of learning. The well-known graceful bridge in Mostar has also been destroyed. Other buildings particularly in Sarajevo, where mosques, churches and synagogues existed side by side, have also been damaged or destroyed.

At the time of writing, many of the Muslim enclaves thought to be under UN protection have been overtaken or threatened by Serb invaders and the threat of a larger civil war also involving Croatia, looms over the region. So far thousands of people have died and many have become refugees.

♦ THE MUSLIM LIFE-CYCLE

Birth and Childhood

When a child is born, the *adhan*, call to prayer, is generally recited in the baby's ear. A traditional ceremony called *aqiqa* is performed on the seventh day, when the child is formally given a name and part of the hair is shaved. The family will at the time perform an act of charity or give a feast.

Children are taught to recite the Quran at an early age so that they will become familiar with the scripture and its teachings. Where possible, children attend *kuttab*, Quranic schools (which are known by different names in the Muslim world). The Prophet Muhammad abolished the practice among certain Arab tribes, of killing new born daughters by burying them alive. He insisted on the education and full participation in religious life of boys and girls and ensured through the example of his daughter Fatima, that girls would be educated and respected in his society which had a strong patriarchal heritage.

Circumcision and Puberty

According to Muslim tradition, the circumcision of boys is a universal requirement. The age when circumcision is performed varies from region to region. It can take place after birth, at the age of seven or at the onset of puberty. In West Africa, for example, as in many other parts of the Muslim world, the traditional initiation ritual becomes blended into the Muslim life-cycle so that initiation also involves the capacity to recite the Quran. Adulthood is thus marked by the acquisition of new responsibilities and by a deeper understanding of the faith. In certain parts of the world, pre-Islamic practices of female circumcision, involving clitoridectomy and mutilation of female genitalia is still carried out. Many Muslims believe that this practice has no Islamic sanction or justification and have struggled to eradicate it.

Marriage

The Quran reformed dramatically and institutionalized the rules governing marriage. Men had great liberty and often abused the institution of marriage in pre-Islamic Arabia, where women were generally endowed with fewer rights and control over marriage.

The major changes instituted under Islam were to convert marriage into an official, binding contract formalized before witnesses and based on mutual agreement. The new rules were established to ensure that the obligation of marriage was taken seriously and the wife was protected, financially, in case of divorce or separation.

In formal terms, the bride and groom are required to be of marriageable age within the permitted categories excluding close relatives or most blood-relatives. The bride is often represented by a guardian, who must insure that she willingly consents to enter into marriage. The parties must agree on a *mahr*, a gift to be given to the bride, the major part of which is held in reserve in the event the marriage is dissolved or the husband dies.

It is necessary that there must be witnesses to the marriage and a judge, or other established representative may often be in attendance to ensure that the contract has been fulfilled.

While the above formalities constitute the basis for the marriage contract, the celebration and ceremonies related to marriage vary from region to region in the Muslim world and are greatly influenced by local tradition and custom. The festivities involve music, dancing, drama and various other types of entertainment and exchange of gifts.

The Quran permits restricted polygamy, up to four wives. The injunction to treat them with strict equality is broadly understood by most modern Muslims to imply that monogamy is preferable and indeed consistent with Quranic teaching. According to tradition, Muslim men may marry women of other faiths, though women may not. In contemporary times, particularly among Muslims living in the West or as minorities in other cultures, there has been an increase in marriages by Muslim women of non-Muslim men.

Islam allows for divorce, insisting that all necessary efforts at reconciliation be made before a divorce is finalized. Divorce is generally by mutual agreement or judicial dissolution. Contemporary legislation in many parts of the Muslim world has sought to protect the rights of both parties and to ensure the curtailing of the possible abuse by husbands of unilaterally declaring divorce in some cases. After divorce, the mother has custody of young children but may lose that right in the event she remarries.

Death and Burial Practices

It is customary to recite the *shahada* to a dying person. After death, the body is given an ablution and wrapped generally in a simple shroud. Where appropriate, it is carried to the cemetery or burial place in a bier. It is regarded as meritorious to assist in carrying the bier to a cemetery and for the body to be buried as soon as possible, generally within a day or so after death.

At the grave, a special prayer is recited and in traditional settings, women are not allowed to be near the grave site to prevent the possibility of loud lamentation, a practice of pre-Islamic times, when women lamented by way of wailing. The body is placed in the grave with the face towards the Kaba and the prayer is recited. The grave is then filled with earth and a small mound raised above ground level. Generally a simple marker, or headstone may be erected. Tombs of individuals who are highly regarded for their scholarship, piety or service to Islam, often have mausoleums erected over their graves.

Visiting of graves and cemeteries are recommended for Muslims and in most Muslim societies, certain days following death are occasions of mourning, remembrance and sharing of food, generally the seventh, fourteenth and fortieth days after death.

It must be noted that customs accompanying burial vary from region to region and the pressures of contemporary life and circumstance, particularly where Muslims live as minorities, have caused certain observances to change over time.

Glossary

Abim This is a Muslim organization in Malaysia founded in 1972 that has played an active role in Muslim revivalism in the country.

adab This is an Arabic term with a wide connotation of meanings. In its practical aspect, it can refer to qualities necessary for proper, personal behavior, upbringing and mode of conduct of daily life and social interaction. It also stands for the cultivation of knowledge and literary learning that signifies humanistic values of individual achievement. In its literary aspect, adab signifies the material and spiritual culture generated in writing and other artistic accomplishments.

adat Particularly in its Indonesian, Malaysian and South Asian contexts, this concept refers to the practices and customs of the region. Such custom and local tradition often complemented the Sharia as a source of practice, establishing mutually enabling frames of reference for personal, social and community life and law.

adhan This is the Muslim call to the daily ritual prayer in Arabic. The adhan consists of the following elements in recitation: a. God is most great (Allahu Akbar), recited four times, b. I affirm that there is no god other than Allah, c. I affirm that Muhammad is the messenger of God, d. come to prayer (recited twice), e. come to acts of goodness (recited twice); to which the Shia and the Zaydis add "come to the best of deeds," f. God is most great (recited twice), g. There is no god other than Allah. The call to prayer is recited by a muezzin or in modern times through a loud speaker.

adl This is the Quranic term signifying justice.

Aga Khan This is the title of the Imam of the Shia Ismaili Muslims.

ahd This is the Quranic term signifying a covenant or pact as between God and human beings or by extension a pact between various parties.

ahl al bayt (Lit. "people of the house") This is a term given to the family of the Prophet. Among the Shia it is applied to the Prophet, his daughter Fatima, her husband Ali and their children Hasan and Husayn.

ahl al-dhimma Those who are protected, that is, non-Muslim religious communities under Muslim rule or within a Muslim majority, whose autonomy and freedom of religious life and institutions are assured by Quranic prescription. Though primarily referring to Jews and Christians in the earlier period, the term also came to be applied to other religious communities throughout Muslim history.

akhbar These are traditions reported from the Prophet and among the Twelver Shia, the term Akhbari was used to designate a school of thought that believed in the primacy of tradition over rational inquiry.

Al-Azhar This is a well-known mosque/institution of learning in Cairo, founded in the tenth century by the Fatimid dynasty. It has served until today as an important place for the study of law and theology.

alam This is a representation of Imam Husayn's standard in battle at Karbala.

Alawi This is the term for a Sufi group in North Africa but more generally refers to Shia groups in the Middle East who gave Ali, the son-in-law of the Prophet, a pre-eminent role in their theology. The Alawis of Syria are also called Nusayris.

Alhamdu lil lah This is an expression meaning "praise be to God."

Aligarh University This is an institution founded under British rule in India to provide education for Muslims in Islam as well as modern subjects.

Aljamiado This is distinctively Muslim literature of Andalusia in the Romance dialect written in Arabic characters.

Ahl al-Kitab (Lit. "people of the book") In the Quran (2.58 and 5.69), a term referring to Jews, Christians and Sabians, and other believers. The application of the term has been extended to include others who were believed to possess sacred scriptures, thereby establishing a commonality among faith communities to whom divine revelation had been granted.

Allah This is the Quranic name in Arabic for God. The use of the name is not confined to Islam alone, as Arabic speaking Christians also use it for God. It carries, therefore, a universal sense of the Supreme Divine Being, common to many religious traditions.

Allahu akbar This is an expression meaning "God is most Great."

amal In the Quran the term refers to morally worthy acts. The concept of amal was developed further in Muslim law, theology and philosophy. In modern times it is the name of a Muslim organization representing a party of the Twelver Shia in Lebanon.

Amir al-Muminin ("commander of the faithful") This is a title used for Muslim rulers.

amr bi'l maruf wa'l nahy an al-munkar This is the principle of promoting the good and negating the evil.

angels Belief in angels is taught by the Quran. These are a separate category of creation from human beings. Angels mentioned in the Quran are Gabriel and Michael. Tradition recognizes two other archangels: Israfil, who will sound the trumpet on the Last Day, and Azrail, the angel of death. Two angels are said to record the good and bad deeds of every life, an account which will be presented on the Day of Judgment.

ansar The Muslims of Medina who are called "helpers" because they came to the aid of the migrants from Mecca in 632.

apostasy It is regarded as a treasonable act and in traditional Islamic law is punishable by confinement, expulsion or in cases where extensive harm is caused to the community, by death. After the death of the Prophet certain tribal chieftains renounced allegiance to Islam and various "fake prophets" arose to lay claim to authority. The events provoked the "wars of apostasy," undertaken by Muslims against these groups.

aql This is the rational or thinking capacity of human beings. In the Muslim intellectual tradition, it became associated with the "intellect." In the Quran, Adam is taught the "names of all things" by God, implying that the composite status of humanity as created beings was accompanied by a capacity to have access through reason to all resources of knowledge. For most Muslim philosophers and thinkers the intellect complemented and interacted with knowledge based on revelation.

Arabic One of the Semitic languages, Arabic, the language of the Quran, is spoken today by more than 150 million people. It developed throughout the history of Islam as one of the world's major languages. Arabic is the primary language of Muslim religious writings, law, theology and philosophy and was adapted by and further enriched local languages such as Hausa, Persian, Swahili, Turkish and Urdu to name a few. All these languages adopted the Arabic script.

asabiya This is a central concept in the philosophy of history of Ibn Khaldun, the 14th century Muslim thinker. It signified for him the quality of bonding and solidarity that bound society in its various formative stages.

Ashura This is the tenth day of the month of Muharram, with particular significance for the Shia, as the day on which Imam Husayn was martyred. In general, it was also a day for voluntary fasting.

Astronomy Muslim scientists in the medieval period built observatories to develop accurate astronomical tables. Muslim astronomy greatly influenced subsequent developments in Europe.

awliya This is an Arabic word (sing. wali), referring to Muslim individuals who, through their devotion and spirituality, have become reference points for others. In mystical and devotional literature, they are referred to as "friends of God."

ayat These are verses in the Quran, also meaning "signs" in Creation, that signify God's power and presence.

Ayatollah (Lit., "sign of God") This is the title used for the most outstanding religious authorities among Imami Shia in Iran and Iraq, a rank based on leadership qualities, knowledge, charisma and standing within the community. The title is generally attributed by a consensus among the scholars and the faithful. The preeminent scholar of the time is also called Marji- taqlid.

Badr, Battle of In 624, the emerging Muslim community fought a much larger and better equipped Meccan force and defeated them in the first and most memorable battle of early Muslim history. In the Quran, the battle is portrayed as a sign of God's support and the eventual triumph of the Prophet's mission.

Bahai This is a modern religious group that in its formative period, developed in Iran as an offshoot of the Twelver Shia. They were treated as heretics and often persecuted. The Bahais regard themselves as members of a new, universal religion.

Bahasa Indonesia　This is the modern lingua franca of Indonesia, which is influenced by the Malay family of languages, spoken in Southeast Asia.

bani Adam　This refers to the human race.

baraka　This is a Quranic term for blessing. Particularly in Shia and Sufi tradition, the quality has come to be associated with the Prophet and his descendants who possess the capacity to transmit such blessing to others. In the Quran it is also associated with the "night of power" (laylat al qadr) during Ramadan.

basmala　This refers to the formula that appears at the beginning of every chapter of the Quran except one, which in its full form: "Bismillah al-Rahman al-Rahim," means "In the name of God, the most Gracious, the most Merciful."

batin　This is an Arabic term in the Quran signifying the inner, spiritual meaning of scripture and of religious acts.

baya　In Muslim tradition this term was used for the formal allegiance accorded by an individual to the Caliph or Imam of the time. When Muhammad's authority was accepted, new Muslims gave him their allegiance.

Bayt al- Hikma　(Lit. the "House of Wisdom") This is the institution established in Baghdad by the Abbasid Caliph, al-Mamun (d. 833) to translate philosophical and scientific works of Antiquity into Arabic. An observatory was also attached to the institution.

Bayt al-Mal　This is the traditional "treasury" of the Muslim community. The wealth flowing into the expanding Muslim State in early history, was deposited for appropriate distribution to serve for the welfare of Muslims.

Bible　Muslims regard certain parts of the Jewish and Christian Bible to have been divinely revealed, in particular, the Pentateuch (Tawrat in Arabic), the Psalms of David (Zabur) and the Gospels (Injil).

bida　This is the notion in Muslim thought, signifying the introduction of something new into practice for which there is no precedent. Developed primarily by Sunni jurists the concept was developed to argue for innovations that might be considered good or bad.

bimaristan　This is a hospital in the Muslim world, traditionally founded to treat all sick people and endowed by charitable funds.

Black Stone　The stone is set within the outside wall of the Kaba (q.v.) and touched or kissed by pilgrims during the Hajj (q.v.).

caliph　(Ar. khalifa) This is used in the Quran in reference to Adam in his custodial capacity on earth (Q2.28) and also to David (Q38.25). In the sense of deputy or successor to the Prophet it was applied to Abu Bakr, who led the Muslim community after the Prophet's death, and his successors Umar, Uthman and Ali. In 1924 following the disintegration of the Ottoman Empire and the creation of the Republic of Turkey, the new Assembly abolished the title.

calligraphy　The aesthetic, artistic rendering of Arabic script is one of the foremost of the fine arts among Muslims. A number of classic styles of calligraphy evolved in different parts of the Islamic world, but the tradition has continued to be inspired by artistic creativity that has generated a myriad of ways and techniques of representing the Arabic script artistically.

caravanserai　These are places along the caravan routes which served as rest stations and sites for commercial transactions on the ancient trading routes of the Muslim world.

circumcision　The practice of circumcision of male children, while not mentioned in the Quran, is generally accepted as being in accord with Prophetic practice. Most modern Muslims oppose and condemn female circumcision, which they argue representshistorically an indigenous custom in some parts of the world to which Islam has spread, but one which has no Islamic sanction.

Companions of the Prophet　(Ar. sahaba) This term is generally applied to those who were closest to the Prophet in his lifetime and in time by extension to the Muslims with him and in time by anyone who had seen him. The interest in knowing about the companions and their role in Muslim history and learning prompted the writing of biographical literature in which a pattern of ranking the companions was developed.

Cordoba　This is a Spanish city, which became a flourishing cultural center and capital of the Ummayad dynasty during Muslim rule in Andalusia. The Great Mosque—La Mezquita begun in 787, and Madinat al Zahra, the administrative city—were important architectural monuments. Noted scholars of all faiths studied in the city, such as Ibn Hazm, Ibn Rushd and the Jewish philosopher, Maimonides.

Crusades　This refers to the European Christian military expeditions undertaken from 1096 onwards with the aim of seizing the "Holy Land and Places" from Muslim rule. While Palestine was recaptured by Saladin after an initial loss, the Crusaders gained Sicily and a majority of the Iberian Peninsula by the thirteenth century. The Crusades, though essentially a military failure, did in effect, have some positive results, in terms of the exchange of knowledge and increase in trade and commerce between Europe and the Muslim world.

Dar al-Islam   This is the space in which Islam predominated, traditionally, the territory and regions in which Muslims exercised rule.

darud   This is a blessing invoked on the Prophet

dawa   (Lit. invitation or call) In the Quran and by certain Muslim groups, it came to signify the summoning of people to the practice of true Islam. Among the Ismailis (q.v.) it also came to refer to the institutional form of the organization, responsible for preaching Islam. Its use has continued to modern times among Muslims to indicate the continuing goal of preaching and inviting to Islam.

Deoband   This is a traditional institution founded by Muslims in British India to train scholars and preserve Muslim learning for contemporary needs.

dhikr   (Lit. remembrance, or recollection) This is a meditation practice involving the rhythmical repetition, "remembrance," of one or more religious phrases invoking the ninety-nine names of God; The practice of remembering God is mentioned often in the Quran as a form of personal devotion and private prayer. Among Sufis and other Muslims who practicecontemplation and personal meditation, the use of dhikr has come to be a means of attaining spiritual experience

dhimmi   These were protected peoples under Muslim rule, who were granted religious freedom and autonomy in their community affairs as well as protection in time of war. They were required to pay a poll tax and exempt from fighting in times of war.

din   This is a term used extensively in the Quran to signify religion in general.

divorce   Islam permits divorce under certain circumstances. The intention to divorce has to take into account a period of waiting known as idda consisting of three menstrual periods to confirm pregnancy. Should the wife be pregnant, the divorce has to be postponed. Divorce by mutual consent is also allowed and a petition of divorce by the wife may include grounds such as cruelty, impotence, apostasy etc. It must be noted that each of the schools of Muslim law have developed varying rules for how divorce is to be effected and in modern times, such aspects of personal law have been integrated and revised differently in different parts of the Muslim world.

diwan   This is a collection of poems. It also refers to an institution created in early Muslim history to organize in a systematic way, the treasury and to disburse funds appropriately.

Dome of the Rock   This is the sacred space on the site of the deserted Temple Mount in Jerusalem. After the Muslim conquest, one of the Caliphs built a sanctuary on the site in 691. The mosque on one end of the site is called Al-Aqsa, the Farthest Mosque referred to in Quran 17:1, from where the Prophet ascended on his journey to the heavens.

dua   These are prayers of supplication and praise said mostly in times of crisis or to fulfil individual and community needs and requests before God.

Druze   This is a group that separated from the Fatimid Ismailis in the eleventh century and formed a new community which has survived to our day in Syria, Lebanon and Israel.

falsafa   This refers to Muslim philosophy, represented by the tradition of Muslim thinkers who integrated Hellenistic and other forms of philosophical thought, into a broadly based rational system of thought.

faqih   This is an expert in Muslim jurisprudence.

fasting   The practice of fasting during the month of Ramadan is enjoined by the Quran and is regarded in Muslim tradition as a major part of the practice of the faith. In addition to the month long fast lasting from dawn to sunset, Muslims fast on other optional days, following the practice of the Prophet.

al-fatiha   This is the opening sura of the Quran and an integral part of daily prayer.

fatwa   This is a formal opinion rendered by a Muslim scholar having appropriate status and training. Such opinions may be sought from scholars who are known as mufti in the Sunni tradition and as mujtahid (q.v.) among the Shia, but are not necessarily binding. The practice of issuing a fatwa has continued in modern times as a mechanism for dealing with personal, social, legal and religious issues.

fiqh   This is the science of jurisprudence, including its logic, methodology, and applicability. The composite body of law produced by the science is referred to as the Sharia. An expert in jurisprudence is called a faqih. (pl. fuqaha)

food   Certain categories of food are prohibited in Islam, among others, the meat of swine and animals not appropriately slaughtered. Also forbidden is alcohol and intoxicating drugs of all kinds, except where their use is medically necessary and supervised.

funduq   These were used for selling goods and products from the countryside or from other countries and were usually built at city gates, a strategic point where merchants had to unload and pay custom duties.

funerals   Muslims are urged to bury the dead as soon as possible. After the ritual bathing of the corpse, a funeral prayer is performed and the body laid to rest in the ground with the face towards the Kaba.

ghayba   This refers to the eschatological idea of the occultation, particularly in Twelver Imami Shiism (q.v.) when the last Imam is believed to have gone into occultation and cannot be seen.

ghazal   This is a mystically-tinged love lyric, originating in Arabic but passing on to become a feature in many other languages of the Muslim world.

ghusl   This is the term for the major ritual act of ablution involving a full bath.

hadith   This term is applied to reports or narratives of the Prophet Muhammad, including his sayings and actions. These accounts were collected and systematized after his death by Muslim scholars specifically devoted to the task. The mode of recording these narratives, which in their earliest settings were oral accounts or living memory, was to precede the narration of the substance by reference to the transmitter or transmitters through whom it was reported. Hadith were put into collections for thepurpose of teaching transmission and application to the daily lives and activities of Muslims and their communities. The most significant collections for the Sunni community are those compiled by al-Bukhari (d. 870), Muslim ibn Hajjaj (d. 875), Abu Daud (d. 888), Ibn Majah (d. 887) and al-Tirmidhi (d. 892). The Shia, who have their own collections, added to their corpus of hadith the sayings of their Imams. The hadith constitutes a major source in the development of Muslim law, through the concept of Sunna which complements the Quran for interpreting, understanding and applying aspects of Muslim belief and practice.

Hajj   This is the annual pilgrimage to the Kaba (q.v.) in Mecca. It takes place during the month of Dhu al-Hijjah, the last month of the calendar.

halal   This is the Quranic term for that which is lawful or allowed. In general, it connotes that which is appropriate for use or practice and in particular refers to the permitted categories of food and drink. Halal food includes the meat of permitted animals that have been ritually slaughtered, hunted game over which the divine name has been invoked and praised, fish and marine life.

hammam   This is a steam bath, an essential public amenity, reinforcing the idea of purification in Islam.

Hanafi   This is the School of Sunni law based on the work of Abu Hanifa.

Hanbali   This is the School of Sunni law, based on the teachings of Ahmad bin Hanbal.

hanif   ("pure person") These are individuals referred to in the Quran, such as Abraham and others who were devoted to God.

haram   This is a sacred space or sanctuary. Harim (harem) refers to the part of the traditional house where women lived.

har m   Certain food, drink and activities that are viewed as forbidden or taboo.

heaven and hell   See janna and jahannum.

hijab   This refers to any local forms of modest dress or covering worn by women.

Hijaz   The region in Arabia that includes the cities of Mecca and Medina.

Hijra   This is the migration of the Prophet and his followers from Mecca to Medina in 622.

hikma   (Lit. wisdom) By extension, it also means science and philosophy.

ibadat   These are legal prescriptions dealing with the practices of the faith, particularly worship.

Ibadi   This is one of the surviving branches of the Khwarij found mostly in Oman, Zanzibar and in parts of North Africa.

iblis   (Satan, the devil) By his disobedience, he fell out of the group of angels. He refused God's command to prostrate himself before Adam, created from clay. For his disobedience he was expelled from heaven, but his punishment was reprieved until the Day of Judgment.

Idd al Adha   This is the Festival of Sacrifice that is commemorated towards the end of the Hajj as a symbol of Abraham's sacrifice.

Idd al Fitr   This is the Festival that follows the end of Ramadan, the month of fasting.

ihram   This is the seamless white garment donned by pilgrims for the Hajj and the Umra. The term also refers to the state of ritual purification entered by the pilgrims as they enter the sacredspace of the Haram. Once in a state of ihram, a number of actions are prohibited, such as wearing perfume, cutting the nails or hair, killing plants or animals, or any kind of sexual activity.

ijaz al Quran   This is the term used for the miraculous, inimitable nature of the Quran.

ijma   This refers to the consensus of the learned community of religious scholars, which is the third foundation of Sunni law, along with the Quran and the Sunna. See also Usul al Fiqh.

ijtihad This refers to independent reasoning concerning a legal or theological question. According to tradition, the legitimacy of ijtihad was recognized by the Prophet. Ijtihad is important in Shia theology and law as a principle. Scholars are referred to as mujtahids, those who exercise their reasoning in matters of faith.

Ikhwan al Muslimin This refers to The Muslim Brotherhood, a modern religious and political movement that arose in Egypt in the twentieth century and spread to other parts of the Middle East.

ilm (lit. "knowledge") It also means, by extension, any science or field of inquiry.

imam This title applied to a religious leader, to the leader of congregational prayer, and to the founders of the schools of Law. The term originally meant "model" or "example" (Q2.118; 17.73; 36.11; 15.79; 25.74). In Shiism the imam is a religious leader, descended from the line of Ali and attributed with spiritual authority, the position being hereditary and based on a specific designation, nass.

Imambara This is the house of the Imam, a space of gathering for Twelver Shia, where devotional exercises in remembrance of the Imams, particularly Imam Husayn, are commemorated.

Imami This is a term used for Shia in general, because of their belief in their imams.

iman "Faith." In addition to faith in God, iman also refers to formal affirmation of belief in the fundamental articles of faith.

Injil This refers to the Quranic term for the revelation granted to Jesus.

In shaa Allah This is an expression meaning "If God wills."

Islamic Banking This is a modern form of Banking practiced in some parts of the Muslim world and elsewhere that seeks to eliminate interest as a component, because it is believed to be totally forbidden by the Quran.

Ismailiyya This is one of the branches of the Shia. The two major groups are the Mustali, who acknowledge a line of Imams, the last of whom is believed to be in a state of concealment and the Nizari Ismailis who acknowledge a living Imam and who currently accept Karim Aga Khan (q.v) as their present Imam.

isnad This refers to the documentation of the chain of persons through whom sayings of the Prophet have

been transmitted, constituting a process of authentication for Hadith. Information was also collected concerning each person in the isnad for the purpose of documenting their degree of reliability.

isra This is the "journey" of the Prophet to the presence of God referred to in the Quran (17:1) from the "Sacred Mosque" to the "Farthest Mosque," i.e. from the Kaba to Jerusalem.

Ithnaashariyya (Lit. "Twelvers") This is the largest branch of Shiism found predominantly in Iraq and Iran but in many other parts of the world, which recognizes twelve Imams, the last of whom withdrew from the world in the 3rd/9th century and has since remained in a state of occultation. He is expected to return as the Mahdi. Acting on his behalf until that time, mujtahids guide the faithful in religious and legal affairs.

iwan This is a feature of architecture in the Muslim world with a vault facing on to a courtyard.

Jafariya This is the Twelver Imami Shia School of law, named after the sixth Shia Imam, Jafar al Sadiq.

jahannum This is the Quranic term for hell, a place of fiery torment for evil-doers and those damned by their actions.

jahilliya This refers to the age of ignorance; the period before the coming of Islam.

Jamaat-i-Islami This is a political party and organization founded by Sayyid Abu al ala Mawdudi (1903-1979), a reformist who advocated the institution of Sharia as a universal system, sufficient as a vehicle for addressing the problems of modernity. As a party, it has, however, never been able to come to power in Pakistan, but in alliance with other parties, continues to be influential in Pakistan.

jamaat khana This is a gathering space for community activities and for devotional practice, among Sufis and other Muslim groups such as the Nizari Ismailis.

Jami This is the Friday mosque; also Jamia as an extension from this form, meaning "university."

janna (Lit. garden) In the Quran it refers to heaven or paradise, a place of joy and tranquility, signifying the attainment of nearness to God, and symbolized by the richness and serenity of a garden.

janaza This is the funeral bier and the performance of rituals accompanying its carriage to a cemetery.

Janissaries This is an elite army recruited to serve the Ottoman Sultan.

Jerusalem Together with Mecca and Medina, it is regarded as a holy site, by virtue of the Prophet's Night Journey when he was brought by the angel Gabriel to "the farthest mosque" and then ascended into heaven (Q17.1) and by its association with monotheism.

jihad   (lit. "striving") This is a Quranic concept which encompasses the idea of a just war as well as other forms of striving by which individuals or the community extends the practice of Islam and safety for Muslims

jinn   ("genie") This is one of the classes of beings created by God. Whereas humankind was created of clay and divine spirit and angels out of light, the jinn are believed to have been created out of smokeless fire. The Quran describes Solomon's use of the jinn to build the temple.

jizya   This is a poll tax for non-Muslims who were included in the category "Ahl al-Kitab," the basis for which is found in Q9.29.

juma   Friday is the day of congregational prayer which is held at noon.

Kaba   (Lit. "cube") This is the structure located in the center of the mosque at Mecca, covered with an embroidered black cloth and containing the Black Stone. Muslims believe that the first Kaba, constructed by Adam as a place of worship was rebuilt by Abraham and his son Ishmael and then restored as a place for the worship of One God by Muhammad.

kafir   This is an unbeliever or infidel, who deliberately rejects faith and belief in a transcendent being.

Kairouan   It is the site of one of the earliest Muslim institutions of learning. It is located today in Tunisia and was founded in 670.

Kalam   This refers to rational theology or religious philosophy in Islam. The science of theology is called Ilm al-Kalam. Karbala This is a city in modern day Iraq, but formerly the site where Imam Husayn, grandson of the Prophet and Shia Imam, was killed along with several members of his family and followers. The site and a shrine are a major center of visitation and a place of historical and religious significance for the Shia.

khanaqa   This is a Sufi place of gathering for devotion and spiritual practice.

khutba   This is a sermon in the mosque generally given during Friday prayer.

Khwarij   This is an early sectarian group that held strictly to views on how to resolve political differences by adherence to their particular interpretation of the Quran. A group of the Khwarij, the Ibadi, survives to this day in Oman and Zanzibar and parts of Algeria with its own legal interpretation and organization.

Kufic   This is a style of calligraphy used in the writing of the Quran.

kulliye   This is a complex in Ottoman times that provides social and housing services linked to a mosque, hospital, school, and library for the benefit of the public.

kuttab   These are places where children receive instruction in the Quran and in Islamic subjects.

laylat al-qadr   ("night of power") This is referred to in Quran, during the night of Ramadan, when individuals may stay up all night in prayer and meditation.

madhhab   (pl. madhahib) These are the schools of law among Muslims that reflect the diversity and richness of Muslim judicial practice.

madrasa   These are the institutions for learning created in Medieval Islam, particularly for training of scholars in religion and law.

Mahdi   The guided one; this is often a title used by those in Muslim history, who sought to replace tyrannical and unjust rulers. The term also carries an eschatological meaning, particularly among the Shia, referring to the awaited Imam who will restore justice at the end of time.

mahr   This is the dower to be paid to the bride by the groom as part of the marriage contract which remains her property in the event of divorce.

majlis   This is a meeting place or gathering, for congregational activities and as centers of learning.

majlis e shura   A consultative assembly; this is a term which is often used for constitutional vehicles in modern times in many Muslim countries.

Maliki   This is the Sunni school of law which is based on teachings of Malik b. Anas.

Mansa   This is the title used by West African Muslim rulers.

marabout   This is a French version of an Arabic word referring to Muslim preachers and teachers, given particularly regard for their spirituality and good works. Their status is remembered and commemorated at their burial place which are considered as places where blessing may be sought.

marifa   This refers to wisdom which is the ultimate goal of spiritual life in mystical literature.

marriage   According to Quranic teaching and Muslim tradition, marriage is established through a mutual contract, consented to and witnessed by the two parties and their representatives. It is not regarded as a sacrament and therefore does not necessarily need to take place in a mosque.

marsiya These are elegies, particularly in celebration or commemoration of heroic figures in Islam, such as Imam Husayn.

masjid (Lit. a place of prostration) It is the term used for a mosque.

al-masjid al-jami This is a mosque for congregational Friday prayer, which in many cases has an institution of learning.

maslaha This refers to the public good, a principle whereby decisions may be taken for the benefit of society.

masnavi This is a rhymed couplet: a form used in poetry. The Mathnawi of Jalal al-din Rumi exemplifies the best example of this form.

Mawlid al-Nabi This is the birthday of the Prophet celebrated on the 12th day of Rabi al- Awwal.

Mecca This is the birthplace of the Prophet, site of the Kaba and the annual pilgrimage and it is regarded as a city containing one of the most important sacred sites in Islam.

Medicine This is an important science, developed in the medieval period by Muslim physicians and scholars from the Classical heritage. It led to the development of a comprehensive science of medicine, the building of hospitals and the writing of medical text-books, all of which had a major influence in the later Middle Ages in Europe.

Medina This is the name of the city in Arabia to which the Prophet migrated and the site of his burial; it is considered with Mecca to be a sacred place by Muslims. In another sense, the word medina is also used to describe the traditional part of major Muslim cities.

mihrab This is the niche in the center of one of the walls of the mosque which marks the Qibla, the direction of Mecca towards which Muslims orient themselves in prayer.

minaret This is the tower of the mosque from which the call to prayer is made.

minbar This is the pulpit in the mosque from which the khutba (sermon) is delivered.

Moors This is the historical European name for the Muslim peoples of Spain and North Africa.

muamalat These are matters in law regarding marriage, family, personal status, including divorce, custody of children, maintenance, testate and intestate succession.

mudaraba This is a traditional Muslim concept of contract incorporated into some contemporary Muslim economic systems reflecting an equity sharing agreement where one part provides capital and the other the labor and enterprise.

Mudejar This is the Spanish name for the Arabs who remained in Spain after the Reconquista. Their presence continued to aspire the "Moorish" style in art and architecture that also influenced the New World.

muezzin Those who call to prayer and recite the adhan, the call to prayer.

mufti This is a recognized authority who renders opinions on legal questions. The opinion is known as a fatwa. (q.v.)

muhajirun This refers to those who left Mecca to migrate with the Prophet to Medina.

Muharram This is the first month of the Islamic year. The first of Muharram is the Muslim New Year but is not generally a day of celebration. The tenth day, however, is observed by both Sunnis and Shia for its significance as the day of mourning the martyrdom of Imam Husayn. See Ashura.

mujaddid This is a person who is regarded as a renewer of intellectual and moral life in Islam.

mujtahid This is the term for a trained religious scholar, capable of instructing Muslims on issues of faith.

mulla This is the term for a religious scholar, used mostly in Persian speaking parts of the Muslim world as well as in South and Central Asia.

muqarnas This is a decorative, geometric form found widely in Muslim architecture, in corners where walls meet ceilings and also as a transition.

Murjia This is the name of a school of theology in early Islamic history.

musharaka This is a legal term in Muslim commercial transactions that has come to be applied to attempts being made in the modern Muslim world to define participation financing. It reflects a contractual partnership.

Muslim A follower of Islam, the word signifies one who has accepted and is committed to Islam.

Mustaliyya These are one of the branches of the Ismailiyya (q.v.) who believe that their Imams are in a state of concealment but guide the community through a representative known as a dai.

Mutazila This is the school of Muslim theology that emphasized the concepts of God's justice supported by the Abbasid Caliph, al-Mamun in the ninth century. They represented a strong commitment to the use of rational tools to understand Islam.

naat This is the a cappella melodic recitation of devotional verse about the Prophet Muhammad in Arabic and other languages.

nabi This is the Quranic term for a prophet. A prophet who is the messenger of a revelation is also known as rasul.

Najaf This is a center of Shia learning and the seat of burial of Imam Ali in Iraq.

nahda (Lit. renaissance) This is a term used for the new thinking among Arabs in the Muslim world.

Nahdat al-Ulama This is the name of a modern Muslim movement in Indonesia.

nass (Lit. designation) Among the Shia, it establishes the formal means by which an Imam designates a successor.

Nation of Islam This is the name used to describe a group of African-Americans who have converted to Islam through the teachings of Elijah Muhammad. The name is currently retained by the followers of Louis Farrakhan.

Nazar fil Mazalim This is a term for institutions for the administration of law.

nazr This refers to the charitable distribution of food.

nikah This is the Quranic term for marriage and the rules governing it.

niya An intention; it refers to the intention for undertaking prayer or generally for the performance of a good deed.

Nur ("Radiant Light") This is a Quranic concept often used as a symbol to represent divine knowledge.

Ojala This is a term representing the corrupted form in Spanish of the familiar: In shaa Allah, "If God wills."

Pancasila This is a concept defining the basis of Indonesia heritage: Muslim, Hindu, Buddhist and Christian and modern which constitutes the five principles underlying the state.

pilgrimage The Hajj is the major pilgrimage to the sites in and near Mecca and Medina. The Quran urges it upon adult Muslims, once in a lifetime, if they are able to afford it. It occurs once each year during the month of Dhu al-Hijjah. The minor pilgrimage, known as the Umra, may be performed at any time.

pesantrens These are traditional Muslim boarding schools in Indonesia where students in residence receive instruction and training.

pir This is the term for a guide in the Sufi path.

polygyny This is the practice of having more than one wife. The Quran allows one to have four wives provided each is treated with complete equity. In modern times many Muslims regard this practice to have been historically necessary and believe on the basis of the Quranis condition for total equity, that monogamy is to be regarded as the norm. Polygyny is, however, still practiced in parts of the Muslim world.

prayer Ritual prayer (salat) is one of the pillars among practices of the faith. It is preceded by ablution of the face, hands and feet and performed facing Mecca. The space in which the prayer is performed must also be ritually clean and for this reason the use of prayer rugs became customary. Before beginning the prayer, the intention to pray must be affirmed (niya). Ritual prayer is in Arabic and is recited to the accompaniment of prescribed sets of physical positions (raka) which involve standing, bowing, reclining on the knees, and prostration. Dua, private prayer may be in any language and performed at any time.

prophets The Quran mentions many prophets, by name, stating, however, that there is no group in history to whom a prophet was not sent (10:48). They are all believed to have been sent to preach the message of the One God to their communities.

qadi This is a judge appointed to implement Muslim law. He was expected to be a well-known scholar and a respected individual in society.

Qarawiyyin This is a famous mosque and university in Fez, Morocco, first built in 859, endowed by Fatima al Fihri, a woman noted for her support of religious and educational institutions.

qasida A poem, in its classical form, which consists generally of a prologue, narrative of a journey and the central theme, with one rhyme and a uniform meter.

qawwali These are popular devotional songs recited at the shrines of many Sufi figures in South Asia.

qibla This is the direction for prayer, and the point of orientation to the Kaba.

qiyas This refers to analogical reasoning; it is a tool of jurisprudential thought in Sunni law.

Quran (lit. "recitation") It is the term for the complete recorded revelation to the Prophet and the sacred scripture of Islam.

Quraysh This was the leading tribe of the Hijaz during the Prophet's time.

Ramadan This is the ninth month of the Islamic year. Ramadan is the month of the annual fast during which all food, drink and sexual activity are avoided during the hours just before sunrise until sunset. Many Muslims devote the entire month to the study of the Quran. They also intensify the practice of good works and philanthropy. Fasting ends upon the sighting of the new moon marking the festival of Id al-Fitr (q.v.) and the congregational prayer on the day following.

rasul This is the Quranic term for God's messenger.

rawda khani This is the commemorative recitation and ritual expression of grief among the Shia on the occasion of Imam Husayn's martyrdom.

revelation According to the Quran, God has revealed himself at various times to human kind through his prophets, for example, revealing the Torah to Moses and the Gospels, Injil to Jesus before revealing the Quran to the Prophet Muhammad. The Quran is said to have been revealed through a process known as tanzil (lit., "sending down") and by inspiring it to the Prophet.

riba Generally defined as "usury" or "interest," it connotes in the Quran, unlawful gain resulting from exploitative charged on accrued debt. This is, however, not meant to preclude lawful profit or gain.

ribat This is an outpost for religious and devotional gatherings.

rida This refers to acceptance and contentment as a result of one's commitment to God.

ruh This is the Quranic term for "spirit."

sadaqa In the Quran, this is another term used for a charitable act of giving.

salaf al salih These are exemplary individuals in early Islam who are considered to be models for later Muslims.

Salafiyya This is a modern movement to replicate the perceived exemplary model of the early Muslim community.

salam alaykum This is the traditional Muslim greeting of peace and salutation. The response is wa alaykum salam (peace be upon you, too).

salat See prayer.

sama This is the act of devotional participation involving listening and/or rhythmical movement to music. The term also refers to centers for recitation of poetry in musical sessions.

sawm See fasting.

say This is the act of running during the Hajj to commemorate Hagar's quest for water; this is an important ritual of the pilgrimage.

shah This is the title used by kings of Iran and nearby regions.

shahada The shahada is the initial witnessing and declaration of one's acceptance of Islam encompassing the foundational belief in the absolute unity of God and in Muhammad as God's messenger. It is also known as the kalima.

Shahnama This is a classic of Persian literature, chronicling the history of ancient history of kings by Firdawsi.

shaykh This is a term of honor for a great scholar or guide in Sufism.

Sharia (Lit. "the way") Muslim schools of law developed over a period of centuries in response to questions that arose as the Umma expanded its territory and encountered other peoples and cultures with established systems of belief and law. There developed over time a methodology of analysis and application through which answers could be obtained. The methodology is known as fiqh (science of jurisprudence), its foundational principles are known as Usul al-fiqh (roots of jurisprudence), and the body of law it produced is collectively called the Sharia. In a certain sense, however, the Sharia is more than the Western understanding of the sum total of its case law. It is for Muslims a way of life, encompassing not only societal and contractual relationships but the private actions of individuals, providing a guide for living in accordance with the will of God. Different schools of Law emerged around geographic centers of the Islamic empire and out of sectarian differences, achieving a systemization which had many common features. The law encompasses every aspect of human action, refusing to dichotomize the religious and the secular, classifying, in legal and ethical terms, actions into five categories known as al-Akham al-Khamsa: (1) fard (obligatory); (2) sunna (recommended); (3) mubah (neutral; (4) makruh (detestable); and (5) haram (forbidden). Alongside the Sharia, there existed the traditionally established customary laws which were not superseded in the conversion process known as adat. (q.v.)

sharif This is a descendant of the Prophet Muhammad through his daughter Fatima and Ali (who was also his cousin), regarded to be endowed with special honor.

shatahat These are mystical utterances and sayings that were often construed to be of a radical nature but in the content of Sufi understanding, reflected the intense devotion of an individual to God, expressing an ecstatic condition.

shaytan   See Iblis.

Shia   These are the "followers of Ali," and the name of one of the major branches of Islam. The Shia believe that Ali succeeded the Prophet, to continue to safeguard and interpret the divine revelation, a role that was to pass on to a designated successor from among his sons and their descendants.

shirk   (Lit. "association") This refers to idolatry represented in the act of associating anything with God.

shura   This means consultation, a process whereby rulers, scholars and others develop a means of consulting with each other on important decisions.

silsila   This is the chain of authority in a Sufi tariqa marking the lineage back to Ali and the Prophet.

sira   This is the term for a lifestory, particularly of the Prophet.

siyasa   This is administrative law that developed in Muslim societies dealing with issues of governance and the administration of the state.

subhanallah   This is an expression meaning "Glory be to God."

Sufi   This is the term used for those who have chosen the path of mystical understanding and devotion to God. Sufism is the dimension of Islamic spirituality.

Sunna   (Lit. "path") This is the term used for the customs, actions and sayings of the Prophet, later documented and collected into an enormous body of material which constitutes a model upon which Muslims pattern their lives.

Sunni   (Lit. from ahl al-sunna "people of the Sunna") This is the large, majority group in Islam. Sometimes described as "orthodox," Sunnis consider themselves traditionalists whose self- definition grew out of their emphasis on the Quran and the Hadith in the development of their four Schools of Law (the Hanafi, the Hanbali, the Maliki and the Shafii). Sunnis recognize the first four caliphs as legitimate rulers and successors to the Prophet.

suq   This is the term used for the market place or bazaar in the Muslim world.

sura   A chapter in the Quran is called a sura.

Swahili   The Muslim peoples and language of the East African coast are collectively known as Swahili.

tafsir   (Lit. "explaining") This is the explanation and commentary on the Quran, a term which refers both to the exercise of Quranic interpretation in general and to a specific explanation of its language and meaning.

tahara   This means purification, in its broadest sense as combining ritual and inner action and thought.

tajwid   (Lit. "making beautiful") This is the art of Quranic recitation which has been developed into a science and covers rules for the proper pronunciation, vocalization and timing of every letter and syllable of the text, including the length of pauses in between. One who has achieved proficiency in such recitation is know as a qari, and one who is able to recite it from memory is called a hafiz. Several styles of recitation exist. Aside from recitation which regularly forms part of ritual and personal prayer, certain occasions call for Quranic recitation, such as weddings, funerals, public ceremonies and the nights during the month of Ramadan. Competitions in recitation are very popular in Muslim countries.

takbir   This is the declaration of the formula Allah-u-Akbar-God is Most Great.

taqiyya   This is the precautionary dissimulation of one's true religious belief in the face of danger or threat to one's life or community.

taqlid   This is the strict adherence to a particular jurist or school of thought.

Tanzimat   (Lit. "regulations") This is the collective title given to a series of reforms enacted by the Ottoman Sultan Abdul Mejid beginning in 1839. The impetus behind the reforms was the perceived need to modernize and reorganize a bureaucracy whose weaknesses had become apparent in its encounter with European expansionism.

tariqa   (Lit. "path") This is a term which refers both to the esoteric expression of Islam in general (i.e., Sufism) and to a specific group organized under a spiritual leader of Shaykh. Among the earliest tariqa was the Qadiriyya, which established the model adopted by subsequent groups. While regarding exoterism as essential to a spiritual life, the tariqa attracts Muslims who seek a deeper level of spirituality than that which is achieved by following the Sharia alone. The spiritual authority of the Shaykh is established through a silsila, a chain of baraka traced back to the Prophet and Ali.

Taurat   This is the Quranic term for the Torah, the revelation to Moses.

tawaf   This refers to the circling of the Kaba during the pilgrimage.

Tawhid   This refers to the unity of God; which is a foundational belief in Islam. It emphasizes both the absolute transcendence and uniqueness of God.

tawil (Lit. "interpretation") This is a term generally referring to interpretation of the Quran but which has specifically come to mean an allegorical interpretation of the inner meaning of the text. Such an interpretation is acceptable in Shiism and Sufism and is particularly important for Ismailis.

tayammum This is a form of symbolic ablution performed in the absence of water by using earth, sand or, in some instances, a stone.

taziya (Lit. "consolation) This is a passion play performed during the first ten days of Muharram in commemoration of the tragic martyrdom of Husayn at Karbala. The term also refers to a model of Husayn's tomb. These models may be elaborate and permanent structures in the home or they may be temporarily constructed for the ashura ceremonies and for use in street processions.

tekke This is a term used for a Sufi gathering place in Turkey.

tilawa This is the reading of the Quran, an activity highly esteemed by Muslims which requires a knowledge of Arabic phonology as well as conventions regarding traditional responses and phrases are appropriate at certain places in the text.

ulama (Lit. "[the] learned") These are the religious and legal scholars particularly in Sunnism, whose respected knowledge and opinion is collectively accepted as the authoritative consensus known as ijma. There are several recognized categories of ulama: (1) faqih. An expert in jurisprudence (2) mufti. A legal expert, sometimes but not always acting in an official capacity, whose rendered opinion (fatwa) is not legally binding but carries considerable authority. (3) Qadi. Judge appointed by a political leader whose opinions are binding. The term mujtahid, is often used for such scholars among the Shia.

Umma (Lit. "people") This term occurs many times in the Quran to refer to people of a religious community, such as the "umma of Abraham." The word has come to represent the concept of the Muslim community as a whole.

Umm al-Kitab (Lit. "Mother of the Book") This is a term used in the Quran to refer to the Quran itself and also taken to mean the original source exists as an archetype of which recorded revelation is a representation.

Umra This is the lesser pilgrimage to Mecca, performed as an act of piety at any time except during Hajj.

urs These are marriage festivities and also, by extension, activities at a Sufi shrine or mausoleum to commemorate the memory of the deceased Sufi.

Usul al-Fiqh (Lit. "roots of understanding") These are the sources of jurisprudence in Sunnism. They are the Quran, Sunna, Ijma and Qiyas. Al-Shafii, the ninth century scholar, is credited with systematizing legal methodology based on sources in the manner that became accepted in Sunni Islam. In Shiism, however, independent reasoning (ijtihad) is accepted as one of the usul al-fiqh when exercised by a mujtahid.

Wahhabi This term is used to designate the dominant group of Muslims in Saudi Arabia. Their interpretation of Islam is based on the teachings of Muhammad ibn Abd al Wahhab (d. 1787).

wahy (Lit. "inspiration") This is a Quranic term which refers to "divine inspiration" as the instrument through which the Quran was revealed to the Prophet Muhammad.

wajib This refers to obligatory acts in Muslim law, which are incumbent on individuals.

Wilayet-i-faqih This is a jurisconsult's trusteeship; an important concept in Twelver Shiism forming the basis of juristic authority.

waqf This is an endowment or trust stipulated for a specific purpose. It represents the manner of institutionalizing the philanthropic spirit in Islam, by which one gives property or wealth to be used in perpetuity for a specified cause such as: a school, mosque, hospital or for any other philanthropic purpose.

wayang This is a theatrical performance including actors, puppets, or use of shadow images from behind a lighted screen in Indonesia.

Wazir (Vizier) This is a minister of government or the state.

wudu This is an act of ablution, generally performed prior to the saying of prayer. Most mosques contain provisions for running water to enable people to perform wudu.

Yawm al-din This is The Day of Judgement referred to in the Quran when all individuals and their actions will be judged by God.

Zabur This is the Quranic term for the Psalms of David which are regarded as a divinely inspired revelation.

zahir This is the formal aspect of religion or scripture.

zakat This refers to a foundational Quranic practice of sharing wealth and property. It is based on the amount of wealth possessed in abundance to the amount needed and designated for use to help the disadvantaged and needy in society. It represents a formal mode of giving in Islam through an Imam or ruler or directly by the individual.

zam-zam   This is the well near the Kaba, which marks a spring which is believed to have appeared to provide water for Hagar and Ishmael in the desert.

zawiya   This is a religious retreat or a meeting place for Sufis where meditation and spiritual discipline are practiced. In Turkey it is called tekke and in Iran and the Subcontinent, khanqa.

Zaydiyya   This is a branch of Shiism which broke off in 122/740 at the death of the fourth Imam Ali Zayn al-Abidin, electing to follow his son Zayd rather than Muhammad al-Baqir, who became the fifth Imam of the rest of the Shia. Zaydi states were established in Tabaristan and in Yemen, the latter surviving until its overthrow in 1963. Zaydis are distinguished from other schools by their own traditions of law, theology and the recognition of a non-dynastic imamat through the lineage of Ali based on the criteria of political and religious competence. As a consequence, Zaydis are willing to recognize more than one imam at a time as well as none at all. Today Zaydis are dominant in North Yemen.

ziyara   (Lit. "visiting") In its widest application, this term refers to visiting the tomb of the Prophet and the holy sites in Mecca and Medina. In Shiism the term also refers to visiting the tombs of imams, saints and martyrs as places of baraka and spiritual intercession.

General Bibliography

◆ A

Abbott, Nabia. *Language and Literature*, vol. 3 of *Studies in Arabic Literary Papyria*. Chicago: University of Chicago Press, 1972.

————. *The Beloved Mohammed*. Chicago: The University of Chicago Press, 1942.

Abun-Nasr, Jamil M. *A History of the Maghrib in the Islamic Period*. Cambridge: Cambridge University Press, 1987.

Aghnides, Nicholas P. *Introduction to Muhammadan Law and a Bibliography*. Lahore, Pakistan: Sange-Meel Publications, 1981.

Ahmad, Aziz. *An Intellectual History of Islam in India, Islamic Survey*. Edinburgh: Edinburgh University Press, 1969.

Ahmad, Khurshid, ed. *Studies in Islamic Economics*. Jeddah, Saudi Arabia: International Center for Research in Islamic Economics, King Abdul Aziz University, 1981.

Ahmed, Akbar S. *Living Islam: From Samarkand to Stornoway*. London: BBC Books, 1993.

Ahmed, Leila. *Women and Gender in Islam: Historical Roots of a Modern Debate*. New Haven: Yale University Press, 1992.

Ajami, Fouad. *The Vanished Imam: Musa al Sadr and the Shia of Lebanon*. Ithaca, N.Y.: Cornell University Press, 1986.

Akarli, Engin Deniz. *Long Peace: Ottoman Lebanon 1861–1920*. Berkeley: University of California Press, 1993.

Akbar, Jamel. *Crisis in the Built Environment*. Singapore: Concept Media; New York: E. J. Brill, 1988.

Akhtar, Shabbir. *A Faith for All Seasons: Islam and Western Modernity*. London: Bellew, 1990.

Al-Attas, Syed Naguib. *The Mysticism of Hamzah Fansuri*. Kuala Lumpur, Malaysia: University of Malay Press, 1970.

Al-Azmeh, Aziz, ed. *Islamic Law: Social and Historical Contexts*. New York: Routledge, 1988.

Al-Baladhuri, Ahmad B. Yahya. *The Origins of the Islamic State: A Translation of Kitab Futuh al-Buldan*. Translated by P. K. Hitti and F. Murgotten. New York: Columbia University Press, January 1970.

Al-Faruqi, I. R., and L. L. Al-Faruqi, eds. *The Cultural Atlas of Islam*. New York: Macmillan, 1986.

Al-Juwayni, Alaaldin Atamalik ibn Muhammad. *The History of the World Conqueror [Tarikh-i Jahangusha]*. Vols 1, 2. Translated by John Andrew Boyle. Cambridge, Mass.: Harvard University Press, 1958.

Al-Nawawi. *Forty Hadith*. Translated by E. Ibrahim and D. Johnson-Davis. Damascus, Syria: Holy Koran Publishing House, 1977.

Al-Shafii, Muhammad Ibn Idris. *Islamic Jurisprudence: Shafii's Risala*. Translated by Majid Khadduri. Baltimore: John Hopkins University Press, 1961.

Algar, Hamid. *Religion and State in Iran, 1785–1906: The Role of the Ulama in the Qajar Period*. Berkeley: University of California Press, 1969.

Ali, Ahmed. *Al-Quran: A Contemporary Translation*. Princeton: Princeton University Press, 1984.

Ali-Ibn al-Husayn and Zayn al-Abidin. *The Psalms of Islam: Al-Sahifat al-Kamilat Al-Sajjadiyya.* Translated by W. C. Chittick. Oxford: Oxford University Press (Muhammadi Trust of Great Britain and Northern Ireland), n.d.

Alvi, S. M. Ziauddin. *Muslim Educational Thought in the Middle Ages.* New Delhi: Atlantic Publishers, 1988.

Amin, Mohamed. *Pilgrimage to Mecca.* London: Macdonald and Jane's, 1978.

Amin, Syed Hassan. *Islamic Law in the Contemporary World.* Glasgow, Scotland: Royston Ltd., 1985.

———. *Islamic Law and Its Implications for the Modern World.* Glasgow, Scotland: Royston Ltd., 1988.

Anderson, James Norman Dalrymple. *Islamic Law in the Modern World.* New York: New York University Press, 1959. Reprint, Westport: Greenwood Press, 1975.

Andric, Ivo. *The Development of Spiritual Life in Bosnia Under the Influence of Turkish Rule.* Durham, N.C.: Duke University Press, 1990.

Antoun, Richard T. *Muslim Preacher in the Modern World.* Princeton: Princeton University Press, 1989.

Arberry, A. J. *An Introduction to the History of Sufism.* London: Longman, 1942.

Arkoun, Mohammed. *Rethinking Islam Today, Occasional Papers Series.* Washington, D.C.: Georgetown University, 1987.

Armstrong, Karen. *Muhammad: A Western Attempt to Understand Islam.* London: Victor Gollancz, 1991.

Ashtiany, Julia. *Abbasid Belles-Lettres. The Cambridge History of Arabic Literature.* Cambridge: Cambridge University Press, 1990.

Attar, Farid al-Din. *The Conference of the Birds, Mantiq ut-Tair: A Philosophical Religious Poem in Prose.* New York: S. Wiser, 1969.

Averroes. *Ibn Rushd's Metaphysics: A Translation with Introduction of Ibn Rushd's Commentary on Aristotle's Metaphysics, Book Lam.* Leiden: E. J. Brill, 1984.

Ayoub, Mahmoud Mustafa. *The Quran and Its Interpreters.* Albany: State University of New York Press, 1984.

Ayoub, Mahmoud. *Islam: Faith and Practice.* Markham, Ont. (Canada): Open Press, 1989.

Ayoub, Mahoud. *Redemptive Suffering in Islam: A Study of the Devotional Aspects of Ashura' in Twelver Shiism.* The Hague, The Netherlands: Mouton, 1978.

Ayubi, Nazih N. *Political Islam: Religion and Politics in the Arab World.* London: Rutledge, 1993.

Azad, Ghulam Murtaza. *Judicial System of Islam.* Islamabad, Pakistan: Islamic Research Institute, 1987.

♦ **B**

Baldick, Julian. *Mystical Islam: An Introduction to Islam.* New York: Columbia University Press, 1989.

Bannerman, Patrick. *Islam in Perspective: A Guide to Islamic Society, Politics and Law.* New York: Routledge, Chapman & Hall, 1988.

Banu, U. A. B., and Razia Akter. *Islam in Bagladesh.* Leiden: E. J. Brill, 1992.

Bayat, Mangol. *Iran's First Revolution: Shiism and the Constitutional Revolution of 1905–1909.* New York: Oxford University Press, 1992.

Beg, Muhammad Abdul Jabbar. *Fine Arts in Islamic Civilization.* Kuala Lumpur, Malaysia: University of Malaysia Press, 1981.

Blair, Sheila S., and Jonathan M. Bloom, eds. *Images of Paradise in Islamic Art.* Hanover, N.H.: Hood Museum of Art and the Trustees of Dartmouth College, 1991.

Blair, Shelia S., and Jonathan M. Bloom. *The Art and Architecture of Islam 1250–1800.* New Haven: Yale University Press, 1994.

Bosworth, C. E. *The Ghaznavids: Their Empire in Afghanistan and Eastern Iran, 944–1040.* 2d ed. Edinburgh: Edinburgh University Press, 1963.

———. *The Islamic Dynasties: A Chronological and Genealogical Handbook.* Edinburgh: Edinburgh University Press, 1967.

Bowen, Donna Lee, and Evelyn A. Early, eds. *Everyday Life in the Muslim Middle East.* Bloomington: Indiana University Press, 1993.

Bowen, John R. *Muslims Through Discourse: Religion and Ritual in Gayo Society.* Princeton: Princeton University Press, 1993.

Brend, Barbara. *Islamic Art.* London: British Museum Press, 1991.

Brenner, Louis. *Muslim Identity and Social Change in Sub-Saharan Africa.* London: C Hurst & Co., 1993.

Brice, William C., ed. *An Historical Atlas of Islam.* Leiden: E. J. Brill, 1981.

Browne, Edward G. *A Literary History of Persia.* Cambridge: Cambridge University Press, 1953.

Burckhardt, Titus. *Art of Islam: Language and Meaning.* London: World of Islam Festival Publishing Co., 1976.

———. *An Introduction to Sufi Doctrine.* Translated by D. M. Matheson. Wellingborough, U.K.: Crucible, 1990.

Burgat, Francois. *The Islamic Movement in North Africa.* Austin, Tex.: Center for Middle Eastern Studies, University of Texas at Austin, 1993.

Burton, J. *Sources of Islamic Law.* Edinburgh: Edinburgh University Press, 1990.

◆ C

Calder, N. *Studies in Early Muslim Jurisprudence.* Oxford: Clarendon Press, 1993.

Cantacuzino, Sherban, ed. *Architecture in Continuity: The Aga Khan Award for Architecture: Building in the Islamic World Today.* New York: Aperture, 1986.

Chaudhri, K. N. *Asia Before Europe: Economy and Civilization of the Indian Ocean Before the Rise of Islam to 1750.* New York: Cambridge University Press, 1990.

Chittick, William C. *The Sufi Path of Knowledge: Ibn al-Arabi's Metaphysics of Imagination.* Albany: State University of New York Press, 1989.

Chittick, William C., ed. and trans. *A Shiite Anthology.* Albany: State University of New York Press, 1981.

Cole, Juan and Nikki R. Keddie, eds. *Comparing Muslim Societies: Knowledge and the State in a World Civilization.* Ann Arbor: University of Michigan Press, 1992.

Collins, Roger. *The Arab Conquest of Spain, 710–797.* New York: B. Blackwell, 1989.

Connors, Jane, ed. *Islamic Family Law: State Identity and Minority Rights.* London: Graham and Trotman, 1989.

Corbin, Henry. *History of Islamic Philosophy.* Translated by Liadain Sherrard and Phillip Sherrard. London: Kegan Paul International, 1992.

Coulson, Noel J. A. *A History of Islamic Law.* Edinburgh: Edinburgh University Press, 1964.

———. *Conflicts and Tensions in Islamic Jurisprudence.* Chicago: University of Chicago Press, 1969.

Cragg, Kenneth. *Readings in the Quran.* London: Collins, 1988.

Cragg, Kenneth, and R. Marston Speight, comp. *Islam from Within: An Anthology of a Religion.* Belmont, Calif.: Wadsworth Publishing. Co., 1980.

Creswell, Keppel Archibald Cameron, Sir. *A Bibliography of the Architecture, Arts and Crafts of Islam.* Cairo: American University of Cairo Press, 1973.

———. *A Short Account of Early Muslim Architecture.* Aldershot, U.K.: Scolar Press, 1989.

Critchlow, Keith. *Islamic Patterns: An Analytical and Cosmological Approach.* New York: Schocken Books, 1976.

Crone, Patricia. *God's Caliph: Religious Authority in the First Centuries of Islam.* New York: Cambridge University Press, 1987.

◆ D

Dabashi, Hamid. *Authority in Islam: From the Rise of Muhammad to the Establishment of the Ummayads.* New Brunswick, N.J.: Transaction Publishers, 1989.

Daniel, Norman. *Islam and the West: The Making of an Image.* Edinburgh: University of Edinburgh Press, 1960.

———. *Islam, Europe and Empire.* Edinburgh: Edinburgh University Press, 1966.

Dennett, D. C. *Conversion and the Poll Tax in Early Islam.* Cambridge, Mass.: Harvard University Press, 1950.

Denny, Frederick M. *An Introduction to Islam.* New York: Macmillan, 1985.

Djait, Hichem. *Europe and Islam.* Berkeley: University of California Press, 1985.

Dodds, Jerrilynn D., ed. *Al-Andalus: The Art of Islamic Spain.* New York: Metropolitan Museum of Art, 1992.

Dodge, Bayard. *Muslim Education in Medieval Times.* Washington, D.C.: Middle East Institute, 1962.

Doi, Abdur Rahman I. *Shariah, The Islamic Law.* London: Ta Ha Publishers, 1984.

Donner, Fred McGraw. *The Early Islamic Conquests.* Princeton: Princeton University Press, 1981.

Dunn, Ross E. *The Adventures of Ibn Battuta: A Muslim Traveler of the 14th Century.* Berkeley: University of California Press, 1987.

Dwyer, Daisy Hilse. *Law and Islam in the Middle East.* New York: Bergin & Garvey, 1990.

♦ E

Eaton, Richard Maxwell. *Islamic History as Global History, Essays on Global and Comparative History.* Washington, D.C.: American Historical Association, 1990.

Edge, Ian D. *Egyptian Legal System.* London: Butterworth, 1992.

Eickelman, Dale F. *Knowledge and Power in Morocco: The Education of a Twentieth-Century Notable.* Princeton: Princeton University Press, 1985.

El-Said, Issam. *Islamic Art and Architecture: The System of Geometric Design.* Edited by Tarek El-Bouri and Keith Critchlow. Reading, Pa.: Garnet Publishing, 1993.

Esposito, John L., ed. *Islam in Asia: Religion, Politics, and Society.* New York: Oxford University Press, 1987.

Esposito, John L. *Islam: The Straight Path.* New York: Oxford University Press, 1961.

Esposito, John L. *Women in Muslim Family Law.* Syracuse, N.Y.: Syracuse University Press, 1982.

Ettinghausen, R., and O. Grabar. *The Art and Architecture of Islam: 650–1250.* Harmondsworth, England: Penguin, 1987.

♦ F

Fakhry, Majid. *A History of Islamic Philosophy.* New York: Columbia University Press: Longman, 1983.

Fathy, Hassan. *Architecture for the Poor: An Experiment in Rural Egypt.* Chicago: University of Chicago Press, 1973.

Fernea, Elizabeth Warnock. *The Arab World: Personal Encounters.* Garden City, N.Y.: Anchor Press/Doubleday, 1985.

Fischer, Michael. *Iran: From Religious Dispute to Revolution.* Cambridge, Mass.: Harvard University Press, 1980.

Fischer, Michael, and Mehdi Abedi. *Debating Muslims: Cultural Dialogues in Tradition and Post Modernity.* Madison: University of Wisconsin Press, 1990.

Freeman-Grenville, G. S. P. *Historical Atlas of the Middle East.* New York: Simon and Schuster, 1993.

———. *The Muslim and Christian Calendars, Being Tables for the Conversion of Muslim and Christian Dates from the Hijra to the Year A.D. 2000.* 2d ed. London: Rex Collings, 1977.

Fyzee, Asaf Ali Asgar. *Outlines of Muhammadan Law.* 4th ed. Delhi, India: Oxford University Press, 1974.

♦ G

Geertz, Clifford. *Islam Observed: Religious Development of Morocco and Indonesia.* New Haven: Yale University Press, 1968.

Gerholm, Tomas, and Yngve Georg Lithman, eds. *The New Islamic Presence in Western Europe.* London and New York: Mansell, 1988.

Gibb, H. A. R. *Modern Trends in Islam.* Chicago: Chicago University Press, 1947.

Gibb, H. A. R., and J. H. Kramers, eds. *Shorter Encyclopaedia of Islam.* Ithaca, N.Y.: Cornell University, 1961.

Gino, A. M. *Jews, Christians, and Muslims in the Mediterranean World After 1492.* Portland, Ore.: Cass, 1992.

Glasse, Cyril. *Concise Encyclopaedia of Islam.* San Francisco: Harper Collins, 1991.

Goitin, S. D. *A Mediterranean Society: The Jewish Communities of the Arab World as Portrayed in the Documents of the Cairo Geniza.* 5 vols. Berkeley: University of California Press, 1967.

Goldziher, Ignaz. *Introduction to Islamic Theology and Law.* Translated by Andras Hamori and Ruth Hamori. Princeton: Princeton University Press, 1981.

Grabar, Oleg. *The Formation of Islamic Art.* 2d ed. New Haven: Yale University Press, 1988.

Graham, William A. *Beyond the Written Word: Oral Aspects of Scripture in the History of Religion.* New York: Cambridge University Press, 1987.

———. *A Divine Word and Prophetic Word in Early Islam.* The Hague, The Netherlands: Mouton & Co., 1977.

Graham, William A., Marilyn M. Waldman, and Miriam Rosen, eds. *Islams-Fiche: Readings from Primary Sources [microform].* Zug, Switzerland: Inter Documentation, 1983.

Grimwood-Jones, Diana, ed. *Middle East and Islam: A Bibliographical Introduction.* 2d ed. Bibliotheca Asiatica; 15. Zug, Switzerland: Inter-Documentation, 1979.

Gross, Joanne. *Muslims in Central Asia: Expressions of Identity and Change.* Durham, N.C.: Duke University Press, 1992.

Grube, Ernst. *Studies in Islamic Painting and Decorative Arts.* London: Pindar Press, 1993.

♦ **H**

Haddad, Yvonne Yazbeck. *Contemporary Islam and the Challenge of History.* Albany: State University of New York Press, 1982.

Haddad, Yvonne Yazbeck, ed. *The Muslims of America.* New York: Oxford University Press, 1991.

Haddad, Yvonne Yazbeck, Byron Haines, and Ellison Findly, eds. *Contemporary Islam and the Challenge of History.* Albany: State University New York Press, 1982.

———. *The Islamic Impact, Contemporary Issues in the Middle East.* Syracuse, N.Y.: Syracuse University Press, 1984.

Haeri, Shahla. *Law of Desire: Temporary Marriage in Shii Iran.* Syracuse, N.Y.: Syracuse University Press, 1989.

Haghayeghi, Mehrdad. *Islam and Politics in Central Asia.* New York: St. Martin's Press, 1995.

Halm, Heinz. *Shiism.* Edinburgh: Edinburgh University Press, 1991.

Hamarneh, Sami Khalaf. *Health Sciences in Early Islam: Collected Papers.* San Antonio, Tex.: Zahra Publications, 1983–1984.

Harvey, L. P. *Islamic Spain 1250–1500.* Chicago: University of Chicago Press, 1990.

Haykal, Muhammad. *The Life of Muhammad.* Translated by Ismail R. al-Faruqi. Indianapolis: American Trust Publications, 1976.

Hillenbrand Robert. *Islamic Architecture: Form, Function and Meaning.* New York: Columbia University Press, 1993.

Hiskett, Mervyn. *The Course of Islam in Africa.* Edinburgh: Edinburgh University Press, 1994.

Hodgson, Marshall G. S. *Venture of Islam: Conscience and History in World Civilization.* 3 vols. Chicago: University of Chicago, 1974.

Homoud, Sami Hassan. *Islamic Banking: The Adaption of Banking Practice to Conform with Islamic Law.* London: Arab Information, 1985.

Hooker, M. B., ed. *Islam in South-East Asia.* Leiden: E. J. Brill, 1983.

Hopwood, Derek, and Diana Grimwood-Jones, eds. *Middle East and Islam: A Bibliographical Introduction.* Zug, Switzerland: Inter Documentation AG [for the Middle East Libraries Committee], 1972.

Hourani, Albert Habib. *A History of the Arab Peoples.* Cambridge, Mass.: Harvard University Press, 1991.

———. *Islam in European Thought and Other Essays.* New York: Cambridge University Press, 1991.

Hourani, George Fadlo. *Arab Seafaring in the Indian Ocean in Ancient and Early Medieval Times.* Princeton: Princeton University Press, 1951.

Houtsma, M. Th., et al., eds. *The Encyclopaedia of Islam.* 9 vols. Leiden: E. J. Brill, 1987.

Hovannisian, R. G., ed. *Ethics in Islam (9th Georgio Levi Della Vida Conference).* Malibu, Calif.: Undena Publications, 1985.

♦ **I**

Ibn Battuta, Muhammad ibn Ali. *The Travels of Ibn Battuta, A.D. 1325–1354.* 3 Vols. Translated by H. A. R. Gibb. Cambridge: Cambridge University Press, 1958–1971.

Ibn Ishaq, Muhammad. *The Life of Muhammad: A Translation of (Ibn) Ishaq's Sirat Rasul Allah.* Translated by Alfred Guillaume. London: Oxford University Press, 1967.

Ibn Khaldun, Abd al-Rahman B. Muhammad. *The Muqaddimah: An Introduction to History.* Translated by F. Rosenthal. London: Routledge & Kegan Paul, 1958.

Ibrahim, Mahmood. *Merchant Capital and Islam.* Austin: University of Texas Press, 1990.

Ilyas, Mohammad, and M. M. Qurashi. *New Moon's Visibility and International Islamic Calendar: For the Afro-Asian and European Region, 147AH–1421AH.* Malaysia: University of Science, 1993.

Inalcik, Halil. *The Ottoman Empire: The Classical Age, 1300–1600.* Translated by Norman Itzokitz and Colin Imber. New Rochelle, N.Y.: Aristide D. Caratzas, 1989.

Inayat, Hamid. *Modern Islamic Political Thought.* Austin: University of Austin Press, 1982.

Iqbal, Safia. *Women and Islamic Law.* Delhi: Al-Asr Publications, 1988.

Iqbal, Sir Muhammad. *The Reconstruction of Religious Thought in Islam.* Lahore, Pakistan: Sh. Muhammad Ashraf, 1951.

Islamic Fundamentalism and the Gulf Crisis. Chicago: Fundamentalism Project, American Academy of Arts and Sciences, 1991.

◆ **J**

Jafri, S. H. M. *The Origins and Early Development of Shia Islam.* London: Longman, 1979.

Jayyusi, S. *The Legacy of Muslim Spain.* Leiden: E. J. Brill, 1992.

Joly, D., and J. Nielsen. "Muslims in Britain: An Annotated Bibliography, 1960–1984." *Bibliographies in Ethnic Relations* No. 6. Coventry, England: Centre for Research in Ethnic Relations, University of Warwick, 1985.

Juynboll, G. H. *Muslim Tradition: Studies in Chronology, Provenance and Authorship of Early Hadith.* Cambridge: Cambridge University Press, 1983.

◆ **K**

Kaptein, N. J. G. *Muhammad's Birthday Festival: Early History in the Central Muslim Lands and Development in the Muslim West Until the 10th/16th Century.* Leiden: E. J. Brill, 1993.

Kassis, H. E. *A Concordance of the Quran.* Berkeley: University of California Press, 1983.

Kerr, Malcolm H. *Islamic Reform: The Political and Legal Theories of Muhammad Abduh and Rashid Rida.* Berkeley: University of California Press, 1966.

Kettani, M. A. *Muslim Minorities in the World Today.* London: Mansell, 1986.

Khadduri, Majid, and Herbert J. Liebesny, eds. *Origin and Development of Islamic Law, Law in the Middle East.* Vol. 1. Washington, D.C.: Middle East Institute, 1955. Reprint, New York: AMS Press, 1984.

Khan, Hasan Uddin and M. Fishman, eds. *The Mosque: History, Architectural Development and Regional Diversity.* New York: Thames and Hudson, 1994.

King, David A. *Astronomy in the Service of Islam.* Brookfield, Vt.: Variorum, 1993.

Knappert, Jan. *Swahili Islamic Poetry.* Leiden: E. J. Brill, 1971.

Kohlberg, Etan. *Belief and Law in Imami Shiism.* Aldershot, U.K.: Varorium, 1991.

The Koran: Text Translation and Commentary. Translated by Yusuf A. Ali. Washington, D.C.: American International Printing, 1946.

Koszegi, Michael S., and J. Gordon Melton, eds. *Islam in North America: A Sourcebook.* Garland Reference Library of Social Sciences, Vol. 258. New York: Garland Publishing, 1992.

Kraemer, J. *Humanism in the Renaissance of Islam: Cultural Revival During the Buyid Age.* 2d ed. Leiden: E. J. Brill, 1992.

Kuban, Dogan. *Muslim Religious Architecture.* Leiden: E. J. Brill, 1974.

◆ **L**

Lapidus, I. M. *A History of Islamic Societies.* New York: Cambridge University Press, 1988.

Lawrence, Bruce B. *Defenders of God: The Fundamentalist Revolt Against the Modern Age.* San Francisco: Harper & Row, 1989.

Lawrence, Bruce B. "Notes from a Distant Flute: The Extant Literature of Pre-Mughal Indian Sufism." *Imperial Iranian Academy of Philosophy* Publication No. 27. Tehran: Imperial Iranian Academy of Philosophy, 1978.

Lawrence, Bruce B., ed. *The Rose and the Rock: Mystical and Rational Elements in the Intellectual History of South Asian Islam*. Durham, N.C.: Duke University University Press, 1979.

Leaman, Oliver. *An Introduction to Medieval Islamic Philosophy*. Cambridge: Cambridge University Press, 1988.

Levy, Reuben. *Persian Literature: An Introduction*. London: Oxford University Press, 1944.

Lewis, Bernard. *Arabs in History*. 4th ed. London: Hutchinson's, 1966.

———. *Islam in History: Ideas, People and Events in the Middle East*. 2d ed. Chicago: Open Court, 1993.

———. *The Political: Language of Islam*. Chicago: University of Chicago Press, 1991.

———. *Islam from the Prophet Muhammad to the Capture of Constantinople*. New York: Harper & Row, 1974.

Lewis, Bernard, and P. M. Holt, eds. *Historians of the Middle East*. London: Oxford, 1962.

Lincoln, C. Eric. *The Black Muslims in America*. 3d ed. Grand Rapids, Mich.: W. B. Eerdmans, 1994.

Lings, Martin. *Muhammad, His Life Based on the Earliest Sources*. New York: Inner Traditions International, 1983.

———. *The Quranic Art of Calligraphy and Illumination*. 2d ed. New York: Interlink Books, 1987.

———. *What is Suffism?* Berkeley: University of California Press, 1975.

Lippman, Thomas W. *Understanding Islam: An Introduction to the Moslem World*. New York: New American Library, 1982.

Loeffler, Reinhold. *Islam in Practice: Religious Beliefs in a Persian Village*. Albany: State University of New York Press, 1988.

Lopez-Baralt, Luce. *Islam in Spanish Literature: From the Middle Ages to the Present*. Leiden: E. J. Brill, 1992.

◆ M

Makdisi, George, ed. *The Rise of the Colleges: Institutions of Learning in Islam and the West*. Edinburgh: Edinburgh University Press, 1981.

Makdisi, George, ed. *The Rise Humanism in Classical Islam and the Christian West*. Edinburgh: Edinburgh University Press, 1990.

Makdisi, George. *Religion, Law and Learning in Classical Islam*. Aldershot, U.K.: Variorum, 1991.

Malti-Douglas, Fadwa. *Women's Word: Gender and Discourse in Arabo-Islamic Writing*. Princeton: Princeton University Press, 1991.

Mardin, Serif. *Religion and Social Change in Modern Turkey*. Albany: State University of New York Press, 1989.

Massignon, Louis. *Hallaj: Mystic and Martyr*. Princeton: Princeton University Press, 1994.

Masters, Bruce. *The Origins of Western Economic Dominance in the Middle East: Mercantilism and the Islamic Economy in Aleppo, 1600–1750*. New York: Columbia University Press, 1988.

Masudi. *The Meadows of Gold: The Abbasids*. Translated and edited by Paul Lunde and Caroline Stone. New York: Kegan Paul, 1989; distributed by Routledge, Chapman and Hall.

Mayer, Ann Elizabeth. *Islam and Human Rights: Tradition and Politics*. Boulder, Colo.: Westview Press, 1991.

McAuliffe, Jane. *Quranic Christians: An Analysis of Classical and Modern Exegesis*. Cambridge: Cambridge University Press, 1991.

McChesney, R. D. *Waqf in Central Asia*. Princeton: Princeton University Press, 1991.

The Meaning of the Glorious Koran: An Explanatory Translation. Translated by Mohammed Marmaduke Pickthall. New York: New American Library and Mentor Books, 1985.

Mernissi, Fatima. *Beyond the Veil: Male-Female Dynamics in a Modern Muslim Society*. Rev. ed. Bloomington, Ind.: Indiana University Press, 1987.

Mernissi, Fatima. *Women and Islam: An Historical and Theological Inquiry*. Oxford: Blackwell, 1991.

Messick, B. *The Calligraphic State: Textural Domination and History in a Muslim Society.* Berkeley: University of California Press, 1993.

Metcalfe, Barbara. *Islamic Revival in British India: Deoband, 1860–1900.* Princeton: Princeton University Press, 1982.

Metcalfe, Barbara. *Perfecting Women: Maulana Ashraf 'Ali Thanawi's Bihishti Zawar.* Berkeley: University of California Press, 1990.

The Middle East Studies Association Bulletin. 1967–. Tuscon: The Middle East Studies Association. University of America, Inc., n.d.

Mir, Mustansir. *Dictionary of Quranic Terms and Concepts.* New York: Garland Publishing, 1987.

Modarressi, Hossein. *An Introduction to Shii Law: A Bibliographical Study.* London: Ithaca Press, 1984.

Momen, Moojan. *An Introduction to Shii Islam: The History and Doctrines of Twelver Shiism.* New Haven, Conn.: Yale University Press, 1985.

Morony, Michael G. *Iraq After the Muslim Conquest.* Princeton: Princeton University Press, 1984.

Mottahedeh, Roy P. *Loyalty and Leadership in an Early Islamic Society.* Princeton: Princeton University Press, 1980.

Mottahedeh, Roy. *The Mantle of the Prophet: Religion and Politics in Iran.* New York: Simon and Schuster, 1985.

Muhammad, Abduh. *The Theology of Unity.* Translated by Ishaq Musaad and Kenneth Cragg. New York: Humanities, 1966.

Munson, Henry Jr. *Islam and Revolution in the Middle East.* New Haven, Conn.: Yale University Press, 1988.

♦ N

Naim, A. A. *Towards an Islamic Reformation: Civil Liberties, Human Rights and International Law.* Syracuse, N.Y.: Syracuse University Press, 1990.

Nanji, Azim, ed. *Building for Tomorrow: The Aga Khan Award for Architecture.* London: Academy Group Ltd., 1994.

Nasr, Seyyed Hossein. *Ideals and Realities of Islam.* Boston: Beacon Press, 1994.

———. *Islamic Art and Spirituality.* Albany: State University of New York Press, 1987.

———. *Islamic Science: An Illustrated Study.* [s.l.]: World of Islam Festival Pub. Co., 1976.

———. *Science and Civilization in Islam.* Cambridge: Harvard University Presss, 1968.

———. *A Young Muslim's Guide to the Modern World.* Cambridge: The Islamic Texts Society, 1994.

Nasr, Seyyed Hossein, ed. "Islamic Spirituality: Foundations." *World Spirituality* 19. New York: Crossroads, 1987.

Nasr, Seyyed Hossein, H. Dabashi, and S. V. R. Nasr, eds. *Shiism: Doctrines, Thought, Spirituality.* Albany: State University of New York Press, 1988.

Necipoglu, Gulru. *Architecture, Ceremonial, and Power: The Topkapi Palace in the Fifteenth and Sixteenth Centuries.* New York: Architectural History Foundation, 1991.

Nelson, Kristina. *The Art of Reciting the Quran.* Austin: University of Texas Press, 1985.

Netton, Ian Richard. *Al-Farabi and His School.* New York: Routledge, 1992.

———. "Muslim Neoplatonists: An Introduction to the Thought of the Brethren of Purity." *Islamic Surveys* 19. Edinburgh: Edinburgh University Press, 1991.

Ngah, Modh Nor Bin. *Kitab Jawi: Islamic Thought of the Malay Muslim Scholars.* Research Notes and Discussions Paper No. 33. Singapore: Institute of Southeast Asian Studies, 1983.

Nicholson, Reynold Alleyne. *A Literary History of the Arabs.* Cambridge: Cambridge University Press, 1969.

Nielsen, Jorgen S. *Muslims in Western Europe.* Edinburgh: Edinburgh University Press, 1992.

♦ O

Ofori, P. E. *Islam in Africa South of the Sahara: A Select Bibliographic Guide.* Nendeln, Liechtenstein: KTO, 1977.

Oxford Encyclopedia of the Modern Islamic World. 4 vols. New York: Oxford University Press, 1995.

◆ P

Pascotori, James P. *Islam in a World of Nation-States.* Cambridge: Cambridge University Press, 1986.

Peters, F. E. *Allah's Commonwealth: A History of the Near East 600–1100 A.D.* New York: Simon and Schuster, 1973.

———. *The Hajj: The Muslim Pilgrimage to Mecca and the Holy Places.* Princeton: Princeton University Press. 1994.

———. *Muhammad and the Origins of Islam.* Ithaca: State University of New York Press, 1994.

———. *A Reader on Classical Islam.* Princeton: Princeton University Press, 1994.

Petrushevsky, I. P. *Islam in Iran.* Translated by Hubert Evans. Albany: State University of New York Press, 1985.

Poston, Larry. *Islamic Dawah in the West: Muslim Missionary Activity and the Dyanmics of Conversion to Islam.* New York: Oxford University Press, 1992.

Pouwels, Randall Lee. *Horn and Crescent: Cultural Change and Traditional Islam on the East African Coast, 800–1900.* New York: Cambridge University Press, 1987.

Powell, J. *Muslims Under Latin Rule.* Princeton: Princeton University Press, 1990.

Powers, David S. *Studies in Quran and Hadith: The Formation of the Islamic Law of Inheritance.* Berkeley: University of California Press, 1986.

◆ R

Rahman, Fazlur. *Health and Medicine in the Islamic Tradition: Change and Identity.* New York: Crossroad, 1987.

———. *Islam.* 2d ed. Chicago: University of Chicago Press, 1979.

———. *Islam and Modernity: The Transformation of an Intellectual Tradition.* Chicago: University of Chicago Press, 1982.

———. *Major Themes of the Quran.* Minneapolis: Bibliotheca Islamica, 1980.

Rahman, Habib Ur. *Islam and Modernity: Transformation of an Intellectual Tradition.* Chicago: University of Chicago Press, 1982.

Reinhart, A. Kevin. *Before Revelation: The Boundaries of Muslim Moral Thought.* Albany: State University of New York Press, 1994.

Richardson, E. Allen. *Islamic Cultures in North America: Patterns of Belief and Devotion of Muslims from Asian Countries in the United States and Canada.* New York: Pilgrim Press, 1981.

Rippin, Andrew, ed. *Approaches to the History of the Interpretation of the Quran.* London: Oxford University Press, 1988.

Rippin, Andrew. *Muslims: Their Religious Beliefs and Practices.* London: Routledge, 1990.

Robinson, Francis. *Atlas of the Islamic World Since 1500.* New York: Facts on File, 1982.

Roded, Ruth. *Women in Islamic Biographical Collections: from Sa'd to Who's Who.* Boulder, Colo.: Lynne Rienner, 1994.

Rodinson, Maxime. *Europe and the Mystique of Islam.* Seattle: University of Washington Press, 1987.

———. *Islam and Capitalism.* Translated by Brian Pearce. London: Pantheon Books, 1973.

Rolf, William, ed. *Islam and the Political Economy of Meaning.* Berkeley: University of California Press, 1987.

Roy, Olivier. *Islam and Resistance in Afghanistan.* 2d ed. New York: Cambridge University Press, 1990.

Rund, Inger Marie. *Women's Status in the Muslim World: A Bibliographical Survey.* Leiden: E. J. Brill, 1981.

Ruthven, Malise. *Islam in the World.* New York: Oxford University Press, 1984.

◆ S

Sachedina, Abdulaziz. *Islamic Messianism: The Idea of Mahdi in Twelver Shiism.* Albany: State University of New York Press, 1981.

———. *The Just Ruler in Shiite Islam: The Comprehensive Authority of the Jurist in Imamite Jurisprudence.* New York: Oxford University Press, 1988.

Sadi. *The Rose-Garden of Shekh Muslihu'd-din Sadi of Shiraz.* London: Octagon Press, 1974.

Said, Edward W. *Culture and Imperialism*. London: Chatto and Windus, 1993.

————. *The Question of Palestine*. New York: Vintage Books, 1980.

Saunders, John Joseph. *A History of Medieval Islam*. New York: Barnes & Noble, 1965.

Sauvaget, J. *Introduction to the History of the Muslim East: A Bibliographical Guide*. Berkeley: University of California Press, 1965.

Savory, R. M., ed. *Introduction to Islamic Civilization*. Cambridge: Cambridge University Press, 1976.

Savory, Roger. *Iran Under the Safavids*. Cambridge: Cambridge University Press, 1980.

Schact, Joseph. *An Introduction to Islamic Law*. 1964. Reprint, Oxford: Clarendon Press, 1982.

Schacht, Joseph, and C. E. Bosworth, eds. *The Legacy of Islam*. 2d ed. Oxford: Clarendon Press, 1974.

Schimmel, Annemarie. *And Muhammad is His Messenger: The Veneration of the Prophet in Islamic Piety*. Chapel Hill: University of North Carolina Press, 1985.

————. *Calligraphy and Islamic Culture*. New York: New York University Press, 1984.

————. *Islam in India and Pakistan*. Leiden: E. J. Brill, 1982.

————. *Islam in the Indian Subcontinent*. Leiden-Köln: E. J. Brill, 1980.

————. *Islam: An Introduction*. (*Der Islam.*) Albany: State University of New York Press, 1992.

Schimmel, Annemarie. *Mystical Dimensions of Islam*. Chapel Hill: University of North Carolina Press, 1975.

Schubel, Vernon. *Religious Performance in Contemporary Islam: Shii Devotional Rituals in South Asia*. Columbia: University of South Carolina Press, 1993.

Schuon, Frithjof. *Understanding Islam*. London: George, Allen & Unwin, 1963.

Sells, Michael. *Mystical Languages of Unsaying*. Chicago: University of Chicago Press, 1994.

Serageldin, Ismail. *Space for Freedom: The Search for Architectural Excellence in Muslim Societies*. Boston: Butterworth Architecture, 1989.

Shaban, M. A. *Islamic History: A New Interpretation*. 2 vols. Cambridge: Cambridge University Press, 1971.

Shaikh, Farzana, ed. *Islam and Islamic Groups: A Worldwide Reference Guide*. Essex, U.K.: Longman Group UK Ltd., 1992; distributed in Canada and the United States by Gale Research.

Siddiqi, Muhammad Zubayr. *Hadith Literature, Its Origin, Development, Special Features, and Criticism*. Cambridge: Islamic Texts Society, 1993.

Sivan, Emmanuel. *Radical Islam: Medieval Theology and Modern Politics*. New Haven, Conn.: Yale University Press, 1990.

Smith, Jane I., ed. *Women in Contemporary Muslim Societies*. Lewisburg, Pa.: Bucknell University Press, 1980.

Smith, Jane I., and Yvonne Haddad. *The Islamic Understanding of Death and Resurrection*. Albany: State University of New York Press, 1981.

Smith, Margaret. *Rabia the Mystic and Her Fellow Saints in Islam*. Cambridge: Cambridge University Press, 1928.

Smith, Wilfred Cantwell. *Islam in Modern History*. Princeton: Princeton University Press, 1957.

————. *On Understanding Islam: Selected Studies*. New York: Mourton, 1981.

Sourdel, Dominique. *Medieval Islam*. London: Routledge and Kegan Paul, 1983.

Steel, James. *Architecture for a Changing World*. New York: St. Martin's Press, 1992.

Stowasser, Barbara Freyer, ed. *The Islamic Impulse*. Washington, D.C.: Georgetown University CCAS, 1987.

♦ T

Tabatabai, Allamah Sayyid Muhammad Husayn. *Shiite Islam*. Translated by Seyed Hossein Nasr. Albany: State University of New York, 1975.

Tibawi, Abdul Latif. *Islamic Education: Its Traditions and Modernization into the Arab National Systems*. London: Luzac, 1972.

Tibi, Bassam. *The Crisis of Modern Islam: A Preindustrial Culture in the Scientific-Technological Age*. Salt Lake City: University of Utah Press, 1988.

Tjandrasamita, Uka. *The Arrival and Expansion of Islam in Indonesia Relating to Southeast Asia.* Jakarta, Indonesia: Masagung Foundation, 1985.

The Translation of the Meanings of Sahih-al Bukhari. 3d ed. Translated by Muhammad Muhsin Khan. Chicago: Kazi Publication; Albany: State University of New York Press, 1979.

Trimingham, J. Spencer. *The Sufi Orders In Islam.* Oxford: Clarendon Press, 1971.

♦ **U**

Udovitch, A. L., ed. *The Islamic Middle East, 700–1900: Studies in Economic and Social History.* Princeton: Darwin Press, 1981.

Ullmann, Manfred. *Islamic Medicine.* Edinburgh: Edinburgh University Press. 1978.

United States. Central Intelligence Agency. *Major Muslim Ethnic Groups in Armenia, Iran, and the Islamic Commonwealth States.* Washington, D.C.: Central Intelligence Agency, 1992.

♦ **V**

Van Donzel, E. *Islamic Desk Reference.* Leiden: E. J. Brill, 1994.

Voll, A. *Eighteenth-Century Renewal and Reform in Islam.* Syracuse, N.Y.: Syracuse University Press, 1987.

Voll, John Obert. *Islam: Continuity and Change in the Modern World.* Boulder, Colo.: Westview Press, 1982.

Von Grunebaum, G. E. *Unity and Variety in Muslim Civilization.* Chicago: University of Chicago Press, 1955.

♦ **W**

Walker, Paul. *Early Philosophical Shiism: The Ismaili Neoplatonism of Abu Yaqub al Sijistani.* Cambridge: Cambridge University Press, 1993.

Walther, Wiebke. *Women in Islam.* Rev. ed. Princeton, N.J.: Weiner Publishing, 1993.

Wan Daud, Wan. *The Concept of Knowledge in Islam and Its Implication for Education in a Developing Country.* London: Mansel, 1989.

Watt, William Montgomery. *The Influence of Islam on Medieval Europe.* Edinburgh: University of Edinburgh Press, 1972.

———. *The Majesty That Was Islam: The Islamic World, 661–1100.* London: Sidgewick and Jackson, 1974.

———. *Muhammad: Prophet and Statesman.* London: Oxford University Press, 1961.

———. *Muslim Intellectual: A Study of al-Ghazali.* Edinburgh, University of Edinburgh Press, 1963.

Waugh, Earl, Abu-Laban, and Regula B. Qureshi, eds. *The Muslim Community in North America.* Edmonton, Alberta (Canada): University of Alberta Press, 1983.

Weekes, Richard V., ed. *Muslim Peoples: A World Ethnographic Survey.* 2d ed. Westport, Conn.: Greenwood Press, 1984.

Wensinck, Arent Jan. *Handbook of Early Muhammadan Tradition Alphabetically Arranged.* Leiden: E. J. Brill, 1960.

Williams, John Alden, ed. *The Word of Islam.* Austin: University of Texas Press, 1994.

Wolfson, Harry Austryn. *The Philosophy of the Kalam.* Cambridge: Harvard University Press, 1976.

Woods, John E. *The Aqquyunlu: Clan, Confederation, Empire: A Study in 15th/9th Century Turko-Iranian Politics.* Minneapolis: Bibliiotheca Islamica, 1976.

♦ **Y**

Young, M. J. L., et al. *Religion, Learning and Science in the Abbasid Period.* New York: Cambridge University Press, 1990.

♦ **Z**

Zebiri, Kate. *Mahmud Shaltut and Islamic Modernism.* Oxford: Oxford University Press, 1993.

Zoghby, S. M. *Islam in Sub-Saharan Africa: A Partially Annotated Guide.* Washington, D.C.: Library of Congress, 1978.

Zubaida, Sami. *Islam, the People and the State: Essays on Political Ideas and Movements in the Middle East.* New York: Routledge, 1989.

Zuhur, Sherifa. *Revealing Reveiling: Islamist Gender Ideology in Contemporary Egypt.* Albany: State University of New York Press, 1992.

Illustrations

1: Courtesy of Frederick M. Denny; 9: Courtesy of The Library, Institute of Ismaili Studies, London; 11: Courtesy of S. Noorani/Aga Khan Trust for Culture; 12: Courtesy of Frederick M. Denny; 13: Courtesy of Frederick M. Denny; 15: Courtesy of *Ahlan Wasahlan* (Saudi Arabian Airlines); 16: Courtesy of *Ahlan Wasahlan* (Saudi Arabian Airlines); 20b: Courtesy of Aga Khan Trust for Culture; 20c: Courtesy of Aga Khan Trust for Culture; 20: Courtesy of Jaques Betrant/Aga Khan Trust for Culture; 21: Courtesy of C. Little/Aga Khan Trust for Culture; 22: Courtesy of Jaques Betrant/Aga Khan Trust for Culture; 23: Courtesy of Aga Khan Trust for Culture; 29: Courtesy of Aga Khan Trust for Culture; 35: Courtesy of John Waterbury; 39: Courtesy of Aga Khan Trust for Culture; 40: Courtesy of Aga Khan Visual Archive, MIT; 42: Courtesy of Hasan-Uddin Khan; 46: Courtesy of Stephen Harmon; 47: Courtesy of Aga Khan Trust for Culture; 48: Courtesy of C. Benedetti/Aga Khan Trust for Culture; 49: Courtesy of Hasan-Uddin Khan; 52: Courtesy of Aga Khan Trust for Culture; 56b: Courtesy of Aga Khan Trust for Culture; 56a: Courtesy of Vasudha Narayanan; 57: Courtesy of Vasudha Narayanan; 58: Courtesy of Hasan-Uddin Khan; 59: Courtesy of Aga Khan Trust for Culture; 63: Courtesy of Vasudha Narayanan; 74: Courtesy of Frederick M. Denny; 77: Courtesy of Frederick M. Denny; 92: Courtesy of C. Little/Aga Khan Trust for Culture; 93: Courtesy of Chi Wa Chan; 96: Courtesy of Aga Khan Trust for Culture; 99: Courtesy of Michael Dillion; 101: Courtesy of Michael Dillion; 102: Courtesy of Michael Dillion; 110: Courtesy of Hasan-Uddin Khan; 112: Courtesy of Aga Khan Trust for Culture; 116a: Courtesy of Stephen Harmon; 116b: Courtesy of Aga Khan Trust for Culture; 117: Courtesy of Aga Khan Trust for Culture; 120: Courtesy of Aga Khan Trust for Culture; 121: Courtesy of Aga Khan Trust for Culture; 122: Courtesy of Aga Khan Trust for Culture; 126: Courtesy of Aga Khan Trust for Culture; 132: Courtesy of Aga Khan Trust for Culture; 133: Courtesy of Aga Khan Trust for Culture; 134: Courtesy of Jaques Betrant/Aga Khan Trust for Culture; 135: Courtesy of Jaques Betrant/Aga Khan Trust for Culture; 136: Courtesy of R. Gunay/Aga Khan Trust for Culture; 136 142: Courtesy of Vernon Schubel; 143: Courtesy of Aga Khan Trust for Culture; 145: Gulzar Haider/Courtesy of Aga Khan Trust for Culture; 147: Courtesy of Hasan-Uddin Khan; 153: Courtesy of UPI/Bettman; 154: Courtesy of Archive Photos; 155: Courtesy of AP/Wide World Photos; 163: Courtesy of T. Kamal-Eldin; 166: Courtesy of Aga Khan Visual Archive, MIT, Walter Denny; 179: Courtesy of Jaques Betrant/Aga Khan Trust for Culture; 182: Courtesy of Jaques Betrant/Aga Khan Trust for Culture; 183: Courtesy of The Library, Institute of Ismaili Studies, London; 184: Courtesy of Aga Khan Trust for Culture; 190: Courtesy of The Library, Institute of Ismaili Studies, London; 199: Courtesy of The Library, Institute of Ismaili Studies, London; 201: Courtesy of Courtesy of the Fogg Art Museum, Harvard University Art Museums, Bequest of Estate of Abby Aldrich

Rockefeller; **216:** Courtesy of Courtesy of the Fogg Art Museum, Harvard University Art Museums; **217:** Courtesy of Jaques Betrant/Aga Khan Trust for Culture; **218:** Courtesy of Courtesy of the Fogg Art Museum, Harvard University Art Museums, Grace Nichols Strong Fund, Francis H. Burr Fund, and Friends of the Fogg Art Museum Fund; **219:** Courtesy of Vasudha Narayanan; **224:** Courtesy of Vasudha Narayanan; **228:** Courtesy of Vernon Schubel; **229:** Courtesy of Aga Khan Trust for Culture; **232–250:** Courtesy of Shakeel Hossain; **254:** Courtesy of Jaques Betrant/Aga Khan Trust for Culture; **256:** Courtesy of Aga Khan Visual Archive, MIT; **257:** Courtesy of K. Adle/Aga Khan Trust for Culture; **272:** Courtesy of John Waterbury; **278:** Courtesy of Freer Galley of Art; **279:** Courtesy of Freer Galley of Art; **280:** Courtesy of Freer Galley of Art; **281:** Courtesy of Freer Galley of Art; **282:** Courtesy of Freer Galley of Art; **283:** Courtesy of Freer Galley of Art; **284:** Courtesy of Musee du Louvre, Paris; **286:** Courtesy of Freer Galley of Art; **287:** Courtesy of Freer Galley of Art; **288:** Courtesy of Freer Galley of Art; **289:** Courtesy of Museum fur Islamische Kunst, Berlin; **290:** Courtesy of Freer Galley of Art; **291:** Courtesy of Freer Galley of Art; **292b:** Courtesy of Freer Galley of Art; **292a:** Courtesy of Freer Galley of Art; **293:** Courtesy of National Library, Cairo; **294b:** Courtesy of Topkapi Palace Museum, Istanbul; **294a:** Courtesy of Freer Galley of Art; **295:** Courtesy of State Hermitage Museum, Petersburg; **296b:** Courtesy of Freer Galley of Art; **296a:** Courtesy of Freer Galley of Art; **297:** Courtesy of Museum of Turkish and Islamic Arts, Istanbul; **298:** Courtesy of Topkapi Palace Museum, Istanbul; **299:** Courtesy of Freer Galley of Art; **300:** Courtesy of Freer Galley of Art; **301:** Courtesy of Freer Galley of Art; **302:** Courtesy of Dar al-Athar al-Islamiyyah, Kuwait; **303a:** Courtesy of Topkapi Palace Museum, Istanbul; **303b:** Courtesy of Topkapi Palace Museum, Istanbul; **304b:** Courtesy of Dar al-Athar al-Islamiyyah, Kuwait; **304a:** Courtesy of Topkapi Palace Museum, Istanbul; **305:** Courtesy of National Museum of Painting and Sculpture; **310:** Courtesy of Aga Khan Visual Archive, MIT; **311:** Courtesy of Aga Khan Visual Archive, MIT; **312:** Courtesy of T. Kamal-Eldin; **312:** Courtesy of Aga Khan Visual Archive, MIT; **313:** Courtesy of Aga Khan Visual Archive, MIT; **316:** Courtesy of C. Little/Aga Khan Trust for Culture; **320:** Courtesy of Aga Khan Visual Archive, MIT; **323:** Courtesy of Aga Khan Trust for Culture; **326:** Courtesy of Aga Khan Visual Archive, MIT; **333:** Courtesy of Hartford Seminary; **338:** Courtesy of Courtesy of the Fogg Art Museum, Harvard University Art Museums, Loan from Private Collection; **347:** Courtesy of Courtesy of the Fogg Art Museum, Harvard University Art Museums, F. H. Burr Memorial Fund; **348:** Courtesy of Courtesy of the Fogg Art Museum, Harvard University Art Museums, Gift of John Goelet; **351:** Courtesy of Courtesy of the Fogg Art Museum, Harvard University Art Museums, Bequest of Estate of Abby Aldrich Rockefeller; **356:** Courtesy of Courtesy of the Fogg Art Museum, Harvard University Art Museums, Loan from Private Collection; **357:** Courtesy of A. Asani; **382:** Courtesy of Aga Khan Foundation; **383:** Courtesy of Aga Khan Visual Archive, MIT; **384:** Courtesy of Michael Dillion; **385:** Courtesy of Aga Khan Trust for Culture; **386:** Courtesy of Aga Khan Foundation; **388:** Courtesy of Aga Khan Foundation; **410a:** Courtesy of Hasan-Uddin Khan; **410b:** Courtesy of Aga Khan Trust for Culture; **414:** Courtesy of Aga Khan Visual Archive, MIT; **415:** Courtesy of Aga Khan Trust for Culture; **416:** Courtesy of Aga Khan Trust for Culture; **417:** Courtesy of Aga Khan Trust for Culture; **425:** Courtesy of Hartford Seminary; **446:** Courtesy of A. Asani; **447:** Courtesy of Aga Khan Trust for Culture; **466:** Courtesy of Aga Khan Trust for Culture; **469:** Courtesy of Aga Khan Foundation; **470:** Courtesy of Aga Khan Trust for Culture; **471:** Courtesy of Aga Khan Trust for Culture; **472:** Courtesy of Aga Khan Trust for Culture; **476:** Courtesy of Jaques Betrant/Aga Khan Trust for Culture; **477:** Courtesy of Aga Khan Trust for Culture; **479:** Courtesy of A. Ippocitti/Aga Khan Trust for Culture.

Index

Page numbers in *italics* denote illustrations; page numbers followed by 't' designate tables.

Names and terms that begin with al-, or an elided form of al- such as an- or as-, are indexed under the letter that follows the hyphen; e.g., al-Ghazali is sorted under 'g.' Names from the early centuries of Islam are indexed in the form in which they are most familiar in the West, that is, under the given name or relationship name: for example, Abu, ibn, and umm. More modern names generally follow the Western system of indexing the surname. Exceptions tend to be geographically linked; Chinese and Indonesian names are not inverted. The indexer has followed the lead of the many authors of this text as well as provided cross references for the reader's benefit.

E

G

U